DATE DUE

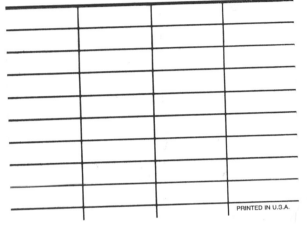

PRINTED IN U.S.A.

Library of Congress
Subject Headings

LIBRARY OF CONGRESS SUBJECT HEADINGS

Principles and Application

Third Edition

Lois Mai Chan

1995
LIBRARIES UNLIMITED, INC.
Englewood, Colorado

ory of

au N. Mark

LIBRARIES UNLIMITED, INC.
P.O. Box 6633
Englewood, CO 80155-6633
1-800-237-6124

Production Editor: Louisa M. Griffin
Copy Editor: D. Aviva Rothschild
Layout and Design: Pamela J. Getchell

Library of Congress Cataloging-in-Publication Data

Chan, Lois Mai.
    Library of Congress subject headings : principles and application
/ Lois Mai Chan. -- 3rd ed.
    xiv, 541 p. 17x25 cm.
    Includes bibliographical references and index.
    ISBN 1-56308-195-4. -- ISBN 1-56308-191-1 (pbk.)
    1. Subject headings, Library of Congress.   I. Title.
Z695.Z8L5226   1995
025.4'9--dc20
                                                                95-2664
                                                                  CIP

CONTENTS

Part 2
Application

Reference Materials 210
    Works About Reference Books 210
    Bibliographies of Reference Books 211
    Reference Works 212
Children's Materials 221
    Topical Juvenile Materials 222
    Juvenile Belles Lettres 223
Nonprint Materials 225
    General 225
    Cartographic Materials 226
    Computer Software and Databases 228
    Films 229
    Microforms 232
Biography 233
    Definition 233
    Types of Headings Assigned to Biography 233
    Subdivisions That Designate Biography 233
    Collective Biography 235
    Individual Biography 243
    Special Types of Biographical Works 251
Works About Corporate Bodies 254
    Corporate Bodies Discussed Collectively 254
    Works About Individual Corporate Bodies 255
    Name Changes in Corporate Bodies 256
Works About Buildings and Other Structures 259
    Works About Specific Types of Buildings or Structures . . 259
    Works About Individual Buildings or Structures 260
Works Involving City Districts, Sections, and Quarters . . . 261
Works Related to Individual Works 263
    Commentary Versus Edition 263
    Supplements to Individual Works 265
    Indexes to Individual Works 265
Notes 266

10 SUBJECT AREAS REQUIRING SPECIAL
    TREATMENT 269
Literature 269
    Types of Headings 269
    Application 272
Music 301
    Types of Headings 301
    Application 305
Fine Arts 321
    Types of Headings 321
    Application 323
Religion 332
    Types of Headings 332
    Application 333

Preface

Because MARC (MAchine-Readable Cataloging) records prepared by the Library of Congress (LC) have served as cataloging copy for most libraries and bibliographic utilities in the United States (as well as in many libraries abroad), and because the entire LC MARC database and the OCLC Union Catalog are accessible through the Internet, the Library of Congress Subject Headings (LCSH) system has become the primary subject retrieval tool worldwide for monographic and serial publications. Its adoption by many commercial online databases has rendered it an important retrieval tool for many other types of materials as well. Thus, it is now playing a retrieval role in an environment that is very different from that for which it was designed and developed.

This third edition of *Library of Congress Subject Headings: Principles and Application* reflects the changes and developments since the second edition appeared in 1986. Since that date, use of LCSH has expanded considerably, not only in the United States but also abroad, and not only for library catalogs and bibliographies but also for online databases. During the same period, most libraries in the United States have converted their catalogs to machine-readable form. The LCSH system has also been adopted or adapted for use by many libraries in other countries. In many respects, the system has become a de facto standard subject access tool.

Like the previous editions, this edition attempts to throw light on the current system. The book is divided into three parts. Part 1 gives a brief history of the system, analyzes its principles, and describes the vocabulary and subject authority control. Part 2 deals with the application of LC subject headings on LC MARC records. It outlines LC policies with regard to the assignment of subject headings in general and the treatment of certain types of materials in particular. The approach here is to describe rather than prescribe. Part 3 discusses the future prospects of the system as an online retrieval tool, drawing on recent literature on the subject. In order to avoid confusing what is with what ought to be, my own opinions are largely limited to parts 1 and 3 of the book. The appendixes contain sample MARC subject authority records and bibliographic records, lists of the most frequently used free-floating subdivisions, patterns and examples of cross references for certain types of name headings, lists of reference sources consulted in establishing headings, rules for capitalization and punctuation, and USMARC coding for subject headings.

The entire book has been rewritten to reflect changes since the second edition. All heading examples have been updated or verified in the latest print and online versions of LCSH. All cataloging examples have been replaced with those taken from the LC MARC database and reflect cataloging since 1990. The examples in the text do not contain MARC codes because many readers of this book are not USMARC users, and many others use this book in a context other than cataloging, for instance, in reference work or training in online searching. Examples of authority and bibliographic records with USMARC codes are included in appendix A. Throughout the book, boldface type is used to indicate valid Library of Congress subject headings, and italics signify unauthorized terms or obsolete headings.

This book is primarily intended for library and information professionals, library and information science educators, and advanced students. Library technicians, paraprofessionals, and beginning students may also find it useful.

I am indebted to many individuals for their help in the preparation of this edition. I wish to acknowledge the following people: Theodora Hodges for her invaluable editorial assistance and for preparing the index; Stella Cottam and Nancy Lewis for bibliographic assistance and proofreading; and Lynn El-Hoshy and Mary K. Pietris, Subject Cataloging Policy Specialists at the Library of Congress, for answering numerous questions regarding application, heading revisions, and recent policy changes.

The preparation of all three editions of this book was supported by grants from the Council on Library Resources, for which I wish to make a special acknowledgment.

PART 1

PRINCIPLES, FORM, AND STRUCTURE

1 Introduction

The subject headings system used at the Library of Congress (LC) was originally intended as a subject cataloging tool for its own use. Over the years, however, it has been adopted widely by libraries and other information services in the United States and abroad, probably because for most of its history LC cataloging has been widely available to other institutions, in recent decades through MARC (MAchine-Readable Cataloging) records. Referred to generally as LCSH,[1] it is now one of the two standard systems used for subject cataloging of general collections in U.S. libraries, and the one preferred for large collections.

LCSH is also used as the indexing vocabulary in a number of published bibliographies, among the best known of which is *Subject Guide to Books in Print*. The adoptions just noted relate to the subject cataloging of books. But the system also functions as a thesaurus for periodical indexing. Modified versions of the list are used in many online databases, among which are Cumulative Book Index, Essays and General Literature Index, and Bibliographic Index. Magazine Index, a computer-based index to popular journals, bases its indexing on LCSH.

LCSH has also become an important online retrieval tool both within the Library of Congress and outside. A number of bibliographic utilities allow searching by subject: OCLC (Online Computer Library Center) and RLIN (Research Libraries Information Network) are prominent examples, and most of the records in those utilities carry LC subject headings. Many libraries have their own online catalogs with access by subject, often with sophisticated search options; most of these libraries use LCSH for subject cataloging. Commercial retrieval services such as WILSONLINE and DIALOG carry the MARC file, bringing LC subject cataloging to their subscribers along with flexible and powerful search capabilities. LCSH also, of course, functions as a retrieval tool in the online databases mentioned earlier.

Internationally, LCSH has gained wide acceptance. As libraries worldwide seek to provide or improve subject access in their catalogs, many have developed or adapted controlled vocabularies based on LCSH.[2] *Canadian Subject Headings* (CSH),[3] the system used by most Canadian libraries, is "largely based on *LCSH* in its underlying principles of organization, structure and vocabulary and is specifically designed as an adjunct list to be used in tandem with *LCSH*."[4] *Répertoire de vedettes-matière* (RVM),[5] an adaptation of both LCSH and CSH, is used in Francophone Canada. RVM, in turn, serves as the basis of the subject indexing system RAMEAU used by libraries in France, Belgium, and Switzerland.[6] Other countries that have adopted or adapted controlled vocabularies based on LCSH include Brazil,[7] Iran,[8] and Portugal.[9] The Bodleian Library at Oxford University has been using LCSH for a number of years. The British Library, which for many years relied on PRECIS for subject access, has discontinued assigning PRECIS strings and decided to include LC subject headings in UKMARC records beginning in 1995.

An important reason for the far-ranging use of LCSH is that Library of Congress cataloging records have been available to other institutions throughout the twentieth century. The Library of Congress began selling its printed catalog cards in 1898 and the service was popular. With the advent of the online age, use of LC cataloging information increased considerably when the Library began distributing its MARC records directly through weekly tapes. Some libraries have subscriptions to the tape service; others access MARC records through bibliographic utilities that in turn have regular MARC tape service. And since 1993, LC MARC records have been accessible online through the Internet.

Responding to such widespread use and interest, the Library of Congress regularly solicits suggestions and recommendations from libraries and other institutions outside its walls when it plans major changes or institutes new policies. The Library of Congress as an institution is aware that its subject headings system has become a de facto standard for subject cataloging and indexing in circumstances far beyond those for which it was originally designed.

In most cases, growth such as has occurred for LCSH is considered a mark of a system's success. Yet it is generally acknowledged by information professionals that LCSH is far from ideal. It shows considerable internal inconsistency. It still exhibits characteristics that cater more to manual than to online systems; however, these are being removed as time goes on. The system has clearly demonstrated its versatility in a wide range of conditions and is not only holding its own, but also growing in popularity. Changes are in order, perhaps far-reaching ones; some, many would claim, are long overdue. But to be effective, changes designed to enhance a system must take all the elements and ramifications of that system into account. A new look at the principles that underlie LCSH features is therefore appropriate.

We turn first to the early history of LCSH for the insights it can provide on its current structure. Then we will look at other factors that have influenced its development and that bear on its potential. Finally, we will look at some of the problems faced in designing any thesaurus or subject headings list intended for general use.

HISTORY

The Beginnings

Shortly after the Library of Congress moved from the capitol to its new building in 1897, its officials faced the question of how the collection should be organized. One major decision, made in late 1897, was to establish a new classification system. Another was to adopt the dictionary form for the main catalog—in other words, to have a catalog with names, titles, and subject headings interfiled alphabetically, a decision made in 1898. Charles A. Cutter's *Rules for a Dictionary Catalog* had been published in 1876, and by 1898 was in its third edition;[10] the dictionary catalog was well on its way to becoming the predominant catalog form in U.S. libraries. The Library's move to such a catalog, plus the effect of its practice of selling its printed cards, put the Library at the forefront of the development of both U.S. cataloging practice in general and the use of the dictionary arrangement as a catalog form in particular. Indeed, according to J. C. M. Hanson (the first chief of the Catalogue Division), one of the reasons for adopting the dictionary form for the catalog was "a desire to be in a position to cooperate with the largest possible number of American libraries."[11]

As LC subject headings came to be used more widely, many librarians asked that its headings list be published. This was done under the title *Subject Headings Used in the Dictionary Catalogues of the Library of Congress*, which first appeared in 1914.[12] There has been a continuing series of editions and supplements ever since (with a title change to *Library of Congress Subject Headings* on the eighth edition in 1975).

The development of the list was the responsibility of the staff of the Catalogue Division. Hanson and Charles Martel (whose tours of duty as virtually successive chiefs of the division spanned 1897 to 1930) have been formally recognized as the individuals who provided its initial guiding principles. In the introduction to the fourth edition (1943) of the list, David Judson Haykin, then chief of the Subject Cataloging Division, presented his view of the beginning of the list:

> There was not, to begin with, a scheme or skeleton list of headings to which additions could be made systematically, completing and rounding out a system of subject headings for a dictionary catalog. Such a scheme could not have been devised at the time the Library's dictionary catalogs were begun, because there was no solid body of doctrine upon which it would be based; the guiding principles which were then in print for all to read and apply were very meager and concerned themselves with the form of headings and their choice. They did not provide the theoretical basis for a system of headings.[13]

Actual work on the new subject catalog began simultaneously with the printing of the first author cards in July 1898,[14] when it was found necessary to begin an authority list of subject headings. Haykin's earlier quoted statement that there was not a "skeleton list of headings to which additions could be made systematically" might give the impression that the LC list was begun *in vacuo*. In fact, a list of subject headings had been published a few years earlier by the American Library Association;[15] this was conceived as an appendix to Cutter's rules and was designed for use by small and medium-sized public libraries.[16] In a paper presented at the American Library Association (ALA) Conference in 1909, Hanson recounted the beginning of the compilation of the Library of Congress list:

> While it was recognized that the ALA list of subject headings had been calculated for small and medium-sized libraries of a generally popular character, it was nevertheless decided to adopt it as a basis for subject headings with the understanding, however, that considerable modification and specialization would have to be resorted to. As a first step preliminary to the real work of compilation, a number of copies of the List were accordingly provided, a number of blank leaves sufficient to treble the size of the original volume were added, and the copies thereupon bound in flexible leather. . . . New subjects as they came up for discussion and decision were noted on slips and filed. If the subject had already been adopted by the ALA committee, i.e., had appeared as a regular printed heading on the List, a check mark was added to indicate regular adoption by the Library of Congress.[17]

Hanson also indicated that other works were consulted in addition to the ALA list. These included the Decimal and Expansive classifications, the Harvard list of subjects, the New South Wales subject index, Forescue's subject index, and numerous other catalogs, bibliographies, encyclopedias, and dictionaries.

It is generally accepted among those interested in subject access provisions that Cutter's work on subject headings was seminal to that aspect of the field. It is therefore of considerable historical interest how much impact his work had on the architecture and construction of the early LC list. At the time that the Library of Congress was making its first decisions on how to structure its dictionary catalog, his *Rules for a Dictionary Catalog* had been in circulation for more than 30 years and was well regarded in the profession. One would expect it to have had considerable influence on what the Library did in setting up headings for its new catalog. Yet, writing considerably later, Haykin talked about the inadequate theoretical basis of "guiding principles" then in print. He appeared to believe that Cutter's rules had not been found sufficient for LC's needs. At any rate, Cutter's influence has never been officially recognized by the Library of Congress. In fact, in Haykin's *Subject Headings: A Practical Guide*,[18] which was published in 1951 and acknowledged as the official guide in subsequent editions of the list, there are only a few passing references to Cutter's rules. Nor was Cutter ever mentioned in the preface or introduction to any edition of the list. It is only many years later, in a paper presented by Richard S. Angell when he was chief of the Subject Cataloging Division, that we find recognition of Cutter's role:

The final formulation of Cutter's objectives and rules was taking place at the same time that the Library of Congress was expanding and reorganizing the collections at the turn of the century. His work had a considerable influence on the founders of the Library of Congress catalog.[19]

Nevertheless, as we shall see in later chapters, Cutter's influence is quite obvious in Haykin's discussion of the fundamental concepts of LC subject headings: the reader as the focus, unity, usage, and specificity. Furthermore, Cutter's subject heading principles are even now reflected in LCSH in spite of the many modifications and compromises that have been made in the face of practical demands. As Francis Miksa puts it, LCSH is a reflection of Cutter's principles "interpreted through Haykin."[20]

Editions and Versions of the Subject Headings List

Almost from the beginning, the Library of Congress took on the responsibility of giving other libraries an account of its cataloging practices. One channel for such information was the introductions to new editions of the list; another was auxiliary publications bearing on the lists themselves and on subject headings practice. These are discussed briefly below for the information they convey on the development of the system.

Preparation for publishing the list began in 1909, and the first edition appeared in 1914 under the title *Subject Headings Used in the Dictionary Catalogues of the Library of Congress*; since the eighth edition in 1975, the title has been *Library of Congress Subject Headings*. Until 1988, the list was revised and published at five- to nine-year intervals, but it is now kept current continuously, with a new print version published annually. In the early days, printed supplements were issued quarterly and then annually between editions.

The notes below show highlights in the list's development.

1914 (1st ed.)—Included *see* and *see also* references, as well as the list itself.

1943 (4th ed.)—Included a separate list of *refer from* tracers.

1948 (5th ed.)—Incorporated *refer from* references into main list; introduced symbols to denote type of reference.

1966 (7th ed.)—Production was automated, making supplements easier to produce.

1975 (8th ed.)—Title changed to *Library of Congress Subject Headings*. Included a long introduction featuring subdivision practice, as well as a separate list of headings for children's literature; first to be available in microform, in which medium it has been cumulated quarterly ever since.

1986 (10th ed.)—The machine-readable version of LCSH, called *SUBJECTS*, became available; updated by weekly tapes that are distributed to subscribers; nonsubscribers can access them through bibliographic utilities.

1988 (11th ed.)—The list began to be issued annually. Currently, LCSH is also available on CD-ROM. This version is called CDMARC Subjects. It is fully cumulated quarterly.

The *SUBJECTS* file and the microfiche version, called *Library of Congress Subject Headings Cumulative Microform Edition*, do not include the front matter (i.e., preface, introduction, and list of major changes) that appears in the printed version. Nor are changes as clearly noted. Furthermore, many catalogers and most users find the printed list easier to use. For many reasons, therefore, the hardcover version remains useful even in situations with computerized access to LCSH. And, of course, it is essential in libraries or other information agencies that do not yet have online systems.

In this book, the following terms are used to refer to the various versions:

LCSH = the Library of Congress Subject Headings system in general and the list in whatever form

SUBJECTS or "the *SUBJECTS* file" = the machine-readable version

Library of Congress Subject Headings = the print version

LCSH-microfiche = the microform version

CDMARC Subjects = the CD-ROM version

Auxiliary Publications

Not all information needed for the application of LCSH appears in *Library of Congress Subject Headings* or its other versions, which contain main headings, some subdivisions, and cross references. Not only do many headings and subdivisions appear elsewhere, but LC policies and instructions on using LCSH are also found in other publications. These publications began appearing in 1906 and continue to the present day, the latest being *Subject Cataloging Manual*, fourth edition (1991).[21] Because most of the information given in the early publications is now incorporated in editions of *Library of Congress Subject Headings* and the *Subject Cataloging Manual*, these early lists are primarily of historical interest. The following publications issued by the Library of Congress on a regular basis also contain information on policies and actions bearing on subject heading changes:

Cataloging Service Bulletin [published quarterly; contains information about changes in policy, headings, subdivisions, and lists of subject headings of current interest and revised subject headings]

Free-Floating Subdivisions: An Alphabetical Index [published annually; lists all subdivisions designated as *free-floating*, a term referring to form and topical subdivisions that may be assigned by subject catalogers under designated subjects without the usage being formally authorized]

LC Period Subdivisions Under Names of Places [lists subject headings for place-names, with date subdivisions arranged chronologically]

LC Subject Headings Weekly Lists [available through the Internet (telnet MARVEL.LOC.GOV); contains new and revised headings approved at weekly editorial meetings]

Library of Congress Subject Headings: Principles of Structure and Policies for Application, annotated version[22] [commissioned and published by the Library of Congress; outlines the structural principles of LCSH and policies on its application, extracted from various LC documents relating to LCSH]

ASSUMPTIONS ABOUT FUNCTION

In any indexing system, policy decisions on structure and applications reflect the system director's ideas of what it should do for its users. Different notions of a system's objectives lead to different results. Since the late nineteenth century, many statements of what a subject catalog should aim at doing have been published, and some have been received with considerable acclaim. Unfortunately, when one analyzes the question of what these statements call for in practical terms, one finds a vague picture that at best reflects conflicting demands on the catalog.

Cutter's 1876 statement of "objects" has been cited often—and is still cited—as an articulation of the functions of subject entries:

1. To enable a person to find a book of which . . . the subject is known [and]
2. To show what the library has . . . on a given subject [and] in a given kind of literature.[23]

When Cutter was writing, his context was books and libraries, and his access system a card catalog. But his comments can be generalized to a wider milieu. For "a book" read "material"; for "the library has" read "is available."

Cutter's two points are deceptive in the simplicity of their wording. However, to the extent that their meaning can be assumed, they make different demands on an access system. His first point calls for a subject catalog to be simply a tool for location—to be a finding list for users who have a particular item in mind and use a subject term for access. His second point, on the other hand, calls for collocation of material by subject and by genre—a much more demanding task, because here one is dealing with a group of entries rather than individual ones.

Seventy-five years later, Jesse H. Shera and Margaret Egan spelled out eight "objectives for any form of subject cataloging."[24] They called for access by subject to all relevant materials, at any level of analysis, under precisely phrased controlled vocabulary headings that are further differentiated by subheadings and that take subject ramifications into account. They also called for a supporting structure of cross references from variant terms and to affiliated subject fields (affiliated in several different ways), plus information that would allow users to make selections by various criteria. Writing when they did, Shera and Egan recognized that it was impractical for all their objectives to be met—that limitations of personnel and finance would force modifications.[25]

Both the Cutter and Shera/Egan statements were well received when they appeared. Yet as guides to policy-making, they leave fundamental questions unanswered. What is meant by the phrases "of which the subject is known" and "what the library has on a subject"? Or by Shera and Egan's "all relevant materials," "affiliations among subject fields," or "criteria for selection"? How far should cross references go in showing affiliations among subjects? To what units should subject cataloging apply: books, parts of books, series, individual titles in series, serials, journal articles, nonprint materials of various types? How exhaustive should the subject analysis be: many headings per item to cover all concepts, or one or two (ideally one) to summarize its content? Except for general agreement on using headings to summarize, there has been little consensus within the profession on the best answers to these questions.

Since the late 1970s, as LCSH has moved into the online age as a tool of subject retrieval, similar questions relating to function have continued to be asked, and some answers have begun to emerge through catalog use studies. But many questions remain. The latest statement published by the Library of Congress states the functions of LCSH in the following terms:

The Library of Congress subject headings system serves both internal and external needs:

(1) As a controlled vocabulary for subject cataloging of the Library of Congress collection:

> The Library of Congress Subject Headings system was originally designed as a controlled vocabulary for representing the subject and form of the books and serials in the Library of Congress collection, with the purpose of providing subject access points to the bibliographic records contained in the Library of Congress catalogs.

(2) As a controlled vocabulary for use in subject cataloging and indexing by other libraries or indexing agencies:

> As an increasing number of other libraries have adopted the Library of Congress subject headings system, it has become a tool for subject indexing of library catalogs in general. In recent years, it has also been used as a tool in a number of online bibliographic databases outside of the Library of Congress.[26]

NEED FOR A CODE

Many information professionals believe that the inconsistencies and irregularities that have crept into LCSH over the years are due to the fact that the system has grown by accretion without the guidance of a specific code or body of rules. It is clear that while the basic principles of the dictionary catalog laid down by Cutter and reinterpreted by Haykin have been adhered to in general, they have often been compromised in the face of practical constraints. In some cases, the same principles have been interpreted differently on different occasions. There has thus been repeated interest in the question of formulating a code for subject cataloging, corresponding to the one for descriptive cataloging. Interestingly, the only codification of subject heading practice for dictionary catalogs since the publication of Cutter's work has been one in Italian, in the Vatican Library's *Rules for the Catalog of Printed Books*, which was completed in the 1930s and translated into English in 1948.[27] In essence, the subject headings portion of the Vatican code reflected the practice of the Library of Congress at that point in time.

In this country, for many years, the closest thing to a set of rules for subject headings since Cutter was Haykin's *Subject Headings: A Practical Guide* (1951). That work was officially acknowledged as a statement of principles for the choice and form of headings and references.[28] It contains an account and exposition of Library of Congress practice, with occasional apologetics, but is not cast in the form of a code. Nonetheless, Haykin's work was a full and consistent treatment of the practice and guiding principles in operation at that time. In the more than 40 years since it was written, there have been many changes in both the theory and practice of subject analysis.

In the 1950s, in spite of Haykin's work, there was a surge of interest and an intensified call for a code. Carlyle Frarey's survey of catalog use studies[29] and other works on subject headings in the 1940s, had provided the impetus and could have laid the groundwork for a code. There is evidence that Haykin began work on a code in the late 1950s, but unfortunately his work was not completed; the remains of his attempt exist in an unpublished document entitled "Project for a Subject Heading Code."[30] From then until the mid-1980s, there was no formal effort by LC either to continue his project or to begin anew.

In the late 1980s, there was a renewed call for a subject cataloging code, both at professional meetings and in the literature.[31] But no official action took place, on the part of either LC or ALA. In 1990, the Library of Congress published the document *Library of Congress Subject Headings: Principles of Structure and Policies for Application*, which represents an effort at articulating the principles of LCSH and LC's policies. On the international front, under the auspices of IFLA,[32] a working group is developing a document entitled "Principles Underlying Subject Heading Languages," a broad statement regarding the construction and application of subject headings.

More and more retrieval options are becoming available to library users and other information consumers. At the same time, online catalog use studies indicate that subject searches make up the greater fraction of all searches,[33] and that users have difficulties performing subject searches in online catalogs.[34] If that is the case, it is more important than ever to understand our current subject headings system. Proposals for changes in LCSH are inevitable and much to be welcomed. If improvements are to be effective, however, it seems they must spring from a thorough understanding of the current system. Furthermore, the same understanding is required to assess the impact of proposed changes.

Thus, this book is an attempt to examine in greater depth the basic principles underlying LCSH in light of past and recent literature on subject access in general and on LCSH in particular, and to describe with examples the policies of its application at the Library of Congress.

NOTES

[1] In this text, the term "LCSH" is used to refer to the Library of Congress's subject headings *system*; the title of the print version of the subject headings list is given as *Library of Congress Subject Headings*.

[2] Robert P. Holley, "Report on the IFLA Satellite Meeting 'Subject Indexing: Principles and Practices in the 90's,' August 17-18, 1993, Lisbon, Portugal," *Cataloging & Classification Quarterly* 18(2):87-95 (1993); and, *Subject Indexing: Principles and Practices in the 90's.* Proceedings of the IFLA Satellite Meeting held in Lisbon, Portugal, 17-18 August 1993, and sponsored by the IFLA Section on Classification and Indexing and the Instituto da Biblioteca

Nacional e do Livro, Lisbon, Portugal, ed. Robert P. Holley, et al. (München: K. G. Saur, 1995).

[3]National Library of Canada, *Canadian Subject Headings*, 2nd ed. (Ottawa: National Library of Canada, 1985).

[4]Alina Schweitzer, "A Balancing Act Between Conformity and Divergence: Subject Access to Library Materials in Canada," in *Subject Indexing*, 18-19.

[5]*Répertoire de vedettes-matière* (Québec: Bibliothèque de l'Université Laval, 1989- , semiannual).

[6]Suzanne Jouguelet, "Evolution of Subject Indexing Practice in France," in *Subject Indexing*, 64-80.

[7]Eugénio Decourt and Sónia Maria Guerreiro Pacheco, "Subject Access in the Brazilian Library Network BIBLIODATA CALCO," in *Subject Indexing*, 3-11.

[8]Poori Soltani, "Subject Access in Iran," in *Subject Indexing*, 94-108.

[9]Inês Lopes, "Subject Indexing in Portuguese Libraries: A New Approach with SIPORbase," in *Subject Indexing*, 121-43.

[10]Charles A. Cutter, *Rules for a Dictionary Catalog*, 4th ed., rewritten (Washington, D.C.: GPO, 1904).

[11]J. C. M. Hanson, "The Subject Catalogs of the Library of Congress," *Bulletin of the American Library Association* 3 (July 1, 1909): 387.

[12]Library of Congress, Catalog Division, *Subject Headings Used in the Dictionary Catalogues of the Library of Congress* (Washington, D.C.: GPO, Library Branch, 1910-1914).

[13]Library of Congress, Subject Cataloging Division, *Subject Headings Used in the Dictionary Catalogs of the Library of Congress*, 4th ed., ed. Mary Wilson MacNair (Washington, D.C.: Library of Congress, Subject Cataloging Division, 1943), iii.

[14]Hanson, "Subject Catalogs," 387.

[15]*List of Subject Headings for Use in Dictionary Catalogs*, prepared by a Committee of the American Library Association (Boston: Published for the ALA Publishing Section by the Library Bureau, 1895; 2nd ed. rev., 1898; 3rd ed. rev., 1911).

[16]Carlyle J. Frarey, *Subject Headings, The State of the Library Art*, vol. 1, pt. 2 (New Brunswick, N.J.: Graduate School of Library Science, Rutgers—The State University, 1960), 17.

[17]Hanson, "Subject Catalogs," 387, 391.

[18]David Judson Haykin, *Subject Headings: A Practical Guide* (Washington, D.C.: GPO, 1951).

[19]Richard S. Angell, "Library of Congress Subject Headings—Review and Forecast," in *Subject Retrieval in the Seventies: New Directions: Proceedings of an International Symposium*, ed. Hans (Hanan) Wellisch and Thomas D. Wilson (Westport, Conn.: Greenwood Publishing, 1972), 143.

[20]Francis Miksa, *The Subject in the Dictionary Catalog from Cutter to the Present* (Chicago: American Library Association, 1983), 365.

[21]Library of Congress, Office of Subject Cataloging Policy, *Subject Cataloging Manual*, 4th ed. (Washington, D.C.: Cataloging Distribution Service, Library of Congress, 1991).

[22]Lois Mai Chan, *Library of Congress Subject Headings: Principles of Structure and Policies for Application*, annotated version, prepared by Lois Mai Chan for the Library of Congress, *Advances in Library Information Technology*, no. 3 (Washington, D.C.: Cataloging Distribution Service, Library of Congress, 1990).

[23]Cutter, *Rules for a Dictionary Catalog,* 12.

[24]Jesse H. Shera and Margaret Egan, *The Classified Catalog: Basic Principles and Practices* (Chicago: American Library Association, 1956), 10.

[25]Shera and Egan, *The Classified Catalog*, 10.

[26]Chan, *Library of Congress Subject Headings* (1990), 1.

[27]Vatican Library, *Rules for the Catalog of Printed Books*, translated from the 2nd Italian edition by Thomas J. Shanahan, Victor A. Schaefer, and Constantin T. Vesselowsky, and ed. Wyllis E. Wright (Chicago: American Library Association, 1948).

[28]Haykin, *Subject Headings*.

[29]Carlyle J. Frarey, "Studies of Use of the Subject Catalog: Summary and Evaluation," in *Subject Analysis of Library Materials*, ed. Maurice F. Tauber (New York: School of Library Service, Columbia University, 1953), 147-65.

[30]David Judson Haykin, "Project for a Subject Heading Code" (revised: Washington, D.C., 1957), 10p.

[31]William E. Studwell, "The 1990s: Decade of Subject Access: A Theoretical *Code* for LC Subject Headings Would Complete the Maturation of Modern Cataloging," *American Libraries* 18:958 (December 1987); and his "On the Conference Circuit: The Subject Heading *Code*: Do We Have One? Do We Need One?" *Technicalities* 10 (October 1990): 10-15.

[32]This work is being done by the Working Group of the Classification and Indexing Section of the IFLA Division of Bibliographical Control.

[33]Karen Markey, *Subject Searching in Library Catalogs: Before and After the Introduction of Online Catalogs*, OCLC Library, Information, and Computer Science Series 4 (Dublin, Ohio: OCLC, 1984), 77.

[34]Karen Markey Drabenstott and Diane Vizine-Goetz, *Using Subject Headings for Online Retrieval: Theory, Practice, and Potential* (San Diego, Calif.: Academic Press, 1994), 124.

2 Basic Principles

Since the mid-1980s, the Library of Congress has published two documents on its subject headings system that draw together information that was previously scattered among various sources. The documents are *Subject Cataloging Manual*[1] and *Library of Congress Subject Headings: Principles of Structure and Policies for Application.*[2] Until these appeared, persons interested in the principles that underlie the Library of Congress subject headings system had to infer them from a variety of sources: LC practice and policy statements; Cutter's writings; statements by Haykin and other chiefs of the Subject Cataloging Division; Haykin's 1951 book, *Subject Headings: A Practical Guide;*[3] and the system itself. Indeed, the first two editions of this book were based on those sources.

This chapter elaborates the principles governing the formation of topical subject headings[4] as they are enunciated in the LC documents. Further, it discusses those principles in the light of past and current literature on subject analysis. In the literature, the terms most commonly used to denote the various principles are *user* and *usage; literary warrant; uniform* and *unique headings; internal consistency; stability; specificity, direct entry,* and *coextensivity;* and *precoordination* and *postcoordination*. These are discussed below.

THE USER AND USAGE

Since the early days of the catalog, meeting the needs of the user has been deemed the most important function of the catalog. For Cutter, this was the foremost principle in cataloging. In the preface to the 4th edition of *Rules for a Dictionary Catalog,* he stated:

> The convenience of the public is always to be set before the ease of the cataloger. In most cases they coincide. A plain rule without exceptions is not only easy for us to carry out, but easy for the public to understand and work by. But strict consistency in a rule and uniformity in its application sometimes lead to practices which clash with the public's habitual way of looking at things. When these habits are general and deeply rooted, it is unwise for the cataloger to ignore them, even if they demand a sacrifice of system and simplicity.[5]

Haykin called this guiding principle "the reader as a focus":

> . . . the reader is the focus in all cataloging principles and practice. All other considerations, such as convenience and the desire to arrange entries in some logical order, are secondary to the basic rule that the heading, in wording and structure, should be that which the reader will seek in the catalog, if we know or can presume what the reader will look under. To the extent that the headings represent the predilection of the cataloger in regard to terminology and are dictated by conformity to a chosen logical pattern, as against the likely approach of the reader resting on psychological rather than logical grounds, the subject catalog will lose in effectiveness and ease of approach.[6]

What this principle means is self-evident, but how to make it operational is not. The problem lies in the difficulty in delineating or typifying the user.

Cutter did not appear to have difficulty knowing users and usage. In his study on the subject, Francis Miksa offers this explanation: "For Cutter, . . . the public was notably regular in its habits. In fact, he spoke of the habits of the public as being prominent enough to be observed and in a certain sense charted."[7] Users of libraries in Cutter's time probably were relatively homogeneous, as Miksa suggests, and fairly easily defined. However, the continuing emphasis on the "convenience of the public" in the face of changing historical contexts has led to difficulty in defining or delineating the user. As users became more diversified, questions concerning them were being asked constantly: Who is the user? Is there such a thing as a typical user? Many writers on the subject catalog have pointed out the difficulty. Two particularly cogent comments follow:

> What is the "public" which we, in general libraries, serve through the catalog? Children, young people, adults; the expert, the inept, the illiterate, the savant; scientists, artists, authors, teachers and— librarians. Once the diverse nature of the users of the catalog is recognized, it becomes a patent absurdity to speak of cataloging according to the "public" mind as if that mind were a single entity.[8]
> —Marie Louise Prevost (1946)

> Is there such a creature as "the public," or are there many publics, each with its individual varieties and needs? Studies will, no doubt, continue as long as cash can be found to pay for them. Suppose some study were to succeed; suppose it were to show that there is only one user and to identify that user and his needs and habits. Would we dare to build a catalog around those habits and needs? Perhaps not. Habits and needs change; this year's man will not be the same man next year. A catalog built on this year's public's habits and needs might hinder next year's public.[9]
> —Paul S. Dunkin (1969)

Over the years, there have been numerous studies of catalog users in general and of use of the subject catalog in particular. Until fairly recently, none of these studies made it clear who and what kind of person this user was, who was supposed to hold such powerful sway over the form and shape of the catalog. Yet the policy of the "convenience of the public" continued to operate, apparently based on the premise that catalogers understand who users are and how they behave. Since the 1980s, however, the online public catalog has afforded a powerful new tool for catalog use studies, and a series of them have been carried out.[10] From these studies, new profiles of users and user searching behavior are emerging. One significant finding is that a majority of users use the online catalog for subject searching.[11] Another is that, although catalog users remain diverse in their backgrounds, needs, and habits, many of them share a common characteristic: Most have difficulty with the subject searching process in online catalogs.[12] As new studies focus on the sources of this difficulty, information is surfacing that may go far in indicating how LCSH might become a more effective search instrument. Thus, new analytical tools are giving new life to the tenet, "Make the reader the focus."

Related to the question of user needs is the issue of linguistic usage. The Library of Congress policy states: "User needs are best met if headings reflect current usage in regard to terminology. Thus, terms in current use are selected in establishing new subject headings."[13] The desirability of this policy has long been recognized. In naming the subjects in the catalog, Cutter proposed usage of the public as the guiding principle:

> General rules, always applicable, for the choice of names of subjects can no more be given than rules without exception in grammar. Usage in both cases is the supreme arbiter, the usage, in the present case, not of the cataloger but of the public in speaking of subjects.[14]

Haykin phrased the principle of usage in similar terms:

> The heading chosen must represent common usage or, at any rate, the usage of the class of reader for whom the material on the subject within which the heading falls is intended. Usage in an American library must inevitably mean current American usage. Unless this principle is adhered to faithfully most readers will not find the material they desire under the heading which first occurs to them, if they find it at all.[15]

At the same time, almost from the beginning, there has been general agreement that "common usage" cannot always be determined.

Basically, there are two different approaches to the problem of meeting user needs. The first, proposed by Cutter and seconded by Haykin, is to consider usage as the supreme arbiter in the choice of form and language, having priority over logic or philosophy. The second is to develop a system that adheres to logic and strictly formed principles, assuming that a logical and consistent system can be learned by the user. Good arguments can be brought forward for either approach.

A system based on the usage of the public is considered more user-friendly. However, there are problems. For one, given the growing segment of the population that uses libraries and other information services today, term usage is even more diverse than it was when Prevost and Dunkin were voicing their objections to making the approach of "the public" a primary guide for subject cataloging. Practices that depend on variable factors cannot be articulated, and it is difficult to maintain consistency. For another, because of recent technological developments in cataloging, there is a need for a system that can be easily adapted to machine manipulation; in this context, there is an increasing demand for consistency and uniformity, goals that can be achieved through the second approach. In the case of the Library of Congress subject headings list, the question of which approach to take to further development is particularly relevant because the list, which was originally designed for the Library's own collection and users, now serves also as a general standard for a variety of libraries and other retrieval systems, including many outside the United States. Features and characteristics that were developed to meet the demands of a large general research collection are not always suitable in other contexts.

LITERARY WARRANT

Early decisions on the basic source of the concepts represented in LCSH had an important influence on the nature of the list. Writers on controlled-vocabulary subject-access systems frequently point out that there are two fundamentally different ways to build such a system: from the top down, so to speak, deciding what topics constitute the universe of discourse and what terms and interconnectors should be used to represent them; and from the bottom up, looking at what is written and selecting terms and interconnectors based on what is found in the literature. The latter approach is spoken of as building on literary warrant, a concept first put forward by E. Wyndham Hulme.[16] It was literary warrant that governed construction of both the Library of Congress classification and LCSH. The subject headings list was developed in especially close connection with LC's collection; it was not conceived at the outset as—nor has it ever been intended to be—a comprehensive system covering the universe of knowledge. The policy of literary warrant is stated in the preface to the early editions of the headings list: "The list covers subjects in all branches of knowledge so far as the cataloguing of the corresponding classes of books in the Library of Congress progressed."[17]

Systems based on literary warrant grow mainly by accretion. As time passes, logic and consistency suffer in spite of conscientious maintenance efforts. As early as 1943, in the preface of the 4th edition of *Subject Headings Used in the Dictionary Catalogs of the Library of Congress*, Haykin notes failures in logic and consistency in the list and attributes them to the way the list grew. "The failures in logic and consistency are, of course, due to the fact that headings were adopted in turn as needed, and that many minds participated in the choice and establishment of headings."[18]

A further result of any list's growth by literary warrant is that it reflects the nature and size of the collection it was designed to serve; for LCSH, the collection is that of the Library of Congress. LCSH has been criticized for showing a strong U.S. bias; this bias simply reflects the fact that the de facto national library of the United States is naturally heavily oriented toward U.S. materials. In recent years, this bias has been reduced because headings contributed by libraries other than the Library of Congress, based on the needs of their collections, have also been included in the list.

UNIFORM HEADING

It has long been a tenet of subject cataloging practice that, in order to show what a library has on a given subject, each subject should be represented in the catalog under only one name and one form of that name. Uniformity of terms was considered a remedy for the scattering that resulted from the earlier practice of catchword title entry, in which entry was made under a term used by the author of the work being cataloged. A true subject heading gathers all works on the same subject together, regardless of the author's choice of terminology. Haykin called this the *principle of unity*: "A subject catalog must bring together under one heading all the books which deal principally or exclusively with the subject."[19]

The English language is rich in synonyms derived from different linguistic traditions. Many things are called by more than one name, and many concepts can be expressed in more than one way. Even within one country, variant names for the same object or concept often occur in different geographic areas. There are also many near-synonyms, so close in meaning that it is impractical to establish them as separate subject headings. In all these cases, one of the several possible terms is chosen as the subject heading. If the term chosen appears in different forms or spellings, only one form is used.

However, it should be noted that the objective of listing all books on the same subject together can also be fulfilled by listing all works on that subject under each possible name or form. In other words, if a collection has 20 items on a subject that can be expressed in five different terms, it is possible to list all the items repeatedly under each heading. However, although this was physically workable, it was not economically feasible in the card catalog; even in the online catalog the practice causes problems because of difficulty in maintaining consistency. Thus, the principle of uniform headings is still honored, with choices among candidate expressions conforming as far as possible to prevailing usage.

In establishing a subject heading, three choices are often required: name (word or word string for the entity or concept), form (grammatical construction), and entry element. When a subject has more than one name, one must be chosen as the heading to represent all materials on that subject, regardless of authors' usage. For example, in LCSH, the heading **Ethics** was chosen from among *Ethics, Deontology, Ethology, Moral philosophy, Moral science, Morality,* and *Morals.* Similarly, **Oral medication** was chosen in preference to *Drugs by mouth, Medication by mouth,* and *Peroral medication.*

Frequently, a word may be spelled in different ways (e.g., *Esthetics* or *Aesthetics, Hotbeds* or *Hot-beds, Marihuana* or *Marijuana).* Again, only one of the spellings is used in a heading.

Another choice is needed when the name chosen for a heading can be expressed in grammatically different forms (i.e., a phrase, a term with a qualifier, or a term with a subdivision or subdivisions). For example, a choice must be made between *Surgical diagnosis* and *Surgery—Diagnosis,* and between *Cookery (Shrimp)* and *Cookery—Shrimp.*

A further decision on the entry element may also be necessary if the term contains two or more elements and both or all could possibly serve as an entry point. For example:

Cookery—Shrimp
Shrimp—Cookery

Diagnosis, Surgical
Surgical diagnosis

Plants, Effect of light on
Effect of light on plants
Light on plants, Effect of

The decision on the entry element is extremely important in a manual catalog in which each heading is accessed by the first word only. In an online catalog, the order of words has little bearing on access and retrieval but is still important in index display.

In LCSH a heading in the form of a phrase may be established in its natural word order or in the inverted form, but not both. In this type of heading, the principle of uniform heading is observed almost without exception. In other forms of headings, especially headings with subdivisions, exceptions to the practice of uniform heading are sometimes made, particularly when the two components of a heading are equally significant. For example:

United States—Foreign relations—France

France—Foreign relations—United States

These are duplicate headings in the true sense of the term; they are identical or reciprocal in wording, though with different entry elements. Such duplicate entries are needed in the manual catalog in order to provide additional access points. Again, the need disappears in online catalogs with search options of any sophistication, but the practice continues to a limited extent. However, no new types of reciprocal headings are being established.

Perhaps the major choice in establishing new headings is the choice among candidate synonyms. As stated earlier, the guiding principle in the choice has been "current American usage."[20] Cutter, Haykin, and other writers have also offered general guidelines regarding choice of terms in the following categories: synonymous terms, variant spellings, English and foreign terms, technical (or scientific) and popular terms, and obsolete and current terms.[21]

Choice Among Synonymous Terms

The Library of Congress' guideline regarding choice among synonyms states:

> When an object or concept may be expressed by synonyms, the term chosen as the heading is the one that represents the best possible balance among the criteria of being unbiased, familiar to users, and unambiguous in meaning (having fewest meanings other than the sense in which it is used).[22]

Near-synonymous terms also present a problem. Thelma Eaton noted: "Much more of a problem than synonyms are the near-synonymous terms. . . . There are other subjects that are not exactly the same, but they are closely related and it is easy to put them together under one heading."[23] Cutter's instruction concerning near-synonymous terms is: "In choosing between two names not exactly synonymous, consider whether there is difference enough to require separate entry; if not, treat them as synonymous."[24] In LCSH, there are many examples of near-synonyms treated as synonyms. For example, *Theological education* is treated as a synonym of **Religious education**, and *Freedom* is treated as a synonym of **Liberty**.

Choice Between Variant Spellings

A special case of synonymy is variation in spelling. Needless to say, a current spelling is preferred to an obsolete one at the time of establishing a heading. If one or more spellings of the same word are equally current, the one most familiar to the largest numbers of users, based on reference sources, is chosen. For variant spellings that are in use concurrently, U.S. spellings are preferred, e.g., **Labor** instead of *Labour*; **Catalog** instead of *Catalogue*. In other cases, the choice follows *Webster's Third New International Dictionary* (e.g., **Aesthetics** instead of *Esthetics*; **Archaeology** instead of *Archeology*).

Choice Between English and Foreign Terms

The choice between an English and a foreign term would appear to be obvious; a system designed to serve English-speaking users should naturally rely on English terms. Yet there are exceptions. Cutter's rule concerning language states: "When possible let the heading be in English, but a foreign word may be used when no English word expresses the subject of a work."[25] Haykin stated the rule as follows:

> Foreign terms should be used only under the following conditions:
> (1) when the concept is foreign to Anglo-American experience and no satisfactory term for it exists, e.g., *Reallast, Précieuses*; and (2) when, especially in the case of scientific names, the foreign term is precise, whereas the English one is not, e.g., *Ophiodon elongatus*, rather than *Buffalo cod* or *Blue cod*; *Pityrosporum ovale*, rather than *Bottle bacillus*. Terms of foreign origin, which retain their foreign form, but which have been incorporated into the English vocabulary are, of course, to be regarded as English words, e.g., *Terrazzo, Sauerkraut*.[26]

The Library of Congress chooses English terms as a matter of general policy.[27] However, in a case where there is no English term for the concept, and the concept is normally expressed in the foreign term even in English-language works and reference sources, the foreign term is chosen, as, for example, with **Coups d'état, Tsunamis,** and **Bonsai**.

Choice Between Technical (or Scientific) and Popular Terms

On the choice between a scientific or popular term for a concept or entity, Cutter stated:

> A natural history society will of course use the scientific name, a town library would equally of course use the proper name—**Butterflies** rather than **Lepidoptera, Horse** rather than *Equus caballus*. But the scientific may be preferable when the common name is ambiguous or of ill-defined extent.[28]

Haykin echoed Cutter's comment:

> Whether a popular term or a scientific one is to be chosen depends on several considerations. If the library serves a miscellaneous public, it must prefer the popular to the scientific term. It may even prefer it, if the proper term is commonly used in the professional or scientific literature; in speaking of the genus bee in general, for example, even the scientists will use the term "bee" rather than *Apis*. However, the popular term must be precise and unambiguous.[29]

On another occasion, Haykin further explained:

> The choice is not difficult because, obviously, in a catalog intended for a miscellaneous public the popular term must be used as the kind most likely to be resorted to by the largest group of users, whereas scientific terms, although usually more precise in their meanings, will be sought by the specialist in each field and are, therefore, suitable for a special library catalog.[30]

The user is the focus in both Cutter's and Haykin's statements. Both allow that the choice must be different in a library serving a general public from that in a library serving specialists. In LCSH popular terms are generally used if they are in common use and unambiguous (e.g., **Cockroaches** instead of *Blattariae*; **Lizards** instead of *Lacertilia*). However, for animals and plants, while the common name is preferred, the Latin name is chosen if the common name represents several levels (e.g., species, genus, family) or is not in general lay usage, or if the organism occurs only in a foreign country or countries.

Choice Between Obsolete and Current Terms

In establishing a new heading, a current term is easily chosen over an obsolete one, provided that one is clearly more current than another. The only problem is, how does one recognize an obsolete term? Personal knowledge of the language is a help but not always a reliable guide. Frequently, outside sources must be consulted. Dictionaries seem to be the natural tool. Haykin, however, noted that dictionaries do not usually indicate a choice on the basis of currentness.[31] He recommended periodicals as the "surest sources" of usage because they carry the most current literature on various subjects. However, in dealing with new subjects, a heading is needed immediately, often before its terminology is settled, as recognized in the *Subject Cataloging Manual*:

> Headings are usually established to reflect current American usage for a concept, but sometimes no consensus has yet developed among the authorities in a given field as to the proper terminology for the concept. When establishing a new heading in such a situation, make an intuitive judgment based on available evidence (in some cases only the work being cataloged) by selecting elements that will allow the heading to express what is intended and at the same time serve as a retrieval term in the system.[32]

A new invention or concept is sometimes called different names by different people, and the cataloger is in the position of having to choose among several possible names without much help or guidance from outside sources. One example is the choice of *Electronic calculating-machines* as the heading for computers when they first appeared, a heading that was later replaced by **Computers**.

The ideal of currentness in a catalog or index requires that terminology be updated when it is no longer current. Haykin pointed out the need for constant revision:

> [The cataloger] must use the term in the sense in which it is currently used, regardless of the older literature in and out of the catalog. This leads inevitably to a policy of constant change in order to maintain the catalog up to date. To put this policy into effect the cataloger must substitute the latest heading for the one which is obsolescent or obsolete and must refer the reader to the current heading from the headings which have fallen into disuse.[33]

Until the mid-1970s the Library of Congress had been rather conservative in revising obsolete headings; indeed, in the 1960s and 1970s, outdated terminology was the most criticized aspect of the list, much more so than its structural aspects. An example of such criticism was Sanford Berman's analysis of subject headings relating to people.[34] In recent years, the Library of Congress has been much more responsive to changing language usage, in part because computer technology has greatly facilitated changes. Nevertheless, because the Library's automated system does not allow global change, many bibliographic records still carry obsolete headings that must be corrected one by one.

UNIQUE HEADING

A corollary to the principle of uniform heading is that of unique heading; that is, the principle that each heading should represent only one subject. Homographs are the issue here. In order to minimize irrelevant documents in retrieval, words that are spelled the same but have different meanings must be distinguished. Cutter's rule states: "Carefully separate the entries on different subjects bearing the same name, or take some other heading in place of one of the homonyms."[35] Frequently, "some other heading" may not be available. In such a case, a modifier is added to differentiate between the homographs, as in **Cold; Cold (Disease)** and **Rings (Algebra); Rings (Gymnastics)**, so that each heading represents only one subject or concept.

SPECIFIC ENTRY AND COEXTENSIVITY

Specific and Direct Entry

In general, each subject in LCSH is represented by the most specific, or precise, term naming the subject, rather than a broader or generic term that encompasses the subject. In other words, the term used to represent a subject is coextensive with the subject. In rare cases, a broader term may be used when the most specific term is considered too narrow and therefore not likely to be sought by catalog users.

In the literature, the concepts of specificity (or specific entry) and direct entry are almost always addressed together. For that reason, they are discussed together here. It is worth noting, however, that the two concepts are quite different in nature. Specificity is a many-faceted notion, used in talking about terms themselves and about the match between the meaning of a given term and the content of the document to which it is applied. The concept of directness involves the way a heading of given specificity is presented, by itself or in context. An entry with the heading **Red fescue** is a direct entry, while an entry with equal specificity in the form of *Plants—Range plants—Grasses—Fescue—Red fescue* is a typical indirect entry one would find in a classed catalog. The difference between the concepts of specificity and directness is not always recognized, a fact that often makes it difficult to ferret out what writers mean when they talk about specificity and specific entry.

Cutter explained the rule of specific entry as: "Enter a work under its subject-heading, not under the heading of a class which includes the subject. . . . Put Lady Cust's book on 'The cat' under **Cat**, not under **Zoology** or **Mammals**, or **Domestic animals**; and put Garnier's 'Le fer' under **Iron**, not under **Metals** or **Metallurgy**."[36] The Vatican code states the principle of specific entry in these terms: "Works are recorded under their specific subjects, and not under the names and designations of the classes and disciplines to which they belong, e.g., **Poll-tax**, not **Taxation** or **Finance**."[37]

From these statements and examples, it would appear that the difference between the classed catalog and the dictionary catalog in the treatment of the subject "cats" represents a choice between **Zoology** and **Cats** as the subject heading. Such is, in fact, not the case. In a classed catalog, the heading for a book on cats would presumably be *Zoology—Vertebrates—Mammals—Domestic animals—Cats*, and not **Zoology** alone. In terms of the degree of specificity, this heading is as specific as the heading **Cats**. The real difference is in the choice of the entry element or the access point in the catalog. In a classed catalog, in order to find the subject "cats," the user must look under **Zoology** (or in an accompanying index), while in the dictionary catalog, the subject is listed under **Cats** without intervening elements. This is what is meant by direct entry: The user looks directly under the term that specifically describes the topic rather than under a broader term that includes the specific term as a subdivision.

In order to achieve the benefit of direct access in the catalog, the advantages of subject collocation must be abandoned. However, in the course of the development of the dictionary catalog in U.S. libraries, there seems to have been a desire to have the best of both worlds, to retain some of the advantages of the classed catalog in grouping related subjects together. This was especially true in the earlier stages, when users as well as makers of subject headings were still accustomed to the classed catalog. As a result, many headings that are characteristic of a classed catalog were introduced into dictionary catalogs over the years.

Concept of Specificity

There is another source of difficulty with the principle of specific entry beyond the fact that it is often confused or melded with the notion of direct entry. This difficulty comes in defining the very concept of specificity. From Cutter on, there have been various attempts at definition.

Cutter: "Enter a work under its subject-heading, not under the heading of a class which includes that subject."[38]

Haykin: "The heading should be as specific as the topic it is intended to cover. As a corollary, the heading should not be broader than the topic."[39]

Oliver Linton Lilley, in an inquiry into the meaning and nature of specificity, identifies at least four types of relationships that determine its nature:

1. Specificity is in part a function of a particular subject area.

2. Specificity is in part a function of a particular library.

3. Specificity is in part a function of a particular book.

4. Specificity is in part a function of a searcher's exact need in a particular moment of time.[40]

Later writers on subject analysis continue to search for a workable definition of specificity. Among the more successful attempts are the studies by John Balnaves and Elaine Svenonius. Balnaves summarizes five interrelated but distinguishable aspects of the term:

1. The manner in which one term can be said to be subordinate to, and more specific than another in a hierarchical arrangement of terms . . .

2. The extent to which a characteristic which distinguishes a document class is precisely labelled by a descriptor . . .

3. The extent to which each descriptor provides direct access to the file for the class of documents which it labels . . .

4. The extent to which each descriptor is a precise and exact label for the smallest class to which a document belongs . . .

5. The extent to which descriptors are assigned to classes to which parts of documents belong, as well as to classes to which the whole document belongs.[41]

His final conclusion is: "Whatever improves precision is specificity."

Svenonius identifies seven types of specificity. They are, in summary:

(i) Formal Specificity: Specificity can be defined in terms of the logical relation of class inclusion.

(ii) Extensional Specificity: In ordinary language the specificity relation (regarded as inclusion) is used with logical precision when it holds between classes that can be clearly defined in extensional or referential terms.

(iii) Phrase-length Specificity: One extension of the inclusion relation into the domain of non-referential language is when specification is regarded as modifying. There are exceptions, but generally it holds that a word modified is more specific than the word unmodified.

(iv) Coercive Specificity: The specificity relation can be defined more or less well by enumerating all the pairs of objects (words) between which the relation is supposed to hold.

(v) Componential Specificity: A quantitative measure of specificity has been developed by Thyllis Williams. Roughly, the specificity of a word is proportional to the complexity of its dictionary definition, where definition complexity is understood in terms of both the descriptive components and the syntax of the definition.

(vi) Consensus Specificity: Presumably there exists some partial consistency in different people's opinions about specificity, a consensus whose bounds are unknown but which might be measurable using sociolinguistic experimental methods.

(vii) Operational Specificity: Operational specificity is defined in the context of indexing, or assigning subject headings to books in a library. The operational specificity of an index term is the number of books in the collection indexed by the term. Operational specificity is decidedly relative, but it is so in a clear, mathematically measurable way. Its relativity reflects the very legitimate variability not of "specific," but of "specific (precise) enough for some purpose." Further, the definition of operational specificity goes some way to make explicit the concept of specificity as it is understood in the application of the specific entry principle. It does this insofar as the function of the principle is to regulate the number of entries that accumulate under any one heading. Moreover, an operational definition of specificity is useful in that it provides a method for systematically varying indexing specificity. That is, the definition makes it possible to approach experimentally the question: "How specific is specific?"[42]

Although these writers differ in their approaches and definitions of the concept of specificity, there appears to be a certain degree of agreement that specificity is a relative term and must be viewed in a particular context. The term takes on different meanings depending on the context. Some of the common frames of reference in which the concept of specificity has been defined are discussed below.

(1) *Specificity in relation to the hierarchical structure of a particular indexing language.* This is sometimes referred to as term specificity, or what Metcalfe calls "subject specification."[43] The specificity of a term is defined in relation to other terms in the same indexing language. In this context, the indexing term on a lower level of a hierarchical chain is said to be more specific than one on a higher level. In this respect, the relationship between general and specific terms is similar to that of broad and narrow terms. Thus, **Cats** is more specific than **Mammals**, which in turn is more specific than **Vertebrates**.

Although the specificity of a term can be easily ascertained in a two-dimensional hierarchical chain containing single-concept terms, problems arise when multidimensional hierarchies containing complex terms are involved. For example, it can be easily recognized that **Stomach** is more specific than **Digestive organs**, and that **Ulcers** is more specific than **Diseases**. It is not easy, however, to determine whether **Stomach—Diseases** or **Digestive organs—Ulcers** is the more specific term. In such cases, the notions of specificity and generality become difficult to define.

Another problem relating to term specificity is how to determine the optimal level of specificity in a particular indexing language. On this question, F. W. Lancaster makes the following observation:

> However often a term is used in indexing, it is unjustified if, over a two-year period (for instance), it has never been used in searching. This might indicate that the term is unnecessarily specific, but indexers use it because it is available and documents exist on the specific topic. Even so, requests are never made this specifically in the particular subject area, so a term at this level of specificity is redundant.[44]

An alternative to relying on frequency of use in searching as the criterion of term specificity is to view specificity in terms of frequency of application in indexing, as suggested by G. Salton and C. S. Yang:

> Term specificity . . . may be assumed to be related to the number of documents to which a given term is assigned in a given collection, the idea being that the smaller the document frequency, that is, the more concentrated the assignment of a term to only a few documents in a collection, the more likely it is that a given term is reasonably specific.[45]

In her discussion of "operational specificity," Svenonius puts forth a similar view: "The operational specificity of an index term or subject heading is defined as the number of items in the collection indexed by the term, that is the number of postings made to the term; or in other words, the specificity of a term is its frequency of occurrence."[46] In this sense, the specificity of any term is relative to a particular collection of documents. As pointed out by Angell, the level of specificity should be determined "by the characteristics of the demands which are made upon an information system in a particular application or installation."[47]

(2) *Specificity in regard to literary warrant.* One can also think of specificity in terms of how closely the terms in the thesaurus or subject headings list match the topics in the collection being indexed. This type of specificity certainly holds for the match between LCSH and the LC collection. The selection of terms for LCSH, in fact, has from the beginning been based on what has been needed to catalog the collection at the Library of Congress. New headings are established as they are required in cataloging the Library's collection, and subdivisions are often developed because of the large number of postings under a particular heading in the catalog. However, as the system has been adopted by many other libraries, the determination of the optimal degree of this type of specificity poses a unique problem for those responsible for its development and maintenance. Because the list has become the standard for all but very small libraries and some specialized libraries, it must now try to perform the impossible task of being all things to all people. The various demands placed on the system by other libraries, many of which are vastly different in size, function, and clientele, are often incompatible and even conflicting. As a result, it has been difficult to achieve consistency and uniformity in term selection.

(3) *Specificity in relation to the document being indexed.* In this case, a specific heading is one that coincides with, or corresponds to, the content of the document being represented. Metcalfe uses the term *document specification*[48] for this aspect of specificity. Another term now often used to express this aspect of specificity is *coextensivity*. The degree to which this kind of specificity is achieved is partly the function of the indexing language and partly that of application in the indexing process. In this respect, the specificity of a particular indexing term is viewed in relation to the document to which it is assigned, not to its place in the hierarchical structure of the indexing language. A specific heading is not necessarily a narrow one, nor a general heading always a broad one. In other words, *general* is not synonymous with *broad*, nor *specific* with *narrow*. For example, the heading **Zoology** is generally considered broad, and the heading **Cats** narrow. **Zoology** is general when applied to a work about cats. However, for a work of zoology, **Zoology** becomes as specific as **Cats** is for a work about cats. On the other hand, **Cats,** when applied to a work about Siamese cats, is a general heading. In this context, a specific heading is one that corresponds to the content of the document to which it is applied, while a general heading is one that represents the class to which the subject content of the document is subordinate. Library of Congress views on this matter appear in the following statements:

> The heading that represents precisely the subject content of the work is assigned as the primary subject heading, unless such a heading does not exist and cannot be established.[49]

> Specificity means that subject headings should exactly cover the topic of the work cataloged, being neither broader [n]or narrower than the topic. . . . Specificity is not a property of an

individual term or subject heading, but is relative to the relationship between the term or subject heading and the work to which it is applied. The "broad" heading "Economics" is specific when applied to a general work on economics.[50]

Whether coextensivity is always desirable is open to question. There seems to be a general assumption that perfectly coextensive headings should be used if possible. However, in practice this assumption has not always held. In fact, Haykin went so far as to write, "there are limits to the principle of specificity . . . beyond which its application does not appear to serve the best interest of the reader."[51] The answers to the coextensivity question must necessarily vary with regard to the nature and extent of the collection and the needs of the users. At the Library of Congress, attempts are generally made to achieve coextensivity by assigning specific headings whenever they are available, by creating such headings, or by assigning several separate headings (each broader than the content of the document being cataloged) in order to cover various aspects of a complex subject. (This last practice is discussed further in chapter 8.)

(4) *Specificity with regard to the depth of indexing*. Frequently, the term *specificity* is used to refer to depth of indexing. Indexing may be at the document level (summarization), where the subject headings represent the overall content of the document, or it may be at a deeper (unit or chapter) level, where the terms chosen represent the individual components. Depth indexing results in a large number of headings assigned to each document in order to cover the individual parts or units within the document. The number of terms assigned depends primarily on indexing policy, not on the nature of the indexing language; the same thesaurus or subject headings list can in most cases be used either way. The degree of the depth of indexing is generally determined by the demands of the users and, not infrequently, by the availability of personnel and resources. The Library of Congress generally follows a policy of summarization rather than indexing in depth. (This aspect of LC practice is discussed in detail in chapter 8.)

INTERNAL CONSISTENCY

It has been an almost tacit assumption from the beginning that a subject catalog should be internally consistent. Predictability is an essential factor in successful subject retrieval, and predictability is higher if, under analogous circumstances, a given heading pattern recurs throughout the system. Thus, consistency as well as stability is a factor in end-user ease of consultation. At the thesaurus construction stage, taking internal consistency as a goal calls for using similar forms and structures in headings for similar topics.

Svenonius, in a discussion on the design of controlled vocabularies, notes a problem with this approach: "Consistency considerations, introduced often for the sake of structure, primarily affect term form and frequently conflict with the dictates of common usage."[52] Cutter and Haykin both claimed that, for subject headings, general usage should take precedence over logic and consistency.[53] In so doing, they seemed to be deviating from the prior claim of logical consistency and arguing for exceptions. Haykin, in a different source,[54] also rationalized "failures in logic and consistency" by the fact that headings were adopted over time and many minds participated in their choice.

At the Library of Congress, wherever feasible, attempts are made to maintain consistency in form and structure among analogous headings through the use of recurring patterns.[55] This is not always possible, however, because for any new heading under consideration, analogous headings may show different patterns. This happens often, especially when a complex heading is proposed. To date, no far-reaching effort has been made to revise existing headings to ensure that analogous headings show the same grammatical structure and form.

STABILITY

One principle underlying LCSH receives little attention in the literature but still must be kept in mind by anyone studying the system with an eye to the future. This principle calls for maintaining as much stability in the system as is compatible with keeping it responsive to changing conditions.

In respect to other institutions using LCSH, taking stability as a goal means that change is gradual enough that they are not often faced with changes that place great demands on their personnel and other resources, either with learning what is new or with doing whatever is needed to bring existing provisions into conformation. Even doing no more than mapping old headings onto new ones and vice versa is a labor-intensive operation, requiring resources that may not easily be spared. In respect to end-users—library patrons or persons using other LCSH-based retrieval tools—keeping LCSH relatively stable means that once they become familiar with the system, they are not faced, on further use, with something that has changed drastically and must be relearned. For them, "convenience of the user" requires that remembered search patterns still work.

As can be seen, stability and responsiveness to changed circumstances are conflicting goals. In the challenge of revision, in the excitement of developing a system that is fully up-to-date, it is easy to overlook the advantages of system stability. The expected benefits of each proposed change must be carefully assessed to take its cost of implementation and its end-user inconvenience (if any) into account. Almost always, changes are improvements and worth their costs. Still, it can be a mistake not to calculate those costs.

PRECOORDINATION AND POSTCOORDINATION

Generally, the content of a document falls into one of the following categories:

(1) a single object or concept, or single objects or concepts treated separately in a work, e.g., *Flowers; Flowers and shrubs*

(2) aspects of an object or concept, e.g., *Fertilization of flowers; Arrangement of flowers; Collecting and preserving flowers*

(3) two or more objects or concepts treated in relation to each other, e.g., *Flowers in art; Flowers and insects*

It is clear from this list that except for single objects or concepts, document content cannot always or even often be represented by single terms or simple adjectival phrases. When this is the case, specificity must be achieved by other means. In this context, Mortimer Taube identifies two types of specificity: "the specificity of a specific word or phrase and whatever degree of subdivision is allowed" and "the specificity achieved by the intersection, coordination, or logical product of terms of equal generality."[56]

Category 1 (single object or concept) above presents a problem only when a document treats a topic at a deeper level of specificity than is allowed for in the indexing vocabulary, or when users are not expected to approach the system at such a level of specificity. Frequently with category 2 (aspects) and always with category 3 (relationships), a single term is not sufficient, so that to achieve the specificity required, two or more terms must be used. In many cases, a phrase is used to combine two or more general terms, either of which is broader than the resulting heading (e.g., *Fertilization of flowers*; *Flowers in art*; *Effect of light on plants*). Another way to represent complexity is to use two or more separate terms without indicating the nature of their relationship; for example, a document might be assigned the two headings *Flowers* and *Fertilization*. Such an approach leaves it to searchers to track down documents indexed with terms reflecting all the aspects of the topics that interest them.

The two different approaches are called *precoordination* and *postcoordination*. In a precoordinate system, terms for a topic and its aspects are linked at the time of indexing, with prepositions or other devices (punctuation or the structure of the string) showing how the terms interrelate. In a postcoordinate system, terms for the main subject and its aspects are simply listed separately. Searchers combine the terms at the point of retrieval. Most modern indexing systems are postcoordinate. LCSH, like many systems originating from the manual environment, is basically precoordinate. Precoordinate headings, when available, are assigned to works on complex subjects, and new precoordinate headings are constantly being established. On the other hand, because no system can be totally precoordinate, catalogers at the Library of Congress often take a postcoordinate approach.

There have been complex headings in the Library of Congress list since the early editions. But because policies regarding their formation have varied, the list as a whole shows many inconsistencies. A statement from the Library of Congress acknowledges this: "Although LCSH is primarily a precoordinate system, practice under many headings requires postcoordination in order to achieve specificity. There are numerous cases in which we do not combine elements in the heading itself or in subdivisions in order to be specific. Decisions can be determined by looking at LC cataloging."[57]

Precoordination

In a precoordinate system, the combination of multiple topics or facets may take place either before the heading enters the vocabulary or before it is assigned to a document. In the former approach, called *enumeration,* complex headings are enumerated in the list; while in the latter, called *synthesis*, individual terms are listed separately to be combined by the cataloger or indexer.

Enumeration

In early editions of *Library of Congress Subject Headings*, almost all precoordinate headings were enumerated (that is, appeared as such) in the list. Over the years, however, the Library of Congress has taken an increasingly analytico-synthetic approach, through subdivisions and phrase patterns that subject catalogers or indexers may freely combine, within guidelines and as appropriate. Enumerated complex headings in LCSH show the following patterns. Some are relatively simple:

- Adjectival phrases

  Economic forecasting
  Plant diseases
  Plant inspection

- Phrases containing conjunctions (representing partial synonymy)

  Boats and boating
  Reporters and reporting

- Phrases containing conjunctions (representing relationships)

  Architecture and solar radiation
  Church and education
  Television and politics

- Phrases containing prepositions

  Choruses, Secular (Unison) with instrumental ensemble
  Fertilization of plants
  Flowers in literature
  Speech perception in children

- Headings with subdivisions

    Church architecture—Italy
    Physics—Research
    Plants—Identification

- Combinations of the forms above

    Church and labor—Italy
    Clocks and watches in art
    Piano, trumpet, viola with orchestra—Scores

Others are highly complex and specific:

Church maintenance and repair (Ecclesiastical law)
Suites (Clarinets (2), horns (2), violins (2), viola, double bass)
Tariff on recreation equipment and supplies

When dealing with complex subjects for which there are precoordinate headings, cataloging consists of finding the best match between the work being cataloged and the available precombined headings.

Synthesis

When a precoordinate heading that would suit a particular work is not enumerated in LCSH, a heading may be synthesized by combining elements according to appropriate procedures. Especially since the mid-1970s, the Library of Congress has relied more on synthesis than enumeration for precoordinate complex headings. This development is consistent with the progress taking place in the field of indexing. As Svenonius states, "Probably the most significant development in index language construction in the twentieth century is the move from largely enumerative index languages to largely synthetic ones."[58]

Synthesis in LCSH is achieved mainly through the use of free-floating subdivisions, a device that allows the combination of a main term with terms representing common aspects of subjects without requiring that each combination be authorized. Typically, such synthesized headings do not appear in the list. Thus, many highly complex headings appear in bibliographic records but not in *Library of Congress Subject Headings*, such as:

France—History—Revolution, 1789-1799—Literature and the revolution

Lawyers—United States—Discipline—Cases

Social studies—Study and teaching (Elementary)—United States

Teenagers—United States—Books and reading

Synthesis renders a precoordinate subject indexing system much more flexible because it allows many more possible combinations than an enumerative system can accommodate. However, LCSH is not totally synthetic, as some systems are. There are stringent limits regarding how elements may be combined, and in learning to use the system, a great deal of effort must be spent on recognizing them. Synthesis of subject strings is discussed in detail in chapter 5.

An important factor in synthesizing precoordinate headings is the order, called *citation order*, in which terms are combined in headings. In LCSH, the increasing reliance on synthesis has not been accompanied by well-established citation order rules. The resulting lack of a predictable order for the elements in a subject string limits retrieval effectiveness, especially when headings are displayed in a list. One source of trouble is that different citation orders for the same terms may result in headings with different meanings, such as **Science—Indexes—Periodicals** (meaning a journal of scientific indexes) and **Science—Periodicals—Indexes** (meaning an index to scientific journals).

In 1991, the Library of Congress took a step towards normalization of the use of subdivisions: the Subject Subdivisions Conference was held in Airlie, Virginia, to discuss the future of subdivisions in the LCSH system. From this conference emerged six recommendations, the first of which concerns a fixed citation order for combining subdivisions.[59] The question of citation order is discussed in detail in chapters 5 and 11.

Postcoordination

In cataloging a work on a complex subject for which there is no coextensive heading in LCSH and for which one cannot be synthesized, the subject cataloger at the Library of Congress may either propose a new heading as required for the work being cataloged (a procedure currently preferred)[60] or choose to use several existing headings (i.e., take the postcoordinate approach), such as:

Title: *Pandaemonium : ethnicity in international politics* / Daniel Patrick Moynihan. 1993

SUBJECTS:
> **World politics—1989-**
> **Ethnicity.**
> **Nationalism.**
> **Ethnic relations.**

In dealing with a complex subject for which no single heading exists, it is sometimes difficult to predict whether the Library of Congress will take the precoordinate or the postcoordinate approach. Catalogers outside the Library of Congress, not knowing whether the Library of Congress will create a specific heading for the complex subject (and, if so, which form it will take), tend to assign several existing headings to cover the various elements and aspects treated in the document. For example, LCSH contains the heading **Nuns as public school teachers**, but no single heading *Public school teachers*. Until such a heading is established—a likely occurrence when a subject cataloger at the Library of Congress encounters a work on that subject— subject catalogers outside of LC will probably assign such a work two headings, **Public schools** and **Teachers**. Currently, with the exception of free-floating subdivisions and phrases, there are yet no established guidelines regarding when terms may be combined to form precoordinate headings and when the cataloger should take the post-coordinate approach. Catalogers either follow existing patterns or determine each case as the question arises.

NOTES

[1]Library of Congress, Office of Subject Cataloging Policy, *Subject Cataloging Manual*, 4th ed. (Washington, D.C.: Library of Congress, 1991), H315.

[2]Lois Mai Chan, *Library of Congress Subject Headings: Principles of Structure and Policies for Application*, annotated version, prepared by Lois Mai Chan for the Library of Congress, *Advances in Library Information Technology*, no. 3 (Washington, D.C.: Cataloging Distribution Service, Library of Congress, 1990).

[3]David Judson Haykin, *Subject Headings: A Practical Guide* (Washington, D.C.: GPO, 1951), 7.

[4]Topical headings are those representing concepts, objects, or forms. Proper names are also used as subject headings. Personal, corporate, and geographic headings representing jurisdictions are governed by *Anglo-American Cataloguing Rules*.

[5]Charles A. Cutter, *Rules for a Dictionary Catalog*, 4th ed., rewritten (Washington, D.C.: GPO, 1904), 6.

[6]Haykin, *Subject Headings*, 7.

[7]Francis Miksa, *The Subject in the Dictionary Catalog from Cutter to the Present* (Chicago: American Library Association, 1983), 74.

[8]Marie Louise Prevost, "An Approach to Theory and Method in General Subject Heading," *Library Quarterly* 16 (2) (April 1946): 140.

[9]Paul S. Dunkin, *Cataloging U.S.A.* (Chicago: American Library Association, 1969), 141-42.

[10]Carol A. Mandel and Judith Herschman, "Subject Access in the Online Catalog" (a report prepared for the Council on Library Resources, August 1981); Charles R. Hildreth, *Online Public Access Catalogs: The User Interface* (Dublin, Ohio: OCLC, 1982); Joseph R. Matthews, Gary S. Lawrence, and Douglas K. Ferguson, eds., *Using Online Catalogs: A Nationwide Study* (New York: Neal-Schuman, 1983); Karen Markey, *The Process of Subject Searching in the Library Catalog* (Dublin, Ohio: OCLC, 1983); Karen Markey, *Subject Searching in Library Catalogs: Before and After the Introduction of Online Catalogs* (Dublin, Ohio: OCLC, 1984); Karen Markey Drabenstott and Diane Vizine-Goetz, *Using*

Subject Headings for Online Retrieval:Theory, Practice, and Potential (San Diego, Calif.: Academic Press, 1994).

[11]Markey, *Subject Searching in Library Catalogs*, 77.

[12]Drabenstott and Vizine-Goetz, *Using Subject Headings for Online Retrieval*, 124.

[13]Chan, *Library of Congress Subject Headings*, 2.

[14]Cutter, *Rules for a Dictionary Catalog*, 69.

[15]Haykin, *Subject Headings*, 8.

[16]E. Wyndham Hulme, "Principles of Book Classification," *Library Association Record* 13 (1911): 445-47.

[17]Library of Congress, Catalog Division, *Subject Headings Used in the Dictionary Catalogues of the Library of Congress*, 3rd ed., ed. Mary Wilson MacNair (Washington, D.C.: Library of Congress, Catalog Division, 1928), iii.

[18]Library of Congress, Subject Cataloging Division, *Subject Headings Used in the Dictionary Catalogs of the Library of Congress*, 4th ed., ed. Mary Wilson MacNair (Washington, D.C.: Library of Congress, Subject Cataloging Division, 1943), iii.

[19]Haykin, *Subject Headings*, 7.

[20]Library of Congress, *Subject Cataloging Manual*, H187.

[21]In the choice of proper names, the problem involves more than usage alone. Because most proper names used as subject headings also serve as main and added entries, a coordination between descriptive cataloging and subject cataloging is necessary. The choice and forms of proper names are discussed in chapter 4.

[22]Chan, *Library of Congress Subject Headings*, 7.

[23]Thelma Eaton, *Cataloging and Classification: An Introductory Manual*, 4th ed. (Ann Arbor, Mich.: Edwards Brothers, 1967), 156.

[24]Cutter, *Rules for a Dictionary Catalog*, 70.

[25]Cutter, *Rules for a Dictionary Catalog*, 69.

[26]Haykin, *Subject Headings*, 9.

[27]Library of Congress, *Subject Cataloging Manual*, H315.

[28]Cutter, *Rules for a Dictionary Catalog*, 70.

[29]Haykin, *Subject Headings*, 9.

[30]David Judson Haykin, "Subject Headings: Principles and Development," in *The Subject Analysis of Library Materials*, ed. Maurice F. Tauber (New York: School of Library Service, Columbia University, 1953), 50.

[31]Haykin, *Subject Headings*, 8.

[32]Library of Congress, *Subject Cataloging Manual*, H187, p. 1.

[33]Haykin, *Subject Headings*, 8.

[34]Sanford Berman, *Prejudices and Antipathies: A Tract on the LC Subject Heads Concerning People* (Metuchen, N.J.: Scarecrow Press, 1971); 1993 ed. (Jefferson, N.C.: McFarland, 1993).

[35]Cutter, *Rules for a Dictionary Catalog*, 71.

[36]Cutter, *Rules for a Dictionary Catalog*, 66.

[37]Vatican Library, *Rules for the Catalog of Printed Books*, translated from the 2nd Italian edition by Thomas J. Shanahan, Victor A. Schaefer, and Constantin T. Vesselowsky, and ed. Wyllis E. Wright (Chicago: American Library Association, 1948), 250.

[38]Cutter, *Rules for a Dictionary Catalog*, 66.

[39]Haykin, *Subject Headings*, 9.

[40]Oliver Linton Lilley, "How Specific Is Specific?" *Journal of Cataloging and Classification* 11 (1955): 4-5.

[41]John Balnaves, "Specificity," in *The Variety of Librarianship: Essays in Honour of John Wallace Metcalfe*, ed. W. Boyd Rayward (Sydney: Library Association of Australia, 1976), 54-55.

[42]Elaine Svenonius, "Metcalfe and the Principles of Specific Entry," in *The Variety of Librarianship: Essays in Honour of John Wallace Metcalfe*, ed. W. Boyd Rayward (Sydney: Library Association of Australia, 1976), 186-87.

[43]John W. Metcalfe, *Subject Classifying and Indexing of Libraries and Literature* (Sydney: Angus and Robertson, 1959), 278.

[44]F. W. Lancaster, *Vocabulary Control for Information Retrieval*, 2nd ed. (Arlington, Va.: Information Resources Press, 1986), 108.

[45]G. Salton and C. S. Yang, "On the Specification of Term Values in Automatic Indexing," *Journal of Documentation* 29 (December 1973): 352.

[46]Svenonius, "Metcalfe and the Principles of Specific Entry," in *The Variety of Librarianship*, 183.

[47]Richard S. Angell, "Standards for Subject Headings: A National Program," *Journal of Cataloging and Classification* 10 (October 1954): 193.

[48]Metcalfe, *Subject Classifying and Indexing*, 278.

[49]Chan, *Library of Congress Subject Headings*, 34.

[50]Material distributed at Regional Institutes on Library of Congress Subject Headings, sponsored by ALA Resources and Technical Services Division, Library of Congress, ALA/RTSD Council of Regional Groups, 1982-1984.

[51]Haykin, *Subject Headings*, 10.

[52]Elaine Svenonius, "Design of Controlled Vocabularies," in *Encyclopedia of Library and Information Science*, ed. Allen Kent, vol. 45, suppl. 10 (New York: Marcel Dekker, 1990), 87.

[53]See the Cutter and Haykin quotes on pages 15-17, under "The user and usage."

[54]Library of Congress, *Subject Headings Used in the Dictionary Catalogs of the Library of Congress*, iii.

[55]Chan, *Library of Congress Subject Headings*, 4.

[56]Mortimer Taube, "Specificity in Subject Headings and Coordinate Indexing," *Library Trends* 1 (October 1952): 222.

[57]Material distributed at Regional Institutes on Library of Congress Subject Headings.

[58]Svenonius, "Design of Controlled Vocabularies," 88.

[59]Subject Subdivisions Conference (1991: Airlie, Va.), *The Future of Subdivisions in the Library of Congress Subject Headings System: Report from the Subject Subdivisions Conference*, ed. Martha O'Hara Conway (Washington, D.C.: Cataloging Distribution Service, Library of Congress, 1992), 6.

[60]Library of Congress, *Subject Cataloging Manual*, H187.

3 Forms of Headings

Two main categories of headings are used in subject cataloging in LCSH: topical/form headings and name headings.[1] Most topical headings represent objects or concepts; a small number of them represent forms or genres. Headings containing proper names, on the other hand, are assigned to works discussing individual persons, corporate bodies, places, and other entities bearing proper names.

Both topical/form and name headings may be extended by subdivisions. Proper names used in subject headings are treated in chapter 4, and subdivisions are discussed in chapter 5. This chapter discusses the terminology and syntax of topical/form headings.

FUNCTIONS OF HEADINGS

The functions of subject headings may be divided into the following three categories: topical, bibliographic form, and artistic or literary form.

A topical heading represents the subject content of a work. The overwhelming majority of subject headings assigned to works fall into this category. For example, a work about clinical chemistry is assigned the heading **Clinical chemistry**; a work on the process of arriving at decisions for action is assigned the heading **Decision-making**.

Some headings indicate the bibliographic form of a work rather than its subject content. Most of these are assigned to works not limited to any particular subject or to works on very broad subjects (e.g., **Encyclopedias and dictionaries; Almanacs; Yearbooks; Devotional calendars**). There are relatively few headings of this type. The same headings are often assigned to works discussing these forms (e.g., a work about compiling almanacs). In these cases, no attempt is made to distinguish works *in* the forms from works *about* the forms.

Some headings representing bibliographic forms are used only as topical headings and are not assigned to individual specimens of the form. For example, the heading **American periodicals** is assigned only to works *about* American periodicals, not to publications such as *Atlantic Monthly*.

Many headings indicate the artistic or literary genre of the work. They are used extensively in three fields in particular: literature, art, and music. In these fields, the forms of the works are considered of greater importance than their subject content. Examples of this type of heading are:

Painting, Chinese
Short stories
Suites (Wind ensemble)

In some cases, a distinction is made between works in a particular genre and works about it (e.g., **Short story** [as a literary form]; **Short stories** [a collection]). Detailed discussions on headings for art, literature, and music will be presented in chapter 10.

SYNTAX

Topical headings in the Library of Congress system represent a mixture of natural and artificial forms of the English language. Single nouns, adjectival phrases, and prepositional phrases are based on natural forms and word order. On the other hand, headings with qualifiers, headings with subdivisions, and inverted headings are special forms that are not used in everyday speech.

Traditionally, forms of subject headings have been viewed in terms of their grammatical or syntactical structure (i.e., the way words are put together to form phrases or sentences). Over the years, these aspects have not changed greatly. Charles A. Cutter names the following categories of subject headings in a dictionary catalog: a single word; a noun preceded by an adjective; a noun preceded by another noun used like an adjective; a noun connected with another by a preposition; a noun connected with another by "and," and a phrase or sentence.[2] In the Library of Congress system, the sentence form mentioned by Cutter is not used. David Judson Haykin identifies seven forms used in *Library of Congress Subject Headings:* noun headings, adjectival headings, inverted adjectival headings, phrase headings, inverted phrase headings, compound headings, and composite forms.[3] Richard S. Angell categorizes the forms as follows:

> Headings proper have the grammatical form of noun or phrase, the principal types of the latter being adjective-noun, phrases containing a preposition, and phrases containing a conjunction. Phrases may be in normal direct order of words, or inverted.

> Headings are amplified as required by 1) the parenthetical qualifier, used principally to name the domain of a single noun for the purpose of resolving homographs; and 2) the subdivision, of which there are four kinds: topic, place, time and form.[4]

The use of nonverbal symbols in conjunction with the words in a heading is relatively simple in the Library of Congress system. The comma is used to separate a series of parallel terms and to indicate an inverted heading. Parentheses are used to enclose qualifiers. The dash is the signal for subdivision (e.g., **Education—Aims and objectives**). The period is used to separate a subheading from the main heading and only appears in a name heading, a uniform title, or a name-title heading used as a subject heading:

> **United States. Air Force**
> **Bible. N.T. Gospels**
> **Aristotle. Poetics**

Each heading or heading string in the bibliographic record is followed by a period. For details of punctuation, see appendix M of this book.

Most topical headings represent single concepts or objects. Compound headings contain more than one concept or object, some expressing an additive relationship, others representing phase relationships (e.g., cause and effect, influence, bias) between concepts and objects. Still other headings represent a particular aspect of a subject, such as form, space, time, process, or property.

In LCSH, there does not seem to be a relationship between grammatical form and semantic function. A heading representing an aspect of a subject is usually in the form of a subdivided heading, but it may also appear as an adjectival phrase (direct or inverted), a prepositional phrase (direct or inverted), or a heading with a qualifier:

> **Factor tables**
> **Multiplication—Tables**
> **Squares, Tables of**
> **Plant inspection**
> **Fertilization of plants**
> **Plants, Effect of solar radiation on**
> **Cookery (Sausages)**

If LCSH is to show more internal coherence in the future in order to increase the predictability factor in ease of use, the problem of determining which forms of heading are or should be used in what situations must be examined. Some aspects of the problem are discussed below.

SINGLE-CONCEPT HEADINGS

Single-concept headings appear in the form of single- or multiple-word terms. All headings consist of nouns or noun-equivalents.

Single-Word Headings

The simplest form of main heading is a noun or substantive. A single noun or substantive is chosen as the heading when it represents the object or concept precisely:

Catalogs
Chemistry
Democracy
Engineering
Pleasure
Teenagers
Women

When adjectives and participles are chosen, they are used as substantives or noun-equivalents:

Advertising
Aged
Poor
Sick

In the past, the article was used in some cases (e.g., *The arts, The West*) but not others, even when grammatical usage would require it. To facilitate machine filing, a decision was later made that no new subject heading is to be established with "the" in the initial position. Many of the original headings with an initial "the" have been converted to the current form:

Original form	*Converted form*
The arts	**Arts**
The Many (Philosophy)	**Many (Philosophy)**
The One (Philosophy)	**One (The One in philosophy)**
The West	**West (U.S.)**

In cases where the article is retained for semantic or grammatical reasons, the heading is inverted (e.g., **State, The**; **Comic, The**).

In general, the plural form of a noun is used for denoting a concrete object or a class of people (e.g., **Airplanes**; **Churches**; **Florists**; **Teachers**). This is not a rigid rule, and there are many exceptions. A deliberate exception is made for names of fruits for which the singular noun denotes both the fruit and the tree (e.g., **Apple**; **Pear**). Headings that represent biological species are generally in the singular (e.g., **Coconut palm**; **Japanese macaque**; **Rhesus monkey**); headings for higher levels are almost always in the plural (e.g., **Palms**; **Macaques**; **Monkeys**).[5] In cases where both the singular and plural forms of a noun have been established as headings, they represent different subjects: Usually the singular form represents a concept or abstract idea and the plural a concrete object (e.g., **Essay** [as a literary form]; **Essays** [for a collection of specimens of this literary form]). However, in newly established headings, this distinction is no longer made. Another way of distinguishing between the concept and the specimens is to use the phrase form in one of the headings (e.g., **Biography** [for collective biographies]; **Biography as a literary form**).

In headings for art, the former practice of using the singular (e.g., *Painting*), to represent the activity and the plural (e.g., *Paintings*), for the objects has been discontinued. Currently the singular noun (e.g., **Painting**; **Watercolor painting**), is used to represent both the activity and the object.[6]

Multiple-Word Headings

When a single object or concept cannot be properly expressed by a single noun, a phrase is used. Multiword terms appear in the form of adjectival or prepositional phrases.

Adjectival Phrase Headings

The most common phrase headings consist of a noun or noun phrase with an adjectival modifier. The modifier takes one of the following forms:

- Common adjective

  Chemical engineering
  Mathematical statistics
  Social workers
  Vocational guidance

- Common noun

  Career plateaus
  Earthquake engineering
  Food service
  Hospitality industry
  Library catalogs
  Student assistance programs

- Ethnic, national, or geographical adjective

  Jewish etiquette
  American drama

- Other proper adjective

  Brownian movements
  Newtonian telescopes

- Present or past participle

  Working class
  Laminated plastics

- Common noun in the possessive case

  Carpenter's square
  Children's art
  Women's rights

- Proper noun in the possessive case

  Halley's comet

- Proper noun

  New Age movement
  Norton motorcycle
  Norway lobster

- Combination

  Real estate office buildings
  Gold-platinum alloys
  Print finishing processes

Prepositional Phrase Headings

Prepositional phrases are used in single-concept headings when the concept is generally expressed in the English language in the form of a prepositional phrase:

Balance of power
Boards of trade
Divine right of kings
Figures of speech
Spheres of influence
Stories without words

A large number of headings in the form of **[Class of people] as [another class of people]** represent the role of a certain class of people in an activity or profession (e.g., **Children as actors**; **Artists as teachers**). Previously, many of these headings referred to women, such as *Women as diplomats* and *Women as missionaries*. They have now been replaced by headings in the adjectival form (e.g., **Women diplomats**; **Women missionaries**).[7] However, headings of this type that refer to groups of people other than women remain valid (e.g., **Physicians as musicians**), as well as headings in the form of **Women in [discipline]** (e.g., **Women in business**).

Choice Between Nouns and Phrases

No satisfactory solution has yet been offered to the problem of what choice to make between a noun and a phrase that both represent the same object or concept, although Cutter wrote that in general phrases "shall when possible be reduced to their equivalent nouns, as **Moral philosophy** to **Ethics** or to **Morals; Intellectual** or **Mental philosophy** to **Intellect** or **Mind**."[8] However, he also recognizes the difficulty in applying such a rule:

> In reducing, for instance, Intellectual philosophy or Moral philosophy, will you say Mind or Intellect, Morals or Ethics? And the reader will not always know what the equivalent noun is,—that Physics = Natural philosophy, for example, and Hygiene = Sanitary science. Nor does it help us at all to decide whether to prefer Botanical morphology or Morphological botany.[9]

In LCSH, the choice in such cases often depends on the judgment of the cataloger who, in proposing the heading, tries to take prevailing usage into account. The same holds for the choice among different types of phrases.

Choice Among Different Types of Phrases

In his rules, Cutter gives examples of the same subject named in different ways:[10]

Capital punishment
Death penalty
Penalty by death

Floral fertilization
Flower fertilization
Fertilization of flowers

He feels that there is no way to formulate an absolute rule to ensure consistency in the choice, and that the best rule of thumb is, "when there is any decided usage (i.e., custom of the public to designate the subjects by one of the names rather than by the others) let it be followed." Here Cutter immediately recognizes a difficulty: "As is often the case in language, usage will be found not to follow any uniform course." As a result of this difficulty, there is little uniformity regarding the choice among different types of phrases in LCSH.

MULTIPLE-CONCEPT HEADINGS

Multiple-concept headings appear as compound phrases, prepositional phrases, or subject heading strings made up of a main heading with one or more subdivisions.

Compound Phrases

Compound phrase headings, consisting of two or more nouns, noun phrases, or both, with or without modifiers, connected by the word *and*, the word *or*, or followed by the word *etc.*, serve various purposes:

(1) to express a reciprocal relationship between two general topics discussed at a broad level from the perspectives of both topics:

> **Art and technology**
> **Education and state**
> **Literature and society**
> **Psychoanalysis and literature**
> **Religion and sociology**
> **Television and children**
> **Women and peace**

(2) to connect subjects that are often treated together in works because they are similar, opposite, or closely associated:

> **Boats and boating**
> **Bolts and nuts**
> **Children's encyclopedias and dictionaries**
> **College student newspapers and periodicals**
> **Debtor and creditor**
> **Emigration and immigration**
> **Good and evil**
> **Lamp-chimneys, globes, etc.**
> **Law reports, digests, etc.**
> **Library institutes and workshops**
> **Open and closed shelves**
> **Reporters and reporting**
> **Skis and skiing**
> **Stores or stock-room keeping**

Library of Congress policy regarding headings of this type has varied over the years, with current policy requiring the establishment of separate headings for each of the elements in a conjunctive phrase heading. Many previously established headings of this type have been replaced by separate headings; for example, the heading *Textile industry and fabrics* was replaced by the two headings **Textile fabrics** and **Textile** industry; the heading *Bicycles and tricycles* was replaced by the two headings **Bicycles** and **Tricycles**.

(3) to connect two nouns when one serves to define the other, more general noun (e.g., **Forces and couples**; **Force and energy**).

Although previously established conjunctive phrase headings listed under (2) and (3) will continue to be used in subject cataloging, no new headings of these types are being established. Newly established conjunctive phrase headings are limited to reciprocal relationships, and only when the subject cannot be expressed in the **[Main heading]—[Subdivision]** form—that is, when the relationship between the two concepts is discussed at a broad level and from the perspectives of both topics (e.g., **Education and crime**; **Feminism and the arts**; but **Body temperature—Effect of drugs on** [not *Drugs and body temperature*]; **American literature—English influences** [not *American literature and English civilization*]).[11]

Prepositional Phrase Headings

Prepositional phrase headings, consisting of nouns, noun phrases, or both, with or without modifiers connected by one or more prepositions, are used to express complex relationships between topics:

Care of sick animals
Child sexual abuse by clergy
Counseling in elementary education
Federal aid to youth services
Fertilization of plants by insects
Taxation of bonds, securities, etc.
Teacher participation in curriculum planning

Free-Floating Phrase Headings

In addition to the prepositional phrase headings listed in LCSH, there are a number of phrases that can be combined with valid headings to form new headings without being officially established or displayed in LCSH. These phrases are referred to as "free-floating." They include **...in art** and certain free-floating elements combined with geographic headings, which are discussed in chapter 4. Examples of free-floating phrase headings are:

Chapels in art
Christian saints in art

Combinations that are used as examples and those requiring unique cross references do appear in LCSH. Others may be formed by catalogers as needed.

The phrase **[Topic] in literature**, previously a free-floating phrase, is no longer freely combined.

Choice Between Phrase Headings and Headings with Subdivisions

Many phrase headings represent an aspect or facet of a subject that could be represented by a subdivided heading (e.g., **Cataloging of art** instead of *Art—Cataloging*; **Taxation of aliens** instead of *Aliens—Taxation*).[12] Haykin recognized the problem of having to choose among forms that have equal standing in current usage, such as *Stability of ships, Ships' stability,* and *Ships—Stability,* but offers no solution.[13] In LCSH, any of three forms may have been chosen with regard to individual headings:

Squares, Tables of
Factor tables
Multiplication—Tables

According to current Library of Congress policy, headings describing certain kinds of relationships are constructed with the use of standardized subdivisions such as **[Main topic]—Effect of [topic] on**; **[Main topic]—[Topic] influences**; **[Main topic]—Psychological aspects**; and **[Main topic]—Social aspects**.[14] Many phrase headings established earlier have been converted to the subdivided form:

Original form	*Converted form*
Social science research	**Social sciences—Research**
Teachers, Certification of	**Teachers—Certification**

Such conversion is ongoing; many more existing phrase headings can be expected to be changed to headings with subdivisions.

However, in many cases, a new phrase heading is constructed when the cataloger proposing the heading believes that the concept is very well known by the public in the phrase form:

Library orientation for engineering students
    [instead of *Engineering students—Library orientation*]
Simulcasting of horse racing
    [instead of *Horse racing—Simulcasting*]

It has been noted that because of the lack of specific rules regulating the choice of forms over the years, and because many people have participated in establishing headings, many inconsistencies exist in LCSH. A few have already been resolved. The publication of *Subject Cataloging Manual,* which began in 1984 and is now in its 4th edition, represents attempts to regularize new heading formation to a greater degree than before.[15] As older headings are revised to make them conform to new heading patterns, the system as a whole should improve, not only in ease of application but also in ease of use by end-users.

SEMANTICS

The principle of unique headings requires that each heading represents only one subject. The problem of multiple meaning is resolved in part by using *qualifiers*, added for the purpose of disambiguation.[16] A qualifier is a word or phrase enclosed within parentheses following the heading. Examples are:

Iris (Eye)
Iris (Plant)

Ordination (Buddhism)
Ordination (Liturgy)

Profession of faith (Islam)
Profession of faith (Canon law)

Rings (Algebra)
Rings (Gymnastics)

A qualifier may also be used to provide context for obscure or technical terms, in which case it usually takes the form of the name of a discipline or of a category or kind of thing:

Assemblage (Art)
Charge transfer devices (Electronics)
Chlorosis (Plants)
Consumption (Economics)
Correlation (Statistics)
Golden age (Mythology) in literature
Imagination (Philosophy)
Résumés (Employment)
Spectral theory (Mathematics)
Twisting machines (Textile machinery)

Over the years, parenthetical qualifiers have been added to subject headings for various purposes: (1) to distinguish between homographs, such as **Pool (Game)**, **Cold (Disease)**, and **Rape (Plant)**; (2) to clarify the meaning of an obscure or foreign term, such as **Extra Hungariam non est vita (The Latin phrase)**; (3) to limit the meaning of a heading in order to render it more specific, such as **Olympic games (Ancient)**; (4) to indicate the genre of a proper name, such as **Banabans (Kiribati people)**, **DECSYSTEM-20 (Computer)**, and **Conquistadora (Statue)**; (5) to designate a special application of a general concept, such as **Cookery (Chicken)**; and (6) to specify the medium of performance in music headings, such as **Concertos (Violin)**.

In a number of cases it is not clear why the qualified form instead of a phrase form or subdivided form was used, or why the qualifier was used at all, as, for example, in **Profession (in religious orders, congregations, etc.)** and **Programming languages (Electronic computers)**.

In many cases, another form would achieve the desired purpose (e.g., *Chicken—Cookery*; *Ancient Olympic Games* [or *Olympic games, Ancient*]).

In regard to qualifiers, as with so many other features of LCSH, practice has not been consistent. In 1978, the Library of Congress began to develop guidelines with regard to qualifiers.[17] The parenthetical qualifier is to be used (a) to specify the intended meaning of the term if several dictionary definitions exist; (b) to resolve ambiguity if the main heading is similar in construction to other existing or possible headings; and (c) to make an obscure term more explicit. Current practice follows these guidelines. The parenthetical qualifier is no longer used to designate a special application of a general concept. For this purpose, the following forms are used instead:

- Headings with subdivisions (preferred form)

  Geography—Network analysis
  [not *Network analysis (Geography)*]
  Public health—Citizen participation
  [not *Citizen participation (Public health)*]

- Adjectival phrase headings

  Industrial design coordination
  [not *Designs (Industrial publicity)*]

- Prepositional phrase headings

  Information theory in biology
  [not *Information theory (Biology)*]
  Anesthesia in cardiology
  [not *Anesthesia (Cardiology)*]
  Abandonment of automobiles
  [not *Abandonment (Automobiles)*]

INVERTED HEADINGS

In the past, many phrase headings were established in the inverted form in order to bring a significant word into a prominent position as the entry element:

Chemistry, Organic
Education, Higher
Philosophy, Modern
Quotations, American
Taxation, Exemption from
Plants, Effects of radioactive pollution on

In a manual catalog or a single-entry listing or display, the inverted form serves the purpose of collocating entry elements when using natural word order—for instance, *Life insurance*—would separate a heading from others related to it. Because LCSH was originally designed for the card catalog, in which each record possessed only a few access points and was filed in the catalog only under them, the choice of the word to be used as the entry element in a phrase heading was a paramount consideration. In online retrieval systems with key-word searching capability, the entry element is no longer an issue. Therefore, newly established headings are in the direct form, except where a pattern of inverted headings exists among similar headings. Nonetheless, while many of the inverted headings have been converted to the direct form over the past few years, many still exist. For this reason, an understanding of the background and rationale for inverted headings is in order.

Because there were no specific guidelines nor discernible patterns for inverting headings in the past, there is no way to predict the form of a heading in LCSH, as the following headings show:

Bessel functions
Functions, Abelian
Abelian groups
Groups, Multiply transitive

Agricultural chemistry
Botanical chemistry
Environmental chemistry
Chemistry, Analytic
Chemistry, Organic
Chemistry, Technical

To normalize word order, the Library of Congress made the decision in 1983 to create new headings in direct form using natural language.[18] However, because of the large number of headings already established in the inverted form, it was decided to retain such headings in the following categories:

(1) headings qualified by time period:
        Logic, Ancient
        Philosophy, Medieval
        History, Modern

(2) headings with modifiers for artistic or musical style:
        Art, Baroque
        Bronzes, Renaissance
        Drawing, Rococo

(3) headings for types of fossils:
        Footprints, Fossil
        Trees, Fossil

(4) music headings with the following qualifiers:
        ..., Arranged
        ..., Unaccompanied

(5) battles (see discussion in chapter 4)

(6) geographic headings (see discussion in chapter 4)

(7) names of fictitious and legendary characters (see discussion in chapter 4)

(8) topical headings qualified by languages, nationalities, and ethnic groups:

> **Art, Mexican**
> **Authors, Spanish**
> **Medicine, Arab**
> **Painting, Brazilian**

However, there are a number of exceptions:

(A) Headings containing these qualifiers followed by the terms terms below are established in the natural word order:

> **... diaries**
> **... drama**
> **... drama (Comedy)**
> **... drama (Tragedy)**
> **... drama (Tragicomedy)**
> **... essays**
> **... farces**
> **... fiction**
> **... imprints**
> **... language**
> **... letters**
> **... literature**
> **... newspapers**
> **... periodicals**
> **... philology**
> **... poetry**
> **... prose literature**
> **... wit and humor**

(B) Topical headings qualified by ethnic groups in the United States are established in natural word order:

> **Afro-American baseball players**
> **Japanese American farmers**
> **Italian American art**

Until all inverted headings are converted to natural word order, users and catalogers should be aware of the patterns of existing inverted headings in LCSH.

NOTES

[1]In *Library of Congress Subject Headings*, headings authorized for use as subject entries are printed in boldface type. In MARC records, they are indicated by appropriate field tags.

[2]Charles A. Cutter, *Rules for a Dictionary Catalog*, 4th ed., rewritten (Washington, D.C.: GPO, 1904), 71-72.

[3]David Judson Haykin, *Subject Headings: A Practical Guide* (Washington, D.C.: GPO, 1951), 21-25.

[4]Richard S. Angell, "Library of Congress Subject Headings—Review and Forecast," in *Subject Retrieval in the Seventies: New Directions: Proceedings of an International Symposium*, ed. Hans (Hanan) Wellisch and Thomas D. Wilson (Westport, Conn.: Greenwood Publishing, 1972), 144.

[5]"Animal and Plant Names," *Cataloging Service Bulletin* 20 (Spring 1983): 42; Library of Congress, Office for Subject Cataloging Policy, *Subject Cataloging Manual*, 4th ed. (Washington, D.C.: Cataloging Distribution Service, Library of Congress, 1991), H1332.

[6]"Art Headings," *Cataloging Service* 121 (Spring 1977): 13-14.

[7]Library of Congress, Office for Subject Cataloging Policy, *Subject Cataloging Manual*, 4th ed. (Washington, D.C.: Library of Congress, 1991), H360.

[8]Cutter, *Rules for a Dictionary Catalog*, 72.

[9]Cutter, *Rules for a Dictionary Catalog*, 74.

[10]Cutter, *Rules for a Dictionary Catalog*, 74.

[11]Library of Congress, *Subject Cataloging Manual*, H310.

[12]Subdivisions are discussed in detail in chapter 5.

[13]Haykin, *Subject Headings*, 23.

[14]Library of Congress, *Subject Cataloging Manual*, H310.

[15]Library of Congress, *Subject Cataloging Manual*, H1332.

[16]Library of Congress, *Subject Cataloging Manual*, H357.

[17]"Parenthetical Qualifiers in Subject Headings," *Cataloging Service Bulletin* 1 (Summer 1978): 15-16; Library of Congress, *Subject Cataloging Manual*, H357.

[18]Library of Congress, *Subject Cataloging Manual*, H306.

4 Proper Names in Subject Headings

Many proper names are used as main subject headings, as parts of subject strings, or as subdivisions. These names include personal names, names of corporate bodies, geographic names, names of works established as uniform titles, and names of individual entities. In the past, most of these headings were not printed in *Library of Congress Subject Headings*. This policy was changed in 1976; since the 10th edition the list has included those name headings that are used as subject entries but not as entries in descriptive cataloging.

At the Library of Congress, headings for proper names that have been or are likely to be used in descriptive cataloging are established according to *Anglo-American Cataloguing Rules*, 2nd revised edition, 1988 revision *(AACR2R)*.[1] These include headings for persons, corporate bodies, jurisdictions, uniform titles, and names of certain types of entities.[2] These headings are currently kept in a name authority file. The machine-readable version is called *NAMES*. It is also available on CD-ROM, called CDMARC Names, and in microform, called Name Authorities Cumulative Microform Edition. These name headings are not included in the *SUBJECTS* file nor printed in *Library of Congress Subject Headings*, except for the few that are included for the purpose of displaying special subdivisions or unique references, or of serving as pattern headings.[3] Also omitted from LCSH are free-floating phrase headings such as those for regions or geographic features, regions of cities, and metropolitan areas.

This chapter discusses and presents numerous examples of the types of proper names used as or in subject headings. Appendix G shows the patterns of cross references for such headings.

PERSONAL NAMES

Names of Individual Persons

Names of individual persons are used as subject headings for biographies, eulogies, festschriften, criticisms, bibliographies, and literary works in which the persons figure. At the Library of Congress, to ensure that the same form of a personal name is used for both author and subject entries, headings consisting of names of persons are established according to *AACR2R*. Following are some examples of personal name headings:

> **Alexander, the Great, 356-323 B.C.**
> **Ambrose, Saint, Bishop of Milan, d. 397**
> **Aristotle**
> **Bernward, Bishop of Hildesheim, ca. 960-1022**
> **Byron, George Gordon, Baron, 1788-1824**
> **Catherine II, Empress of Russia, 1729-1796**
> **Charlemagne, Emperor, 742-814**
> **Charles, Prince of Wales, 1948-**
> **Columbus, Christopher**
> **Devonshire, Andrew Robert Buxton Cavendish, Duke of, 1920-**
> **Franz Joseph I, Emperor of Austria, 1830-1916**
> **John Paul II, Pope, 1920-**
> **Kennedy, John F. (John Fitzgerald), 1917-1963**
> **Mullett, A. B. (Alfred Bult), 1834-1890**
> **Nicholas, of Cusa, Cardinal, 1401-1464**

Subdivisions used under name headings are discussed in chapter 5.

Names of Families, Dynasties, Royal Houses, Etc.[4]

The heading for a family appears in the form of **[Proper name] family** (e.g., **Rockefeller family**). The older form with a qualifier, such as *Smith family (William Smith, 1669-1743)*, has been discontinued. No effort is made to distinguish between families with the same surname. The heading **Kennedy family,** for example, is used for works about any family with the surname Kennedy. Examples of family name headings include:

> **Adams family**
> **Cook family**
> **Gookin family**
> **Koch family**

If the same family has been known by different names, the most common form of the name is chosen as the heading, with cross references from other forms. Variants are usually determined from the work being cataloged and from standard reference works. Another source of variants is references to surnames already used as catalog entries.

Similar family names from different ethnic backgrounds and family names that have been changed as the result of emigration are established as separate headings, connected by related references.

Names of dynasties and royal houses are established in the following forms: **[Name] dynasty** (for non-European royal houses); **[Name], House of** (for European royal houses). Dates indicating the span of years of a particular dynasty are added to the heading whenever possible. Examples include:

Hoysala dynasty, ca. 1006-ca. 1346
Habsburg, House of
Saxe-Coburg-Gotha, House of
Vasa, House of
Orange-Nassau, House of

USE references are made from variant forms of the name, and BT (broader term) references are made from appropriate history headings for dynasties and from **[Country (or region)]—Kings and rulers** for royal houses. A discussion and examples of cross references appear in chapter 6.

Headings for individually named houses of dukes, counts, or earls are established in the form of **[Name], [Title of rank in English] of**:

Celje, Counts of
Derby, Earls of
Leinster, Dukes of

Headings for other aristocratic or noble families are established in the form of **[Name] family**:

Tokugawa family

Names of Mythological, Legendary, or Fictitious Characters

Names of mythological, legendary, or fictitious characters are not covered by *AACR2R*. However, they are often required as subject headings. Headings for mythological characters that are not gods or goddesses are established in the form of **[Name of character] ([Ethnic adjective] mythology)**:

Draupadī (Hindu mythology)
Lilith (Semitic mythology)

The qualifier **(Legendary character)** is used with headings for legendary characters:

Aeneas (Legendary character)
Anansi (Legendary character)
Bunyan, Paul (Legendary character)
Hector (Legendary character)
Pecos Bill (Legendary character)
Robin Hood (Legendary character)
Roland (Legendary character)

The qualifier **(Fictitious character)** is used with names of characters of literary or artistic invention, as opposed to legendary characters originating from legends, myths, or folklore. Examples of headings for fictitious characters include:

    Bond, James (Fictitious character)
    Hamete Benengeli, Cide (Fictitious character)
    Holmes, Sherlock (Fictitious character)
    Tarzan (Fictitious character)

Names of comics characters are also established in the form of **[Name of character] (Fictitious character)**:

    Felix the Cat (Fictitious character)
    Snoopy (Fictitious character)

Biblical figures are established with appropriate qualifiers:

    Abraham (Biblical patriarch)
    Adam (Biblical figure)
    Moses (Biblical leader)

Names of Gods and Goddesses

Names of gods and goddesses are established in the form of **[Name of god or goddess] ([Ethnic adjective] deity)**:

    Amon (Egyptian deity)
    Apollo (Greek deity)
    Krishna (Hindu deity)

Previously, names of gods and goddesses of classical mythology were usually established only in the Latin form, with *see* references from the names of their Greek counterparts. Charles A. Cutter defends the use of the Latin form for the reasons "(1) that the Latin names are at present more familiar to the majority of readers; (2) that it would be difficult to divide the literature, or if it were done, many books must be put both under **Zeus** and **Jupiter**, **Poseidon** and **Neptune**, etc., filling considerable room with no practical advantage."[5] This policy has been changed. The current policy requires that the heading be established as required by the work being cataloged:[6]

    Hermes (Greek deity)
    Cacus (Roman deity)

When equivalencies can be determined between Greek and Roman gods and goddesses, reciprocal RT (related-term) references are made between them.

Minerva (Roman deity)
  RT   Athena (Greek deity)

Athena (Greek deity)
  RT   Minerva (Roman deity)

For a discussion of related-term references, see chapter 6.

NAMES OF CORPORATE BODIES

Works related to the origin, development, activities, and functions of individual corporate bodies are assigned subject entries under their names. Headings for corporate bodies, like personal name headings, are established according to *AACR2R* and kept in the *NAMES* file.

Corporate bodies include public and private organizations, societies, associations, institutions, government agencies, commercial firms, churches, and other groups identified by a name, such as conferences and exploring expeditions. Examples of corporate names used as subject headings are given below. Some of the headings are qualified by generic terms or names of places, as required according to *AACR2R* and Library of Congress descriptive cataloging policies.[7] The forms of geographic names used as qualifiers are discussed on pages 69-74 of this chapter.

Aberdeen (Ship)
Alberta. Premier's Council on Science and Technology
Colonial Williamsburg Foundation
Conference on Security and Cooperation in Europe (1972 :
    Helsinki, Finland)
First Baptist Church (Bloomington, Ill.)
Freer Gallery of Art
Golden State Warriors (Basketball team)
Indian Hills Community Church (Lincoln, Neb.)
Metropolitan Museum of Art (New York, N.Y.)
Michigan State University. Libraries. Special Collections
    Division
Museum of International Folk Art (N.M.)
Museum of Modern Art (New York, N.Y.)
Rand Corporation
United Nations. Armed Forces
United States. European Command
University of Nebraska-Lincoln. Cooperative Extension
Teens (Musical group)

Name Changes in Corporate Bodies

When the name of a corporate body is changed, successive entries are established according to *AACR2R* for use in descriptive cataloging.[8] For subject cataloging purposes, the heading for the name used by the body during the latest period covered by the work is assigned.[9]

OTHER INDIVIDUAL ENTITIES BEARING PROPER NAMES

In addition to the proper names discussed above, many other individual entities that bear proper names also serve as subject headings. Headings for which there are no provisions in *AACR2R* are established and displayed in LCSH. Some of the categories are given below with examples.

Historical Events

Historical events identified by specific names are entered under their names, usually accompanied by dates:

Anthracite Coal Strike, Pa., 1887-1888[10]
Bookbinders' Strike, London, England, 1901
Canadian Invasion, 1775-1776
Canadian Spy Trials, Canada, 1946
Chrysler Corporation Slowdown Strike, 1939
King Philip's War, 1675-1676
Louisiana Purchase
Northwestern Conspiracy, 1864
Pacific Coast Indians, Wars with, 1847-1865
Waterloo, Battle of, 1815
World War, 1939-1945

Names of other events may also be used as headings:

Brighton Run (Antique car race)
National Library Week

Animals[11]

Subject headings are required for works about individual famous animals. The heading consists of the name of the animal qualified by type of animal, with a cross reference from the broader, generic term, such as:

Princess (Cat)
   BT   Cats

Seattle Slew (Race Horse)
    BT   Horses

Squirt (Dolphin)
    BT   Dolphins

For a detailed discussion of cross references, see chapter 6.

Prizes, Awards, Scholarships, Etc.

Individual prizes, awards, scholarships, and so on are represented by specific headings:

Congressional Award
Erasmus Prize
Father of the Year
International Simón Bolívar Prize
Maryland Hunt Cup

Holidays, Festivals, Etc.

Examples of headings for holidays, festivals, etc., are:

Ascension Day
Bastille Day
Christmas
Feast of Fools
Good Friday
Halloween
Hanukkah
Memorial Day
Mid-autumn Festival
Ramadan
Thanksgiving Day

Ethnic Groups, Nationalities, Tribes, Etc.

Until 1981, many headings for individual nationalities were established in the form of *[National group] in [Place]* (e.g., *Poles in Austria*; *Russians in France*). All such headings in LCSH have been converted to the form of **[National group]—[Place]** (e.g., **Poles—Austria**; **Russians—France**; **Americans—Foreign countries**).[12] On most of LC MARC records, the former headings have been converted to the current form. However, some still remain and are converted when the records are revised for other reasons.

Headings for groups of individual nationalities living in the United States as permanent residents or naturalized citizens are established in the composite form [Qualifier designating country of origin] Americans (e.g., Japanese Americans). These headings may be further subdivided by locality (e.g., Japanese Americans—California). Headings such as Japanese—United States and Germans—United States are used for aliens living in the United States, students from abroad, and the like. For groups of Americans already identified with ethnic groups whose names are in composite form (e.g., Russian Germans in the United States), headings such as Russian Germans—United States are used instead of *Russian German Americans*.

For a specific nationality in a foreign country, headings of the type [Nationality]—[Place] are used whether these people reside in the country permanently or temporarily.

Examples of headings for ethnic groups and the like are:

Arabs
Indians of North America
Italians
Italian Americans   [for residents and citizens]
Italians—Foreign countries
Italians—United States   [for aliens]
Japanese Americans—California—San Francisco [for residents and citizens]
Japanese—California   [for aliens]
North Africans
North Africans—Belgium
Nzakara (African people)

Religions, Philosophical Systems, Etc.

Examples of headings for individual religions, philosophical systems, and so forth are:

Buddhism
Christianity
Confucianism
Islam
Neoplatonism

Objects Bearing Proper Names

Specific name headings are also established for objects bearing proper names:

Bury Saint Edmunds Cross
Conquistadora (Statue)

GEOGRAPHIC NAMES[13]

Geographic names are used widely in both subject and descriptive cataloging. In subject headings, they may be the main heading or part of a heading phrase; they may be used as subdivisions; or they may figure as qualifiers.[14] Examples include:

Jamaica—Description and travel
Paris (France) in motion pictures
Library finance—United States
Building permits—Belgium
First Baptist Church (Bloomington, Ill.)

Names of countries and political or administrative divisions within countries, such as provinces, states, and cities are referred to as *jurisdictional names*. Such names are used very heavily in descriptive cataloging as entries in themselves, as parts of corporate names, or as additional designations or qualifiers. Such headings are established according to the provisions of *AACR2R* for geographic names. Other geographic names, such as those for natural features and man-made structures associated with places, are referred to as *non-jurisdictional names*. With few exceptions, non-jurisdictional headings are established and maintained in LCSH. Attempts are made to ensure compatibility with *AACR2R* whenever possible.

The following sections discuss general aspects of geographic heading formation and usage. Because the distinction between jurisdictional and non-jurisdictional names comes into the discussion at many points, the first two sections extend and give examples for the brief definitions presented above. Later sections treat language, choice of entry element, qualifiers, free-floating phrase headings, and changes of name. A final section deals with categories of geographic headings that require special treatment.

Jurisdictional Headings

Entities that can be called jurisdictions include countries, principalities, territories, states, provinces, counties, administrative districts, cities, archdioceses, and dioceses. When names for these entities figure in subject cataloging, the *AACR2R* forms are used. Examples of jurisdictional names are:

Bavaria (Germany)[15]
Berlin (Germany)[16]
Bourbon County (Ky.)
Brittany (France)
Dorset (England)
Glasgow (Ky.)
Glasgow (Scotland)
Great Britain

London (England)
Ontario
Pennsylvania
Provence (France)
Sardinia (Kingdom)
Vienna (Austria)

Non-Jurisdictional Headings[17]

Many headings for geographic areas or entities are not jurisdictional units. As noted above, these headings are established in LCSH, with the exception of those formed by using free-floating terms (a matter that is covered on pages 75-77 of this chapter). Types of places with non-jurisdictional names include:

archaeological sites, historic cities, etc.
areas and regions (when not free-floating)
canals
city sections
dams
extinct cities (pre-1500)
farms, ranches, gardens
forests, grasslands, etc.
geographic features (e.g., caves, deserts, non-jurisdictional islands,
    lakes, mountains, plains, ocean currents, rivers, seas, steppes)
geologic basins, geologic formations, etc.
mines
parks, reserves, refuges, recreation areas, etc.
reservoirs
roads, streets, trails
valleys (when not free-floating)

Examples of headings for non-jurisdictional place-names are:

Africa, Southern
Arroyo Hondo Site (N.M.)
Big Bend National Park (Tex.)
Big Cypress National Preserve (Fla.)
Big Sur Coast National Scenic Area (Calif.)
Black Hills National Forest (S.D. and Wyo.)
Gateway National Recreation Area (N.J. and N.Y.)
Glacier Bay (Alaska)
Grand Canyon (Ariz.)
Gulf Region (Tex.)
Himalaya Mountains
Knossos (Extinct city)
Lehigh Canal (Pa.)
Missouri River
North End (Boston, Mass.)

Oregon Trail
South Philadelphia (Philadelphia, Pa.)
Tahoe, Lake (Calif. and Nev.)

Language

The language of jurisdictional names is determined by *AACR2R* and *Library of Congress Rule Interpretations*.[18] The English form of the name, particularly a conventional name, is preferred, unless there is no English name in common use. Examples include:

South America
[not Sudamerica; America del sur]
Germany
[not Deutschland]
Spain
[not España]
Bavaria (Germany)[19]
[not Bayern]
Vienna (Austria)
[not Wien]

The vernacular form is chosen when there is no English form in general use or when the vernacular form is widely accepted in English-language works, as with **Rio de Janeiro (Brazil)**.

In determining the language of a non-jurisdictional name to be used in a heading, the Library of Congress usually gives priority to the decisions of the U.S. Board on Geographic Names (BGN) as a favored authority. The decisions made by BGN are evaluated in connection with other reference sources used as authorities for establishing geographic names (see appendix H for a list of these authorities) to determine if there are any conflicts with existing headings and to aid in the preparation of cross references.

Naturally, for places in English-speaking regions, English names are used. For places in non-English-speaking regions, on the other hand, a choice must often be made between English and vernacular names. In cases where the BGN has approved both an English and a vernacular form of a name, the English form, if it is in general use, is chosen as the heading.[20] In certain cases, even when the name approved by BGN is in the vernacular form, an English name is used in the heading if it is a conventional name justified by reference sources.[21] Based on these policies, the following forms are used in headings:

Japanese Alps (Japan)
[not Nihon arupusu]
Rhine River
[not Rhein]
West Lake (China)
[not Hsi-hu]

The vernacular form of the name is chosen if the entity in question is best known by its vernacular name among English-speaking users, when the generic term in the name is an integral part of the name, and for names in certain categories, such as city sections, parks, and streets. When the vernacular name is chosen as the heading for a non-jurisdictional entity, the generic term in the name is translated into English, unless the vernacular form is better known in the English-speaking world or is part of the conventional name:

Fontainebleau, Forest of (France)
 [not Forêt de Fontainebleau (France)]

Steinhuder Lake (Germany)
 [not Steinhuder Meer (Germany)]

Rio de la Plata (Argentina and Uruguay)
 [not Plate River (Argentina and Uruguay)]

Tien Shan
 [not Tien Mountains]

Vernacular names in non-roman scripts are transliterated according to Library of Congress transliteration tables. Occasionally these forms may not agree with the transliterated forms approved by BGN. For example, for names in the Chinese script, the Library of Congress uses the Wade-Giles romanization rather than the pinyin system followed by BGN:[22]

Peking (China)
 [not Beijing (China)]
Yangtze River (China)
 [not Yangzi River (China)]

Entry Element

When a geographic name contains more than one word, there is also the problem of choice of entry element. With few exceptions, names of political jurisdictions generally appear in their natural word order without inversion, such as **South Africa**; **North Carolina**; **Lake Forest (Ill.)**. This holds even for names of foreign places beginning with an article, for example, **El Salvador.**

Initial articles in non-jurisdictional geographic names for places located in English-speaking countries are retained. The heading is inverted if the initial article is *The*.[23] Examples include:

El Dorado Lake (Kan.)
El Rancho Gumbo (Mont.)
Mall, The (Washington, D.C.)

Initial articles in non-jurisdictional geographic names for places located in non-English-speaking countries are omitted unless the initial article is *The* and forms an integral part of the name. In such cases, the heading is inverted:

Bierzo (Spain)
[not El Bierzo (Spain)]

Sound, The (Denmark and Sweden)

The inverted form is used when the name of a natural feature begins with a generic term with a proper name in a later position. The proper name is used as the entry word:

Berkeley, Vale of (England)
Blanc, Mont (France and Italy)
Dover, Strait of
Hood, Mount (Or.)
Mexico, Gulf of
Michigan, Lake

In a small number of cases in which a foreign-language generic term has little generic significance for most English-speaking users and when the vernacular form is well known, the direct form is retained:

Costa del Sol (Spain)

Geographic names that contain adjectives indicating directions or parts and are not considered proper names are generally inverted:

Africa, East
Africa, Central
Africa, North
Alps, Eastern
Asia, Central
Asia, Southeastern
California, Southern
Tennessee, East

Compare, however:

Central America
East End (Long Island, N.Y.)
South China Sea
West Indies
East Asia
South Asia

Qualifiers[24]

For jurisdictional names, qualifiers are added to geographic names according to *AACR2R*. In accordance with *AACR2R*, a parenthetical qualifier is frequently added to a geographic name to identify it more clearly or to distinguish it from another place or other places with the same name. Qualifiers added to non-jurisdictional names are formulated in a way compatible with jurisdictional names where feasible.

For geographic names, Haykin identifies three types of qualifiers: generic (e.g., *Dover, Strait of; Faroe Islands*), geographic (e.g., *Saint-Dizier, France; Athens, Ga.*), and political or jurisdictional (e.g., *New York (State); Mexico (Viceroyalty)*).[25] In current practice, the qualifier is placed within parentheses after the name. If two or more types of qualifiers are required for a heading, they are enclosed within a single set of parentheses and separated by the sequence space-colon-space. Examples include:

Naples (Italy)
Naples (Kingdom)
Union (Pa. : Township)
Cape of Good Hope (South Africa : Cape)
Dolores River (Colo. and Utah)
Mackinac Island (Mich. : Island)

The name of a city used as a qualifier takes the form of the established heading for the city reformulated by (a) placing it within a single set of parentheses, (b) separating the city name from the name of its own larger qualifying jurisdiction with a comma, and (c) omitting any additional information that is part of the established heading for the city unless there is a conflict. Examples include:

Florence (Italy)	[form of heading for city]
(Florence, Italy)	[form when used as qualifier]
Richmondville (N.Y. : Village)	[form of heading for city]
(Richmondville, N.Y.)	[form when used as qualifier]

The following discussion treats current Library of Congress policies regarding different types of qualifiers for geographic headings: generic, geographic, and political or type-of-jurisdiction qualifiers.

Generic Qualifiers

The names of many natural features contain generic terms as an integral part:

Mississippi River Valley
Rocky Mountains

When there are two or more geographic entities with the same name, and the conflict cannot be resolved by geographic qualifiers, a generic qualifier is added in parentheses, even if it repeats a generic term in the place-name:

Cold Lake (Alta.) [the city]
Cold Lake (Alta. : Lake)

Grand Island (N.Y. : Island)
Grand Island (N.Y. : Town)

Geographic Qualifiers

Geographic qualifiers for jurisdictional headings are formulated according to *AACR2R*. They are used when it is appropriate to add the name of a place to a heading as shown below.

Names used as geographic qualifiers include those of countries, regions, provinces, states, islands, counties, and cities. Names of continents are not used as qualifiers, nor are names of sections within cities (e.g., Brooklyn, Georgetown), except in cases of conflict.

The following discussion of geographic qualifiers for jurisdictional headings is based on *AACR2R* and on Library of Congress policies regarding options; the discussion of geographic qualifiers for non-jurisdictional headings is based on policies established by the Cataloging Policy and Support Office of the Library of Congress and published in *Subject Cataloging Manual* and *Cataloging Service Bulletin*.

(1) *Geographic qualifiers for jurisdictional headings*. According to Rule 23.4 in *AACR2R*, the name of a larger place is added as a qualifier to the name of a place other than a country or, in certain cases, a state or province.[26] In general, all places below the national level require qualifiers, with the following exceptions to which *no* geographic qualifier is added:

states of Australia, Malaysia, and the United States

provinces of Canada

republics of Yugoslavia (i.e., Serbia and Montenegro)

constituent countries of Great Britain

islands that are jurisdictions

the city of Jerusalem

Hong Kong and Vatican City

Examples include:

New South Wales
Vermont
Pinang
Ontario
Scotland
Jerusalem

In order to understand the extent of the application of the option and the forms of the qualifier, it may be useful to become familiar with the types of geographic names used as qualifiers. Normally, the qualifier is the name of a country (e.g., **Paris (France)**; **Tokyo (Japan)**; **Rome (Italy)**; **Leipzig (Germany)**; **Seoul (Korea)**).[27] However, there are a number of notable exceptions. For places in the United States, Canada, Australia, Great Britain, Malaysia, and Yugoslavia, and certain places on islands, the primary qualifiers are the first-order political divisions or the island or island group. Types of qualifiers used with jurisdictional headings are listed below:

Heading Being Established	*Qualifier*[28]
Cities, counties, etc.	
in United States	Name of state
in Canada	Name of province
in Australia	Name of state
in Northern Ireland	Northern Ireland
in Malaysia	Name of state
in Yugoslavia	Name of constituent republic
Cities in the British Isles (except Northern Ireland)	Name of region, or island area
All other places below the national level[29]	Name of country

Examples of headings with geographic qualifiers include:

Aberdeen (Scotland)
Bourbon County (Ky.)
Cairo (Egypt)
Dorset (Vt. : Town)
Dorset (England)
Edinburgh (Scotland)
Georgetown (Washington, D.C.)
Kiev (Ukraine)
Nagasaki-ken (Japan)
Newcastle (N.S.W.)
        [not Newcastle (Australia)]
North Holland (Netherlands)
Oxford (England)

Palma (Majorca)
Palma (Spain)
San Francisco (Calif.)
Split (Croatia)
Toronto (Ont.)
Washington (D.C.)

The names of many of the first-order political jurisdictions and some of the countries are abbreviated according to *AACR2R* when used as qualifiers but are spelled out in full when used as main headings:

Minnesota [the state]
Alberta (Minn.)

Alberta [the province]
  · **Edmonton (Alta.)**

A list of first-order political divisions and their appropriate abbreviations appears in appendix I of this book.

If the name of a larger place used as a qualifier has changed, the current name is used:

Kinshasa (Zaire)
    [not Kinshasa (Congo)]

(2) *Geographic qualifiers for non-jurisdictional headings.* In general, the Library of Congress also follows *AACR2R* in establishing non-jurisdictional headings. However, there are a number of variations because of the different nature of such headings. The variations and situations not covered by *AACR2R* are discussed below.

(a) *Entities located wholly within a single country or first-order political division.* The qualifier used is the same as that used for jurisdictional headings. For example:

Okeechobee Lake (Fla.)
Great Barrier Reef (Qld.)
Asama Mountain (Japan)
Lake District (England)
Tay River (Scotland)

(b) *Entities located in two jurisdictions.* For an entity located in two jurisdictions, the names of both are added as qualifiers. The names are added in alphabetical order unless the entity is located principally in one of the jurisdictions, which then will be the one listed first. For a river, however, the place of origin is always listed first:

Everest, Mount (China and Nepal)
Neusiedler Lake (Austria and Hungary)

Wye, River (Wales and England)
Black Creek (N.M. and Ariz.)

This policy, however, does not apply to international bodies of water, which are not qualified unless there is a conflict:

Bering Strait
English Channel

(c) *Entities located in more than two jurisdictions.* For an entity that spreads over three or more jurisdictions, no qualifier is added unless there is a conflict or the name is ambiguous:

Appalachian Region
Gaza Strip
Caribbean Sea
Amazon River
West (U.S.)

(d) *Conflicts between geographic entities.* In cases of conflicts between headings representing the same type of geographic entity, one or more narrower jurisdictions are added, followed by a comma, before the regular qualifier within the same set of parentheses:

Pelican Lake (Otter Tail County, Minn.)
Pelican Lake (Saint Louis County, Minn.)

Paraná River (Brazil-Argentina)
Paraná River (Goiás, Brazil)

Rio Negro (Amazonas, Brazil)
Rio Negro (Brazil and Uruguay)

If the conflict involves a river located in more than two jurisdictions, a qualifier containing the name of the jurisdiction in which the river originates and the name of the jurisdiction where the mouth is located is added. In this case, the two names are joined with a hyphen instead of with *and:*

Red River (Tex.-La.)
Coon Creek (Monroe County-Vernon County, Wis.)

If the conflict exists between headings representing different types of geographic entities, a generic qualifier is added after the regular qualifier in the same set of parentheses and separated by the sequence space-colon-space:

Mecklenburg (Germany : Castle)
Mecklenburg (Germany : Region)

Cape of Good Hope (South Africa)   [the city]
Cape of Good Hope (South Africa : Cape)

(e) *Individual non-jurisdictional islands or island groups.*[30] Individual non-jurisdictional islands or island groups that lie near a land mass and are under its jurisdiction, as well as individual islands that form part of a jurisdictional island cluster, are qualified by the name of the country, the first-order political division, or the jurisdictional island cluster:

Aegina Island (Greece)
Elizabeth Islands (Mass.)
Hawaii Island (Hawaii)
Izu Islands (Japan)
Nantucket Island (Mass.)
Santa Catalina Island (Calif.)
        [not Santa Catalina Island (Channel Islands, Calif.)]
Palma (Canary Islands)
Madeira (Madeira Islands)
Pulap Island (Micronesia)
Rota Island (Northern Mariana Islands)
Shortland Islands (Solomon Islands)

The name of the city is used as the qualifier if the island is a city section or if the city name is needed to resolve a conflict:

Ile de la Cité (Paris, France)

Qualifiers are not used with isolated islands or island groups that are not associated with a mainland country, or with islands that comprise more than one autonomous jurisdiction:

Borneo
Islands of the Pacific
Midway Islands

(f) *Natural features within cities.* Lakes, hills, and the like located within cities are qualified by the name of the larger jurisdiction rather than by the name of the city, except in cases of conflict:

Corpus Christi, Lake (Tex.)

(g) *Other entities within cities.* Headings for city districts, quarters, sections, and other entities located within a city (e.g., buildings, parks, streets, plazas, bridges, monuments) are qualified by the name of the city in the established form. Examples include:

Georgetown Square (Washington, D.C.)
Quartier des Halles (Paris, France)
Times Square (New York, N.Y.)

Sunset Boulevard (Los Angeles, Calif.)
Hôtel de Ville (Lausanne, Switzerland)
Roman Forum (Rome, Italy)
Golden Gate Bridge (San Francisco, Calif.)
Park Avenue (New York, N.Y.)

The name of a borough, city section, or city district is used as a qualifier only if it is necessary to resolve a conflict between entities with identical names located in the same city.

(h) *Entities on islands.* Headings for entities on islands are qualified by the name of the island established either as a jurisdictional or non-jurisdictional heading:

Tan-shui River (Taiwan)
Hellshire Hills (Jamaica)
Teide, Pico de (Tenerife, Canary Islands)
Werner Mountain (Greenland)

Headings for entities on islands in Hawaii, Japan, or New Zealand are qualified by **(Hawaii), (Japan),** or **(N.Z.),** instead of the names of the individual islands, which are used only in cases of conflict. Examples include:

Kaneohe Bay (Hawaii)
Fuji, Mount (Japan)
Taupo, Lake (N.Z.)
Kailua Bay (Hawaii Island, Hawaii)

(i) *Other qualifiers.* Places in Antarctica are qualified by **(Antarctica),** and places on the moon are qualified by **(Moon):**

Transantarctic Mountains (Antarctica)
Victoria Land (Antarctica)
Mare Crisium (Moon)

Type-of-Jurisdiction Qualifiers

When two or more places belonging to different types of jurisdictions bear the same name, a qualifier indicating the type of jurisdiction is added, in accordance with *AACR2R*. The type-of-jurisdiction qualifier follows the geographic qualifier if there is one. Because headings for all modern cities now carry geographic qualifiers, the qualifier *(City)* used with some of the pre-1981 headings, such as *New York (City)*; *Rome (City)*, is no longer used. The type-of-jurisdiction qualifier is usually an English term, if available. The vernacular term is used when there is no equivalent in English. Examples include:

Québec (Province)
Québec (Québec)

Naples (Italy)
Naples (Kingdom)
Poznań (Poland : Voivodeship)
Poznań (Poland)

The type-of-jurisdiction qualifier is omitted when the name of the jurisdiction itself is used as a qualifier:

Washington (State) [form of heading]
(Wash.) [form when used as qualifier]

Micronesia (Federated States) [form of heading]
(Micronesia) [form when used as qualifier]

Arequipa (Peru : Dept.) [form of heading]
(Arequipa, Peru) [form when used as qualifier]

Free-Floating Phrase Headings
Involving Names of Places[31]

A number of free-floating phrases may be combined with certain types of geographic names to form valid headings. The term *free-floating* means that a word or phrase may be combined with a valid main heading without the usage being authorized formally. Headings resulting from free-floating combinations do not appear in LCSH unless they carry unique references or subdivisions or are used as examples.

(1) *Geographic regions*. The word **Region** may be added to a valid heading for a geographic feature (including parks, roads, mines, etc., but not islands, river valleys, or watersheds) to form a subject heading:

Geographic heading	*Heading for region*
Caspian Sea	Caspian Sea Region
Danube River	Danube River Region[32]
Death Valley (Calif. and Nev.)	Death Valley Region (Calif. and Nev.)[33]
Himalaya Mountains	Himalaya Mountains Region
Rocky Mountain National Park (Colo.)	Rocky Mountain National Park Region (Colo.)
Saint Helens, Mount (Wash.)	Saint Helens, Mount, Region (Wash.)
Sandia Mountains (N.M.)	Sandia Mountains Region (N.M.)

Regions that are well known by alternative name forms and those having unique names are entered under those names instead of names constructed as above:

Caribbean Area
      [not Caribbean Sea Region]
Mediterranean Region
      [not Mediterranean Sea Region]
Sierra Nevada Region (Calif. and Nev.)
      [not Sierra Nevada Mountains Region (Calif. and Nev.)]
Black Country (England)
Midlands (England)
Innviertel (Austria)
Texas Hill Country (Tex.)

The terms **Watershed, Delta**, and **Estuary** were previously free-floating. Their use as free-floating elements has been discontinued; all headings for watersheds, deltas, and estuaries are now authorized and displayed in LCSH, for example:

Loch Vale Watershed (Colo.)
Po River Delta (Italy)
Potomac River Estuary

(2) *River valleys.* The word **Valley**, which designates the flatlands extending along the course of a river and its tributaries, is free-floating and may be added to the valid heading for a river to form a subject heading.

Heading for river	*Heading for valley*
Po River (Italy)	**Po River Valley (Italy)**
Connecticut River	**Connecticut River Valley**
Tombigbee River	**Tombigbee River Valley**
(Miss. and Ala.)	**(Miss. and Ala.)**

However, headings for valley regions not associated with a river are formed by using the free-floating phrase **...Valley Region** in the heading:[34]

Death Valley (Calif. and Nev.)
Death Valley Region (Calif. and Nev.)

(3) *River regions.* Headings for river regions or watershed regions are formed by adding the free-floating term **Region** to the river name, rather than the name of the valley or watershed:

Potomac River Region
      [not Potomac River Valley Region or Potomac River
        Watershed Region]

(4) *Metropolitan areas and city regions.* These are discussed on pages 80-81.

(5) *Places "in art."* The free-floating phrase **... in art** may be added to an established geographic heading to form a phrase heading:

Long Island (N.Y.) in art
Pompeii (Extinct city) in art
Québec (Québec) in art

Because these are free-floating combinations, they are normally not listed in LCSH except when unique cross references are required or when they are used as examples.

The phrase *[Place] in literature*, as in *Spain in literature* and *Greenwich Village (New York, N.Y.) in literature*, which was previously free-floating, is no longer used. The form currently used is **[Place]—In literature**.

Changes of Name

Names of places change frequently. In such cases a decision must be made on which name or names to use as headings. There are two types of changes: linear name changes and mergers and/or splits. Following is a discussion of Library of Congress policies regarding changes of jurisdictional names used in subject entries.

Linear Name Changes[35]

When the change of the name of a country, state, city, and the like does not affect its territorial identity, all new subject headings appear under the new name—with USE references from earlier names—regardless of the period covered by the works being cataloged, and all subject headings under the old name are changed to the new name. Examples of linear name changes include:

Former name(s)	Latest name
Congo, Belgian	
Congo Free State	Zaire
Congo (Democratic Republic)	
British Honduras	Belize
Ceylon	Sri Lanka
Rhodesia, Northern	Zambia
Rhodesia, Southern	Zimbabwe

While both the earlier and later names are used as valid headings for main entries and added entries in descriptive cataloging, only the latest name is used in subject entries, both as a main heading and as a geographic qualifier, such as **(Zimbabwe)** instead of *(Rhodesia, Southern)*.[36]

The practice of using a uniform heading as the subject entry for a place regardless of name changes has the advantage of collocating material about a particular place. The policy is, however, at variance with descriptive cataloging practice, as *AACR2R* specifies successive entries rather than a uniform heading for works issued under different names of a government.

Merger or Split

When the change of name involves substantial changes affecting territorial identity, the latest form of name is used except when the following conditions *all* apply:

(1) The work cataloged deals with the time period prior to the merger or split

(2) The work is limited to historical, political, or cultural matters pertaining to the earlier jurisdictions

(3) The name is to be applied in the initial part of the subject heading and not in a subdivision

In these cases, an earlier name may be used as the subject heading instead of the latest form.

An example of a merger is the joining of the Territory of Papua and the Territory of New Guinea in 1945 to form the administrative unit of the Territory of Papua New Guinea, which became self-governing in 1973 as Papua New Guinea. The following headings are used in cataloging works about this place as appropriate:

Papua
New Guinea (Territory)
Papua New Guinea

Example of a split is the two Koreas:

Korea
Korea (North)
Korea (South)

Example of a split and merger is the two Germanies:[37]

Germany
     [pre-1949]
Germany (East)
Germany (West)
Germany
     [1990-]

Geographic Headings Requiring
Special Treatment

Some types of geographic headings are given special treatment because of their unique nature. These include names of ancient or early cities and archaeological sites; areas associated with cities; entities within cities; parks, reserves, and so forth; and other man-made structures associated with places.

Extinct Cities and Archaeological Sites[38]

Previously, the names of ancient or early cities and archaeological sites were not printed in *Library of Congress Subject Headings*. Since 1976, newly established headings in this category have been included in LCSH. Because cities that went out of existence before the creation of modern states (ca. A.D. 1500) are rarely required for descriptive cataloging, these headings are generally established as subject headings. If there is evidence that the exact original site of the ancient or early city has been continuously or recurrently occupied until modern times, however, the heading established for the modern city is used:

London (England) [instead of *Londinium*]
Vienna (Austria) [instead of *Vindobona*]

General guidelines for establishing ancient or early cities that no longer exist are described below.

(1) Use the form of the name most commonly found in standard reference sources (e.g., encyclopedias, gazetteers).

(2) Add the qualifier **(Extinct city)** to a city in Europe, Africa, or Asia if it existed only before medieval times.[39] Examples include **Pompeii (Extinct city)**; **Troy (Extinct city)**. The name of the larger jurisdiction in which the city would be located today is added if there are two cities by the same name, such as **Thebes (Egypt : Extinct city)** and **Thebes (Greece)**.

(3) When the name of an extinct city is used as a qualifier for another heading, the qualifier **(Extinct city)** is omitted:

Angkor (Extinct city)   [heading for city]
Angkor Wat (Angkor)   [form used as qualifier]

Memphis (Extinct city)   [heading for city]
Temple of Hathor (Memphis)   [form used as qualifier]

(4) For an archaeological site, the heading is established on the basis of the work being cataloged. The term **Site** and the appropriate geographic qualifier are added to the name. Examples include:

Cobá Site (Mexico)
Copan Site (Honduras)
Duke I Site (Tenn.)
Fourth of July Valley Site (Colo.)
Masada Site (Israel)

If the site is located in a modern city, the name of the city is used as the qualifier:

Roman Forum Site (London, England)
Lewis-Weber Site (Tucson, Ariz.)
Kami Site (Osaka, Japan)

If the site is a cave or mound that has been named, the name of the cave or mound is used as the site name:

Texcal Cave (Mexico)
Shanidar Cave (Iraq)

Areas Associated with Cities[40]

Four kinds of headings designate the various areas associated with an individual city, as shown in these examples based on Chicago:

Chicago (Ill.)
Chicago Metropolitan Area (Ill.)
Chicago Region (Ill.)
Chicago Suburban Area (Ill.)

In terms of territory, these four types of headings have been defined as follows:

(1) **[City name]**: the city jurisdiction itself.

(2) **[City] Metropolitan Area**: a designated area consisting of the city itself and those densely populated territories immediately surrounding it that are socially and economically integrated with it.

(3) **[City] Suburban Area**: the territory associated with the city, including neighboring residential areas lying outside the city and nearby smaller satellite jurisdictions, but not the city itself.

(4) **[City] Region**: an area including the city itself and its surrounding territory, the exact size and boundaries of which are not defined and may vary according to the work being cataloged.

The phrases **Metropolitan Area**; **Suburban Area**; and **Region** are free-floating; they may he combined with the name of a city and its qualifier to form valid headings.

Headings for metropolitan and suburban areas and city regions are qualified in the same manner as cities:

Boston Suburban Area (Mass.)
Pensacola Metropolitan Area (Fla.)
Montréal Metropolitan Area (Québec)
Binghamton Metropolitan Area (N.Y.)
        [not *Binghamton Metropolitan Area (N.Y. and Pa.)*]
Binghamton Region (N.Y.)
Jerusalem Region

Metropolitan and suburban areas and regions associated with the cities of Washington and New York are not qualified even though the headings for the cities are; thus:

New York Metropolitan Area
Washington Suburban Area

A metropolitan or suburban area or a region involving two cities is represented by two separate headings:

Dallas Metropolitan Area (Tex.)
Fort Worth Metropolitan Area (Tex.)
        [not *Dallas-Fort Worth Metropolitan Area (Tex.)*]

Names of metropolitan and suburban areas and city regions may be used as main headings or subdivisions.

Entities Within Cities[41]

Headings for districts, quarters, sections, and other entities located within a city, such as buildings, streets, plazas, parks, bridges, and monuments, consist of the name of the entity qualified by the name of the city.[42] The name of the entity is normally in the vernacular form of the country in which it is located, except for pre-1500 buildings and structures that have well-established English names. Examples include:

2040 Union Street (San Francisco, Calif.)
Balboa Park (San Diego, Calif.)
Boulevard du Temple (Paris, France)
Brooklyn (New York, N.Y.)
Brooklyn Bridge (New York, N.Y.)
City Park (New Orleans, La.)
Cleveland Municipal Stadium (Cleveland, Ohio)
Edinburgh Castle (Edinburgh, Scotland)
Federal Hill (Baltimore, Md.)

Fontana di Trevi (Rome, Italy)
Fort Worth Water Garden (Fort Worth, Tex.)
Gateway Arch (Saint Louis, Mo.)
Glaspalast (Munich, Germany)
Hauptbahnhof (Hamburg, Germany)
Hôtel de ville (Lyon, France)
Library of Congress James Madison Memorial Building
    (Washington, D.C.)
Mount Clare (Baltimore, Md. : Building)[43]
North End (Boston, Mass.)
Pont-Neuf (Paris, France)
Promenade du Peyrou (Montpellier, France)
Schloss Richmond (Braunschweig, Germany)
Stalag 12 D (Trier, Germany : Concentration camp)
Vestvolden (Copenhagen, Denmark)
Western Wall (Jerusalem)

Parks, Reserves, Etc.

At the Library of Congress, the following types of entities are established as non-jurisdictional headings:

public and private parks of all kinds

nature conservation areas, natural areas, natural history reservations, nature reserves

wild areas, wilderness areas, roadless areas

forests, forest reserves and preserves

seashores, marine parks and reserves, wild and scenic rivers

wildlife refuges, bird reservations and sanctuaries, game ranges and preserves, wildlife management areas

historic sites, national monuments, etc.

trails

Headings for individual parks, reserves, and the like, including those located within cities, consist of the names of the entities with appropriate geographic qualifiers. The previous practice of entering the name of a city park under the name of the city as the main heading has been discontinued. As a general rule, headings for parks, reserves, trails, streets, and roads are established in the vernacular form.[44]

Examples of headings for individual parks, reserves, and so forth include:

Bandelier National Monument (N.M.)
Fortress of Louisbourg National Historic Park (N.S.)

Hiawatha National Forest (Mich.)
Ice Age National Scientific Reserve (Wis.)
Mesa Verde National Park (Colo.)
Mount Saint Helens National Volcanic Monument (Wash.)
Naturpark Hohe Mark (Germany)
North York Moors National Park (England)
Palos Forest Preserve (Ill.)
Spruce Knob-Seneca Rocks National Recreation Area (W. Va.)

Other Man-Made Structures Associated with Places[45]

Other man-made structures include physical plants, roads, bridges, monuments, and the like not located within a particular city. They are normally entered directly under their own names, with the addition of geographic and generic qualifiers as appropriate (see discussion of geographic qualifiers on pages 69-74). Examples include:

Arkport Dam (N.Y.)
Balmoral Castle (Scotland)
Battle Road (Mass.)
Blenheim Palace (England)
EPCOT Center (Fla.)
Great Point Light (Mass.)
Great Pyramid (Egypt)
Great Wall of China (China)
Grini (Norway : Concentration camp)
Harry S. Truman Reservoir (Mo.)
Hearst-San Simeon State Historical Monument (Calif.)
Mount Vernon (Va. : Estate)
Overland Telegraph Line (N.T. and S. Aust.)
Silver Bluff (S.C.)
Sturgeon Fort (Sask.)
Three Mile Island Nuclear Power Plant (Pa.)

NOTES

[1]*Anglo-American Cataloguing Rules*, 2nd ed., 1988 revision, prepared under the direction of the Joint Steering Committee for Revision of AACR, a committee of the American Library Association, the Australian Committee on Cataloguing, the British Library, the Canadian Committee on Cataloguing, the Library Association, and the Library of Congress, eds. Michael Gorman and Paul W. Winkler (Chicago: American Library Association, 1988).

[2]For a list of such entities, consult Library of Congress, Office of Subject Cataloging Policy, *Subject Cataloging Manual*, 4th ed. (Washington, D.C.: Cataloging Distribution Service, Library of Congress, 1991), H405.

[3]Categories of unprinted headings are listed in chapter 8.

[4]Library of Congress, *Subject Cataloging Manual*, H1574, H1631.

[5]Charles A. Cutter, *Rules for a Dictionary Catalog*, 4th ed. rewritten. (Washington, D.C.: GPO, 1904), 69.

[6]Library of Congress, *Subject Cataloging Manual*, H1636.

[7]*Library of Congress Rule Interpretations*, 2nd ed. (Washington, D.C.: Cataloging Distribution Service, Library of Congress, 1989).

[8]Successive entry refers to the practice, in descriptive cataloging, of establishing both former and current names as valid headings.

[9]For the assignment of subject headings to works about a corporate body, see chapter 9.

[10]For instruction concerning the forms of headings for strikes, consult the note under the heading **Strikes and Lockouts** in LCSH.

[11]"Animal and Plant Names," *Cataloging Service Bulletin* 20 (Spring 1983): 44; Library of Congress, *Subject Cataloging Manual*, H1332.

[12]Library of Congress, *Subject Cataloging Manual*, H1919.5.

[13]Library of Congress, *Subject Cataloging Manual*, H690-H1050.

[14]Geographic subdivisions are discussed in detail in chapter 5.

[15]A discussion of geographic qualifiers appears on pages 69-74.

[16]The formations **Berlin (Germany : East)** and **Berlin (Germany : West)** are used only as parts of headings for corporate bodies located in the former East or West Berlin, e.g, **Berlin (Germany : West). Abgeordenetenhaus; Berlin (Germany : West). Senat**.

[17]Library of Congress, *Subject Cataloging Manual*, H690.

[18]*Library of Congress Rule Interpretations*, 2nd ed.

[19]A discussion of geographic qualifiers appears on pages 69-74.

[20]Library of Congress, *Subject Cataloging Manual*, H690.

[21]Library of Congress, *Subject Cataloging Manual*, H690, p. 3.

[22]Library of Congress, *Subject Cataloging Manual*, H690.

[23]Library of Congress, *Subject Cataloging Manual*, H690.

[24]Library of Congress, *Subject Cataloging Manual*, H810.

[25]David Judson Haykin, *Subject Headings: A Practical Guide* (Washington, D.C.: GPO, 1951), 49-53.

[26]*Anglo-American Cataloguing Rules*, 435-38.

[27]Note that the qualifier **(Korea)** is used for places in both North and South Korea.

[28]Appendix I of this book provides a list of qualifiers for exceptional countries.

[29]Qualifiers for non-jurisdictional islands or island groups are discussed on pages 73-74 of this book.

[30]Library of Congress, *Subject Cataloging Manual*, H807; H810, pp. 5-6.

[31]Library of Congress, *Subject Cataloging Manual*, H760, H790, H800.

[32]A river region differs from a river in that the region includes the drainage basin and other adjacent territories beyond the basin.

[33]For valley regions associated with a river, see page 76.

[34]Library of Congress, *Subject Cataloging Manual*, H800, p. 9.

[35]Library of Congress, *Subject Cataloging Manual*, H708.

[36]Information concerning such subject cataloging usage is carried in field 667 in the USMARC format for authority records.

[37]Library of Congress, *Subject Cataloging Manual*, H945.

[38]Library of Congress, *Subject Cataloging Manual*, H715, H1225.

[39]Cities of the Americas that ceased to exist by 1500 are treated as archaeological sites. Until 1991, the qualifier (*Ancient city*) was used for cities that existed only before 1500 and the qualifier (*City*) was used for cities that existed during medieval times.

[40]Library of Congress, *Subject Cataloging Manual*, H790.

[41]Library of Congress, *Subject Cataloging Manual*, H720, H1334.

[42]Note that the names of city sections and districts may be used as main headings but are not used as geographic subdivisions. They are used as qualifiers only if necessary to resolve a conflict between entities with identical names located in the same city.

[43]Details of buildings that bear proper names are represented by headings in the form **[Name of detail] ([Name of structure])**. For example:

Hyman Liberman Memorial Door (South African National Gallery)
Saito (Yakushiji, Nara-shi, Japan)

[44]Library of Congress *Subject Cataloging Manual*, H690, p. 5.

[45]Library of Congress, *Subject Cataloging Manual*, H1334.

5 Subdivisions

In the Library of Congress subject headings system, a main heading may be subdivided by one or more elements. The concept embodied in the subdivision usually reflects a secondary emphasis with relation to the topic of the main heading.[1] Subdivisions are used extensively to subarrange a large file or bring out aspects of a topic.

The decision whether to subdivide a subject depends to a large extent on one's perception of the purpose of subdivision. If subdivision is used solely as a means of subarrangement, as David Judson Haykin believed, it is called for only if there is a substantial amount of material on a subject.[2] But if subdivision is used for the purpose of rendering a subject more specific, which is by and large the current philosophy of the Library of Congress, a heading is subdivided whenever there are documents in the collection that focus on a specific aspect of the subject. The subdivided heading thus serves to maintain coextensivity between the heading and the document, as stated in the current policy: "Subdivisions should be assigned to reflect the contents of the work, without regard to the size of the file under the basic heading."[3]

There are four types of subdivisions in the Library of Congress subject headings system: topical, geographic, chronological, and form. Topical subdivisions have always been used to achieve specificity as well as to provide for subarrangement. Current policy requires the use of form subdivisions when applicable and appropriate. On the other hand, chronological subdivisions are still used mainly as a device for subarranging large files. Many subjects that lend themselves to chronological treatment are not subdivided by period (e.g., **Satire, English**). Likewise, the histories of many small countries are not divided chronologically. In the past, form and geographic subdivisions were also used mainly as a means of subarrangement. This is why many headings have not been subdivided by place even though some of the library materials on the subject are limited to a certain locality. Newly established headings indicate a trend toward greater use of geographic subdivision even where the size of the file would not require it; the criterion followed now is suitability of geographic qualification to the literature of the subject.

TOPICAL SUBDIVISION

A topical subdivision represents an aspect of the main heading other than space, time, or form. Examples of topical subdivisions are:

Auditing—Standards
Geology—Mathematics
Venice (Italy)—Buildings, structures, etc.

In appearance, a main subject heading subdivided by a topical subdivision resembles an entry in a classed catalog, where entries typically follow a genus-species, thing-part, or class-inclusion pattern. Cutter's rules do not treat subdivision, and Haykin believed that classed entries should be avoided in a dictionary catalog. It is still accepted policy that such headings are inappropriate in a subject catalog.[4]

However, there are different types of topical subdivisions, some of which are not of the genus-species or class-inclusion type; these resemble classed entries in their outward form only. For example, the relationship between the main heading and the topical subdivision in headings such as **Heart—Diseases** or **Agriculture—Taxation** is not that of genus-species or thing-part type. Haykin wrote: "CONSTRUCTION INDUSTRY—TAXATION is another way of saying 'taxation of the construction industry', and obviously not 'taxation as a division of the subject CONSTRUCTION INDUSTRY'."[5] He stated that topical subdivision is used "only where the broad subject forms part of the name of the topic and a convenient phrase form sanctioned by usage is lacking, or, for the purpose of the catalog, where it is desirable to conform to an existing pattern."[6] For example, *legal research* is a commonly accepted phrase, while *physical research* is not. Therefore, the headings that were established for these subjects are **Legal research** and **Physics—Research**. However, in order to ensure greater uniformity, current policy requires the use of the form **[Topic]—Research** for newly established headings.

In LCSH, topical subdivisions are most often used to bring out aspects or facets of the main subject, such as concepts, methods, or techniques, rather than to indicate its kinds or parts.[7] Nonetheless, a small number of headings characteristic of classed entries have been introduced into the list. The following examples are of the genus-species type:

Shakespeare, William, 1564-1616—Characters—Children
Shakespeare, William, 1564-1616—Characters—Fathers
Wages—Minimum wage

In the first two, the genus-species relationship occurs between the subdivision and the sub-subdivision. While these headings bring together all types of characterization in Shakespeare's works—an advantage of the classed catalog—the practice results in inconsistency, because this form is not used regularly with similar or related headings, such as:

Children in literature
[not *Literature—Characters—Children*]
Retirement income
[not *Income—Retirement income*]

In these examples, the principle of specific entry is observed.

There is also a small number of headings of the thing-part type:

Airplanes—Motors—Carburetors
Airplanes—Motors—Mufflers
Airplanes—Wings

The purpose of this form is subject collocation (i.e., the grouping of different parts of an airplane together). Again, there is the problem of maintaining consistency and predictability in similar headings. Although **Motors** and **Wings** are entered as subdivisions under **Airplanes**, other parts of the airplane are entered in the direct form: **Ailerons**; **Flaps (Airplanes)**; **Tabs (Airplanes)**. Fortunately, references are made from the forms not used, and the user is guided to the forms used:

Aircraft carburetors
USE **Airplanes—Motors—Carburetors**

Airplanes—Flaps
USE **Flaps (Airplanes)**

GEOGRAPHIC SUBDIVISION

Many subjects lend themselves to geographic treatment. When the geographic aspect of the subject is of significance, geographic (also called place or local) subdivisions are often used. The policies regarding geographic subdivision have varied over the years. Until 1981, a heading that was limited to a geographic area might appear in one of two forms:

- **[Topic]—[Place]**

    Churches, Catholic—Italy
    Education—Japan

- *[Topic] in [Place]*

    Church and education in Connecticut [*Italy, United States, etc.*]
    Germans in Poland

Beginning in 1981, the type of heading *[Topic] in [Place]* was discontinued and replaced by the **[Topic]—[Place]** type of heading.[8]

In LCSH, not all headings may be subdivided geographically; the designation *(May Subd Geog)* following a heading is used to indicate that the heading may be subdivided by place. Previously, only topics that lend themselves particularly to geographic treatment and headings under which there was a large file of material could be so divided. Current policy allows a greater degree of geographic subdivision; all newly established headings for subjects that can be treated from a geographic point of view are subdivisible by place. The designation *(Not Subd Geog)* follows headings on which the Library of Congress has made a decision not to subdivide by place, as with **Applegate family** *(Not Subd Geog)*. Headings without either designation are currently not subdivided by place but may be so in the future.

For a given place, when the inverted form is used in a main heading, the same form is generally used when the place appears as a subdivision under another heading:

Asia, Southeastern—Economic conditions
Social service—Asia, Southeastern
Africa, Northeast—Strategic aspects
United States—Relations—Africa, Northeast

There are two forms of geographic subdivisions: direct and indirect. In direct geographic subdivision, the name of the place in question follows immediately a topical main heading or topical subdivision (e.g., **Art—California**); in indirect geographic subdivision, the form used with local places, the name of a larger geographic place is interposed between the topical element and the local place in question (e.g., **Art—France—Normandy**). With the exception of Antarctic regions and the names of certain island groups, no geographical name higher than the level of a country is used as an interposing element, and none below the level of a city or town is used as a geographic subdivision. Furthermore, no geographic subdivision may contain more than two levels of geographic elements. For example:

Music—Europe
Music—Germany
[not *Music—Europe—Germany*]

Music—Germany—Bavaria
Music—Germany—Munich
[not *Music—Germany—Bavaria—Munich*]

The following sections discuss direct and indirect geographic subdivision in detail. The procedures described below represent current Library of Congress policy regarding geographic subdivision.[9]

Direct Subdivision

If the place in the geographic subdivision is at the country level or above, the name of the place follows the main heading or main heading-topical subdivision combination immediately:

Benedictine nuns—Europe
Catholic Church—Belgium
Geology—Antarctica
Monarchy—Great Britain
Teachers—Training of—United States
Economic stabilization—Middle East
Peace Corps (U.S.)—Ghana
Post-communism—Former Soviet republics
Soil chemistry—Arctic regions

In addition, the types of places listed below also follow the topical element directly:

(1) the first-order political divisions of the following three countries:[10]

Country	*First-order divisions*	*Examples*
Canada	provinces	**Ontario; Alberta**
Great Britain	constituent countries	**England; Scotland**
United States	states	**Alaska; Montana**

Examples of headings include:

Animal industry—Alberta
Energy policy—Scotland
Historic buildings—England
Architecture—Massachusetts
Coastal ecology—Alaska

(2) places located in more than a single country (or first-order political division of the three exceptional countries listed above), including:

places in the three exceptional countries noted above (e.g., **Southern States; New England**)

historical kingdoms, empires, etc. (e.g., **Holy Roman Empire**)

geographic features and regions, such as continents and other major regions, bodies of water, mountain ranges, etc. (e.g., **Europe; Great Lakes; West (U.S.); Mexico, Gulf of; Rocky Mountains; Nile River Valley**)

Examples of headings include:

Earth movements—Sierra Nevada (Calif. and Nev.)
Oceanography—Baltic Sea
Art—Mediterranean Region

In such cases, any geographic qualifier normally accompanying the name is retained.[11]

(3) the cities New York, Washington, and Jerusalem:[12]

Education—New York (N.Y.)
Commuting—Washington Metropolitan Area
Art—Washington (D.C.)
Armenians—Jerusalem

Hong Kong and Vatican City are also used without interposing elements:[13]

Export marketing—Hong Kong
Christian art and symbolism—Vatican City

(4) Islands. The following types of islands or island groups are assigned directly after the heading:[14]

(a) Islands or island groups located some distance away from the controlling jurisdiction:

Crabs—Easter Island
Meteorology— Falkland Islands
Mollusks—Galapagos Islands

(b) Islands or island groups that are autonomous or comprise more than one autonomous jurisdiction:

Natural history—Borneo
Reptiles—Hispaniola
Botany—Islands of the Pacific

(c) Names of individual Caribbean islands south of the Virgin Islands. These islands are assigned directly after the heading regardless of their present political status, the reason being that most of these islands have achieved independence or appear likely to do so relatively soon. Examples of headings include:

Ethnology—Grenada
       [not *Ethnology—West Indies—Grenada*]
Marine algae—Bonaire
       [not *Marine algae—Netherlands Antilles—Bonaire*]

All other places below the country level are entered indirectly.

Indirect Subdivision

When a heading is subdivided by a place within a country, the name of the relevant country or the name of the first-order political division (in Canada, Great Britain, or the United States) is interposed between the subject heading and the name of any subordinate political, administrative, or geographical division. Although the interposition of the name of the larger geographic entity renders the heading a blatantly classed entry, the benefit of collocating materials relating to the larger area has been considered important enough by the Library of Congress to suspend the principle of specific and direct entry.

General Procedure for Indirect Subdivision

Places below the national level are normally assigned indirectly. With the exceptions noted above, a heading is subdivided locally by interposing the name of the country between the heading and the name of any geographic entity contained wholly within the country. These geographic entities include:

subordinate political jurisdictions, such as provinces, districts, counties, cities, etc.

historic kingdoms, principalities, etc.

geographic features and regions, such as mountain ranges, bodies of water, lake regions, watersheds, metropolitan areas, etc.

islands situated within the territorial limits of the country in question

Examples:

Agriculture—Brazil—Parana (State)
Architecture—Belgium—Flanders
Architecture, Gothic—Italy—Venice
Elephants—Tunisia—Carthage (Extinct city)
Excavations (Archaeology)—Greece—Athens
Geology—Turkey—Taurus Mountains
Spanish language—Dialects—Spain—Leon (Kingdom)
Upper class—France—Aix-en-Provence

The local place-name used in an indirect subdivision is not qualified by the name of a larger geographic entity if the qualifier (abbreviated or spelled out) is the same as the interposing element:[15]

Paris (France)
Art—France—Paris
        [not *Art—France—Paris (France)*]

Sacramento River (Calif.)

Eutrophication—California—Sacramento River
  [not *Eutrophication—California—Sacramento River (Calif.)*]

Vienna (Austria)
Music—Austria—Vienna

Chicago Suburban Area (Ill.)
Reference services (Libraries)—Illinois—Chicago Suburban Area

If the geographic entity in question is below the level of a first-order political division of Canada, Great Britain, or the United States, it is entered as a sub-subdivision under the name of the first-order political division.[16] In other words, the names of the first-order political divisions instead of the names of the countries are used as interposing elements:

Architecture—British Columbia—Vancouver
Architecture—England—Cambridge
Art, American—Illinois—Chicago
Cliff-dwellings—Colorado—Mesa Verde

It should be noted that, for Canada, Great Britain, and the United States, the first-order political divisions used in indirect subdivision are the same as the qualifiers used in establishing geographic headings according to the current *Anglo-American Cataloguing Rules (AACR2R)*.

Vancouver (B.C.)—Buildings, structures, etc.
Architecture—British Columbia—Vancouver

Cambridge (England)—Social conditions
Social classes—England—Cambridge

It may therefore appear that *AACR2R* governs subject cataloging policies for indirect subdivision. This is not the case; the coincidence is limited to the three countries just mentioned. This fact should be borne in mind particularly in dealing with places in Australia, Malaysia, and Yugoslavia; places within these countries are assigned through the names of the countries.

Sydney (N.S.W.)—Buildings, structures, etc.
Architecture—Australia—Sydney (N.S.W.)

In the latter example, the qualifier **(N.S.W.)** is retained in the local subdivision because it differs from the interposing element.
  In the case of a single island that is part of an island group located some distance away from its controlling jurisdiction, the name of the island group of which it is a part is interposed:

Water-supply—Canary Islands—Tenerife

An island that is part of a jurisdiction is divided indirectly through the country or first order political division:[17]

Streets—New York (State)—Long Island

When areas associated with cities are used as geographic subdivisions, they are assigned indirectly (with the exceptions noted below) through the jurisdiction in which the city proper is located, even if the area or region spreads over more than one jurisdiction (e.g., **Minorities—Missouri—Saint Louis Metropolitan Area**). By way of exception, areas and regions associated with New York City, Washington, and Jerusalem are used as direct subdivisions (e.g., **Minorities—New York Metropolitan Area; Minorities—Washington Suburban Area; Minorities—Jerusalem Region**).

No level lower than that of a city or town is used in an indirect subdivision.[18] Thus, *Tourist trade—California—Chinatown (San Francisco)* is not a valid heading. Such a topic can, however, be expressed by assigning two headings, such as **Tourist trade—California—San Francisco** and **Chinatown (San Francisco, Calif.)**.

Changes of Name or Jurisdiction

As discussed in chapter 4, when the name of the place in question has changed during the course of its existence, the latest name is always used in the subdivision, regardless of the form of the name or period covered in the work being cataloged. For example, as a geographic subdivision, **Zimbabwe** is used instead of *Southern Rhodesia*.

If a region or jurisdiction has existed under various sovereignties in its history, the name of the country currently in possession of the place is interposed, regardless of past territorial arrangements described in the work cataloged, as long as the region or jurisdiction is now wholly contained in that country:

Title: *Bibliographie der deutschsprachigen Gegenwartsliteratur im Elsass* / Bernard Bach. c1992
    SUBJECTS:
      German literature—France—Alsace—Bio-bibliography.
      German literature—20th century—Bio-bibliography.

Title: *L'Alsace autrefois* / Marie-José Strich ; préface de Auguste Wackenheim. [1992]
    SUBJECTS:
      Alsace (France)—History.
      Postcards—France—Alsace.

Extinct cities are assigned indirectly through the appropriate modern jurisdiction. For example:

Coins, Roman—Bulgaria—Abrittus (Extinct city)

Summary of Procedures
for Geographic Subdivision

Because of the complexity of geographic subdivision, the following summary of guidelines for direct and indirect geographic subdivision may be helpful.

(1) Direct subdivision

    (a) Countries or places not wholly within a country
        —France; —Europe; —Himalaya Mountains;
        —Andes Region; —Bering Sea; —Pacific Ocean

    (b) Place in two or more countries
        —Gobi Desert (Mongolia and China)

    (c) First-order political divisions (provinces, constituent countries, and states) in Canada, Great Britain, or United States
        —British Columbia; —Scotland; —Illinois

    (d) Places in two or more first-order political divisions in Canada, Great Britain, or United States
        —Severn River (Wales and England);
        —Rocky Mountains

    (e) Places with names containing name of country or first-order political division in inverted form
        —California, Southern; —Italy, Northern;
        —Tennessee, East

    (f) Three exceptional cities:
        —New York (N.Y.); —Washington (D.C.); —Jerusalem

    (g) Two city-states: **—Hong Kong** and **—Vatican City**

    (h) Islands at a distance from "owning" land mass
        —Falkland Islands

(2) Indirect subdivision

    (a) Places within a country, assigned indirectly through name of country or through first-order political division of Canada, Great Britain, or United States; only two levels permitted:
        —France—Paris; —Argentina—Buenos Aires;
        —Italy—Rome; —Illinois—Chicago; —British
        Columbia—Vancouver; —Scotland—Edinburgh

    (b) Metropolitan areas
        —Massachusetts—Boston Metropolitan Area

        If in several states, divided through the state the city is in
        —Missouri—Saint Louis Metropolitan Area

    (c) Island in a group distant from "owners," assigned indirectly through the island group

    (d) Islands close to owning jurisdiction, assigned indirectly through country or first-order political division

    (e) Latest form of name used in case of name changes
        —Sri Lanka— [not *—Ceylon—*]; **—Zimbabwe—**
        [not *—Rhodesia, Southern—*]

    (f) Present territory used as interposing element in case of territorial changes

    (g) Qualifier for local place-name omitted if the same as interposing element

  (3) City sections not used in geographic subdivision, lowest level being the city

  (4) Common citation order of local subdivision
      **[Topical main heading—Topical subdivision
      —Geographic subdivision—Chronological
      subdivision—Form subdivision]**

  (5) Indirect subdivision involving places in Malaysia, Yugoslavia, and Australia not affected by *AACR2R* rules for qualifiers

CHRONOLOGICAL SUBDIVISION

A chronological subdivision brings out the time period of the subject represented by the main heading. Such a subdivision may follow the main heading directly or appear after another subdivision. Not all headings are subdivided chronologically. For the most part, chronological subdivision is used with main headings that lend themselves to chronological treatment, most frequently in the social sciences or humanities, and particularly in history. The chronological subdivisions used under a heading either correspond to epochs generally recognized in the literature of the field or represent spans of time frequently treated in books. Formerly, many chronological subdivisions used in cataloging did not appear in the printed list. This policy was changed in 1975, and now all established chronological subdivisions appear in LCSH.

General Principles of Chronological Subdivision

A chronological subdivision under a heading denotes a certain point in time or a span of time. The division into chronological periods varies according to place and to subject: Scholarly consensus is the general guide.

Chronological subdivisions under the history of a given country are not always mutually exclusive. As Haykin pointed out, "the presence in the catalog of broad subdivisions does not preclude the use of subdivisions covering events or lesser epochs falling within the broad period."[19] In application, however, a broad chronological subdivision and a more specific chronological subdivision falling within it are not usually used together for the same work. Prior to the eighth edition of *Library of Congress Subject Headings*, when two or more chronological subdivisions began with the same date, greater periods were placed before lesser periods:

> France—History—1789-1900
> —1789-1815
> —Revolution
> —Revolution, 1789-1793
> —Revolution, 1789

This, of course, is a logical arrangement reflecting the principle of general before specific. However, since the eighth edition, in order to facilitate computer filing, a strictly numerical arrangement has been adopted, resulting in shorter periods being filed before broad periods:

> France—History—Revolution, 1789
> —Revolution, 1789-1793
> —Revolution, 1789-1799
> —1789-1815
> —1789-1900

In chronological subdivisions under the name of a country that has undergone one or more name changes, the latest name of the country is used as the main heading; occasionally, this practice produces anachronistic headings (e.g., **United States—History—Colonial period, ca. 1600-1775**). The advantage of collocating the history of a particular country under the same heading has outweighed logical considerations.

Chronological subdivisions under subjects other than countries are usually mutually exclusive:

> **English literature—Middle English, 1100-1500**
> **—Early modern, 1500-1700**
> **—18th century**
> **—19th century**
> **—20th century**

Corporate headings for chiefs of state that are used as main or added entries, such as *Great Britain. Sovereign (1558-1603: Elizabeth)*, are not used as subject headings except when they are needed as name-title subject entries.

Title: *In Congress. December 6, 1775 : We the delegates of the thirteen United Colonies in North America have taken into our most serious consideration a proclamation issued from the Court of St. James's on the twenty-third day of August last. ...* [1775]
SUBJECTS:

> **Great Britain. Sovereign (1760-1820 : George III). By the King. A proclamation for suppressing rebellion and sedition.**
> **United States—History—Revolution, 1775-1783 —Causes.**

For a work about the reign or administration of a chief of state, a counterpart in the form of **[Name of jurisdiction]—History— [Chronological subdivision]** is used.

One peculiarity in the treatment of wars and battles has been pointed out by Haykin.[20] Wars, other than civil wars, are entered under their own names with references from the names of participating countries followed by the appropriate periods of their history, and from variant names that have been applied to the wars:

> **Austro-Prussian War, 1866**
> > [with references from the following:
> > **Austria—History—Austro-Prussian War, 1866**
> > **Austro-German War, 1866**
> > **Prussia (Germany)—History—Austro-Prussian War, 1866**
> > **Seven Weeks' War**]
> **Spain—History—Civil War, 1936-1939**

Exceptions are made for wars, other than those of worldwide scope, in which the United States (or the American colonies) participated; these are entered under **United States**:

> **United States—History—King George's War, 1744-1748**
> **United States—History—Tripolitan War, 1801-1805**
> **World War, 1914-1918**

Battles, on the other hand, are entered under their own names rather than under the war headings, with cross references from the latter:

> **Trafalgar, Battle of, 1805**
> **Lenino, Battle of, 1943**

Forms of Chronological Subdivisions

Before describing the various forms of chronological subdivisions, it is important to note that such subdivision is not the only device in the Library of Congress system for representing the chronological aspects of a topic. Some main headings denote both subject and chronological characteristics; their most common form is an inverted adjectival phrase:

Art, Ancient
Art, Baroque
Art, Gothic
Art, Medieval
Art, Renaissance
Art, Rococo
Art, Romanesque

There are several different forms for true chronological subdivisions. Furthermore, different forms may appear under the same heading, depending on which form is most appropriate for representing a particular period.

(1) A main heading may be followed by a subdivision containing the beginning and ending dates or the beginning date alone (also called an open-ended date):

Egypt—Economic conditions—332 B.C.-640 A.D.
Japan—Economic conditions—1989-
United States—Social life and customs—1783-1865
World politics—1945-

(2) A main heading may be followed by a subdivision containing the name of a monarch, a historical period, or an event, followed by dates:

Christian art and symbolism—Medieval, 500-1500
English drama—Restoration, 1660-1700
German poetry—Middle High German, 1050-1500
China—History—Ming dynasty, 1368-1644
Germany—History—Ferdinand I, 1556-1564
Germany—History—Unification, 1990
Japan—History—Meiji period, 1868-1912
United States—History—King William's War, 1689-1697
United States—History—Colonial period, ca. 1600-1775
United States—History—Revolution, 1775-1783

This form is mostly used with the subdivision **—History** under names of places. The same periods, when applied under topical subdivisions such as —**Foreign relations** and —**Politics and government**, usually appear without the descriptive terms or phrases:

> **Great Britain—History—Puritan Revolution, 1642-1660**
> **Great Britain—Politics and government—1642-1660**
>
> **Great Britain—History—Victoria, 1837-1901**
> **Great Britain—Foreign relations—1837-1901**

(3) A main or subdivided heading may be followed by the name of the century as a subdivision:

> **Europe, Eastern—Church history—20th century**
> **Italian poetry—15th century**
> **Netherlands—Church history—17th century**

This form of chronological subdivision is usually adopted when there is no distinctive name for the period or event, when a longer period of time than a single event or movement has to be covered, or when only very broad chronological subdivisions are required.

(4) A main heading may be followed by a chronological subdivision constructed with the preposition **To** followed by a date:

> **Sicily (Italy)—Politics and government—To 1282**
> **Great Britain—Civilization—To 1066**
> **Rome—History—To 510 B.C.**

This type of chronological subdivision usually appears as the first of the chronological subdivisions under a subject or place. It is used when the beginning date is uncertain or cannot be determined.

(5) A main heading may be followed by a subdivision in the form —**Early works to [date]**. While chronological subdivisions usually indicate the periods covered in works, this type of chronological subdivision represents the date of publication (e.g., **Aeronautics—Early works to 1900**; **Geometry—Early works to 1800**). This type is used most frequently with headings in scientific or technical fields, because scholars often want to separate recent works from earlier literature.

Many headings with the subdivision —**Description and travel** were further subdivided by date of publication (e.g., *Germany—Description and travel—1919-1944*). This type of chronological subdivision is being phased out in favor of simply —**Description and travel** or —**Description and travel—Early works to 1800**.[21]

FORM SUBDIVISION

Haykin defined the term *form subdivision* and explained its nature and function in the following words: "Form subdivision may be defined as the extension of a subject heading based on the form or arrangement of the subject matter in the book. In other words, it represents what the book is, rather than what it is about, the subject matter being expressed by the main heading."[22]

Form subdivisions include those that indicate either the physical or the bibliographical form of a work, such as —**Bibliography**; —**Maps**; —**Encyclopedias**; —**Pamphlets**; —**Periodicals**; —**Pictorial works**; —**Software**. They may follow any type of main heading or heading string, such as:

Art, Medieval—Congresses
Cosmology—Encyclopedias
Minorities—Massachusetts—Bibliography
Great Britain—History—Civil War, 1642-1649—Pamphlets

Traditionally, certain subdivisions that indicate intended audiences, forms of presentation, or authors' approaches to their subjects are also considered to be form subdivisions, occasionally referred to as inner forms (e.g., —**Biography**; —**History**; —**Juvenile literature**; —**Study and teaching**).

In some cases, a form subdivision may be further subdivided by one or more additional form subdivisions:

Great Plains—History—Sources—Bibliography—Catalogs
France—Industries—Statistics—Periodicals

Form subdivisions appear under all types of headings, including topical, geographic, corporate, and personal name headings. Previously, use of form subdivisions under corporate and name headings was restricted. This policy has been changed, and now form subdivisions are used under these headings where appropriate.[23] One area still not fully developed in regard to form subdivisions is nonprint media. In the treatment of subject content, there should not be any difference between book and nonbook materials. Because the main difference between them is the physical format or media, it would appear that using form subdivisions indicating the media to bring out the differences would be appropriate. In practice, however, there are relatively few subdivisions representing nonprint media in LCSH so far. Those that exist include:

—**Juvenile films**
—**Juvenile software**
—**Juvenile sound recordings**
—**Microform catalogs**
—**Software**
—**Video catalogs**

Many form subdivisions are used to represent both works *in* the form and those *about* the form.[24] In the latter case, they function as topical subdivisions. For example, in **Medicine—Periodicals**, meaning a general medical journal, the subdivision indicates the bibliographic form, whereas in **Medicine—Periodicals—History**, the subdivision **—Periodicals** is part of the subject. In other words, it is the function of the subdivision in a string that determines whether a subdivision is a topical or form subdivision.

In some cases, works *in* a particular form and works *about* that form are represented by different subdivisions or combinations. For example, **—Abstracts** and **—Indexes** are used for works *in* those forms, while **—Abstracting and indexing** is used for works *about* the preparation of abstracts and indexes in a particular field.

FREE-FLOATING SUBDIVISIONS[25]

Definition and Application

At the Library of Congress, each time a subdivision is used under a heading for the first time, its usage must be established editorially (i.e., authorized), in the same manner that a new heading is established. (This procedure is described in chapter 7.) There are, however, certain exceptions to this pattern of practice. A number of subdivisions, generally of wide application, have been designated as "free-floating." A free-floating subdivision is defined as a "form or topical subdivision that may be assigned by the subject cataloger without the usage being established editorially, and, as a consequence, without the usage appearing in the *SUBJECTS* file under each individual subject heading."[26] As a result, many subject strings found in bibliographic records do not appear in LCSH.

Although the official designation of a large number of subdivisions as free-floating did not take place until 1974, limited use of such subdivisions dated back to the second edition (1919) of *Subject Headings Used in the Dictionary Catalogues of the Library of Congress*, in which certain form subdivisions were omitted from the printed list but were used in cataloging. In the fourth edition, the concept of pattern headings—meaning the use of certain headings as patterns or models for subdivisions for headings in the same subject category—was introduced through the inclusion of the headings for four persons (Abraham Lincoln, Napoleon Bonaparte, William Shakespeare, and George Washington) as models for personal name headings. In subsequent editions, common form subdivisions and pattern headings continued to expand until 1974, when a large number of commonly used subdivisions were declared free-floating.[27]

The increased use of free-floating subdivisions and pattern headings has contributed toward the transformation of LCSH from a basically enumerative system into an increasingly analytico-synthetic one. In a way, these subdivisions are analogous to the standard subdivisions in the *Dewey Decimal Classification*, which reflect the principle of facet analysis and provide for freedom of synthesis.

Most of the **[Heading]—[Free-floating subdivision]** combinations that were established in the past and enumerated in the printed list have been gradually removed. Some are kept in the list because they require unique cross references or serve as examples.

In application, although free-floating subdivisions may be assigned freely by catalogers, they should not be used without regard for appropriateness or for established principles governing the use of a particular subdivision. In determining the appropriateness of using a free-floating subdivision for the first time under a subject heading, the following considerations should be borne in mind.

(1) *Correct usage.* The cataloger should consider the compatibility of the subdivision with the subject heading to which it is being attached. Many free-floating subdivisions have restricted usage; they are used under specific types of main headings or under certain circumstances. Information regarding their proper usage is found in three sources: scope notes and general references in LCSH, free-floating lists and instructions in *Subject Cataloging Manual*, and the publication *Free-Floating Subdivisions: An Alphabetical Index*.[28] Any limitations in scope and application accompanying the subdivision should be observed.

(2) *Conflict.* Before assigning a free-floating subdivision, the cataloger should first determine whether the use under consideration conflicts with a previously established heading. If there is a conflict, the subdivision should not be assigned. Frequently, there already exists a phrase heading carrying the same meaning as the heading with subdivision being considered. For example, because the heading **Library administration** already exists, the subdivision **—Administration** should not be used under **Libraries**. Also **Electronic apparatus and appliances** is used instead of *Electronics—Equipment and supplies*; **Christmas music** instead of *Christmas—Songs and music*.

Categories of Free-Floating Subdivisions

There are six categories of free-floating subdivisions. These are discussed below.

Free-Floating Form and Topical Subdivisions of General Application

A large number of common subdivisions have been designated free-floating. They include common form subdivisions that can be used under virtually all types of headings and those topical subdivisions that are widely used across many subject areas or disciplines, for example, **—Bibliography**; **—Dictionaries**; **—Periodicals**. Some of them are further subdivided by other form, topical, or, in a few cases, chronological sub-subdivisions. Usage of these subdivisions is explained in the scope notes that appear in the *Subject Cataloging Manual* as well as in the introduction to the print version of *Library of Congress Subject Headings* and under individual entries in LCSH. Appendix B of this book contains a list of free-floating form and topical subdivisions used under main headings that represent topics.

Many of the free-floating subdivisions may be further subdivided by place, as instructed by the designation *(May Subd Geog)* after the subdivision.[29]

Free-Floating Subdivisions Under Specific Types of Headings

The Library of Congress has developed separate lists of free-floating subdivisions used under headings of the following types: classes of persons, ethnic groups, corporate bodies, names of persons, names of places, and bodies of water. (For selective lists of these subdivisions, see appendixes C and E.)[30] Among these, subdivisions used under the names of persons and places merit special attention.

Free-Floating Subdivisions Under Individual Name Headings

(1) *Persons.* Headings for individual persons other than literary authors (discussed further below) may be subdivided by the terms appearing in the list of free-floating subdivisions used under headings for persons.[31]

Previously, a number of personal headings were designated as pattern headings for subdivisions in several broad categories of persons: rulers and statespeople, musicians, philosophers, founders of religions, and literary authors. Free-floating subdivisions were established and printed in *Library of Congress Subject Headings* under these pattern name headings. In 1985 the separate lists of free-floating subdivisions used under personal names were consolidated into one list for all personal headings except those of literary authors, for which the heading **Shakespeare, William, 1564-1616** continues to serve as the pattern heading.

The following examples show combinations of personal name headings with free-floating subdivisions:

Alexander, the Great, 356-323 B.C.—Friends and associates
Kennedy, John F. (John Fitzgerald), 1917-1963—Assassination
Mozart, Wolfgang Amadeus, 1756-1791—Homes and haunts

The list of free-floating subdivisions used under headings for persons appears in appendix E of this book. Among the subdivisions listed, four relate the person to specific disciplines, fields, or topics:

—Career in [specific field or discipline]
—Contributions in [specific field or topic]
—Knowledge—Agriculture, [America, etc.][32]
—Views on [specific topic]

These subdivisions are to be completed on a free-floating basis:

Jefferson, Thomas, 1743-1826—Career in agriculture
Jefferson, Thomas, 1743-1826—Contributions in architecture
Debussy, Claude, 1862-1918—Knowledge—Literature
John Paul II, Pope, 1920-   —Views on Judaism.

(2) *Families.* A short list of free-floating subdivisions used under names of families appears in the instruction sheet on genealogical materials in *Subject Cataloging Manual.*[33] Examples include:

—Archives
—Correspondence
—Homes and haunts (*May Subd Geog*)
—Photograph collections
—Political activity
—Registers

(3) *Corporate bodies.*[34] Free-floating subdivisions appearing in this list may be used under headings for individual corporate bodies covering a large variety: businesses and corporations, nonprofit institutions, voluntary associations, cultural institutions, religious organizations, political parties, fraternal groups, labor organizations, professional societies, clubs, international agencies, government agencies on all levels, and more. Also included are individual exhibitions, fairs, expositions, and the like. However, individual corporate bodies covered by pattern headings, such as individual educational institutions and legislative bodies, are excluded; so are jurisdictions that are covered in the list for places.
Examples include:

—Buildings
—By-laws
—Corrupt practices
—Officials and employees

Free-Floating Subdivisions Under Geographic Headings

The following lists of free-floating subdivisions have been prepared for different types of geographic headings:

(1) *Subdivisions used under headings for places.* Earlier, two separate lists of subdivisions were used under headings for places—one for cities and one for regions, countries, and so forth; but in 1985 the two lists were consolidated. (For a complete listing, see appendix F.)

These subdivisions may be used, within stated limitations, under the following types of geographic name headings that have been established either as valid *AACR2R* name headings or as subject headings: continents; regions; islands; countries; states, provinces, and equivalent jurisdictions; counties and other local jurisdictions larger than cities; metropolitan areas, suburban areas, and regions based on names of cities; cities; extinct cities; and city sections, districts, or quarters. Examples of headings include:

> **Antarctica—Description and travel**
> **Asia—Foreign relations—United States**
> **Athens (Greece)—Antiquities**
> **Bermuda Islands—History—Sources**
> **Boston (Mass.)—Officials and employees—Salaries, etc.**
> **Carthage (Extinct city)—Social life and customs**
> **Hong Kong—Description and travel**
> **Rive gauche (Paris, France)—Description and travel**
> **Washington Suburban Area—Intellectual life**

Appropriate subdivisions from this list may also be used under headings for geographic features or for regions based on geographic features (e.g., **Indian Ocean Region—Emigration and immigration—History —Congresses**).

(2) *Subdivisions used with names of bodies of water.*[35] For a complete listing of these subdivisions, see appendix F. These subdivisions may be used under names of individual bodies of water, including rivers, man-made lakes, reservoirs, and canals.[36] For example:

> **California, Gulf of (Mexico)—Shorelines**
> **Colorado River (Colo.-Mexico)—Navigation**
> **Suez Canal (Egypt)—Water-rights**
> **Superior, Lake—Climate**
> **Tug Fork—Name**
> **Wolfgangsee (Austria)—Poetry**

Free-Floating Subdivisions Under Headings for Classes of Persons and Ethnic Groups

Although many of the free-floating subdivisions used under headings for classes of persons and those for ethnic groups are similar, they are established in two separate lists because each category has certain unique subdivisions not applicable to the other.[37]

> Examples: Classes of persons
> **—Bonding**
> **—Conduct of life**
> **—Medals**

Examples: Ethnic groups
    —Agriculture
    —Census
    —Missions

Free-Floating Form and Topical Subdivisions Controlled by Pattern Headings[38]

There are often subdivisions of common application for headings in a particular subject category. In order to avoid repeating these subdivisions under each heading in that category, they are listed under one or occasionally several representative headings, which then serve as patterns or models. Subdivisions under pattern headings then become free-floating and can be used with all headings of the same subject category, if appropriate, and when there is no conflict. For example, the heading **German language—Grammar, Historical** is a valid heading, even though it does not appear in LCSH, because the subdivision **—Grammar, Historical** appears under the pattern heading **English language**. Likewise, the heading **Milton, John, 1608-1674—Political and social views** is a valid heading following the pattern of Shakespeare.

Table 5.1 shows the pattern headings designated by the Library of Congress as of 1995.[39] Lists of free-floating subdivisions under many of the pattern headings listed in Table 5.1, on pages 108-109, appear in *Subject Cataloging Manual*. Lists of subdivisions used with some of the more common pattern headings are included in appendix C of this book. Where there is a discrepancy or conflict between the subdivisions appearing in one of these lists and those listed under the pattern heading in LCSH, the source that bears a later date has precedence since it represents more recent revisions.

As noted earlier, personal name headings for literary authors may be subdivided according to the pattern heading **Shakespeare**. Examples include:

Eliot, T. S. (Thomas Stearns), 1888-1965—Criticism and interpretation
Dickens, Charles, 1812-1870—Technique

Note that a number of subdivisions that appear under the heading for Shakespeare are not applicable to works about him, for example: **Shakespeare, William, 1564-1616—Political activity**. Because the heading for **Shakespeare** serves as the pattern for subdivisions under the headings for other literary authors, such subdivisions are included for use as needed.

Table 5.1.

Pattern Headings Established by the Library of Congress as of 1995.

Subject Field	Category	Pattern Heading(s)	
RELIGION	Religious and monastic orders	Jesuits	H1186
	Religions	Buddhism	H1185
	Christian denominations	Catholic Church	H1187
	Sacred works (including parts)	Bible	H1188

Subject Field	Category	Pattern Heading(s)	
HISTORY AND GEOGRAPHY	Colonies of individual countries	Great Britain— Colonies	H1149.5
	Legislative bodies (including individual chambers)	United States. Congress	H1155
	Military services (including armies, navies, marines, etc.)	United States— Armed Forces	H1159
		United States. Air Force	
		United States. Army	
		United States. Marine Corps	
		United States. Navy	
	Wars	World War, 1939-1945	H1200
		United States— History—Civil War, 1861-1865	

Subject Field	Category	Pattern Heading(s)	
SOCIAL SCIENCES	Industries	Construction industry	H1153
		Retail trade	
	Types of educational institutions	Universities and colleges	H1151.5
	Individual educational institutions	Harvard University	H1151
	Legal topics	Labor laws and legislation	H1154.5

Subject Field	Category	Pattern Heading(s)	
THE ARTS	Groups of literary authors (including authors, poets, dramatists, etc.)	Authors, English	H1155.2
	Individual literary authors	Shakespeare, William, 1564-1616	H1155.4
	Literary works entered under author	Shakespeare, William, 1564-1616. Hamlet	H1155.6
	Literary works entered under title	Beowulf	H1155.8
	Languages and groups of languages	English language French language Romance languages	H1154
	Literatures (including individual genres)	English literature	H1156
	Music compositions	Operas	H1160
	Musical instruments	Piano	H1161

Subject Field	Category	Pattern Heading(s)	
SCIENCE AND TECHNOLOGY	Land vehicles	Automobiles	H1195
	Materials	Concrete Metals	H1158
	Chemicals	Copper Insulin	H1149
	Organs and regions of the body	Heart Foot	H1164
	Diseases	Cancer Tuberculosis	H1150
	Plants and crops	Corn	H1180
	Animals	Fishes Cattle	H1147

Free-floating subdivisions that may be used with headings control-led by pattern headings are not limited to those appearing in the pattern headings lists. The general free-floating subdivisions (discussed above), although not listed under pattern headings, may also be applied as appropriate.

Birds—Poetry
[—**Poetry** is a general free-floating subdivision, although it is not listed under either the heading **Birds** or the pattern heading for animals, **Fishes**]
German language—Periodicals

They may also be further subdivided by place or common free-floating form subdivisions when appropriate:

**English language—Rhetoric—Study and teaching
—United States
Spanish language—Semantics—Bibliography**

Free-Floating Chronological Subdivisions

In general, chronological subdivisions are not free-floating because period divisions are unique under individual topics and regarding specific places. In the list of free-floating subdivisions of general application, there are a number of broad chronological subdivisions used as sub-subdivisions under the free-floating subdivision **—History**:

**—History—16th century
—17th century
—18th century
—19th century
—20th century**

Their use is restricted to topical headings to which the free-floating subdivision **—History** can be assigned appropriately. However, they are not used with headings that begin with the name of a region, country, or the like. For example, *America—History—19th century* is not a valid heading.

In addition, a limited number of free-floating chronological subdivisions are included under the pattern headings for music compositions and under certain headings in literature.

Chronological subdivisions under headings for places are enumerated in LCSH and *LC Period Subdivisions Under Names of Places*.[40]

Subjects or Topics As Free-Floating Subdivisions

According to Library of Congress practice, under certain headings, names of subjects may be assigned as subdivisions whenever appropriate without establishing the usage editorially. These headings are indicated by means of a "multiple" subdivision, such as:[41]

**Baptism—Anglican Communion, [Catholic Church, etc.]
Mysticism—Brahmanism, [Judaism, Nestorian Church, etc.]
English language—Dictionaries—French, [Italian, etc.]
Bibliography—Bibliography—Agriculture, [America,
    Botany, Shakespeare, William, 1564-1616, etc.]
Reference books—Chemistry, [San Francisco (Calif.),
    Journalism, Shakespeare, William, 1564-1616, etc.]**

The following headings may be generated from headings with the multiple subdivisions listed above:

Baptism—Armenian Church
Mysticism—Eastern Orthodox Church
French language—Dictionaries—Sango

(Further details on multiple subdivisions are given in chapter 8.)

In addition to the free-floating subdivisions discussed above, LCSH includes some free-floating phrases. These include free-floating combinations of certain words or phrases with geographic names and with headings used in art. Such phrase headings are discussed in chapters 4 and 10.

ORDER OF SUBDIVISIONS

In the early stages of the development of LCSH, subdivisions were relatively simple. Usually, a subject was divided by a form, chronological, place, or topical aspect. Gradually, more and more subdivisions were introduced, and various kinds of subdivisions were sanctioned as applicable to the same heading, to form a string of terms. Furthermore, in many cases, more than one subdivision of the same kind may now be used under a particular heading. The string in some cases can be quite elaborate, such as:

United States—History—Civil War, 1861-1865—Secret
    service—Juvenile literature
Mathematics—Study and teaching (Secondary)
    —Illinois—Chicago

Order of Main Heading and Subdivision

In the formation of headings with numerous subdivisions, the order of elements in the string is important. Until recently, there were few stated instructions concerning this order. Modern classification schemes contain such instructions, called *citation formulae*. But in most cases, subject catalogers have had to rely on arrangements already established in the list as a guide. New headings were generally established according to existing patterns. Even so, what was done over the years was not always consistent. Thus, there is considerable variation on this score in LCSH as it stands now.

The matter is not simply the question of the optimal order of subdivisions under a heading. When a subject for which a heading is to be devised contains a topical element and another element representing place or another topical aspect, it is often necessary to determine which is to be the main heading and which the subdivision—in other words, which should be the entry element.

Topic Versus Form

On the whole, the topic serves as the main heading, with the form as a subdivision, such as **Chemistry—Bibliography**; **Library science—Periodicals**. There are a few exceptions to this pattern (e.g., **Reference books—Chemistry**).

Topic Versus Period

Like the form subdivision, the chronological division does not usually stand alone without first conceding the subject. Rather, topics are divided by time periods (e.g., **Drama—18th century**). There is, however, an exception to this pattern. Widely used names of historical periods may appear as main headings. In such cases, they are not usually subdivided by topic, although they are often subdivided by form of material (e.g., **Renaissance—Juvenile literature**; **Middle Ages—Bibliography**).

Topic Versus Topic

In LCSH, the term representing a concrete subject generally serves as the main heading, and the term indicating an action serves as the subdivision; the usage is similar to the key system/action arrangement in many indexing systems. This concrete/action citation order is in line with modern theories of facet analysis and synthesis, which have been expounded over time by Julius O. Kaiser (concrete/process), Marie Louise Prevost (noun rule), Brian C. Vickery (substance/action), S. R. Ranganathan (personality/energy), Derek Austin (key system/action), and E. J. Coates (thing/action).[42] In LCSH, this citation pattern is generally observed:

> **Kidneys—Surgery**
> **Kidneys—Diseases—Diagnosis**
> **Automobiles—Taxation**

However, there are exceptions:

> **Advertising—Cigarettes**
> **Classification—Books**

Topic Versus Place

Place-names are used widely as subdivisions under a topic to indicate the geographical aspect from which a subject is treated, just as chronological and form subdivisions show time and literary approach or physical form. In contrast with period or form, place may also be the main subject of a work, particularly in the fields of history and geography. In many fields of social sciences, in fact, place may be considered of greater significance than topic even when it is not featured as such. In such cases, a place-name may be used as the main heading, with subdivisions for topical and other elements as appropriate (e.g., **United States—History**; **United States—Social life and customs**). In some cases, the distinction or emphasis is not so obvious, as in works on geology.

Because of the principle of uniform heading, catalogers do not have free rein to use reciprocal place/topic and topic/place headings for the same concept. What principles can they then follow in reaching a decision on whether to favor place or topic?

In an attempt to solve the topic/place problem, Coates proposed ranking the main areas of knowledge according to the extent to which they appear to be significantly conditioned by locality: (1) geography and biological phenomena, (2) history and social phenomena, (3) language and literature, (4) fine arts, (5) philosophy and religion, (6) technology, and (7) phenomena of physical sciences. He suggests that subjects near the top of this list be entered under the place subdivided by the subject and those at the bottom be treated in reverse, but recognizes that the "problem is at what point in the middle of the list should the change be made."[43]

As it stands now, LCSH reflects these difficulties. Some headings are in the form of topics subdivided by place, while others have place-names subdivided by topic. As there have been no clear-cut criteria for determination, it is difficult for users or catalogers to predict which form should be used in each case. Fortunately, the list of free-floating subdivisions under place-names (see appendix F) indicates which topics are used as subdivisions under place-names. Furthermore, for each topic used as a subdivision under place-names, an SA (*see also*) reference is given under the name of the topic in LCSH:

Boundaries
> SA *subdivisions* Boundaries *under names of countries, states, etc.*

Industry
> SA *subdivision* Industries *under names of countries, cities, etc.*

As was seen to be the case for other entry element questions, the choice of the order of elements in a subdivided heading is not as important in most online systems as it is for card catalogs or printed indexes. In online systems where main heading and subdivision are equally accessible, the terms arranged in either order, **[Topic]—[Place]** or **[Place]—[Topic]**, are retrievable. However, it has an effect on browsing the index display.

Order of Subdivisions Under the Same Main Heading

When there are two or more subdivisions under the same main heading, the citation order—the order in which the elements in the heading string are arranged—can affect the meaning. As an example, take the two pairs of headings:

Science—Study and teaching—History
> [meaning the history of science education]

Science—History—Study and teaching
　　[meaning the study and teaching of science history]
Medicine—Research—United States
　　[meaning research conducted in the United States about
　　medicine anywhere]
Medicine—United States—Research
　　[meaning research on medicine as practiced in the United
　　States]

It is clear that each of these headings represents a distinct subject. The citation order should be determined by the meaning of the string. However, a predetermined order facilitates heading construction and consistency among catalogers. For this consideration and in the interest of facilitating machine validation of subject headings, the Airlie House Conference recommended that, in the case of a topical main heading with numerous subdivisions, a consistent citation order be established in the following form regardless of its impact on the meaning: *[Topic]—[Topical subdivision]—[Geographic subdivision]—[Chronological subdivision]—[Form subdivision].*[44] Until a decision is made concerning the implementation of this recommendation, current guidelines regarding citation order prevail. Currently, there are two basic patterns for citation order:[45]

(1) When the string begins with a geographic heading, the elements are generally arranged in the following citation order:

[Place]—[Topic]—[Time]—[Form]

For example:

England—Civilization—16th century—Sources
Great Britain—Colonies—Administration—History—20th
　　century—Sources[46]

(2) When the string begins with a topical heading, the following citation order prevails:

[Topic]—[Place]—[Time]—[Form]

For example:

Nobility—Great Britain—History—16th century—Sources
Plantation life—Georgia—History—19th century

When the string contains another topical element, the elements may be arranged in one of the following citation orders:

(A)　**[Topic]—[Topic]—[Place]—[Time]—[Form]**
(B)　**[Topic]—[Place]—[Topic]—[Time]—[Form]**

Currently, the choice of citation order depends on whether or not the designation *(May Subd Geog)* follows the topical subdivision in LCSH or in the free-floating subdivisions lists. When a heading contains a geographic subdivision and one or more of the other subdivisions, the geographic subdivision is normally placed between the main heading and the other subdivision(s):

> **Education** *(May Subd Geog)*
>   **—Finance**
> **Education—Florida—Finance**
> **Education—New Jersey—Finance—Statistics**

However, a number of subdivisions are themselves further subdivided by place. In such cases, the designation *(May Subd Geog)* appears after the topical subdivision. (A list of these subdivisions, called "Free-Floating Subdivisions Further Subdivided by Place,"[47] appears in appendix D of this book.) In such cases, the geographic subdivision follows the topical subdivision.

> **Education** *(May Subd Geog)*
>   **—Economic aspects** *(May Subd Geog)*
> **Education—Economic aspects—Finland**
> **Education—Economic aspects—United States**

> **Land titles** *(May Subd Geog)*
>   **—Registration and transfer** *(May Subd Geog)*
> **Land titles—Registration and transfer—California**
>   **—Popular works**

> **Christian art and symbolism** *(May Subd Geog)*
>   **—Medieval, 500-1500** *(May Subd Geog)*
> **Christian art and symbolism—Medieval, 500-1500**
>   **—Greece—Guidebooks**

Furthermore, to the basic patterns of citation order discussed above, there are minor variations when the string contains more than one subdivision of a particular type (i.e., a string with more than one topical element and/or more than one form subdivision):

> **Railroads—France—Cars—History—19th century**
>   **—Pictorial works**
> **Tuberculosis—Patients—Hospital care—Maryland**
>   **—Baltimore—History—20th century—Bibliography**
> **United States—History—Civil War, 1861-1865—Sources**
>   **—Juvenile literature**

The order shown in (2A) on page 114 is, of course, the one recommended by the Airlie House Conference. In preparation for implementing the recommended citation order, the Library of Congress has issued a new policy: "new topical subdivisions for which geographic orientation is logical are now established with the designation *(May Subd Geog)*. On a case-by-case basis, subdivisions not previously divided by place are being authorized for geographic subdivision."[48] As time goes on, more and more topical subdivisions will be further subdivisible by place.

NOTES

[1]Lois Mai Chan, *Library of Congress Subject Headings: Principles of Structure and Policies for Application*, annotated version. Prepared by Lois Mai Chan for the Library of Congress. *Advances in Library Information Technology*, no. 3. (Washington, D.C.: Cataloging Distribution Service, Library of Congress, 1990), 16.

[2]David Judson Haykin, *Subject Headings: A Practical Guide* (Washington, D.C.: GPO, 1951), 27.

[3]Library of Congress, Office of Subject Cataloging Policy, *Subject Cataloging Manual*, 4th ed. (Washington, D.C.: Cataloging Distribution Service, Library of Congress, 1991), H180, p. 4.

[4]Haykin, *Subject Headings*, 35-36.

[5]David Judson Haykin, "Subject Headings: Principles and Development," in *The Subject Analysis of Library Materials*, ed. Maurice F. Tauber (New York: School of Library Service, Columbia University, 1953), 51.

[6]Haykin, *Subject Headings: A Practical Guide*, 36.

[7]Lynn M. El-Hoshy, "Introduction to Subdivision Practice in the Library of Congress Subject Headings System," in Subject Subdivisions Conference (1991: Airlie, Va.), *The Future of Subdivisions in the Library of Congress Subject Headings System* (Washington, D.C.: Cataloging Distribution Service, Library of Congress, 1992), 117.

[8]Library of Congress, *Subject Cataloging Manual*, H900.

[9]Library of Congress, *Subject Cataloging Manual*, H830.

[10]For a complete list of the first-order political divisions of these countries, see appendix I.

[11]For an explanation of geographic qualifiers, see chapter 4.

[12]Library of Congress, *Subject Cataloging Manual*, H1050.

[13]Library of Congress, *Subject Cataloging Manual*, H1045.

[14]Library of Congress, *Subject Cataloging Manual*, H807.

[15]For a discussion of qualifiers for geographic names, see chapter 4.

[16]If the name of the local place is in the form of the name of the country (or the name of a first-order political division in Canada, Great Britain, or the United States) followed by an adjectival qualifier, no interposing element is required:

Nutrition surveys—Italy, Southern
   [not *Nutrition surveys—Italy—Italy, Southern*]
Hot tubs—California, Southern
   [not *Hot tubs—California—California, Southern*]

[17]Library of Congress, *Subject Cataloging Manual*, H807, p. 5.

[18]Library of Congress, *Subject Cataloging Manual*, H830, p. 3.

[19]Haykin, *Subject Headings*, 34.

[20]Haykin, *Subject Headings*, 34-35.

[21]"Subdivision Simplification Progress," *Cataloging Service Bulletin* 61 (Summer 1993): 13.

[22]Haykin, *Subject Headings*, 27.

[23]"Form Subdivisions," *Cataloging Service Bulletin* 3 (Winter 1979): 13-14.

[24]El-Hoshy, "Introduction to Subdivision Practice in the Library of Congress Subject Headings System," 117.

[25]Library of Congress, *Subject Cataloging Manual*, H1095.

[26]Library of Congress, *Subject Cataloging Manual*, H1095, p. 1.

[27]A list of most commonly used subdivisions, with scope notes, appeared in *A Guide to Subdivision Practice* (Washington, D.C.: Library of Congress, 1981).

[28]Library of Congress, Cataloging Policy and Support Office, *Free-Floating Subdivisions: An Alphabetical Index*, 6th ed. (Washington, D.C.: Cataloging Distribution Service, Library of Congress, 1994).

[29]A list of subdivisions to be further subdivided by place appears in appendix D of this book.

[30]For complete lists, consult Library of Congress, *Subject Cataloging Manual*.

[31]Library of Congress, *Subject Cataloging Manual*, H1110.

[32]Represents the person's knowledge of a particular topic as well as the person's educational background in a specific topic.

[33]Library of Congress, *Subject Cataloging Manual*, H1631, p. 8.

[34]Library of Congress, *Subject Cataloging Manual*, H1105.

[35]Library of Congress, *Subject Cataloging Manual*, H1145.5.

[36]The list does not apply to generic headings for types of bodies of water such as **Lakes; Saline waters; Sounds (Geomorphology).**

[37]Library of Congress, *Subject Cataloging Manual*, H1100, H1103.

[38]Library of Congress, *Subject Cataloging Manual*, H1146-H1200.

[39]Library of Congress, *Subject Cataloging Manual*, H1146.

[40]Library of Congress, Office of Subject Cataloging Policy, *LC Period Subdivisions Under Names of Places*, 5th ed. (Washington, D.C.: Cataloging Distribution Service, Library of Congress, 1994).

[41]Library of Congress, *Subject Cataloging Manual*, H1090.

[42]Julius O. Kaiser, *Systematic Indexing*, Card System Series, vol. 2 (London: Pitman, 1911), 300-303; Marie Louise Prevost, "An Approach to Theory and

Method in General Subject Heading," *Library Quarterly* 16, no. 2 (April 1946): 140-51; Brian C. Vickery, "Systematic Subject Indexing," *Journal of Documentation* 9, no. 1 (1953): 48-57; S. R. Ranganathan, *Elements of Library Classification*, 3rd ed. (Bombay: Asia Publishing House, 1962), 82-89; Derek Austin with Mary Dykstra, *PRECIS: A Manual of Concept Analysis and Subject Indexing*, 2nd ed. (London: British Library, Bibliographic Services Division, 1984), 107-21; E. J. Coates, *Subject Catalogues: Headings and Structure* (London: Library Association, 1960, reissued with new preface 1988), 50-58.

[43]Coates, *Subject Catalogues*, 61.

[44]Subject Subdivisions Conference (1991 : Airlie, Va.): *The Future of Subdivisions in the Library of Congress Subject Headings System: Report from the Subject Subdivisions Conference*, edited by Martha O'Hara Conway. Washington, D.C.: Cataloging Distribution Service, Library of Congress, 1992.

[45]Library of Congress, *Subject Cataloging Manual*, H180, pp. 4-5.

[46]The subdivision —**History** is frequently used to introduce a time period; in such cases the combination —**History—[Time]** may be considered the chronological element.

[47]Library of Congress, *Subject Cataloging Manual*, H860.

[48]"Subdivisions Simplification Progress," *Cataloging Service Bulletin* 66 (Fall 1994): 43.

6 Cross References

In retrieval, cross references carry a great deal of the burden of leading users to desired material. In LCSH and in most indexing systems that adhere to the principle of uniform heading, a given subject is represented by only one term. Users, however, cannot always be expected to know which of several synonyms or near-synonymous terms, or which of several possible forms, has been chosen as the valid heading. Furthermore, under the principle of specific and direct entry, material on a subject is listed under a specific term even though many users may look for it under a more general term. Finally, users need to be made aware of headings that are related to the subject being sought. Therefore, it is in the best interest of users if the system provides linkages between related terms and from terms that are not used as headings to those that are. Both objectives are achieved by means of cross references.

Three types of relationships are represented in the cross-reference structure of LCSH: equivalence, hierarchical, and associative. These relationships are expressed in terms of USE and UF (used for), BT (broader term) and NT (narrower term), RT (related term), and SA (see also) references.[1] Each reference links a term or heading with another heading or with a group of headings.

Patterns and examples of cross references for various types of proper name headings in the Library of Congress system are given in appendix G of this book.

EQUIVALENCE RELATIONSHIPS[2]

References among equivalent terms link those not used as headings to the term chosen as the valid heading. Such references allow the user to access materials on a particular subject by inputting (or looking under) any term that is synonymous with the uniform heading under which all such materials are listed. In LCSH, a USE reference guides the user from a term that is not used as a heading to the term that is. USE references are made from synonymous terms, variant spellings, alternative forms, different entry elements, opposite terms, and "overly" narrow terms. Thus, USE references provide an entry vocabulary for the system. A subject heading enables retrieval of a subject through one term only, while a subject heading with, for example, four

USE references allows retrieval through five different terms. In other words, the user is able to access the subject through any of five possible synonymous or variant terms instead of one.

In some online systems, such referencing is automatic and transparent; searchers inputting any one of several equivalent terms are given all the material the system has on the topic to which the term refers. No matter how sophisticated the system, however, this can only happen if equivalent terms are linked at both the thesaurus construction and system design stages.

The following discussion focuses on Library of Congress cataloging practice. But what is said applies equally to other situations in which LCSH or a variant of it is used in indexing or cataloging.

In *Library of Congress Subject Headings* and its counterparts, instructions for making USE references are given under both the unused term and the valid heading. The symbol UF means a USE reference is to be made from the term or terms that follow. For example:

Archaeology
    UF   Prehistory
             Ruins

In the printed list and in a catalog or index based on LCSH, reciprocal entries appear under the UF terms:

Prehistory
    USE   **Archaeology**
Ruins
    USE   **Archaeology**

In MARC formats for authorities, the synonymous terms not used as headings are indicated by appropriate field tags.[3]

USE references from synonymous terms and variant spellings are generally made in most indexing systems. The other types of USE references in the Library of Congress system are provided because of the principle of uniform heading and the unique features of specific and direct entry discussed in chapter 2.

Synonymous Terms

When a heading has been chosen from two or more synonymous terms, USE references are made from the unused terms to the heading. Charles A. Cutter's rule states: "Of two exactly synonymous names choose one and make a reference from the other."[4] In practice, this kind of reference is extended to near-synonymous terms when it is considered impractical to distinguish between them. David Judson Haykin notes that the basic significance of such references is that "the subject matter is entered not under the heading which occurred to the reader, but under the one chosen by the cataloger even when the terms are not completely synonymous."[5]

Examples of USE references from synonymous and near-synonymous terms are:

Appetite depressants
UF   Appetite suppressing drugs

Audiobooks
UF   Cassette books
          Recorded books

Big bang theory
UF   Big bang cosmology
          Superdense theory

Ethics
UF   Morals

Fitness walking
UF   Exercise walking
          Health walking
          Healthwalking

Fuzzy logic
UF   Nonlinear logic

Greenhouses
UF   Hothouses

Liberty
UF   Emancipation
          Freedom
          Liberation

Oral medication
UF   Drugs by mouth
          Peroral medication

Overpopulation
UF   Population explosion

Urban hospitals
UF   City hospitals
          Metropolitan hospitals

Variant Spellings

USE references are made from different spellings and different grammatical structures, as well as canceled headings:

Aeolian harp
    UF   Eolian harp

Aesthetics
    UF   Esthetics

Airplanes
    UF   Aeroplanes

Archaeology
    UF   Archeology

Audiobooks
    UF   Audio books

Dialing
    UF   Dialling

Dogs
    UF   Dog

Fishing nets
    UF   Fish nets
           Fishnets

Geoduck
    UF   Goeduck
           Gooeyduck

Microcrystalline polymers
    UF   Microcrystal polymers
           Polymer microcrystals

Seafood
    UF   Sea food

Abbreviations, Acronyms, Initials, Etc.

If the heading has been established in the spelled-out form, USE references from abbreviated forms are not generally made unless such forms are well known to the general public:

Adenylic acid
    UF   AMP (Biochemistry)

Ammonium nitrate fuel oil
    UF   AN-FO
          ANFO

Electronic mail systems
    UF   Email systems

If the heading has been established in the form of an abbreviation, an acronym, or initials, a USE reference is made from the spelled-out form:

CPR (First aid)
    UF   Cardiopulmonary resuscitation

MARC formats
    UF   Machine-readable cataloging formats

Different Language Terms

USE references are generally not made from equivalent terms in foreign languages to topical headings that are established in English, unless the foreign terms are well known to English-speaking users:

Carnival
    UF   Mardi Gras

Free enterprise
    UF   Laissez-faire

USE references from vernacular names are regularly made to English-language headings representing named entities. For example:

Aizu Region (Japan)
    UF   Aizu-bonchi (Japan)

Cubagua Island (Venezuela)
    UF   Isla Cubagua (Venezuela)

Texcal Cave (Mexico)
    UF   Cueva del Texcal (Mexico)

Yellow River (China)
    UF   Huang He (China)

USE references are also made from English translations to headings established in the vernacular:

Yangtze River (China)
    UF   Long River (China)

Popular and Scientific Terms

USE references are made from popular terms to the scientific term chosen as the heading, and from scientific terms to the popular term if the latter has been chosen as the heading:

Cockroaches
    UF   Blattaria
            Blattoidea

Medusahead wildrye
    UF   Elymus caput-medusae
            Taeniatherum asperum

Prosencephalon
    UF   Forebrain

Vitamin C
    UF   Ascorbic acid

Alternative Forms

Because of the principle of uniform heading, which requires that a heading appear in the catalog in only one form, other forms of the same heading likely to be consulted by users are referred to the form chosen as the heading. It should be pointed out, however, that in LCSH this is true in principle but not always consistent in practice, particularly among headings established some time ago. Newly established headings show greater consistency. For example:

Aerobic exercises
    UF   Aerobics

Aged—Education
    UF   Education of the aged

Banks and banking—Accounting
    UF   Bank accounting

Cataloging of Arabic imprints
    UF   Arabic imprints—Cataloging

Federal aid to private schools
    UF   Private schools—Federal aid

Foreign exchange—Accounting
    UF   Foreign exchange accounting

Galaxies—Evolution
UF   Galactic evolution

Glass—Research
UF   Glass research

Cataloging of rare books
[No UF references]

Hospitals—Accounting
[No UF references]

Different Entry Elements

When a heading is inverted, a USE reference is generally provided from the direct form:

Art, French
UF   French art

Art, Medieval
UF   Medieval art

Chemistry, Organic
UF   Organic chemistry

Education, Higher
UF   Higher education

USE references are made from inverted forms to direct headings if they are considered to provide useful access points:

Aerospace planes
UF   Planes, Aerospace

Fuzzy logic
UF   Logic, Fuzzy

Mexican American arts
UF   Arts, Mexican American

Popular music
UF   Music, Popular

The inverted UF reference is not made if there is a BT reference that begins with the same word or words as the UF reference:

Talking birds
BT   Birds   [the reference *UF Birds, Talking* is not made]

When a compound heading expresses a relationship between two objects or concepts, a USE reference is made from the form with the terms in reverse order:[6]

Computers and family
    UF   Family and computers

Architecture and state
    UF   State and architecture

In cases of previously established compound headings that connect two parallel or opposite objects or concepts that are often treated in the same work but not necessarily in relationship to each other, a USE reference is made from the second term in the heading:

Cities and towns
    UF   Towns

Emigration and immigration
    UF   Immigration

Encyclopedias and dictionaries
    UF   Dictionaries

Compound headings of this type are no longer being established; separate headings are made instead.

If the heading is in the form of a topic subdivided by other topics, a UF reference is sometimes made from the reversed form:

Advertising—Newspapers
    UF   Newspapers—Advertising

Opposite Terms Not Used As Headings

In the past, when a heading was established under one of two opposite terms, a USE reference was made from the one not chosen:

Literacy
    UF   Illiteracy

Militarism
    UF   Antimilitarism

Temperance
    UF   Intemperance

This practice is now rare. Current policy is to establish each term as a separate heading when required.

Narrow Terms Not Used As Headings

When a term is considered too narrow to be useful as a separate heading, a USE reference, also called an *upward reference*, is sometimes made from the narrow term to a broader one that is used as a heading:

Children as authors
UF   Children as poets

Liberty
UF   Civil liberty
        Personal liberty

Pollution
UF   Pollution—Control
        Pollution—Prevention

Popular music
UF   Popular songs
        Popular vocal music

Schools—Accounting
UF   High schools—Accounting
        Public schools—Accounting

Occasionally a USE reference is made from a narrower term not used as a heading to a broader heading and to other related headings at the same time:

Christmas books
    USE   **Christmas**
              Christmas plays
              Christmas stories
              Christmas—Exercises, recitations, etc.
              Gift books

In recent years, fewer and fewer upward-pointing USE references have been added to the list. Current policy favors establishing the narrower terms as separate headings.

General USE References

There are several circumstances when a general USE reference, which links an unauthorized or nonpreferred term to a group of related headings, is used: (a) when there is no heading equivalent to the term in question; (b) when it is considered impractical to list as specific references all relevant individual headings, and (c) when it is desirable to explain free-floating subdivision usage. For example:

> Amateurs' manuals
>> USE   *subdivision* Amateurs' manuals *under technical topics for works of instruction for nonprofessionals on how to acquire a skill or perform an operation, e.g.* Radio—Amateurs' manuals

> Military reform
>> USE   *subdivision* Reorganization *under individual military services, e.g.* United States—Armed Forces—Reorganization

> Office, Appointment to
>> USE   *subdivision* Officials and employees—Selection and appointment *under names of countries, cities, etc. and names of individual government agencies; and subdivision* Selection and appointment *under types of officials*

HIERARCHICAL RELATIONSHIPS[7]

Hierarchical references and *related-term references*, connect two or more terms that are both (or all) valid subject headings. They usually express certain kinds of subject relationships. Cutter's rule states: "Make references from general subjects to their various subordinate subjects and also to coordinate and illustrative subjects."[8] Haykin rephrases the rule in these terms:

> In binding related headings together the basic rule is that a "see also" reference be made from a given subject: 1) to more specific subjects or topics comprehended within it, or to an application of the subject; and 2) to coordinate subjects which suggest themselves as likely to be of interest to the user seeking material under the given heading, because they represent other aspects of the subject, or are closely related to it.[9]

In LCSH, headings related hierarchically are connected by reciprocal BT and NT references. In earlier editions of the list, *see also* references were used to provide links among related terms and from broader terms to narrower terms but not vice versa. Similarly, in LCMARC subject authority records, BT and RT references appear in the 5xx fields. NT references are generated for display in the catalog but do not appear in the authority records. For each BT reference, a reciprocal NT reference is made under the broader heading in the printed list.

Under each valid heading, other headings representing concepts on a level immediately above in the hierarchy are listed as BT, except when the heading in question represents the "top term" in the hierarchy, or when the broader term cannot be readily identified. Other exceptions include headings for geographic regions, family names, and inverted headings qualified by names of languages, nationalities, ethnic groups, or terms that designate time periods. In such cases, the only appropriate BT is the identical heading without the qualifier. When a heading belongs to more than one hierarchy, multiple BT references may be made. In complex situations such as compound headings, prepositional phrase headings, and headings with subdivisions, BT references are made in selective cases even when the relationships so expressed are not truly hierarchical.

Using the subject **Cats** as an example, Phyllis A. Richmond demonstrated the "hidden classification" in the cross-reference structure of LCSH. She concluded that even though the structure is imperfect and could be improved, the potential is there.[10] In an examination of the relationship between LC subject headings and classification for Judaica, Bella Hass Weinberg also noted the "hidden classification," or hierarchical structure, embodied in the BT and NT references in LCSH.[11]

In LCSH, each term in a chain of subjects from a hierarchy is usually connected to the one immediately above it and the one below it by BT and NT references. For example:

Chordata
  NT   Vertebrates

Vertebrates
  BT   Chordata
  NT   Mammals

Mammals
  BT   Vertebrates
  NT   Primates

Primates
  BT   Mammals
  NT   Monkeys

Monkeys
  BT   Primates
  NT   Cercopithecidae

Cercopithecidae
  BT   Monkeys
  NT   Macaques

Macaques
  BT   Cercopithecidae
  NT   Japanese macaque

Japanese macaque
  BT   Macaques

Figure 6.1, on page 130, illustrates part of a classificatory structure based on the hierarchical references in LCSH. The hierarchical structure is embodied in the references, with occasional irregularities.

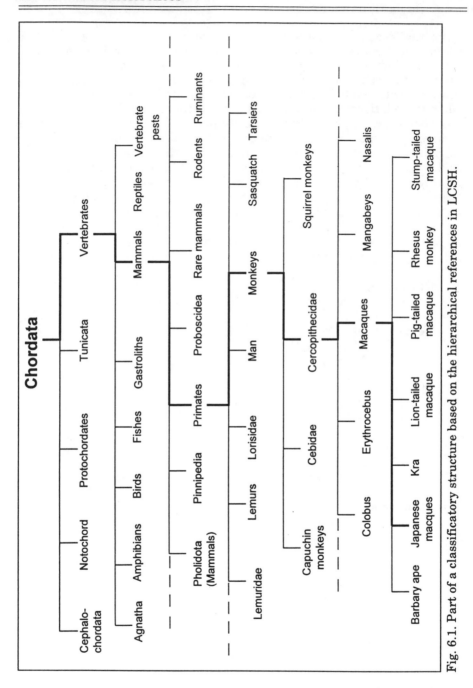

Fig. 6.1. Part of a classificatory structure based on the hierarchical references in LCSH.

For instance, the subject **Chordata** is not connected to any subject superordinate to it, e.g., **Animals.**

Theoretically, an alphabetical subject catalog with a thorough, systematically constructed network of cross references can provide the best of both worlds by combining the advantages of the alphabetical and classified approaches. Tying a controlled vocabulary to a classificatory structure facilitates the making of proper cross references, ensuring that term relationships are well defined and well represented. Many modern indexing vocabularies are built on classified structures. An example is *Medical Subject Headings* with its attendant tree structures.

Policies for making hierarchical and related references in LCSH have varied over the years, resulting in irregular and imperfect term relationships. In recent years, efforts have been made to normalize cross references. Currently, hierarchical references are made between headings having the relationships delineated below.

(1) Genus/species (or class/class member). Examples include:

Apes
    NT   Gorilla

German fiction
    NT   Science fiction, German

Motor vehicles
    NT   Automobiles

Sheep dogs
    NT   Belgian sheepdog

The NT reference is not made, however, in cases of inverted headings qualified by names of languages, nationalities, or ethnic groups when the broader term is identical to the narrower heading without the qualifier. References such as the following are *not* made:

Art
    NT   Art, German
          Art, Japanese

(2) Whole/part. Examples include:

Hand
    BT   Arm
    NT   Fingers

Fingers
    BT   Hand
    NT   Finger joint
          Fingernails
          Thumb

When a heading belongs to more than one hierarchy, a reference is made from the next broader heading in each hierarchy:

Causeways
    BT   Bridges
           Roads

(3)   Instance (or generic topic/entity name heading).[12] Examples include:

Buildings—Texas
    NT   Old Stone Fort (Nacogdoches, Tex.)

Botanical gardens—California
    NT   Huntington Herb Garden (San Marino, Calif.)

Dwellings—Georgia
    NT   Chief Vann House (Spring Place, Ga.)
           Plum Orchard (Ga.)
           Robert Toombs House (Washington, Ga.)
           Stafford Plantation (Ga.)

Mountains—France
    NT   Vanoise Mountains (France)

Palaces—England
    NT   Blenheim Palace (England)
           Hampton Court (Richmond upon Thames, London, England)

Palaces—Spain
    NT   Alcázar (Madrid, Spain)
           Alcázar (Seville, Spain)
           Alhambra (Granada, Spain)

Rivers—Colorado
    NT   Gunnison River (Colo.)
           North Platte River
           Piedra River (Colo.)

Streets—France
    NT   Boulevard du Temple (Paris, France)

World War, 1939-1945—Campaigns—Italy
    NT   Cassino (Italy), Battle of, 1944

The geographic subdivision in the generic heading is at the level of the country or first-order political division in the case of Canada, Great Britain, and the United States. This level is often broader than that represented by the qualifier of the individual name heading.

The previous practice of making subject-to-name references, including personal names, corporate names, jurisdictional names, and uniform titles, has been discontinued because authority records for these names, established according to *AACR2R*, now reside in the *NAMES* file.[13]

(4) Compound and complex relationships. For headings containing multiple topics or concepts, BT references are made from those topics or concepts not used as the entry element. Such topics, which often represent generic concepts with regard to the compound or complex headings, are presented in their established heading form:

Music and anthropology
    BT   Anthropology

Education and crime
    BT   Crime

Hydrogen as fuel
    BT   Fuel

Aerial photography in city planning
    BT   City planning

Surrealism in motion pictures
    BT   Motion pictures

Domestic relations (Roman law)
    BT   Roman law

BT references are also made from headings that correspond to subdivisions, such as **—Contracting out** and **—Election,** unless the terms are too broad or general, such as **[Topic]—Application** and **[Topic]—Utilization.** For example:

County services—Contracting out
    BT   Contracting out

Judges—Election
    BT   Elections

ASSOCIATIVE RELATIONSHIPS

RT references are made between terms that are related other than hierarchically; that is, related topics that do not constitute a genus/species or whole/part relationship. These references appear under both headings involved:

Religion
    RT   Theology

Theology
    RT   Religion

Comprehension	Memory
RT Memory	RT Comprehension

RT references are now required in the cases discussed below, unless they share a common BT or begin with the same word or word stem. To avoid subjective judgments in making RTs, the Library of Congress has established the following guidelines, with deliberate effort to limit their number.[14] RT references are made:

- to link two terms with overlapping meanings

  Ships
  RT   Boats and boating

  Boats and boating
  RT   Ships

- to link a discipline and the object studied

  Earthquakes
  RT   Seismology

  Epithelial cells
  RT   Exfoliative cytology

  Entomology
  RT   Insects

- to link a class of persons and their fields of endeavor

  Physicians
  RT   Medicine

- to link other closely related terms

  Drugs—Overdosage
  RT   Medication errors

  Clinical sociology
  RT   Social psychiatry

  Longevity
  RT   Old age

  Purchasing power
  RT   Income

SA (GENERAL *SEE ALSO*) REFERENCES[15]

For reasons of economy, a general SA reference is sometimes made from a heading to a group of headings, frequently listing one or more individual headings by way of example. Such a reference suggests to the user the pattern of the heading under which a particular class or group of topics is entered, alerts users to the existence of more specific headings, and provides guidance as to the type of heading more appropriate to their search. Currently, specific references are preferred.

SA references represent an open-ended approach, in that no exhaustive list of headings referred to is given, and the user is left to formulate the terms to be searched. In the past, a type of general *see also* reference frequently used was one made from the generic heading to its members named collectively, with one or more specific examples given:

> *Tools*
>   SA   individual specific tools, e.g. Files and rasps; Saws

The policy of making this type of general *see also* reference has now been largely abandoned by the Library of Congress in favor of making specific references, such as:[16]

> **Tools**
>   NT   Agricultural implements
>   Artists' tools
>   Axes
>   Bench vises
>   Carpentry—Tools

Still, there are situations under which it is impractical or redundant to make specific references. In such cases, general *see also* references are still being made. Currently there are three types of such references:

(1) General *see also* references to free-floating subdivisions. Many headings carry SA references to free-floating subdivisions:

> **Economic history** (*Not Subd Geog*)
>   SA   *subdivision* Economic conditions *under names of countries, cities, etc.*

However, a number of such references are also made to non-free-floating subdivisions. Therefore, the presence of such a reference does not indicate the free-floating status of a particular subdivision.

(2) General SA references from a subject heading to a category or a type of name heading that is normally not included in the *SUBJECTS* file:

Bible—Biography
    SA   *names of individuals mentioned in the Bible, e.g.* Mary, Blessed Virgin, Saint

(3) General *see also* references to headings beginning with the same word or word stem:

Heart
    SA   *headings beginning with the words* Cardiac *or* Cardiogenic

Strictly speaking, these references are not open-ended, in that the headings referred to are enumerated in LCSH. Because they can be readily identified and located, it would be redundant to list them in the reference.

CROSS REFERENCES FOR PROPER NAME HEADINGS

Certain types of name headings require special cross references. These are discussed below. Patterns of cross references and examples for various types of names are shown in appendix G.

Personal Names

Individual Persons

Cross-references for headings of individual persons are made according to *AACR2R* and maintained in the *NAMES* file. Examples include:

Lewis, C. S. (Clive Staples), 1898-1963
    See references from:
        Lewis, Jack, 1898-1963
        Hamilton, Clive, 1898-1963
        Clerk, N. W., 1898-1963
        Lewis, Clive Staples, 1898-1963

Onassis, Jacqueline Kennedy, 1929-
    See references from:
        Kennedy, Jacqueline Bouvier, 1929-
        Bouvier, Jacqueline, 1929-

For contemporary authors or authors with separate bibliographic identities who have multiple headings, only the "basic heading" established according to *Library of Congress Rule Interpretations* is used as the subject heading for works about the person:[17]

Twain, Mark, 1835-1910
> For works of this author written under other names, search also under Clemens, Samuel Langhorne, 1835-1910, Snodgrass, Quintus Curtius, 1835-1910

Clemens, Samuel Langhorne, 1835-1910
> Works by this author are usually entered under Twain, Mark, 1835-1910. For a listing of other names used by this author, search also under Twain, Mark, 1835-1910[18]
> SUBJECT USAGE: This heading is not valid for use as a subject. Works about this person are entered under Twain, Mark, 1835-1910[19]

Snodgrass, Quintus Curtius, 1835-1910
> Works by this author are usually entered under Twain, Mark, 1835-1910. For a listing of other names used by this author, search also under Twain, Mark, 1835-1910
> SUBJECT USAGE: This heading is not valid for use as a subject. Works about this person are entered under Twain, Mark, 1835-1910

References for headings of fictitious and mythological characters are established and maintained in LCSH. UF or RT references are made from variant names and different entry clements. Examples include:

Finn, Huckleberry (Fictitious character)
> UF   Huckleberry Finn (Fictitious character)

Randolph, Snooky (Fictitious character)
> UF   Snooks (Fictitious character)
> Snooky (Fictitious character)

Zeus (Greek deity)
> BT   Gods, Greek
> RT   Jupiter (Roman deity)

Family Names

For headings of family names, UF references are made from different spellings not used as headings, and RT references are made from each known variant of the family name that has been established as a valid heading:

Adams family
UF   Adam family
       Adamson family
       Addams family
       Adems family
       Adom family
RT   Ade family

Goodenough family
UF   Goodenow family
       Goodnough family

Cook family
RT   Koch family

Koch family
RT   Cook family

Gregory family
RT   McGregor family

McGregor family
RT   Gregory family

Dynasties

USE references are made from variant forms of the name, and BT references are made from **[Country (or region)]—Kings and rulers**. Examples include:

Hoysala dynasty, ca. 1006-ca. 1346
BT   India—Kings and rulers

Habsburg, House of
UF   Austria, House of
       Hapsburg, House of
BT   Austria—Kings and rulers

Saxe-Coburg-Gotha, House of
UF   Coburg, House of
BT   Bavaria (Germany)—Kings and rulers

Savoy, House of
BT   Italy—Kings and rulers

Noble Houses

For names of noble houses, USE references from variant names, forms, and entry elements are made, as well as BT references from **Nobility—[Country]**. Examples include:

Leinster, Dukes of
UF   Dukes of Leinster
BT   Nobility—Ireland

Toulouse, Counts of
UF   Counts of Toulouse
BT   Nobility—France

Derby, Earls of
UF   Earls of Derby
BT   Nobility—Great Britain

Corporate Names

Like headings for individual persons, headings for individual corporate bodies are established according to *AACR2R* and maintained in the *NAMES* file.

For corporate bodies that have changed their names, successive headings—headings under both earlier and later names—are made:

American Library Association. Information Science and Automation Division
Search also under the later heading:
Library and Information Technology Association (U.S.)

Library and Information Technology Association (U.S.)
Search also under the earlier heading:
American Library Association. Information Science and Automation Division

For discussions on the use of earlier and later name headings in cataloging, see chapters 4 and 9.

Geographic Names

Jurisdictional Names

Jurisdictional headings and cross references are made according to the provisions of *AACR2R* and maintained in the *NAMES* file. Examples include:

Austria
   See references from:
      Ostmark
      Alpen- und Donau-Reichsgaue
      Ausztria
      Österreich
   See also references from:
      Austro-Hungarian Monarchy
      Holy Roman Empire

George Town (Pinang)
   See references from:
      Georgetown (Pinang)
      George Town, Pulau Pinang
      Pinang (Pinang)
      Penang (Pinang)
      George Town (Malaysia)

Non-Jurisdictional Names

Non-jurisdictional headings and cross references are established and maintained in LCSH. UF references are made from variant (including former) names, different language forms, and different entry elements. BT references are made from generic headings subdivided by country or first-order political division to specific non-jurisdictional geographic headings, if appropriate. For example:

Berkeley, Vale of (England)
   UF   Vale of Berkeley (England)
   BT   Valleys—England

Bierzo (Spain)
   UF   El Bierzo (Spain)

Costa del Sol (Spain)
   UF   Sol, Costa del (Spain)
   BT   Coasts—Spain

Cumberland River (Ky. and Tenn.)
   BT   Rivers—Kentucky
   BT   Rivers—Tennessee

El Rancho Gumbo (Mont.)
UF   Rancho Gumbo (Mont.)
BT   Ranches—Montana

Gallipoli Peninsula (Turkey)
UF   Gelibolu Peninsula (Turkey)
BT   Peninsulas—Turkey

Geysers, The (Calif.)
UF   Big Geysers (Calif.)
       The Geysers (Calif.)
BT   Geysers—California

Mojave Desert (Calif.)
UF   Mohave Desert (Calif.)
BT   Deserts—California

Mississippi River
BT   Rivers—United States
NT   Mississippi Embayment
       Saint Anthony Falls (Minn.)

Pompeii (Extinct city)
UF   Pompei (Extinct city)
       Pompeii (Ancient city)
BT   Extinct cities—Italy
       Italy—Antiquities

Texas Panhandle (Tex.)
UF   Panhandle (Tex. : Region)

BT references from generic headings subdivided by country or first-order political division are not made if the place is located in more than three jurisdictions.

Changes in Geographic Names

In the case of name changes from mergers or splits in which different names of the same place are used as headings for works covering different periods, *RT* references are made between the successive (i.e., earlier and later) headings. These references are traced in the name authority records but do not necessarily appear in LCSH. Following are examples of authority records showing the changes:

Rhodesia
Here are entered works limited in subject coverage to the historical, political, or cultural aspects of the two former British colonies of Northern and Southern Rhodesia combined for the pre-1953 period. Works dealing with these same aspects of the

Federation of Rhodesia and Nyasaland for the 1953-1963 period are entered under Rhodesia and Nyasaland. All works covering the same area for which these limitations do not apply are entered under the name or names of the current jurisdictions, Zambia and/or Zimbabwe.

Zambia
UF   Northern Rhodesia
       Rhodesia, Northern

Zimbabwe
UF   Rhodesia, Southern
       Southern Rhodesia
       Zimbabwe, Southern Rhodesia

Germany
Here are entered works on Germany for the pre-1949 period, the Territories under Allied Occupation, and East Germany and West Germany, collectively, for the post-1949 period, as well as works on Germany since reunification in 1990.

NT   Germany (East)
       Germany (West)

Germany (East)
Here are entered works on the Democratic Republic established in 1949, and works on the eastern part of Germany before 1949 and since reunification in 1990.

UF   East Germany
       Eastern Germany
       German Democratic Republic
       Germany (Democratic Republic, 1949-)
       Germany (Territory under Allied occupation, 1945-1955)
       Germany, Democratic Republic of
       Germany, East
       Germany, Eastern
BT   Germany

Germany (West)
Here are entered works on the Federal Republic established in 1949, and works on the western part of Germany before 1949 and since reunification in 1990.

UF   German Federal Republic
       Germany (Federal Republic, 1949-)
       Germany (Territory under Allied occupation, 1945-1955)
       Germany, Federal Republic of
       Germany, West

```
            Germany, Western
            West Germany
            Western Germany
    NT      Ruhr (Germany : Region)
    BT      Germany
```

Headings for Other Named Entities and Events

Appropriate cross references are made for headings of other types of named entities and events. Examples include:

London and Port Stanley Railway
    BT   Railroads—Canada

London Bridge (London, England)
    BT   Bridges—England

Persian Gulf War, 1991
    UF   Desert Storm, Operation, 1991
          Gulf War, 1991
          Operation Desert Storm, 1991
          War in the Gulf, 1991
    RT   Iraq-Kuwait Crisis, 1990-1991
    BT   Iraq—History—1958-
          Persian Gulf Region—History
          United States—History, Military—20th century

United States—History—King George's War, 1744-1748
    UF   Governor Shirley's War
          King George's War, 1744-1748
    BT   Austrian Succession, War of, 1740-1748
          Indians of North America—Wars—1600-1750
    NT   Minas (N.S.) Expedition, 1747

World War, 1914-1918
    UF   European War, 1914-1918
          First World War
          World War I
    BT   History, Modern—20th century

CONCLUSION

Cross references provide a useful structure of relationships among subject headings. In practice, however, it has not been demonstrated that the effectiveness and usefulness of these references have been fully realized in actual use. In many libraries, it is a question as to whether all appropriate references have been provided in the catalog. To ensure that all suggested references are made requires a great deal of effort and time. At a time when fast cataloging is of first priority and online cataloging is often performed by technicians at the terminal, one wonders how many libraries are actually able to follow up on all the references each time a new heading is introduced into the catalog or a new reference has been suggested by the Library of Congress. On the other hand, both the principle of specific entry and the principle of uniform heading rely heavily on cross references for subject collocation. Omission or negligence in the provision of cross references reduces access points and greatly lessens the effectiveness of the LCSH list as a tool for subject retrieval.

Because many online catalogs do not have extensive browsing capability, and some do not have any, it is particularly important to provide cross references that can link the user's input terms to those used in subject access fields in bibliographic records. Such provisions may take the form of online browsing of the subject index, the online version of LCSH, or a local authority file.

Together, different kinds of references help in identifying valid access points and navigating the search through terms that are related hierarchically or otherwise. The importance of cross references cannot be over-emphasized.

NOTES

[1]Before the 11th edition (1988) of *Library of Congress Subject Headings*, the symbols *see*, *x* (*see from*), *see also* and *xx* (*see also from*) were used.

[2]Library of Congress, Office of Subject Cataloging Policy, *Subject Cataloging Manual*, 4th ed. (Washington, D.C.: Cataloging Distribution Service, Library of Congress, 1991), H373.

[3]In the USMARC authorities format, the synonymous terms not used as headings are included in the 4xx fields, *cf. USMARC Format for Authority Data, Including Guidelines for Content Designation*, prepared by Network Development and MARC Standards Office (Washington, D.C.: Cataloging Distribution Service, Library of Congress, 1987).

[4]Charles A. Cutter, *Rules for a Dictionary Catalog*, 4th ed., rewritten (Washington, D.C.: GPO, 1904), 70.

[5]David Judson Haykin, *Subject Headings: A Practical Guide* (Washington, D.C.: GPO, 1951), 14.

[6]Library of Congress, *Subject Cataloging Manual*, H310.

[7]Library of Congress, *Subject Cataloging Manual*, H370, H375.

[8]Cutter, *Rules for a Dictionary Catalog*, 79.

[9]Haykin, *Subject Headings*, 14.

[10]Phyllis Allen Richmond, "Cats: An Example of Concealed Classification in Subject Headings," *Library Resources & Technical Services* 3 (Spring 1959): 102-12.

[11]Bella Hass Weinberg, "The Hidden Classification in Library of Congress Subject Headings for Judaica," *Library Resources & Technical Services* 37 (October 1993): 369-79.

[12]Forms of name headings and their qualifiers are discussed in detail in chapter 4.

[13]Examples of subject-to-name references included:

Architects, British
    sa   Wren, Sir Christopher, 1632-1723
Soft drink industry—Great Britain
    sa   Schweppes (Firm)
International airports—New York (State)
    sa   John F. Kennedy International Airport
Television programs—Canada
    sa   Connections (Television program)
Confucianism—Sacred books
    sa   Shih san ching

[14]Library of Congress, *Subject Cataloging Manual*, H370, p. 2.

[15]Library of Congress, *Subject Cataloging Manual*, H371.

[16]"General See Also References," *Cataloging Service Bulletin* 19 (Winter 1982): 15.

[17]*Library of Congress Rule Interpretations*, 2nd ed. (Washington, D.C.: Cataloging Distribution Service, Library of Congress, 1989), 22.2B, p. 2.

[18]On an LC name authority record, this note is found in field 663.

[19]On an LC name authority record, this note is found in field 667.

7 Subject Authority Control and Maintenance

Because the Library of Congress Subject Headings system is based on a controlled vocabulary, only authorized terms are used in or as subject headings.[1] Among the principles governing LCSH is that of specificity, which requires that a heading or headings closest to the contents of the work being cataloged be assigned. As knowledge grows, new subjects—for which no adequate subject headings yet exist—are constantly emerging. Therefore, any topic encountered in cataloging but not yet represented in LCSH may be proposed as a new subject heading so long as it represents a "discrete, identifiable concept."[2] Furthermore, because terminology changes and the list must reflect current usage to be effective, modifications of established headings may also be proposed.

Developing and maintaining a list of controlled vocabulary is often referred to as *thesaurus construction and maintenance*. The vehicle for thesaurus construction and maintenance at the Library of Congress is an editorial group within the Cataloging Policy and Support Office, which meets weekly. Attendants at the meetings include a Subject Cataloging Policy Specialist, representatives from the editorial team and cooperative cataloging teams, and interested catalogers. The group considers all proposals for changes: additions to, alterations in, or deletions of existing headings, heading/subdivision combinations, cross references, or free-floating subdivisions. For new headings, the group deliberates on terminology (wording), cross references, notes, compatibility with descriptive headings (if applicable), and conformity to existing patterns and broad policies governing LCSH. A change that is approved by this group is said to be editorially established.

New headings proposed and examined at an editorial meeting are generally of five types: headings representing new objects or concepts, combinations (coordinations) of existing headings, new subdivisions under existing headings, new free-floating subdivisions, and cross references. Headings proposed for revision and updating are handled in the same way—they must be reviewed by the editorial group before they are formally established in their new form. Guidelines for establishing new headings are given in the *Subject Cataloging Manual*.[3]

All new and revised headings are incorporated into the *SUBJECTS* file, the CD-ROM and microfiche versions of the full list (which is fully cumulated and issued quarterly), and the next edition of *Library of Congress Subject Headings*.

ESTABLISHING NEW HEADINGS[4]

Procedure

Most proposals for new subjects originate with catalogers who discover the need for a new or changed heading in the course of their everyday work. When a subject that is not yet represented in LCSH is found in a work being cataloged, the cataloger usually proposes a new heading. A new subject heading may also be proposed for a topic needed as a BT reference for an existing heading, to complete its hierarchical chain.

After editorial approval, an authority record for the new heading is prepared and entered into the *SUBJECTS* file. The procedure for creating subject authority records is discussed below.

Authority Records

It has long been a part of thesaurus maintenance to create subject authority records for new (or changed) headings and to keep these records in a subjects authority file—the set of current authority records. A subject authority file contains records for topical headings, nonjurisdictional headings, headings for named objects and entities (with a few exceptions), headings for families, and headings for fictitious or legendary persons. At the Library of Congress, records for names that are also used in descriptive cataloging have traditionally been kept in a separate name authority file.

A subject authority record contains the established heading, information on the sources used in establishing the heading, and other matters related to the heading, including scope note (if any) and cross references.

Authority Research

In proposing a new subject heading, and as preparation for the authority record that will be made if the heading is established, catalogers have to do considerable research. A subject authority record contains information regarding the following aspects of the subject heading:

the exact form of the approved subject heading

scope note, if appropriate

instruction for geographic subdivision and Library of Congress classification numbers, if any

references: UF, BT, RT, and general references

authorities or sources consulted in determining the choice of the heading and references

Catalogers proposing new headings must therefore document all of the above elements that apply to the proposal at issue.

Their first step is the identification of a new concept in a work being cataloged. This concept is then verified in reference sources. If the proposed heading is analogous to an existing heading or a pattern, the heading or pattern may be cited as one of the authorities on which the proposed heading is based.

Sources consulted as authorities for establishing new headings are recorded on the proposed authority record, regardless of whether the term sought appears in them. To guard against later duplication of effort, information on such "empty" sources is particularly important in cases where the cataloger fails to find the term in question in any likely source outside the work being cataloged.

The most frequently consulted sources include the following:[5]

work being cataloged

existing LC subject headings

records in the MARC database

general dictionaries, especially *Webster's Third New International Dictionary* (Web. 3), which is always cited when applicable

general encyclopedias (e.g., *Encyclopedia Americana, Encyclopaedia Britannica, Collier's*)

general indexes and thesauri (e.g., *New York Times Index, Legislative Indexing Vocabulary* [LIV], *Readers' Guide to Periodical Literature*)

bibliography in the work being cataloged

topical reference sources and other authoritative works in the field in question, if the topic is peculiar to a particular discipline

When needed, Library of Congress catalogers may also consult appropriate individuals or agencies by telephone.

Figures 7.1-7.5, on pages 149-54, are examples of subject authority records retrieved from LOCIS, the online system of Library of Congress, showing the heading, cross references, and types of authorities consulted. For fully coded USMARC authority records, see appendix A.

Text continues on page 154.

```
11/26/93      SUBJECTS    FIND   MUMS      PAGE  1 OF  1
0*FAC* DISPLAYED RECORD HAS BEEN VERIFIED.                    112

VERIFIED                    EVAL          SU

  001  sh93-7668
  040  DLC DLC
  150  Tailhook Scandal, 1991-1993
  550  Sexual harassment of women—United States broader term
  670  Work cat.: 93-138159: Women in the military : the Tailhook affair the
       problem of sexual harassment, 1992.
  670  Wash. Post index, 1992 (Tailhook Association ... sexual harassment
       scandal)
  670  NYT index, Jan.-Mar. 1993.
  670  MAGS (Tailhook scandal scars Naval aviation)
  670  LC data base, 10/5/93 (Tailhook Association)
```

```
05/18/94      SUBJECTS    PCRD   MUMS      PAGE  1 OF  1
0*FAC* DISPLAYED RECORD HAS BEEN VERIFIED.                    112

VERIFIED                    EVAL          SU
              MAY SUBD GEOG

  001  sh94-2701
  040  DLC DLC
  150  Golden parachutes (Executive compensation)
  680  Here are entered works on severance benefits paid to executives in
       the event of a corporate takeover.
  450  Golden umbrellas (Executive compensation) used for
  550  Executives—Salaries, etc. broader term
  550  Severance pay broader term
  550  Consolidation and merger of corporations related term
  670  UMI business vocab.
  670  LIV.
  670  Scott, D.L. Wall Street words, 1988: (Golden parachutes, also known
       as Golden umbrellas)
```

Fig. 7.1. Topics in the news.

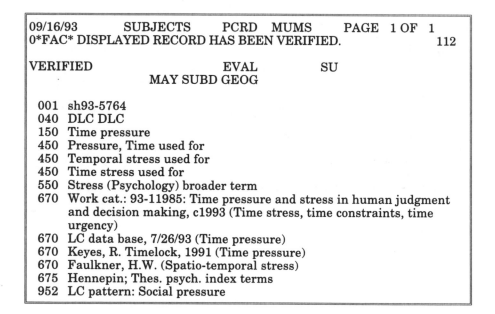

```
11/26/93        SUBJECTS      PCRD   MUMS       PAGE  1 OF  1
0*FAC* DISPLAYED RECORD HAS BEEN VERIFIED.                  112

VERIFIED                      EVAL           SU
                    MAY SUBD GEOG

  001  sh93-7525
  040  DLC DLC
  150  Health care reform
  450  Health reform used for
  450  Health system reform used for
  450  Medical care reform used for
  450  Reform of health care delivery used for
  450  Reform of medical care delivery used for
  550  Medical policy broader term
  550  Insurance, Health related term
  670  Work cat.: 93-35883: Domestic Policy Council (U.S.). Health security,
       c1993 (health care reform)
  670  MESH 1994 (Health care reform)
  670  Washington Post (health care reform, health reform)
  670  IAC (health care reform)
```

```
09/16/93        SUBJECTS      PCRD   MUMS       PAGE  1 OF  1
0*FAC* DISPLAYED RECORD HAS BEEN VERIFIED.                  112

VERIFIED                      EVAL           SU
                    MAY SUBD GEOG

  001  sh93-5764
  040  DLC DLC
  150  Time pressure
  450  Pressure, Time used for
  450  Temporal stress used for
  450  Time stress used for
  550  Stress (Psychology) broader term
  670  Work cat.: 93-11985: Time pressure and stress in human judgment
       and decision making, c1993 (Time stress, time constraints, time
       urgency)
  670  LC data base, 7/26/93 (Time pressure)
  670  Keyes, R. Timelock, 1991 (Time pressure)
  670  Faulkner, H.W. (Spatio-temporal stress)
  675  Hennepin; Thes. psych. index terms
  952  LC pattern: Social pressure
```

Fig. 7.2. Topics about public affairs issues.

```
01/19/93       SUBJECTS    PCRD   MUMS      PAGE  1 OF  1
0*FAC* DISPLAYED RECORD HAS BEEN VERIFIED.                    112

VERIFIED                    EVAL            SU
                MAY SUBD GEOG

   001  sh92-6456
   040  DLC DLC
   150  Bossa nova (Music)
   550  Jazz—Brazil broader term
   550  Popular music—Brazil broader term
   670  Work cat.: 92-832395: Suzigan, G. Bossa nova, 1990.
   670  New Grove dict. jazz, 1988 (A musical style of Brazilian origin blending
        elements of the samba and cool jazz)
   670  New Grove.
   670  New Harvard dict. mus., 1986.
   675  Web. 3
```

```
05/28/93       SUBJECTS    PCRD   MUMS      PAGE  1 OF  1
0*FAC* DISPLAYED RECORD HAS BEEN VERIFIED.                    112

VERIFIED                    EVAL            SU

   001  sh93-2569
   040  MnMHCL DLC
   150  World music
   680  Here are entered popular musical works combining traditional
        rhythms from around the world with elements of jazz and rock.
   450  World beat music used for
   550  Popular music broader term
   670  Work cat.: Spencer, P. World beat, 1992 : a listener's guide
        contemporary world music on CD, 1992 (World music)
   670  BDNE (World Beat)
   670  Hennepin (World beat music)
   670  Ox. dict. new world (World music)
   670  M. Ziomek visited Tower Records, 5/18/93 (World music)
```

Figure 7.3 is continued on page 152.

```
02/24/93        SUBJECTS     PCRD   MUMS      PAGE  1 OF 1
0*FAC* DISPLAYED RECORD HAS BEEN VERIFIED.                112

VERIFIED                       EVAL        SU
                    MAY SUBD GEOG

  001  sh93-146
  040  DLC DLC
  150  Lost architecture
  053  NA209 (General)
  680  Here are entered works on buildings, structures, etc., that were
       accidentally or purposefully destroyed or demolished.
  450  Lost architectural heritage used for
  450  Lost buildings used for
  550  Architecture broader term
  670  Work cat.: 92-43452: Jones, C. Lost Baltimore, c1993.
  670  92-73620: DeAngelo, D. The law offices of Shook ... Kansas City as
       seen through its lost architecture, c1992.
  670  LC data base, 12/15/92 (lost architecture; lost architectural heritage)
  670  Art. human. cit. index (lost architecture)
  675  Bibl. guide art arch.; Hennepin; LIV; IAC; Readers' guide; NYT
       index; Random House; Art index
  952  LC pattern: Vernacular architecture
```

Fig. 7.3. Topics in humanities.

```
02/18/93        SUBJECTS     PCRD   MUMS      PAGE  1 OF  1
0*FAC* DISPLAYED RECORD HAS BEEN VERIFIED.                112

VERIFIED                       EVAL        SU
                    MAY SUBD GEOG

  001  sh93-98
  040  DLC DLC
  150  Crop circles
  450  Circle formations in crops used for
  450  Circles, Corn used for
  450  Circles, Crop used for
  450  Corn circles used for
  450  Crop circle formations used for
  450  Crop field circles used for
  450  Cropfield circles used for
  450  Formations, Crop circle used for
  550  Curiosities and wonders broader term
  670  Hennepin (Crop circles x Crop field circles; Cropfield circles)
  670  LC data base, 1/8/93 (crop circles)
  670  Ox. dict. new words (crop circle: a (usually circular) area of standing
       crops which has been inexplicably flattened, apparently by a swirling,
       vortex-like movement (sometimes also called corn circles))
  670  Crop circle enigma, 1990: pp. 10, 12 (Circle formations in crops, corn circles)
  675  IAC
```

Fig. 7.4. Topics in technology.

```
01/17/91        SUBJECTS     PCRD   MUMS      PAGE   1 OF   1
0*FAC* DISPLAYED RECORD HAS BEEN VERIFIED.                    112

VERIFIED                           SU
                      NOT SUBD GEOG

  001  sh85-54468
  040  DLC DLC DLC
  151  Germany
  680  Here are entered works on Germany for the pre-1949 period, the
       Territories under Allied Occupation, and East Germany and West
       Germany, collectively, for the post-1949 period, as well as works on
       Germany since reunification in 1990.
```

```
01/17/91        SUBJECTS     PCRD   MUMS      PAGE   1 OF   3
0*FAC* DISPLAYED RECORD HAS BEEN VERIFIED.                    112

VERIFIED                    EVAL        SU
                      NOT SUBD GEOG

  001  sh85-54663
  040  DLC DLC DLC
  151  Germany (East)
  680  Here are entered works on the Democratic Republic established in
       1949, and works on the eastern part of Germany before 1949 and
       since reunification in 1990.
  451  East Germany used for
  451  Eastern Germany used for
  451  German Democratic Republic used for
  451  Germany (Democratic Republic, 1949- ) used for
  451  Germany (Territory under Allied occupation, 1945-1955) used for
  451  Germany, Democratic Republic of used for
  451  Germany, East used for
  451  Germany, Eastern used for
  551  Germany broader term


                             * * *
```

Figure 7.5 is continued on page 154.

```
01/17/91        SUBJECTS      PCRD   MUMS        PAGE  1 OF  1
0*FAC* DISPLAYED RECORD HAS BEEN VERIFIED.                  112

VERIFIED                      EVAL          SU
                   NOT SUBD GEOG

001  sh85-54668
040  DLC DLC DLC
151  Germany (West)
680  Here are entered works on the Federal Republic established in 1949,
     and works on the western part of Germany before 1949 and
     since reunification in 1990.
451  German Federal Republic used for
451  Germany (Federal Republic, 1949-  ) used for
451  Germany (Territory under Allied occupation, 1945-1955) used for
451  Germany, Federal Republic of used for
451  Germany, West used for
451  Germany, Western used for
451  West Germany used for
451  Western Germany used for
551  Germany broader term
```

Fig. 7.5. Places.

In formulating cross references, subject catalogers are instructed to ensure that the terms in the proposed USE references do not conflict with existing headings or other existing USE references, and that hierarchical and related term references connect valid headings and conform to established patterns for cross references, if any.

REVISING AND UPDATING HEADINGS
AND SUBDIVISIONS

A subject entry standing by itself fulfills the finding function of the catalog, but only in the way it stands as part of a larger whole in relation to other entries can it fulfill the catalog's collocation function. For this latter function, there are two requirements: The entry must be compatible with analogous entries, and there must be cross references to related entries.

A major requirement in ensuring a logically structured subject catalog is to reconcile the conflicts that result from heading changes. Each change of heading affects not only the actual entries in the catalog under the old heading, but also all cross references that involve that heading. The magnitude of the work involved can be enormous. When resources are limited, large-scale revision and updating can only be performed gradually.

Changes in subject headings generally fall into the following six categories:

(1) Simple one-to-one changes for the purpose of updating terminology or spelling. Examples include:

Old heading	Current heading
Baseball players' wives	**Baseball players' spouses**
Charwomen and cleaners	**Cleaning personnel**
Human ecology—Moral and ethical aspects	**Environmental ethics**
Marihuana	**Marijuana**

(2) Changes in headings containing proper names to conform to *AACR2R*. Examples include:

Old heading	Current heading
Kronshtadt (R.S.F.S.R.) —History	**Kronshtadt (Russia)** **—History**
Moravia (Czechoslovakia) —History	**Moravia (Czech Republic)** **—History**

(3) Changes in form or entry element. Examples include:

Old heading	Current heading
Dolls, Amish	**Amish dolls**
Schoharie Creek (N.Y.) —Bridges	**Bridges—New York (State)** **—Schoharie Creek**

(4) Changes resulting from splitting a compound heading or a heading containing two or more concepts into separate headings. Examples include:

Old heading	Current heading
Hunting, Primitive	**Hunting** **Hunting, Prehistoric** **Hunting and gathering societies**
Great Britain—Princes and princesses	**Princes—Great Britain** **Princesses—Great Britain**

(5) Changes resulting from merging overlapping headings into a single heading. Examples include:

Old heading	Current heading
MARC System MARC System—Format	**MARC formats**

(6) Changes involving subdivisions. Examples include:

Old heading	*Current heading*
America—Description and travel—1981-	**America—Description and travel**
Napoleon I, Emperor of the French, 1769-1821, in fiction, drama, poetry, etc.	**Napoleon I, Emperor of the French, 1769-1821—In literature**

When a subject heading containing an obsolete term is updated, all existing LCSH headings containing the obsolete term are revised to reflect the current term. All cross references related to the obsolete heading are also revised. In addition, a USE reference is made from the obsolete term to the new heading.

In addition to obsolete headings, many other headings have been or are being removed from LCSH. Each time a subdivision is declared free-floating, an effort is made to remove the subdivision under existing headings in LCSH, unless the heading—subdivision combinations contain unique cross references or their own subdivisions, or are used as examples.

In the LC's MARC database, each time a change in a subject heading takes place, an attempt is made to revise all bibliographic records bearing the heading. However, because the LC's automated cataloging system does not have a global change capability, subject heading changes must be performed on a record-by-record basis, a very labor-intensive operation. Changes involving large files of records can thus be effected only gradually. For example, when the decision was made in 1992 to change the free-floating subdivision —*Description* under names of cities to —**Description and travel**, bibliographic records as well as authority records containing the subdivision had to be changed one by one.

THE *SUBJECTS* FILE

For many years, the printed version of the LC subject headings list served as the subject authority file. Various supplementary lists were published, and a number of card files were created and maintained for internal use by the Subject Cataloging Division. Later, a subject authority card file was set up, and, later still, the automated *SUBJECTS* file. For other libraries using the system, LCSH is often the sole subject authority file. Some libraries also maintain a local authority file for subject headings.

The first application of automation to subject headings at the Library of Congress was the conversion of the subject headings list into machine-readable form to enable the Government Printing Office to print the 7th (1966) edition by photocomposition. The system used until 1985 was developed and implemented by the Library of Congress between 1969 and 1972—that is, while the list was in its 7th edition and not too long after the Library began inputting its new English-language cataloging into the MARC database. It was thus one of the oldest of the Library's automation efforts.

In 1986, the conversion of subject authority records according to the specifications in *Authorities: A MARC Format* was completed, and the *SUBJECTS* file was implemented.[6] Current subject authority records are kept in this file, which is used as the basis for generating LCSH in other formats.

Authority records for name headings established according to *AACR2R* are kept in the corresponding *NAMES* file. Most but not all of the headings in the *NAMES* file may be used as subject headings.[7] Also, in some cases, the form of a name assigned as a subject heading may be different from the one used in descriptive cataloging; when this is the case, the subject form is given in field 667 of the name authority record. For an example, see page 421 of appendix A.

NOTES

[1]Some LC MARC records contain uncontrolled subject terms coded in the 653 field. These terms are outside of the scope of LCSH and are "used under exceptional circumstances to provide supplementary subject access from natural language terms that are not included as headings or UF references in *LCSH* because of editorial policies, do not have precise English equivalents, and do not duplicate headings in any of the other searchable fields" (Library of Congress, Office of Subject Cataloging Policy, *Subject Cataloging Manual*, 4th ed. [Washington, D.C.: Cataloging Distribution Service, Library of Congress, 1991], H160, p. 1).

[2]Library of Congress, *Subject Cataloging Manual*, H187.

[3]Library of Congress, *Subject Cataloging Manual*, H180-H203.

[4]Library of Congress, *Subject Cataloging Manual*, H200-H202.

[5]For certain categories of headings, the subject catalogers have been instructed to consult specific references. For a list of general reference sources, see appendix H.

[6]*USMARC Format for Authority Data, Including Guidelines for Content Designation*. Prepared by Network Development and MARC Standards Office (Washington, D.C.: Cataloging Distribution Service, Library of Congress, 1987).

[7]Library of Congress, *Subject Cataloging Manual*, H430.

PART 2

APPLICATION

8 Subject Cataloging

Part 1 of this book discusses Library of Congress subject headings from the standpoint of their principles, form, and structure, all of which affect the ultimate purpose of subject headings—their function as subject access points in retrieval. This chapter and the ones that follow in part 2 treat the practical aspect of subject heading assignment. The discussions are based largely on information published in *Subject Cataloging Manual*, *Cataloging Service Bulletin*, and *Free-Floating Subdivisions: An Alphabetical Index*, on consultation with the staff of the Cataloging Policy and Support Office of the Library of Congress, and on examination of LC MARC records.[1]

Effective subject cataloging depends in large part on the individuals who assign subject headings. Their familiarity and understanding of the nature and structure of subject headings, their interpretation of a given work, their ability to coordinate headings with that work—all affect the quality and effectiveness of subject access. Were all these factors optimum for all works cataloged, the resulting records would show a high degree of uniformity and consistency—except, of course, for the dissonances that spring from changing approaches to a subject over time. But the optimum is rarely achieved, and no subject catalog is as internally consistent as one might wish. Over the years, many theorists in the field have speculated that consistency would be greater if there were a code to govern subject heading work. However, it is extremely difficult to codify the procedures for assigning subject headings to specific works because of the inevitable subjective element that operates in subject cataloging. There are naturally differences from cataloger to cataloger in interpretation of content, and sometimes even the same individual reading the same work at two different times will not make the same judgment on its content.

It may also happen that some works are cataloged under different assumptions about the appropriate depth of subject indexing than are other works in the same catalog. Depth of cataloging for a document may vary from summarization, which aims to express only the document's overall subject content, to exhaustive or in-depth indexing, which aims to enumerate all its significant concepts or aspects or to represent individual components of the work. The following examples demonstrate two approaches to similar works.

161

(1) Example of summarization:

Title: *At the limits of romanticism : essays in cultural, feminist, and materialist criticism* / edited by Mary A. Favret & Nicola J. Watson. c1994
  SUBJECTS:
  English literature—19th century—History and criticism.
  Great Britain—Civilization—19th century.
  Romanticism—Great Britain.

(2) Example of exhaustive cataloging:

Title: *British romantic writers and the East : anxieties of empire* / Nigel Leask. 1992
  SUBJECTS:
  English literature—Oriental influences.
  English literature—19th century—History and criticism.
  East and West in literature.
  Romanticism—Great Britain.
  Imperialism in literature.
  Exoticism in literature.
  Orient in literature.
  Asia—In literature.

The few headings in the first example summarize the overall subject of the work. In the second example, the eight subject headings bring out individual topics within the work on British romanticism. The difference between the two examples lies in the exhaustivity of analysis.

Another concept related to depth of cataloging is level of cataloging: whether subject headings are assigned on the basis of the overall content of an entire work or on the content of individual units, such as chapters or articles, within a work.

It is the cataloging policy of a given library or information agency that primarily governs both depth and level of analysis, though individual judgments may vary considerably even under a given policy. Library of Congress policy has leaned toward summarization, particularly in its earlier years.

In situations where summarization is considered insufficient, additional subject headings may be assigned. Or, terms from the work itself may be used to bring out individual topics or aspects of the work. One might, for example, augment cataloging records with additional subject access points based on words and phrases found within the index or table of contents of the work being analyzed. This device would increase the number of subject access points and allow a measure of free-text access to terms used in the document cataloged.

The discussion in part 2 of this book is based on Library of Congress practice, and examples are taken from LC MARC records. Individual libraries may establish their own policies with regard to the exhaustiveness and levels of subject cataloging.

GENERAL CONSIDERATIONS

General Policy

The general policy of assigning subject headings at the Library of Congress has been stated in *Subject Cataloging Manual* in the following words: "Assign to the work being cataloged one or more subject headings that best summarize the contents of the work and bring to the attention of the catalog user the most important topics discussed. Assign headings only for topics that comprise at least 20% of the work."[2] This policy provides guidelines for assigning headings that are considered essential. These are sometimes referred to as *primary headings*. In practice, the policy has been interpreted loosely. While most LC catalogers follow it, many have regularly assigned additional headings to enhance access.

Sources of Headings Used in Subject Entries

As discussed in part 1 of this book, subject headings appearing in LC MARC records are not limited to those included in LCSH. Following is a list of sources of headings that may be used as subject entries.[3]

Headings in LCSH

LCSH, in its various formats (paper, microfiche, CD-ROM, and online), contains all topical/form headings (except those formed by free-floating phrases) and proper name headings not residing in the *NAMES* file. The *SUBJECTS* file, the online version of LCSH, constitutes the most current authority because it is brought up to date most frequently. The *SUBJECTS* file is a working file and therefore includes not only authorized headings but also headings being proposed or updated. Such headings carry the notation "PROPOSED," "BEING UPDATED," or "REVISED HDG," as well as the status notation "VERIFIED" or "UNVERIFIED." The print and microfiche versions of LCSH do not contain unverified headings.

Headings Residing in the *NAMES* file

Headings in the *NAMES* file are established according to *AACR2R*. These include headings for persons, corporate bodies, and jurisdictions; the *NAMES* file also includes uniform titles.

Free-Floating Provisions in *Subject Cataloging Manual*

Free-floating subdivisions and other elements found in *Subject Cataloging Manual* may be combined with headings in LCSH or the *NAMES* file. The combinations resulting from main headings and free-floating subdivisions or phrases appear in bibliographic records but are not enumerated in LCSH or in the *NAMES* files except when they serve as examples or when unique cross references or further subdivisions are required.

Headings with Multiple Subdivisions[4]

Headings with "multiple" subdivisions were introduced in the 5th edition of the LC subject headings list as a device to save space in the printed list.[5] Currently, there are four types of multiple subdivisions in LCSH, all of which are free-floating:

(1) Multiple subdivisions under established headings, e.g.,

Subject headings—Aeronautics, [Education, Latin America, Law, etc.]
Names, Personal—Scottish, [Spanish, Welsh, etc.]

With headings like these, any topic or qualifier falling into the categories indicated in the brackets may be combined with the main heading:

Subject headings—Psychology
Names, Personal—Hungarian

(2) Multiple subdivisions under pattern headings:

World War, 1939-1945—Personal narratives, American, [French, German, etc.]
English language—Dictionaries—French, [Italian, etc.]
Shakespeare, William, 1564-1616—Contemporary England, [Contemporary America, Contemporary France, etc.]
United States—Foreign public opinion, Austrian, [British, etc.]

Because the multiple subdivisions are free-floating, the following headings, though not listed in LCSH, are valid:

Korean War, 1950-1953—Personal narratives, Korean
Chinese language—Dictionaries—Latin
Goethe, Johann Wolfgang von, 1749-1832—Contemporary Germany
France—Foreign public opinion, American
United States—Foreign public opinion, Latin American

(3) Multiple free-floating subdivisions under place-names (e.g., **[Place]—History—Blockade, [date]; [Place]—History—Siege, [date]**). The following heading is valid as a result:

Port Hudson (La.)—History—Siege, 1863

(4) Multiple subdivisions displayed by means of instructional scope notes:

Solar eclipses
Subdivided by date, e.g. Solar eclipses—1854

Scope notes, which allow for free-floating subdivision as described, should not be confused with general *see also* references, which do not necessarily authorize free-floating use of a subdivision:

Pamphlets
SA *subdivision* Pamphlets *under 16th, 17th and 18th century period subdivisions of European and American history, e.g.* Germany—History—1517-1648—Pamphlets; *and under individual wars, e.g.* United States—History—Civil War, 1861-1865—Pamphlets

In this case, the subdivision **—Pamphlets** is not free-floating under period subdivisions. However, it is a free-floating subdivision under names of individual wars, because it is listed under the pattern heading for wars.

MARC Codes for Subjects

In a bibliographic record, subject headings are tagged according to the specific MARC format used. In the USMARC format, for instance, subject headings are coded as follows:

600 Subject added entry - Personal name
610 Subject added entry - Corporate name
611 Subject added entry - Meeting name
630 Subject added entry - Uniform title
650 Subject added entry - Topical term
651 Subject added entry - Geographic name

Each of these fields may be repeated, as there is often more than one subject entry in a given category in a particular record. For more details about the USMARC codes for subject, see appendix J of this book. These coded MARC fields are often referred to as *subject entry tracings*, a term that stems from card catalog practice.

Order of Headings on Bibliographic Records[6]

In a bibliographic record, an attempt is made to match the LC Classification (LCC) number with the first subject heading assigned. Both are based on the predominant topic of the work. However, it is not always possible to achieve a perfect match, because LCC and LCSH often differ in specificity. When two or more headings are assigned to a bibliographic record, the following policies regarding the order of subject headings prevail.

(1) The first subject heading represents the predominant topic of the work.

(2) If the predominant topic is represented by two or more headings, these headings precede any headings for secondary topics. Among two or more predominant headings, the one more closely approximating the class number is assigned first.

(3) Headings for secondary topics and headings assigned as enhanced access points follow the primary headings, in no particular order.

In the case of individual biography, for instance, the first subject heading assigned is the personal name heading for the biographee. Those headings assigned to bring out subsidiary aspects or to reflect local interests, such as other biographical headings or extra local history headings, are given last.

ASSIGNING SUBJECT HEADINGS

Scope Notes[7]

Scope notes are provided under many headings in LCSH to help users determine the scope of the material covered by a particular heading and to enable catalogers to maintain consistency in assigning headings to works being cataloged. Scope notes generally provide information concerning one or more of the following aspects of the headings under which they appear: definition, relation to other headings, and application. Examples are given below.

(1) Definition. This type of note is particularly helpful in situations in which the heading represents a new concept for which the name has not yet been firmly established in usage and for which there is no dictionary definition, and in which reference sources fail to agree completely on the meaning of the term used. It is also helpful when the LCSH term is used in a somewhat different sense than generally prevails. Examples include:

Host countries (Business) *(Not Subd Geog)*
> Here are entered works on the countries, other than the home country, where the activities of an international business enterprise take place.

Lost architecture *(May Subd Geog)*
> Here are entered works on buildings, structures, etc., that were accidentally or purposefully destroyed or demolished.

Self-efficacy *(May Subd Geog)*
Here are entered works on the belief that people can bring about desired changes through their own efforts.

No first use (Nuclear strategy)
Here are entered works on the principle that a military power, in the event of war, would not be the first to resort to the tactical or strategic use of nuclear weapons. . . .

Western and Northern Territories (Poland)
Here are entered works which discuss the former German areas of Poland that lie east of the Oder-Neisse Line.

(2) Relation to other headings. Notes of this type indicate the scope of the headings in question and call attention to overlapping or more specific headings. Examples include:

Amateur plays *(May Subd Geog)*
Here are entered collections of plays, skits, recitations, etc. for production by nonprofessionals. Works about, including history and criticism of, such plays are entered under Amateur theater.

Amateur theater *(May Subd Geog)*
Here are entered works about, including history and criticism of, productions of plays, skits, recitations, etc. for production by nonprofessionals. Collections of such plays are entered under Amateur plays.

Multiculturalism *(May Subd Geog)*
Here are entered works on policies or programs that foster the preservation of different cultural identities, including customs, languages, and beliefs, within a unified society such as a state or nation. Works on the condition in which numerous distinct ethnic, religious, or cultural groups coexist within one society are entered under Pluralism (Social sciences).

World War, 1939-1945—Occupied territories
Here are entered works on enemy occupied territories discussed collectively. Works on the occupation of an individual country are entered under the name of the country with appropriate period subdivision, e.g., Belgium—History—German occupation, 1940-1945; Norway—History—German occupation, 1940-1945.

(3) Instructions, explanations, referrals, etc. Notes of this type provide information about making additional entries, about subdivisions used under the heading, and about general references to other headings. Examples include:

School prose
> For works limited to one school, the heading is qualified by nationality and subdivided by place, and an additional subject entry is made under the name of the school.

Developing countries *(Not Subd Geog)*
> Here are entered comprehensive works on those countries having relatively low per capita incomes in comparison with North American and Western European countries. This heading may be subdivided by those topical subdivisions used under names of regions, countries, etc., e.g., Developing countries—Economic conditions, and may be used as a geographic subdivision under those topics authorized for local subdivision, e.g., Technology—Developing countries.

General Versus Specific

The principle of specific entry requires that a work be assigned a specific heading that ideally represents the contents of the work exactly. This principle originated with Charles A. Cutter and has been the guiding principle of subject catalogs in this country for more than a century.

At the Library of Congress, subject catalogers are instructed to propose a new heading for each new topic encountered in cataloging but not yet represented in the subject headings list. In practice, however, there are occasions when it is considered impossible or impractical to establish a new concept or topic as a heading. In such cases, the subject content of the work is brought out either through a general heading or through several related headings.

Under the policy of specific entry, the question arises whether, after assigning a specific heading such as **Cats** to a work about cats, one should also assign one or more general headings, such as **Domestic animals** and **Pets**. Normally, a general heading and a specific one comprehended within it are not assigned to a work dealing with a specific subject. A work on algebra is given the heading **Algebra**, not **Mathematics** as well; a work about cataloging is given the heading **Cataloging**, but not also **Library science**. Similarly, a work on algebra is not usually given additional headings for various branches of algebra. In other words, under a strict policy of specific entry, when a heading that is coextensive with the overall content of a work is assigned, neither more specific headings subsumed under the given heading nor more general headings that comprehend the given heading are assigned in addition. This means neither exhaustive indexing nor generic posting is done as a matter of general LC policy.

In recent years, the Library of Congress has relaxed its general policies of not assigning a generic heading in addition to the specific heading coextensive with the content of the work and of not assigning a specific heading to a part of a work. This is evident in its treatment of individual biographies, analytical entries, and doubling.

(1) Individual biographies. For individual biographies, a generic heading representing the class of persons to which the individual belongs is assigned in addition to the personal name heading. (For a more detailed discussion, see chapter 9.)

(2) Analytical entries. When a work on a general topic devotes 20 percent or more of its space to a specific topic, two headings are assigned: one to cover the overall content of the work and the other to represent the specific topic. The first heading in the following example is assigned to represent a part of the content:

Title: *Gardening for the small property* / Jack Kramer. c1994
    SUBJECTS:
        Landscape gardening.
        Gardening.

The two headings are assigned even though there is an NT reference from **Gardening** to **Landscape gardening**. It is LC policy that the presence of a hierarchical reference between two headings should not preclude the use of both headings for the same work as long as the two headings represent the actual content of the work.

(3) Doubling in specific cases. The term *doubling* refers to the practice of assigning bilevel (generic and specific) headings to the same work. Bilevel headings are assigned in the cases described below.[8]

(a) If the work being cataloged deals with a topic in general and also applies to a particular locality, two headings are assigned as follows:

Title: *Longman's economics : our American economy* / E.L.
       Schwartz. c1994
    SUBJECTS:
        Economics.
        United States—Economic conditions.

(b) If the heading appropriate for the work being cataloged contains a heading in the form of **[Place]—Description and travel— Early works to 1800**, an additional heading in the form of **[Place]— History—[Chronological subdivision]** is assigned.[9]

(c) Bilevel headings are assigned by tradition to certain subjects, such as **World War, 1939-1945**; **Paleontology**.

(d) Works of interest to local historians and genealogists are assigned headings of the type **[City]—[Topic]** in addition to other appropriate headings.

(e) Works discussing buildings or structures within a city are assigned additional headings in the form of **[City]—Buildings, structures, etc.**

(f) Frequently, when a heading assigned to a work contains a free-floating subdivision named in a multiple subdivision (see discussion on pages 164-65), an additional heading representing the topic named in the subdivision is also assigned:[10]

> Title: *Nomes proprios* / Ana Belo. 1992
> SUBJECTS:
> > **Names, Personal—Portuguese—Dictionaries —Portuguese.**
> > (Authorized by: **Names, Personal—Scottish, [Spanish, Welsh, etc.]**)
> > **Portuguese language—Etymology—Names.**

> Title: *Women in development thesaurus* / editors, Zurniaty Nasrul ... [et al.]. 1991
> SUBJECTS:
> > **Subject headings—Women.**
> > **Subject headings—Developing countries.**
> > (Authorized by: **Subject headings—Aeronautics, [Education, Latin America, Law, etc.]**)
> > **Women—Developing countries—Abstracting and indexing.**
> > **Developing countries—Abstracting and indexing.**

(g) In addition to headings representing the central subject of the work, headings broader than or related to the central subject are often assigned as additional access points. With the relaxation on the number of headings allowed for each record, this practice is particularly evident in recently created records.

Duplicate Entries

As discussed in chapter 2, exceptions are sometimes made to the principle of uniform heading (one topic/one heading) in cases in which two elements in a heading are of equal significance and it is therefore desirable to provide access to both. In such cases, specific instructions are given in LCSH to assign both headings to the same work, even though they consist of the same elements and have identical meanings:

Title: *Oldest allies, guarded friends : the United States and France since 1940* / Charles G. Cogan. 1994
SUBJECTS:
United States—Foreign relations—France.
France—Foreign relations—United States.

Duplicate entries of this type are particularly helpful in manual catalogs. They are not necessary in online catalogs, but the practice persists because there are still systems that do not have keyword search capabilities. It is also helpful in online browsing of the alphabetical subject index.

Number of Headings for Each Record

It is difficult, and perhaps not practical, to regulate the number of subject headings to be assigned to each work. In general, such a decision is based on the requirements of the work in hand, with consideration given to the general policy of summarization. In the past, the Library of Congress restricted the number of headings for each record in order to save space in the card catalog, and the library was often criticized for assigning too few headings. A study published in 1979 estimated that the average number of subject headings assigned to an LC cataloging record was less than two,[11] and many considered this finding an indication of deficiency in LC practice.

In recent years, the Library of Congress has relaxed its rules on coextensivity and summarization. Current guidelines state:

The number of headings required varies with the work being cataloged. Sometimes one heading is sufficient. Generally a maximum of six is appropriate. In special situations as many as ten may be required. Do not assign more than ten headings to a work.[12]

As a result of this policy change, many more records carry multiple subject headings. Because these additional headings are assigned according to the judgment of individual catalogers, practice varies from case to case. The following examples show records to which multiple headings have been assigned.

Title: *In the company of scholars : the struggle for the soul of higher education* / Julius Getman. 1992
SUBJECTS:
Education, Higher—United States—Philosophy.
Education, Higher—Political aspects—United States.
Education, Humanistic—United States.
Elites (Social sciences)—United States.
Universities and colleges—United States—Faculty.

Title: *Cultural diversity and the schools* / edited by James Lynch,
Celia Modgil, and Sohan Modgil. 1992
SUBJECTS:
   Multicultural education.
   Pluralism (Social sciences)
   Discrimination in education.
   Prejudices.
   Racism.
   Group work in education.

Title: *The graphic unconscious in early modern French writing* /
Tom Conley. 1992
SUBJECTS:
   French literature—16th century—History and criticism.
   Type and type-founding—France—History—16th century.
   Visual poetry, French—History and criticism.
   Printing—France—History—16th century.
   Psychoanalysis and literature.
   Reader-response criticism.
   Semiotics and literature.

Title: *Celebration & renewal : rites of passage in Judaism* / edited
by Rela M. Geffen. 1993
SUBJECTS:
   Judaism—Customs and practices.
   Life cycle, Human—Religious aspects—Judaism.
   Life change events—Religious aspects—Judaism.
   Judaism—20th century.
   Judaism—United States.
   Jewish way of life.

Title: *Colonialism and gender relations from Mary Wollstonecraft
to Jamaica Kincaid : East Caribbean connections* / Moira
Ferguson. c1993
SUBJECTS:
   English literature—Caribbean influences.
   **English literature—Women authors—History and
      criticism.**
   Women and literature—Caribbean Area—History.
   Women and literature—Great Britain—History.
   Slavery and slaves in literature.
   Caribbean Area in literature.
   Race relations in literature.
   Imperialism in literature.
   Colonies in literature.
   Sex role in literature.

SPECIAL CONSIDERATIONS

As has been noted above, even under a policy of summarization, it is not always possible to give each work a heading that is coextensive with its content. Many works deal with multiple topics or complex subjects and so require more than one heading. Even works dealing with a single subject may occasionally require more than one heading. The following comments summarize subject heading assignment practice in terms of the types of documents encountered.

Works on a Single Topic

The heading that exactly represents the content, if available, is assigned to a work on a single topic:

Title: *Beyond the hype : rediscovering the essence of management /* Robert G. Eccles and Nitin Nohria, with James D. Berkley. c1992
SUBJECTS:
Management.

Title: *Your child's development : from birth through adolescence : a complete guide for parents /* by Richard Lansdown and Marjorie Walker. 1991
SUBJECTS:
Child development.

Title: *The education of desire : Marxists and the writing of history /* Harvey J. Kaye. 1992
SUBJECTS:
Marxian historiography.

Title: *Granitoid rocks /* D.B. Clarke. 1992
SUBJECTS:
Granite.

Title: *Quality management : implementing the best ideas of the masters /* Bruce Brocka and M. Suzanne Brocka. 1992
SUBJECTS:
Total quality management.

Title: *Dead reckoning : calculating without instruments /* Ronald W. Doerfler. 1993
SUBJECTS:
Ready-reckoners.

Title: *Sampling /* Steven K. Thompson. c1992
SUBJECTS:
Sampling (Statistics)

Title: *Stratigraphy* / Pierre Cotillon. c1992
SUBJECTS:
Geology, Stratigraphic.

In cases where the topic of the work being cataloged is not represented in LCSH, and for various reasons it is considered impractical to establish the concept as a new heading, a more general heading or several related headings—whichever designates more closely the topic of the work—are assigned:

Title: *Land-mobile radio system engineering* / Gary C. Hess. 1993
SUBJECTS:
Mobile communication systems.
Mobile radio stations.

Title: *Particulate two-phase flow* / edited by M.C. Roco, with 50
        contributing authors. c1993
SUBJECTS:
Two-phase flow.
Particles.

Title: *Feminist epistemologies* / edited and with an introduction by
        Linda Alcoff and Elizabeth Potter. 1993
SUBJECTS:
Feminist theory.
Knowledge, Theory of.

Title: *A postmodern Tao : a guide to apprehending ways of meaning
        in pathless lands : seven contemplations with review / re-
        flection exercises for geography, philosophy, and science
        students* / Jim Norwine ; edited by Linda Ford Winans ;
        foreword by Steven Bindeman. c1993
SUBJECTS:
Postmodernism.
Tao.

Multitopical Works

Works on Two or Three Topics

For a work covering two or three topics treated separately, a heading representing precisely each of the topics is assigned. The two or three specific headings are assigned in favor of a general heading if the latter includes in its scope more than three subtopics. This is called the "rule of three."[13]

Title: *Gems and jewelry : all color guide* / by Joel Arem. c1992
SUBJECTS:
   Gems.
   Jewelry.

Title: *Creating letterforms : calligraphy and lettering for beginners* /
   Rosemary Sassoon, Patricia Lovett. 1992
SUBJECTS:
   Calligraphy.
   Lettering.

Title: *Embeddings and immersions* / Masahisa Adachi ; translated
   by Kiki Hudson. 1993
SUBJECTS:
   Embeddings (Mathematics)
   Immersions (Mathematics)

Title: *Integrated production and inventory management : revital-
   izing the manufacturing enterprise* / Thomas E. Vollmann,
   William L. Berry, D. Clay Whybark. c1993
SUBJECTS:
   Production management.
   Inventory control.

Title: *The economics of money, banking, and financial markets* /
   Frederic S. Mishkin. 1992
SUBJECTS:
   Finance.
   Money.
   Banks and banking.

Works on Four or More Topics

Some works on four topics are assigned a general heading, and
others are assigned four individual headings.

Title: *A brief look at our social, political, educational, cultural
   heritage* / [commentaries by] Eustace Usher, J.P. 1992
SUBJECTS:
   Belize.

Specific headings are preferred when the work being cataloged deals
with four topics, each of which forms only a small portion of a general
topic. This is called the "rule of four."[14]

Title: *Joyce's grandfathers : myth and history in Defoe, Smollett,
   Sterne, and Joyce* / John M. Warner. c1993
SUBJECTS:
   English fiction—18th century—History and criticism.

> *Smollett, Tobias George, 1721-1771—Criticism and interpretation.
> *Sterne, Laurence, 1713-1768—Criticism and interpretation.
> *Defoe, Daniel, 1661?-1731—Criticism and interpretation.
> Influence (Literary, artistic, etc.)
> *Joyce, James, 1882-1941. Ulysses.
> History in literature.
> Myth in literature.

For a work treating five or more related topics, a single generic heading that encompasses all the topics treated is used if one exists or can be established, even if the generic heading includes other topics not present in the work being cataloged.

> Title: *Eight American poets : twentieth-century voices : Theodore Roethke, Elizabeth Bishop, Robert Lowell, John Berryman, Anne Sexton, Allen Ginsberg, Sylvia Plath, James Merrill : an anthology* / edited by Joel Conarroe. 1994
> SUBJECTS:
> American poetry—20th century.

If a generic heading does not exist or cannot be established, either several very broad headings or one or more form headings (e.g., **American essays**) are assigned:

> Title: *The Great American Bologna Festival and other student essays : a celebration of writing by students using The St. Martin's Guide* / edited by Elizabeth Rankin. c1991
> SUBJECTS:
> College prose, American.
> American essays—20th century.
> College readers.

> Title: *The Hutchinson book of essays* / chosen and introduced by Frank Delaney ; with engravings by Reynolds Stone. 1990
> SUBJECTS:
> English essays.
> American essays.
> Essays—Translations into English.

> Title: *The Norton sampler : short essays for composition* / [edited by] Thomas Cooley. 1993
> SUBJECTS:
> College readers.
> English language—Rhetoric.
> Essays.

Aspects of Main Topics

Many works treat topics with regard to one or more of their aspects, such as subtopic, time, or place. Others are presented in a specific form: a dictionary, an index, a manual. In most cases, these aspects are represented by subdivisions. In others, they are represented by a complex heading (a phrase heading or a heading with a qualifier) that combines an aspect with the main topic. In these cases, the elements are precoordinated.

Subtopic

Title: *Strategic management in the hospitality industry* / Michael D. Olsen, Eliza Ching-Yick Tse, Joseph J. West. 1992
SUBJECTS:
Hospitality industry—Management.

Title: *Assessing sport skills* / Bradford N. Strand, Rolayne Wilson. c1993
SUBJECTS:
Athletic ability—Testing.

Title: *Data analysis for the chemical sciences : a guide to statistical techniques* / Richard C. Graham. 1993
SUBJECTS:
Chemistry—Statistical methods.

Title: *The Global media debate : its rise, fall, and renewal* / edited by George Gerbner, Hamid Mowlana, and Kaarle Nordenstreng. 1993
SUBJECTS:
Communication—International cooperation.

Title: *Broadband network analysis and design* / Daniel Minoli. 1993
SUBJECTS:
Broadband communication systems—Design.

Title: *Deciding what to teach and test : developing, aligning, and auditing the curriculum* / Fenwick W. English. c1992
SUBJECTS:
Curriculum planning.

Title: *Administration of the small public library* / Darlene E. Weingand. 1992
SUBJECTS:
Public libraries—Administration.
Small libraries—Administration.

Title: *After the war was over : Hanoi and Saigon* / Neil Sheehan. 1992
SUBJECTS:
Hanoi (Vietnam)—Description and travel.
Ho Chi Minh City (Vietnam)—Description and travel.

Title: *Jewish civilization : the Jewish historical experience in a comparative perspective* / S.N. Eisenstadt. c1992
SUBJECTS:
Jews—Civilization.
Jews—History.

In some cases, the subtopics in a complex subject are brought out by means of two or more headings:

Title: *Broadband telecommunications technology* / Byeong Gi Lee, Minho Kang, Jonghee Lee. 1993
SUBJECTS:
Broadband communication systems.
Integrated services digital networks.

Title: *Thermal properties and temperature-related behavior of rock/fluid systems* / W.H. Somerton. 1992
SUBJECTS:
Petroleum—Geology.
Rocks—Thermal properties.
Fluids—Migration.
Soil porosity.

In these cases, each of the headings assigned is broader than the subject treated in the work. Specificity is achieved only through post-coordination (i.e., combining the heading being consulted with other headings during the process of searching). This is a more powerful device in automated information retrieval systems than in manual ones, but it is effective in both.

Place

The geographic aspect of a work is normally brought out by means of a geographic subdivision or a geographic heading:

Title: *Italy from the air* / text by Franco Lefevre ; photographs by Guido Rossi. 1993
SUBJECTS:
Italy—Pictorial works.
Italy—Aerial photographs.

Title: *Researching women in Latin America and the Caribbean* /
   edited by Edna Acosta-Belen and Christine E. Bose. 1993
SUBJECTS:
   Women—Research—Latin America.
   Women—Research—Caribbean Area.

Title: *Change and challenge in library and information science
   education* / Margaret F. Stieg. 1992
SUBJECTS:
   Library education—United States.
   **Information science—Study and teaching—United
   States.**

Title: *The evolution of mobile communications in the U.S. and
   Europe : regulation, technology, and markets* / Michael
   Paetsch. 1993
SUBJECTS:
   Telecommunication—United States.
   Telecommunication—Europe.
   Mobile communications systems—United States.
   Mobile communications systems—Europe.

Because geographic subdivisions are generally not provided under
names of species, breeds of animals, specific musical instruments, and
certain other specific subjects, the geographic aspect is brought out by
assigning, in addition to the specific heading, a broader heading under
which geographic subdivisions are provided:

Title: *Several complex variables in China* / Chung-Chun Yang,
   Sheng Gong, editors. c1993
SUBJECTS:
   Functions of several complex variables.
   Mathematics—Research—China.

Title: *Historia de una guitarra : Teatro Albeniz, mayo 1991* /
   Comunidad de Madrid, Consejeria de Cultura, Centro de
   Estudios y Actividades Culturales. [1991]
SUBJECTS:
   Guitar—Exhibitions.
   Musical instruments—Spain—Exhibitions.

Time

The time, or chronological, aspect of a subject is usually brought out by means of chronological subdivisions:

Title: *Performing baroque music* / Mary Cyr ; Reinhard G. Pauly, general editor. c1992
SUBJECTS:
Performance practice (Music)—17th century.
Performance practice (Music)—18th century.

Title: *The mid-Tudor crisis, 1545-1565* / David Loades. 1992
SUBJECTS:
Great Britain—History—Edward VI and Mary, 1547-1558.
Great Britain—History—Tudors, 1485-1603.
Tudor, House of.

Title: *Cultural transformations in the new Germany : American and German perspectives* / edited by Friederike Eigler and Peter C. Pfeiffer. 1993
SUBJECTS:
Germany—Intellectual life—20th century.
Arts, Modern—20th century—Germany.
German literature—20th century—History and criticism.
Arts and society—Germany—History—20th century.
German literature—Appreciation—United States.

If the specific heading, assigned to a work treating the subject with respect to a period, does not provide for period subdivisions, an additional, broader heading that allows for period subdivision is sometimes assigned to bring out the chronological aspect:

Title: *The formation of a society on Virginia's Eastern Shore, 1615-1655* / James R. Perry. c1990
SUBJECTS:
Virginia—History—Colonial period, ca. 1600-1775.
Eastern Shore (Md. and Va.)—History.

In some cases, the time aspect of a work is ignored in cataloging if it is considered insignificant.

Form

Form subdivisions, most of which are free-floating (see chapter 5), are used when appropriate. They may be assigned under all types of headings—personal names, corporate names, meetings and conferences, uniform titles, geographic headings, and topical headings:

Title: *The Cambridge history of Southeast Asia* / edited by Nicholas
    Tarling. 1992
SUBJECTS:
    Asia, Southeastern—History.

Title: *Population structure* / by Shigemi Kono. [1993]
SUBJECTS:
    Population—Statistics.
    Population forecasting—Statistics.

Title: *McGraw-Hill encyclopedia of chemistry* / Sybil P. Parker,
    editor in chief. c1993
SUBJECTS:
    Chemistry—Encyclopedias.

Title: *Handbook of practical coal geology* / Larry Thomas. 1992
SUBJECTS:
    Coal—Geology—Handbooks, manuals, etc.

When a form subdivision is used under a heading for a work
assigned more than one heading, the same form subdivision should be
used with all the headings if it is applicable. Exceptions are naturally
made for cases in which different parts of the work are in different
forms.

Title: *Bibliography of law and economics* / edited by Boudewijn
    Bouckaert and Gerrit de Geest. c1992
SUBJECTS:
    Law—Bibliography.
    Law—Europe—Bibliography.
    Economics—Bibliography.
    Economics—Europe—Bibliography.

Title: *Companion to medieval and renaissance music* / edited by
    Tess Knoghton and David Fallows. 1992
SUBJECTS:
    Music—500-1400—History and criticism.
    Music—15th century—History and criticism.
    Music—16th century—History and criticism.

Title: *Proceedings of the Second International Symposium [on]*
    Particles, Strings, and Cosmology, Northeastern Univer-
    sity, Boston, 25-30 March 1991 / editors, Pran Nath and
    Stephen Reucroft. c1992
SUBJECTS:
    Particles (Nuclear physics)—Congresses.
    String models—Congresses.
    Cosmology—Congresses.

Title: *Gardeners delight : gardening books from 1560 to 1960* /
Martin Hoyles. 1994
SUBJECTS:
Horticultural literature—History.
Gardening—Bibliography.

Multiple Aspects

Many complex subjects contain multiple aspects, or facets. These
are often precoordinated in a single heading string:

Title: *Neo furniture* / Claire Downey. 1992
SUBJECTS:
**Furniture design—Europe—History—20th century—
Themes, motives.**

Title: *Doctors and the law : medical jurisprudence in nineteenth-
century America* / James C. Mohr. 1993
SUBJECTS:
**Medical jurisprudence—United States—History—
19th century.**

Title: *Inventing the Middle Ages : the lives, works, and ideas of the
great medievalists of the twentieth century* / Norman F.
Cantor. 1991
SUBJECTS:
Middle Ages—Historiography—History—20th century.

When a single heading or heading string cannot express all the aspects
in the subject, multiple headings are assigned:

Title: *The end of the Salon : art and the state in the early Third
Republic* / Patricia Mainardi. 1993
SUBJECTS:
Salon (Exhibition : Paris, France)
Art and state—France—History—19th century.

Title: *Outsiders : class, gender, and nation* / Dorothy Thompson. 1993
SUBJECTS:
Chartism—History.
**Working class—Great Britain—Political activity—
History—19th century.**

This approach is taken most frequently when a large number of concepts are involved:

Title: *Teacher-parent partnerships to enhance school success in early childhood education* / Kevin J. Swick. 1991
SUBJECTS:
Early childhood education—United States—Parent participation.
Parent-teacher relationships—United States.

Title: *Handbook of paleolithic typology* / Andre Debenath, Harold L. Dibble. 1993-
SUBJECTS:
Paleolithic period—Europe.
Stone implements—Europe—Classification.
Tools, Prehistoric—Europe—Classification.
Europe—Antiquities.

Title: *Roofed theaters of classical antiquity* / George C. Izenour. c1992
SUBJECTS:
Theaters—Greece.
Classical antiquities.
Architecture—Greece.
Architecture—Rome.
Theaters—Rome.
Roofs—Greece.
Roofs—Rome.

As a result of the relaxation of the restriction on the number of headings assigned to each item, additional headings may be used to bring out other aspects of the work:

Title: *Replanning the blitzed city centre : a comparative study of Bristol, Coventry, and Southampton, 1941-1950* / Junichi Hasegawa. 1992
SUBJECTS:
Urban renewal—England—Bristol—History.
Urban renewal—England—Coventry—History.
Urban renewal—England—Southampton—History.
Central business districts—England—Bristol—Planning—History.
Central business districts—England—Coventry—Planning—History.
Central business districts—England—Southampton—Planning—History.
Bristol (England)—History—Bombardment, 1940-1941.
Coventry (England)—History—Bombardment, 1940-1941.
Southampton (England)—History—Bombardment, 1940-1944.

Title: *Rocks and minerals for the collector. Estrie and Gaspesie, Quebec, and parts of New Brunswick* / Ann P. Sabina. 1992
SUBJECTS:
Rocks—Collectors and collecting—Quebec—Estrie (Administrative region)
Minerals—Collectors and collecting—Quebec—Estrie (Administrative region)
Rocks—Collectors and collecting—Quebec—Gaspe Peninsula.
Minerals—Collectors and collecting—Quebec—Gaspe Peninsula.
Rocks—Collectors and collecting—New Brunswick.
Minerals—Collectors and collecting—New Brunswick.

Title: *Jasper Johns, Brice Marden, Terry Winters : drawings.* c1992
SUBJECTS:
Drawing, American—Exhibitions.
Drawing—20th century—United States—Exhibitions.
Johns, Jasper, 1930- —Exhibitions.
Marden, Brice, 1938- —Exhibitions.
Winters, Terry—Exhibitions.

Phase Relations

Many works treat subjects in relation to each other; in cataloging, most intersubject relationships are referred to as *phase relations*, and include general relations, influence, tool or application, comparison, and bias. When appropriate, headings representing such relations are assigned, if available (e.g., **Body temperature—Effect of drugs on**; **Fungi in agriculture**; **Plants, Effects of electricity on**; **Television and politics**).[15] If such headings do not exist, LC subject catalogers may propose new headings if the relationship is considered significant, or they may use separate headings for each topic involved:

Title: *Floquet theory for partial differential equations* / Peter Kuchment. c1993
SUBJECTS:
Differential equations, Partial.
Floquet theory.

Title: *Classroom management for secondary teachers* / Edmund T. Emmer ... [et al.]. 1994
SUBJECTS:
Classroom management.
Education, Secondary.

Title: *Application of neural networks to modelling and control* /
     edited by G.F. Page, J.B. Gomm, and D. Williams. 1993
SUBJECTS:
Neural networks (Computer science)
Computer simulation.
Automatic control.

Title: *Application of crop simulation models in agricultural re-
     search and development in the tropics and subtropics* /
     Philip Thornton. [1991]
SUBJECTS:
Agriculture—Research—Mathematical models.
Crops—Mathematical models.
Agriculture—Research—Tropics—Mathematical
    models.
Tropical crops—Mathematical models.

The author's or publisher's viewpoint is often brought out in the
subject heading, particularly the intended readership (if juvenile) and
the approach (e.g., fact or fiction):

Title: *Bringing up parents : the teenager's handbook* / by Alex J.
     Packer ; edited by Pamela Espeland ; illustrated by Harry
     Pulver, Jr. c1992
SUBJECTS:
Parent and teenager—Juvenile literature.
Conflict of generations—Juvenile literature.
Interpersonal relations—Juvenile literature.
Family—Juvenile literature.

On the other hand, the level of textbooks is generally ignored.

Title: *Elementary hydrology* / Vijay P. Singh. c1992
SUBJECTS:
Hydrology.

Topics Without Representation in LCSH

Even after multiple headings have been assigned to a work, all
aspects of a work may still not be totally covered. For example:

Title: *Intentionality and the new traditionalism : some liminal
     means to literary revisionism.* 1991
SUBJECTS:
**English literature—17th century—History and criticism
    —Theory, etc.**
English literature—History and criticism—Theory, etc.
Intentionalism.
Literary form.

Title: *The third force in seventeenth century thought* / by Richard
      H. Popkin. 1992
    SUBJECTS:
      Philosophy, Modern—17th century.

In the first example above, the topics "new traditionalism" and "revisionism" are not represented by the subject headings assigned; neither is the topic "the third force" in the second example. In an online catalog, the topics can be retrieved through keyword searching in the title field, an advantage of online systems not present in manual catalogs. In card catalogs, however, partial-title added entries (discussed below) were previously used to provide access not possible through titles or subject headings. The practice of assigning partial-title added entries has been discontinued.

In other cases, if the topic of the work being cataloged is not represented in LCSH and cannot be established as a valid subject heading (because of various factors such as uncertain terminology) it is LC practice to assign a more general heading or several related headings—whichever designates more accurately the topic of the work in view of the various headings available.

Subject Headings Identical to Descriptive Access Points[16]

Previously, the Library of Congress had a policy of not assigning to a work a subject heading that exactly matched a name heading. This policy was discontinued in 1972. Currently, an appropriate subject heading is assigned to a work even though the heading may duplicate a main or added entry assigned in descriptive cataloging. This happens often with works entered under corporate bodies, with autobiographical works, with nontopical compilations of general laws, and with artistic reproductions that have commentary.[17] It also occurs when a valid heading is identical to the title of work. Such duplicate access points were considered unnecessary in a manual dictionary catalog. They are, however, important in an online catalog because of the nature of online searching. Author and title entries are not retrieved in subject searches, only in searches for authors or titles, and a user wanting material about a given corporate body, for instance, would probably not make an author search for it. The following examples illustrate duplicate access points:

Title: *Barbara Bush : a memoir* / Barbara Bush. c1994
    SUBJECTS:
      Bush, Barbara, 1925-
      Bush, George, 1924-
      Presidents' spouses—United States—Biography.
    MAIN ENTRY:
      Bush, Barbara, 1925-

Title: *Iconographic index to New Testament subjects represented in photographs and slides of paintings in the visual collections, Fine Arts Library, Harvard University* / Helene E. Roberts and Rachel Hall. 1992-
SUBJECTS:
    Bible. N.T.—Illustrations—Slides—Catalogs.
    Bible. N.T.—Illustrations—Photographs—Catalogs.
    Painting—Slides—Catalogs.
    Painting—Photographs—Catalogs.
    Harvard University. Fine Arts Library—Catalogs.
ADDED ENTRIES:
    Hall, Rachel, 1905-
    Harvard University. Fine Arts Library.

NOTES

[1]Library of Congress, Office of Subject Cataloging Policy, *Subject Cataloging Manual*, 4th ed. (Washington, D.C.: Cataloging Distribution Service, Library of Congress, 1991).; *Cataloging Service Bulletin* 1- (Summer 1978-); Library of Congress, Cataloging Policy and Support Office, *Free-Floating Subdivisions: An Alphabetical Index*, 6th ed. (Washington, D.C.: Cataloging Distribution Service, Library of Congress, 1994).

[2]Library of Congress, *Subject Cataloging Manual*, H180, p. 1.

[3]Library of Congress, *Subject Cataloging Manual*, H200, p. 1.

[4]Library of Congress, *Subject Cataloging Manual*, H1090.

[5]The practice of "multiple" headings such as *Authors, American, [English, French, etc.]*; *Coins, Arab, [Austrian, French, etc.]*, which were printed in *Library of Congress Subject Headings* until 1981, has been discontinued.

[6]Library of Congress, *Subject Cataloging Manual*, H80.

[7]Library of Congress, *Subject Cataloging Manual*, H400.

[8]Library of Congress, *Subject Cataloging Manual*, H870.

[9]"Description and Travel," *Cataloging Service Bulletin* 63 (Winter 1994): 28.

[10]Library of Congress, *Subject Cataloging Manual*, H1090.

[11]Edward T. O'Neill and Rao Aluri, *Research Report on Subject Heading Patterns in OCLC Monographic Records*. OCLC Research Report Series OCLC/RDD/RR 79/1. (Columbus, Ohio: Ohio College Library Center, 1979), 7.

[12]Library of Congress, *Subject Cataloging Manual*, H180, p. 1.

[13]Library of Congress, *Subject Cataloging Manual*, H180, p. 1.

[14]Library of Congress, *Subject Cataloging Manual*, H180, p. 2.

[15]Library of Congress, *Subject Cataloging Manual*, H1580.

[16]Library of Congress, *Subject Cataloging Manual*, H184.

[17]A more detailed discussion and examples of these types of materials appear in chapters 9 and 10.

9 Subject Cataloging of Special Types of Materials

The discussion in the last chapter concerns subject cataloging in general. In the Library of Congress subject headings system, several types of materials and special subject areas receive special or unique treatment. These are discussed in chapters 9 and 10.

SERIALS

Subject headings for serial publications in general, and for periodicals and journals in particular, are based on the subject range of a publication over its expected life, not the subjects in individual issues. Topical and geographical headings are assigned as appropriate, with a form subdivision used to show the material's bibliographical form. Most Library of Congress form subdivisions are free-floating; the following list shows those that are most frequently used for serials:

—**Congresses**
—**Directories**
—**Indexes**
—**Periodicals**
—**Societies, etc.**

Of these, the one in widest use is —**Periodicals**. It is used as a form subdivision under topical, personal name, corporate name, and geographic headings. A periodical is defined as "a publication other than a newspaper that is actually or purportedly issued according to a regular schedule (monthly, quarterly, three times a year, etc.) in successive parts, each of which bears a numerical or chronological designation and that is intended to be continued indefinitely."[1]

The subdivision —**Periodicals** may be combined with other form headings or form subdivisions when appropriate:

(1) It may be used with form headings such as

French poetry—Periodicals

189

(2) It may be further subdivided by other form subdivisions such as

—Periodicals—Indexes
—Periodicals—Juvenile literature

(3) It may be used as a further subdivision under most other free-floating form subdivisions, such as

—Abstracts—Periodicals
—Biography—Periodicals
—Statistics—Periodicals

However, it is *not* used as a further subdivision under the following form subdivisions:[2]

—Amateurs' manuals
—Atlases
—Calendars
—Cases
—Congresses
—Dictionaries
—Directories
—Encyclopedias
—Gazetteers
—Guidebooks
—Handbooks, manuals, etc.
—Juvenile films
—Juvenile literature
—Juvenile sound recordings
—Laboratory manuals
—Maps
    {also **—Maps, Comparative**; **—Maps, Manuscript**; etc.}
—Observers' manuals
—Outlines, syllabi, etc.
—Photo maps
—Registers
—Road maps
—Telephone directories
—Zoning maps

As a result, headings such as *[Topic]—Congresses—Periodicals* are not authorized for use.

In choosing a form subdivision, the cataloger should be guided by both the nature of the publication in question (not just what is suggested by the wording of the title) and the scope notes in *Subject Cataloging Manual* that apply to form subdivisions.

The following examples reflect current LC subject cataloging practice for various types of serial publications. When discussion of a given publication type is better suited to a different section of this book, a cross reference to the relevant pages is given.

Abstracts

See the discussion and examples on page 199.

Annual Reports

See the discussion and examples on pages 195-96.

Biographical Reference Works

Title: *Almanac of famous people.* c1989-
  SUBJECTS:
    Biography—Periodicals.
    Biography—Indexes—Periodicals.

Title: *Who's who in America. Junior & senior high school version.*
    c1989-
  SUBJECTS:
    United States—Biography—Dictionaries.

Title: *Nigeria who's who in business, including investment directory.*
    1992-
  SUBJECTS:
    Businessmen—Nigeria—Biography—Periodicals.
    Industrialists—Nigeria—Biography—Periodicals.
    Nigeria—Economic conditions—1970- —Periodicals.

Book and Media Reviews

Title: *Booklist's guide to the year's best books : definitive reviews of
    over 1,000 fiction and nonfiction titles in all fields.* c1992-
  SUBJECTS:
    Books—Reviews—Periodicals.
    Best books.

Title: *New letters review of books.* c1987-
  SUBJECTS:
    Books—Reviews—Periodicals.
    American literature—Book reviews—Periodicals.
    English literature—Book reviews—Periodicals.

Title: *The Music independent.* c1989-
  SUBJECTS:
    Sound recording industry—United States—Periodicals.
    Sound recordings—Reviews—Periodicals.

Title: *Roger Ebert's video companion.* c1993-
   SUBJECTS:
       Motion pictures—Reviews—Periodicals.
       Video recordings—Periodicals.

Conference (Congress, Symposium, Etc.) Publications

Publications emanating from conferences, congresses, symposia, and the like are assigned topical headings with the subdivision **—Congresses**. Such headings are not further subdivided by form, except for the subdivision **—Juvenile literature**, even when the publication in question consists of collected papers issued in condensed form; in other words, the form *[Topic]—Congresses—Abstracts* is not used. Examples include:

Title: *Annual conference* / the African Society of International and
       Comparative Law = *Congrès annuel* / La Société africaine
       de droit international et comparé. c1989-
   SUBJECTS:
       Law—Africa—Congresses.
       Comparative law—Africa—Congresses.
       International law—Africa—Congresses.

Title: *UIST : proceedings of the ACM Symposium on User Interface
       Software and Technology.* c1991-
   SUBJECTS:
       User interfaces (Computer systems)—Congresses.
       Interactive computer systems—Congresses.

Title: *Transactions of the American Association of Cost Engineers.*
       c1990-
   SUBJECTS:
       Costs, Industrial—Congresses.
       Industrial engineering—Congresses.
       Cost control—Congresses.

Directories

See the discussion on pages 218-19.

Government Publications

Serially issued government publications are assigned subject headings appropriate to their subject content and form. In other words, no subdivision is used to bring out the fact that a publication is issued by a government.

Title: *Aviation system capital investment plan : report of the Federal Aviation Administration to the U.S. Congress pursuant to Section 504 (b) (1) of the Airport and Airway Improvement Act of 1982 (Title V, P.L. 97-248).* [1991]-
SUBJECTS:
Airways—United States—Planning—Periodicals.
Aeronautics, Commercial—Capital investments— United States—Periodicals.

Title: *By the year 2000 : report of the FCCSET Committee on Education and Human Resources.* 1991-
SUBJECTS:
Science—Study and teaching—United States—Periodicals.
Mathematics—Study and teaching—United States— Periodicals.
Engineering—Study and teaching—United States— Periodicals.
Education and state—United States—Periodicals.

Title: *Critical technologies plan* / the Department of Defense for the Committees on Armed Services, United States Congress. 1989-
SUBJECTS:
Military research—United States—Periodicals.
United States—Armed Forces—Equipment—Periodicals.

Indexes

See the discussion and examples on pages 202-4.

Monographic Series

When a monographic series is cataloged as a whole, one or more topical headings (generally with the subdivision **—Periodicals)** representing the overall subject of the entire series are assigned:

Title: *Publications in natural science* / *the New Brunswick Museum = Publications de sciences naturelles* / le Musée du Nouveau-Brunswick. [1983?]-
SUBJECTS:
Natural history—New Brunswick—Periodicals.

Until early 1988, collections of independent works published together in one or more volumes were assigned headings with the subdivision *—Collected works*. This subdivision is now obsolete.[3]

Periodicals and Journals

Periodicals that cover very broad or general subjects are not assigned subject headings. Headings such as **American periodicals** indicate topic, not form; in other words, the heading **American periodicals** is assigned to a work *about* American periodicals, but is not used with periodicals such as *Saturday Evening Post* or *Atlantic Monthly*. Examples include:

Title: *Journal of mathematical sciences.* c1994-
SUBJECTS:
Mathematics—Periodicals.

Title: *Macromolecular rapid communications.* c1994-
SUBJECTS:
Macromolecules—Periodicals.
Polymers—Periodicals.
Chemistry—Periodicals.

Title: *International review of economics & finance.* 1992-
SUBJECTS:
Economics—Periodicals.
Finance—Periodicals.

Title: *Journal of computer and software engineering.* 1993-
SUBJECTS:
Computers—Periodicals.
Software engineering—Periodicals.

Title: *Advances in genome biology.* c1992-
SUBJECTS:
Genetics—Periodicals.
Molecular biology—Periodicals.
Genomes—Periodicals.

Title: *The Sandhills review.* c1992-
SUBJECTS:
Literature—Periodicals.

Title: *Journal of strength and conditioning research.* c1993-
SUBJECTS:
Physical education and training—Periodicals.
Weight training—Physiological aspects—Periodicals.
Physical fitness—Periodicals.

Title: *Fitness and sports review international.* c1992-
   SUBJECTS:
      Physical education and training—Periodicals.
      Sports—Periodicals.
      Sports medicine—Periodicals.

Title: *Sport science review.* 1992-
   SUBJECTS:
      Sports sciences—Periodicals.

Title: *The Atlantic monthly.* c1993-
      [No subject headings]

Reports

For serially issued reports by government agencies or other corporate bodies that contain substantive subject information, one or more topical headings, with the subdivision **—Periodicals**, are assigned.

Title: *Biennial report* / Virginia Workers' Compensation Commission. 1992-
   SUBJECTS:
      Workers' compensation—Virginia—Periodicals.
      Reparation—Virginia—Periodicals.

If the publication contains information about the corporate body as well as substantive information, an additional heading under the name of the corporate body is assigned:

Title: *Annual report* / Royal Commission on the Historical Monuments of England. 1992-
   SUBJECTS:
      Royal Commission on Historical Monuments (England)—Periodicals.
      Historic buildings—Great Britain—Conservation and restoration—Periodicals.
      Historic sites—Great Britain—Conservation and restoration—Periodicals.

Title: *Committee on Institutional Cooperation : [biennial report].* 1989-
   SUBJECTS:
      Committee on Institutional Cooperation—Periodicals.
      University cooperation—United States—Periodicals.

If the publication contains only information about the corporate body, only the heading under the name of the body is assigned.

Title: *Calvin Coolidge Memorial Foundation annual report of ...*
SUBJECTS:
Calvin Coolidge Memorial Foundation—Periodicals.

Title: *Biennial report* / Mechanical Department, [County of Los Angeles]. 1961-
SUBJECTS:
Los Angeles County (Calif.). Mechanical Dept.
—Appropriations and expenditures—Periodicals.

Serial Publications Devoted to Individual Persons

For a serial publication devoted to one person, a heading in the form of **[Name of person]—Periodicals** is assigned.

Title: *Shakespeare yearbook.* c1990-
SUBJECTS:
Shakespeare, William, 1564-1616—Periodicals.

Title: *Faulkner studies.* 1980-
SUBJECTS:
Faulkner, William, 1897-1962—Criticism and interpretation—Periodicals.
Faulkner, William, 1897-1962—Periodicals.

Society Publications

Publications issued serially by societies are assigned subject headings appropriate to their subject content and form.

Title: *Current directions in psychological science : a journal of the American Psychological Society.* c1992-
SUBJECTS:
Psychology—Periodicals.

Title: *Bulletin of the Natural History Museum. Geology series.* c1993-
SUBJECTS:
Geology—Periodicals.
Paleontology—Periodicals.

Title: *Memoirs of the Faculty of Science, Kyushu University. Series D, Earth and planetary sciences.* 1991-
SUBJECTS:
Geology—Periodicals.
Earth sciences—Periodicals.

For reports *of* societies, see the discussion above. For works *about* societies, see the discussion on pages 254-56.

Statistics

Title: *The Knight-Ridder CRB commodity yearbook statistical supplement.* 1993-
SUBJECTS:
Commodity futures—Statistics—Periodicals.
Futures—Statistics—Periodicals.
Commodity exchanges—Statistics—Periodicals.

Title: *Market share reporter.* 1991-
SUBJECTS:
Market share—Statistics—Periodicals.
Marketing—Statistics—Periodicals.
Corporations—Statistics—Periodicals.
Commercial products—Statistics—Periodicals.
International business enterprises—Statistics—Periodicals.
Service industries—Marketing—Statistics—Periodicals.

Title: *States in profile : the state policy reference book.* 1990-
SUBJECTS:
United States—States—Statistics—Periodicals.

Title: *Rand McNally sales & marketing planning atlas city / county data.* 1990-
SUBJECTS:
Retail trade—United States—States—Statistics —Periodicals.
Income—United States—States—Statistics—Periodicals.
Cities and towns—United States—Maps.
United States—States—Statistics—Population— Periodicals.
United States—Administrative and political divisions— Periodicals.

Title: *State rankings : a statistical view of the 50 United States.* 1990-
SUBJECTS:
United States—Statistics—Periodicals.

Title: *Statistical abstract of the United States.* Reference Press ed. [1992]-
SUBJECTS:
United States—Statistics—Periodicals.

Union Lists

See the discussion on pages 206-7.

Yearbooks

The subdivision —*Yearbooks* is no longer valid; the subdivision —**Periodicals** is now used for yearbooks.

Title: *Liao-ning nien chien = Liaoning yearbook* / [Liao-ning nien chien pien wei hui pien]. 1992-
SUBJECTS:
Liaoning Province (China)—Periodicals.

Title: *International artist profile yearbook* / Wildlife Art News. c1987-c1990
SUBJECTS:
Wildlife artists—United States—Biography— Periodicals.
Artists—United States—Biography—Periodicals.
Wildlife artists—Canada—Biography—Periodicals.
Artists—Canada—Biography—Periodicals.

Title: *Annual review* / Idaho Racing Commission. 1991-
SUBJECTS:
Pari-mutuel betting—Idaho—Periodicals.

Title: *The Annual review of European Community affairs.* c1991-
SUBJECTS:
European Economic Community—Periodicals.
European Economic Community countries—Foreign relations—Periodicals.

LISTS OF PUBLICATIONS

Lists of publications appear in various forms, such as abstracts, bibliographies, and catalogs. These are normally brought out by free-floating form subdivisions such as:

—**Abstracts**
—**Bibliography**
—**Catalogs**
—**Imprints** [under names of places]
—**Indexes**
—**Union lists**

The following discussion and examples illuminate LC treatment of various types of lists and the proper use of relevant form subdivisions.

Abstracts[4]

Both —**Abstracts** and —**Bibliography** are free-floating form subdivisions that may be used under topical, geographic, corporate, or personal headings to bring out the form of a publication. However, some publications, such as lists of publications with annotations, may not clearly fall into one of the two categories. To assist the cataloger, the Library of Congress has provided the following guidelines. The subdivision —**Abstracts** is used when a work lists publications and provides full bibliographical information together with substantive summaries or condensations of the facts, ideas, or opinions for each publication listed.[5] The nature of the annotations or summaries is the criterion. The following characteristics are considered to be typical of abstracts:

> They present briefly the essential points made in the original publication, usually including the conclusion, if any, drawn by its author.

> They provide enough detail to enable the user to decide whether or not to refer to the original publication.

> They evaluate or criticize the publication.[6]

Examples of abstracts include:

> Title: *Current awareness abstracts of library and information science.* c1993-
> SUBJECTS:
> **Information science—Abstracts—Periodicals.**
> **Library science—Abstracts—Periodicals.**

> Title: *NTIS alert. Medicine & biology.* c1992-
> SUBJECTS:
> **Medicine—Abstracts—Periodicals.**
> **Biology—Abstracts—Periodicals.**

> Title: *Subject coverage and arrangement of abstracts by sections in Chemical abstracts.* c1992
> SUBJECTS:
> **Chemical abstracts—Outlines, syllabi, etc.**
> **Chemistry—Abstracts—Outlines, syllabi, etc.**

Bibliographies

The free-floating subdivision —**Bibliography** is used for unannotated or annotated lists of publications. Annotations are distinguished from abstracts in that they give an indication of the general nature of each publication listed rather than distill its content, and they are seldom critical in nature.

Two subdivisions that seem especially difficult to distinguish are —**Indexes** and —**Bibliography**. (Indexes as a form of publication are discussed below.) The Library of Congress offers the following usage criteria for —**Bibliography** and —**Indexes**:

> —**Indexes** is used under subject headings for works that provide a comprehensive subject approach to printed materials published in a specific field of knowledge....
>
> The subdivision —**Bibliography** is used for works that merely list publications. Many bibliographies, however, are themselves indexed by subject. When a subject-indexed bibliography is judged to be sufficiently comprehensive in scope as to be usable as a general index to the publications in a field, the subdivision —**Indexes** is used instead of —**Bibliography**.[7]

Examples of bibliographies include:

> Title: *Dinosaurs : a guide to research* / Bruce Edward Fleury. 1992
> SUBJECTS:
> **Dinosaurs—Bibliography.**

> Title: *American higher education : a guide to reference sources* / Peter P. Olevnik ; with the assistance of Betty W. Chan, Sarah Hammond, and Gregory M. Toth ; foreword by Philip G. Altbach. 1993
> SUBJECTS:
> **Education, Higher—United States—Bibliography.**

The combination —*Bibliography—Indexes* is not authorized for use. On the other hand, the subdivision —**Bibliography** may be combined with another form subdivision to indicate specific types of bibliography.

> —**Bibliography—Catalogs**
> —**Bibliography—Exhibitions**
> —**Bibliography—Microform catalogs**
> —**Bibliography—Periodicals**
> —**Bibliography—Union lists**

> Title: *Recent Department of Education publications in ERIC* / Education Resources Information Center (ERIC), Office of Research, Office of Educational Research and Improvement, U.S. Department of Education. [1992]-
> SUBJECTS:
> **Education—United States—Bibliography—Periodicals.**
> **United States. Dept. of Education—Periodicals.**
> **ERIC (Information retrieval system)—Periodicals.**

Library of Congress policies require that whenever one of the following types of headings is assigned to a work, a duplicate entry be made under **[Topic]—Bibliography**:[8]

Best books [when assigned to a work involving a specific topic]
Bibliography—Bibliography—[Topic]

Examples include:

Title: *Let the authors speak : a guide to worthy books based on historical setting* / Carolyn Hatcher. c1992
SUBJECTS:
History—Bibliography.
Historical fiction, English—Bibliography.
Best books.
Children—Books and reading.

Title: *The environmentalist's bookshelf : a guide to the best books* / Robert Merideth. c1993
SUBJECTS:
Human ecology—Bibliography.
Environmental protection—Bibliography.
Environmental policy—Bibliography.
Best books.

Title: *A world bibliography of geographical bibliographies* / Takashi Okuno. 1992-
SUBJECTS:
Bibliography—Bibliography—Geography.
Geography—Bibliography.

Title: *A Bibliography of Latin American and Caribbean bibliographies, 1985-1989 : social sciences and humanities* / Lionel V. Loroña, editor. 1993
SUBJECTS:
Bibliography—Bibliography—Latin America.
Latin America—Bibliography.

For a bibliography that lists works by or about an individual person or work, a personal name heading or a name/title heading for the original work with the free-floating subdivision **—Bibliography** is used.[9]

Title: *Shakespeare : an annotated bibliography* / Joseph Rosenblum. c1992
SUBJECTS:
Shakespeare, William, 1564-1616—Bibliography.

Title: *The taming of the shrew : an annotated bibliography* / Nancy
  Lenz Harvey. 1994
  SUBJECTS:
  **Shakespeare, William, 1564-1616. Taming of the shrew—
  Bibliography.**

If the work has a topical orientation, an additional heading in the form
of **[Topic]—Bibliography** is also assigned:

Title: *Henry IV, Parts 1 and 2 : an annotated bibliography* /
  compiled by Catherine Gira, Adele Seeff. 1994
  SUBJECTS:
  **Shakespeare, William, 1564-1616. King Henry IV—
  Bibliography.**
  **Henry IV, King of England, 1367-1413—In literature—
  Bibliography.**

Title: *King John : an annotated bibliography* / compiled by Deborah
  T. Curren-Aquino. 1994
  SUBJECTS:
  **Shakespeare, William, 1564-1616. King John—
  Bibliography.**
  **John, King of England, 1167-1216—In literature—
  Bibliography.**
  Kings and rulers in literature—Bibliography.
  Historical drama, English—Bibliography.

Indexes

The free-floating form subdivision —**Indexes** is used under subject
headings for "works that provide a comprehensive subject approach to
printed materials published in a specific field of knowledge."[10] The
treatment of various kinds of indexes is illustrated below.

(1) *General indexes and indexes limited to books*:

Title: *Subject index to feature articles and special reports in ency-
  clopedia yearbooks, 1975-1991* / edited by Sheila Dilbert.
  1992
  SUBJECTS:
  Encyclopedias and dictionaries—Indexes.
  Reference books—Indexes.

Title: *Guide to 1990 U.S. decennial census publications : detailed
  abstracts and indexes derived from the American statistics
  index : publications issued through 1992.* c1993
  SUBJECTS:
  United States—Census, 21st, 1990—Indexes.
  United States—Census, 21st, 1990—Abstracts.

United States—Statistics—Abstracts.
United States—Statistics—Indexes.

Title: *Vermont philatelic index* / by Karl E. Henson. c1993
  SUBJECTS:
    Postal service—Vermont—History—Indexes.
    Postage-stamps—Vermont—Indexes.
    Postal service—Vermont—Indexes.

(2) *Indexes limited to specific forms of materials other than books.*
A subdivision representing the specific form of material (except for indexes to films on a topic) is used. This subdivision is interposed between the topical heading and the subdivision **—Indexes.**[11]

Title: *Accounting literature index* / Jean Louis Heck, Robert P.
  Derstine, Ronald J. Huefner. c1994
  SUBJECTS:
    Accounting—Periodicals—Indexes.

Title: *People in world history.* c1989-
  SUBJECTS:
    World history—Periodicals—Indexes.
    Biography—Periodicals—Indexes.
    Dissertations, Academic—Indexes.

(3) *Indexes to works of an individual author.* A heading in the form of **[Name of author]—[Form of publication, if appropriate]—Indexes** is assigned:

Title: *Hugo Schuchardt Nachlass : Schlüssel zum Nachlass des
  Linguisten und Romanisten Hugo Schuchardt (1842-
  1927)* / Michaela Wolf. c1993
  SUBJECTS:
    **Schuchardt, Hugo Ernst Mario, 1842-1927—Corre-
      spondence—Indexes.**
    Linguists—Austria—Correspondence—Indexes.

Title: *The Thaddeus Stevens papers : guide and index to the
  microfilm edition* / Beverly Wilson Palmer, editor ; Holly
  Byers Ochoa, assistant editor. 1994
  SUBJECTS:
    **Stevens, Thaddeus, 1792-1868. Thaddeus Stevens
      papers—Indexes.**
    Stevens, Thaddeus, 1792-1868—Archives—Indexes.
    Legislators—United States—Archives—Indexes.
    **United States—Politics and government—1849-1877—
      Sources —Indexes.**

(4) *Indexes to individual monographic works or individual serials.*
See the discussion on pages 265-66.

The subdivision —**Indexes** may be further subdivided by another form subdivision representing the form of the index.

Title: *Biblio list updates in print.* [1991-]
SUBJECTS:
    Finance—Periodicals—Indexes—Periodicals.
    Economics—Periodicals—Indexes—Periodicals.

Title: *EconLit* [computer file]. 1990-
SUBJECTS:
    Economics—Periodicals—Indexes—Databases.

Catalogs of Publications[12]

Catalogs of Library Materials[13]

The following types of headings are assigned to catalogs of library materials:

    [Topic of works listed]—[Form of works listed]—Catalogs
    [Name of institution, if any]—Catalogs
    [Name of collection, if any]—Catalogs

The most commonly used subdivisions for the forms of works are:

    —**Audio-visual aids—Catalogs**
    —**Bibliography—Catalogs**
    —**Bibliography—Microform catalogs**
    —**Discography**
    —**Film catalogs**
    —**Manuscripts—Catalogs**
    —**Manuscripts—Microform catalogs**
    —**Video catalogs**
    —**Periodicals—Bibliography—Catalogs**

Examples include:

Title: *Hidden research resources in the Dutch-language collections of the Library of Congress : a selective bibliography of reference works = Verborgen onderzoeks-bronnen in de nederlandstalige collectie van de Library of Congress /* Margrit B. Krewson. 1993
SUBJECTS:
    Benelux countries—Bibliography—Catalogs.
    Dutch literature—Bibliography—Catalogs.
    Library of Congress—Catalogs.

Title: *A bibliography of African language texts in the collections of the School of Oriental and African Studies University of London to 1963* / compiled by Michael Mann and Valerie Sanders. 1994
SUBJECTS:
University of London. School of Oriental and African Studies. Library—Catalogs.
African languages—Texts—Bibliography—Catalogs.

Title: *Censored Japanese serials of the pre-1946 period: a checklist of the microfilm collection = Kenétsu Wazasshi (1945-nen izen) : maikurofirumu chekkurisuto* / compiled by Yoshiko Yoshimura (Japanese Section, Asian Division). 1994
SUBJECTS:
Japanese periodicals—Bibliography—Microform catalogs.
Japanese periodicals—Censorship—Japan— Bibliography—Microform catalogs.
Censorship—Japan—History—Sources—Bibliography— Microform catalogs.
Periodicals in microform—Catalogs.
Library of Congress—Microform catalogs.

Title: *Catalogue of census returns on microfilm = Catalogue de recensements sur microfilm, 1901* / Thomas A. Hillman. c1993
SUBJECTS:
Canada—Census, 1901—Bibliography—Microform catalogs.
Canada—Population—Statistics—Bibliography— Microform catalogs.
National Archives of Canada—Microform catalogs.

Title: *The Nathan Axelrod collection* / edited by Amy Kronish, Edith Falk, Paula Weiman-Kelman. 1994-
SUBJECTS:
Jews—Palestine—History—20th century—Film catalogs.
Palestine—History—1917-1948—Film catalogs.
Zionism—History—Film catalogs.
Israel—History—Film catalogs.
Newsreels—Catalogs.
Centre for Preservation of Israeli and Jewish Film (Jerusalem)—Catalogs.

Title: *Imperial War Museum film catalogue I* / edited by Roger Smither. 1994
SUBJECTS:
World War, 1914-1918—Sources—Film catalogs.
World War, 1914-1918—Film catalogs.
Imperial War Museum (Great Britain)—Film catalogs.
World War, 1914-1918—Great Britain—Film catalogs.

Title: *Duke Ellington, day by day and film by film* / Klaus Stratemann. c1992
SUBJECTS:
Ellington, Duke, 1899-1974—Chronology.
Ellington, Duke, 1899-1974—Film catalogs.

Title: *Screen studies catalogue* / Film and Video Lending Collection, National Library of Australia. 1992-
SUBJECTS:
National Library of Australia. Film and Video Lending Collection—Film catalogs.
National Library of Australia. Film and Video Lending Collection—Video catalogs.
Motion pictures—Catalogs.

Union Lists

For union lists or catalogs, a heading in the form of **Catalogs, Union—[Place]** (referring to the location of the union list or catalog) is assigned in addition to other appropriate headings subdivided by **—Union lists**:

Title: *Union list of periodicals in Kenyan libraries.* 1993
SUBJECTS:
Periodicals—Bibliography—Union lists.
Serial publications—Kenya—Bibliography—Union lists.
Catalogs, Union—Kenya.

Title: *Guide to railroad historical resources, United States and Canada* / compiled by Thomas T. Taber III. c1993
SUBJECTS:
Railroads—United States—History—Sources—Bibliography—Union lists.
Railroads—Canada—History—Sources—Bibliography—Union lists.
Catalogs, Union—United States.
Catalogs, Union—Canada.

Title: *A bibliography of Florida* / by James A. Servies and Lana D. Servies. 1993-
SUBJECTS:
Florida—Bibliography—Union lists.
Florida—Imprints—Union lists.
Catalogs, Union—United States.

Title: *The French image of America : a chronological and subject bibliography of French books printed before 1816 relating to the British North American colonies and the United States* / by Durand Echeverria and Everett C. Wilkie, Jr. 1993
SUBJECTS:
America—Early works to 1800—Bibliography—Union lists.
America—Bibliography—Union lists.
North America—History—Colonial period, ca. 1600-1775 —Bibliography—Union lists.
Great Britain—Colonies—America—Early works to 1800—Bibliography—Union lists.
Bibliography—Early printed works—Union lists.
French imprints—Union lists.
Catalogs, Union.

Publishers' Catalogs[14]

The following types of headings are assigned to catalogs of individual publishing houses:

[Name of publishing house]—Catalogs
Catalogs, Publishers'—[Country]

and one of the following three:

[Country]—Imprints—Catalogs
Government publications—[Country]—Bibliography—Catalogs
[Topic]—Bibliography—Catalogs

If the publications listed are in a specific form, headings similar to the following are assigned in addition:

Microforms—Catalogs   [only for general microform catalogs]
Pamphlets in microform—Catalogs
Books on microfilm—Catalogs
Periodicals on microfiche—Catalogs

Examples include:

Title: *Microfiche catalog : publications of the Summer Institute of Linguistics.* 1993
SUBJECTS:
Linguistics—Bibliography—Microform catalogs.
Summer Institute of Linguistics—Microform catalogs.
Catalogs, Publishers'—United States.

Title: *Heritage Press catalog and checklist* / Michael C. Bussacco.
c1993-
SUBJECTS:
Heritage Press (New York, N.Y.)—Catalogs.
Bibliography—United States—Fine editions—Catalogs.
Literature—Bibliography—Catalogs.
Catalogs, Publishers'—United States.

Title: *The Corvinus Press : a history and bibliography* / by Paul W.
Nash and A.J. Flavell. c1994
SUBJECTS:
Corvinus Press—Catalogs.
Privately printed books—Bibliography—Catalogs.
Private presses—England—London—History—20th
century.
Great Britain—Imprints—Catalogs.
Catalogs, Publishers'—Great Britain.

Imprints[15]

The following types of headings are assigned to lists of works
published in a particular place or language:

[Place of origin]—Imprints
[Language] imprints—[Place]
[not assigned if the language is predominant in the place
of question]
[Name of library]—Catalogs
[for a listing of a library's special collection of imprints]
[Topic]—Bibliography

If the work lists imprints existing at a specific locality or available from
a specified source, the subdivision **—Catalogs** is added to the headings
above. Headings of the type **[Language] imprints** and **[Place]—Imprints** are not further subdivided by **—Bibliography**, because the
term *imprints* already implies lists of publications.

Title: *Swedish polar bibliography : a guide to Swedish literature on
polar research 1945-1988, with supplement, 1989-1992* [1993]
SUBJECTS:
Polar regions—Bibliography.
Sweden—Imprints.

Title: *Dizionario dei dizionari : stampati in Italia dal Millenove-
cento ai giorni nostri* / cercati, trovati, sistemati da
Eugenio Cascone e Giampaolo Mascheroni. 1993
SUBJECTS:
Encyclopedias and dictionaries, Italian—Bibliography.
Italy—Imprints.

Lists and Abstracts of Dissertations and Theses[16]

The following types of headings are assigned to lists and abstracts of dissertations and theses:

[Topic]—Bibliography [or —Abstracts]
[Institution]—Dissertations—Bibliography [or —Abstracts]
Dissertations, Academic—[Country]—Bibliography
[or —Abstracts]

Examples include:

Title: *Primer tesauro de tesis profesionales de la Facultad de Ciencias de la Conducta* / Adolfo López Suárez, Luis A. Guadarrama Rico, y Benjamín Lovera Estévez. 1991
SUBJECTS:
Psychology—Bibliography.
Universidad Autónoma del Estado de México. Facultad de Ciencias de la Conducta—Dissertations—Bibliography.
Dissertations, Academic—Mexico—Bibliography.

Title: *Keeping the faith : the clinical tradition in organizational behavior at Yale, 1962-1988* / David N. Berg, editor. c1992
SUBJECTS:
Organizational behavior—Abstracts.
Yale University. School of Organization and Management—Dissertations—Abstracts.
Dissertations, Academic—United States—Abstracts.

The third type of heading listed above is assigned to all lists of dissertations and theses. If the list is not limited to a specific institution, the first and third types are used:

Title: *Bibliography of geoscience theses of the United States and Canada.* 1993
SUBJECTS:
Earth sciences—United States—Bibliography.
Earth sciences—Canada—Bibliography.
Dissertations, Academic—United States—Bibliography.
Dissertations, Academic—Canada—Bibliography.

Title: *Theses and dissertations relevant to Virginia archaeology, architecture, and material culture* / J. Mark Wittkofski. 1991
SUBJECTS:
Virginia—Antiquities—Bibliography.
Architecture—Virginia—Bibliography.
Material culture—Virginia—Bibliography.
Dissertations, Academic—United States—Bibliography.

Title: *Index of graduate theses in Baptist Theological seminaries, 1963-1965* / compiled by Lynn E. May, Jr. 1965
SUBJECTS:
Religion—Bibliography.
Dissertations, Academic—United States—Bibliography.

If the list is not limited to a specific topic, the second and third heading types are used:

Title: *Theses and dissertations accepted at the University of Idaho arranged by major/department, 1985-1989* / compiled by J. Muriel Saul. c1991
SUBJECTS:
University of Idaho—Dissertations—Bibliography— Catalogs.
Dissertations, Academic—United States—Bibliography —Catalogs.

REFERENCE MATERIALS

Works About Reference Books[17]

Works about reference books are assigned the heading **Reference books**. This is a topical heading; it is not used for reference books per se, which are simply assigned topical headings as appropriate. The heading **Reference books** is used without subdivision when the work being cataloged is not limited by topic; it may, however, be qualified by language other than English (e.g., **Reference books, German**). Examples include:

Title: *Reference interviews, questions, and materials* / by Thomas P. Slavens. 1994
SUBJECTS:
Reference services (Libraries)—United States.
Reference books.

To a work about reference works in a particular field, a heading of the type **Reference books—[Topic]** is assigned. The **—[Topic]** subdivision is free-floating, provided that the topic is a valid heading. Examples include **Reference books—Chemistry; Reference books— Canada; Reference books— Shakespeare, William, 1564-1616**.

Title: *Political science : illustrated search strategy and sources : with an introduction to legal research for undergraduates* / by Roger C. Lowery, Sue A. Cody. 1993
SUBJECTS:
Political science—Research.
Reference books—Political science.
Legal research.

Bibliographies of Reference Books

Nontopical Bibliographies

The heading **Reference books—Bibliography** or **Reference books, [Language]—Bibliography** is assigned to a nontopical bibliography of reference books:

Title: *Walford's concise guide to reference material* / edited by Anthony Chalcraft ... [et al.]. 1992
SUBJECTS:
    Reference books—Bibliography.

Title: *Introduction to reference work* / William A. Katz. c1992
SUBJECTS:
    Reference services (Libraries).
    Reference books—Bibliography.

Title: *Recommended reference books in paperback* / Andrew L. March, editor. 1992
SUBJECTS:
    Reference books—Bibliography.
    Paperbacks—Bibliography.
    Best books.

Title: *Best reference books, 1986-1990 : titles of lasting value selected from American reference books annual* / compiled by G. Kim Dority ; edited by Bohdan S. Wynar. 1992
SUBJECTS:
    Reference books—Bibliography.
    Best books.

Title: *A guide to the college library : the most useful resources for students and researchers* / Christopher Lee Philips. 1993
SUBJECTS:
    Academic libraries—United States.
    Academic libraries—Canada.
    Reference books—Bibliography.

Topical Bibliographies

To a bibliography of the reference sources in a particular field, two types of headings are assigned:

[Topic]—Bibliography
Reference books—[Topic]—Bibliography

Examples include:

Title: *Introduction to reference sources in the health sciences /* [compiled] by Fred W. Roper and Jo Anne Boorkman. 1994
SUBJECTS:
Reference books—Medicine—Bibliography.
Medicine—Bibliography.
Medicine—Information services.

Title: *Australian sourcebooks : social sciences* / compiled by Barbara Brady. [1992]
SUBJECTS:
Reference books—Social sciences—Bibliography.
Social sciences—Australia—Bibliography.

If the reference sources listed in the bibliography are limited to a language other than English, an additional heading in the form of **Reference books, [Language]—Bibliography** is also assigned.

Title: *A guide to reference books for Japanese studies* / [compiled by International House of Japan Library = Nihon kenkyu no tame sanko tosho / Kokusai Bunka Kaikan Toshoshitsu henshu]. 1989.
SUBJECTS:
Japan—Bibliography.
Reference books—Japan—Bibliography.
Reference books, Japanese—Bibliography.

Reference Works

In LCSH, several categories of reference works are given special treatment or represented by special subdivisions. These include almanacs, catalogs of objects, dictionaries, directories, and handbooks and manuals.

Almanacs

Form headings such as **Almanacs, American** and **Almanacs, Children's** are used to bring out the form of publication.

Title: *The information please kids' almanac* / Alice Siegel and Margo McLoone Basta. 1992
SUBJECTS:
Almanacs, Children's.

Title: *Chinese almanacs* / Richard J. Smith. 1992
SUBJECTS:
Almanacs, Chinese.

Topical headings are assigned to bring out the subject of the almanac.

Title: *The World Almanac : the complete 1868 original and selections from 25, 50, and 100 years ago* / edited by June Foley, Mark Hoffman, and Tom McGuire. 1992
SUBJECTS:
Almanacs, American.
History, Modern.

Title: *The east Tennessee almanac* / Robert Beverley. 1992
SUBJECTS:
Tennessee, East.
Almanacs, American—Tennessee, East.

Title: *The complete golfer's almanac 1995* / James M. Lane. 1995
SUBJECTS:
Golf—Miscellanea.
Almanacs, American.

Title: *Chicago sun-times metro Chicago almanac : fascinating facts and offbeat offerings about the Windy City* / Don Hayner and Tom McNamce. c1993
SUBJECTS:
Chicago (Ill.)—Miscellanea.
Almanacs, American—Illinois—Chicago.
Chicago Region (Ill.)—Miscellanea.
Almanacs, American—Illinois—Chicago Region.

Catalogs of Objects[18]

The free-floating subdivision **—Catalogs** is used under headings for listings of various types of objects, including merchandise, art objects, products, publications,[19] collectors' items, and technical equipment, that are available or are located at particular places or are offered on a particular market, often systematically arranged with descriptive details, prices, and the like. The following types of headings are assigned:

[Objects]—Catalogs
[Kind of institution]—Catalogs
[Name of institution or collection]—Catalogs

Title: *The Frederick C. Crawford Collection : the automobile in American culture.* c1991
SUBJECTS:
Frederick C. Crawford Auto-Aviation Museum—Catalogs.
Automobiles—Catalogs.
Crawford, Frederick C., b. 1891.

Title: *Collecting world coins : a century of monetary issues* / Colin
R. Bruce II, editor ; Marian Moe, associate editor. c1992
SUBJECTS:
Coins—Catalogs.

For catalogs of natural objects and musical instruments, the subdivision **—Catalogs and collections** instead of **—Catalogs** is used:

Title: *The insect and spider collections of the world* / by Ross H.
Arnett, Jr., G. Allan Samuelson, and Gordon M. Nishida.
c1993
SUBJECTS:
Insects—Catalogs and collections—Directories.
Spiders—Catalogs and collections—Directories.
Arachnida—Catalogs and collections—Directories.

Dictionaries[20]

The subdivision **—Dictionaries** is the most frequently used subdivision for both language and subject dictionaries. However, many different kinds of dictionaries and dictionary-like publications exist. There is, therefore, a considerable list of free-floating subdivisions that may be applied to particular dictionaries or dictionary-like publications. These are listed below; full information on their use may be found in *Subject Cataloging Manual*.

—Abbreviations
—Acronyms
—Concordances
—Dictionaries
—Dictionaries, Juvenile
—Directories
—Encyclopedias
—Encyclopedias, Juvenile
—Gazetteers
—Glossaries, vocabularies, etc.
—Language—Glossaries, etc.
—Language (New words, slang, etc.)
—Nomenclature
—Registers
—Slang
—Terminology
—Terms and phrases

LC guidelines for the major categories of dictionary-like materials are briefly summarized below.

(1) *Language dictionaries.* For a comprehensive dictionary in one language, a heading of the type **[Name of language]—Dictionaries** is used:

Title: *Webster's dictionary.* c1991
SUBJECTS:
English language—Dictionaries.

For a bilingual dictionary that gives the terms of one language in terms of the other, a heading of the type **[Name of first language]—Dictionaries—[Name of second language** (adjective only)**]** is used. If the second language is also given in terms of the first, a duplicate heading with the languages reversed is also assigned:

Title: *Living language French dictionary : French-English, English-French* / revised by Liliane Lazar based on the original by Ralph Weiman. c1993
SUBJECTS:
French language—Dictionaries—English.
English language—Dictionaries—French.

Title: *The Oxford German minidictionary : German-English, English-German = Deutsch-Englisch, Englisch-Deutsch* / Gunhild Prowe, Jill Schneider. 1993
SUBJECTS:
German language—Dictionaries—English.
English language—Dictionaries—German.

For a polyglot dictionary, when each language in a polyglot dictionary is given in terms of the others, the general heading **Dictionaries, Polyglot** is assigned. If one language is given in terms of more than one other language, a heading of the type **[Name of language]—Dictionaries—Polyglot** is assigned.

Title: *Illustrated international dictionary* / by Claude O. Proctor. c1990
SUBJECTS:
English language—Dictionaries—Polyglot.

The subdivision **—Glossaries, vocabularies, etc.** is used for a dictionary containing a subset of individual words in a language, with or without definitions, arranged alphabetically or otherwise:

Title: *The words you should know : 1200 essential words every educated person should be able to use and define* / David Olsen. c1991
SUBJECTS:
Vocabulary.
English language—Glossaries, vocabularies, etc.

The subdivision **—Terms and phrases** is used if the work contains a list of expressions, phrases, and the like found in a particular language:

Title: *The Cassell dictionary of word and phrase origins* / Nigel Rees. 1992
SUBJECTS:
English language—Etymology—Dictionaries.
English language—Terms and phrases.

Title: *A shorter dictionary of catch phrases : based on the work of Eric Partridge and Paul Beale* / Rosalind Fergusson. 1994
SUBJECTS:
English language—Terms and phrases.
English language—Slang—Dictionaries.

(2) *Subject dictionaries.* If the dictionary is limited to a subject field, a heading of the type **[Topic]—[Place, if appropriate]—Dictionaries— [Name of language]** (other than English) is assigned. For a subject dictionary in the English language, the subdivision by language is omitted. Examples include:

Title: *The encyclopedia of the New York stage, 1940-1950* / Samuel L. Leiter. 1992
SUBJECTS:
Theater—New York (N.Y.)—Dictionaries.

Title: *Dictionary of image technology* / BKSTS. 1994
SUBJECTS:
Audio-visual equipment—Dictionaries.

The subdivision **—Terminology** instead of **—Dictionaries** is used if the work contains a noncomprehensive list of terms on the topic, or if the comprehensive list is not arranged alphabetically:

Title: *Grand slams, hat tricks, and alley-oops : a sports fan's book of words* / Robert Hendrickson. c1994
SUBJECTS:
Sports—Terminology.
Sports—Slang.

For a bilingual or polyglot subject dictionary, language headings are assigned in addition to the topical headings:

Title: *Major laws of the Republic of China on Taiwan : with practical legal English and vocabularies* / compiled by James C. Liu ... [et al.]. 1991
SUBJECTS:
Law—Taiwan.
Law—Taiwan—Dictionaries.
English language—Dictionaries—Chinese.

Title: *Literaturwissenschaftliches Wörterbuch : Deutsch-Englisch, Englisch-Deutsch* / James Fanning. c1993
SUBJECTS:
Literature—Terminology—Dictionaries.
Criticism—Terminology—Dictionaries.
German language—Dictionaries—English.
English language—Dictionaries—German.

Title: *A glossary of Zen terms* / by Hisao Inagaki. [1991]
SUBJECTS:
Zen Buddhism—Dictionaries—Japanese.
Japanese language—Dictionaries—English.

Title: *Elsevier's dictionary of biometry : in English, French, Spanish, Dutch, German, Italian, and Russian* / edited by D. Rasch, M.L. Tiku, and D. Sumpf. 1994
SUBJECTS:
Biometry—Dictionaries—Polyglot.
Dictionaries, Polyglot.

Title: *The International dictionary of heating, ventilating, and air conditioning* / compiled by the Publishing Committee of REHVA (Federation of European Heating and Airconditioning Associations). 1994
SUBJECTS:
Heating—Dictionaries—Polyglot.
Ventilation—Dictionaries—Polyglot.
Air conditioning—Dictionaries—Polyglot.
Dictionaries, Polyglot.

Title: *Elsevier's dictionary of climatology and meteorology : in English, French, Spanish, Italian, Portuguese, and German* / compiled by J. L. de Lucca. 1994
SUBJECTS:
Meteorology—Dictionaries—Polyglot.
Climatology—Dictionaries—Polyglot.
Dictionaries, Polyglot.

(3) *Biographical dictionaries.* A heading in the form of **Biography— Dictionaries** or **[Class of persons, organizations, place, etc.]— Biography—Dictionaries** is assigned to biographical dictionaries. The previous practice of *not* further subdividing **—Biography** by **—Dictionaries** has been discontinued. Examples include:

Title: *Webster's New World pocket biographical dictionary* / Donald Stewart, project editor; Laura Borovac, biography editor. c1994
SUBJECTS:
Biography—Dictionaries.

Title: *Basketball biographies : 434 U.S. players, coaches, and contributors to the game, 1891-1990* / by Martin Taragano. c1991
SUBJECTS:
  Basketball players—United States—Biography— Dictionaries.
  Basketball coaches—United States—Biography— Dictionaries.

Title: *Old worlds to new : the age of exploration and discovery* / Janet Podell and Steven Anzovin. 1993
SUBJECTS:
  Biography—Dictionaries.
  Explorers—Biography—Dictionaries.
  Scientists—Biography—Dictionaries.

Directories[21]

The free-floating subdivision **—Directories** may be used under the following categories of headings:

names of countries, cities, etc., for lists of names and addresses of the inhabitants or organizations of a place

classes of persons, ethnic groups, and names of individual families

types of organizations

individual corporate bodies

individual Christian denominations

topical headings, including headings for disciplines, industries and activities, and headings for particular kinds of newspapers

Examples include:

Title: *How to buy American books in Latin America* / William M. Childs. c1990
SUBJECTS:
  Booksellers and bookselling—Latin America—Directories.
  Publishers and publishing—United States—Directories.
  United States—Imprints—Marketing—Latin America —Directories.

Title: *The hotel/motel special program and discount guide* / compiled by Beverly Boe and Phil Philcox. c1994
SUBJECTS:
  Hotels—United States—Directories.
  Hotels—Canada—Directories.
  Motels—United States—Directories.
  Motels—Canada—Directories.

Title: *Eating out in Barcelona & Catalunya : a personal guide to over 75 local restaurants* / Craig Allen. 1994
SUBJECTS:
Restaurants—Spain—Barcelona—Directories.
Restaurants—Spain—Catalonia—Directories.

If a list contains names of persons without addresses or other identifying data, the subdivision **—Registers** is used instead:

Title: *The Fiji School of Medicine : a brief history and list of graduates* / Harry Lander and Virginia Miles. c1992
SUBJECTS:
Fiji School of Medicine—History.
Fiji School of Medicine—Alumni—Registers.

Title: *The Roxbury Latin School, 1645-1987 : quinquennial catalogue and alumni directory for the three hundred and forty-second year.* [1987?]
SUBJECTS:
Roxbury Latin School (Mass.)—Registers.

Handbooks and Manuals[22]

The free-floating subdivision **—Handbooks, manuals, etc.** may be used under topical headings and under names of regions, countries, and the like for concise reference works in which facts and information pertaining to a subject field or place are arranged for ready-reference and consultation rather than continuous reading and study. The presence of the words *handbook* or *manual* in the title does not necessarily require the use of the subdivision.

Title: *The graduate research guidebook : a practical approach to doctoral/masters research* / Edward S. Balian. c1994
SUBJECTS:
Dissertations, Academic—United States—Handbooks, manuals, etc.
Report writing—Handbooks, manuals, etc.
Research—Handbooks, manuals, etc.

Title: *The whole library handbook : current data, professional advice, and curiosa about libraries and library services* / compiled by George M. Eberhart. 1991
SUBJECTS:
Library science—United States—Handbooks, manuals, etc.
Libraries—United States—Handbooks, manuals, etc.

Title: *Manual on exercise testing : a training handbook* / by Donald
C. Zavala. c1993
SUBJECTS:
Exercise tests—Handbooks, manuals, etc.
Pulmonary function tests—Handbooks, manuals, etc.
**Respiratory organs—Diseases—Diagnosis—Handbooks,
manuals, etc.**

Title: *Manufacturing engineer's reference book* / edited by Dal
Koshal ; with specialist contributors. 1993
SUBJECTS:
Production engineering—Handbooks, manuals, etc.

Title: *The Education evaluator's workbook : how to assess educa-
tion programs* / Leslie A. Ratzlaff, editor. c1987-c1990
SUBJECTS:
**Educational evaluation—United States—Handbooks,
manuals, etc.**
**Education—Research—United States—Methodology—
Handbooks, manuals, etc.**

For specialized manuals, the following subdivisions are used where
appropriate: **—Amateurs' manuals; —Guidebooks; —Laboratory
manuals; —Observers' manuals; —Tables**. Examples include:

Title: *Caribbean ports of call : a guide for today's cruise passenger*
/ Kay Showker. 1993
SUBJECTS:
Caribbean Area—Guidebooks.
Ocean travel—Guidebooks.

Title: *Manual for physical agents* / Karen W. Hayes. c1993
SUBJECTS:
Physical therapy—Laboratory manuals.

Title: *Immunochemical techniques laboratory manual* / John Goers.
c1993
SUBJECTS:
Immunochemistry—Laboratory manuals.
Immunoassay—Laboratory manuals.

Title: *All thumbs guide to home security* / by Robert W. Wood ;
illustrated by Steve Hoeft. 1993
SUBJECTS:
Dwellings—Security measures—Amateurs' manuals.

Title: *The art of fine furniture building* / Kathy Prochnow and
Dave Prochnow. c1993
SUBJECTS:
Furniture making—Amateurs' manuals.

CHILDREN'S MATERIALS[23]

In 1965 the Library of Congress initiated the Annotated Card (AC) Program for children's materials. The purpose of the program was to provide more appropriate and extensive subject cataloging of juvenile titles through more liberal application of subject headings and through the use of headings better suited to juvenile users. In some cases, existing LC subject headings were reinterpreted or modified; in others, new headings were created. As a result, a list of headings that represent exceptions to the master LC list was compiled. This list was first issued as a separate publication entitled *Subject Headings for Children's Literature*. With the 8th edition of *Library of Congress Subject Headings*, the list was included in the main publication and also published separately. After 1979 the children's list was no longer published separately. Since its March 1983 issue, the LCSH microfiche edition has included a fiche containing the complete list of subject headings for children's literature.[24]

The term *annotated card* comes from the practice of providing a summary of the content of the work in a note. In subject cataloging, two sets of headings are assigned: (1) regular headings with appropriate subdivisions, such as —**Juvenile literature**, and headings for children's literature, such as **Children's poetry**, without the juvenile subdivisions, and (2) headings from the children's list.

Subdivisions used to indicate children's materials include:

—**Dictionaries, Juvenile**
—**Juvenile drama**
—**Juvenile fiction**
—**Juvenile films**
—**Juvenile humor**
—**Juvenile literature**[25]
—**Juvenile poetry**
—**Juvenile software**
—**Juvenile sound recordings**

Many juvenile works are designated as such by their publishers, through such phrases as "K-3" (kindergarten through third grade), "10 up," "14+," and so on. At the Library of Congress, all materials intended primarily for children through the age of 15 (or the ninth grade) are treated as juvenile material and included in the AC Program. In addition, general or adult works that are suitable for children and young adults may also be included. Fiction for high school students or young adults (often designated as "young adult" or YA) is also included; nonfiction works intended solely or primarily for high school age and above, on the other hand, are treated as adult materials. For works in which the intended age is not explicitly stated, determination of level is based on content, format, publisher, treatment of previous works in the same series, and so on.

Juvenile headings on LC MARC records are distinguished by the second indicator "1" in the subject (6xx) fields and the omission of juvenile subdivisions. In addition, records for juvenile works typically include a summary.[26]

Topical Juvenile Materials

Following are examples of nonfiction juvenile works, with AC headings enclosed in square brackets:

Title: *Merriam-Webster's elementary dictionary.* c1994
SUBJECTS:
 English language—Dictionaries, Juvenile.
 [English language—Dictionaries.]

Title: *Bringing up parents : the teenager's handbook* / by Alex J.
  Packer ; edited by Pamela Espeland ; illustrated by Harry
  Pulver, Jr. c1992
SUBJECTS:
 Parent and teenager—Juvenile literature.
 Conflict of generations—Juvenile literature.
 Interpersonal relations—Juvenile literature.
 Family—Juvenile literature.
 [Parent and child.
 Conduct of life.]

Title: *Patterns of work* / Judith Condon. c1992
SUBJECTS:
 Labor market—Juvenile literature.
 Unemployment—Juvenile literature.
 Technological innovations—Juvenile literature.
 Family—Juvenile literature.
 Longevity—Juvenile literature.
 [Work.
 Labor.]

Title: *Cheering for the home team* / Dan Quello ; [illustrations by
  Lynda Adkins]. c1992
SUBJECTS:
 Sibling rivalry—Juvenile literature.
 Brothers and sisters—Juvenile literature.
 Competition (Psychology)—Juvenile literature.
 Family—Juvenile literature.
 [Brothers and sisters.
 Sibling rivalry.]

Title: *Skating* / [Donna Bailey]. c1991
SUBJECTS:
    Skating—Juvenile literature.
    [Ice skating.]

Title: *The name of the game : how sports talk got that way* / Lafe
    Locke. c1992
SUBJECTS:
    Sports—Miscellanea—Juvenile literature.
    Sports—Terminology—Juvenile literature.
    [Sports—Terminology.
    Sports—Miscellanea.]

Title: *Michael Jordan : basketball skywalker* / Thomas R. Raber.
    c1992
SUBJECTS:
    Jordan, Michael, 1963- —Juvenile literature.
    Basketball players—United States—Biography—
        Juvenile literature.
    [Jordan, Michael, 1963-
    Basketball players.
    Afro-Americans—Biography.]

Juvenile Belles Lettres

For drama, fiction, poetry, or other literary works written for children, by one author or several authors, headings from the main list, such as **Children's poetry**; **Children's poetry, [Language/nationality]**, are always assigned in addition to other required form and topical headings for literature (see the discussion on pages 273, 277-79).[27] These form headings are not assigned to belles lettres for young adults. If juvenile literary form headings are not available, regular literary form headings without juvenile subdivisions are used (e.g., **Detective and mystery stories; Fairy tales**).

Topical headings assigned to literature for children are subdivided by **—Juvenile poetry**; **—Juvenile drama**; and **—Juvenile fiction**.

The following examples show subject headings for juvenile literary works, with AC headings enclosed in square brackets:

Title: *Fathers, mothers, sisters, brothers : a collection of family
    poems* / poems by Mary Ann Hoberman ; illustrations by
    Marylin Hafner. 1993
SUBJECTS:
    Family—Juvenile poetry.
    Children's poetry, American.
    [Family life—Poetry.
    American poetry.]

Title: *Primula the non-sheepdog and the great grey wolf : a play
        for young people* / Graham Holliday. c1991
    SUBJECTS:
        Animals—Juvenile drama.
        Children's plays, English.
        [Animals—Drama.
        Plays.]

Title: *Silly animal jokes* / by Gary Perkins ; illustrated by Dan
        Nevins. c1993
    SUBJECTS:
        Riddles, Juvenile.
        Animals—Juvenile humor.
        [Jokes.
        Riddles.
        Animals—Wit and humor.]

Title: *50 Years of Little golden books, 1942-1992 : a commemora-
        tive set of the first twelve Little golden books.* c1992
    SUBJECTS:
        Children's stories.
        Tales.
        Nursery rhymes.
        Children's poetry.
        [Animals—Fiction.
        Folklore.
        Nursery rhymes.]

Title: *Little pig goes to market* / Heather S. Buchanan. 1992
    SUBJECTS:
        [Nursery rhymes—Adaptations.
        Folklore.]

For fiction in particular, the use of topical headings from the
children's list, subdivided by **—Fiction**, and headings representing the
form of literature is often more liberal in the AC Program than in
regular subject cataloging practice:

Title: *The prince and the pauper* / Mark Twain. 1994
    SUBJECTS:
        **Edward VI, King of England, 1537-1553—Juvenile
            fiction.**
        [Edward VI, King of England, 1537-1553—Fiction.
        Adventure and adventurers—Fiction.
        England—Fiction.]

Title: *The night crossing* / by Karen Ackerman ; illustrated by
    Elizabeth Sayles. 1994
  SUBJECTS:
    Holocaust, Jewish (1939-1945)—Juvenile fiction.
    [Holocaust, Jewish (1939-1945)—Fiction.
    Jews—Austria—Fiction.
    Austria—Fiction.]

Title: *Young Wolf's first hunt* / by Janice Shefelman ; illustrated
    by Tom Shefelman. 1994
  SUBJECTS:
    Indians of North America—Juvenile fiction.
    [Indians of North America—Fiction.
    Bison—Fiction.]

Title: *The ballad of the pirate queens* / written by Jane Yolen ;
    illustrated by David Shannon. c1995
  SUBJECTS:
    Bonny, Anne, b. 1700—Juvenile fiction.
    Read, Mary, d. 1720?—Juvenile fiction.
    [Bonny, Anne, b. 1700—Fiction.
    Read, Mary, d. 1720?—Fiction.
    Pirates—Fiction.]

Title: *Eagle Feather* / by Clyde Robert Bulla ; illustrated by Tom
    Two Arrows. 1994
  SUBJECTS:
    Navajo Indians—Juvenile fiction.
    [Navajo Indians—Fiction.
    Indians of North America—Southwest, New—Fiction.]

NONPRINT MATERIALS

General

In LC practice, the same types and forms of headings are assigned
to works on the same subject whether they are in book form or not.
With a few exceptions, the medium of publication of a work is not
brought out in its subject headings. There are only a few free-floating
subdivisions for nonprint materials: **—Maps** [and various types of
cartographic materials]; **—Juvenile films**; **—Juvenile sound recordings**;
—Software; **—Juvenile software**; and **—Databases**.[28]
The sections below include discussion and examples of how the
Library of Congress catalogs the following types of nonbook materials:
cartographic materials, computer software and databases, films, and
microforms.

Cartographic Materials

The subdivision —**Maps** is free-floating under names of places, corporate bodies, and topical headings for individual maps, collections of maps, or atlases. When used under names of places, this subdivision may be qualified by terms indicating the nature or kinds of maps:

—Maps, Comparative
—Maps, Manuscript
—Maps, Mental
—Maps, Outline and base
—Maps, Physical
—Maps, Pictorial
—Maps, Topographic
—Maps, Tourist
—Photo maps
—Road maps

Examples include:

Title: *New York road map* / American Map Corporation. 1992
  SUBJECTS:
  New York (State)—Road maps.
  New York Metropolitan Area—Road maps.

Title: *I [heart symbol] NY tourism map : a travel guide* / H. M. Gousha. 1992
  SUBJECTS:
  New York (State)—Maps, Tourist.
  New York (State)—Road maps.
  New York State Thruway (N.Y.)—Maps.

Title: *New Jersey* / Rand McNally. c1993
  SUBJECTS:
  New Jersey—Road maps.

Title: *New Mexico state map : including Albuquerque, El Paso, TX, Farmington, Las Cruces, Roswell, Santa Fe* / Rand McNally. c1993
  SUBJECTS:
  New Mexico—Road maps.
  New Mexico—Maps, Tourist.

Title: *New York State map : map : including New York City and vicinity, Buffalo-Niagara Falls, Rochester ... plus New York City-Long Island area ... city-to-city mileage log* / Rand McNally. c1993
  SUBJECTS:
  New York (State)—Road maps.
  New York Metropolitan Area—Road maps.

Long Island (N.Y.)—Road maps.

Title: *Washington, D.C.* / Capitol Reservations. c1993.
  SUBJECTS:
  Washington (D.C.)—Maps, Tourist.
  Central business districts—Washington (D.C.)—Maps.

Title: *United States of America* / Rand McNally. [1992]
  SUBJECTS:
  United States—Maps.

Title: *Mapsco Dallas 1993 : a routing and delivery system for
  metropolitan Dallas : including Lewisville, McKinney,
  Plano and Rockwall.* c1993
  SUBJECTS:
  Dallas Metropolitan Area (Tex.)—Maps.
  Delivery of goods—Texas—Dallas Metropolitan
  Area—Maps.

Title: *Dallas & vicinity : zip code boundaries.* 1992
  SUBJECTS:
  Dallas (Tex.)—Maps
  Dallas Metropolitan Area (Tex.)—Maps.
  Zip code—Texas—Dallas—Maps.

Title: *Buena Park* / Map Masters. c1992
  SUBJECTS:
  Buena Park (Calif.)—Maps.

Form headings are assigned to world atlases. For example:

Title: *World atlas.* [1994]
  SUBJECTS:
  Atlases.

If the atlas pertains to a particular area, a geographic heading with the
subdivision —Maps is assigned:

Title: *Atlas of Palm Beach, Florida* / Robert E. Owen & Associates,
  Inc. [1984]
  SUBJECTS:
  Palm Beach (Fla.)—Maps.

For an atlas on a particular subject, the appropriate topical heading
with the subdivision —Atlases is used:

Title: *An atlas of myocardial infarction : and related cardiovascu-
  lar complications* / Duncan S. Dymond. c1994
  SUBJECTS:
  Heart—Infarction—Atlases.

Computer Software and Databases

The same principles and policies for assigning subject headings to books are applied to computer software and computer files. Headings for such materials carry the following subdivisions:[29]

—Software or **—Juvenile software**   [for computer software]
—Databases   [for computer files or databases]
—Computer programs [for works *about* computer software or programs]

Examples of subject headings assigned to computer software and files and to works about them are shown below:

(1) Computer software:

Title: *RegisterPlus* [computer file]. c1991
   SUBJECTS:
      Point-of-sale systems—Software.

Title: *Microsoft Mail remote for Windows* [computer file]. c1993
   SUBJECTS:
      Electronic mail systems—Software.
      Microcomputer workstations—Software.

Title: *Microsoft MS-DOS 6.2 upgrade* [computer file]. c1993
   SUBJECTS:
      Operating systems (Computers)—Software.

(2) Computer databases:

Title: *Ei page one* [computer file].
   SUBJECTS:
      Engineering—Bibliography—Databases.
      Engineering—Indexes—Databases.
      Engineering—Periodicals—Bibliography—Databases.
      Engineering—Periodicals—Indexes—Databases.

Title: *Current contents on diskette. Engineering, technology & applied sciences* [computer file]. Began with: Vol. 20, issue 1 (Jan. 1, 1990).
   SUBJECTS:
      Technology—Periodicals—Indexes—Databases.
      Engineering—Periodicals—Indexes—Databases.

Title: *General periodicals ondisc* [computer file].
   SUBJECTS:
      Periodicals—Indexes—Databases.
      Periodicals—Abstracts—Indexes—Databases.

Title: *The PsycLit database* [computer file].
SUBJECTS:
Psychology—Abstracts—Databases.
Psychology—Indexes—Databases.

(3) Works about software:

Title: *Microsoft Access for Windows : step-by-step* / Margaret D. McGee, Judy Boyce. c1993
SUBJECTS:
Database management.
Microsoft Access.

Title: *A list guide to personal computer programs for spreadsheets for the public administrator : a selected bibliography* / Anthony G. White. [1990]
SUBJECTS:
Public administration—Software—Catalogs.
Electronic spreadsheets—Software—Catalogs.

(4) Works about individual computer programs:

Title: *Looking at Lotus 1-2-3 (version 2.2)* / Bruce J. McLaren. c1992
SUBJECTS:
Lotus 1-2-3 (Computer file)
Business—Computer programs.
Electronic spreadsheets.

(5) Works about databases:

Title: *Using online scientific & engineering databases* / Harley Bjelland. c1992
SUBJECTS:
Online data processing.
Science—Databases.
Engineering—Databases.

Films

The term *film* is defined by the Library of Congress as "any type of visual material, including motion pictures, filmstrips, videorecordings, slides, etc."[30]

LC subject catalogers follow certain guidelines for films, which are summarized below.

Topical (Nonfiction) Films

At least one subject heading is assigned to each topical film, and in general the rules governing the assignment of subject headings to books also apply to topical films.

However, as in the case of other nonbrowsable materials, the Library of Congress often provides fuller information on the subject content of films than it does for books. For instance, a summary statement is usually included as a note on cataloging records for films. The treatment of topical or nonfiction films is described below.

(1) Each important topic mentioned in the summary statement on the cataloging record receives a subject heading. In particular, if one specific topic is especially emphasized in the summary in order to illustrate a more general concept, both the specific topic and the general concept are assigned subject headings.

(2) If a topic is treated in conjunction with a place, subject headings for both the topic and the place are provided.

(3) If a film uses a particular person as a representative of a particular profession in order to describe the profession, entries are made under both the name of the individual and the professional activity. (Such films will normally not be regarded as biographies.)

(4) A commercial for a particular brand of product is assigned a subject heading under the generic name of the product. Subject headings are also assigned for particular types of commercials, such as television commercials.

Examples of subject cataloging for topical films include:

Title: *Anything for jazz* / by Visual and Environmental Studies 150 at the Carpenter Center for the Visual Arts, Harvard University ; directed by Dan A. Igrant ; produced by Peter Hutton and Alex Griswold. 1979
SUBJECTS:
Byard, Jaki—Criticism and interpretation.
Jazz—1971-1980.

Title: *Astronomers* [Television program]. Part 2, Searching for black holes / production of KCET-Los Angeles ; directed and produced by James F. Golway ; written by James F. Golway and Donald Goldsmith. 1991-04-22.
SUBJECTS:
Black holes (Astronomy)
Big bang theory.
Quasars.
Galaxies.

Fiction Films

The following types of headings are assigned to fiction films:

[Topic]—Drama or **—Juvenile films**
[Headings expressing genre or technique], e.g., **Comedy films**;
    Experimental films
[Form heading], e.g., **Feature films**; **Short films** {for films lasting
    less than 60 minutes}

Fiction films are treated in the same way their scripts (or any drama in book form) would be handled, with the appropriate topical headings plus the subdivision **—Drama** (e.g., **Baseball—Drama**; **World War, 1939-1945—Drama**; **Merlin—Drama**). The form subdivision **—Drama** is used only in connection with fiction films, with the connotation "dramatization of"; it does not apply to topical films, such as documentaries, as a means of bringing out the medium.

Title: *A Midnight clear* / Beacon presents an A&M Films produc-
    tion ; directed and written for the screen by Keith Gordon ;
    produced by Dale Pollock and Bill Borden. 1992
  SUBJECTS:
    World War, 1939-1945—Campaigns—Ardennes—Drama.

Title: *Beauty and the beast* / Walt Disney Pictures in association
    with Silver Screen Partners IV ; directed by Gary Trous-
    dale and Kirk Wise ; produced by Don Hahn ; animation
    screenplay, Linda Woolverton. 1991
  SUBJECTS:
    Love—Drama.
    Ugliness—Drama.
    Magic—Drama.

Title: *Poker* [videorecording] / Six Bells Productions presents a
    Gaspar Hernandez III film ; producers Gaspar Hernandez
    III, Sandra M. Tracy ; director, writer, Gaspar Hernandez
    III. 1990, c1988.
  SUBJECTS:
    Poker—Drama.
    Life on other planets—Drama.
    Short films.

Title: *The Firm* / a John Davis/Scott Rudin/Mirage production ;
    directed by Sydney Pollack ; produced by Sydney Pollack,
    Scott Rudin and John Davis ; screenplay by David Rabe,
    Robert Towne, & David Rayfiel. 1993
  SUBJECTS:
    Corporation law—Drama.

Title: *The Babe* / a Waterhorse-Finnegan-Pinchuk production ; directed by Arthur Hiller ; produced and written by John Fusco. 1992
SUBJECTS:
Ruth, Babe, 1895-1948—Drama.
Baseball players—United States—Drama.

Juvenile Films[31]

A juvenile film is defined as a film intended for persons through the age of 15. The subdivision **—Juvenile films** instead of **—Drama** is used for juvenile fiction films on particular subjects:

Washington, George, 1732-1799—Drama [adult film]
Washington, George, 1732-1799—Juvenile films [juvenile film]

In addition to the normal LC subject headings indicated above, all juvenile films, both topical and nontopical, receive bracketed children's literature subject headings in the same manner as do juvenile books.

Microforms

Works published in microform are assigned the same types of headings as their print counterparts.

Title: *Life and letters* [microform]. 1922-1925
SUBJECTS:
Biography—Periodicals.

Title: *Comment* [microform] : *Communist fortnightly review*. 1963-1982
SUBJECTS:
Communism—Great Britain—Periodicals.

Title: *Jewish genealogical consolidated surname index* [microform]. c1992
SUBJECTS:
Jews—Genealogy.
Names, Personal—Jewish—Registers.

Title: *The register of St. Oswald's, Winwick, Lancashire. Marriages, 1813-1841, baptisms & burials, 1807-1837* [microform] / transcribed, edited, and indexed by J.R. Bulmer. [1992?]
SUBJECTS:
Marriage records—England—Winwick (Cheshire)
Registers of births, etc.—England—Winwick (Cheshire)
Church records and registers—England—Winwick (Cheshire)

Winwick (Cheshire, England)—Genealogy.
St. Oswald's (Church : Winwick, Cheshire, England)—
Registers.

BIOGRAPHY

Definition

For the purpose of cataloging, *biography* (including *autobiography*) has been defined as "a narrative work more than fifty percent of which recounts the personal aspects of the life of one or more individuals.... **Personal aspects** include such details as the individual's early years, education, marriage and other personal relationships, personal habits and personality, family life, travels, personal experiences and tragedies, last years and death, etc."[32]

A biography of two or more individuals is called a *collective biography*, and a biography of one person an *individual biography*. A work of which less than 50 percent is biographical material is referred to as a *partial biography*.

Types of Headings Assigned to Biography

The types of headings generally used with biography are listed below.

(1) Personal name heading for the biographee (For forms of personal name headings, see chapter 4.)

(2) "Class of persons" heading with the subdivision —**Biography**; also called "biographical heading"

(3) Headings representing the person's association with a place or organization, or involvement with a specific event

(4) Topical headings, as appropriate

Subdivisions That Designate Biography

The Library of Congress uses the free-floating subdivisions listed in table 9.1 to designate biography. They are used with main headings denoting classes of persons, disciplines, organizations, ethnic groups, places, and events. Subdivisions used under names of individuals are listed in appendix E. For special meanings and uses of the listed subdivisions, consult *Subject Cataloging Manual*.

Table 9.1.
Subdivisions Designating Biography

	Class of persons	Topics	Corporate bodies	Ethnic groups	Places	Events, wars
—Anecdotes	X	X	X	X	X	X
—Bio-bibliography		X			X	
—Biography	X		X	X	X	X
—Biography—Diction-aries	X		X	X	X	X
—Biography—Por-traits			X		X	
—Correspondence	X			X		
—Diaries	X			X		
—Genealogy	X		X	X	X	
—Interviews	X			X		
—Personal narratives						X
—Portraits	X			X		X

The Subdivision —Biography

The subdivision —**Biography** is used as the generic subdivision for the concept of biography, designating not only individual and collective biography but also autobiography, personal reminiscences, and personal narratives. If a choice is possible, it is used under the heading for the pertinent class of persons rather than that for the corresponding field or discipline.

Artists—Biography
Musicians—Biography
Musicians—Bolivia—Biography

A [**Topic**]—**Biography** heading is established if a heading representing a class of persons does not exist and cannot be formulated. For example:

Art—Biography
[for a collective biography of persons associated with art, including artists, art dealers, collectors, museum personnel, etc.]

The Subdivision —Correspondence[33]

The subdivision —**Correspondence** is free-floating under headings representing classes of persons, ethnic groups, families, and individual persons:

> **Theologians—Great Britain—Correspondence**
> **Periodical editors—United States—Correspondence**
> **Poets, American—20th century—Correspondence**
> **Watson, James S. (James Sibley), 1894- —Correspondence**

For correspondence carried on by types of organizations or for the correspondence of individual organizations, the subdivision —**Records and correspondence** is used.

The Subdivision —Personal Narratives[34]

The subdivision —**Personal narratives**, previously also used under headings for classes of persons, is now used only under names of events and wars as a form subdivision for eyewitness reports or autobiographical accounts of experiences in connection with these events or wars.

Collective Biography

At the Library of Congress, a collective biography containing the life histories of up to four individuals is assigned a personal name heading for each individual. The following discussion concerns collective biographies of more than four persons.

Collective Biography of a Group of Persons Not Associated with a Particular Field or Discipline

The form heading **Biography**, with or without bibliographical form subdivisions, is assigned to a work containing biographies of persons not limited to a particular period, place, organization, ethnic group, gender, or specific field or discipline:

> Title: *A dictionary of universal biography of all ages and of all peoples* / by Albert M. Hyamson. 1993
> SUBJECTS:
> **Biography—Dictionaries.**

> Title: *The Random House biographical dictionary.* c1992
> SUBJECTS:
> **Biography—Dictionaries.**

The main heading **Biography** is subdivided by period if the biographees belong to a specific period:

Title: *Men, women, and history : a biographical reader in Western civilization since the sixteenth century* / Roland N. Stromberg. c1995
SUBJECTS:
Civilization, Western—History.
Biography—17th century.
Biography—18th century.
Biography—19th century.
Biography—20th century.

If a collective biography does not pertain to a special field or discipline but involves an organization, an ethnic or national group, a place, an event, or a war, the appropriate heading (indicating the special aspect) is followed by the subdivision **—Biography** (or a more specific subdivision such as **—Genealogy; —Interviews**):

Title: *Mountain of fame : portraits in Chinese history* / John E. Willis, Jr. 1994
SUBJECTS:
China—Biography.

Title: *Struggle and survival in the modern Middle East* / edited by Edmund Burke III. c1993
SUBJECTS:
Middle East—Biography.

Title: *California biographical dictionary : people of all times and places who have been important to the history and life of the state.* 1994
SUBJECTS:
California—Biography—Dictionaries.

Title: *American lives : an anthology of autobiographical writing* / edited by Robert F. Sayre. c1994
SUBJECTS:
Autobiographies—United States.
United States—Biography.

Title: *Native American autobiography : an anthology* / edited by Arnold Krupat. 1994
SUBJECTS:
Indians of North America—Biography.
Autobiographies—Indian authors.
Indians of North America—History.
American literature—Indian authors.

Title: *Bearing witness : selections from African-American autobi-
ography in the twentieth century* / edited by Henry Louis
Gates, Jr. c1991
SUBJECTS:
Afro-Americans—Biography.
Autobiographies—United States.
United States—Biography.

If a work focuses on a specific place during a particular historical
period, two headings are assigned: (1) the place with the subdivision
—Biography, and (2) the main heading **Biography** with a period
subdivision.

Title: *Many faces : an anthology of Oregon autobiography* / [edited
by] Stephen Dow Beckham. c1993
SUBJECTS:
Oregon—Biography.
Biography—20th century.

Title: *Zeitportrats* / Raimund Hoghe. c1993
SUBJECTS:
Europe—Biography.
Europe—Biography—Portraits.
Biography—20th century.
Biography—20th century—Portraits.

For a collective biography of spouses who have no special careers
of their own, headings denoting specific groups of spouses (e.g., **Army
spouses; Diplomats' spouses; Teachers' spouses; Wives**), subdivided by **—Biography**, are used.

Title: *Old Adam, new Eves* / by Richard Grunberger. c1991
SUBJECTS:
Women—Biography.
Wives—Biography.
Biography—19th century.
Biography—20th century.
Sex role.

Title: *Private lives of pastors' wives* / Ruth A. Tucker. [1992?]
SUBJECTS:
Spouses of clergy—Biography.
Evangelists' spouses—Biography.

Title: *First ladies* / Betty Boyd Caroli. c1993
SUBJECTS:
Presidents' spouses—United States—Biography.

There are also headings for various other classes of persons not limited to a field or discipline, such as **Men; Women; Children; Teenage boys; Teenage girls; Young men**.

Collective Biography of Persons Belonging to a Particular Field or Discipline

For collective biographies of persons belonging to a particular field or discipline, headings in the form of [**Class of persons]—Biography** are used. The geographic subdivision, if applicable, is interposed between the main heading representing the class of persons and the biographical subdivision.

Title: *Outstanding women athletes : who they are and how they influenced sports in America* / by Janet Woolum. 1992
SUBJECTS:
Women athletes—United States—Biography—Dictionaries.
Sports for women—United States—History.

Title: *Biographical dictionary of the extreme right since 1890* / Philip Rees. c1990
SUBJECTS:
Statesmen—Biography—Dictionaries.
Intellectuals—Biography—Dictionaries.
Right-wing extremists—Biography—Dictionaries.
Biography—20th century—Dictionaries.
Biography—19th century—Dictionaries.

Title: *The golden legend : readings on the saints* / Jacobus de Voragine. 1993
SUBJECTS:
Christian saints—Biography.

Title: *Biographical dictionary of geography* / Robert P. Larkin and Gary L. Peters. 1993
SUBJECTS:
Geographers—Biography—Dictionaries.

Title: *Portraits, creative conversations with celebrities* / Cork Millner. 1994
SUBJECTS:
Celebrities—Interviews.
United States—Biography.
Biography—20th century.

If appropriate for the work being cataloged, a more specific form subdivision is used instead of —**Biography** (e.g., **Entertainers—Interviews; Poets, English—Correspondence; Afro-American artists—Portraits**).

If a biographical work on persons associated with a field or discipline also involves an organization, an ethnic group, a place, or an event, headings indicating the other aspects as well as those indicating the fields, or headings combining both, are assigned as shown below.

Title: *West Pointers and early Washington : the contributions of U.S. Military Academy graduates to the development of the Washington Territory, from the Oregon Trail to the Civil War, 1834-1862* / edited by Major General John A. Hemphill, USA-ret. and Robert C. Cumbow. 1992
SUBJECTS:
Washington (State)—History—To 1889.
Washington (State)—History, Military.
Soldiers—Washington (State)—History—19th century.
United States Military Academy—Biography.

Title: *Five brave explorers* / by Wade Hudson ; illustrated by Ron Garnett. 1995
SUBJECTS:
Afro-American explorers—Biography—Juvenile literature.

Title: *Black stars in orbit : NASA's African-American astronauts* / by Khephra Burns and William Miles. c1994
SUBJECTS:
Afro-American astronauts—United States—Biography—Juvenile literature.

Title: *Jews in the American academy, 1900-1940 : the dynamics of intellectual assimilation* / Susanne Klingenstein. c1991
SUBJECTS:
Jews—United States—Biography—Dictionaries.
Jewish college teachers—United States—Biography.
Jews—Cultural assimilation—United States.
United States—Ethnic relations.

Title: *Brevet brigadier generals in blue* / Roger D. Hunt & Jack R. Brown. c1990
SUBJECTS:
United States—History—Civil War, 1861-1865—Biography.
Generals—United States—Biography.
United States. Army—Biography.

Title: *Nine men in gray* / Charles L. Dufour ; introduction to the Bison Book edition by Gary W. Gallagher. [1993]
SUBJECTS:
United States—History—Civil War, 1861-1865—Biography.
Confederate States of America—Biography.

Title: *Swamp angels : a biographical study of the 54th Massachu-setts Regiment : true facts about the black defenders of the Civil War* / Robert Ewell Greene. 1990
SUBJECTS:
    United States. Army. Massachusetts Infantry
        Regiment, 54th (1861-1865)—Biography.
    Afro-American soldiers—Massachusetts—Biography.
    Massachusetts—History—Civil War, 1861-1865—
        Biography.
    United States—History—Civil War, 1861-1865—
        Biography.

If the biographical work covers other topics not designated by the biographical headings, additional topical headings, generally without biographical subdivision, are assigned:

Title: *From these beginnings : a biographical approach to Ameri-can history* / Roderick Nash, Gregory Graves. c1994
SUBJECTS:
    United States—History.
    United States—Biography.

Title: *Women at war : a record of their patriotic contributions, heroism, toils, and sacrifice during the Civil War* / by L.P. Brockett and Mary C. Vaughan ; with an introduction by Henry W. Bellows. 1993
SUBJECTS:
    United States—History—Civil War, 1861-1865—Women.
    United States—History—Civil War, 1861-1865—Hospitals.
    United States—History—Civil War, 1861-1865—
        Biography.
    Women—United States—Biography.
    Hospitals, Military—United States—History—19th
        century.

Family Histories[35]

For the history of an individual family, the following types of headings are assigned:

[Surname] family
[Place]—Genealogy

Examples:

Title: *The Kennedys.* [1992]
SUBJECTS:
    Kennedy family.
    Kentucky—Genealogy.

Title: *History and genealogy of the Greever / Griever / Greaver / Grever*
        family of Virginia / by John Greever. c1992
     SUBJECTS:
        Greever family.
        Virginia—Genealogy.

Title: *Identifying the Wrights in Goochland County, Virginia : tithe*
        lists / by Robert N. Grant. [1993]
     SUBJECTS:
        Wright family.
        Goochland County (Va.)—Genealogy.
        Virginia—Genealogy.
        Tithes—Virginia—Goochland County.

Title: *The Nickens family : how to trace a non-slave African Ameri-*
        can lineage from Virginia to Maryland and back / Karen
        E. Sutton. c1993
     SUBJECTS:
        Nickens family.
        Afro-Americans—Genealogy.
        Virginia—Genealogy.
        Maryland—Genealogy.

The heading under place is omitted in the case of **United States—
Genealogy**.

Title: *Kennedys : the next generation* / Jonathan Slevin and Maureen
        Spagnolo. 1992
     SUBJECTS:
        Kennedy family.

Title: *Those who served : biographical sketches of Orrell soldiers*
        who fought in the War Between the States / by Robert
        Stanley Orrell. c1992
     SUBJECTS:
        Orrell family.
        United States—History—Civil War, 1861-1865—
           Biography.

If more than one family is named on the title page, each family is
designated by a separate heading if there are no more than three:

Title: *The Fitzgeralds and the Kennedys : an American saga* / Doris
        Kearns Goodwin. 1991
     SUBJECTS:
        Fitzgerald family.
        Kennedy family.
        United States—Biography.

If more than three families are named, subject headings are assigned for them individually or collectively, based on the cataloger's judgment.

If one or more of the members of the family are given prominent treatment in the work, a heading or headings under the personal names are also assigned:

> Title: *The descendants of William Brown (1819-1908) and Isabella Kennedy (1820-1894) of Ireland, Scotland, and Hampton Falls, New Hampshire* / by Wilma T. Regan and Laird C. Towle. 1992
> SUBJECTS:
> **Kennedy family.**
> **Brown, William, 1819-1908—Family.**

> Title: *Our McGinnis family : the story of James and Sarah Davis McGinnis and their descendants* / by Irma McGinnis Dotson. 1993
> SUBJECTS:
> **Guinness family.**
> **McGinnis, James, ca. 1750-ca. 1832—Family.**
> **Virginia—Genealogy.**
> **West Virginia—Genealogy.**

> Title: *Vendetta : the Kennedys* / Matthew Smith ; foreword by Jim Marrs. 1993
> SUBJECTS:
> **Kennedy, John F. (John Fitzgerald), 1917-1963—Assassination.**
> **Kennedy, Robert F. (Robert Francis), 1925-1968—Assassination.**
> **Kennedy, Edward Moore, 1932-**
> **Kennedy family.**
> **Political crimes and offenses—United States.**

Previously established headings in a form such as *Smith family (William Smith, 1669-1743)* are no longer used.

For the history of a royal or noble family, an additional heading under the name of the relevant place is always assigned:[36]

> Title: *Auf den Spuren der Habsburger* / Gerhard Totschinger ; mit einem Geleitwort von Otto Von Habsburg. c1992
> SUBJECTS:
> **Habsburg, House of.**
> **Austria—History.**
> **Austria—Kings and rulers.**
> **Holy Roman Empire—History.**

Title: *The Lancastrian affinity : 1361-1399* / Simon Walker. 1990
SUBJECTS:
John, of Gaunt, Duke of Lancaster, 1340-1399.
Great Britain—History—House of Lancaster, 1399-1461.
England—Social conditions—1066-1485.
England—Economic conditions—1066-1485.
Great Britain—History—14th century.
Lancaster, House of.
Feudalism—England.

Individual Biography

Personal Name Headings

The name of the biographee serves as the primary heading for an individual biography. The form of the heading is the same as that used for main or added entries (see chapter 4 on name headings). The personal name heading is assigned even when it duplicates the main entry or an added entry.

Title: *Giambattista Tiepolo* / by William L. Barcham. 1992
SUBJECTS:
Tiepolo, Giovanni Battista, 1696-1770.
Artists—Italy—Venice—Biography.
ADDED ENTRIES:
Tiepolo, Giovanni Battista, 1696-1770.
Tiepolo.

In general, a work containing the lives of up to four persons treated either collectively or separately is not treated as a collective biography, but is assigned an individual heading for each person.[37]

Subdivisions Under Personal Names

Appropriate subdivisions are added to a name heading if the biography deals with specific aspects of the person's life. A list of free-floating subdivisions used under names of persons (other than literary authors) appears in appendix E of this book.[38] Those used under names of literary authors are listed under the pattern heading **Shakespeare, William, 1564-1616** (see appendix C). Note that the subdivision **—Biography** is used under headings for individual literary authors, but not under headings for other persons.

When a person with a multifaceted career belongs in more than one category, the subdivisions appropriate to the category emphasized in the work being cataloged are used. For example, if a person who is well known as a literary author is treated as a statesperson in the work, the subdivisions from the list of free-floating subdivisions used under names of persons are used. On the other hand, if another work deals with the same person as a literary author, the appropriate literary subdivisions are used. When there is a direct conflict between the two free-floating subdivision lists, the subdivisions belonging to the category in which the person is better known are used.

Additional Headings for Individual Biography

(1) *Biographical headings*. In addition to the personal name heading of the biographee, the same biographical headings assigned to a collective biography on the same topic are assigned to an individual biography.[39] In effect, the biographical heading in these cases represents generic posting, (i.e., listing under a generic heading that encompasses the personal heading). Such treatment is a deliberate departure from the general policy of not assigning both a general and a specific heading to the same body of material. The policy was probably adopted in the interest of collocating biographies of persons in the same field or sharing the same characteristics. These biographical headings are particularly useful in generic searches because subject-to-personal-name references are no longer being made.

The types of biographical headings assigned to individual biographies are discussed below.

(a) *Biographical headings for persons associated with a field or discipline*. To a biography of a person associated with a field or discipline, headings of the following types are assigned in addition to the personal name heading:

[Class of persons]—[Place]—[Biographical subdivision][40]
[Discipline]—Biography
    [if the class-of-persons heading is not available]
[Organization, ethnic group, place, event, or gender]—
    [Biographical subdivision]
        [The heading designating an ethnic group is assigned only
        if the point of the work is personal identification with
        the group. The place heading is assigned only when the
        person has local significance or when the class-of-persons
        heading is not available.]

Examples include:

Title: *Judy Garland : the secret life of an American legend* / David
    Shipman. 1993
SUBJECTS:
    Garland, Judy.
    Singers—United States—Biography.
    Motion picture actors and actresses—United States—
        Biography.

Title: *John Wayne : a bio-bibliography* / Judith M. Riggin. 1992
    SUBJECTS:
        Wayne, John, 1907-1979.
        Wayne, John, 1907-1979—Bibliography.
        Motion picture actors and actresses—United States—
            Biography.

Title: *Dress gray : a woman at West Point* / by Donna Peterson.
        c1990
    SUBJECTS:
        Peterson, Donna.
        United States Military Academy—Biography.
        United States. Army—Biography.
        United States. Army—Women.
        Women soldiers—United States—Biography.

Title: *The definitive Diana* / Sally Moore. 1991
    SUBJECTS:
        Diana, Princess of Wales, 1961-
        Princesses—Great Britain—Biography.

Title: *The generals : Ulysses S. Grant and Robert E. Lee* / Nancy Scott
        Anderson, Dwight Anderson. 1994
    SUBJECTS:
        United States—History—Civil War, 1861-1865—
            Biography.
        Generals—United States—Biography.
        United States. Army—Biography.
        Grant, Ulysses S. (Ulysses Simpson), 1822-1883.
        Lee, Robert E. (Robert Edward), 1807-1870.
        United States—History—Civil War, 1861-1865—
            Campaigns.
        United States—History, Military—To 1900.

Title: *J. Edgar Hoover : the man and the secrets* / Curt Gentry.
        c1991
    SUBJECTS:
        Hoover, J. Edgar (John Edgar), 1895-1972.
        United States. Federal Bureau of Investigation—
            Biography.
        Police—United States—Biography.
        Government executives—United States—Biography.

Title: *Colin Powell : a biography* / Jim Haskins. c1992
    SUBJECTS:
        Powell, Colin L.
        Generals—United States—Biography.
        Afro-American generals—Biography.
        United States. Army—Biography.

For a person who is active in several fields, multiple biographical headings are used to bring out those careers described in the work in hand. No attempt is made to name every activity in which the person was engaged. It should rarely be necessary to assign more than two or three such headings. Examples include:

Title: *Albert Schweitzer : friend of all life* / by Carol Greene. c1993
SUBJECTS:
    Schweitzer, Albert, 1875-1965—Juvenile literature.
    Missionaries, Medical—Gabon—Biography—
        Juvenile literature.
    Theologians—Europe—Biography—Juvenile literature.
    Musicians—Europe—Biography—Juvenile literature.

If the work being cataloged focuses only on one career aspect, only the heading for that one aspect is assigned:

Title: *Albert Schweitzer, musician* / by Michael Murray. c1993
SUBJECTS:
    Schweitzer, Albert, 1875-1965.
    Organists—Biography.

Title: *Schweitzer : shadow of a star* / Gene Schulze. c1993
SUBJECTS:
    Schweitzer, Albert, 1875-1965.
    Missionaries, Medical—Gabon—Biography.

Catalogers are advised not to make value judgments in the selection of the class of persons to which the biographee belongs. Headings that represent career, profession, or special pursuit are selected. For example, Hitler is described as a head of state, not as a war criminal, dictator, or National Socialist.

Title: *Hitler : the missing years* / Ernst Hanfstaengl ; introduction
      by John Toland ; afterword by Egon Hanfstaengl. 1994
SUBJECTS:
    Hitler, Adolf, 1889-1945.
    Heads of state—Germany—Biography.
    Germany—Politics and government—1918-1933.

Title: *Josef Stalin : Verwandler der Welt* / Adolf von Thadden.
      c1991
SUBJECTS:
    Stalin, Joseph, 1879-1953.
    Heads of state—Soviet Union—Biography.
    Soviet Union—History—1925-1953.

(b) *Biographical headings for persons belonging to no particular field or discipline.* If the individual biography does not pertain to a special field or discipline, biographical headings in the form of **[Organization, ethnic group, place, event, or war]—Biography** are assigned, in order to bring out any and all important associations by which the person may be identified:

Title: *Always running : la vida loca, gang days in L.A.* / by Luis J.
      Rodriguez. 1993
SUBJECTS:
    Rodriguez, Luis J., 1954-
    Gangs—California—Los Angeles—Biography.
    Mexican American youth—California—Los Angeles—
      Biography.

Title: *A trip through hell : an autobiography* / Hattie M. Cousain.
      c1991
SUBJECTS:
    Cousain, Hattie M., 1933-
    Afro-American women—Biography.
    California—Biography.

(2) *Topical headings.* If the biographical work also contains discussions on special topics not designated by the biographical headings, they are brought out by regular topical headings without biographical subdivisions:

Title: *Challenge and change : the story of civil rights activist, C.T.*
      Vivian / by Lydia Walker. c1993
SUBJECTS:
    Vivian, C. T.
    Civil rights workers—United States—Biography.
    Afro-Americans—Biography.
    Civil rights movements—Southern States—History—
      20th century.
    Afro-Americans—Civil rights.
    Southern States—Race relations.

Title: *Mary Dyer : biography of a rebel Quaker* / by Ruth Talbot
      Plimpton. 1994
SUBJECTS:
    Dyer, Mary, d. 1660.
    Quakers—Massachusetts—Boston—Biography.
    Christian martyrs—Massachusetts—Boston—Biography.
    Freedom of religion—Massachusetts—History—
      17th century.
    Boston (Mass.)—Biography.

Individual Biography of Specific Classes of Persons

Biographies of certain classes of persons are given special treatment, as delineated below.

(1) Artists. See the discussion on pages 330-31.

(2) Founders of religions. A personal name heading is assigned without the accompanying class-of-persons heading. The subdivision **—Biography** is not used under the personal name unless established in LCSH.

Title: *Buddha* / by Susan L. Roth. 1994
SUBJECTS:
Gautama Buddha—Juvenile literature.

Title: *The life of Christ* / Howard F. Vos. c1994
SUBJECTS:
Jesus Christ—Biography.

(3) Literary authors. See the discussion on pages 293-94.

(4) Music composers and musicians. See the discussion on pages 316-17.

(5) Statespeople or heads of state. When the work being cataloged presents personal facts concerning the life of a politician, statesperson, or ruler, two headings are assigned: the personal name with topical subdivision, if appropriate, and the biographical heading with an appropriate subdivision (e.g., **Great Britain—Kings and rulers—Biography**; **Presidents—United States—Biography**; **Emperors—Rome—Biography**). Examples include:

Title: *JFK, reckless youth* / Nigel Hamilton. 1992
SUBJECTS:
Kennedy, John F. (John Fitzgerald), 1917-1963—
Childhood and youth.
Presidents—United States—Biography.

Title: *The man who would be president : Dan Quayle* / by David S. Broder, Bob Woodward. 1992
SUBJECTS:
Quayle, Dan, 1947-
Vice-Presidents—United States—Biography.

If, in addition to personal facts, the work also discusses political affairs or events in which the biographee participated during a period of the country's history, a heading for this special aspect is also assigned (e.g., **[Place]—History—[Period subdivision]; [Place]—Politics and government—[Period subdivision]**). Examples include:

Title: *Alexander I, Emperor of Russia : a post-Communism reap-praisal* / by Ludmila Evreinov. 1995
SUBJECTS:
Alexander I, Emperor of Russia, 1777-1825.
Russia—Kings and rulers—Biography.
Russia—History—Alexander I, 1801-1825.

Title: *Franz Joseph* / Jean-Paul Bled ; translated by Teresa Bridgeman. 1992
SUBJECTS:
Franz Joseph I, Emperor of Austria, 1830-1916.
Austria—Kings and rulers—Biography.
Austria—History—Francis Joseph, 1848-1916. [dates of reign]

For a work that describes the times in which a politician, or statesperson, lived and the person's relationship to those times, but that contains few or no biographical details about the person, the biographical heading is omitted:

Title: *The bully pulpit : the presidential leadership of Ronald Reagan* / William Ker Muir, Jr. 1992
SUBJECTS:
Reagan, Ronald.
United States—Politics and government—1981-1989.
Political leadership—United States—History—
20th century.

Title: *With Reagan : the inside story* / Edwin Meese III. 1992
SUBJECTS:
Reagan, Ronald—Friends and associates.
Presidents—United States—Staff.
United States—Politics and government—1981-1989.
Meese, Edwin.

Title: *Liberty, retrenchment, and reform : popular liberalism in the Age of Gladstone, 1860-1880* / Eugenio F. Biagini. 1992
SUBJECTS:
Great Britain—Politics and government—1837-1901.
Liberalism—Great Britain—History—19th century.
Gladstone, W. E. (William Ewart), 1809-1898.
Liberal Party (Great Britain)

Title: *President John Fitzgerald Kennedy's grand and global alliance : world order for the new century* / edited by Joseph A. Bagnall. 1992
SUBJECTS:
United States—Foreign relations—1961-1963.
Kennedy, John F. (John Fitzgerald), 1917-1963.

Title: *Saddam Hussein's Gulf wars : ambivalent stakes in the Middle East* / Miron Rezun. 1992
SUBJECTS:
Iraq—Politics and government.
Hussein, Saddam, 1937-
United States—Foreign relations—Iraq.
Iraq—Foreign relations—United States.

Title: *Inner circles : how America changed the world : a memoir* / Alexander M. Haig, Jr., with Charles McCarry. 1992
SUBJECTS:
United States—Foreign relations—1945-1989.
United States—Foreign relations—1989-1993.
Haig, Alexander Meigs, 1924-

(6) Travelers. Biographical headings are not assigned to personal accounts of travel unless the journey described in the work is intimately associated with the career of the traveler (as in the case of statespeople, animal collectors, or musicians who travel) or unless the traveler is a literary author:

Title: *Balkan ghosts : a journey through history* / Robert D. Kaplan. 1993
SUBJECTS:
Kaplan, Robert D., 1952- —Journeys—Balkan Peninsula.
Balkan Peninsula—Description and travel.
Balkan Peninsula—History.

(7) Spouses. A biography or autobiography of a famous person's spouse or family member who is active in a special field is treated in the normal manner. However, if the spouse or family member has no special career, or if his or her career is not emphasized, a biographical work that relates personal experiences in association with the famous person is assigned the following types of headings: **[Name of person]**; **[Name of famous person]**; **[Class-of-persons heading]**. Examples include:

Title: *First Lady from Plains* / Rosalynn Carter. 1994
SUBJECTS:
Carter, Rosalynn.
Carter, Jimmy, 1924-
Presidents' spouses—United States—Biography.

Title: *Mila* / Sally Armstrong. 1992
SUBJECTS:
Mulroney, Mila, 1953-
Mulroney, Brian, 1939-
Prime ministers' spouses—Canada—Biography.

Title: *Nelly Custis : child of Mount Vernon* / by David L. Ribblett.
1993
SUBJECTS:
Lewis, Nelly Custis, 1779-1852.
Grandchildren—United States—Biography.
Presidents—United States—Family.
Washington, George, 1732-1799—Family.
Washington family.

Special Types of Biographical Works

Autobiographies and Autobiographical Writings

The personal name heading is assigned to an autobiography even though it duplicates the main entry:

Title: *Barbara Bush : a memoir* / Barbara Bush. c1994
SUBJECTS:
Bush, Barbara, 1925-
Bush, George, 1924-
Presidents' spouses—United States—Biography.
MAIN ENTRY:
Bush, Barbara, 1925-

Other autobiographical writings, such as memoirs, journals, and diaries, are treated similarly:

Title: *The Shah and I : the confidential diary of Iran's royal court, 1969-1977* / Asadollah Alam. 1992
SUBJECTS:
Alam, Asadollah, 1919-1978—Diaries.
Statesmen—Iran—Diaries.
Mohammed Reza Pahlavi, Shah of Iran, 1919-
Iran—Politics and government—1941-1979.

Title: *Diaries* / Alan Clark. 1994
SUBJECTS:
Clark, Alan, 1928- —Diaries.
Statesmen—Great Britain—Diaries.
Great Britain—Politics and government—1979-
Great Britain—Social life and customs—1945-

Title: *The same river twice : a memoir* / Chris Offutt. 1993
SUBJECTS:
Offutt, Chris, 1958-
United States—Biography.

Title: *Martyrs' Day : chronicle of a small war* / Michael Kelly. 1993
SUBJECTS:
Persian Gulf War, 1991—Personal narratives.
Kelly, Michael, 1957- —Journeys—Middle East.

Title: *The Haldeman diaries* / H.R. Haldeman. c1994
SUBJECTS:
United States—Politics and government—1969-1974.
Nixon, Richard M. (Richard Milhous), 1913- —Friends
    and associates.
Haldeman, H. R. (Harry R.), 1926- —Diaries.

Correspondence[41]

To a collection of personal correspondence, the following complex of headings is assigned:

[Name(s) of the letter writer(s) (if no more than three)]—
    Correspondence
[Name(s) of the addressee(s) (if no more than two)]—
    Correspondence
[Class of persons or ethnic group]—Correspondence
[Special topics discussed in the letters]

Examples include:

Title: *To his excellency Thomas Jefferson : letters to a president* /
    selected and edited by Jack McLaughlin. 1991
SUBJECTS:
Jefferson, Thomas, 1743-1826—Correspondence.
Working class—United States—Correspondence.
Presidents—United States—Correspondence.

Title: *The correspondence of Sigmund Freud and Sandor Ferenczi*
    / edited by Eva Brabant, Ernst Falzeder, and Patrizia
    Giampieri-Deutsch, under the supervision of Andre Hay-
    nal ; transcribed by Ingeborg Meyer-Palmedo ; translated
    by Peter T. Hoffer ; introduction by Andre Haynal. 1993-
SUBJECTS:
Freud, Sigmund, 1856-1939—Correspondence.
Ferenczi, Sandor, 1873-1933—Correspondence.
Psychoanalysts—Correspondence.
Psychoanalysis.

Partial Biography[42]

A partial biography—a work about a person's life and work with at least 50 percent of the content devoted to personal details (except for people from ancient times about whom few personal details are known)—is treated like an individual biography by assigning a personal heading and additional biographical headings as appropriate. Additional headings are assigned to bring out the topical aspects if they have not been represented by the biographical headings. If a work about a person contains few or no personal details, biographical headings are not assigned. The personal heading is assigned in all cases. Examples include:

Title: *Matters of principle : an insider's account of America's rejection of Robert Bork's nomination to the Supreme Court* / Mark Gitenstein. 1992
SUBJECTS:
Bork, Robert H.
United States. Supreme Court—Officials and employees —Selection and appointment.
Judges—United States—Selection and appointment.

Title: *Storming the statehouse : running for governor with Ann Richards and Dianne Feinstein* / Celia Morris. 1992
SUBJECTS:
Richards, Ann, 1933-
Feinstein, Dianne, 1933-
Governors—Texas—Election.
Governors—California—Election.
Texas—Politics and government—1951-
California—Politics and government—1951-

Title: *Schwarzkopf : an insider's view of the commander and his victory* / Robert D. Parrish and N.A. Andreacchio. 1991
SUBJECTS:
Persian Gulf War, 1991—Campaigns.
Persian Gulf War, 1991—Biography—Miscellanea.
Schwarzkopf, H. Norman, 1934- —Miscellanea.
United States. Army—Biography—Miscellanea.
Generals—United States—Biography—Miscellanea.

Title: *Thought and faith in the philosophy of Hegel* / edited by John Walker. 1991
SUBJECTS:
Hegel, Georg Wilhelm Friedrich, 1770-1831—Religion— Congresses.
Religion—Philosophy—History—19th century— Congresses.

Title: *Nietzsche and Emerson : an elective affinity* / George J.
Stack. c1992
SUBJECTS:
Nietzsche, Friedrich Wilhelm, 1844-1900.
Emerson, Ralph Waldo, 1803-1882—Philosophy.
Emerson, Ralph Waldo, 1803-1882—Influence.

True Stories About Animals and Pets[43]

To a work containing true-life stories about animals, a heading in
the form of **[Type of animal]—[Place** (if appropriate)]—**Biography**
[or **—Anecdotes]** is assigned:

Title: *Waiting for Billy* / Martin Jacka. 1990
SUBJECTS:
Bottlenosed dolphins—Anecdotes—Juvenile literature.
Race horses—Anecdotes—Juvenile literature.
Dogs—Anecdotes—Juvenile literature.

To a true-life story of an animal or pet that has an established name,
the name heading is also assigned.

Title: *Good dog, Millie* / story by Andy Mayer and Jim Becker ;
illustrations by Mary Kittila. c1993
SUBJECTS:
Millie (Dog)
Bush, George, 1924-
Bush, Barbara, 1925-
Dogs—United States—Biography.

For fictional accounts of animals, see the discussion on pages 276 and
282.

WORKS ABOUT CORPORATE BODIES

The treatment of works about corporate bodies is similar in many
ways to that of biography.

Corporate Bodies Discussed Collectively

For a work about a specific type of corporate body, the generic term
is assigned as the heading (e.g., **Libraries; Trade and professional
associations; Trade-unions, Catholic**). Many of the headings for
corporate bodies are subdivided by place (e.g., **Libraries—Finland;
Libraries—Alaska**). Examples include:

Title: *The lessons of change : Baltimore schools in the modern era* / commissioned by the Fund for Educational Excellence and written by Mike Bowler. c1991
SUBJECTS:
Public schools—Maryland—Baltimore—History.

Title: *Academia's golden age : universities in Massachusetts, 1945-1970* / Richard M. Freeland. 1992
SUBJECTS:
Education, Higher—Massachusetts—Boston—History.
Universities and colleges—Massachusetts—Boston—History.

Title: *Standard & Poor's 500 guide* / Standard & Poor's Corporation. 1994
SUBJECTS:
Stocks—United States—Directories.
Corporations—United States—Finance—Directories.

Works About Individual Corporate Bodies

The name of the corporate body, as established according to *Anglo-American Cataloguing Rules*, 2nd edition, 1988 revision (*AACR2R*) (see the discussion on pages 59-60), is assigned as the subject heading for a work about an individual corporate body, even if the subject entry duplicates the main entry or an added entry.[44] Generic headings representing types of corporate bodies are not assigned. Examples include:

Title: *Strategic planning for the United States Army personnel function* / William M. Hix, Ronald E. Sortor. 1992
SUBJECTS:
United States. Army—Personnel management.

Title: *Contributions to Cornell history, portraits, memorabilia, plaques and artists : 1990 addendum to the revised 1984 edition by Elizabeth Baker Wells, Cornell 1928* / Diane B. Nelson, compiler and editor. [1990].
SUBJECTS:
Cornell University—History.
Cornell University—Collectibles.
Cornell University—Benefactors.

Title: *Wedge : the secret war between the FBI and CIA* / by Mark Ribling. 1994
SUBJECTS:
Intelligence service—United States.
United States. Central Intelligence Agency.
United States. Federal Bureau of Investigation.

Title: *The College of Earth and Mineral Sciences at Penn State* / E. Willard Miller. c1992
SUBJECTS:
Pennsylvania State University. College of Earth and Mineral Sciences—History.

Title: *Museum of Science, Boston : the founding and formative years : the Washburn era, 1939-1980* / by Mary Desmond Rock. 1989.
SUBJECTS:
Boston Museum of Science—History.

Title: *Eclipse : the last days of the CIA* / Mark Perry. 1992
SUBJECTS:
United States. Central Intelligence Agency.
Intelligence service—United States.

Title: *A tradition of distinction : Alfred University, 1836-1991* / Edward G. Coll, Jr. 1990
SUBJECTS:
Alfred University—History.

For the proceedings of meetings of a society or institution dealing with a specific topic, a heading in the form of **[Topic]—Congresses** is assigned. However, for the annual meetings that deal with the internal affairs of the corporate body, a heading in the form of **[Name of corporate body]—Congresses** is used.

Name Changes in Corporate Bodies

When a corporate body changes its name, the present policy in accordance with *AACR2R* is to provide headings for all the names and link them with *see also* references. In assigning subject headings to corporate bodies that have changed their names, two different policies are in effect: one for corporate bodies in general, and one specifically for political jurisdictions.

For a work about a non-jurisdictional corporate body that has had a linear name change, a merger, or a split, the name current during the latest period covered by the work is assigned:[45]

Title: *The Ringling Brothers : circus family* / by Richard and Sally Glendinning ; illustrated by William Hutchinson. 1991
SUBJECTS:
Ringling Brothers—History—Juvenile literature.
Circus performers—United States—Biography—Juvenile literature.

Title: *The great Hartford circus fire : creative settlement of mass disasters* / Henry S. Cohn and David Bollier. c1991
SUBJECTS:
Ringling Brothers Barnum and Bailey Combined Shows—Trials, litigation, etc.
Torts—Connecticut—Hartford—History—20th century.
Dispute resolution (Law)—Connecticut—Hartford— History—20th century.
Receivers—Connecticut—Hartford—History— 20th century.
Hartford Circus Fire, Hartford, Conn., 1944.

Title: *"Achievements and challenges" : the HEW forum papers, second series, 1968-69.* [1969]
SUBJECTS:
United States. Dept. of Health, Education, and Welfare.

Title: *Education Department 1990 : a resource manual for the Federal Education Department* / David T. Chester. [1990]
SUBJECTS:
Federal aid to education—United States—Directories.
United States. Dept. of Education—Directories.

Title: *America 2000 : an education strategy.* 1991
SUBJECTS:
Educational planning—United States.
Education and state—United States.
United States. Dept. of Education.

For a work about a political jurisdiction that has changed its name without involving territorial changes, the latest name is used as the subject heading or subdivision regardless of the period treated in the work:[46]

Title: *From civilization to segregation : social ideals and social control in southern Rhodesia, 1890-1934* / Carol Summers. c1994
SUBJECTS:
Zimbabwe—History—1890-1965.
Zimbabwe—Social conditions—1890-1965.
Zimbabwe—Race relations.

Title: *'Rhodesians never die' : the impact of war and political change on White Rhodesia, c. 1970-1980* / Peter Godwin and Ian Hancock. 1993
SUBJECTS:
Zimbabwe—History—Chimurenga War, 1966-1980.
Whites—Zimbabwe—Politics and government.
Zimbabwe—Ethnic relations.

If the change is a complicated one, such as one involving territorial boundaries, the name or names used during the periods covered by the work are assigned:

Title: *DDR : Grundriss der Geschichte* / von Hermann Weber. 1993
  SUBJECTS:
    Germany (East)—History.

Title: *A history of West Germany* / Dennis L. Bark and David R. Gress. c1993
  SUBJECTS:
    Germany (West)—History.

Title: *Die Deutschen vor ihrer Zukunft* / Christian Graf von Krockow. 1993
  SUBJECTS:
    Germany—History—Philosophy.

Title: *Germany at the crossroads : the costs of reunification* / Mike Wilson. c1991
  SUBJECTS:
    Germany—Economic conditions—1990-
    Germany—Economic policy—1990-
    Germany—Economic conditions—Regional disparities.
    Germany—Industries.
    Germany—History—Unification, 1990.

Title: *Russia in the age of reaction and reform 1801-1881* / David Saunders. 1992
  SUBJECTS:
    Russia—History—Alexander I, 1801-1825.
    Russia—History—Nicholas I, 1825-1855.
    Russia—History—Alexander II, 1855-1881.

Title: *Twentieth century Russia* / Donald W. Treadgold. 1994
  SUBJECTS:
    Russia—History—1801-1917.
    Soviet Union—History.
    Former Soviet republics—History.

Title: *Russia and the Soviet Union : an historical introduction from the Kievan state to the present* / John M. Thompson. 1994
  SUBJECTS:
    Russia—History.
    Soviet Union—History.
    Russia (Federation)—History.

Title: *Russian Federation* / prepared under the direction of John Odling-Smee, by an IMF staff team comprising Ernesto Hernandez-Cata ... [et al.]. [1993]
SUBJECTS:
Russia (Federation)—Economic conditions—1991-
Russia (Federation)—Economic policy—1991-

WORKS ABOUT BUILDINGS AND OTHER STRUCTURES[47]

Works About Specific Types of Buildings or Structures

To a work that collectively discusses a certain type of building or structure, topical headings, with appropriate geographic subdivisions if applicable, are assigned:

Title: *Cathedrales* / auteur, Michel Bouttier. c1990-
SUBJECTS:
Cathedrals—France.

Title: *Europe's castle and palace hotels* / Carole Chester. c1989.
SUBJECTS:
Hotels—Europe—Guidebooks.
Castles—Europe—Guidebooks.
Palaces—Europe—Guidebooks.
Europe—Guidebooks.

Title: *L'eau et la vie : fontaines de Meurthe-et-Moselle* / Philippe Duley, Serge Gouvenel. [1991]
SUBJECTS:
Meurthe-et-Moselle (France)—Description and travel.
Fountains—France—Meurthe-et-Moselle—
  Pictorial works.
Water use—France—Meurthe-et-Moselle—History.

If the work discusses a type or class of building or structure within a city from an architectural point of view, or if the work describes members of the class as physical entities, an additional heading in the form of **[City]—Buildings, structures, etc.** is assigned:[48]

Title: *Cityscapes of Boston : an American city through time* / text by Robert Campbell ; photographs by Peter Vanderwarker. 1992
SUBJECTS:
Architecture—Massachusetts—Boston.
Boston (Mass.)—Buildings, structures, etc.

Title: *San Francisco architecture : the illustrated guide to over 1000 of the best buildings, parks, and public artworks in the Bay Area* / Sally B. Woodbridge and John M. Woodbridge ; design and illustration, Chuck Byrne ; editing, Elizabeth Douthitt Byrne. c1992

SUBJECTS:

Architecture—California—San Francisco—Guidebooks.
Parks—California—San Francisco—Guidebooks.
Public art—California—San Francisco—Guidebooks.
San Francisco (Calif.)—Buildings, structures, etc.

Title: *The Loop : where the skyscraper began* / Judith Paine McBrien ; illustrated by Victoria Behm ; edited by Joan C. Pomaranc. c1992

SUBJECTS:

Tall buildings—Illinois—Chicago—Guidebooks.
Architecture, Modern—19th century—Illinois—Chicago—Guidebooks.
Architecture, Modern—20th century—Illinois—Chicago—Guidebooks.
Loop (Chicago, Ill.)—Guidebooks.
Chicago (Ill.)—Buildings, structures, etc.—Guidebooks.

Works About Individual Buildings or Structures

For a work about an individual building, the following types of headings are used:

[Name of structure]
[Name of city]—Buildings, structures, etc.
    [If the building or structure is located within a city and the work discusses it from an architectural point of view]
[Name of architect]
[Name of owner, resident, etc.]—Homes and haunts—[Place]
[Special feature or topic]

Examples include:

Title: *Presidio of San Francisco, Golden Gate National Recreation Area, California* / Erwin N. Thompson, Sally B. Woodbridge. [1992]

SUBJECTS:

Presidio of San Francisco (Calif.)—History.
Golden Gate National Recreation Area (Calif.)
San Francisco (Calif.)—Buildings, structures, etc.

Title: *Cow Palace, great moments : Cow Palace tales* / by Edward
Diran ; edited by Tony Compagno. 1991
SUBJECTS:
Cow Palace (San Francisco, Calif.)
San Francisco (Calif.)—Buildings, structures, etc.
San Francisco (Calif.)—Social life and customs.

Title: *The White House : the first two hundred years* / edited by
Frank Freidel, William Pencak. c1994
SUBJECTS:
White House (Washington, D.C.)
Presidents—United States.
Washington (D.C.)—Social life and customs.
Washington (D.C.)—Buildings, structures, etc.

Title: *The Lincoln Memorial* / by Catherine Reef. c1994
SUBJECTS:
Lincoln Memorial (Washington, D.C.)—Juvenile
literature.
Washington (D.C.)—Buildings, structures, etc.—
Juvenile literature.
Lincoln, Abraham, 1809-1865—Monuments—
Washington (D.C.)—Juvenile literature.

Title: *Dana-Thomas House : Frank Lloyd Wright, architect.* c1992
SUBJECTS:
Dana House (Springfield, Ill.)
Prairie school (Architecture)—Illinois—Springfield.
Wright, Frank Lloyd, 1867-1959—Criticism and
interpretation.
Springfield (Ill.)—Buildings, structures, etc.

WORKS INVOLVING CITY DISTRICTS, SECTIONS, AND QUARTERS[49]

When a work deals with a topic in a city district, section,[50] or
quarter, the following types of headings are assigned:

[Topic]—[Larger entity]—[City]
[Name of district, section, or quarter]—[Subdivision, if
appropriate]
[City]—[Subdivision]

This approach is taken because the lowest level of geographic subdivision in the LC subject headings system is the city. In other words,
subjects are not subdivided by city districts, sections, or quarters.

Title: *The secret gardens of Georgetown : behind the walls of Washington's most historic neighborhood* / Adrian Higgins ; photographs by Mick Hales. c1994
SUBJECTS:
Gardens—Washington (D.C.)
Georgetown (Washington, D.C.)

Title: *The insider's guide to Manhattan bars : the prices, the settings, and the people you'll find at more than two hundred drinking spots* / Eric Zicklin. c1993
SUBJECTS:
Bars (Drinking establishments)—New York (N.Y.)—Guidebooks.
Manhattan (New York, N.Y.)—Guidebooks.

Title: *The Black churches of Brooklyn* / Clarence Taylor. 1994
SUBJECTS:
Afro-American churches—New York (N.Y.)
Brooklyn (New York, N.Y.)—Church history.
Afro-Americans—New York (N.Y.)—Religion.

If the topic involved corresponds to one of the concepts represented by the free-floating subdivisions under names of places, the same subdivision is used under the heading for the district and the heading for the city. Examples include:

Title: *The impact of the 1906 earthquake on San Francisco's Chinatown* / Erica Y.Z. Pan. 1995
SUBJECTS:
Chinatown (San Francisco, Calif.)—History.
San Francisco (Calif.)—History.
Earthquakes—California—San Francisco—History—20th century.

Title: *Brooklyn : people and places, past and present* / Grace Glueck, Paul Gardner. 1991
SUBJECTS:
Brooklyn (New York, N.Y.)—History—Pictorial works.
Brooklyn (New York, N.Y.)—Pictorial works.
New York (N.Y.)—History—Pictorial works.
New York (N.Y.)—Pictorial works.

Title: *Generations romantiques : les etudiants de Paris & le Quartier latin, 1814-1851* / par Jean-Claude Caron ; preface de Maurice Agulhon. c1991
SUBJECTS:
Paris (France)—Intellectual life—19th century.
College students—France—Paris—Political activity.
Latin Quarter (Paris, France)—Social conditions.

Paris (France)—Social conditions.
Revolutions—France—History—19th century.

Title: *Chinatown no more : Taiwan immigrants in contemporary New York* / Hsiang-Shui Chen. 1992
SUBJECTS:
Chinese Americans—New York (N.Y.)—Social conditions.
Taiwanese Americans—New York (N.Y.)—Social conditions.
Queens (New York, N.Y.)—Social conditions.
New York (N.Y.)—Social conditions.

WORKS RELATED TO INDIVIDUAL WORKS

To a work related to another work—a commentary or criticism, an index, or a supplement—a heading representing the original work is generally assigned in addition to other appropriate headings.

Commentary Versus Edition[51]

Commentaries are sometimes published separately as independent works and sometimes published along with the text of the original work. In the latter case, the subject headings assigned vary, depending on whether the work as a whole is treated as a commentary or as an edition. The decision on the way to treat such a work generally parallels the decision made in descriptive cataloging according to *AACR2R*. If main entry is under the author or the uniform title of the original work, it is treated as an edition. On the other hand, if main entry is under the name of the commentator, it is treated as a commentary.

Commentaries on Individual Works

To a commentary on an individual work, two types of headings are assigned: a name/title heading (or uniform title for a work entered under title) for the original work, and the same topical headings that were assigned to the original work.[52] Examples of subject headings assigned to commentaries include:

Title: *Kant's Critique of pure reason* / edited by Ruth F. Chadwick and Clive Cazeaux. 1992
SUBJECTS:
Kant, Immanuel, 1724-1804. Kritik der reinen Vernunft.
Knowledge, Theory of.
Causation.
Reason.

Original text:
Title: *Critique of pure reason* / Immanuel Kant ; introduced by A.D.
       Lindsay ; translated by J.M.D. Meiklejohn. 1991
    SUBJECTS:
       Knowledge, Theory of.
       Causation.
       Reason.

Title: *Freud's wishful dream book* / Alexander Welsh. 1994
    SUBJECTS:
       Freud, Sigmund, 1856-1939. Traumdeutung.
       Dream interpretation.
       Psychoanalysis.

Original text:
Title: *Die Traumdeutung* / von Sigm. Freud. 1919
    SUBJECTS:
       Dream interpretation.
       Psychoanalysis.

The title in the subject heading is the uniform title, and not necessarily the title as it appears in the commentary. The reason for using the uniform title is to group together all commentaries about a particular work regardless of variant titles or titles in the different languages under which the work has appeared. The topical headings used are those that have been assigned to the original work. However, if the headings assigned to the text are only used as form headings, such as **Agriculture—Periodicals** or **Egypt—History—Fiction**, they are converted to their topical equivalents, such as **Agriculture—Periodicals—History** and **Egypt—In literature**.

The topical headings are assigned even if the commentary does not contain the original text. If, however, the commentary consists purely of textual criticism (i.e., commentary on the text as text and not the substantive matter of the original work), the topical headings assigned to the original work are not assigned.

Variant Editions of a Work[53]

To each variant edition (the term *edition* includes issues, reprints, and translations, but not adaptations) of a previously cataloged work, the Library of Congress assigns the same subject headings that were assigned to the original edition, provided that the contents of the variant edition do not vary significantly from the original.

Title: *The Republic* / Plato ; translated by A.D. Lindsay ; intro-
       duced by Terence Irwin. c1992
    SUBJECTS:
       Political science—Early works to 1800.
       Utopias.

Different or additional headings are assigned if variations in content are significant.

If the edition of a work contains a substantial amount of commentary (e.g., at least 20 percent of the work), a subject heading in the form of **[Name. Title]** or **[Uniform title]** is assigned, even though it may duplicate the main entry or an added entry of the work.

Supplements to Individual Works

The same subject headings assigned to the original work are used for its separately published supplementary works. If a supplement treats other topics as well, additional headings are assigned. Examples include:

Title: *American drama criticism : interpretations, 1890-1977 /* compiled by Floyd Eugene Eddleman. 2nd ed. 1979.
SUBJECTS:
American drama—History and criticism—Bibliography.
Theater—United States—Reviews—Bibliography.
Dramatic criticism—United States—Bibliography.

Title: *American drama criticism : supplement II to the second edition /* compiled by Floyd Eugene Eddleman. 1989
SUBJECTS:
American drama—History and criticism—Bibliography.
Theater—United States—Reviews—Bibliography.
Dramatic criticism—United States—Bibliography.

Title: *American drama criticism : supplement III to the second edition /* compiled by Floyd Eugene Eddleman. 1992
SUBJECTS:
American drama—History and criticism—Bibliography.
Theater—United States—Reviews—Bibliography.
Dramatic criticism—United States—Bibliography.

Indexes to Individual Works

Two types of headings are assigned to an index of an individual work:

[Name. Title or Uniform title]—Indexes
or **[Uniform title]—Indexes**
[Same heading assigned to original work]—Indexes

Examples include:

Title: *Index to Saccardo's Sylloge fungorum, volumes I-XXVI in XXIX, 1882-1972* / by Clyde F. Reed and David F. Farr. 1993
SUBJECTS:
    Saccardo, P. A. (Pier Andrea), 1845-1920. Sylloge fungorum omnium hucusque cognitorum—Indexes.
    Fungi—Nomenclature—Indexes.
    Fungi—Indexes.

Title: *Die Wiener Weltbühne, Wien, 1932-1933, Die Neue Weltbühne, Prag/Paris, 1933-1939 : Bibliographie einer Zeitschrift* / bearbeitet von Jörg Armer. 1992
SUBJECTS:
    Die Wiener Weltbühne—Indexes.
    Die Neue Weltbühne—Indexes.

Title: *Composite index to volumes XIV-XVII (Revolutionary War rolls) of the New Hampshire state papers* / Frank C. Mevers, compiler. c1993
SUBJECTS:
    New Hampshire state papers—Indexes.
    New Hampshire—History—Revolution, 1775-1783—Registers.
    United States—History—Revolution, 1775-1783—Registers.
    New Hampshire—Genealogy.
    Soldiers—New Hampshire—Registers.
    New Hampshire—Registers.

Title: *Who was who : a cumulated index, 1897-1990.* 1991
SUBJECTS:
    Who was who—Indexes.
    Great Britain—Biography—Indexes.
    Biography—Dictionaries—Indexes.

NOTES

[1]Library of Congress, Office of Subject Cataloging Policy, *Subject Cataloging Manual*, 4th ed. (Washington, D.C.: Cataloging Distribution Service, Library of Congress, 1991), H1927, p. 1.

[2]Library of Congress, *Subject Cataloging Manual*, H1927, p. 2.

[3]Library of Congress, *Subject Cataloging Manual*, H1425.

[4]Library of Congress, *Subject Cataloging Manual*, H1205.

[5]For summaries of the proceedings of a congress or conference, the subdivision **—Congresses** is used instead of **—Abstracts**.

[6]Library of Congress, *Subject Cataloging Manual*, H1205, p. 2.

[7]Library of Congress, *Subject Cataloging Manual*, H1670, p. 1.

[8]Library of Congress, *Subject Cataloging Manual*, H1325.

[9]Library of Congress, *Subject Cataloging Manual*, H1322.

[10]Library of Congress, *Subject Cataloging Manual*, H1670, p. 1.

[11]The subdivision **—Film catalogs** is used for indexes to films on a topic.

[12]For catalogs of objects, see discussion on pages 213-14.

[13]Library of Congress, *Subject Cataloging Manual*, H1361.

[14]Library of Congress, *Subject Cataloging Manual*, H1965.

[15]Library of Congress, *Subject Cataloging Manual*, H1660.

[16]Library of Congress, *Subject Cataloging Manual*, H1570.

[17]Library of Congress, *Subject Cataloging Manual*, H1980.

[18]Library of Congress, *Subject Cataloging Manual*, H1360.

[19]Catalogs of publications are discussed on pages 204-6. Art catalogs are discussed on pages 325-26.

[20]Library of Congress, *Subject Cataloging Manual*, H1540.

[21]Library of Congress, *Subject Cataloging Manual*, H1558.

[22]Library of Congress, *Subject Cataloging Manual*, H1646.

[23]Library of Congress, *Subject Cataloging Manual*, H1690.

[24]"Library of Congress Subject Headings in Microfiche, 1983- ," *Cataloging Service Bulletin* 25 (Summer 1984): 82.

[25]Note that the subdivision **—Juvenile literature** is used under topical headings but not for juvenile belles lettres, for which juvenile headings such as **Children's stories; Nursery rhymes; Children's poetry;** or headings with the subdivisions **—Juvenile drama; —Juvenile fiction; —Juvenile humor; —Juvenile poetry** are used.

[26]On LC catalog cards, juvenile headings were distinguished by (a) bracketed subject headings without juvenile subdivisions, (b) the presence of the summary, and (c) the designation AC in the lower right-hand corner of the card.

[27]Library of Congress, *Subject Cataloging Manual*, H1780, H1790, H1800.

[28]Library of Congress, *Subject Cataloging Manual*, H1690, p. 2.

[29]Library of Congress, *Subject Cataloging Manual*, H2070.

[30]Library of Congress, *Subject Cataloging Manual*, H2230.

[31]Library of Congress, *Subject Cataloging Manual*, H1690, p. 2.

[32]Library of Congress, *Subject Cataloging Manual*, H1330, p. 1.

[33]Library of Congress, *Subject Cataloging Manual*, H1480.

[34]Library of Congress, *Subject Cataloging Manual*, H1928.

[35]For treatment of genealogical materials in general, see pages 376-78.

[36]Library of Congress, *Subject Cataloging Manual*, H1574.

[37]Library of Congress, *Subject Cataloging Manual*, H1330, p. 1.

[38]Library of Congress, *Subject Cataloging Manual*, H1110.

[39]Additional biographical headings are not assigned to lives of legendary or fictitious characters.

[40]For different types of biographical subdivisions, see pages 233-34.

[41]Library of Congress, *Subject Cataloging Manual*, H1480.

[42]Library of Congress, *Subject Cataloging Manual*, H1330.

[43]Library of Congress, *Subject Cataloging Manual*, H1720.

[44]Library of Congress, *Subject Cataloging Manual*, H184.

[45]Library of Congress, *Subject Cataloging Manual*, H460.

[46]Library of Congress, *Subject Cataloging Manual*, H708, p. 1; H830, p. 3.

[47]Library of Congress, *Subject Cataloging Manual*, H1334, H1334.5.

[48]Library of Congress, *Subject Cataloging Manual*, H1334.5.

[49]Library of Congress, *Subject Cataloging Manual*, H720.

[50]Boroughs of New York (N.Y.) are treated as city sections.

[51]Library of Congress, *Subject Cataloging Manual*, H1435.

[52]Commentaries on certain types of literary works receive special treatment. For a discussion of these, see pages 295-301. For works about sacred scriptures and liturgical works, see pages 339-43, 349-50.

[53]Library of Congress, *Subject Cataloging Manual*, H175.

10 Subject Areas Requiring Special Treatment

LITERATURE

Types of Headings

Four types of headings are used for works in the field of literature (belles lettres): literary form headings; topical headings representing themes, characters, or features in literary works; headings combining form and topic; and other topical headings. These are discussed below.

Literary Form Headings

(1) *Headings representing literary forms or genres*. Examples include:

Drama
Poetry
Fiction
Romances
Satire

(2) *Headings indicating language or nationality*. Examples include:

American literature
Japanese literature
French literature
Hindu literature

(3) *Headings that combine language/nationality and form*. Examples include:

American poetry
English drama (Comedy)
Epic poetry, Italian
Prose poems, American
French drama
African drama (English)
Ghanaian poetry (English)

The heading **English literature** serves as the pattern heading for subdivisions that may be used under headings for individual literatures and under genres of those literatures (e.g., **Swedish literature**;

269

French drama; German essays; Epic poetry, Finnish; Short stories, Chinese). A list of these free-floating subdivisions appears in appendix C. Period subdivisions listed under the pattern heading are not used under headings for minor genres (i.e., genres other than fiction, drama, poetry, essays, and prose literature) or under inverted headings, and they are not free-floating under headings with qualifiers, such as **Nigerian fiction (English)**. Needless to say, period subdivisions that are unique to English literature (e.g., **—Old English, ca. 450-1100**) are not used under headings for other literatures. Period subdivisions that are unique to a particular literature are established separately and displayed under the appropriate heading in LCSH.

In using free-floating subdivisions under literary form headings, Library of Congress policy does not authorize the combination of a period subdivision with a geographic subdivision that brings out a specific place of origin (e.g., **American literature—Southern States**) or with topical subdivisions such as **— . . . authors** (e.g., **American poetry—Women authors**). The main heading is doubled (i.e., by assigning an additional heading with chronological subdivision), in order to bring out the time aspect. For example, for a collection of twentieth-century American poetry by women authors from the south, the following headings are used:

American poetry—20th century
American poetry—Southern States—Women authors

The period subdivision may be followed by a form subdivision (e.g., **American poetry—20th century—History and criticism**).

When the language and nationality of a specific body of literature are represented by two different terms, or when a body of literature within a country is written in a nonindigenous language, one must choose which term to feature in the heading—the one for the language or the one for the nationality or place. Over the years, both approaches have been taken by the Library of Congress, as in **English literature—Irish authors** and **Algerian poetry (French)**. Current policy favors stressing country or region, with the nationality term first and the name of the language appearing as a parenthetical qualifier. With such headings, a USE reference is routinely made from the alternative approach:

Israeli poetry (English)
    UF   English poetry—Israeli authors
Moroccan literature (French)
    UF   French literature—Moroccan authors

New headings are established according to the pattern above, and many headings of the type **[Language] literature—[Nationality] authors** have been changed to the current pattern. Nevertheless, many headings like **English literature—Chinese authors** remain in LCSH and continue to be used.

An exception is made for the literatures of Arabic-speaking countries. The Arabic literature of a particular country is represented by the heading **Arabic literature** with a local subdivision, and a USE reference is made from the alternative form:

Arabic literature—Lebanon
UF   Lebanese literature (Arabic)

The writings of authors belonging to particular nonlinguistic subgroups within a country (e.g:, Jewish authors, Catholic authors, women authors) are designated by means of a subdivision under the pertinent literature, such as **South African literature (English)—Women authors**. Literature written in a language indigenous to a country is represented by the literature heading without qualifiers (e.g., **Urdu literature**). When the use of an indigenous language by a subgroup extends to neighboring countries or areas, local subdivisions are added (e.g., **Urdu literature—Pakistan**).

Topical Headings Representing Themes, Characters, or Features in Literary Works

For literary works the following types of headings are used:

[Topic or Name]—Drama
[Topic or Name]—Fiction
[Topic or Name]—Literary collections
[Topic or Name]—Poetry

Examples include:

Columbus, Christopher—Poetry
Lincoln, Abraham, 1809-1865—Drama
Presley, Elvis, 1935-1977—Fiction
America—Discovery and exploration—Spanish—Poetry
Horses—Fiction
World War, 1939-1945—Literary collections

For works *about* literature the following types of headings are used:[1]

[Topic] in literature[2]
[Personal name, family, place, corporate body, or sacred books]—In literature[3]
[Name of event or war]—Literature and the war, [revolution, etc.]

Examples include:

Social problems in literature
Animals in literature
Shakespeare, William, 1564-1616—In literature
Lincoln, Abraham, 1809-1865—In literature

Roosevelt family—In literature
Chicago (Ill.)—In literature
Bible—In literature
Cuba—History—Revolution, 1959—Literature and the revolution
World War, 1914-1918—Literature and the war

Headings Combining Form and Topic

Examples include:

Christmas plays
Patriotic poetry
Detective and mystery stories, English
Western stories

Other Topical Headings

Examples include:

Criticism, Textual
Literary forgeries and mystifications
Literature—Research
Literature and medicine
Literature and society
Religion and literature

Application[4]

Works in the field of literature fall into two broad categories: (1) literary works (or specimens) and (2) works *about* literature in general or *about* individual authors or individual works. Their treatment is described in the following pages.

Literary Works

Collections of Two or More Independent Works By Different Authors

(1) *Literary form headings.* Literary form headings are assigned to collections of two or more independent works by different authors:

Title: *Modern French short fiction* / edited by Johnnie Gratton and
Brigitte Le Juez. 1994
SUBJECTS:
Short stories, French.

Title: *A nation's voice : an anthology of American short fiction* /
[edited by] John Timmerman. 1994
SUBJECTS:
Short stories, American.

Title: *Eight American poets : twentieth-century voices : Theodore
Roethke, Elizabeth Bishop, Robert Lowell, John Berry-
man, Anne Sexton, Allen Ginsberg, Sylvia Plath, James
Merrill : an anthology* / edited by Joel Conarroe. 1994
SUBJECTS:
American poetry—20th century.

Title: *The Penguin book of Renaissance verse* / selected and with an
introduction by David Norbrook ; edited by H. R. Woud-
huysen. 1993
SUBJECTS:
English poetry—Early modern, 1500-1700.

Title: *The Divided home/land : contemporary German women's
plays* / edited by Sue-Ellen Case. c1992
SUBJECTS:
German drama—20th century—Translations into English.
**German drama—Women authors—Translations into
English.**

Title: *The Gymnasium of the imagination : a collection of children's
plays in English, 1780-1860* / [compiled by] Jonathan Levy.
1992
SUBJECTS:
English drama—19th century.
English drama—18th century.
Children's plays, English.

Title: *Favorite poems for children* / edited by Holly Pell McConnaughy.
1993
SUBJECTS:
Children's poetry, American.
Children's poetry, English.

When the works in a collection belong to a minor literary form and the
form heading has no provision for period subdivisions, a second,
broader form heading with the appropriate period subdivision is also
assigned in order to represent the time aspect:

Title: *Two Tudor tragedies* / edited with an introduction and notes
by William Tydeman. 1992
SUBJECTS:
English drama—Early modern and Elizabethan, 1500-1600.
English drama (Tragedy)

The subdivision —**Collections** is not free-floating. It is established under the following literary headings only:[5] **Drama**; **Fiction**; **Literature**; **Poetry**:

Title: *The McGraw-Hill introduction to literature* / [selection and introductions by] Gilbert H. Muller, John A. Williams. c1995
SUBJECTS:
Literature—Collections.

(2) *Topical headings.* If the collection is centered on a theme, person, place, or event, a topical heading subdivided by either —**Literary collections** (when the works in the collection are written in two or more literary forms) or one of the major literary forms (—**Drama**; —**Fiction**; —**Poetry**), is assigned in addition to the appropriate literary form headings.[6] The form subdivisions —**Drama**; —**Fiction**; —**Poetry** are used under an identifiable topic for a collection of literary works on that topic. However, topical headings are not assigned to collections on vague and general topics such as fate, belief, malaise, and mankind. Examples include:

Title: *It's not quiet anymore : new work from the Institute of American Indian arts* / senior editors, Heather Ahtone, Allison Hedge Coke ; editors, Milton Apache . . . et al. c1993
SUBJECTS:
American literature—Indian authors.
Indians of North America—Literary collections.
American literature—20th century.

Title: *An Anthology of Canadian literature in English* / edited by Russell Brown, Donna Bennett and Nathalie Cooke. c1990
SUBJECTS:
Canadian literature.
Canada—Literary collections.

Title: *Gothic high* / Goldian VandenBroeck. c1992
SUBJECTS:
Architecture, Gothic—France—Poetry.
Cathedrals—France—Poetry.
Sonnets, American.

Title: *Eternal light : grandparent poems : a twenty-century selection* / edited by Jason Shinder. c1994
SUBJECTS:
Grandparents—Poetry.
American poetry—20th century.

Title: *Bless me, father : stories of Catholic childhood* / edited by Amber Coverdale Sumrall and Patrice Vecchione. c1994
SUBJECTS:
Short stories, American—Catholic authors.
Catholics—United States—Fiction.
Children—United States—Fiction.

Title: *Centers of the self : stories by black American women from the nineteenth century to the present* / edited and with an introduction by Judith A. Hamer and Martin J. Hamer. 1994
SUBJECTS:
Short stories, American—Afro-American authors.
Short stories, American—Women authors.
Afro-American women—Social life and customs—Fiction.
Afro-Americans—Social life and customs—Fiction.

Title: *Where past meets present : modern Colorado short stories* / edited by James B. Hemesath. c1994
SUBJECTS:
Short stories, American—Colorado.
American fiction—20th century.
Colorado—Social life and customs—Fiction.

Some phrase headings combine topical and form aspects, such as **Detective and mystery stories, American; Science fiction, American; Sea stories; Christmas plays; Ghost plays; Political plays**. When such headings exist, they are used instead of separate topic and form headings:

Title: *Poems of the five mountains : an introduction to the literature of the Zen monasteries* / [introduction, notes, and translation by] Marian Ury. 1992
SUBJECTS:
Chinese poetry—Japan—Translations into English.
Zen poetry, Chinese—Japan—Translations into English.

Title: *The Goodnight Trail* / Ralph Compton. c1992
SUBJECTS:
Western stories.

Title: *Quest to Riverworld* / edited by Philip Jose Farmer. c1993
SUBJECTS:
Science fiction, American.

Title: *365 love poems* / compiled by John Gabriel Hunt. c1993
SUBJECTS:
Love poetry, English.
Love poetry, American.

Title: *All I want for Christmas is you : a collection of love poems from Blue Mountain Arts.* c1993
    SUBJECTS:
        Love poetry, American.
        Christmas—Poetry.

If, however, a heading is assigned for a very specific topic, the topic/form heading for a more general topic is not used. Instead, a literary form heading is assigned. For example, the following headings are assigned to a collection of American drama on the theme of Trinity:[7]

American drama.
Trinity—Drama
    [not *Christian drama, American*]

In the case of fiction about animals, the heading **Animals [or Kind of animals]—Fiction** or **Animals [or Kind of animals]—Juvenile fiction** is used.[8]

Works By Individual Authors[9]

Collected Works

(1) *Literary form headings.* In general, literary form headings are not assigned to collected works in a major form by an individual author. In other words, the heading **English drama—Early modern and Elizabethan, 1500-1600** is not used with the complete plays of Shakespeare.

Title: *Postmortem : poems* / by Maurice Kilwein Guevara. 1994
    [No subject headings assigned]

Title: *Selected poems* / John Keats. 1993
    [No subject headings assigned]

Title: *Novels 1942-1954* / William Faulkner. 1994
    [No subject headings assigned]

However, there are two exceptions to this general rule. The literary form heading is assigned if it combines form and topic in one heading, such as **Detective and mystery plays; Sea poetry, English; Love poetry; War poetry;** and **Western stories**:

Title: *Gifts of love* / Helen Steiner Rice ; compiled by Virginia J. Ruehlmann. c1992
    SUBJECTS:
        Christian poetry, American.
        Love poetry, American.

Title: *Selected stories and sketches* / Bret Harte ; edited with an introduction by David Wyatt. 1995
SUBJECTS:
Western stories.

The form heading is also assigned if the form is highly specific, such as **Allegories**; **Fairy tales**; **Radio stories**; **Carnival plays**; **Children's plays**; **College and school drama**; **Concrete poetry, German**; **Didactic drama**; **Radio plays**; and **Sonnets, American:**

Title: *Emily Dickinson : poetry for young people* / edited by Frances S. Bolin ; illustrated by Chi Chung. c1994
SUBJECTS:
Children's poetry, American.

Title: *Grover's just so-so stories* / by Nancy Hall ; illustrated by Rick Wetzel. c1992
SUBJECTS:
Children's stories, American.

Title: *The runaway soup and other stories* / Michaela Muntean ; illustrated by Tom Cooke ; featuring Jim Henson's Sesame Street Muppets. c1992
SUBJECTS:
Children's stories, American.

Headings of the following types are *not* considered to be "highly specific": **American fiction**; **Short stories**; **English drama**; **English drama (Comedy)**; **Comedy**; **Farces**; **Melodrama**; **One-act plays**; **Tragedy**; **Tragicomedy**; **English diaries**.

(2) *Topical headings.* If the works in the collection are centered on an identifiable topic or based on an event or on the life of an individual, a topical heading with an appropriate literary form subdivision (**—Fiction**; **—Drama**; **—Poetry**; **—Literary collections**) is assigned.[10] A phrase heading combining form and topic is used if it is available. Topical headings are not usually assigned for vague and general topics such as fate, mankind, belief, and malaise. Examples include:

Title: *Pangs of love : stories* / by David Wong Louie. 1992
SUBJECTS:
Asian Americans—Fiction.

Title: *Tales from the tropics : seven sea stories* / by C. H. Scott. 1992
SUBJECTS:
Sailing—Fiction.
Sea stories, American.
Caribbean Area—Fiction.

Title: *Men of the sea* / Robert Carl ; illustrations by Eileen Lauden-
slager. c1992
SUBJECTS:
Sea stories.

Title: *Oddly enough* / stories by Bruce Coville ; illustrations by
Michael Hussar. c1994
SUBJECTS:
Horror tales, American.
Children's stories, American.

Title: *An ark for the next millennium : poems* / by José Emilio
Pacheco ; drawings by Francisco Toledo ; translations by
Margaret Sayers Peden from Album de zöología, selected
by Jorge Esquinca. 1993
SUBJECTS:
Animals—Poetry.

Individual Works

(1) *Literary form headings*. Headings representing major literary
forms, such as **English drama** and **American fiction**, are *not* assigned to individual literary works. For example:

Title: *The tragicall historie of Hamlet, Prince of Denmarke* / edited
and introduced by Graham Holderness and Bryan
Loughrey. 1992
[No subject headings assigned]

Title: *Absalom, Absalom : the corrected text* / William Faulkner. 1993
[No subject headings assigned]

However, form headings of the types listed below are assigned.

(a) Form headings for children's literature, such as **Children's
plays, American; Children's poetry, English;** and **Children's stories,
German**, are assigned to individual literary works for children:[11]

Title: *Hamlet for young people* / by William Shakespeare ; edited
and illustrated by Diane Davidson. c1993
SUBJECTS:
Children's plays, English.

Title: *The horse and his boy* / by C. S. Lewis ; adapted by Glyn
Robbins. c1992
SUBJECTS:
Children's plays, English.

Title: *Wisdom from Nonsense Land* / by R. and L. Page ; afterword by P. K. Page. c1991
SUBJECTS:
Children's poetry, Canadian.

(b) Form headings that include a topical aspect, such as **Detective and mystery plays, American**; and **War poetry, American**, are assigned to individual works of drama and poetry, but not to individual works of fiction:

Title: *Twenty years* / John C. Harrell ; with art by Philip L. "Moki" Martin. 1992
SUBJECTS:
War poetry, American.

Title: *Wings of fire* / Mattie Shavers Johnson. c1993
SUBJECTS:
Persian Gulf War, 1991—Poetry.
War poetry, American.

(c) Headings representing highly specific forms, such as **Carnival plays**; **Nonsense verses**; and **Nursery rhymes, American, [English, etc.]**, are assigned to individual works of drama and poetry, but not to individual works of fiction:

Title: *There was an old man— : a gallery of nonsense rhymes* / by Edward Lear ; illustrated by Michele Lemieux. c1994
SUBJECTS:
Children's poetry, English.
Nonsense verses, English.
Limericks, Juvenile.

(2) *Topical headings*. An individual work of drama or poetry that focuses on an identifiable topic or is based on the life of a person is assigned a topical or name heading with the subdivision **—Poetry** or **—Drama**. Such headings are not assigned for very general or vague topics such as mankind, fate, belief, and malaise. Examples include:

Title: *The man of destiny* / by George Bernard Shaw. 1991
SUBJECTS:
Napoléon I, Emperor of the French, 1769-1821—Drama.

Title: *The magical voyage of Ulysses : a play for young people* / John Wiles. c1991
SUBJECTS:
Odysseus (Greek mythology)—Juvenile drama.
Children's plays, English.

Title: *We say we love each other : poetry* / by Minnie Bruce Pratt. 1992
SUBJECTS:
Lesbians—Poetry.

Title: *Adonais : 1821* / Percy Bysshe Shelley. 1992
SUBJECTS:
Keats, John, 1795-1821—Poetry.

Title: *Amadeus : a drama* / by Peter Shaffer. c1993
SUBJECTS:
Salieri, Antonio, 1750-1825—Drama.
Mozart, Wolfgang Amadeus, 1756-1791—Drama.

Title: *The little people's guide to the big world* / written and
illustrated by Trevor Romain. c1993
SUBJECTS:
Children—Conduct of life—Juvenile poetry.
Children's poetry, American.

Title: *The night before Christmas* / Clement C. Moore ; photography,
Paul and Charles Esselburn ; concept, Regena Smith Gregory.
c1993
SUBJECTS:
Santa Claus—Juvenile poetry.
Christmas—Juvenile poetry.
Children's poetry, American.

Title: *Uncle's South China Sea blue nightmare* / Lamont B. Steptoe.
c1994
SUBJECTS:
Vietnamese Conflict, 1961-1975—Afro-Americans—Poetry.
Afro-American soldiers—Poetry.
War poetry, American.

For individual works of fiction, topical headings are assigned to
biographical fiction, historical fiction, and animal stories only, as
delineated below.[12]

(a) For biographical fiction, examples include:

Title: *Napoleon, chronique romanesque* / Michel Peyramaure. c1991
SUBJECTS:
Napoléon I, Emperor of the French, 1769-1821—Fiction.
France—History—Consulate and Empire, 1799-1815—
Fiction.

Title: *Lincoln* / Gore Vidal. 1993
SUBJECTS:
Lincoln, Abraham, 1809-1865—Fiction.

Title: *Camille and the sunflowers* / Laurence Anholt. 1994
    SUBJECTS:
        Gogh, Vincent van, 1853-1890—Juvenile fiction.

      (b) A heading representing the specific historical event or period with the subdivision **—Fiction** is assigned to a historical novel or story.[13] The topical heading is not assigned when the event or period is merely the backdrop to the actual story; it is assigned only when the event or period is the principal focus of the work. Examples include:

Title: *Scales of gold* / Dorothy Dunnett. 1992
    SUBJECTS:
        Fifteenth century—Fiction.
        Belgium—History—To 1555—Fiction.
        Vander Poele, Nicholas (Fictitious character)—Fiction.

Title: *Sacred hunger* / Barry Unsworth. 1992
    SUBJECTS:
        Slave-trade—History—18th century—Fiction.

Title: *Death in the off-season : a Merry Folger mystery* / Francine
        Mathews. 1994
    SUBJECTS:
        Women detectives—Massachusetts—Nantucket Island—
            Fiction.
        Nantucket Island (Mass.)—Fiction.

Title: *An ancient hope* / Caroline Strickland. 1994
    SUBJECTS:
        Brothers—England—Dorset—History—Fiction.
        Family—England—Dorset—History—Fiction.
        Dorset (England)—History—Fiction.

Title: *Gulf stream* / Marie Stanley ; preface by Caldwell Delaney ;
        introduction by Philip D. Beidler. [1993]
    SUBJECTS:
        Women—Alabama—Mobile—Fiction.
        Mulattoes—Alabama—Mobile—Fiction.

Title: *Nightfall* / Katharine Marlowe. 1993
    SUBJECTS:
        Women—Connecticut—Crimes against—Fiction.
        Connecticut—Fiction.

(c) For a fictional work about animals in general or about a particular kind of animal, a heading in the form of **Animals—Fiction** or **[Kind of animal]—Fiction** is assigned:[14]

Title: *The ice at the end of the world* / Robert Siegel. c1994
  SUBJECTS:
    Whales—Fiction.

Medieval Legends and Romances[15]

To literary versions of legendary tales, including individual works and collections in prose, verse, or dramatic form, headings designating the dominant character or motif, with the form subdivision **—Legends** or **—Romances,** are assigned. Additional headings appropriate for folklore materials or for individual works of drama, fiction, or poetry may also be assigned.

The subdivision **—Legends** is used under names of individual persons, legendary characters, and uniform titles of sacred works, and under religious topics for literary versions of legendary tales, including sagas, about them.[16]

The subdivision **—Romances** is used under names of individual persons and legendary characters for texts of medieval (i.e., pre-1501) European tales based chiefly on legends of chivalric love and adventure in which these persons or characters are dominant characters.

Alexius, Saint—Legends
Faust, d. ca. 1540—Legends
Grail—Legends
Charlemagne, Emperor, 742-814—Romances
Arthurian romances
  [an exception to the usual form, which would be *Arthur, King—Romances*]
Lancelot (Legendary character)—Romances.

Examples of medieval legends and romances include:

Title: *The English Faust book : a critical edition, based on the text of 1592* / edited by John Henry Jones. 1994
  SUBJECTS:
    Faust, d. ca. 1540—Legends.

Title: *The Romance of Arthur : an anthology of medieval texts in translation* / edited by James J. Wilhelm. 1994
  SUBJECTS:
    Arthurian romances.

Title: *Three Middle English Charlemagne romances* / edited by
Alan Lupack. 1990
SUBJECTS:
Charlemagne, Emperor, 742-814—Romances.
English poetry—Middle English, 1100-1500.
Romances, English.

Title: *La Vie de Saint Alexis : the Old French text and its transla-
tion into English and modern French as The life of Saint
Alexis* / with an introduction, critical notes and commen-
tary, and a bibliography by Guy R. Mermier. 1994
SUBJECTS:
Alexius, Saint—Legends—Poetry.
Christian poetry, French—Translations into English.
Christian saints—Legends—Poetry.

Title: *The Complete works of the Pearl poet* / translated with an
introduction by Casey Finch ; Middle English texts edited
by Malcolm Andrew, and Ronald Waldron, Clifford Peterson.
c1993
SUBJECTS:
**English poetry—Middle English, 1100-1500—Modernized
versions.**
Manuscripts, English (Middle)—England—West Midlands.
Gawain (Legendary character)—Romances.
Arthurian romances.

The same headings and subdivisions assigned to medieval legends
and romances are used for modern versions (after 1501) of legends and
romances, provided that the characters and plots are essentially unal-
tered from their original.

Title: *Le morte d'Arthur* / Sir Thomas Malory. 1994
SUBJECTS:
Arthurian romances.
[not Arthur, King—Poetry]
Romances, English.

Modern versions of legends and romances that have been altered to the
extent that they are no longer recognizable as a retelling of their
medieval origins are treated as literary works. The subdivisions **—Fiction, —Drama**, and **—Poetry** are used as they normally would be for
works of this kind written after 1501. Examples include:

Title: *The oak above the kings : a book of the Keltiad* / Patricia
Kennealy-Morrison. c1994
SUBJECTS:
Arthurian romances—Adaptations.
Arthur, King—Fiction.

Title: *The misfortunes of Arthur : a critical, old-spelling edition* /
edited by Brian Jay Corrigan. 1992
SUBJECTS:
Arthurian romances—Adaptations.
Arthur, King—Drama.

Title: *Merlin's bones* / Fred Saberhagen. 1995
SUBJECTS:
Merlin (Legendary character)—Fiction.
Arthurian romances—Adaptations.

For the treatment of works about legends and romances, see pages
290-91.

Works About Literature

Works about literature in general, exclusive of those about individual
authors and their works, are assigned headings that represent their
subject content:

Title: *Re-thinking theory : a critique of contemporary literary theory
and an alternative account* / Richard Freadman, Seumas
Miller. 1992
SUBJECTS:
Criticism.
Literature, Modern—History and criticism—Theory, etc.

Title: *Von Homer bis Hemingway : Einzelanalysen zu Erzählstil und
Erzähldynamik in der Weltliteratur* / Hermann Wiegmann.
c1992
SUBJECTS:
Narration (Rhetoric)
Discourse analysis, Narrative.
Style, Literary.
Literature—History and criticism.

Title: *A critic's notebook : essays* / by Irving Howe ; with an
introduction by Nicholas Howe. 1994
SUBJECTS:
Criticism.
Literature—History and criticism.

If the work focuses on a particular literature or form, one or more
literary form headings, with the subdivision **—History and criticism**
or another appropriate subdivision, are assigned:

Title: *The Cambridge history of Russian literature* / edited by
      Charles A. Moser. 1992
  SUBJECTS:
  Russian literature—History and criticism.

Title: *American short story writers : a collection of critical essays* /
      edited by Julie Brown. 1994
  SUBJECTS:
  Short stories, American—History and criticism.

Title: *Melodrama.* 1992
  SUBJECTS:
  Melodrama—History and criticism.

Title: *Drama in early Tudor Britain, 1485-1558* / Howard B. Norland.
      c1995
  SUBJECTS:
  English drama—Early modern and Elizabethan,
    1500-1600—History and criticism.
  English drama—Middle English, 1100-1500—
    History and criticism.

Title: *Twentieth-century German dramatists, 1919-1992* / edited
      by Wolfgang D. Elfe and James Hardin. c1992
  SUBJECTS:
  German drama—20th century—Bio-bibliography.
  Dramatists, German—20th century—Biography.

Title: *The short story in English : Britain and North America : an
      annotated bibliography* / by Dean Baldwin and Gregory L.
      Morris. 1994
  SUBJECTS:
  Short stories, English—Bibliography.
  Short stories, American—Bibliography.
  Short stories, Canadian—Bibliography.
  Short story—Bibliography.

Title: *The Shaping of text : style, imagery, and structure in French
      literature : essays in honor of John Porter Houston* / edited
      by Emanuel J. Mickel, Jr. 1992
  SUBJECTS:
  French literature—History and criticism.
  French language—Figures of speech.
  French language—Style.
  Literary form.

Title: *Staging the Renaissance : essays on Elizabethan and Jacobean drama* / edited by David Scott Kastan and Peter Stallybrass. 1991
SUBJECTS:
English drama—17th century—History and criticism.
English drama—Early modern and Elizabethan, 1500-1600—History and criticism.
Theater—England—History—17th century.

Title: *Deutsches Drama der 80er Jahre* / herausgegeben von Richard Weber. 1992
SUBJECTS:
German drama—20th century—History and criticism.

Title: *Classic science fiction writers* / edited and with an introduction by Harold Bloom. c1994
SUBJECTS:
Science fiction, English—History and criticism.
Science fiction, American—History and criticism.
Science fiction, American—Bio-bibliography.
Science fiction, English—Bio-bibliography.

The subdivision **—History and criticism** may be further subdivided:

Title: *The psychoanalytic theory of Greek tragedy* / C. Fred Alford. 1992
SUBJECTS:
Greek drama (Tragedy)—History and criticism—Theory, etc.
Psychoanalysis and literature.

Title: *Swedish non-academic criticism in the era of freedom, 1718-1772* / Hans Ostman. [1993]
SUBJECTS:
Swedish literature—History and criticism—Theory, etc.
Criticism—Sweden—History—18th century.

Title: *What about murder?. 1981-1991 : a guide to books about mystery and detective fiction* / by Jon L. Breen. 1993
SUBJECTS:
Detective and mystery stories—History and criticism—Bibliography.
Detective and mystery stories—Technique—Bibliography.

As noted earlier, the heading **English literature** serves as the pattern heading for subdivisions that may be used under headings for individual literatures and under genres of those literatures, such as **Swedish literature; French drama; German essays; Epic poetry, Finnish; Short stories, Chinese.** A list of these free-floating subdivisions appears in appendix C.

Frequently, when a work deals with a minor form of a particular period but the relevant literary form heading has no provision for period subdivisions, a second, broader heading with the appropriate period subdivision is also assigned:

Title: *The German Nachspiel in the eighteenth century* / David G. John. c1991
SUBJECTS:
    German drama—18th century—History and criticism.
    German drama (Comedy)—History and criticism.

Title: *Aspects of fifteenth-century society in the German carnival comedies : speculum hominis* / Edelgard E. DuBruck. c1993
SUBJECTS:
    German drama—To 1500—History and criticism.
    Carnival plays—Germany—Nuremberg—History and criticism.
    Nuremberg (Germany)—Social life and customs.

For discussions about particular themes with regard to a particular literature or form, paired headings are assigned:

**[Literary form heading]—History and criticism
[Topic] in literature**[17]

Title: *Modern black American poets and dramatists* / edited and with an introduction by Harold Bloom. c1994
SUBJECTS:
    American literature—Afro-American authors—History and criticism.
    American literature—Afro-American authors—Bio-bibliography.
    Afro-Americans in literature.

Title: *Bloody murder : from the detective story to the crime novel* / Julian Symons. c1992
SUBJECTS:
    Detective and mystery stories—History and criticism.
    Crime in literature.

Title: *Seeing together : friendship between the sexes in English writing from Mill to Woolf* / Victor Luftig. c1993
SUBJECTS:
    English literature—19th century—History and criticism.
    English literature—20th century—History and criticism.
    Man-woman relationships in literature.
    Friendship in literature.
    Sex role in literature.
    Women in literature.
    Men in literature.

Title: *The African American short story, 1970-1990 : a collection of critical essays* / edited by Wolfgang Karrer and Barbara Puschmann-Nalenz. 1993

SUBJECTS:

Short stories, American—Afro-American authors—History and criticism.
American fiction—20th century—History and criticism.
Afro-Americans in literature.

Title: *Black American women fiction writers* / edited and with an introduction by Harold Bloom. c1994

SUBJECTS:

American fiction—Afro-American authors—History and criticism.
American fiction—Afro-American authors— Bio-bibliography.
American fiction—Women authors—History and criticism.
American fiction—Women authors—Bio-bibliography.
Women and literature—United States.
Afro-American women in literature.
Afro-Americans in literature.

For discussions of the theme of wars in literature, the headings assigned are in the form of **[Name of war or event]—Literature and the war, [revolution, etc.]**:

Title: *Levitating the Pentagon : evolutions in the American theatre of the Vietnam War era* / J. W. Fenn. 1992

SUBJECTS:

American drama—20th century—History and criticism.
Vietnamese Conflict, 1961-1975—Literature and the conflict.
Literature and society—United States—History— 20th century.
Theater and society—United States—History— 20th century.
Peace movements in literature.
War in literature.

Title: *Nigerian writers on the Nigerian Civil War : anguish, commitment, catharsis* / by Olu Obafemi. c1992

SUBJECTS:

Nigerian literature (English)—History and criticism.
Nigeria—History—Civil War, 1967-1970—Literature and the war.

Title: *Radical visions : poetry by Vietnam veterans* / Vince Gotera.
    c1994
SUBJECTS:
  American poetry—20th century—History and criticism.
  Vietnamese Conflict, 1961-1975—Literature and the conflict.
  Veterans' writings, American—History and criticism.
  War poetry, American—History and criticism.
  Radicalism in literature.

Title: *A gulf so deeply cut : American women poets and the Second World War* / Susan Schweik. c1991
SUBJECTS:
  American poetry—20th century—History and criticism.
  World War, 1939-1945—Literature and the war.
  Women and literature—United States—History—20th century.
  American poetry—Women authors—History and criticism.
  War poetry, American—History and criticism.

A heading that combines form and topic may also be subdivided by **—History and criticism**, such as **Detective and mystery stories, American—History and criticism**; **Religious drama—History and criticism**. An example is:

Title: *Christi Himmelfahrt : ihre Darstellung in der europäischen Literatur von der Spatantike bis zum ausgehenden Mittelalter* / Karin Wilcke. 1991
SUBJECTS:
  Religious drama—History and criticism.
  Jesus Christ—Ascension—Drama—History and criticism.
  Drama, Medieval—History and criticism.

For a work that discusses the portrayal of a person (including literary authors) or place in literature, a heading in the form of **[Name of person or place]—In literature** is assigned in addition to one or more literary form headings:

Title: *Writing Illinois : the prairie, Lincoln, and Chicago* / James Hurt. c1992
SUBJECTS:
  American literature—Illinois—History and criticism.
  Lincoln, Abraham, 1809-1865—In literature.
  Chicago (Ill.)—In literature.
  Illinois—Intellectual life.
  Illinois—In literature.
  Prairies in literature.

Title: *Being English : narratives, idioms & performances of national identity from Coleridge to Trollope* / Julian Wolfreys. 1994
SUBJECTS:
English literature—19th century—History and criticism.
National characteristics, English, in literature.
England—In literature.
Narration (Rhetoric)

The history and criticism of medieval legends and romances in general (and indexes, concordances, etc., to them) require a heading subdivided by **—History and criticism**; **—Dictionaries**; **—Indexes**; or whatever other subdivision is appropriate:[18]

Title: *The Grail : quest for the eternal* / John Matthews. 1991
SUBJECTS:
Grail—Miscellanea.
Grail—Legends—History and criticism.

Title: *Index des motifs narratifs dans les romans arthuriens français en vers : XIIe-XIIIe siècles = Motif-index of French Arthurian verse romances : XIIth-XIIIth cent.* / Anita Guerreau-Jalabert. 1992
SUBJECTS:
Arthurian romances—Themes, motives—Indexes.
French poetry—To 1500—Themes, motives—Indexes.
Narrative poetry, French—Themes, motives—Indexes.

Title: *Figuren der Unruhe : Faustdichtungen* / Karl-Heinz Hucke. 1992
SUBJECTS:
German literature—History and criticism.
European literature—History and criticism.
Faust, d. ca. 1540—Legends—History and criticism.

Title: *The lady of the lake in Arthurian legend* / Christopher Dean. c1993
SUBJECTS:
Lady of the Lake (Legendary character)—Romances—History and criticism.
Arthurian romances—History and criticism.
English literature—History and criticism.

Title: *Artus : Biographie einer Legende* / Heinz Ohff. c1993
SUBJECTS:
Arthur, King—Legends.
Arthurian romances—History and criticism.
Literature, Medieval—Themes, motives.

If the work focuses on a specific character rather than on the legends or romances, the heading for the character without literary form subdivision is assigned.

Title: *The real King Arthur : a history of post-Roman Britannia, A.D. 410-A.D. 593* / by P. F. J. Turner. c1993
SUBJECTS:
    Arthur, King.
    Great Britain—Civilization, Celtic.
    Great Britain—History—To 1066.
    Britons—Kings and rulers.
    Britons—History.

Works About Individual Authors[19]

Works about individual authors are assigned headings in the form of the name of the author with appropriate subdivisions. The heading **Shakespeare, William, 1564-1616** serves as the pattern heading for subdivisions; the subdivisions listed under it may be used under any literary author, as appropriate. This is the reason why a number of subdivisions not applicable to Shakespeare are listed under his name (e.g., **—Exile**). The Shakespeare list showing free-floating subdivisions for use under literary authors is included in appendix C. Topical headings with appropriate subdivisions are assigned to bring out themes, style, characters, and other aspects of the author's works.
Examples of works about individual authors include:

Title: *Christopher Marlowe : the plays and their sources* / edited by Vivien Thomas and William Tydeman. 1994
SUBJECTS:
    Marlowe, Christopher, 1564-1593—Sources.
    English drama—Early modern and Elizabethan, 1500-1600—Sources.

Title: *A concordance to the poems and plays of Robert Browning* / compiled by Richard J. Shroyer and Thomas J. Collins. 1993
SUBJECTS:
    Browning, Robert, 1812-1889—Concordances.

Title: *The Shakespeare name dictionary* / by J. Madison Davis and A. Daniel Frankforter. 1994
SUBJECTS:
    Shakespeare, William, 1564-1616—Dictionaries.
    Names, Geographical, in literature—Dictionaries.
    Names, Personal, in literature—Dictionaries.

Title: *A dictionary of quotations from Shakespeare : a topical guide to over 3,000 great passages from the plays, sonnets, and narrative poems* / selected by Margaret Miner and Hugh Rawson. c1992
SUBJECTS:
Shakespeare, William, 1564-1616—Indexes.
Shakespeare, William, 1564-1616—Quotations.
Quotations, English—Indexes.

Title: *Conditions handsome and unhandsome : the constitution of Emersonian perfectionism* / Stanley Cavell. c1990
SUBJECTS:
Emerson, Ralph Waldo, 1803-1882—Philosophy.
Emerson, Ralph Waldo, 1803-1882—Ethics.
Perfection—Moral and ethical aspects.

For a work of criticism or interpretation of an author's works, a heading in the form of the name of the author with the subdivision **—Criticism and interpretation** or another more specific subdivision is assigned:[20]

Title: *Faulkner's families : a southern saga* / Gwendolyn Chabrier. 1993
SUBJECTS:
Faulkner, William, 1897-1962—Criticism and interpretation.
Domestic fiction, American—History and criticism.
Faulkner, William, 1897-1962—Characters.
Southern States—In literature.
Family—Southern States.
Family in literature.

Title: *The Critical response to Eudora Welty's fiction* / edited by Laurie Champion. 1994
SUBJECTS:
Welty, Eudora, 1909-   —Criticism and interpretation.

Title: *The empty garden : the subject of late Milton* / Ashraf H. A. Rushdy. 1992
SUBJECTS:
Milton, John, 1608-1674—Criticism and interpretation.

Title: *Literate culture : Pope's rhetorical art* / Ruben Quintero. 1992
SUBJECTS:
Pope, Alexander, 1688-1744—Technique.
Rhetoric—1500-1800.

Title: *Gerard Manley Hopkins and critical discourse* / edited by
Eugene Hollahan. 1993
SUBJECTS:
**Hopkins, Gerard Manley, 1844-1889—Criticism and
interpretation—History—20th century.**

If the work contains biographical information (at least 50 percent
of the work) as well as criticism of the author's literary efforts, two
headings are assigned: the name of the author without subdivision, and
a biographical heading:[21]

Title: *C. S. Lewis at the breakfast table, and other reminiscences* /
edited by James T. Como. 1992
SUBJECTS:
Lewis, C. S. (Clive Staples), 1898-1963.
Authors, English—20th century—Biography.

To a true biography of a literary author, two headings are assigned:
the name of the author with a biographical subdivision such as
—Biography, as well as the biographical heading:

Title: *Thomas Carlyle's Life of Friedrich Schiller.* 1992
SUBJECTS:
Schiller, Friedrich, 1759-1805—Biography.
Authors, German—18th century—Biography.

Title: *Henry James : the imagination of genius : a biography* / Fred
Kaplan. 1992
SUBJECTS:
James, Henry, 1843-1916—Biography.
Authors, American—19th century—Biography.
Authors, American—20th century—Biography.

Title: *One writer's beginnings* / Eudora Welty. 1991
SUBJECTS:
Welty, Eudora, 1909- —Childhood and youth.
Authors, American—20th century—Biography.

Title: *A Keats chronology* / F. B. Pinion. 1992
SUBJECTS:
Keats, John, 1795-1821—Chronology.
Poets, English—19th century—Chronology.

Title: *The Thoreau log : a documentary life of Henry David
Thoreau, 1817-1862* / [compiled by] Raymond R. Borst.
1992
SUBJECTS:
Thoreau, Henry David, 1817-1862—Chronology.
Authors, American—19th century—Chronology.

In the case of a partial biography or a biography in a special form or on a special aspect or theme, the required headings specified above with appropriate subdivisions, and any additional appropriate headings, are assigned:

Title: *The honest courtesan : Veronica Franco, citizen and writer in sixteenth-century Venice* / Margaret F. Rosenthal. 1992
SUBJECTS:
    Franco, Veronica, 1546-1591.
    Venice (Italy)—Intellectual life.
    Courtesans—Italy—Biography.
    Authors, Italian—16th century—Biography.

Title: *Fanny Fern : an independent woman* / Joyce W. Warren. 1992
SUBJECTS:
    Fern, Fanny, 1811-1872—Biography.
    Feminism and literature—United States—History—19th century.
    Novelists, American—19th century—Biography.
    Journalists—United States—Biography.

Title: *Wandering ghost : the odyssey of Lafcadio Hearn* / Jonathan Cott. 1992
SUBJECTS:
    Hearn, Lafcadio, 1850-1904—Biography.
    Authors, American—19th century—Biography.
    Americans—Japan—History—19th century.
    Journalists—United States—Biography.

Title: *A world of my own : a dream diary* / Graham Greene. 1994
SUBJECTS:
    Greene, Graham, 1904- —Diaries.
    Novelists, English—20th century—Diaries.
    Dreams.

Title: *James Kirke Paulding : the last republican* / Lorman Ratner. 1992
SUBJECTS:
    Paulding, James Kirke, 1778-1860.
    Authors, American—19th century—Biography.
    Frontier and pioneer life in literature.
    Social problems in literature.

Title: *Dead secrets : Wilkie Collins and the female gothic* / Tamar Heller. 1992
SUBJECTS:
    Collins, Wilkie, 1824-1889—Criticism and interpretation.
    Horror tales, English—History and criticism.
    Gothic revival (Literature)—Great Britain.
    Women and literature—Great Britain.

Title: *Imagination and myths in John Keats's poetry* / Diane
      Brotemarkle. c1993
  SUBJECTS:
    Keats, John, 1795-1821—Criticism and interpretation.
    Imagination in literature.
    Mythology in literature.
    Myth in literature.

Title: *The characters in the novels of Thomas Love Peacock (1785-*
      1866) : with bibliographical lists / Claude A. Prance. 1992
  SUBJECTS:
    Peacock, Thomas Love, 1785-1866—Characters
    —Dictionaries.
    Characters and characteristics in literature—Dictionaries.

Works About Individual Literary Works

For a work about an individual literary work, a [**Name. Title**]
heading is used. Literary form headings such as **American poetry** or
German drama are not assigned to individual works, except for
special forms such as **Children's poetry**.

Title: *The fall : a matter of guilt* / Brian T. Fitch. 1994
  SUBJECTS:
    Camus, Albert, 1913-1960. Chute.

Title: *Emile Zola, L'assommoir* / David Baguley. 1992
  SUBJECTS:
    Zola, Emile, 1840-1902. Assommoir.

Title: *Regaining paradise lost* / Thomas Corns. 1994
  SUBJECTS:
    Milton, John, 1608-1674. Paradise lost.

Title: *Go down, Moses* / annotated by Nancy Dew Taylor. 1994
  SUBJECTS:
    Faulkner, William, 1897-1962. Go down, Moses.

For a work about an individual literary work with special themes,
additional headings designating the themes are assigned:

Title: *Blowing the bridge : essays on Hemingway and For whom*
      the bell tolls / edited by Rena Sanderson. 1992
  SUBJECTS:
    Hemingway, Ernest, 1899-1961—Criticism and
      interpretation.
    Hemingway, Ernest, 1899-1961. For whom the bell tolls.
    Spain—History—Civil War, 1936-1939—Literature
      and the war.

Title: *A farewell to arms : the war of the words* / Robert W. Lewis. c1992
SUBJECTS:
Hemingway, Ernest, 1899-1961. Farewell to arms.
World War, 1914-1918—Literature and the war.

Title: *Troilus and Criseyde : the poem and the frame* / Allen J.
Frantzen. c1993
SUBJECTS:
Chaucer, Geoffrey, d. 1400. Troilus and Criseyde.
Troilus (Legendary character)—In literature.
Frame-stories—History and criticism.
Trojan War in literature.

Title: *A glossarial concordance to the Riverside Chaucer* / Larry D.
Benson. 1993
SUBJECTS:
Chaucer, Geoffrey, d. 1400—Language—Glossaries, etc.
English language—Middle English, 1100-1500
—Glossaries, vocabularies, etc.
Chaucer, Geoffrey, d. 1400—Concordances.
Chaucer, Geoffrey, d. 1400. Works. 1987.

If a work contains both a text and commentaries, subject headings appropriate for both are assigned.

Title: *Paradise lost : an authoritative text, backgrounds and
sources, criticism* / John Milton ; edited by Scott Elledge.
c1993
SUBJECTS:
Fall of man—Poetry.
Milton, John, 1608-1674. Paradise lost.
Fall of man in literature.

If appropriate, the following subdivisions may be used with a **[Name. Title]** heading:[22]

—Bibliography
—Concordances
—Congresses
—Criticism, Textual
—Exhibitions
—Illustrations
—Indexes
—Juvenile films
—Juvenile literature
—Juvenile sound recordings
—Pictorial works
—Sources

Examples include:

Title: *A complete concordance to Gottfried von Strassburg's Tristan* /
Clifton D. Hall. c1992
SUBJECTS:
**Gottfried, von Strassburg, 13th cent. Tristan
—Concordances.**

Title: *The play behind the play : Hamlet and quarto one* / Maxwell
E. Foster ; edited by Anne Shiras. 1991
SUBJECTS:
**Shakespeare, William, 1564-1616. Hamlet—Criticism,
Textual.
Shakespeare, William, 1564-1616—Bibliography—Quartos.**

Title: *The Hamlet : a concordance to the novel* / edited by Noel Polk
and John D. Hart. 1990
SUBJECTS:
Faulkner, William, 1897-1962. Hamlet—Concordances.

Title: *Cojimar : Ernest Hemingway e Il vecchio e il mare : album
fotografico* / foto di Raul Corrales . . . [et al.] ; introduzione
di Fernanda Pivano. c1990
SUBJECTS:
**Hemingway, Ernest, 1899-1961. Old man and the sea
—Pictorial works.**

If the original work is entered under title, as in the case of
anonymous or multiauthored works, the subject entry consists of the
uniform title:

Title: *"Waz sider da geschach" : American-German studies on the
Nibelungenlied* / edited by Werner Wunderlich and Ulrich
Muller with the assistance of Detlef Scholz. 1992
SUBJECTS:
Nibelungenlied.

Title: *Sir Gawain and the Green Knight and the idea of righteousness*
/ Gerald Morgan. c1991
SUBJECTS:
**Gawain and the Grene Knight.
Gawain (Legendary character)—Romances—History
and criticism.
Manuscripts, English (Middle)—England—West Midlands.
Christian ethics in literature.
Pentacles in literature.**

The uniform title may be subdivided by the following free-floating subdivisions when appropriate:[23]

—Adaptations
—Authorship
—Bibliography
—Characters
—Concordances
—Congresses
—Criticism, Textual
—Dictionaries
—Dramatic production
—Exhibitions
—Illustrations
—Indexes
—Juvenile films
—Juvenile literature
—Juvenile sound recordings
—Language
—Language—Glossaries, etc.
—Manuscripts
—Manuscripts—Facsimiles
—Parodies, imitations, etc.
—Periodicals
—Sources
—Style
—Translations
—Translations—History and criticism
—Translations into French, [German, etc.]
—Translations into French, [German, etc.]—History and criticism
—Versification

Title: *Beowulf scholarship : an annotated bibliography, 1979-1990* / Robert J. Hasenfratz. 1993
SUBJECTS:
Beowulf—Bibliography.
Epic poetry, English (Old)—History and criticism—Bibliography.

Title: *Story-telling techniques in the Arabian nights* / by David Pinault. 1992
SUBJECTS:
Arabian nights—Style.
Narration (Rhetoric)
Storytelling.

Title: *A concordance to the Qian zuo du* / compiled by Bent Nielsen. 1992
SUBJECTS:
Ch'ien tso tu—Concordances.
I ching.

The subdivision **—Criticism and interpretation** is not used under name-title or uniform title heading for a literary work. For a work of general criticism and interpretation or a discussion combining the approaches represented by several of these subdivisions, the name-title or uniform title heading is assigned for the literary work without subdivision. If another aspect of the work not represented in the lists is to be brought out, a separate heading is assigned in addition to the name-title or uniform title heading:

Title: *Approaches to teaching Joyce's Ulysses* / edited by Kathleen McCormick and Erwin R. Steinberg. 1993
SUBJECTS:
Joyce, James, 1882-1941. Ulysses.
Joyce, James, 1882-1941—Study and teaching.

Title: *Rhetoric, comedy, and the violence of language in Aristophanes' Clouds* / Daphne Elizabeth O'Regan. 1992
SUBJECTS:
Aristophanes. Clouds.
Aristophanes—Technique.
Violence in literature.
Rhetoric, Ancient.
Comedy.

For an index to a literary work, the following types of headings arc used:

[Name. Title]—Indexes
[Uniform title]—Indexes

An example is:

Title: *The Mystery fancier : an index to volumes I-XIII, November, 1976-Fall, 1992* / by William F. Deeck. 1993
SUBJECTS:
Mystery fancier—Indexes.
Detective and mystery stories—History and criticism—Periodicals—Indexes.

Works About Individual Medieval Legends and Romances[24]

To a work that discusses a single legend or romance, or a specific version of it, two types of headings are assigned: the heading for the specific legend or romance (i.e., the uniform title or the name-title entry) and the form heading assigned to the texts subdivided by **—History and criticism** or another appropriate subdivision, such as **—Concordances** or **—Indexes**:

Title: *Knighthood in the Morte D'Arthur* / Beverly Kennedy. 1992
SUBJECTS:
Malory, Thomas, Sir, 15th cent. Morte d'Arthur.
Arthurian romances—History and criticism.
Knights and knighthood in literature.

Title: *T. H. White's The once and future king* / Elisabeth Brewer. 1993
SUBJECTS:
White, T. H. (Terence Hanbury), 1906-1964. Once and future king.
Arthurian romances—Adaptations—History and criticism.

Title: *Sir Gawain and the Green Knight : sources and analogues* / compiled by Elisabeth Brewer. 1992
SUBJECTS:
Gawain and the Grene Knight—Sources.
Gawaine (Legendary character)—Romances—Sources.
Arthurian romances—Sources.
Literature, Medieval.

Title: *La Geste de Roland* / Robert Lafont. c1991
SUBJECTS:
Chanson de Roland.
Roland (Legendary character)—Romances—History and criticism.
Epic poetry, French—History and criticism.

Title: *Oaths, vows and promises in the first part of the French prose Lancelot romance* / Lisa Jefferson. c1993
SUBJECTS:
Lancelot (Prose romance)
Lancelot (Legendary character)—Romances—History and criticism.
Oaths in literature.
Vows in literature.
Promises in literature.

Title: *Tristan in the underworld : a study of Gottfried von Strass-
burg's Tristan together with the Tristan of Thomas* / Neil
Thomas. 1992
SUBJECTS:
Gottfried, von Strassburg, 13th cent. Tristan—Sources.
Thomas (Anglo-Norman poet). Tristan.
**Tristan (Legendary character)—Romances—History
and criticism.**
Arthurian romances—History and criticism.
Knights and knighthood in literature.

Title: *An annotated bibliography and study of the contemporary
criticism of Tennyson's Idylls of the king, 1859-1886* /
Aletha Andrew. c1993
SUBJECTS:
**Tennyson, Alfred Tennyson, Baron, 1809-1892. Idylls
of the king—Bibliography.**
**Tennyson, Alfred Tennyson, Baron, 1809-1892—Criticism
and interpretation—History.**
**Arthurian romances—Adaptations—History and
criticism—Bibliography.**

MUSIC

Types of Headings

Various types of headings are used in the subject cataloging of
music. Some represent music in general; others indicate various kinds
or aspects of music, such as genre, style, medium of performance,
ethnicity, musical form, and musical settings.

Current LC policies and practice regarding subject headings used
for music are discussed below.

Music Headings[25]

In the past, almost all music headings were printed in *Library of
Congress Subject Headings*. In the mid-1970s, the Library of Congress
established standard citation patterns for music headings with qualifiers
specifying instrumental or vocal parts. With these patterns, subject
catalogers could formulate such headings as required. From then on,
headings so constructed have been included in LCSH only when unique
cross references or subdivisions are required for them; thus, many valid
LC headings for music do not appear in the list. By category, these are:

- Headings for instrumental chamber music not entered under
  musical form

  Trios; Quartets; Quintets [etc.]
  Brass trios [etc.]

String trios [etc.]
Wind trios [etc.]
Woodwind trios [etc.]

- Headings for musical forms that take qualifiers for instrumental medium

Canons, fugues, etc.
Chaconnes
Chorale preludes
Marches
Minuets
Monologues with music
Overtures
Passacaglias
Polkas
Polonaises
Potpourris
Rondos
Sacred monologues with music
Sonatas
Suites
Symphonic poems
Symphonies
Trio sonatas
Variations
Waltzes

- Certain headings for vocal music

Choruses
Choruses, Sacred   } [qualified by number of vocal parts and accompanying medium]
Choruses, Secular

Songs   } [qualified by voice range and accompanying medium]
Sacred songs

When the headings in the categories listed above are qualified by instruments, the specified order of instruments is:[26]

(1) keyboard instruments

(2) wind instruments

(3) plectral instruments

(4) percussion and other instruments

(5) bowed stringed instruments

(6) unspecified instruments

(7) continuo

Instruments within each category are given in alphabetical order, with the exception of bowed string instruments, which are given in score order (e.g., **Violin, viola, violoncello, double bass**). The number of each instrument, if more than one, is indicated by an Arabic number enclosed in parentheses following the name of the instrument. However, the number of percussion players is not indicated.

Headings for duets do not always follow the same citation order. All headings for duets are enumerated in LCSH because USE references from the alternative form are required. Catalogers should consult LCSH for these headings.

Following are examples of headings formulated according to the established citation patterns:

> **Trios (Piano, clarinet, violoncello)**
> **Trios (Bass guitar, electric guitar, electronics)**
> **Quartets (Harpsichord, piano, harp, cimbalom)**
> **Octets (Recorder, percussion, violins (2), viola, violoncello, double bass)**
> **Octets (Bassoon, clarinet, horn, violins (2), viola, violoncello, double bass)**
> **Octets (Organ, horn, trombone, trumpets (2), tuba, percussion)**
> **Brass octets (Trombones (8)), Arranged—Scores and parts**
> **Brass quartets (Horn, trombone, trumpets (2))**
> **Wind octets (Bassoons (2), clarinets (2), horns (2), oboes (2))**
> **Overtures (Horns (2), trombones (2), trumpets (3), tuba)**
> **Suites (Bassoon, violins (2), viola, violoncello, double bass)**
> **Songs (High voice), Unaccompanied**
> **Choruses, Sacred (Mixed voices) with instrumental ensemble**
> **Choruses, Secular (Men's voices, 4 parts)**

Free-Floating Phrase Headings

The phrase heading **[Medium or form for instrumental music], Arranged** is free-floating, as in **Guitar music, Arranged; Waltzes (Saxophone and piano), Arranged; Violoncello and guitar music, Arranged**.

Free-Floating Subdivisions Under Pattern Headings[27]

Operas and **Piano** have been designated as pattern headings for subdivisions in the field of music. The heading **Operas** provides the pattern for musical compositions, including headings for form, medium, style, music for special seasons or occasions, musical settings of special texts, and the like, including **Concertos (Piano); Trios (Piano, flute, violin); Rock music; Easter music; Magnificat (Music)**. **Piano** serves as the pattern for musical instruments, either specific instruments or groups of instruments (e.g., **Flute; Wind instruments**). The free-floating subdivisions listed under **Piano** are not applicable to the general heading

Musical instruments. Lists of free-floating subdivisions used under the headings for musical compositions and musical instruments mentioned above appear in appendix C of this book.

Period Subdivisions[28]

The following period subdivisions are free-floating under headings for music compositions:

—To 500
—500-1400
—15th century
—16th century
—17th century
—18th century
—19th century
—20th century

Period subdivisions are used for textual works about music (including headings used solely for such works, e.g., **Choral music**; **Symphony**; **Concerto**) and collections of Western art music by two or more composers emphasizing a particular period. They are not used for: (1) a work in which a period is emphasized only in a series statement, (2) collections of compositions by only one composer, (3) separate music compositions, or (4) folk, popular, and non-Western music. Under headings for popular music, period subdivisions are individually established in LCSH.

When a collection of music has been assigned multiple headings, period subdivisions are used only under those headings that refer to the works of two or more composers.

The period subdivision is placed after the geographic subdivision and before other free-floating subdivisions:

Music—France—Nice—19th century—History and criticism
Choruses with orchestra—20th century—Bibliography
Choruses—20th century—Bibliography
Songs—Austria—19th century—History and criticism
Symphonies—18th century—Bibliography
Symphonies—19th century—Thematic catalogs

Topical Headings with Subdivisions Indicating Music

In addition to the music headings discussed above, other topical headings with music subdivisions are also used in cataloging music. Examples of such headings are:

Catholic Church—United States—Hymns
Marriage—Songs and music

Narcotic habit—Songs and music
Pound, Ezra, 1885-1972—Musical settings
Tipperary (Ireland : County)—Songs and music
Vietnamese Conflict, 1961-1975—Songs and music

Application

Works in the field of music may be divided into two broad categories: (1) music scores and texts and (2) works about music. As in the field of literature, specimens and works *about* the subject are treated differently in subject cataloging.

Music Scores and Texts

Works containing scores and texts, including instrumental and vocal music, are assigned form headings (i.e., headings that describe what the works *are* rather than what the works are *about*) as appropriate.

Instrumental Music

For instrumental music, subject headings bring out the following aspects: musical form (e.g., **Canons, fugues, etc.**; **Overtures**; **Sonatas**; **Symphonies**), medium of performance (e.g., **Guitar music**; **Hu ch'in music**; **Piano music**), and performing group (e.g., **Trios**; **Octets**; **String quartets**; **Woodwind septets**; **Band music**; **Orchestral music**). Other topical headings with music subdivisions are also assigned as appropriate. Examples include:

Title: *Fantasia para guitarra y arpa* / Xavier Montsalvatge. c1990
 SUBJECTS:
 Guitar and harp music—Scores.

Title: *The second collection of pieces for the harpsichord* / taken from different works of F. Geminiani, and adapted by himself to that instrument. [1993?]
 SUBJECTS:
 Harpsichord music, Arranged.

Title: *Conversation : between mandolin & viola* / Eileen Pakenham. c1990
 SUBJECTS:
 Viola and mandolin music—Scores and parts.

Title: *Werke für zwei Klaviere* / W. A. Mozart ; nach den Autographen, Abschriften, und Erstausgaben herausgegeben von Wolf-Dieter Seiffert ; mit Ergänzungen und einer Übertragung von Franz Beyer ; Fingersatz [von] Andreas Groethuysen. 1992

SUBJECTS:

Piano music (Pianos (2))—Scores.

Title: *Sonata in G major, K. 301 for cello and piano* / Mozart ; [transcribed and edited by] Valter Dešpalj, Arbo Valdma. c1991

SUBJECTS:

Sonatas (Violoncello and piano), Arranged—Scores and parts.

Title: *The piano concertos* / Frederic Chopin ; arranged for two pianos ; piano arrangement by Jerzy Lefeld. 1993

SUBJECTS:

Concertos (Piano)—2-piano scores.

Title: *Sonate sei per chiesa e da camera : a tre per due violini e basso continuo* / Leopold Mozart ; nach der Erstausgabe (1740) neu herausgegeben und mit Continuobegleitung versehen von Georg Steinschaden. c1991

SUBJECTS:

Trio sonatas (Violins (2), continuo)—Scores and parts.

Title: *Sonata in D major, K. 381 for 4 cellos* / Mozart ; [transcribed and edited by] Valter Dešpalj. c1991

SUBJECTS:

String quartets (Violoncellos (4)), Arranged—Scores and parts.

Title: *Harmonie in D, 2 oboes, 2 clarinets (A), 2 horns (D) & 2 bassoons* / Joseph Anton Steffan ; edited by David J. Rhodes. c1993

SUBJECTS:

Wind octets (Bassoons (2), clarinets (2), horns (2), oboes (2))—Scores.

Title: *Streichquintettsatz in a-Moll für zwei Violinen, zwei Violen und Violoncello, K.V. Anhang 79 (515c)* / Wolfgang Amadeus Mozart ; erganzt und herausgegeben von Franz Beyer. 1992?, c1989.

SUBJECTS:

String quintets (Violins (2), violas (2), violoncello)—Scores and parts.

Title: *Musik für Streichorchester oder Streichquintett* / Dietrich
   Erdmann. c1992
   SUBJECTS:
   Erdmann, Dietrich—Manuscripts—Facsimiles.
   String-orchestra music—Scores.
   **String quintets (Violins (2), viola, violoncello, double
      bass)—Scores.**
   Music—Manuscripts—Facsimiles.

Title: *Images ; Jeux ; and, The martyrdom of St. Sebastian. Suite* /
   Claude Debussy. 1992
   SUBJECTS:
   Orchestral music—Scores.
   Ballets—Scores.
   Suites (Orchestra)—Scores.
   Incidental music—Excerpts—Scores.

Vocal Music

For vocal music, headings that bring out the form, voice range,
number of vocal parts, and accompanying medium are used.[29] Typical
headings for vocal music are:

- Secular vocal music

   Ballads
   Cantatas, Secular (Equal voices)
   Choruses, Secular (Men's voices) with accordion
   Madrigals
   Operas
   Part-songs
   Polyphonic chansons
   Polyphonic lieder
   Song cycles
   Songs
      [also headings for various kinds of songs, e.g., **Children's
         songs; War songs**]
   Vocal trios, Unaccompanied

- Sacred vocal music

   Cantatas, Sacred (Women's voices)
   Carols
   Chants
   Chorales
   Choruses, Sacred (Mixed voices, 4 parts) with organ
   Hymns
   Masses
   Motets
   Oratorios
   Part-songs, Sacred

> Psalms (Music)
> Requiems (Unison)
> Sacred songs (Medium voice) with harpsichord
> Vespers (Music)

Following are examples of subject headings assigned to works containing vocal music:

Title: *Il trovatore* / Giuseppe Verdi ; libretto by Salvatore Cammarano, based on the play El trovador by Antonio Garcia Gutierrez. 1994
SUBJECTS:
Operas—Scores.

Title: *The anvil chorus : [from] Il trovatore* / music by Giuseppe Verdi ; [arranged by Greg Pliska ; edited by David Dik]. 1993
SUBJECTS:
Choruses, Secular (Women's voices, 2 parts) with instrumental ensemble.
Operas—Excerpts—Vocal scores with piano.

Title: *Can you love? : soprano and baritone* / music by Leonard Bernstein ; lyric by Alan Jay Lerner; [edited by Erik Haagensen]. 1993
SUBJECTS:
Vocal duets with piano.

Title: *James Joyce's Chamber music : the lost song settings* / [musical settings by G. Molyneux Palmer ; foreword by Harry Levin ; musical foreword by Robert White] ; edited and with an introduction by Myra Teicher Russel. c1993
SUBJECTS:
Songs (High voice) with piano.

Title: *The Southern harmony & musical companion : containing a choice collection of tunes, hymns, psalms, odes, and anthems, selected from the most eminent authors in the United States and well adapted to Christian churches of every denomination, singing schools, and private societies : with a musical anthology on compact disc* / [compiled] by William Walker ; edited by Glenn C. Wilcox. [1993]
SUBJECTS:
Hymns, English.
Psalms (Music)
Anthems.
Tune-books.
Choruses, Sacred (Mixed voices), Unaccompanied.
Shape note hymnals.

Whenever appropriate, topical headings with music subdivisions are assigned in addition to the music headings discussed above.

Title: *The dimension of stillness : 1988 : quartet for soprano, flute, cello and guitar* / Lars Hegaard ; [text], Ezra Pound, "Canto 49". c1991.
SUBJECTS:
Songs (High voice) with instrumental ensemble—Scores.
Pound, Ezra, 1885-1972—Musical settings.

Title: *Beginnings : for solo voice and piano or chamber orchestra* / text by Eudora Welty ; music by Luigi Zaninelli. c1992
SUBJECTS:
Songs (High voice) with chamber orchestra—Vocal scores with piano.
Welty, Eudora, 1909- —Musical settings.

Title: *The perfect rose : a Christmas cantata* / by John Leavitt ; text by Phil Speary. c1993.
SUBJECTS:
Cantatas, Sacred—Scores.
Christmas music.
Speary, Phil—Musical settings.

Title: *Windsongs : poetry by children at Terezin, Czechoslovakia, who were prisoners of the Nazis in the concentration camp of Thereisienstadt i.e. Theresienstadt : song cycle for voice and piano* / by Larry Zimmerman. c1992.
SUBJECTS:
Song cycles.
Songs with piano.
**Terezin (Czech Republic : Concentration camp)
—Poetry—Musical settings.**
Holocaust, Jewish (1939-1945)—Czech Republic—Songs and music.
World War, 1939-1945—Children—Czech Republic —Songs and music.

Title: *Tears, idle tears : for soprano, bassoon, and piano* / by Willard Elliot ; from the poem of Alfred, Lord Tennyson. c1990.
SUBJECTS:
Songs (High voice) with instrumental ensemble— Scores and parts.
Tennyson, Alfred Tennyson, Baron, 1809-1892—Musical settings.

Title: *American Catholic hymnbook : a new edition of The Johannine hymnal, in memory of Pope John XXIII.* c1992
SUBJECTS:
Catholic Church—United States—Hymns.
Hymns, English.

Title: *Jesu meine Freude* / Buxtehude ; prepared by Robert Illing. c1992
SUBJECTS:
Cantatas, Sacred—Scores and parts.
Franck, Johann—Musical settings.

Title: *Santa Beatrice d'Este : Vienna, 1707* / Camilla de Rossi, musica ; Cardinal Benedetto Pamphili, poesia ; edited and translated by Barbara Garvey Jackson. c1993
SUBJECTS:
Beatrice I, d'Este, 1206-1226—Songs and music.
Oratorios—Scores.

Sound Recordings

Sound recordings of music are treated in the same manner as other musical works. No special subdivisions are used to bring out the format:

Title: *Cembalo Konzerte ; Sinfonia* [sound recording] / Wilhelm Friedemann Bach. [1990?]
SUBJECTS:
Concertos (Harpsichord with string orchestra)
Symphonies.

Title: *Black gipsy 1927 / 1941* [sound recording]. p1993.
SUBJECTS:
Jazz.
Violin music (Jazz)

Title: *Jelly's last jam* [sound recording]. p1992.
SUBJECTS:
Morton, Jelly Roll, d. 1941—Biography.
Musicals.
Jazz.

Title: *Scandinavian suite* [sound recording]. p1991.
SUBJECTS:
Suites (String orchestra)
Suites (String orchestra), Arranged.
String-orchestra music.

Title: *Rural voices* [sound recording]. 1990
SUBJECTS:
Rural development—Wisconsin.
Wisconsin—Songs and music.

Title: *Popular Gipsy melodies* [sound recording] = *Beliebte Zigeunerweisen.* p1992
SUBJECTS:
Gypsies—Hungary—Music.
Popular instrumental music—Hungary.

Title: *Le reniement de saint Pièrre* [sound recording] ; *Méditations pour le Carême* / Marc-Antoine Charpentier. p1993
SUBJECTS:
Oratorios.
Motets.
Choruses, Sacred (Men's voices, 3 parts), Unaccompanied.
Lenten music.
Peter, the Apostle, Saint—Songs and music.

Title: *Quattro cantate da camera* [sound recording] / Giovan Battista Pergolesi. p1993
SUBJECTS:
Solo cantatas, Secular (High voice) with continuo.
Solo cantatas, Secular (High voice) with instrumental ensemble.

If a recording contains works in more than one form, separate headings are assigned to represent the forms of individual works:

Title: *Flute sonata ; Woodwind quintet no. 1 ; Quartet for piano and winds* [sound recording] / Robert Baksa. 1991
SUBJECTS:
Sonatas (Flute and piano)
Wind quintets (Bassoon, clarinet, flute, horn, oboe)
Quartets (Piano, bassoon, clarinet, oboe)

Title: *Piano quintet in G minor ; String quartet no. 2 in E minor* [sound recording] / Arnold Bax. p1990
SUBJECTS:
Piano quintets.
String quartets.

Dance Music

A work containing music for a specific dance form is assigned a heading for the name of the dance form. Previously, headings for dance forms were qualified with names of instruments when appropriate. Currently, headings for dance forms (with the exception of **Minuets;**

312 / 10—Subject Areas Requiring Special Treatment

Polkas; **Polonaises**; and **Waltzes**) are no longer qualified. Additional headings may be assigned for the medium and other aspects or topics.

> Title: *Andante, Variationen und Bolero : für Flöte und Orchester* / Peter Joseph von Lindpaintner ; herausgegeben von Dieter H. Förster. c1992
> SUBJECTS:
> **Variations (Flute with orchestra)—Scores.**
> **Boleros.**

> Title: *Mazurek, op. 39, für Violine und Klavier* / Antonin Dvorak ; herausgegeben von Klaus Doge. c1992
> SUBJECTS:
> **Violin and piano music—Scores.**
> **Mazurkas.**

Examples of exceptions are:

> Title: *Opera overtures* [sound recording] / Stanisław Moniuszko. p1993
> SUBJECTS:
> **Overtures.**
> **Polonaises (Orchestra)**
> **Mazurkas.**
> **Operas—Excerpts.**

> Title: *International Chopin piano competitions* [sound recording] : *best polonaise performances.* p1990
> SUBJECTS:
> **Polonaises (Piano)**

> Title: *The rootbeer barrel polka : for string orchestra, piano, and percussion* / by John O'Neill. c1992
> SUBJECTS:
> **Polkas (String orchestra)—Juvenile—Scores and parts.**

> Title: *Polkas and waltzes for accordion : Slovenian style* / written by George Staiduhar. c1991
> SUBJECTS:
> **Polkas (Accordion)**
> **Waltzes (Accordion)**

> Title: *Tioga waltz : for flute quartet or flute choir* / by Steven i.e. Stephen Foster ; arranged by Janice Boland. c1993
> SUBJECTS:
> **Waltzes (Flutes (4))—Scores and parts.**

Title: *Twilight waltzes : solos for pedal harp* / by Nancy Gustavson.
c1993
SUBJECTS:
Waltzes (Harp)

Music of Ethnic and National Groups[30]

The following types of headings are assigned to works that consist of the music of ethnic groups, music that has a national emphasis, and non-Western art music:

[Ethnic or national group]—[Place]—Music
[Headings for musical genre or style, or for ballads and
songs with national emphasis]
[Headings for language, i.e., Ballads, Folk songs, or **Songs**
with language qualifier]
Musical instruments—[Place]
[Other topical headings, as applicable]

The first two types of headings are assigned to a work of music wherever possible; the others are assigned as appropriate. Examples include:

Title: *La Perla de Cadiz* [sound recording]. 1992
SUBJECTS:
Folk songs, Spanish—Spain—Andalusia.
Folk music—Spain—Andalusia.
Flamenco music.

Title: *Alhucema* / [creación y escenografía] Salvador Tavora ;
[música, Vicente Sanchis, Salvador Távora]. 1991
SUBJECTS:
Revues—Spain—Andalusia—Librettos.
Folk music—Spain—Andalusia.

Title: *Navajo songs from Canyon de Chelly* [sound recording]. 1990
SUBJECTS:
Navajo Indians—Music.
Folk music—Arizona.

Title: *Navajo songs* [sound recording] / recorded by Laura Boulton
in 1933 and 1940. p1992
SUBJECTS:
Navajo Indians—Music.
Folk songs, Navajo.

For works consisting of the texts of ballads, folk songs, or songs of ethnic groups, a heading in the form of **[Heading with language qualifier]—Texts** is used.

Works About Music

Works about music are assigned topical headings that reflect the subject content of the works. The subdivision —**Instruction and study** is used with headings for musical compositions and instruments instead of —**Study and teaching**, and —**History and criticism** instead of —**History** for musical compositions.

Following are examples of works about music:

Title: *Living sounds : a music appreciation anthology* / [edited by] Stephen Schultz. c1993
SUBJECTS:
Music appreciation.

Title: *The joy of music* / Leonard Bernstein. 1994
SUBJECTS:
Music—History and criticism.

Title: *The symphony* / Preston Stedman. c1992
SUBJECTS:
Symphony.

Title: *The early flute* / by John Solum. 1992
SUBJECTS:
Flute.
Flute music—Bibliography.

Title: *Ensemble! : a rehearsal guide to thirty great works of chamber music* / by Abram Loft ; Reinhard G. Pauly, general editor. c1992
SUBJECTS:
Chamber music—Analysis, appreciation.

Title: *Walls of circumstance : studies in nineteenth-century music* / by Eric Frederick Jensen. 1992
SUBJECTS:
Music—19th century—History and criticism.

Title: *Western plainchant : an introduction* / David Hiley. 1993
SUBJECTS:
Chants (Plain, Gregorian, etc.)—History and criticism.

Title: *The Cambridge companion to the violin* / edited by Robin Stowell. 1992
SUBJECTS:
Violin.
Violin music—History and criticism.

Title: *Mandolin music in America : 3800 pieces for mandolin and where to find them* / ed., Joshua Bell. c1993
SUBJECTS:
Mandolin music—Bibliography.
Chamber music—Bibliography.
Instrumental music—Bibliography.
Music—United States—Bibliography.

Title: *El bolero : historia de un amor* / Iris M. Zavala. c1991
SUBJECTS:
Boleros—History and criticism.
Popular music—Latin America—Texts.

Title: *Woodwind anthology : a compendium of woodwind articles from the Instrumentalist.* 1992
SUBJECTS:
Woodwind instruments—Instruction and study.

Title: *Romantic music : sound and syntax* / Leonard G. Ratner. 1992
SUBJECTS:
Music—19th century—History and criticism.
Romanticism in music.
Musical analysis.

Title: *The Who in print : an annotated bibliography, 1965 through 1990* / by Stephen Wolter and Karen Kimber. 1992
SUBJECTS:
Who (Musical group)—Bibliography.
Rock musicians—England—Bibliography.

Title: *Saxophone recital music : a discography* / compiled by Stanley L. Schleuter. 1993
SUBJECTS:
Saxophone music—Discography.
Chamber music—Discography.

Works About the Music of Ethnic and National Groups

Works about the music of ethnic and national groups, and about their musical instruments, are assigned the same headings that are used for the music itself, with the addition of subdivisions such as **—History and criticism;**[31] **—Bibliography; —Discography:**

Title: *The twist : the story of the song that changed the world* / Jim Dawson. [1995]
SUBJECTS:
Popular music—United States—1961-1970—History and criticism.

Twist (Dance).
Afro-Americans—Music—History and criticism.

Title: *Wade in the water : the wisdom of the spirituals* / Arthur C.
Jones. c1993
SUBJECTS:
Spirituals (Songs)—History and criticism.
Afro-Americans—Music—History and criticism.

Title: *Musica y tradiciones populares* / Antonio Vallejo Cisneros.
1990
SUBJECTS:
Folk music—Spain—Mancha—History and criticism.

Title: *Traditional Anglo-American folk music : an annotated dis-
cography of published sound recordings* / Norm Cohen.
1994
SUBJECTS:
Folk music—United States—Discography.
Folk songs, English—United States—Discography.

Title: *Northward bound : the Mexican immigrant experience in
ballad and song* / Maria Herrera-Sobek. c1993
SUBJECTS:
Mexican Americans—Music—History and criticism.
Folk songs, Spanish—United States—History and
criticism.
Folk music—United States—History and criticism.
Folk music—Mexico—History and criticism.

Works About Individual Composers and Musicians

Personal name headings and biographical (class-of-persons) headings are assigned to works about the lives, or lives and works, of
individual composers or musicians, in accordance with the general
guidelines for biography (see the discussion on pages 243-46).

Title: *Beethoven : his life, work and world* / compiled and edited by
H. C. Robbins Landon. 1993
SUBJECTS:
Beethoven, Ludwig van, 1770-1827.
Composers—Austria—Biography.

Title: *The memory of all that : the life of George Gershwin* / Joan
Peyser. c1993
SUBJECTS:
Gershwin, George, 1898-1937.
Composers—United States—Biography.

Title: *Leonard Bernstein : a life* / by Meryle Secrest. 1994
SUBJECTS:
Bernstein, Leonard, 1918-
Musicians—United States—Biography.

Title: *Elton John* / Philip Norman. 1993
SUBJECTS:
John, Elton.
Rock musicians—England—Biography.

Title: *Hammerstein and Lerner : the great wordsmiths* / Stephen
Citron. 1995
SUBJECTS:
Hammerstein, Oscar, 1895-1960.
Lerner, Alan Jay, 1918-
Librettists—United States—Biography.

Headings for names of musicians and composers may be subdivided by
the free-floating subdivisions used under names of persons. (A list of
these free-floating subdivisions is given in appendix E.)

Title: *The Beethoven encyclopedia : his life and art from A to Z* / by
Paul Nettl. 1994
SUBJECTS:
Beethoven, Ludwig van, 1770-1827—Encyclopedias.

Title: *Madonna, the early days : 65 classic photographs of Madonna
and friends* / Michael McKenzie. c1993
SUBJECTS:
Madonna, 1959- —Portraits.
Rock musicians—United States—Portraits.

Title: *Mozart in Belgien : ein Wunderkind unterwegs durch die
Südlichen Niederlande, 1763-1766* / herausgegeben von Fons
de Haas und Irène Smets ; Pieter Andriessen . . . [et al.] ; mit
einem Vorwort von Gerard Mortier ; [Übersetzung, Hans
Jurgen Terjung]. c1990
SUBJECTS:
**Mozart, Wolfgang Amadeus, 1756-1791—Childhood
and youth.**
Music—Belgium—18th century—History and criticism.

Title: *Mozart Briefe : mit zahlreichen Abbildungen* / neu ausgewählt,
eingeleitet und kommentiert von Wolfgang Hildesheimer.
1991
SUBJECTS:
Mozart, Wolfgang Amadeus, 1756-1791—Correspondence.
Composers—Austria—Correspondence.

More specific subdivisions are provided for special topics under headings for composers:

   —**Appreciation**
   —**Discography**
   —**Harmony**
   —**Performances**
   —**Stories, plots, etc.**
   —**Thematic catalogs**

Examples are:

   Title: *Mozart & posterity* / Gernot Gruber ; translated by R. S. Furness. 1994
   SUBJECTS:
   Mozart, Wolfgang Amadeus, 1756-1791—Appreciation.

   Title: *The complete Elton John discography* / by John DiStefano ; with additional research by Peter Dobbins. c1993
   SUBJECTS:
   John, Elton—Discography.

   Title: *Thematisch-systematisches Verzeichnis der musikalischen Werke von Johann Sebastian Bach : Bach-Werke-Verzeichnis (BWV)* / herausgegeben von Wolfgang Schmieder. 1990
   SUBJECTS:
   Bach, Johann Sebastian, 1685-1750—Thematic catalogs.

If the work does not pertain to the personal life of the composer or musician, the biographical heading (**[Class of persons]—Biography**) is not assigned:

   Title: *Wolfgang Amade Mozart* / Georg Knepler ; translated by J. Bradford Robinson. 1994
   SUBJECTS:
   Mozart, Wolfgang Amadeus, 1756-1791—Criticism and interpretation.
   [for a comprehensive discussion or criticism]

   Title: *The music of Chopin* / Jim Samson. 1994
   SUBJECTS:
   Chopin, Frederic, 1810-1849—Criticism and interpretation.

   Title: *Aspects of Verdi* / George Martin. 1993
   SUBJECTS:
   Verdi, Giuseppe, 1813-1901—Criticism and interpretation.

Works About Individual Musical Works[32]

Name-title headings are assigned to works about individual musical compositions. Other music or topical headings are assigned as appropriate:

Title: *Haydn, string quartets, op. 50* / W. Dean Sutcliffe. 1992
SUBJECTS:
 Haydn, Joseph, 1732-1809. Quartets, strings, H. III, 44-49.

Title: *Schumann, Fantasie, op. 17* / Nicholas Marston. 1992
SUBJECTS:
 Schumann, Robert, 1810-1856. Fantasie, piano, op. 17, C major.

Title: *Wolfgang Amadeus Mozart, Klavierkonzert D-Dur KV 451* / Rudolf Bockholdt. c1991
SUBJECTS:
 Mozart, Wolfgang Amadeus, 1756-1791. Concertos, piano, orchestra, K. 451, D major.

Title: *Culture and the creative imagination : the genesis of Gustav Mahler's Third symphony* / Morten Solvik Olsen. 1992
SUBJECTS:
 Mahler, Gustav, 1860-1911. Symphonies, no. 3, D minor.
 Symphonies—Analysis, appreciation.

Title: *Tosca* / volume a cura di Achille Bonito Oliva. [c1990]
SUBJECTS:
 Puccini, Giacomo, 1858-1924. Tosca.
 Opera programs.
 Operas—Librettos.

Title: *De opera "Die Zauberflöte" van Mozart : het libretto verklaard uit de geest der muziek* / F. de Graaff. c1990
SUBJECTS:
 Mozart, Wolfgang Amadeus, 1756-1791. Zauberflöte.
 Operas—Librettos.

Title: *The magic flute unveiled : esoteric symbolism in Mozart's masonic opera : an interpretation of the libretto and the music* / Jacques Chailley. 1992
SUBJECTS:
 Mozart, Wolfgang Amadeus, 1756-1791. Zauberflöte.
 Mozart, Wolfgang Amadeus, 1756-1791—Symbolism.

For a work about the compositions by one composer in a specific form or medium, a heading in the form of [**Name of composer. Subheading**] is used:

Title: *Hugo Wolf : the vocal music* / Susan Youens. 1992
SUBJECTS:
Wolf, Hugo, 1860-1903. Vocal music.
Vocal music—19th century—History and criticism.

Title: *Edvard Grieg, chamber music : nationalism, universality, individuality* / Finn Benestad and Dag Schjelderup-Ebbe. c1993
SUBJECTS:
Grieg, Edvard, 1843-1907. Chamber music.
Chamber music—Analysis, appreciation.

Title: *The Beethoven sonatas and the creative experience* / Kenneth Drake. c1994
SUBJECTS:
Beethoven, Ludwig van, 1770-1827. Sonatas, piano.
Sonatas (Piano)—Analysis, appreciation.

Title: *Formale Aspekte des ersten Allegros in Mozarts Konzerten* / von Konrad Küster. 1991
SUBJECTS:
Mozart, Wolfgang Amadeus, 1756-1791. Concertos.
Concertos—Analysis, appreciation.

Title: *The Cambridge companion to Chopin* / edited by Jim Samson. 1992
SUBJECTS:
Chopin, Frederic, 1810-1849—Criticism and interpretation.
Chopin, Frederic, 1810-1849. Piano music.

Title: *Mozarts Kirchenmusik* / Harald Schützeichel (Hg.) ; mit Beiträgen von Martin Haselböck . . . [et al.]. 1992
SUBJECTS:
Mozart, Wolfgang Amadeus, 1756-1791. Vocal music—Congresses.
Church music—Austria—18th century—Congresses.

Title: *The Verdi baritone : studies in the development of dramatic character* / Geoffrey Edwards and Ryan Edwards. c1994
SUBJECTS:
Verdi, Giuseppe, 1813-1901. Operas.
Verdi, Giuseppe, 1813-1901—Dramaturgy.

The subheading used after the name of the composer corresponds to the uniform title used in cataloging the music of individual composers according to *Anglo-American Cataloguing Rules*, 2nd edition, 1988 revision (*AACR2R*).[33] Examples of authorized subheadings used in subject cataloging include:

- Subheadings for general and specific mediums of performance

  Brass music
  Chamber music
  Choral music
  Instrumental music
  Keyboard music
  Orchestra music
  Piano music
  String quartet music
  Violin, piano music
  Vocal music

- Subheadings for types of compositions with qualifiers for medium, as appropriate

  Concertos
  Operas
  Overtures
  Polonaises, piano
  Quartets
  Quartets, strings
  Sonatas
  Sonatas, violin, piano
  Songs
  Symphonies

FINE ARTS[34]

At the Library of Congress, a distinction is made between the "fine" arts and the "useful" or "decorative" arts. Works in the fields of fine arts receive certain special treatment, while those pertaining to decorative arts (with the exception of works related to bronzes, porcelain, and pottery) are assigned headings according to general LC practice.[35] The following discussion focuses on the treatment of fine arts.

Types of Headings

The following types of subject headings are assigned to represent various topics or aspects of art:

[Name of artist or Group of artists]
[Art form], [National, ethnic, or religious background]
   —[Place of origin]

[Art form with period qualifier and/or century subdivision]
    —[Place of origin]
[Style, movement, etc.]—[Place of origin]
[Theme]
[Art form]—[Present location]
[Owner]
[Other headings as appropriate]

Form subdivisions are not used to bring out the fact that the work consists of photographic reproductions or illustrations of works of art.

Free-Floating Subdivisions

Many of the general free-floating subdivisions (see the discussion in chapter 5) may be used with art headings, with the exceptions noted in *Subject Cataloging Manual*. Some of the most commonly used subdivisions under headings for art or artists are:

—**Biography**
        [Free-floating only when used under headings for groups of
            people, e.g., Painters]
—**Catalogs**
        [For exhibition catalogs, the subdivision —**Exhibitions**
            rather than —**Catalogs** is used]
—**Collectors and collecting** *(May Subd Geog)*
—**Exhibitions**
—**Themes, motives**

Geographic Subdivisions[36]

In art headings, the concepts of national, ethnic, or religious background are normally expressed by national adjectives (e.g., **Painting, Italian**; **Painting, Japanese**), while the concept of the place where the art originates from or where the art is kept now is represented by geographic subdivisions (e.g., **Painting—Italy—Florence**; **Painting—Japan—Tokyo**). The two concepts of place may be combined in the same heading (e.g., **Painting, Italian—Italy—Florence**).

Period Subdivisions

Period subdivisions are provided under many of the art headings:

Art, Modern—20th century
Drawing—16th century
Painting, Modern—19th century
Engraving—14th century

These headings may be further subdivided by place to indicate the location of the art (e.g., **Art, Modern—20th century—United States; Engraving—16th century—Italy**).

Chronological subdivisions are not provided under fine art headings with ethnic, national, or religious qualifiers indicating the origin of the art, with the exception of headings for Oriental (Chinese, Japanese, and Korean) art. Examples include:

> **Art, Jewish**
> **Painting, American**
> **Engraving, English**
> **Art, Chinese—T'ang-Five dynasties, 618-960**
> **Painting, Japanese—Meiji period, 1868-1912**

Because period subdivisions are normally not free-floating and are editorially established, catalogers are advised to consult LCSH when considering period subdivisions of a given art heading.

Multiple headings are used to bring out various aspects when necessary. For example, for a work on eighteenth-century Italian painting in Rome, the following headings are used:

> **Painting, Italian—Italy—Rome**
> **Painting—18th century—Italy—Rome**

but,

> **Painting, Chinese—Ming-Ch'ing dynasties, 1368-1912— China—Peking**

Free Floating Phrase Headings

The phrase **. . . in art** may be combined with the following types of headings to form valid subject headings: **[Topic] in art**; **[Descriptive name** (*except personal name*) **heading in *AACR2R* form] in art**.[37] Examples include: **History in art**; **Birds in art**; **Cities and towns in art**; **New York (N.Y.) in art**.

Application

Subject headings assigned to works containing examples of art (normally in the form of photographic reproductions) and those assigned to works about art (appreciation, history, and criticism) are in the same form. The subdivision **—History** is used only for very general, all-inclusive works. The subdivision **—History and criticism** is not used with art headings.

If the work treats a particular kind of art with regard to a specific period and a special locality, two headings, one bringing out the period and the other the locality, are assigned:

Title: *Peindre à Paris au XVIIIe siècle* / Jean Chatelus. c1991
    SUBJECTS:
        Painting, French—France—Paris.
        Painting, Modern—17th-18th centuries—France—Paris.
        Art and society—France—Paris—History—18th century.

Works of Art By More Than One Artist Treated Collectively

Books or other materials containing reproductions of works of art by more than one artist, and books about such art, are assigned headings of the following types:[38]

    [Art form], [National, ethnic, or religious background]—
        [Place of origin]
    [Art form with period qualifier and/or century subdivision]—
        [Place of origin]
    [Style, movement, etc.]—[Place of origin]
    [Theme]
    [Art form]—[Present location]
    [Owner]
    [Other headings as appropriate]

Examples include:

Title: *Birds : an illustrated treasury* / compiled by Michelle Lovric.
       c1992
    SUBJECTS:
        Birds in art.
        Painting.

Title: *Landscape and power* / edited by W. J. T. Mitchell. 1994
    SUBJECTS:
        Landscape in art.
        Pastoral art.

Title: *The impressionists* / Steven Adams. 1990
    SUBJECTS:
        Impressionism (Art)—France.
        Painting, French.
        Painting, Modern—19th century—France.
        Impressionist artists—France—Biography.
        France—Intellectual life—19th century.

Place in Art[39]

A heading in the form of **[Place] in art** is assigned to a book consisting of reproductions of art works with a specific place as a theme and to a work discussing the treatment of a specific place in art. The phrase **[Place] in art** is free-floating.

Title: *Paintbrush in Paris : the artistic adventures of an American cat in Paris* / written and illustrated by Jill Butler. 1994
SUBJECTS:
Butler, Jill.
Paris (France) in art.

Title: *California's name : three WPA-sponsored murals* / by Lucile Lloyd. [1992]
SUBJECTS:
Lloyd, Lucile.
California in art.
Mural painting and decoration—20th century—California —Los Angeles.

Title: *Paintings of California* / edited by Arnold Skolnick ; introduction by Ilene Susan Fort. c1993
SUBJECTS:
California in art.
California—In literature.
Landscape painting, American.
Landscape painting—19th century—United States.
Landscape painting—20th century—United States.

A heading in the form of **[Place]—Pictorial works** is assigned to works consisting of photographs of a place, or of paintings made before the invention of photography that present views of a place.

Catalogs of Art Museums, Collections, and Exhibitions[40]

The catalog of an unnamed art collection that is permanently housed in an individual museum is assigned the following types of headings:

[Type of object]—Catalogs
[Type of object]—[Place]—Catalogs
[Name of museum]—Catalogs
[Type of object]—[Period subdivision]—[Place, if applicable]— Catalogs

Examples include:

Title: *La Gravure d'illustration en Alsace au XVIe siècle* / Bibliothèque nationale et universitaire de Strasbourg. 1992-
SUBJECTS:
Wood-engraving, French—France—Alsace—Catalogs.
Wood-engraving—16th century—France—Alsace—Catalogs.
Illustration of books—16th century—France—Alsace—Catalogs.

Title: *The new nineteenth-century European paintings and sculpture galleries* / by Gary Tintero. c1993
SUBJECTS:
Art, European—Catalogs.
Art, Modern—19th century—Europe—Catalogs.
Art—New York (N.Y.)—Catalogs.
Metropolitan Museum of Art (New York, N.Y.)—Catalogs.

Title: *German paintings of the fifteenth through seventeenth centuries* / John Oliver Hand with the assistance of Sally E. Mansfield. 1993
SUBJECTS:
Painting, German—Catalogs.
Painting, Renaissance—Germany—Catalogs.
Painting, Modern—17th-18th centuries—Germany—Catalogs.
Painting—Washington (D.C.)—Catalogs.
National Gallery of Art (U.S.)—Catalogs.

Title: *Sculpture in the Rijksmuseum Kroller-Muller : catalogue of the collection* / compiled and edited by Marianne Brouwer and Rieja Brouns ; [translation, Ruth Koenig]. 1992
SUBJECTS:
Sculpture, Modern—19th century—Catalogs.
Sculpture, Modern—20th century—Catalogs.
Sculpture—Netherlands—Amsterdam—Catalogs.
Rijksmuseum Kroller-Muller—Catalogs.

Title: *Catalogue of the Amon Carter Museum photography collection* / [compiled by] Carol E. Roark, Paula Ann Stewart, and Mary Kennedy McCabe. c1993
SUBJECTS:
Amon Carter Museum of Western Art—Photograph collections—Catalogs.
Photography, Artistic.

The subdivision —**Exhibitions** is used instead of —**Catalogs** for the catalog of an exhibition:

Title: *Crosscurrents : Americans in Paris, 1900-1940* / Ann Yaffe Phillips. 1993
SUBJECTS:
Art, American—Exhibitions.
Art, Modern—20th century—United States—Exhibitions.
Expatriate artists—France—Exhibitions.
Artists—United States—Exhibitions.

Title: *The artist as native : reinventing regionalism* / Alan Gussow ; John Driscoll, introduction ; and statements by fifty-three artists. c1993
SUBJECTS:
Regionalism in art—United States—Exhibitions.
Painting, American—Exhibitions.
Painting, Modern—20th century—United States—Exhibitions.

Title: *French master drawings from the Pierpont Morgan Library* / Cara Dufour Denison. c1993
SUBJECTS:
Drawing, French—Exhibitions.
Drawing—New York (N.Y.)—Exhibitions.
Pierpont Morgan Library—Exhibitions.

Title: *In the sculptor's landscape : celebrating twenty-five years of the Franklin D. Murphy Sculpture Garden* / edited by Cynthia Burlingham and Elizabeth Shepherd. c1993
SUBJECTS:
Sculpture, Modern—19th century—Exhibitions.
Sculpture, Modern—20th century—Exhibitions.
Sculpture—California—Los Angeles—Exhibitions.
Franklin D. Murphy Sculpture Garden—Exhibitions.

Private Art Collections

For catalogs of private art collections, including those that have been donated or sold to public institutions but are still known by their original names, the following types of headings are used in addition to the headings discussed above.

[Name of owner]—Art collections—Catalogs [or —Exhibitions]
[Topical or form heading]—Private collections [or another appropriate subdivision]—[Place]—Catalogs [or —Exhibitions]

Examples include:

Title: *Four icons in the Menil Collection* / edited by Bertrand
    Davezac. 1992
  SUBJECTS:
    Icons, Byzantine—Themes, motives.
    Christian saints in art.
    Uspenie (Icon)
    Mary, Blessed Virgin, Saint—Art.
    Icons, Russian—Themes, motives.
    Orthodox Eastern Church and art.
    Menil Collection (Houston, Tex.)

Title: *Looking for Leonardo : native and folk art objects found in
    America by Bates and Isabel Lowry* / text by Bates Lowry.
    c1993
  SUBJECTS:
    Outsider art—United States—Catalogs.
    Folk art—United States—Catalogs.
    Lowry, Bates, 1923- —Art collections—Catalogs.
    Lowry, Isabel—Art collections—Catalogs.
    **Outsider art—Private collections—United States—
      Catalogs.**

Title: *A catalogue of the Devonshire Collection of European drawings
    before 1800* / Michael Jaffe. 1993
  SUBJECTS:
    Drawing, European—Catalogs.
    **Devonshire, Andrew Robert Buxton Cavendish, Duke
      of, 1920- —Art collections—Catalogs.**
    **Drawing—Private collections—England—Derbyshire—
      Catalogs.**
    Chatsworth (England)—Catalogs.

Title: *Splendid legacy : the Havemeyer collection* / Alice Cooney
    Frelinghuysen . . . [et al.] ; with contributions by Maryan
    W. Ainsworth . . . [et al.]. c1993
  SUBJECTS:
    **Havemeyer, Henry Osborne, 1847-1907—Art collec-
      tions—Catalogs.**
    **Havemeyer, Louisine Waldron Elder—Art collections—
      Catalogs.**
    Art—Private collections—New York (N.Y.)—Catalogs.
    Art—New York (N.Y.)—Catalogs.
    Metropolitan Museum of Art (New York, N.Y.)—Catalogs.

Title: *Pathways to the Afterlife : early Chinese art from the Sze
    Hong Collection* / Julia M. White, Ronald Y. Otsuka. 1993
  SUBJECTS:
    Art, Chinese—To 221 B.C.—Catalogs.

Art, Chinese—Ch'in-Han dynasties, 221 B.C.-220
A.D.—Catalogs.
Art, Chinese—Three kingdoms-Sui dynasty, 220-618—
Catalogs.
Art, Chinese—T'ang-Five dynasties, 618-960—Catalogs.
King, Warren—Art collections—Catalogs.
King, Shirley—Art collections—Catalogs.
Art—Private collections—Colorado—Denver—Catalogs.

Title: *The Dutch and Flemish drawings in the collection of Her
Majesty the Queen at Windsor Castle* / Christopher White
and Charlotte Crawley. 1994
SUBJECTS:
Drawing, Dutch—Catalogs.
Drawing, Flemish—Catalogs.
Elizabeth II, Queen of Great Britain, 1926-   —Art
collections—Catalogs.
Drawing—England—Windsor (Berkshire)—Catalogs.
Windsor Castle. Royal Library—Catalogs.

Works By and About Individual Artists

Works containing reproductions of an artist's works (with main
entry or added entry under the artist's name) and works about an
individual artist's work (with main entry other than the artist) are
assigned a subject heading under the name of the artist, regardless of
the main or added entry. The artist's name may be subdivided by the
free-floating subdivisions used under names of persons (see appendix
E) in order to bring out other aspects of the work. Additional headings
are assigned to bring out style or movement, theme, location, and
ownership. Examples include:

Title: *Poussin's paintings : a study in art-historical methodology* /
David Carrier. c1993
SUBJECTS:
Poussin, Nicolas, 1594?-1665—Criticism and
interpretation.
Classicism in art—France.

Title: *Goya, la decada de los Caprichos : retratos, 1792-1804* / Nigel
Glendinning. 1992
SUBJECTS:
Goya, Francisco, 1746-1828—Exhibitions.
Nobility—Spain—Portraits—Exhibitions.

Title: *Monet paintings.* c1992
SUBJECTS:
Monet, Claude, 1840-1926—Catalogs.
Miniature books—Catalogs.

Title: *Reaching for the sky : New York, 1928-1932 : drawings and prints* / Mark Freeman. c1992
SUBJECTS:
Freeman, Mark, 1908-   —Catalogs.
New York (N.Y.) in art—Catalogs.

Title: *Expressions of place : the art of William Stanley Haseltine* / Marc Simpson, Andrea Henderson, Sally Mills. 1992
SUBJECTS:
Haseltine, William Stanley, 1835-1900—Exhibitions.
Landscape in art—Exhibitions.
ADDED ENTRIES:
Haseltine, William Stanley, 1835-1900.

Title: *Remington & Russell : the Sid Richardson collection* / by Brian W. Dippie. 1994
SUBJECTS:
Remington, Frederic, 1861-1909—Catalogs.
Russell, Charles M. (Charles Marion), 1864-1926—Catalogs.
West (U.S.) in art—Catalogs.
Richardson, Sid, 1891-1959—Art collections—Catalogs.
Art—Private collections—Catalogs.

Title: *Max Beckmann prints from the Museum of Modern Art* / James L. Fisher. 1992
SUBJECTS:
Beckmann, Max, 1884-1950—Exhibitions.
Museum of Modern Art (New York, N.Y.)—Exhibitions.

A biography of an individual artist is assigned a personal name heading without the subdivision **—Biography** and one or more biographical headings:

Title: *Manet* / Patricia Wright. 1993
SUBJECTS:
Manet, Edouard, 1832-1883.
Painters—France—Biography.

Title: *My fourscore years : autobiography* / by sculptor Thomas Ball ; epilogue by Greta Elena Couper. 1993
SUBJECTS:
Ball, Thomas, 1819-1911.
Sculptors—United States—Biography.

Title: *Manet by himself : correspondence & conversation, paintings, pastels, prints & drawings* / edited by Juliet Wilson-Bareau. c1991
SUBJECTS:
Manet, Edouard, 1832-1883—Correspondence.

Painters—France—Correspondence.
Manet, Edouard, 1832-1883—Interviews.
Painters—France—Interviews.

The biographical heading is not assigned to a work containing reproductions of an artist's works unless the work contains substantial information (at least 50 percent of the text) about the artist's personal life:

Title: *Salvador Dalí, das Rätsel der Begierde* / Einführung von Wieland Schmied. 1991
SUBJECTS:
Dalí, Salvador, 1904-1989.

Works About Individual Works of Art

The following types of headings are assigned to works discussing individual works of art:

[Name of artist. English title of work]
[Vernacular title of work] ([Type of art])
  {for a work by an unknown artist}
[Heading for style, movement, theme, etc.]

Examples of works about individual works of art include:

Title: *Auguste Rodin : die Burger von Calais : eine Kunst-Monographie* / von Roland Bothner. 1993
SUBJECTS:
Rodin, Auguste, 1840-1917. Burghers of Calais.
ADDED ENTRIES:
Rodin, Auguste, 1840-1917.

Title: *La Mona Lisa : una fascinante historia* / Eulalio Ferrer Rodriguez. c1990
SUBJECTS:
Leonardo, da Vinci, 1452-1519. Mona Lisa.
Leonardo, da Vinci, 1452-1519—Influence.

Title: *Manet, the execution of Maximilian : painting, politics, and censorship* / Juliet Wilson-Bareau ; with essays by John House and Douglas Johnson. 1992
SUBJECTS:
Manet, Edouard, 1832-1883. Execution of the emperor Maximilien.
Manet, Edouard, 1832-1883—Political and social views.
France—History—Second Empire, 1852-1870.

Title: *Los desastres de la guerra* / Goya ; [Katalog, Eckhard Schaar ; Mitarbeit, Jenns Howoldt]. [1992]
SUBJECTS:
    Goya, Francisco, 1746-1828. Disasters of war—Exhibitions.

RELIGION

Types of Headings

Headings Representing Religions or Religious Concepts[41]

A large number of Library of Congress subject headings represent religions or religious concepts. Some examples are:

Buddhism
Catholic Church
Christianity
Church and state
Church history
Islam
Meditation
Muslims
Mysticism
Ordination
Salvation

Many of these headings may be subdivided according to the pattern headings listed below:

Category	*Pattern heading*
Religious and monastic orders	**Jesuits**
Religions	**Buddhism**
Christian denominations	**Catholic Church**
Sacred works (including parts)	**Bible**

There are also a number of headings that may be subdivided by religion or denomination. These are usually indicated in LCSH by means of multiple subdivisions:

Baptism—Anglican Communion, [Catholic Church, etc.]
Lord's Supper—Catholic Church, [Presbyterian Church, etc.]
    [may be subdivided by the name of any Christian denomination]
Mysticism—Brahmanism, [Judaism, Nestorian Church, etc.]
    [may be subdivided by the name of any religion]
Mysticism—Catholic Church, [Orthodox Eastern Church, etc.]
    [may be subdivided by the name of any denomination]

Headings for Nonreligious Topics with Religious Subdivisions[42]

Many nonreligious topics are subdivided by the subdivision —**Religious aspects** or —**Mythology** to represent a religious or mythological point of view. These subdivisions are not free-floating. The subdivision —**Moral and ethical aspects**, on the other hand, is free-floating. Examples include:

Marriage—Religious aspects
Falkland Islands War, 1982—Moral and ethical aspects
Stars—Mythology

The subdivision —**Religious aspects** may be further subdivided by —**[Religion or denomination]** on a free-floating basis. Examples include:

Birth control—Religious aspects
    — —Baptists, [Catholic Church, etc.]
    — —Buddhism, [Christianity, etc.]

The multiple subdivisions shown above authorize the following headings:

Birth control—Religious aspects—Islam
Marriage—Religious aspects—Catholic Church

The subdivision —**Religious aspects** is not used under headings for classes of persons or ethnic groups.

Geographic subdivisions are not interposed between the topic and the subdivisions —**Religious aspects**; —**Mythology**; or —**Moral and ethical aspects**. An additional heading in the form of **[Topic]— [Place]** is assigned to bring out the geographical aspect.

Application

Works on Religious Topics

Appropriate topical headings are assigned according to the normal procedures for subject cataloging:

Title: *The ground we share : everyday practice, Buddhist and Christian* / Robert Aitken and David Steindl-Rast ; conversations edited by Nelson Foster. c1994
SUBJECTS:
    Spiritual life—Comparative studies.
    Christianity and other religions—Buddhism.
    Buddhism—Relations—Christianity.

· Title: *In the lap of the Buddha* / Gavin Harrison ; foreword by
Joseph Goldstein. 1994
SUBJECTS:
Meditation—Buddhism.
Meditation—Therapeutic use.

Title: *The awakening of the west : the encounter of Buddhism and
Western culture* / Stephen Batchelor. 1994
SUBJECTS:
Buddhism—Europe—History.
Buddhism—Study and teaching—Europe—History.

Title: *Encyclopedia of Hasidism* / edited by Tzvi M. Rabinowicz. c1994
SUBJECTS:
Hasidism—Encyclopedias.
Hasidim—Encyclopedias.

Title: *An introduction to Islam* / David Waines. 1995
SUBJECTS:
Islam.

Title: *A brief history of the Episcopal Church : with a chapter on
the Anglican Reformation and an appendix on the annul-
ment of Henry VIII* / David L. Holmes. c1993
SUBJECTS:
Episcopal Church—History.
Anglican Communion—United States—History.

When a heading of the type **[Topic]—[Church or denomina-
tion]** is assigned to a work, an additional heading under **[Religion or
denomination]—[Topical subdivision]** is often assigned:

Title: *By water and the Spirit : a study of baptism for United
Methodists* / [Dwight Vogel]. c1993
SUBJECTS:
Baptism—Methodist Church.
Baptism—United Methodist Church (U.S.)
United Methodist Church (U.S.)—Doctrines.

Title: *Holy Communion* / from the French of Saint Peter Julian
Eymard ; translated by Clara Morris Rumball. [1992?]
SUBJECTS:
Lord's Supper—Catholic Church.
Catholic Church—Doctrines.

Title: *Corpus Christi : an encyclopedia of the Eucharist* / by Michael
O'Carroll. [1993]
SUBJECTS:
Lord's Supper—Catholic Church—Encyclopedias.
Catholic Church—Doctrines—Encyclopedias.

Title: *The sacraments* / Inos Biffi ; illustrations by Franco
    Vignazia. c1994
SUBJECTS:
    Sacraments—Catholic Church—Juvenile literature.
    Catholic Church—Doctrines—Juvenile literature.
    Catholic Church—Liturgy—Juvenile literature.

Works on Nonreligious Topics Treated from a Religious Point of View

When assigning a nonreligious topical heading with the subdivision
—Religious aspects, —Moral and ethical aspects, or **—Mythology,**
the following guidelines should be observed:

The subdivision **—Religious aspects** is used under headings for
nonreligious topics for works that discuss the topic from a religious
standpoint (e.g., how it occurs as a theme in religious beliefs and
practices, its importance in religious doctrines, the relationship in
general between the topic and religion):

Title: *Liquid life : abortion and Buddhism in Japan* / William R.
    LaFleur. c1992
SUBJECTS:
    Abortion—Religious aspects—Buddhism.
    Abortion—Japan.

Title: *Catholic women and abortion : stories of healing* / edited by
    Pat King. c1994
SUBJECTS:
    Abortion—Religious aspects—Catholic Church.
    Women, Catholic—Psychology.

Title: *The evolution of an earthly code : contraception in Catholic
    doctrine* / [Maggie Hume]. c1991
SUBJECTS:
    Birth control—Religious aspects—Catholic Church.
    Sex—Religious aspects—Catholic Church.

Title: *Meeting the Great Bliss Queen : Buddhists, feminists, and
    the art of the self* / Anne Carolyn Klein. 1994
SUBJECTS:
    Woman (Buddhism)
    Ye-ses-mtsho-rgyal, 8th cent.
    Feminism—Religious aspects—Buddhism.
    Buddhism—Social aspects—China—Tibet.

When a heading of the type **[Topic]—Religious aspects—[Name
of religion or denomination]** is assigned to a work, an additional
heading in the form of **[Religion or denomination]—[Topical sub-
division]** is often assigned. The subdivisions that may be used in this

way, however, are restricted to those under the relevant pattern headings or under the heading for the specific religion or denomination in question. For this reason, the topic expressed in the **[Religion or denomination]—[Topical subdivision]** headings is often more general than the one expressed in the **[Topic]—Religious aspects** heading:

> Title: *Marriage and sacrament : a theology of Christian marriage /*
> Michael G. Lawler. c1993
> SUBJECTS: ·
> **Marriage—Religious aspects—Catholic Church.**
> **Catholic Church—Doctrines.**

> Title: *Mystical passion : the art of Christian loving /* William
> McNamara. 1991
> SUBJECTS:
> **Spiritual life—Catholic Church.**
> **Emotions—Religious aspects—Catholic authors.**
> **Love—Religious aspects—Catholic Church.**
> **Catholic Church—Doctrines.**

If the work being cataloged discusses the topic from a moral or ethical standpoint as well as a religious point of view, an additional heading with the subdivision **—Moral and ethical aspects** is assigned:

> Title: *Abortion—my choice, God's grace : Christian women tell*
> *their stories /* Anne Eggebroten, editor. c1994
> SUBJECTS:
> **Abortion—United States—Moral and ethical aspects.**
> **Abortion—United States—Religious aspects.**

> Title: *Against nature? : types of moral argumentation regarding*
> *homosexuality /* Pim Pronk ; translated by John Vriend ;
> foreword by Hendrik Hart. c1993
> SUBJECTS:
> **Homosexuality—Religious aspects—Christianity.**
> **Homosexuality—Moral and ethical aspects.**

> ·Title: *Aids, ethics & religion : embracing a world of suffering /*
> Kenneth R. Overberg, editor. c1994
> SUBJECTS:
> **AIDS (Disease)—Moral and ethical aspects.**
> **AIDS (Disease)—Religious aspects—Christianity.**
> **AIDS (Disease)—Social aspects.**

The subdivision **—Mythology** is used to represent the topic as a theme in mythology. Additional headings may be assigned to bring out types of mythology (e.g., **Mythology, Greek**; **Mythology, Jewish**). Example:

Title: *The Greek plant world in myth, art, and literature* / Hellmut Baumann ; translated and augmented by William T. Stearn and Eldwyth Ruth Stearn. 1993
SUBJECTS:
   Botany—Greece—Mythology.
   Plants in art.
   Plants in literature.
   Botany—Greece—Folklore.
   Mythology, Greek.
   Ethnobotany—Greece.

If the work discusses the religious implications of the theme in mythology from the standpoint of a particular religion or denomination, an additional heading of the type **[Topic]—Religious aspects—[Religion or denomination]** is assigned. This heading is not necessary unless a particular religion or denomination is involved.

Sacred Scriptures

The Bible

Biblical Texts

Subject headings are not assigned to biblical texts except in the cases listed below. Examples include:

Title: *The Bible for today's family : Contemporary English Version : New Testament.* c1991
   [No subject headings]

Title: *The King and the Beast : a student New Testament : Contemporary English Version.* c1991
   [No subject headings]

Title: *Proverbs : 75 proverbs from the Living Bible* / calligraphic illustration and prayers by Timothy R. Botts. c1994
   [No subject headings]

Exceptions:

(1) *Paraphrases of biblical texts*. Because paraphrases of biblical texts are entered under the name of the paraphraser according to *AACR2R*, form headings are assigned as follows:

Bible—Paraphrases
[used for texts of paraphrases in two or more languages]
Bible—Paraphrases, English, [French, German, etc.]
[used for texts of paraphrases in a particular language]

Paraphrases of parts of the Bible follow the same pattern (e.g., **Bible. O.T. Psalms—Paraphrases, German**). Examples include:

Title: *Psalms for teens* / Eldon Weisheit. c1992
SUBJECTS:
Bible. O.T. Psalms—Paraphrases, English.
Bible. O.T. Psalms—Paraphrases.
Prayer books and devotions.
Christian life.

(2) *Harmonies*. The pattern for paraphrases of Biblical texts is followed for harmonies:

Title: *Records of the life of Jesus : Revised Standard Version* / [as arranged by] Henry Burton Sharman. c1991
SUBJECTS:
Bible. N.T. Gospels—Harmonies, English.

Title: *New Gospel parallels* / Robert W. Funk. c1990-
SUBJECTS:
Bible. N.T. Gospels—Harmonies, English.

(3) *Translations of early versions*.[43] In descriptive cataloging the main entry for the translation of a version of a biblical text is under the uniform title containing the name of the modern version but ignoring the version from which the translation is made. Thus, a subject heading of the type **[Uniform title for the early version]—Translations into [name of language]** (e.g., **Bible. O.T. Pentateuch. Aramaic. Targum Pseudo-Jonathan—Translations into English**) is assigned to bring out the earlier version. For example,

Title: *Targum Onkelos to Leviticus : an English translation of the text with analysis and commentary (based on A. Sperber and A. Berliner editions)* / by Israel Drazin. c1994
SUBJECTS:
Bible. O.T. Leviticus. Aramaic. Onkelos—Translations into English.
Bible. O.T. Leviticus. Aramaic. Onkelos—Commentaries.

MAIN ENTRY:
> *Bible. O.T. Leviticus. Aramaic. Onḳelos. 1993.*

Title: *Targum Pseudo-Jonathan, Genesis* / translated, with introduction and notes by Michael Maher. 1992
SUBJECTS:
> **Bible. O.T. Genesis. Aramaic. Targum Pseudo-Jonathan—Translations into English.**
> **Bible. O.T. Genesis. Aramaic. Targum Pseudo-Jonathan—Criticism, interpretation, etc.**

MAIN ENTRY:
> *Bible. O.T. Genesis. English. Maher. 1992.*

Works About the Bible[44]

Works about the Bible or its parts receive subject headings in the form of the uniform title used in descriptive cataloging, except that designations for the language, version, and date are omitted. Appropriate subdivisions are added:

Title: *The gospel according to Job* / Mike Mason. c1994
SUBJECTS:
> **Bible. O.T. Job—Meditations.**

Title: *The journey isn't over : the pilgrim Psalms for life's challenges and joys* / Walter C. Kaiser, Jr. c1993
SUBJECTS:
> **Bible. O.T. Psalms CXX-CXXXIV—Meditations.**

Title: *Song of the self : biblical spirituality and human holiness* / by Carol Ochs. 1994
SUBJECTS:
> **Bible. O.T. Genesis—Criticism, interpretation, etc.**
> **Bible. O.T. Job—Criticism, interpretation, etc.**
> **Self—Biblical teaching.**

Title: *The Babylonian Esther midrash : a critical commentary* / by Eliezer Segal. c1994
SUBJECTS:
> **Bible. O.T. Esther—Commentaries.**
> **Talmud. Megillah I, 10b-17a—Criticism, Redaction.**
> **Midrash—History and criticism.**

Title: *The Targum sheni to the book of Esther : a critical edition based on MS. Sassoon 282 with critical apparatus* / by Bernard Grossfeld. 1994
SUBJECTS:
> **Bible. O.T. Esther—Paraphrases, Aramaic.**

Targum sheni—Criticism, Textual.

Title: *In sovereign hands* / James T. Dyet and Larry D. Green. c1992
SUBJECTS:
Bible. O.T. Ezra—Study and teaching.
Bible. O.T. Esther—Study and teaching.

Title: *Commentary on Ezra, Nehemiah, and Esther* / by James
Burton and Thelma B. Coffman. 1993
SUBJECTS:
Bible. O.T. Ezra—Commentaries.
Bible. O.T. Nehemiah—Commentaries.
Bible. O.T. Esther—Commentaries.

However, if the work is about a particular version or translation of the
Bible, it is specifically designated.[45] The following types of headings
with appropriate subdivisions are used:

[Uniform title]—Versions (e.g., **Bible—Versions**; **Bible. N.T.
—Versions**)
[For general works collectively discussing translations of
the Bible]
[Uniform title]—Versions, [Name of language group] (e.g.,
Bible—Versions, Slavic)
[For works collectively discussing the translations of the
Bible or its parts into a particular language group]
[Uniform title]. [Language of translation]—Versions (e.g.,
Bible. English—Versions—Authorized; **Bible. N.T.
Latin—Versions—Vulgate**)
[For works on the translations of the Bible or its parts into
a particular language]

For example:

Title: *Defending the King James Bible : a four-fold superiority :
texts, translators, technique, theology* / D. A. Waite. c1992
SUBJECTS:
Bible. English—Versions—Authorized.

Title: *Die Bugenhagenbibel : Untersuchungen zur Übersetzung
und Textgeschichte des Pentateuchs* / von Ingrid Schröder.
1991
SUBJECTS:
**Bible. O.T. Pentateuch—Translating—History—16th
century.**
**Bible. O.T. Pentateuch—Criticism, Textual—
History—16th century.**
Bugenhagen, Johann, 1485-1558.
Bible. German—Versions—Luther.

Title: *Analytical lexicon to the Septuagint : a complete parsing guide* / Bernard A. Taylor. 1994
SUBJECTS:
    Bible. O.T. Greek—Versions—Septuagint—Language, style.
    Greek language, Biblical—Parsing.
    Greek language, Biblical—Dictionaries.

Title: *Structure, role, and ideology in the Hebrew and Greek texts of Genesis 1:1-2:3* / William P. Brown. c1993
SUBJECTS:
    Bible. O.T. Genesis I, 1-II, 3—Criticism, interpretation, etc.
    Bible. O.T. Greek—Versions—Septuagint—Criticism, Textual.
    Water in the Bible.

Title: *Notes on the Greek text of Genesis* / John William Wevers. c1993
SUBJECTS:
    Bible. O.T. Genesis. Greek—Versions—Septuagint.
    Bible. O.T. Genesis—Translating.

Works about paraphrases of the Bible or its parts are assigned headings such as

    Bible—Paraphrases—History and criticism
    Bible—Paraphrases, English—History and criticism
    Bible. O.T. Psalms—Paraphrases, English—History and criticism

Special themes in the Bible are brought out by headings of the type **[Topic] in the Bible** (not free-floating).

Apocryphal Books

The headings **Apocryphal books; Apocryphal books (New Testament); Apocryphal books (Old Testament)**, with appropriate subdivisions, are assigned to works collectively dealing with apocryphal books. Subdivisions follow the pattern established under the Bible:

    Apocryphal books—Introductions
    Apocryphal books (New Testament)—Commentaries
    Apocryphal books (New Testament)—Theology
    Apocryphal books (Old Testament)—Criticism, interpretation, etc.

Examples of apocryphal books and works about them include:

Title: *The Apocryphal New Testament : a collection of apocryphal Christian literature in an English translation* / [edited by] J. K. Elliott. c1993
    SUBJECTS:
      Apocryphal books (New Testament)
      Apocryphal books (New Testament)—Criticism, interpretation, etc.

Title: *Divine disclosure : an introduction to Jewish apocalyptic* / D. S. Russell. c1992
    SUBJECTS:
      Apocalyptic literature—History and criticism.
      Apocryphal books (Old Testament)—Criticism, interpretation, etc.
      Bible. O.T. Apocrypha—Criticism, interpretation, etc.

Title: *The Armenian apocryphal Adam literature* / by W. Lowndes Lipscomb. c1990
    SUBJECTS:
      Apocryphal books (Old Testament)—Criticism, interpretation, etc.
      Adam (Biblical figure)

Other Sacred Scriptures

The heading **Bible** serves as the pattern for subdivisions for other sacred scriptures (e.g., **Vedas. Atharvaveda—Criticism, interpretation, etc.; Koran—Commentaries**). Examples include:

Title: *Atharva-Veda samhita = Atharvaveda samhita ; with English translation* / by Satya Prakash Sarasvati. [1992?]
    [No subject headings]

Title: *The essential Koran : the heart of Islam : an introductory selection of readings from the Qur'an* / translated and presented by Thomas Cleary. c1993
    [No subject headings]

Title: *The Talmud of Babylonia : an academic commentary* / by Jacob Neusner. c1994-
    SUBJECTS:
      Talmud—Commentaries.

Title: *The Qur'an : an introductory essay* / by Theodor Noldeke ; edited by N. A. Newman. c1992
    SUBJECTS:
      Koran.

Title: *Insight into the Qur'an = Tafseer.* c1992-
SUBJECTS:
  Koran—Commentaries.

Title: *Qur'an : selected commentaries : the Qur'an as explained by the Qur'an : a new reading of the Holy Qur'an in modern English* / translation and notes by Muhammad M. Al-Akili. c1993
SUBJECTS:
  Koran. Sūrat al-Baqarah—Commentaries.

Title: *Approaches to the Qur'an* / edited by G. R. Hawting and Abdul-Kader A. Shareef. 1993
SUBJECTS:
  Koran—Criticism, interpretation, etc.—History.
  Koran—Hermeneutics.

Title: *The Hindu ethics of Holy Veda as found in Bali : Sanskrit texts with English and Indonesian translations* / by I. B. Oka Punia Atmaja. [1992]
SUBJECTS:
  Vedas—Criticism, interpretation, etc.
  Hindu ethics.

Title: *God, rebirth, and the Vedas* / Swami Paramananda Bharathi ; translated by B. G. Sreelakshmi. c1993
SUBJECTS:
  God (Hinduism)
  Soul (Hinduism)
  Reincarnation.
  Vedas—Criticism, interpretation, etc.

Title: *The ancillary literature of the Atharva-Veda : a study with special reference to the Parisistas* / B. R. Modak. 1993
SUBJECTS:
  Vedas. Atharvaveda—Criticism, interpretation, etc.

Liturgy[46]

Liturgical texts and works about liturgy or about liturgical books are assigned similar headings with different form subdivisions. Examples are given below.

Texts of Liturgical Books

To a collection of liturgies, an individual liturgical book, or a selection from one or more liturgical books, one or more headings of the following types are assigned:

[Name of Christian denomination]—Liturgy—Texts
Judaism—Liturgy—Texts
[Type of liturgical book]—Texts

Examples include:

Title: *The book of common prayer and administration of the sacraments and other rites and ceremonies of the church according to the use of the Church of England.* 1992
SUBJECTS:
   Church of England—Liturgy—Texts.
   Anglican Communion—Liturgy—Texts.

Title: *Celebrating common prayer : a version of the Daily Office, SSF.* c1992
SUBJECTS:
   Breviaries—Texts.
   Divine office—Texts.
   Church of England—Liturgy—Texts.
   Anglican Communion—Liturgy—Texts.
   Society of St. Francis—Prayer-books and devotions—English.

Title: *Service hymnal* / produced by the Commission on Worship of the Lutheran Church—Missouri Synod in cooperation with the Ministry to the Armed Forces, Board for Mission Services. c1993
SUBJECTS:
   Lutheran Church—Missouri Synod—Hymns.
   Lutheran Church—Hymns.
   Lutheran Church—Missouri Synod—Liturgy—Texts.
   Lutheran Church—Liturgy—Texts.
   Hymns, English.

Title: *The Monastic diurnal revised : a breviary based upon the 1932 Monastic diurnal and the 1979 Book of common prayer for the recitation of the divine office* / edited by Community of St. Mary, Eastern Province. 1989-1990
SUBJECTS:
   Breviaries—Texts.
   Divine office—Texts.
   Episcopal Church—Liturgy—Texts.

> **Anglican Communion—Liturgy—Texts.**
> **Community of St. Mary (Peekskill, N.Y.)—**
> **Prayer-books and devotions—English.**

Title: *Sing praise : morning prayer and evening prayer.* c1992
SUBJECTS:
> **Franciscan Sisters of Perpetual Adoration (La Crosse,**
> **Wis.)—Prayer-books and devotions—English.**
> **Divine office—Texts.**
> **Catholic Church—Liturgy—Texts.**

Title: *The Psalter : a faithful and inclusive rendering from the
Hebrew into contemporary English poetry, intended primarily for communal song and recitation . . . /* offered for
study and for comment by the International Commission
on English in the Liturgy ; [art, Linda Ekstrom]. 1994
SUBJECTS:
> **Psalters—Texts.**
> **Catholic Church—Liturgy—Texts.**
> **Bible. O.T. Psalms—Liturgical use.**

Title: *Thank you, God : a Jewish child's book of prayers /* Judyth
Groner and Madeline Wikler ; illustrated by Shelly O.
Haas. c1993
SUBJECTS:
> **Jewish children—Prayer-books and devotions.**
> **Benedictions—Texts.**
> **Judaism—Liturgy—Texts.**

If the work is limited to a particular ceremony, ritual, holiday, or the
like, an additional heading in the form of **[Type of ceremony, etc.]—
Liturgy—Texts** is also assigned:

Title: *The Prefaces of the Roman Missal : a source compendium
with concordance and indices /* Anthony Ward, Cuthbert
Johnson. 1989
SUBJECTS:
> **Prefaces (Liturgy)—Catholic Church—Texts.**
> **Catholic Church—Liturgy—Texts.**

Title: *Jerusalem gates Haggadah /* design by Haim Ron. c1993
SUBJECTS:
> **Haggadot—Texts.**
> **Seder—Liturgy—Texts.**
> **Judaism—Liturgy—Texts.**

Title: *Children's Haggadah = [Hagadah la-yeladim]* / text by
   Howard Bogot and Robert Orkand ; illustrated and de-
   signed by Davis Grebu. c1994
SUBJECTS:
   Haggadot—Texts—Juvenile literature.
   Seder—Liturgy—Texts—Juvenile literature.
   Judaism—Liturgy—Texts—Juvenile literature.

Title: *Becoming free : a biblically oriented Haggadah for Passover :
   the permanent relevance of the ancient lesson = [Hagadah
   shel Pesah]* / adapted and with notes [by] Howard S.
   Rubenstein and Judith S. Rubenstein. c1993
SUBJECTS:
   Haggadot—Texts.
   Seder—Liturgy—Texts.
   Judaism—Liturgy—Texts.
   Haggadah (Rubenstein)

Title: *The promise of His glory : services and prayers for the season
   from All Saints to Candlemas* / commended by the House
   of Bishops of the General Synod of the Church of England.
   1991
SUBJECTS:
   Church of England—Liturgy—Texts.
   Anglican Communion—Liturgy—Texts.
   All Saints' Day—Prayer-books and devotions—English.
   Advent—Prayer-books and devotions—English.
   Christmas—Prayer-books and devotions—English.
   Epiphany—Prayer-books and devotions—English.

Works About Liturgy

   A heading of the type **Judaism—Liturgy** or **[Name of Christian
denomination]—Liturgy** is assigned to a general work about Judais-
tic liturgy or the liturgy of a particular Christian denomination. The
subdivision **—Liturgy** may be further subdivided by other free-floating form subdivisions.

Title: *The origins of the Roman rite* / edited and translated by
   Gordon P. Jeanes. c1991
SUBJECTS:
   Catholic Church—Liturgy—History.

Title: *Luah 5754 : table of prayers, blessings, and rituals* / by
   Kenneth S. Goldrich. c1993
SUBJECTS:
   Judaism—Liturgy—Handbooks, manuals, etc.

Title: *Liturgical inculturation in the Anglican Communion : including the York statement "Down to earth worship"* / edited by David R. Holeton. c1990
SUBJECTS:
Anglican Communion—Liturgy.
Christianity and culture.

Title: *From "bounden duty" to a "joyful thing" : development of the language of the principal liturgies of the Episcopal Church* / introduction by David G. Robinson, Jr. ; edited by Alan J. Bouffard. c1992-
SUBJECTS:
Episcopal Church—Liturgy—History.
Anglican Communion—Liturgy—History.

For a work discussing the liturgy of a particular ceremony, ritual, holiday, or the like, headings of the following types are assigned:

[Name of religion or Christian denomination]—Liturgy
[Type of ceremony, etc.]—[Name of religion or denomination (if appropriate)]

Examples include:

Title: *Entering Jewish prayer : a guide to personal devotion and the worship service* / Reuven Hammer. c1994
SUBJECTS:
Judaism—Liturgy—History.
Prayer—Judaism.
Siddur.

Title: *Kos Eliyahu : insights on the Haggadah and Pesach* / Eliyahu Safran. c1993
SUBJECTS:
Haggadah.
Judaism—Liturgy.
Passover.

Title: *And you shall be a blessing : an unfolding of the six words that begin every brakhah* / Joel Laurie Grishaver. c1993
SUBJECTS:
Benedictions—Sources.
Barukh atah Adonai Elohenu Melekh ha-'olam (The Hebrew phrase)
Judaism—Liturgy—Texts—History and criticism.
Rabbinical literature—History and criticism.

Title: *Prayer and penitence : a commentary on the High Holy Day Machzor* / Jeffrey M. Cohen ; foreword by Immanuel Jakobovits ; preface by Jonathan Sacks. 1994
SUBJECTS:
Mahzor. High Holidays.
Judaism—Liturgy.
High Holidays—Liturgy.

Title: *Real food : a spirituality of the Eucharist* / Robert Fabing. c1994
SUBJECTS:
Lord's Supper—Catholic Church.
God—Love.
Spiritual life—Catholic Church.
Catholic Church—Doctrines.
Catholic Church—Liturgy.

Title: *Sacramental theology* / Herbert Vorgrimler ; translated by Linda M. Maloney. c1992
SUBJECTS:
Sacraments—Catholic Church.
Catholic Church—Doctrines.
Catholic Church—Liturgy.

Title: *The complete training course for altar guilds* / B. Don Taylor. c1993
SUBJECTS:
Altar guilds—Episcopal Church.
Episcopal Church—Liturgy.
Anglican Communion—Liturgy.

Title: *A Baptism sourcebook* / edited by J. Robert Baker, Larry J. Nyberg, Victoria M. Tufano ; art by G. E. Mullan. 1993
SUBJECTS:
Baptism—Catholic Church.
Baptism (Liturgy)
Catholic Church—Liturgy.

Title: *Infant baptism : a parish celebration* / Timothy Fitzgerald. c1994
SUBJECTS:
Infant baptism.
Baptism—Catholic Church.
Baptism (Liturgy)
Catholic Church—Liturgy.

Works About Liturgical Books

For a work about a type of liturgical book or an individual liturgical book, one or more headings of the following types are used:

Judaism—Liturgy—Texts—History and criticism
[Name of Christian denomination]—Liturgy—Texts—History and criticism
[Type of liturgical book]
[Type of ceremony, ritual, holiday, etc.]
[Uniform title of the individual book]

Examples include:

Title: *The 1892 Book of common prayer* / Lesley Armstrong Northup. c1993
SUBJECTS:
Episcopal Church. Book of common prayer (1892)
Episcopal Church—Liturgy—History—19th century.

Title: *O marvelous exchange : daily reflections for Christmas and Epiphany* / John J. McIlhon. c1991
SUBJECTS:
Christmas—Meditations.
Epiphany season—Meditations.
Catholic Church. Liturgy of the hours (U.S., et al.)— Meditations.

Title: *Welcoming the light of Christ : a commentary on the promise of His glory : services and prayers for the season from All Saints to Candlemas* / Michael Perham and Kenneth Stevenson. 1991
SUBJECTS:
Church of England. Promise of His glory.
Church of England—Liturgy.
Anglican Communion—Liturgy.
All Saints' Day—Prayer-books and devotions—English.
Advent—Prayer-books and devotions—English.
Christmas—Prayer-books and devotions—English.
Epiphany—Prayer-books and devotions—English.

Title: *The art of Jewish prayer* / by Yitzchok Kirzner with Lisa Aiken. c1991
SUBJECTS:
Amidah.
Judaism—Liturgy—Texts—History and criticism.
Prayer—Judaism.

If the work contains the text as well as commentary of a liturgical book, subject headings for both aspects are assigned:

Title: *A Feast of history : the drama of Passover through the ages : with a new translation of the Haggadah for use at the Seder* / Chaim Raphael. [1993]
SUBJECTS:
  Haggadot—Texts—History and criticism.
  Seder—Liturgy—Texts—History and criticism.
  Judaism—Liturgy—Texts—History and criticism.
  Haggadah—Illustrations.
  Illumination of books and manuscripts, Jewish.
  Haggadot—Texts.
  Seder—Liturgy—Texts.
  Judaism—Liturgy—Texts.

LAW[47]

Types of Headings

Legal Headings

Law headings represent different forms of legal texts, systems and branches of law, and specific legal topics:

Charters
Commercial law
Common law
Constitutional amendments
Constitutional law
Deeds
Habeas corpus
Insurance law
Law
Law, Maya
Law, Medieval
Law, Slavic
Liens
Ordinances, Municipal
Roman law
Treaties

The heading **Labor laws and legislation** serves as the pattern heading for subdivisions.[48]

Topical Headings with Legal Subdivisions

Legal texts and works about law are often assigned topical headings with legal subdivisions such as the following:

—**Law and legislation** (*May Subd Geog*)
[free-floating under specific categories]
—**Legal status, laws, etc.** (*May Subd Geog*)
[free-floating under classes of persons and ethnic groups]
—**Safety regulations** (*May Subd Geog*)
[free-floating under general topics and industries]

These subdivisions may be further divided by the subdivisions listed under the pattern heading **Labor laws and legislation** (see appendix C).

The subdivision —**Law and legislation** (*May Subd Geog*) is used under topical headings:

Firearms—Law and legislation—United States
Income tax—Law and legislation—United States—History
Smoking—Law and legislation—Canada

If the topical heading represents a group of people, the subdivision —**Legal status, laws, etc.** (*May Subd Geog*) is used:

Afro-Americans—Legal status, laws, etc.
Minorities—Legal status, laws, etc.—United States
Children—Legal status, laws, etc.
Artists—Legal status, laws, etc.—Chile
Japanese Americans—Legal status, laws, etc.—United States

The free-floating subdivision —**Safety regulations** (*May Subd Geog*) is used under headings for types of objects, chemicals, materials, machines, installations, industries, or activities, or under names of disciplines for safety rules or orders that have the force of law:

Coal mines and mining—Safety regulations—India
Pipelines—Safety regulations—Great Britain
Plutonium—Safety regulations—United States

Legal headings and headings of the type **[Topic]—Law and legislation** may be subdivided by special form subdivisions such as:

—**Digests**[49]
[for monographic or serial works consisting of systematically
arranged compilations of brief summaries of individual
statutes, regulations, court decisions, or regulatory
agency decisions on particular topics, e.g., **Criminal
law—United States—Digests**]

—Legal research[50]
> [for works discussing the use of legal research tools such as court reports, codes, digests, citators, etc., in determining the status of statutory, regulatory, or case law on a legal topic, e.g., **Taxation—Law and legislation—United States—Legal research**]

Application

Legal Texts

General Laws (Nontopical Compilations)

A subject heading in the form of **Law—[Place]** is assigned to a nontopical compilation of laws when main entry has been made under the name of a jurisdiction:

Title: *Illinois compiled statutes annotated* / prepared by the editorial staff of the publisher. 1993
  SUBJECTS:
  Law—Illinois.

Title: *The statute law of the Bahamas, 1799-1987 : in force on the 30th June, 1987, as amended by the Statute Law Revision Act, 1987. Rev. ed.* / by Sir Gordon Bryce. 1988
  SUBJECTS:
  Law—Bahamas.

Title: *Logbok fyri Foroyar* / lagt til raettis hava Johan Djurhuus . . . [et al.]. 1992-
  SUBJECTS:
  Law—Faroe Islands.

Title: *Den danske rigslovgivning 1513-1523* / udgivet af det Danske sprog- og litteraturselskab og Selskabet for udgivelse af kilder til danske historie ved Aage Andersen. 1991
  SUBJECTS:
  Law—Denmark.
  Law—Denmark—Sources.

General Laws (Topical Compilations)

If the laws pertain to a particular topic, a topical heading subdivided by the jurisdiction is assigned:

Title: *Compilation of basic banking laws : revised through July 1, 1992* / Committee on Banking, Finance, and Urban Affairs, House of Representatives. 1992
SUBJECTS:
Banking law—United States.

Title: *Regulations of the State Bank Commissioner, Title 5, Delaware code* / issued by State Bank Commissioner. [1991]
SUBJECTS:
Banking law—Delaware.

Title: *Aktiengesetz* / erlautert von Uwe Huffer. 1993
SUBJECTS:
Corporation law—Germany.

Title: *Ley del impuesto sobre la renta y su reglamento : Decreto numero 26-92.* [1992]
SUBJECTS:
Income tax—Law and legislation—Guatemala.

Title: *State of Maine laws relating to public schools, 1990 : through the first special session of the 114th Maine Legislature, 1989.* [1990]
SUBJECTS:
Educational law and legislation—Maine.

Constitutions[51]

The heading **Constitutions** is used for a general collection of texts of constitutions. The heading is subdivided by place if the collection contains the texts of constitutions of a particular region.

Title: *Les Constitutions de l'Europe des douze* / textes et documents rassemblés et présentés par Henri Oberdorff, avec la participation de l'Université Jean Monnet de Saint-Etienne. c1992
SUBJECTS:
Constitutions—Europe.

To a collection of texts of constitutions or an individual constitution of a particular country, state, province, or the like, a heading in the form of **[Jurisdiction]—Constitution** is assigned.

Title: *Draft constitution for the Cayman Islands, July 1992.*
[1992]
SUBJECTS:
Cayman Islands—Constitution.

Title: *Constitution of the Islamic Republic of Pakistan, 1973 /*
[compiled] by Sh. Shaukat Mahmood, Sh. Nadeem
Shaukat. 1992
SUBJECTS:
Pakistan—Constitution.

For a collection of texts of the constitutions of various states, a
heading in the form of **Constitutions, State—[Place]** is used:

Title: *Constitutions of the states of Malaysia /* compiled by Legal
Research Board. 1991
SUBJECTS:
Constitutions, State—Malaysia.

Title: *Das Verfassungsrecht der österreichischen Bundesländer /*
herausgegeben von Heinz Schäffer. [1991-]
SUBJECTS:
Constitutions, State—Austria.
Austria—Constitutional law, State.

Title: *The Federal and state constitutions, colonial charters, and
other organic laws of the states, territories, and colonies
now or heretofore forming the United States of America /*
compiled and edited under the act of Congress of June 30,
1906 by Francis Newton Thorpe. 1993
SUBJECTS:
Constitutions, State—United States.
United States—Constitution.
United States—Constitutional history—Sources.

Title: *Index digest of state constitutions /* prepared for the New
York State Constitutional Convention Commission by the
Legislative Drafting Research Fund of Columbia University.
1993
SUBJECTS:
Constitutions, State—United States—Digests.

A heading in the form of **[Jurisdiction]—Constitution—
Amendments** is assigned to a collection containing texts of constitutional amendments of a particular jurisdiction. Texts of particular
constitutional amendments are assigned headings of the type **[Juris-
diction]—Constitution—Amendments—1st, [2nd, 3rd, etc.].**

Ordinances

A heading of the type **Ordinances, Municipal—[Place]** is assigned to the text of a nontopical compilation of ordinances:

Title: *Los Angeles municipal code. 5th ed.* / compiled under the direction of James K. Hahn. c1990-
SUBJECTS:
Ordinances, Municipal—California—Los Angeles.

Title: *The Ordinances of Bristol, 1506-1598* / edited by Maureen Stanford. 1990
SUBJECTS:
Ordinances, Municipal—England—Bristol.
Bristol (England)—History—Sources.

Title: *Reglamentos municipales : Ayuntamiento de Campeche, 1989-1991.* 1990
SUBJECTS:
Ordinances, Municipal—Mexico—Campeche (Campeche)

Charters

One or more of the following types of headings are assigned to the text of a compilation of published charters: **Charters; County charters—[Place]; Municipal charters—[Place].** Examples include:

Title: *Municipal charters of Maryland* / compiled by the Dept. of Legislative Reference, General Assembly of Maryland. 1990-
SUBJECTS:
Municipal charters—Maryland.

For the text of a single charter, the following types of headings are used:

[City]—Charters
[for an American city]
[City]—Charters, grants, privileges
[for a foreign city]

Examples include:

Title: *Rules and orders of the Common Council of the city of Boston. The city charter, the city ordinances, and the laws of the commonwealth relating to the city, passed since the publication of the volume of ordinances. Together with a list of the city officers.* 1832
SUBJECTS:
Ordinances, Municipal—Massachusetts—Boston.
Boston (Mass.)—Charters.
Boston (Mass.). Common Council—Rules and practice.

Title: *Chancelarias portuguesas. D. Afonso IV* / organizador A. H. de Oliveira Marques. 1990-1992
SUBJECTS:
Portugal—Charters, grants, privileges.
Law—Portugal—Sources.

Title: *Pre-conquest charter-bounds of Devon and Cornwall* / Della Hooke. 1994
SUBJECTS:
Devon (England)—Charters, grants, privileges.
Cornwall (England : County)—Charters, grants, privileges.
Cornwall (England : County)—Boundaries.
Anglo-Saxons—England—Cornwall (County)
Anglo-Saxons—England—Devon.
Devon (England)—Boundaries.

Title: *Facsimiles of Anglo-Saxon charters* / edited by Simon Keynes. c1991
SUBJECTS:
England—Charters, grants, privileges.
Law, Anglo-Saxon—Sources.
Great Britain—History—Anglo-Saxon period, 449-1066—Sources.
Manuscripts, English (Old)—Facsimiles.

Court Rules

Title: *General rules of practice annotated* / by David F. Herr. 1993
SUBJECTS:
Court rules—Minnesota.

Title: *Federal rules of civil procedure* / [edited] by Thomas A. Coyne. 1994-
SUBJECTS:
Court rules—United States.
Civil procedure—United States.

Works About Law

Works about law in general are assigned the heading **Law** with appropriate subdivisions:

Title: *Your handbook of everyday law* / George Gordon Coughlin, Jr. c1993
SUBJECTS:
Law—United States—Popular works.

Title: *English law and its background* / C. H. S. Fifoot. 1993
SUBJECTS:
Law—Great Britain—History.

Title: *Legal system of Bangladesh* / A. B. M. Mafizul Islam Patwari ;
with foreword by Dorothy W. Nelson. 1991
SUBJECTS:
Law—Bangladesh.
Law—Bangladesh—History.

Title: *Rhode Island practice.* c1990-
SUBJECTS:
Law—Rhode Island.

Title: *Nolo's pocket guide to California law* / by Lisa Guerin & Nolo
Press editors. 1994
SUBJECTS:
Law—California—Popular works.

Title: *Law in everyday life* / edited by Austin Sarat and Thomas R.
Kearns. c1993
SUBJECTS:
Law—United States—Popular works.
Law—Philosophy.

Works on specific branches or topics of law are assigned appropriate
headings, with form subdivisions if applicable.

Title: *California performance test workbook : California bar exam
performance test questions (1986-1989) with model answers.*
c1990
SUBJECTS:
Bar examinations—California.
Law—California—Examinations, questions, etc.

Title: *Between a rock and a hard place : law for school administrators* /
by Lillian Lee Port. c1992
SUBJECTS:
Educational law and legislation—California.
School administrators—California—Handbooks,
manuals, etc.

Title: *West's California code forms with practice commentaries.*
Education / by Jay E. Grenig. 1992
SUBJECTS:
Educational law and legislation—California—Forms.

Title: *Company law of Canada* / by Harry Sutherland ; together
     with David B. Horsley . . . [et al.]. 1993
  SUBJECTS:
  Corporation law—Canada.

Title: *Banking regulation and supervision : a comparative study of*
     the UK, USA, and Japan / Maximilian J. B. Hall. c1993
  SUBJECTS:
  Banking law—Great Britain.
  Banking law—United States.
  Banking law—Japan.

Title: *Federal income taxation of corporations and shareholders* /
     Boris I. Bittker, James S. Eustice ; with the collaboration
     of Jasper L. Cummings, Jr. c1994
  SUBJECTS:
  Corporations—Taxation—Law and legislation—United
   States.
  Income tax—Law and legislation—United States.

Title: *Problems, cases and materials on federal income taxation* /
     by Laurie L. Malman, Lewis D. Solomon, Jerome M.
     Hesch. 1994
  SUBJECTS:
  Income tax—Law and legislation—United States—Cases.

Title: *Smoking by-laws in Canada 1991* / Environment Health
     Directorate, Health Protection Branch. [1991]
  SUBJECTS:
  Smoking—Law and legislation—Canada.
  Ordinances, Municipal—Canada.

Title: *Draft calendar of patent rolls, 28-29 Elizabeth I, 1585-1587*
     (C66/1271 - 1291) : (continuing the calendar of patent
     rolls Elizabeth I). 1991
  SUBJECTS:
  Letters patent—Great Britain—Indexes.
  Great Britain—Charters, privileges, etc.—Indexes.
  Great Britain. Court of Chancery—Bibliography—
   Catalogs.

For a periodical or journal of law pertaining to a particular jurisdiction, a heading in the form of **Law—[Place]—Periodicals** is assigned:

Title: *Lawyer's weekly USA.* 1993-
  SUBJECTS:
  Law—United States—Periodicals.

Title: *The William and Mary Bill of Rights journal : a student publication of the Marshall-Wythe School of Law.* c1992-
SUBJECTS:
Civil rights—United States—Periodicals.
Law—United States—Periodicals.
Law reviews—Virginia.

To a work that discusses constitutions or constitutional law in general, the heading **Constitutional law** is assigned. Works that discuss the constitutions or constitutional law of particular regions, countries, states, provinces, and other such areas are assigned headings in the form of **[Jurisdiction]—Constitutional law**. Examples include:

Title: *Control in constitutional law* / edited by Carla M. Zoethout, Ger van der Tang, Piet Akkermans. c1993
SUBJECTS:
Europe—Constitutional law—Congresses.

Title: *Original intent & the framers of the Constitution : a disputed question* / Harry V. Jaffa, with Bruce Ledewitz, Robert L. Stone, George Anastaplo ; foreword by Lewis E. Lehrman. c1993
SUBJECTS:
United States—Constitutional law—Interpretation and construction.
United States—Constitutional history.

Title: *Constitutional and legal systems of ASEAN countries* / Carmelo V. Sison, editor ; Roshan T. Jose, associate editor. c1990
SUBJECTS:
Constitutions—Asia, Southeastern.
Asia, Southeastern—Constitutional law.

Title: *Constitutional law of Canada* / by Peter W. Hogg. 1992
SUBJECTS:
Canada—Constitutional law.

Title: *State constitutional law : cases and materials* / Robert F. Williams. c1993
SUBJECTS:
Constitutions, State—United States—Cases.
United States—Constitutional law—Cases.

Comparative works discussing state constitutions or the state constitutional law of a region or country are assigned headings in the form of **[Region or country]—Constitutional law, State**. Works discussing constitutional amendments and the amending process in general are assigned the heading **Constitutional amendments**. Works discussing constitutional amendments or state constitutional amendments of a country, state, or province are assigned headings in the form

of [Jurisdiction]—Constitutional law—Amendments or [Juris-
diction]—Constitutional law, State—Amendments:

> Title: *State constitutional conventions, commissions & amend-*
> *ments, 1979-1988 : an annotated bibliography.* c1989
> SUBJECTS:
> > Constitutional conventions—United States—States—
> > Bibliography.
> > Constitutions, State—United States—Amendments—
> > Bibliography.

Works discussing a specific constitutional amendment are assigned a
heading in the form of [Jurisdiction]—Constitution—Amendments—1st, [2nd, 3rd, etc.] or [Jurisdiction]—Constitutional
law—Amendments—1st, [2nd, 3rd, etc.].

> Title: *The First Amendment in the balance* / Joseph F. Schuster.
> > c1993
> SUBJECTS:
> > United States—Constitutional law—Amendments—1st.
> > Freedom of speech—United States.
> > Freedom of the press—United States.
> > Freedom of religion—United States.

> Title: *America's real religion : separation between religion and*
> > *government in the United States of America* / Gene Garman.
> > c1991
> SUBJECTS:
> > Freedom of religion—United States.
> > Religion and state—United States.
> > United States—Constitution—Amendments—1st.

> Title: *Conscience and the Constitution : history, theory, and law of*
> > *the Reconstruction amendments* / David A. J. Richards.
> > c1993
> SUBJECTS:
> > United States—Constitutional law—Amendments—
> > 13th—History.
> > United States—Constitutional law—Amendments—
> > 14th—History.
> > United States—Constitutional law—Amendments—
> > 15th—History.
> > Civil rights—United States—History.
> > Abolitionists—United States.
> > Reconstruction.

For works about specific branches of law or specific legal topics, the same headings assigned to the texts of such laws are used:

Title: *The law and finance of corporate insider trading : theory and evidence* / Nasser Arshadi, Thomas H. Eyssell. c1993
SUBJECTS:
Insider trading in securities—Law and legislation—United States.

Title: *Media law* / Ralph L. Holsinger, Jon Paul Dilts. c1994
SUBJECTS:
Mass media—Law and legislation—United States.
Press law—United States.

Title: *The Supreme Court bar : legal elites in the Washington community* / Kevin T. McGuire. 1993
SUBJECTS:
United States. Supreme Court.
Judicial process—United States.
Lawyers—United States—Interviews.
Law and politics.

Title: *Environmental diplomacy : negotiating more effective global agreements* / Lawrence E. Susskind. 1994
SUBJECTS:
Environmental law, International.
Sustainable development—Law and legislation.

Form subdivisions may be added when appropriate:

Title: *The paths to privity : the history of the third party beneficiary contracts at English law* / Vernon Valentine Palmer. c1992
SUBJECTS:
Contracts—Great Britain—History.
Third parties (Law)—Great Britain—History.

Title: *The law of sex discrimination* / J. Ralph Lindgren, Nadine Taub. c1993
SUBJECTS:
Sex discrimination against women—Law and legislation—United States—Cases.
Sex discrimination in employment—Law and legislation—United States—Cases.
Women—Legal status, laws, etc.—United States—Cases.

Title: *Compendio de legislación bancaria : anotada y concordada* / ASELEX, S. A. 1990
SUBJECTS:
Banking law—Costa Rica—Digests.

A work about a particular law is assigned a heading under the uniform title of the law in addition to other appropriate topical headings assigned to the original text:

Title: *The Health Care Quality Improvement Act of 1986 : a legislative history of Pub. L. No. 99-660 /* [compiled] by Bernard D. Reams, Jr. 1990
SUBJECTS:
    United States. Health Care Quality Improvement act of 1986.
    Medical care—Law and legislation—United States.
    Physicians—Malpractice—United States.

Treaties[52]

Texts of Treaties

(1) For general (nontopical) collections of treaties, general form headings are used as appropriate (e.g., **Peace treaties; Treaties—Collections; [Place]—Foreign relations—Treaties**).[53] Examples include:

Title: *Compendio de tratados internacionales.* [1993?]
SUBJECTS:
    Treaties—Collections.

Title: *International law & world order : basic documents /* edited by Burns H. Weston. c1994-
SUBJECTS:
    International law—Sources.
    Treaties—Collections.

Title: *Treaties and alliances of the world /* [compiled by] N. J. Rengger. 1990
SUBJECTS:
    Alliances.
    Treaties—Collections.

Title: *Arabian treaties, 1600-1960 /* editors, Penelope Tuson and Emma Quick. 1992
SUBJECTS:
    Arabian Peninsula—Foreign relations—Treaties—Collections.

(2) For topical collections of treaties, the appropriate topical headings are assigned (e.g., **Environmental law, International; Human rights; Postal conventions; Commercial treaties; Sex discrimination against women—Law and legislation; World War, 1939-1945—Treaties**). Examples include:

Title: *International conventions on protection of humanity and environment* / edited by Gunter Hoog, Angela Steinmetz. 1993
SUBJECTS:
Human rights.
War (International law)
Environmental law, International.
Treaties—Collections.

Title: *Text of the General Agreement* / General Agreement on Tariffs and Trade. [1986] (1990 printing)
SUBJECTS:
Tariff—Law and legislation.
Foreign trade regulation.

Title: *EEC legislation and agreements : the texts of leading regulations, directives, and international agreements* / edited by Gabriel M. Wilner, Kent S. Karlsson. 1992
SUBJECTS:
Trade regulation—European Economic Community countries.
Commercial law—European Economic Community countries.
European Economic Community countries— Commercial treaties.

If the purpose of the collection is to present the treaties to which a particular country is a party, a general heading without local subdivision is used to bring out the international aspect. In addition, geographic headings with appropriate subdivisions are assigned to bring out the countries involved. For example:

Title: *Internationale Verträge, Europarecht : Textausgabe mit Anmerkungen und Verweisungen sowie einem systematischen und einem alphabetischen Inhaltsverzeichnis und einem ausführlichen Sachverzeichnis.* 1991-
SUBJECTS:
Germany—Foreign relations—Treaties—Collections.
Treaties—Collections.
International law.

Title: *Derecho internacional publico* / Jose Joaquin Caicedo Perdomo, Jorge Dario Garzon Diaz. [1991-]
SUBJECTS:
Colombia—Foreign relations—Treaties—Collections.
International law—Sources.

If the collection is limited to only two countries, the general heading is omitted, and reciprocal headings are used to bring out both parties:

Title: *Textos básicos para el estudio de las relaciones Panamá-EE.UU. : edición, cronología, índice temático de los tratados de 1977 y notas a cargo de Virgilio Araúz.* 1993
SUBJECTS:
United States—Foreign relations—Panama—Sources.
Panama—Foreign relations—United States—Sources.
United States—Foreign relations—Treaties.
Panama—Foreign relations—Treaties.

(3) For individual treaties, the types of headings used for topical collections of treaties are assigned in addition to the uniform title for the treaty:

Title: *North American Free Trade Agreement between the government of the United States of America, the government of Canada, and the government of the United Mexican States.* 1992
SUBJECTS:
Canada. Treaties, etc. 1992 Oct. 7.
Tariff—Law and legislation—North America.
Free trade—North America.
Foreign trade regulation—North America.
Free trade—United States.
Free trade—Canada.
Free trade—Mexico.

The heading for the name of the treaty is not assigned to a work that contains only the text of the treaty.

Works About Treaties

The types of headings assigned to texts of treaties are also used for works about treaties treated collectively:

Title: *United States treaty index : 1776-1990 consolidation* / compiled and edited by Igor I. Kavass. 1991-1993
SUBJECTS:
United States—Foreign relations—Treaties—Indexes.

Title: *The states system of Europe, 1640-1990* / Andreas Osiander. 1994
SUBJECTS:
Europe—Politics and government.
Peace treaties.

Title: *United States investment treaties : policy and practice* / by
Kenneth J. Vandevelde. 1992
SUBJECTS:
**Investments, Foreign—Law and legislation—United
States.**
Investments, Foreign—Law and legislation.
United States—Commercial treaties.

Title: *E visa form book : treaty trader and investor (E) visa ques-
tionnaires and supplemental information forms required
by U.S. Consular posts abroad* / edited by Richard S.
Goldstein. c1991
SUBJECTS:
Admission of nonimmigrants—United States—Forms.
**Emigration and immigration law—United States—
Forms.**
Visas—United States—Forms.
United States—Commercial treaties—Forms.

A work about a particular treaty is assigned the same types and
forms of headings as those used with the text of the treaty:

Title: *NAFTA schedule of Mexico.* [1993]
SUBJECTS:
Canada. Treaties, etc. 1992 Oct. 7.
Tariff—Law and legislation—Mexico.
Foreign trade regulation—Mexico.
Free trade—United States.

Trials[54]

The same types of headings are assigned to the proceedings of a
trial or trials as are assigned to works discussing them.

General Works

The heading **Trials—[Place]** is assigned to a nontopical collection
of proceedings of trials and to a work describing various trials:

Title: *Great American trials* / Edward W. Knappman, editor ;
Stephen G. Christianson and Lisa Paddock, consulting
legal editors ; contributors, Stephen G. Christianson . . .
[et al.]. 1994
SUBJECTS:
Trials—United States.

Title: *Famous trials* / by the First Earl of Birkenhead. 1991
SUBJECTS:
> **Trials—Great Britain.**
> **Trials.**

Title: *On trial* / by Gerald Dickler. 1993
SUBJECTS:
> **Trials.**

Particular Types of Trials

A heading of the type **Trials ([Topic])—[Place]** is assigned to a collection of proceedings of a particular type of civil or criminal trial or to a work describing several trials of a specific type:

Title: *Famous trials* / by John T. Morse, Jr. 1993
SUBJECTS:
> **Trials.**
> **Orton, Arthur, 1834-1898—Trials, litigation, etc.**
> **Doughty-Tichborne, Roger Charles, 1829-1854.**
> **Trials (Impostors and imposture)—Great Britain.**
> **Trials—France.**
> **Trials—United States.**

Title: *Final report of the Independent Counsel for Iran/Contra Matters* / Lawrence E. Walsh, independent counsel. [1993]
SUBJECTS:
> **Trials (Contempt of legislative bodies)—United States.**
> **Trials (Conspiracy)—United States.**
> **Trials (Perjury)—United States.**
> **Iran-Contra Affair, 1985-1990.**
> **Special prosecutors—United States.**

Title: *Salem story : reading the witch trials of 1692* / Bernard Rosenthal. 1993
SUBJECTS:
> **Witchcraft—Massachusetts—Salem.**
> **Trials (Witchcraft)—Massachusetts—Salem.**
> **Salem (Mass.)—Church history.**

Title: *The costs of processing murder cases in North Carolina* / Philip J. Cook, Donna B. Slawson ; with the assistance of Lori A. Gries. c1993
SUBJECTS:
> **Trials (Murder)—North Carolina—Costs.**
> **Prosecution—North Carolina—Costs.**
> **Criminal justice, Administration of—North Carolina—Costs.**

Individual Trials

The following types of headings are used for works containing the proceedings of a trial and for works about a particular trial:

[Name of defendant]—Trials, litigation, etc.[55]
[Name of party initiating civil action]—Trials, litigation, etc.
[Name(s) of major party or parties]—Trials, litigation, etc.
[Name of the trial] [if it has been established as a heading]
Trials ([Topic])—[Place]
[Topical headings, as appropriate]

Examples are:

Title: *The Greig affair : an 1859 tragedy* / by Matthew J. Conway. 1992
    SUBJECTS:
        Budge, Henry H.—Trials, litigation, etc.
        Trials (Murder)—New York (State)—Greig.

Title: *Redrum the innocent* / Kirk Makin. 1992
    SUBJECTS:
        Murder—Ontario—Queensville.
        Morin, Guy Paul—Trials, litigation, etc.
        Trials (Murder)—Ontario.
        Jessop, Christine, 1974-1984.

Title: *Unequal verdicts : the Central Park jogger trials* / Timothy
      Sullivan. c1992
    SUBJECTS:
        Central Park Jogger Rape Trial, New York, N.Y., 1990.
        Trials (Rape)—New York (N.Y.)
        Trials (Assault and battery)—New York (N.Y.)

Title: *A Documentary history of the legal aspects of abortion in the
      United States : Roe v. Wade* / compiled by Roy M. Mersky,
      Gary R. Hartman. 1993
    SUBJECTS:
        Roe, Jane, 1947- —Trials, litigation, etc.
        Wade, Henry—Trials, litigation, etc.
        Trials (Abortion)—Washington (D.C.)
        Abortion—Law and legislation—United States—History—Sources.

Title: *American grotesque : an account of the Clay Shaw-Jim Garrison Kennedy assassination trial in the city of New Orleans* / James Kirkwood. 1992
SUBJECTS:
Shaw, Clay, 1912?- —Trials, litigation, etc.
Trials (Conspiracy)—Louisiana—New Orleans.
Trials (Assassination)—Louisiana—New Orleans.
Garrison, Jim, 1921-
Kennedy, John F. (John Fitzgerald), 1917-1963
—Assassination.

Title: *Cold War casualty : the court-martial of Major General Robert W. Grow* / George F. Hofmann. c1993
SUBJECTS:
Grow, Robert W., 1895-1985—Trials, litigation, etc.
Grow, Robert W., 1895-1985—Diaries.
Trials (Military offenses)—Maryland—Fort George G. Meade.
Courts-martial and courts of inquiry—United States.

Title: *The People v. Clarence Darrow : the bribery trial of America's greatest lawyer* / Geoffrey Cowan. c1993
SUBJECTS:
Darrow, Clarence, 1857-1938—Trials, litigation, etc.
Trials (Bribery)—California—Los Angeles.
Lawyers—United States—Biography.

Title: *L'affaire Canson* / Laura Fairson et Alauzen Di Genova. c1990
SUBJECTS:
Pesnel, Joelle—Trials, litigation, etc.
Trials (Larceny)—France—Toulon.
Trials (Fraud)—France—Toulon.
Art—France—Forgeries.

Title: *The trial of the Templars* / Malcolm Barber. 1993
SUBJECTS:
Templars—Trials, litigation, etc.
Trials (Heresy)—France.
Inquisition—France.

Title: *Skin tight : the bizarre story of Guess v. Jordache—glamour, greed, and dirty tricks in the fashion industry* / by Christopher Byron. c1992
SUBJECTS:
Guess (Firm)—Trials, litigation, etc.
Jordache (Firm)—Trials, litigation, etc.
Trials (Fraud)—California—Los Angeles.
Clothing trade—United States—Corrupt practices.

Title: *Undue influence : the epic battle for the Johnson & Johnson fortune* / David Margolick. c1993
SUBJECTS:
Johnson, J. Seward, d. 1983—Will.
Johnson, Barbara Piasecka—Trials, litigation, etc.

War Crime Trials

To proceedings of and works about a war crime trial, the following types of headings are assigned in addition to other topical headings: **[Name of defendant or trial]; War crime trials—[Place]**. Examples include:

Title: *The trial of Adolf Eichmann : record of proceedings in the District Court of Jerusalem.* 1992-
SUBJECTS:
Eichmann, Adolf, 1906-1962—Trials, litigation, etc.
War crime trials—Jerusalem.
Holocaust, Jewish (1939-1945)—Sources.

Title: *Days of judgment : the World War II crimes trials* / by Isobel V. Morin. c1995
SUBJECTS:
War crime trials.
World War, 1939-1945—Atrocities.

Title: *Proposal for an international war crimes tribunal for the former Yugoslavia* / by rapporteurs (Corell Turk-Thune) under the CSCE Moscow human dimension mechanism to Bosnia-Herzegovina and Croatia. [1993]
SUBJECTS:
International courts.
War crime trials—Yugoslavia.
Yugoslav War, 1991- —Atrocities.

Title: *Remembering in vain : the Klaus Barbie trial and crimes against humanity* / Alan Finkielkraut ; translated by Roxanne Lapidus with Sima Godfrey ; introduction by Alice Y. Kaplan. c1992
SUBJECTS:
Barbie, Klaus, 1913- —Trials, litigation, etc.
War crime trials—France—Lyon.
Holocaust, Jewish (1939-1945)—France.
World War, 1939-1945—France—Lyon—Atrocities.

Title: *The Tokyo trial and beyond : reflections of a peacemonger /*
B. V. A. Roling ; edited and with an introduction by Antonio
Cassese. 1993
SUBJECTS:
Tokyo Trial, Tokyo, Japan, 1946-1948.

SOURCE MATERIALS IN THE FIELDS OF HISTORY AND GENEALOGY[56]

In the past, many publications of interest to genealogists and
historians, especially local historians, were assigned headings of the
type **[Topic]—[Place]**. Since December 1975, such materials have
been given an additional heading of the type **[Place]—[Topic]** if the
place is below the country level. The topical subdivision in this case is
chosen from the following list:

—**Antiquities**
—**Biography**
—**Church history**
—**Description and travel**
—**Economic conditions**
—**Ethnic relations**
—**Genealogy**
—**History**
> [including the various modifications of the subdivision,
> e.g., —**History, Local;** —**History, Military**]
—**Race relations**
—**Religion**
—**Religious life and customs**
—**Social conditions**
—**Social life and customs**

All these are free-floating subdivisions. The subdivision —**Genealogy**
or —**History** is used when none of the others listed above seems
particularly appropriate to the work in hand.

The Subdivision —History[57]

The subdivision —**History** is a free-floating subdivision that is
widely used under a variety of topics to designate historical treatment.
However, certain restrictions to its use have developed over the years,
as explained in the following discussion.

General Use

The subdivision —**History** is used under subjects (including the names of places or organizations) for descriptions and explanations of past events concerning the topic, place, or organization, such as **Aeronautics— History; Indians of North America—History; Washington (D.C.)— History; Catholic Church—History; General Motors Corporation —History**.

Exceptions

The subdivision —**History** is not used:

(1) under literary, music, or film form headings; in these cases, the subdivision —**History and criticism** is used instead (e.g., **English poetry—History and criticism; Music—19th century—History and criticism; Western films—History and criticism**)

(2) under subjects for which phrase headings have been provided (e.g., **Church history; Military history; Social history**)

(3) under uniform titles or name-title headings, which are assigned without subdivision to historical treatments of the work in question

(4) under art genre headings qualified by names of national, ethnic, or religious groups (e.g., **Painting—History** but not *Painting, French—History*)

(5) under historical headings or headings with an obvious historical connotation (e.g., **Migrations of nations; Reformation; Discoveries in geography; [Names of individual events or wars]**)

(6) under topical subdivisions considered historical in intent. These include all subdivisions that are obviously historical in nature (e.g., —**Discovery and exploration; —Territorial expansion**) and subdivisions that imply history by designating special kinds of conditions (e.g., —**Economic conditions**), special customs (e.g., —**Social life and customs**), and political affairs (e.g., —**Foreign relations; —Politics and government**). Following is a list of the subdivisions of this type that are not further subdivided by —**History**:[58]

—**Administrative and political divisions**
—**Aerial exploration**
—**Annexation to [. . .]**
—**Anniversaries, etc.**
—**Antiquities**
—**Art**
—**Autonomous communities**

—Boundaries
—Cantons
—Centennial celebrations, etc.
—Chronology
—Church history
—Civilization
—Constitutional history
—Constitutional law
—Court and courtiers
—Cult
—Departments
—Description and travel
—Discovery and exploration
—Economic conditions
—Economic policy
—Ethnic relations
—Exhibitions
—Exiles
—Foreign economic relations
—Foreign relations
—Gold discoveries
—Government relations
—Heraldry
—Historical geography
—Historiography
—History
—Illustrations
—Intellectual life
—Kings and rulers
—Military policy
—Military relations
—Origin
—Politics and government
—Portraits
—Prophecies
—Provinces
—Queens
—Race relations
—Regions
—Relations
—Religion
—Religious life and customs
—Republics
—Rites and ceremonies
—Rural conditions
—Sieges
—Social conditions
—Social life and customs
—Social policy
—States

—Territorial expansion
—Union territories

Period Subdivisions

Under certain headings, especially names of places, the subdivision —**History** is further subdivided by period when there is sufficient material to warrant it. If one of the exceptional headings or subdivisions noted under points 5 and 6 above (see page 371) is to be further subdivided by period, the period subdivision follows immediately after the heading or the topical subdivision, as in **Social history—19th century**; **Great Britain—Economic conditions—20th century**; **Chicago (Ill.)—Politics and government—To 1950**.

Historical Source Materials

The subdivision —**Sources** follows directly after the exceptional headings and subdivisions noted in points 2, 5, and 6 above (see page 371) without the interposition of the subdivision —**History** (e.g., **Reconstruction—Sources**; **World War, 1914-1918—Sources**; **China—Foreign relations—Sources**; **United States—Politics and government—1783-1789—Sources**). Examples include:

Title: *The nation divides : the Civil War, 1820-1880* / Richard
   Steins. c1993
 SUBJECTS:
   **Slavery—United States—History—Sources—Juvenile
   literature.**
   **United States—History—1815-1861—Sources—Juvenile
   literature.**
   **United States—History—Civil War, 1861-1865—Sources—
   Juvenile literature.**
   Reconstruction—Sources—Juvenile literature.

Title: *The Allies against the Axis : World War II (1940-1950)* /
   Richard Steins. c1993
 SUBJECTS:
   World War, 1939-1945—Sources—Juvenile literature.

Archives and Archival Resources[59]

The free-floating subdivision —**Archives** is used with collections or discussions of documentary material, such as manuscripts, household records, diaries, correspondence, photographs, or memorabilia. It can be used as either a form or topical subdivision under headings for types of corporate bodies and educational institutions, for classes of persons, and for ethnic groups, as well as under names of individual corporate bodies, educational institutions, persons, and families. In addition, topical headings are assigned to bring out any subject content of the documents. Examples include:

Title: *The F.B.I. files on the assassination of President Kennedy* [microform]. 1993
SUBJECTS:
  Kennedy, John F. (John Fitzgerald), 1917-1963— Assassination—Sources.
  Oswald, Lee Harvey.
  Ruby, Jack.
  United States. Warren Commission.
  United States. Federal Bureau of Investigation—Archives.

Title: *The Churchill war papers* / [compiled by] Martin Gilbert. c1993-
SUBJECTS:
  World War, 1939-1945—Naval operations, British—Sources.
  Great Britain. Admiralty—History—Sources.
  World War, 1939-1945—Sources.
  Churchill, Winston, Sir, 1874-1965—Archives.

The free-floating subdivision **—Archival resources** is used under topical headings and names of places for brief descriptions of available types of documents and historical records that pertain to the topic or place in question. For example:

Title: *Les Fonds musicaux anciens en Midi-Pyrénées : pré-inventaire.* [1992]
SUBJECTS:
  Music—France—Midi-Pyrénées—Archival resources.
  Archival resources—France—Midi-Pyrénées.

The subdivision **—Archival resources** may be further subdivided by **—Directories** for works containing the names, addresses, and brief descriptions of institutions housing archival materials on a particular topic:

Title: *The St. Martin's guide to sources in contemporary British history* / compiled for the British Library of Political and Economic Science by Chris Cook and David Waller. 1993-
SUBJECTS:
  Great Britain—History—20th century—Sources— Directories.
  Great Britain—History—Elizabeth II, 1952- —Sources —Directories.
  Great Britain—History—Elizabeth II, 1952- —Archival resources— Directories.
  Archives—Great Britain—Directories.

Title: *Maine's historical records : a guide to collections of original, unpublished materials.* [1992]
    SUBJECTS:
        Maine—History—Library resources—Directories.
        Maine—History—Archival resources—Directories.

Title: *First guide to Civil War genealogy* / by G. R. Post. c1993
    SUBJECTS:
        United States—History—Civil War, 1861-1865—Archival resources—Directories.
        United States—Genealogy—Archival resources—Directories.

Title: *Historical and genealogical holdings in the state of Florida* / gathered and compiled for the Genealogy and Local History Caucus, Florida Library Association. [1992]
    SUBJECTS:
        Florida—Genealogy—Library resources—Directories.
        Florida—Genealogy—Archival resources—Directories.
        Florida—History, Local—Library resources—Directories.
        Florida—History, Local—Archival resources—Directories.

Form Subdivisions

To bring out the bibliographic or physical form of a work, the subdivision **—History** may be subdivided by an appropriate free-floating form subdivision:

Science—History—Miscellanea
Science—History—Outlines, syllabi, etc.
Science—History—Popular works

Title: *Marvels of science : 50 fascinating 5-minute reads* / Kendall Haven. 1994
    SUBJECTS:
        Discoveries in science—History.
        Science—History.
        Science—History—Miscellanea.

Title: *The universe and eye : making sense of the new science* / text by Timothy Ferris ; illustrations by Ingram Pinn ; foreword by John Gribbin ; in association with New Scientist. 1993
    SUBJECTS:
        Science—History—Popular works.
        Technology—History—Popular works.
        Science—Philosophy—Popular works.
        Scientists—Popular works.

Genealogical Materials[60]

For works of interest to genealogists and local historians, topical headings are assigned according to general guidelines. The following types of headings are generally assigned:

[Topic]—[Place]
[Place]—[Topic]
[Place]—Genealogy
[Form headings]

Topical headings with appropriate subdivisions are assigned according to general guidelines. If the work pertains to a particular place and the topical heading is in the form of [Topic]—[Place], an additional heading under the name of the place with one of the following topical subdivisions is assigned:

—Antiquities
—Biography
—Church history
—Description and travel
—Economic conditions
—Ethnic relations
—Genealogy
—History [or one of its variations, e.g., —History, Military]
—Race relations
—Religion
—Religious life and customs
—Social conditions
—Social life and customs

The subdivision —History or —Genealogy is used if none of the more specific subdivisions applies.

For works of value in the study of the origin, descent, and relationship of named families, especially those works that assemble such information from family papers, deeds, wills, public records, parish registers, cemetery inscriptions, ship lists, and the like, a heading in the form of [Place]—Genealogy is always assigned even if the place is a country or a larger region.

When appropriate, a form heading is also assigned. Typical headings of this nature are:

Archives
Business records
Church records and registers
Court records
Criminal registers
Deeds
Epitaphs

Families of royal descent
Heraldry
Inscriptions
Inventories of decedents' estates
Land grants
Land titles
Marriage licenses
Mining claims
Names
Obituaries
Probate records
Public land records
Public records
Registers of births, etc.
Slave records
Titles of honor and nobility
Trials
Voting registers
Wills

All these may be subdivided by place.

Examples include:

Title: *Gone to the world : vital statistics on individuals in the Shaker community at Pleasant Hill, Kentucky* / Marc Alan Rhorer. 1992
SUBJECTS:
Pleasant Hill (Ky.)—Genealogy.
Shakers—Kentucky—Pleasant Hill—Genealogy.

Title: *Everyname index to 1860 census of Guthrie County, Iowa.* 1993
SUBJECTS:
Guthrie County (Iowa)—Genealogy.
Registers of births, etc.—Iowa—Guthrie County.
Guthrie County (Iowa)—Census, 1860—Indexes.
United States—Census, 8th, 1860—Indexes.

Title: *Pleasantville Union Cemetery, 1714-1993* / compiled and edited by Richard H. Yoder. [1994?]
SUBJECTS:
Oley (Pa. : Township)—Genealogy.
Registers of births, etc.—Pennsylvania—Oley (Township)
Yoder family.
Pleasantville Union Cemetery (Pa.)
Inscriptions—Pennsylvania—Oley (Township)

Title: *Africans in Georgia, 1870* / compiled by Roma Jones Stewart.
c1993
SUBJECTS:
Georgia—Genealogy.
Afro-Americans—Georgia—Genealogy.
Registers of births, etc.—Georgia.
Georgia—Census, 1870.
United States—Census, 9th, 1870.

Title: *California residents statewide lists of school-land warrants,
1852-1858* / [compiled by the Pomona Valley Genealogical
Society]. 1991
SUBJECTS:
California—Genealogy.
Land titles—California.
Landowners—California—Registers.

Title: *A closer look at Worcester County wills* / David V. Heise. 1991
SUBJECTS:
Worcester County (Md.)—Genealogy.
Wills—Maryland—Worcester County.

For a discussion and examples of works about individual families, see
pages 240-43.

Other Works of Interest to Historians[61]

The following types of materials are also considered of interest to
historians

(1) *Activities*. Typical headings include:
Cattle trade
Country life
Frontier and pioneer life
Fur trade
Mountain life
Plantation life
Printing—History
Ranch life

(2) *Archaeological evidence*.[62] Typical headings include:
Christian antiquities
Earthworks (Archaeology)
Excavations (Archaeology)
Industrial archaeology
Kitchen-middens
Mounds

(3) *Classes of persons.* Typical headings include:
Cowboys
Lawyers
Minorities
Physicians
Pirates
Politicians

(4) *Monuments and memorials.* Typical headings include:
Cemeteries
Epitaphs
Historical markers
Inscriptions
Memorials
Monuments
Sepulchral monuments
Soldiers' monuments
Statues
Tombs
War memorials

(5) *Particular uses of land; historic structures.* Typical headings include:
Bridges
Churches
Farms
Fountains
Historic sites
Hotels
Taverns (Inns)
Mines and mineral resources
Parks
Roads

(6) *Historic events.* Typical headings include:
Battles
Earthquakes
Epidemics
Fires
Storms

If a work is historical in nature and requires one of the headings of the types listed above, the additional heading **[Place]—[Topic]** is usually assigned.

Title: *Gila Cliff Dwellings National Monument : an administrative history* / by Peter Russell. 1992
    SUBJECTS:
        Gila Cliff Dwellings National Monument (N.M.)—History.
        Mogollon culture.

Archaeological surveying—New Mexico—Gila Cliff
Dwellings National Monument—History.
New Mexico—Antiquities.

Title: *Aztec Ruins National Monument* / [written by Scott Thybony].
c1992
SUBJECTS:
Aztec Ruins National Monument (N.M.)
Pueblo Indians—Antiquities.
New Mexico—Antiquities.

Title: *Crooked trails* / written and illustrated by Frederic Remington.
[1992]
SUBJECTS:
Frontier and pioneer life—West (U.S.)
West (U.S.)—Social life and customs.
Cowboys—West (U.S.)
Folklore—West (U.S.)
Cowboys—Florida.
Frontier and pioneer life—Florida.
Florida—Social life and customs.
Folklore—Florida.

Title: *Frontierswomen : the Iowa experience* / Glenda Riley. 1994
SUBJECTS:
Women pioneers—Iowa—History.
Frontier and pioneer life—Iowa.
Iowa—History.

Title: *German pioneer life : a social history* / edited by Don Heinrich
Tolzmann. c1992
SUBJECTS:
German Americans—Pennsylvania—Social life and
customs.
Frontier and pioneer life—Pennsylvania.
Pennsylvania—Social life and customs.

Title: *Indian mounds you can visit : 165 aboriginal sites of west
coast Florida* / by I. Mac Perry. c1993
SUBJECTS:
Indians of North America—Florida—Antiquities—
Guidebooks.
Mounds—Florida—Guidebooks.
Kitchen-middens—Florida—Guidebooks.
Florida—Antiquities—Guidebooks.
Florida—Guidebooks.

Title: *The pirates of the New England coast, 1630-1730* / by George
Francis Dow and John Henry Edmonds ; introduction by
Ernest H. Pentecost. 1993
SUBJECTS:
Pirates—New England—History.
New England—History—Colonial period, ca. 1600-1775.

Title: *The complete guide to Boston's Freedom Trail* / by Charles
Bahne. 1993
SUBJECTS:
Freedom Trail (Boston, Mass.)—Guidebooks.
Boston (Mass.)—Guidebooks.
Historic sites—Massachusetts—Boston—Guidebooks.

The prescribed extra heading **[Place]—[Topic]** is assigned to
works of interest to historians only when the place in question is at a
lower level than a country (e.g., a city, county, state, region of a
country). It is not assigned when the place in question corresponds to
a country or a larger region, except for works classed in D, E, and F at
the Library of Congress.

An example of a work to which the additional heading **[Place]—
[Topic]** is *not* assigned is shown below:

Title: *The fallen : a photographic journey through the war cemeteries
and memorials of the Great War, 1914-18* / John Garfield ;
with an introduction by Gavin Stamp. 1990
LC CALL NUMBER: TR654 .G343 1990
SUBJECTS:
Photography, Artistic.
World War, 1914-1918—Monuments—Europe—Pictorial
works.
World War, 1914-1918—Battlefields—Europe—Pictorial
works.
War memorials—Europe—Pictorial works.
World War, 1914-1918—Europe—History.

An example of a work classed in D requiring the additional heading
[Place]—[Topic] follows. (The heading with an asterisk **[*]** listed in
the example is the prescribed extra heading.)

Title: *Pyramids of ancient Egypt* / John D. Clare, editor. 1992
LC CALL NUMBER: DT61 .P97 1992
SUBJECTS:
*Egypt—Social life and customs—To 332 B.C.—Juvenile
literature.
Pyramids—Egypt—Design and construction—Juvenile
literature.

ARCHAEOLOGICAL WORKS[63]

Types of Headings

For works on the archaeology of particular places, one or more of the following types of headings are used:

[Name of site]   [if the work is about a specific site]
[Place]—Antiquities
    or [Place]—Antiquities, Roman, [etc.][64]
[Name of people, prehistoric culture or period, etc.][65]
Excavations (Archaeology)—[Place]
[Other special topics, as needed]

Application

Works Not Limited to a Single Site

The heading for the place and the heading for the people are assigned to an archaeological work if both a single area (but not a single site) and a single people are under discussion. If two peoples are involved, a separate heading for each is assigned. If more than two peoples are involved or if the names of the peoples cannot be identified from the work being cataloged, headings for the people are not used. If the name of the relevant jurisdiction corresponds closely to that of the people (e.g., **Egypt** and **Egyptians**), only the heading for the place is assigned.[66]

Examples of works *not* limited to a single site include:

Title: *China's buried kingdoms* / by the editors of Time-Life Books. c1993
    SUBJECTS:
        China—Antiquities.
        Excavations (Archaeology)—China.
        China—Civilization.
        Tombs—China.

Title: *Greece : temples, tombs, and treasures* / by the editors of Time-Life Books. 1994
    SUBJECTS:
        Greece—History—To 146 B.C.
        Greece—Antiquities.
        Excavations (Archaeology)—Greece.

Title: *Ancient Jerusalem revealed* / edited by Hillel Geva ; [English version, Joseph Shadur]. 1994
    SUBJECTS:
        Jerusalem—Antiquities.
        Excavations (Archaeology)—Jerusalem.

Title: *The Northern Tucson Basin survey : research directions and background studies* / John H. Madsen, Paul R. Fish, and Suzanne K. Fish, editors; contributions by James Bayman . . . [et al.]. 1993
SUBJECTS:
Hohokam culture.
Indians of North America—Arizona—Tucson Basin.
Excavations (Archaeology)—Arizona—Tucson Basin.
Arizona—Antiquities.
Tucson Basin (Ariz.)—Antiquities.

Title: *Upland adaptations in Lower Glen Canyon during the Archaic and Pueblo periods : archaeological data recovery at 20 sites along the Antelope Point Road (Route N22B) near Page, Arizona* / by Paul F. Reed. [1992]
SUBJECTS:
Indians of North America—Arizona—Antiquities.
Excavations (Archaeology)—Arizona.
Glen Canyon (Utah and Ariz.)—Antiquities.

Title: *The Yucatan : a guide to the land of Maya mysteries plus sacred sites at Belize, Tikal & Copan* / by Antoinette May. 1993
SUBJECTS:
Yucatán Peninsula—Guidebooks.
Yucatán Peninsula—Antiquities—Guidebooks.
Mayas—Antiquities—Guidebooks.
Indians of Mexico—Mexico—Yucatán Peninsula—Antiquities—Guidebooks.

Title: *The jade lords* / O. L. González Calderón. c1991
SUBJECTS:
Olmecs sculpture.
Olmecs pottery.
Olmecs—Antiquities.
Jade—Mexico.
Mexico—Antiquities.

Title: *The ancient Maya* / [edited by] Robert J. Sharer. 1994
SUBJECTS:
Mayas.
Mayas—Antiquities.
Mexico—Antiquities.
Central America—Antiquities.

Works on Individual Sites

A work about an individual archaeological site is assigned one or more of the following types of headings:

[Name of site]
[Place]—Antiquities
[Special topics]

Examples include:

Title: *The Temple of Apollo Bassitas* / by Frederick A. Cooper. [1992]
SUBJECTS:
Temple of Apollo (Bassai)
Bassai (Extinct city)
Greece—Antiquities.

Title: *Lithic analysis of Acheulean assemblages from the Avivim sites, Israel* / Milla Y. Ohel. 1990
SUBJECTS:
Avivim Sites (Israel)
Acheulian culture—Israel.
Israel—Antiquities.

Title: *Megiddo : a city-state and royal centre in north Israel* / by Aharon Kempinski. [c1989]
SUBJECTS:
Megiddo (Extinct city)
Excavations (Archaeology)—Israel.
Israel—Antiquities.

Title: *Excavations in the south of the Temple Mount : the Ophel of Biblical Jerusalem* / Eilat Mazar and Benjamin Mazar ; with appendices by Yonatan Nadelman . . . [et al.]. 1989
SUBJECTS:
Excavations (Archaeology)—Jerusalem.
Jerusalem—Antiquities.
Ophel (Jerusalem)—Antiquities.
Temple Mount (Jerusalem)—Antiquities.

Title: *The Damascus Gate, Jerusalem : excavations by C.-M. Bennett and J.B. Hennessy at the Damascus Gate, Jerusalem, 1964-66* / G. J. Wightman. 1989
SUBJECTS:
Damascus Gate (Jerusalem)
Gates—Jerusalem.
Jerusalem—Antiquities.
Excavations (Archaeology)—Jerusalem.

Title: *Yaxchilán* / Laura Elena Sotelo Santos ; presentación por
José Patrocinio González B. Garrido. 1992
SUBJECTS:
Yaxchilán Site (Mexico)
Mayas—Antiquities.

NOTES

[1]"[Topic] in literature; The Subdivision —In literature," *Cataloging Service Bulletin* 63 (Winter 1994): 28-29.

[2]The phrase **[Topic] in literature**, previously a free-floating phrase, is no longer so. Each such heading is now established separately and displayed in LCSH.

[3]The type of heading *[Personal name] in fiction, drama, poetry, etc.*, previously used for works about persons as themes or characters in literature, is now obsolete.

[4]Library of Congress, Office of Subject Cataloging Policy, *Subject Cataloging Manual*, 4th ed. (Washington, D.C.: Cataloging Distribution Service, Library of Congress, 1991), H1780, H1790, H1800.

[5]The only other headings that may be subdivided by **—Collections** are **Autographs**; **Charters**; **Manuscripts**; **Playbills**; **Treaties**.

[6]The subdivision *—Stories* used under topical headings has been discontinued. However, there still exist a few phrase headings that are used for certain kinds of stories (e.g., **Sea stories**; **Detective and mystery stories**).

[7]Library of Congress, *Subject Cataloging Manual*, H1780, p. 1.

[8]The subdivision *—Legends and stories*, previously used under types of animals, is no longer valid. The subdivision **—Folklore** is now used under the heading **Animals** or type of animal (e.g., **Dogs**) for one or more legends about them. The subdivision **—Anecdotes** is used for anecdotal accounts, and the subdivision **—Biography** is used for true accounts about animals.

[9]Works by joint authors, such as *The Maid's Tragedy* by Beaumont and Fletcher, are treated in the same manner as works by individual authors.

[10]The subdivisions **—Juvenile fiction** ; **—Juvenile drama**; **—Juvenile poetry** are used for juvenile belles lettres. The subdivision **—Juvenile literature**, on the other hand, is used with headings assigned to nonliterary work for children. Note also specific juvenile headings such as **Children's stories** and **Nursery rhymes**. For literature written for children, see also the discussion on pages 223-25.

[11]Not assigned to fiction for young adults.

[12]From March to June 1993, the Library of Congress initiated a "fiction project" to assign additional topical headings to fiction. As a result, many LC MARC records produced during that period carry topical headings not called for in the policy stated in Library of Congress, *Subject Cataloging Manual*.

[13]The term *historical fiction* is defined broadly to include fiction about entities such as movements, corporate bodies other than jurisdictions, camps, parks, structures, geographical features other than regions, ethnic groups, disasters, and categories of events. (cf. Library of Congress, *Subject Cataloging Manual*, H1790, p. 3).

[14]Library of Congress, *Subject Cataloging Manual*, H1720.

[15]Library of Congress, *Subject Cataloging Manual*, H1795.

[16]Library of Congress, *Subject Cataloging Manual*, H1095.

[17]**[Topic] in literature**, previously a free-floating form, is no longer free-floating; each heading of this type is now established separately and included in LCSH.

[18]For works about an individual legend or romance, see the discussions on pages 300-301.

[19]For works about an individual literary work, see the discussion on pages 295-99.

[20]For works about an individual literary work, see the discussion on pages 295-99.

[21]Library of Congress, *Subject Cataloging Manual*, H1330.

[22]Library of Congress, *Subject Cataloging Manual*, H1155.6.

[23]Library of Congress, *Subject Cataloging Manual*, H1155.8.

[24]Library of Congress, *Subject Cataloging Manual*, H1795, pp. 3-4.

[25]Library of Congress, *Subject Cataloging Manual*, H1160.

[26]Library of Congress, *Subject Cataloging Manual*, H1917.5.

[27]Library of Congress, *Subject Cataloging Manual*, H1160, H1161.

[28]Library of Congress, *Subject Cataloging Manual*, H1160, p. 2.

[29]Medium not specified for larger works, such as operas and oratorios.

[30]Library of Congress, *Subject Cataloging Manual*, H1917.

[31]Not applicable under the heading **Musical instruments** or names of musical instruments.

[32]Library of Congress, *Subject Cataloging Manual*, H1438, pp. 2-3.

[33]*Anglo-American Cataloguing Rules,* 2nd ed., 1988 revision, prepared under the direction of the Joint Steering Committee for Revision of AACR, a committee of the American Library Association, the Australian Committee on Cataloguing, the British Library, the Canadian Committee on Cataloguing, the Library Association, the Library of Congress, eds. Michael Gorman and Paul W. Winkler (Chicago: American Library Association, 1988), 534-35.

[34]Library of Congress, *Subject Cataloging Manual*, H1250.

[35]Bethany Mendenhall, "Implications for Art Subject Headings," paper prepared for the ALCTS Subject Analysis Committee, Subcommittee on the Order of Subdivisions, November 1993.

[36]Mendenhall, "Implications for Art Subject Headings."

[37]For personal names, the form **[Person]—Art** [for persons who lived before 1400] or **[Person]—Portraits** is used. For proper uses of these subdivisions, consult *Subject Cataloging Manual*.

[38]Library of Congress, *Subject Cataloging Manual*, H1250, p. 2.

[39]Library of Congress, *Subject Cataloging Manual*, H910.

[40]Library of Congress, *Subject Cataloging Manual*, H1427.

[41]Library of Congress, *Subject Cataloging Manual*, H1997, H2015.

[42]Library of Congress, *Subject Cataloging Manual*, H1998.

[43]Library of Congress, *Subject Cataloging Manual*, H1300, p. 2.

[44]Library of Congress, *Subject Cataloging Manual*, H1295, H1300, H1435, pp. 3-4.

[45]Library of Congress, *Subject Cataloging Manual*, H1300.

[46]The term *liturgy* refers to services such as prayers, ritual, acts, and ceremonies used in public worship in accordance with the authorized or standard forms of a religion or denomination.

[47]Library of Congress, *Subject Cataloging Manual*, H1154.5, H1550, H1705, H1710.

[48]Library of Congress, *Subject Cataloging Manual*, H1154.5.

[49]Library of Congress, *Subject Cataloging Manual*, H1550.

[50]Library of Congress, *Subject Cataloging Manual*, H1710.

[51]"Constitutions in Subject Heading Practice," *Cataloging Service Bulletin* 24 (Spring 1984): 56-57.

[52]Library of Congress, *Subject Cataloging Manual*, H2227.

[53]The subdivision **—Treaties** is used only with the names of wars and Indian tribes, and with headings of the type **[Jurisdiction]—Foreign relations**.

[54]Library of Congress, *Subject Cataloging Manual*, H2228.

[55]For a work about the trial of Jesus, the heading **Jesus Christ—Trial** is used.

[56]Library of Congress, *Subject Cataloging Manual*, H1845.

[57]Library of Congress, *Subject Cataloging Manual*, H1647.

[58]Library of Congress, *Subject Cataloging Manual*, H1647, p. 5.

[59]Library of Congress, *Subject Cataloging Manual*, H1230.

[60]Library of Congress, *Subject Cataloging Manual*, H1845.

[61]Library of Congress, *Subject Cataloging Manual*, H1845, pp. 3-5.

[62]For works on the archaeology of particular places, see the section on archaeological works beginning on page 382.

[63]Library of Congress, *Subject Cataloging Manual*, H1225.

[64]The subdivision **—Antiquities** is qualified by one of the following adjectives if applicable: **Byzantine; Celtic; Germanic; Phoenician; Roman; Slavic; Turkish**.

[65]This heading is subdivided by **—Antiquities** if the people are still extant in modern times, e.g., **Mayas—Antiquities**.

[66]The heading **Romans** is not assigned if the work is assigned one of the following headings: **Rome—Antiquities; Italy—Antiquities; [Place within Italy]—Antiquities, Roman**.

PART 3

FUTURE PROSPECTS

11 Library of Congress Subject Headings As an Online Retrieval Tool

Over the last 25 years, there have been major advances in the retrieval options available to online catalog users. The first online catalogs were, in retrospect, rather primitive, especially in the ways the subject fields in a record could be searched. Current systems are much more sophisticated. This chapter will discuss the likely future prospects of the Library of Congress subject headings system in the context of a retrieval environment in which a very large segment of the information-seeking community has access to quite sophisticated online retrieval systems.

As we look into the next century, we cannot help asking whether there is a future for LCSH. The central issue is whether a system originally designed for the manual catalog can continue to be a viable tool in the online environment.

Many factors will determine what system will be the favored tool for subject access in the coming decades, and not the least among these is economics. Maximum possible effectiveness is, of course, essential, and logical, philosophical, and theoretical considerations also apply. It cannot be denied that systems that are theoretically more satisfying than LCSH have been devised. However, the question of whether to continue the present system or adopt another system is not purely academic.

In the mid-1980s, the debate on the future of LCSH suggested three possible alternatives:

(1) abandon the system completely in favor of natural language or of another system such as PRECIS (Preserved Context Index System), which was then in use in *British National Bibliography*;

(2) let LCSH continue on the present course and see what happens, a sort of *que sera, sera* approach; and

(3) try to improve the current system and render it more logical and consistent, with rigorously defined rules that rest on an understanding of user needs and behavior, of the nature of catalogs, and of the principles of information retrieval.[1]

As we entered the 1990s, the debate appeared to come to a halt, with general agreement that the third approach represented the most viable course. There are numerous reasons for this consensus. William E. Studwell offers three arguments for not discarding LCSH:

> First, the other systems really have not proven themselves on a long-term basis and in a wide-scale environment. Second, LC is improving at an accelerating rate. . . . And third, the economic, administrative, intellectual, and psychological disadvantages of replacing the widely-used and long-established LC system would be enormous.[2]

Going even further, Karen Markey Drabenstott and Diane Vizine-Goetz offer the following reasons for predicting the continuing use of LCSH in libraries throughout North America:

> Public catalog users with varying levels of subject knowledge can find materials on the topics they seek using LCSH.
>
> In terms of subject retrieval, a better system has not been devised, nor will be in the near future.
>
> Online systems have capitalized on some desirable features of the LCSH system.
>
> Online systems have overcome some limitations of the LCSH system.
>
> Improvements can be made to LCSH.
>
> Tens of millions of bibliographic records are available to the users of online bibliographic systems through LCSH.[3]

The prospect of a new system designed totally for the online environment and soundly grounded on theoretical and logical bases is tantalizing, but at present such a system is inconceivable on financial grounds. The resources that would be needed for its development and implementation would be staggering: The costs of converting extant records would have to be added, as would the hidden cost of the confusion caused by a changeover. It is worth noting that changes in LCSH carry international implications, because it has become the de facto standard for subject access in online catalogs almost worldwide. For the time being, therefore, maintaining and improving the current LCSH system seems to be the most viable course. The question now raised is not whether LCSH should continue to be used, but how the system can best be improved.

AGENDA FOR CHANGE

In discussing ways in which the effectiveness of LCSH may be improved, we should be aware that there are three different elements affecting how well any indexing system performs in a retrieval environment. One element is the vocabulary: its terminology, its formal structure, and its syndetic apparatus. Another is the set of policies governing how terms in the thesaurus should be assigned to documents. The third is the existence and eventual enhancement of those online capabilities that affect subject searching.

For LCSH, the first concerns the construction and maintenance of the list itself, and includes terminology, forms of headings and subdivisions, citation order, and cross-reference structure—in other words, all aspects of the vocabulary.

The second concerns how LCSH should be applied in subject cataloging. This element encompasses questions on depth and exhaustivity of indexing, degree of coextensivity, when to use subdivisions, whether to do generic posting, and (especially for individual libraries) how extensive cross references should be. While at given levels of subject analysis the question of coextensivity is determined by available vocabulary, the other aspects of application are mainly a matter of cataloging and indexing policy. This may vary among the libraries or agencies that use the system. Nonetheless, LC policies regarding assignment of subject headings set the patterns for subject cataloging in many libraries and cataloging centers because so many of them make use of LC MARC records.

The third element is the degree to which current and anticipated features of online systems affect either of the other two aspects. For instance, when subject strings can be searched by key words, there is little justification for inverted headings. Similarly, without the bulk restrictions of card or book catalogs, there is less reason to restrict the number of headings assigned a given record.

In view of these considerations, in the past few years the Library of Congress has been implementing gradual changes at an accelerated pace. There is no shortage in the literature of suggestions for improvements in either LCSH itself or in policies for its application. Even those changes found highly desirable by policy-makers at LC, however, cannot always be brought about within a short time frame. The implementation of almost any change is time-consuming and costly; availability of personnel and other resources is always a determining factor. Furthermore, not all changes are of equal urgency or significance; the Library of Congress, with the assistance of the profession, is working out priorities. The Subject Subdivisions Conference, convened by the Library of Congress in 1991, was an important step in a cooperative effort to improve LCSH.[4] Some of the recommendations from this conference will be discussed later in this chapter.

In the pages that follow, many suggestions regarding one or another aspect of the LC subject headings system are discussed, and further questions are raised. Whenever appropriate, recommendations are presented.

Principles of Structure

Terminology

* Terminology is the aspect of LCSH that has received the severest criticism over the years. The four main issues are specificity, currentness, term sensitivity, and common usage (i.e., how well a heading for a topic matches the terms chosen by most users for that topic).

Specificity

The word *specificity* is used in two different senses in discussions of subject catalogs and indexes. For one, it refers to the closeness of match between a term or heading and the document to which it is assigned. For the other, it refers to where a given term lies within a hierarchy of related terms—whether it is near the top and thus fairly general, or fairly far down and thus quite specific. The first sense has to do with how a thesaurus is used, how its terms are applied to documents. It is the second sense that is used when thesaurus construction is the topic of discussion, as it is here.

As discussed in chapter 2, in LCSH, individual term specificity is determined largely by literary warrant; new terms are introduced into the system as required for cataloging or for preparing cross references. Because headings are used to represent the overall contents of books, few highly specialized and narrow terms are needed. As a result, the degree of term specificity in LCSH is, in many areas, broader than that in an indexing vocabulary designed for use with journal articles in a specialized field (e.g., *Medical Subject Headings; Thesaurus of ERIC Descriptors*).

Term specificity in a system is related to the policy on depth or levels and exhaustivity of subject cataloging, not simply a matter of thesaurus construction. If the Library of Congress were to begin indexing individual units, such as chapters, within a document, and the specific concepts within a work in addition to its overall content, the specificity of its terms would have to change accordingly, through literary warrant.

Currentness

There are two aspects to currentness of terminology: whether new terms are added as appropriate, and whether obsolete terms remain. In the past there has been vociferous criticism of the Library of Congress because of the apparent prevalence of obsolete terms in the list and on bibliographic records. In recent years the Library of Congress has increased its rate of updating LCSH terminology. However, its own automated system does not provide for global substitutions in its database, so that each change must be made in the bibliographic file on a record-by-record basis—a labor-intensive operation for which there is rarely sufficient funding. For this reason, obsolete headings sometimes remain in many LC MARC records long after changes in those headings have been announced by the Library of Congress. For the present, therefore, the problem of obsolete terminology is primarily technical and financial, not philosophical. With more sophisticated computer software, it is safe to predict that the situation will improve.

Term Sensitivity

One aspect of terminology that has received a great deal of attention in recent years is the sensitivity of LCSH headings with regard to specific groups of persons.[5] In recent years, the Library of Congress has made many changes to remove bias; a recent example is the replacement of the term "wives" with the term "spouses" in many headings. The Library's automated system may still require records to be changed one by one, but at least it confers the ability to easily identify those records that carry the headings that are to be changed—a capability that has facilitated heading revision.

Nevertheless, as Margaret N. Rogers comments, ". . . subtler forms of gender bias remain in the headings and in the ways they are applied."[6] She also makes a point on which there is yet no consensus in the field:

> A larger question is involved here as well: Is it the library's role to educate users by raising their consciousness, or merely to provide easy access to what they want? In formulating and using subject headings, should LC lead or follow the public? The recent furor over political correctness has highlighted the difficulty—perhaps the impossibility—of formulating any terms that will be truly free of political bias. . . . The difficulty lies in striking a reasonable balance between following traditional prejudices on the one hand and overly politicizing the catalog on the other hand.[7]

On this question, William Studwell offers the following comment: "Terminology in LC subject headings must be sensitive to social issues and other potentially delicate matters, but at the same time 'trendy' terminology must be avoided."[8]

Common Usage

Another aspect of terminology is how well the terms used in a subject headings system match the terms most likely to be sought by users. Both earlier and recent online catalog studies indicate that users experience considerable difficulty with online searching.[9] Several factors may account for search failures. One is that users often submit terms that are either too general or too specific. Another is obsolete headings. Yet another is the fact that, among synonymous terms, the term the user submits does not match the one used in the heading.

The problem of matching terms is an old one: Charles A. Cutter, writing more than 100 years ago, was deeply concerned that subject heading vocabulary should reflect common usage, "the supreme arbiter."[10] More recently, this principle of user-centered approach is reflected in Dagobert Soergel's concept of "request-oriented indexing" and in Elaine Svenonius's discussion of "use warrant."[11] The underlying problem remains: With a highly diverse population of library or information system users, there may be a large spread in the vocabulary used for a given concept or entity.

The power of free-text searching on words in titles and other subject-indicative fields, such as notes (particularly contents notes) and summaries, alleviates to a certain extent the subject access problems that are due to lack of currentness or failure to reflect common usage. Many subject indexes, in fact, rely entirely on the keyword display of terms derived from article titles or abstracts. Of course, only document titles that are expressive of content are effective in keyword retrieval. Still, keyword access to terms in titles can often be a helpful adjunct to systematic indexing and can complement controlled vocabulary in retrieval.

Main Headings

Forms of Headings

Making all usage consistent and uniform renders an information system easier to apply in cataloging and easier to use in retrieval. Such consistency seems particularly desirable for forms of headings. But in LCSH, a given aspect or facet of a subject is not always represented by the same form of heading. Phrase headings, headings with qualifiers, and headings with subdivisions have been used in some cases for the same sort of information. The time facet is usually expressed by means of a period subdivision, but sometimes by an adjectival modifier. The qualifier is most frequently used for distinguishing between homographs or to give context for an obscure term, but it has also been used in place of a subject subdivision or an inverted adjectival heading, such as **Infants (Newborn)**. Syntactical relationships are sometimes expressed by relational words such as *and*, *of*, *in*, *for*, or *as*, and sometimes by subdivisions or adjectival phrases (e.g., **Grooming for men**; **Sheep— Grooming**).

Although in recent years the Library of Congress has taken steps to tighten or normalize the forms of headings—for example, eliminating *[Topic] in [Place]* headings, limiting the use of qualifiers, and cutting down on the use of conjunctive phrases such as *Hotels, taverns, etc.*—many inconsistent patterns remain. A systematic review is needed to determine how different subjects and different sorts of information pertaining to subjects are best reflected in heading forms. For example, subdivisions may be the best way to represent time and space facets. The same is probably true for some aspects such as processes or actions on the subject, and also for phase relationships such as effect or influence, application or tool, and bias or point of view.

Entry Element in Main Headings

In the manual environment the order of words in a heading is important because it is the first word that provides access to the heading. From the inception of LCSH, therefore, for user convenience, inverted headings have been used in many cases to bring the "significant" word forward (e.g., **Chemistry, Organic**; **Plants, Effect of light on**). In an automated system offering keyword searching—which almost every system does—there is no longer a need to construct headings on the basis of the need to bring a "significant" term into filing position. In other words, with individual word access, there is no longer a question of relative significance, because all words in a string are accessible. Thus, headings may be based on logical or syntactical considerations. However, there is a caveat: A significant term as the entry element is still helpful in the online display of subject headings, particularly in systems that do not have KWIC (key-word-in-context) display.

Currently, at the Library of Congress, all new headings are established in natural word order except where there is a pattern of inverted form for similar headings, and many inverted headings have been converted to the direct form. Nonetheless, a large number of inverted headings remain in the system because of the enormous labor that would be required to convert the headings in the bibliographic records and because of the impact that the changes would have on local systems that do not have global change capability.

Distinguishing Between Topical and Form Headings

In LCSH, there are a number of main headings that, in their definitions, could represent either form or topic. Three patterns can be distinguished:

(1) In some cases a distinction is made between form and topic. **Biography** is used as a genre indicator for a work that *is* a biography, but **Biography as a literary form** is used for a work *about* biography; **Essays** is used as a genre indicator, while **Essay** is the term for works *about* essays. In each case, the first is a form heading, the second a topical heading.

(2) Occasionally a heading is used only as a topical heading and not as a form heading. For example, the headings **Bibliography** and **Periodicals** are assigned to works discussing these forms, but not to individual specimens of such forms.

(3) In still other cases, identical headings are used to represent works about a particular bibliographic or artistic form and individual specimens of such forms. For example, the heading **Trials** is used for trial proceedings as well as for works discussing trials, and the heading **Subject headings** is used for general works *on* subject headings as well as *lists of* subject headings in the English language. In this case, the failure to make the distinction between form and topic is a violation

of the principle of unique headings, which states that each heading should represent only one subject or concept. In retrieval, using a heading of this sort will call up works both *in* and *about* the particular form; thus, the search results will rank low in precision.

The lack of a clear pattern regarding the distinction between topic and form headings, in both terminology and assignment policies, creates confusion for catalogers and users. A further difficulty, noted by Barbara L. Berman, is lack of representation for certain forms; for example, there is no LC heading or subdivision for "public opinion polls."[12]

Recently, the Library of Congress has been working on normalizing form headings, with a special effort to distinguish between form and topic. It seems important that form headings should be carefully studied, preferably in connection with form subdivisions. Indeed, the latter were a major topic of discussion at the Subject Subdivision Conference held in 1991.[13] The problem of distinguishing between topic and form could possibly be solved as a matter of application policy rather than the vocabulary per se. Form data might be indicated through fixed field codes or placed in a separate field from the topical elements. For example, in the USMARC format, field 655 is designated for form/genre, although not used by the Library of Congress. Berman also supports the consideration of form headings in conjunction with the 655 field.[14] LCSH users who are not also USMARC users will, of course, resolve the problem within the context of individual cataloging environments.

Subdivisions

Functions

Among the four types of subdivisions used in LCSH, topical subdivisions have been used regularly over the years to make headings more specific, thus increasing their expressivity. Most of the subdivisions in LCSH exist for the purpose of showing topical breakdowns; they represent subtopics of the subject covered by the main heading.

Initially at least, the other three types were used mainly as a device to partition large files under main headings. Many represent aspects of the subject that are not purely topical: the historical time period treated or the geographical setting. Finally, some subdivisions do not have to do with topics at all; they may show language of the text; document type (e.g., abstract, bibliography, specifications); publication form (e.g., facsimiles, juvenile films, slides); and time period of publication (e.g., **—Early works to 1800**). These will be referred to as *nontopical subdivisions*.

In online retrieval, subdivisions are also important because they provide additional access points. For this reason especially, the use of geographic and form subdivision has expanded rapidly in recent years. Most newly established headings are subdivisible by place, if appropriate, and commonly used form subdivisions are applied regularly as free-floating subdivisions. The use of chronological subdivisions, on the other hand, is still quite limited, curtailing their effectiveness in online retrieval. As Marcia Bates notes, "any kind of direct search on dates in subject headings will be thwarted if period subdivisions are added only to subdivide large files. All those other cases where the period is applicable but has not been so indexed will be lost to the searcher."[15]

Functional Overlap with Fixed Field Information

In retrieval, too-high recall is a significant problem, noted in online catalog studies and by scholars in the field.[16] As early as a decade ago, Gerard Salton and Michael J. McGill commented on the "need to reduce to a manageable size the number of items that are to be examined. . . . Even in specialized, relatively narrow topic areas, one tends to become overloaded with information very rapidly."[17] When recall is too high, it can be reduced by various means. One is using subdivisions; the other is limiting through the use of data coded in fixed fields in the MARC record. The limiting feature is a means of avoiding the retrieval of too much material by circumscribing searches in one or more of several predefined ways—for instance, to a given language, type of publication, span of time, or even geographic area.

In LC MARC records, certain information that has traditionally been represented in subdivisions, particularly those relating to form, place, and time of publication, is also carried in fixed fields. In such cases, limiting by fixed fields is a possibility worth exploring. For one thing, the device is machine-efficient: much less central processing unit capacity is needed for sorting on fixed fields than on elements in variable fields. For another, for any given publication, there may be considerably more relevant fixed-field information than is carried in subject headings. Most MARC records are fully coded; any applicable category of information for which there is fixed-field provision is included. On the other hand, subdivisions for language and period (by date of publication) are permissible only under some headings; free-floating form subdivisions may not be applied universally; and not all headings are authorized for geographic division, even though such division might be relevant. The existence in a record of coded information that duplicates what is shown by subdivision thus calls into question the continued value of nontopical subdivisions in headings in machine-accessible records.

Of course, in order to make use of the fixed-field information in MARC records, those fields must be searchable in the online system. Currently, not all systems have such capability, which, for public-access catalogs, must be paired with a querying program. Nevertheless, it is reasonable to expect that in the near future, as library catalogs migrate to ever-more sophisticated systems, this will no longer be an obstacle.

One of the initial proposals presented at the Subject Subdivisions Conference deals with limiting searches by fixed-field codes.[18] However, the recommendations of the conference did not address it.

Citation Order

Even if the functions of some categories of subdivisions were taken over by fixed-field codes, many headings with multiple subdivisions would remain. It might appear that, with keyword access to subject headings, the question of the optimal citation order for the elements of a string is now moot. But in LCSH, citation order within a subject string often plays an important semantic role. Because subject strings rarely include the linking words that provide relational information in ordinary discourse—words such as *of, by, about,* and *on*—the order in which the terms in a string are put together often determines its meaning. For example, the heading **Law—Periodicals—History** is used for a history of law journals, and **Law—History—Periodicals** is used for journals about legal history.

Does the citation order of subdivisions matter for such headings? As LCSH becomes increasingly complex and places a great deal of reliance on synthesis through the use of many free-floating subdivisions, the fact that the same terms can be coordinated in different orders creates a consistency problem. Citation order in a string does not always determine meaning, of course; where it does, the question of appropriate order remains. No viable solution has yet been found. The instructions given in *Subject Cataloging Manual* alleviate the problem to a large extent, but they have become so detailed and voluminous that they are difficult for many outside the Library of Congress to apply. When meaning is not the issue, however, it could be argued that citation order in multiple subdivisions is less significant. In terms of expressiveness, on the other hand, there is no question that the order matters when it affects meaning.

Citation order was one of the main issues discussed at the Subject Subdivisions Conference, and in fact the first recommendation of the conference proposes the establishment of a fixed citation order for subdivisions under topical headings: [Main heading]—[Topical subdivision]—[Place]—[Time]—[Form].[19] In order to implement the proposed citation order, the MARC format must be amended to provide a subfield code for form subdivision that did not previously exist. A proposal for a separate subfield for form subdivision in the USMARC format was approved in 1995.

Nevertheless, although in general a fixed citation order is easy to apply and decreases inconsistency in synthesis, in cases where a predetermined citation order can distort the meaning of a string or fail to distinguish strings with different meanings, some exceptions should be built into the citation formula to maintain needed semantic distinctions.

Free-Floating Subdivisions

The number of subdivisions declared to be free-floating has grown over the years to the point where they are difficult to apply properly—their complexity is one of the reasons for the huge size of the *Subject Cataloging Manual.* Furthermore, some inconsistencies have crept in, as when the same concept is expressed by different subdivisions under different pattern headings. The Subject Subdivisions Conference addressed this problem and recommended the simplification of such subdivisions.[20] Consequently, LC's Cataloging Policy and Support Office has been revamping many free-floating subdivisions, normalizing those that represent the same or similar concepts, and converting many topical subdivisions into topical headings.

Precoordination or Postcoordination

As discussed in chapter 2, there are three alternative approaches for representing complex subjects: precoordination, postcoordination, and a combination of the two. There are few totally precoordinated systems. Many online databases are almost solely postcoordinate; the ERIC database is one example. Some systems, like MeSH (Medical Subject Headings), rely on both precoordination and postcoordination. LCSH is basically a precoordinate system; nonetheless, multiple headings are often used to represent a single, complex subject. In such cases, the system is postcoordinate. Postcoordination of multiple headings requires a lot of mental juggling for users of a manual catalog. But in an online system, it can be achieved easily through Boolean operations. In many cases, postcoordination provides satisfactory retrieval for both recall and precision. Of course, postcoordination, or the simple association of terms, cannot express relationships beyond what can be specified with proximity limits. When linking words or the order of terms in a string affects meaning, precoordinated strings are necessary for precision. *Chemicals and adulterants* as a search statement will not distinguish material on chemical substances deliberately used as adulterants *from* material on foreign adulterating substances found in chemical solutions. Nor will *Grasses and culture* separate materials on lawn and pasture care *from* those on the impact of grasslands on cultural history. Such a list of examples can be easily continued. *Poison and plants* will get material on poisonous plants as well as that indexed under the heading **Plants, Effect of poisons on**; *Art and music* is not the same as *Music in art*. Obviously, one cannot go so far as to claim that the ease of postcoordination in online systems removes the justification for precoordination in headings. But it can at least be said that a complex topic does not necessarily have to be represented by a precoordinated heading.

For online catalogs, postcoordination is often the preferred route for cases in which the specificity of a complex subject can be achieved with equal ease through precoordinated headings or through separate headings. However, cases in which a postcoordinate search would be ambiguous because relationship information is lost should be an exception. Should LCSH move toward greater reliance on postcoordination, it would be desirable to have a set of stated guidelines indicating when precoordination is important.

In either precoordination or postcoordination, a rigorous faceted approach is recommended. When facets are well defined and consistent, and rules of synthesis are logical and clear, both indexing and searching will improve in efficiency and effectiveness. As Bates notes, "faceted indexing seems to be emerging as one of the most effective indexing techniques in online systems."[21]

In the future, the developers of the LC system might consider placing greater reliance on postcoordination. To overcome lower precision in postcoordinate searches, however, a set of guidelines indicating when postcoordination would or would not be desirable would be helpful. Compiling a list of roles that cannot be expressed by a simple juxtaposition of terms could be a start.

Length of Headings

An aspect of subject heading structure that has received little attention in the literature is the desirable lengths of subject strings. Most LC subject headings are relatively short, but there are many long ones. From the user's point of view, there are two serious disadvantages to long strings: the need for those who want to submit exact searches to rely on the thesaurus, and the large likelihood of input error.

In addition to alleviating the problems relating to citation order in long subject strings, there are other advantages of using shorter strings. One argument for shorter headings is that most initial user queries in topical searches are short—an average of 1.8 words.[22] The chances of exact matches between user queries and subject headings are greater when the latter are also shorter. Another argument is that many current online systems, including the Library of Congress's SCORPIO system, limit the string length that can be shown in thesaurus or index displays. Thus, users who consult these displays are denied the screening value of the information at the end of a long string. It is likely that such limits will eventually be raised, but in the meantime, any steps taken to shorten string length also reduce the amount of information lost in truncated displays.

The problem of long headings may be dealt with in a number of ways that do not result in the loss of significant retrieval information:

(1) eliminate subdivisions whose functions can be taken over by fixed field information

(2) treat certain subdivisions as independent specific terms by separating them from main headings and making them into separate headings (e.g., *Great Blood Purge, 1934* instead of **Germany—History—Great Blood Purge, 1934**)

(3) rely more heavily on postcoordination by breaking up a complex subject string and representing individual concepts or elements as separate headings.

Further study should be undertaken to determine the optimal balance between comfortable string length and factors such as specificity and expressivity.

Cross References

Of the two main types of cross references in controlled vocabularies, those that indicate synonymous or equivalent terms and those that connect related concepts, equivalence (USE) references are considered mandatory in all controlled vocabularies. With regard to LCSH, online catalog studies indicate that users need more USE references than currently exist.[23]

The policies governing hierarchical and related references in LCSH in the past were not rigorously defined, nor were existing policies consistently followed. For hierarchically related terms, references were usually made from the more-general to the more-specific terms, but not always. References between coordinate terms (those related in other ways than general/specific) were relatively sparse. Since 1984, however, the Library of Congress has regularized its practice for both hierarchical and related-term references, an important step toward normalizing the cross-reference structure. Even so, the approach so far has apparently been to create cross references on a heading-by-heading basis without attempting to fit concepts into a systematic structure.

Properly structured hierarchical references have great potential. Carried to perfection, they superimpose a classified structure on an alphabetical thesaurus and thereby provide searchers with the best of both worlds. Because devices like the tree structures in MeSH and the hierarchical clusters in ERIC Descriptors are apparently very useful to persons using indexes with such provisions, it would be desirable if something analogous could eventually be developed for searching files of records indexed by LCSH.

An ideal syndetic structure must be as tightly and logically constructed as a classification scheme; only with such a structure can one be sure that the hierarchy is complete and that there are no missing links or elements. To achieve this, one possible approach is to use a classification scheme as a guide in making an overall hierarchical map of the LC system. The profession, most particularly its researchers and theoreticians, should give serious consideration to the question of whether a classification scheme—extant, or to be adapted or even constructed—could function as a workable pattern for linking hierarchically related LCSH terms.

Subject Authority File

A subject authority file is a tool for catalog or database management. Ideally, it should contain a subject authority record for every complete heading that appears on an extant bibliographic record. A thesaurus, on the other hand, serves as a source of indexing terms. For a system that allows free combination of specified elements or categories of elements, as the LC system does to an increasing extent, a thesaurus lists individual index terms and gives the conditions for synthesis. To help the indexer or searcher select appropriate terms, each index term is accompanied by appropriate cross references, definition or scope notes if any, and a history of the term if appropriate. However, a thesaurus does not normally list all the strings actually used.

From the beginning, LCSH, with some auxiliary tools, has served as both thesaurus and subject authority file for LC's subject headings system. The distinction between the two has not been clearly made. The list has included some headings (e.g., established name headings; synthesized heading strings) which a thesaurus would not list; and it has omitted many entries (e.g., headings with free-floating subdivisions) that appear on LC cataloging records, which a true subject authority file would include.

As a source of controlled terms used in subject cataloging, LCSH, in print and machine-readable versions, has fulfilled its thesaural function. For copy cataloging and database maintenance, on the other hand, a file containing complete strings would be desirable. By providing a means for validating and verifying current valid subject heading strings, it would be very useful in database quality control, in retrospective conversion, and in copy cataloging. Furthermore, for searchers of any online database, a complete file of headings used on records in the system would be enormously helpful. At this writing, this matter is under study by the Cooperative Cataloging Council (CCC).[24] In addition, OCLC is conducting research on the feasibility of generating such a file by computer.

In efforts to improve subject authority control, the following questions warrant consideration:

(1) Should an authority record be created for each subject string, including those resulting from the combination of free-floating subdivisions?

(2) Should a separate authority record be created for each free-floating subdivision?

(3) Should history notes, which explain changes that have occurred to the heading, be provided?

The Library of Congress has not felt the need for history notes on changed subject headings, because its policy is to revise all MARC records with superseded headings. But for libraries and databases with split files (i.e., some records under the old heading and some under the new), history notes would be helpful in both cataloging and searching. History notes could take the form of either *see also* or explanatory references.

Several suggestions to remedy omissions in the current *SUBJECTS* file come from Drabenstott. She recommends the creation of a new file of subject authority records for period subdivisions that would, with limited assistance by human intermediaries, assist in the formulation and verification of subject headings with period subdivisions.[25] She also recommends the creation of authority records for indirect forms of geographic names, because with these records, "catalogers could 'cut' indirect subdivisions out of authority records and 'paste' them into the assigned topical subject headings they are formulating."[26] Finally, based on a study of subdivided subject headings in a large bibliographic database, she recommends "a new machine-readable file of authority records for topical subdivisions and for enhancements to the existing subject authority file."[27]

Revamping LCSH

Short of replacing or redesigning LCSH, scholars in the field have suggested revamping the current list. Mary Dykstra suggests recasting LCSH in the form of a true thesaurus, one based on individual *terms* rather than subject heading strings, as a "model, rule-based thesaurus, carefully conforming to the present national and international standards."[28] Drabenstott and Vizine-Goetz also discuss the possibility of a "thorough revamping of LCSH" but stop short at offering specific details. They recognize, however, the commitment and effort required for such an undertaking: "Libraries must make a concerted effort to convince the Library of Congress that they will support a reordering of priorities. This will curtail certain products and services that the library community currently depends on, and the costs of these products and services may be passed onto libraries to enable the Library of Congress to seek alternatives from the private sector."[29]

Such a prospect, though seemingly unfeasible financially under the current circumstances, is intellectually conceivable. In view of current and future environments in which LCSH operates, revamping LCSH to achieve a rich vocabulary, a simple syntax, and logical syndetic structure would render the system more effective for retrieval and more efficient for cataloging and database maintenance.

Application Policies

Because the Library of Congress has been responsible for the development and maintenance of LCSH, and because its cataloging records are used widely by other libraries, the way subject headings are applied at the Library of Congress has become the de facto standard for subject cataloging. Increasingly over the years, other libraries have been working directly with the Library of Congress on subject cataloging matters. For instance, the Subject Authority Cooperative Program (SACO), a cooperative project between the Library of Congress and a number of other libraries, enables the latter to contribute subject authority records to the *SUBJECTS* file. Thus, a function fulfilled until recently by the Library of Congress with minimum input from other institutions is now carried out in a cooperative environment where non-LC libraries not only contribute bibliographic records but also participate in establishing subject authority records.

LC policies and practices regarding application have changed to some extent in recent years, as the Library of Congress has adapted to a new retrieval environment. The following pages discuss some of the ongoing changes and possible future directions.

Dissemination of Policy Information

In a cooperative environment, it is essential that clear and concise guidelines on subject heading establishment and assignment be made available to enable the shared work to be done efficiently and with consistency. The *Subject Cataloging Manual* is a help in this regard, and its availability is an enormous improvement over what existed before it was published. The *Manual*, however, is quite forbidding in its size and complexity, mirroring the size and complexity of the LC system itself. Changes made in the system and in application policies are, of course, eventually reflected in the *Manual*. Insofar as those changes are in the direction of greater simplicity and consistency, there should be less need for complicated, hard-to-follow instructions. Recent efforts by the Library of Congress to consolidate and streamline overlapping free-floating subdivisions are steps in the right direction.

Depth of Indexing

An area of subject cataloging policy that has been sharply criticized in the past is the scarcity of subject headings assigned to each cataloging record. The general policy of summarization (i.e., assigning subject headings to cover the overall content of a book instead of individual parts of it) results in relatively few headings per document. With regard to the manual environment, this economy of subject headings reflected the constraints of the card catalog. As Bates pointed out, "With more than one or two subject entries per book, card catalogs would have become cumbrously large—hard to use, hard to file in, hard to find room for. In the early days, catalog entries often had to be handwritten. The current subject heading system, therefore, was deliberately developed to be minimally redundant."[30] In online systems, on the other hand, additional access points do not measurably affect the bulk of the catalog. They do, however, quite definitely improve recall in searching. The depth of indexing (i.e., the representation of subunits [individual chapters, articles, etc.]) in a bibliographic item is an area that warrants attention.

Exhaustivity of Indexing

Exhaustivity of indexing refers to the representation of individual facets and elements of a complex subject as well as aspects such as literary and artistic genre. Over the years, many writers and critics of LCSH have urged the Library of Congress to increase the number of headings assigned to each record. As a result, the Library of Congress has relaxed its headings limit: Up to 10 headings per record are now allowed. With this relaxation, recent LC MARC records do show greater exhaustivity of subject analysis. The practice does not, however, appear to be consistent among catalogers.

One suggestion in respect to exhaustivity, put forth by many professionals, including Sanford Berman, is to assign additional headings for literary genres and themes to individual novels, plays, and other forms of literature.[31] As an experiment, during 1993, the Library of Congress initiated a six month "fiction project," providing additional topical headings to fictional works. Full implementation was not carried out because of budgetary and workload considerations.

Ultimately, fuller indexing of Library of Congress material, depth and exhaustivity both, is to be desired. How best to achieve this is a theoretical matter and should be addressed. A central question is, "What is the optimal depth and exhaustivity of indexing for increasing recall without sacrificing precision?" In this connection, the problem of information overload should not be overlooked. Users must be able to retrieve manageable sets on broad subjects as well as on specific, narrow topics. Another question is, "Are there aspects of some materials, such as literary genre or thematic topics, that many information seekers would find useful if they were indexed?"

Generic Posting

Generic posting refers to the practice of assigning to a document a heading that is broader than its subject. It is used when a larger context for a given heading is considered desirable, as in the case of assigning biographical headings such as **[Class of persons or Discipline]—Biography** to individual biographies in addition to personal name headings.

While the policy of generic posting adds many more access points, there is a drawback: Many of the additional headings are more general than warranted by the content of the item. The result is an increased number of postings under broad topics. For example, the heading **United States—Social conditions** has been assigned to books on specific kinds or aspects of social conditions in the United States, so that the heading itself is virtually useless as an access point for books about U.S. social conditions in general. Furthermore, the practice of assigning additional or enhancement headings has not been consistent, because there are no specific guidelines on the matter in the *Subject Cataloging Manual*. Such guidelines would help in achieving consistency in application and precision in retrieval.

New guidelines might address questions like those that follow:

> With regard to the depth of cataloging, on what basis are the additional subject headings to be assigned? On individual chapters in the book? Individual units in a collection of writings? Individual articles in a journal? Or detailed analysis similar to back-of-the-book indexing?

> Should all materials in the collection receive the same depth of treatment? Of course, the answer will have enormous financial implications.

If multilevel subject analysis is adopted, how should the subject headings assigned to each level (the entire work, parts of the work, sections within a part, etc.) be labeled? Should they be stored in separate fields?

With regard to exhaustivity, should all facets and aspects of the subject be represented? Should concepts narrower than the overall content be included? In providing more subject access points to individual records, headings more specific than the one that summarizes the overall content of the item are probably more helpful than generic headings. Specific headings improve precision and recall where they are needed, while generic posting tends to overload broad general headings.

To what extent should generic posting be allowed? Should a work on beagles receive the headings **Hounds**; **Hunting dogs**; **Dogs**; and **Canis** in addition to the heading **Beagles (Dogs)**? Or should reliance be placed on hierarchical references, with generic posting reserved for cases in which context cannot easily be denoted any other way, such as through generic qualifiers?

Studwell recommends that "secondary headings, normally more general headings, should be extensively utilized in the application of LC subject headings."[32] However, he has not addressed the problem, alluded to earlier, of overloading general headings such as **[Place]—Social conditions** and **[Place]—History**, which he recommends for every work on every aspect of social conditions or history of a place. Such headings would become useless as access points for general works because they would have so many postings. One way to alleviate the overload problem is the ability to designate major and minor or primary and secondary headings—a capability available in many online databases, such as MEDLINE and ERIC, but not yet implemented in the OCLC or LC online catalogs.

The capability of searching individual words in a heading provides an interesting dimension to headings with parenthetical qualifiers. Generic qualifiers are added to headings for the purpose of distinguishing homographs and identifying obscure or highly technical terms. They are also added to certain categories of name headings, such as names of legendary, fictitious, or mythological characters and names of gods and goddesses. Examples include: **Sequences (Music)**; **Crowns (Dentistry)**; **Fasciae (Anatomy)**; **Manus (Hindu mythology)**; **Snoopy (Fictitious character)**; **Lancelot (Legendary character)**; and **Apollo (Greek deity)**. For geographic and corporate headings, three types of qualifiers are used: generic, type of jurisdiction, and geographic. Examples are **Schweppes (Firm)**; **Pompeii (Extinct city)**; **Naples (Kingdom)**; **Rive gauche (Paris, France)**; and **Auschwitz (Poland : Concentration camp)**.

Because the qualifiers are normally generic concepts that encompass the specific terms in the headings, and because both the headings and the qualifiers are accessible in online retrieval, such headings in effect become reversed classed entries. A heading that contains a local place qualifier, such as **Rive gauche (Paris, France)**; provides in effect a trilevel approach (i.e., the city section, the city, and the country). A heading that contains different types of qualifiers, such as **Auschwitz (Poland : Concentration camp)**, represents a multidimensional classed entry (i.e., Auschwitz as a part of Poland and Auschwitz as an instance of concentration camps).

This fact, though interesting, has no implications for manual systems because of the limitations of linear access. But with multidirectional access in online retrieval, material can be gathered through the qualifier, thus providing what amounts to limited (i.e., bilevel) classed access for those topics covered by headings that include generic qualifiers. As scarce as such headings are, the thought of having any classed entries in a system based on the principle of specific entry is tantalizing. The theory of the alphabetical subject catalog normally prohibits classed entries; now, online access provisions permit the benefits of limited classed approach to material indexed with LCSH without substantial change in the system itself. The benefits could be great: for users who enter query terms that are broader than the topics sought, the generic qualifiers may provide access to the specific topics. While one would hesitate to recommend the increasing use of qualifiers on a large scale because of the enormous implications for implementation, it would be helpful to normalize the forms of qualifiers and render their application more consistent. Furthermore, in cases where the specific headings include generic qualifiers, there is less need for generic posting.

Online Catalog Design

It will take more than improvements in the indexing language and changes in policies on application to give users optimal online subject access through LCSH. A great deal of the effectiveness of subject access depends on the features and capabilities of the online systems that accommodate the subject retrieval apparatus.

Traditionally, library catalogs have been limited to entries for books and runs (not individual issues) of serials; in some cases, even whole sets of books have been treated as if they were a single entity. There have often been separate catalogs for different types of materials, such as children's books or government publications. Records of material in the process of being added to the collection were not part of the catalog, nor was availability data. In the manual environment, such arrangements are advantageous. For special materials, limited-scope catalogs are easier to consult, and a manual catalog that mixed in-process and circulation records with cards for cataloged books would be cumbrous and well-nigh incomprehensible to anyone but librarians—besides being virtually impossible to maintain.

The picture is very different in the online environment. Because records do not have to be consulted serially, a very large file does not present the same sort of hindrance to efficient searching as it would in card form. Different kinds of entries—in-process information or availability data, for instance, or material in other libraries—can be easily identified, and the limiting feature can be used to confine searches to a given category or to refine or expand searches. Furthermore, as local systems are incorporating more and more remote resources—including online reference services and the online catalogs of distant libraries or resources available through networks, particularly the Internet—a user employing a local system could access almost the whole universe of publicly available information.

The larger question here is what the online age implies for the nature of the catalog and the information services libraries should try to provide. Online retrieval capabilities have afforded many advantages not available in the manual environment. Such capabilities include keyword or component word searching, limiting, truncation, Boolean and proximity operators, and automatic term switching or matching. In considering the future of LCSH, such capabilities should be harnessed for the greatest and most effective improvements in subject access. Therefore, in addition to the aspects discussed above, a source of improvement is online offerings and interface features. Some of these are discussed below.

Online Index Browsing

The high rate of less-than-optimum retrieval for people making subject searches in online catalogs can be lowered if system users who were disappointed in their subject search results could turn to an alphabetical index display and browse in the area closest to the terms they first submitted. This is because the alphabetical array of headings often suggests more effective terms or search strategies.

It was noted earlier that LCSH does not list headings that result from the application of the various free-combining principles—subdivisions under pattern headings or in the free-floating lists, for instance, or headings of the form [Topic] in art. This is a particularly serious omission from the point of view of searchers: People accessing large files need to know how they are subdivided if they are to winnow them down efficiently. It is somewhat ironic to note that skipping to promising subdivisions is not as easy in online searching as it is in traditional catalogs that are well provided with guide cards. Incompleteness here is one problem, but even more serious is the implication that because a synthesized heading is not listed, it is not used. Fuller information on what headings might exist, therefore, is an apparent need. An online index display allows users whose input terms do not match any heading exactly and therefore fail to retrieve anything to browse headings in the vicinity of the entry term.

While many online systems, such as the LOCIS system at the Library of Congress, provide online browsing of the subject index that lists complete strings assigned to bibliographic records, there are still systems, such as NOTIS, that do not allow subject index browsing. Those that do might increase consultation of the display if they automatically suggested use of the index whenever a search delivered zero or very few postings. Systems that do not should try to do so.

Online Thesaurus Display

In addition to online alphabetical index scanning, browsing of synonymous and related terms through online thesaurus display can help users identify valid terms or focus on terms more relevant to their topic of interest. Because simple mismatches of vocabulary account for a large proportion of search failures, users particularly need USE references. And because searches on terms that are too broad or too narrow are very common, users need hierarchical references. Online catalog studies indicate the desirability of online vocabulary display to help users choose appropriate and properly formulated search terms.[33]

Many online catalogs still do not have LCSH online; adding it should be the first step. There are different ways to incorporate LCSH in a local system, varying in both cost and sophistication. The least costly and perhaps simplest is to mount the *SUBJECTS* file. Another helpful feature, keyword display of the list, would increase its potential usefulness. Some online systems provide keyword-in-context display of assigned subject headings, listing each heading under all of its terms no matter where they occur in the heading.

Automatic Term Matching

Even when a user has chosen a valid term, problems can still occur when the form of the word or phrase does not match exactly that used in the authorized heading. According to Drabenstott and Vizine-Goetz, such variant forms include spelling errors, singular and plural forms (e.g., *X-ray* instead of **X-rays**), inclusion of initial articles, inclusion or omission of punctuation, abbreviations, and different suffixes (e.g., *Computer programming* instead of **Computer programs**).[34] Online system devices such as keyword access, truncation, an implicit Boolean *and* operator, automatic detection and correction of spelling errors, and tolerance of variations in punctuation can improve term matching significantly.

None of these, however, goes far enough in solving the entry vocabulary problem. A sophisticated and very user-friendly way of helping users with entry vocabulary in an online system is to make the process transparent. In some online systems, the function of equivalence references (*see* or USE references) is taken over by automatic substitution. Synonyms are identified within the system, and the output when any of them is used is the same as if the user had input the "right" or authorized term. This operation requires that the bibliographic records in a system be linked to its thesaurus or authority file. Not many early systems had such linkage, but many current ones do.

Online User Assistance

Online user assistance is an area in which there is room for improvement. In addition to on-screen tutorials that explain what a given system includes (e.g., types of materials it covers, sorts of information provided in its records, commands, retrieval parameters, output formats), assistance in selection of search terms and guidance in case of too few or too many retrieved items is also needed.

To assist users in matching their input terms with subject headings, Bates proposes a "superthesaurus," a front-end database, separate from LCSH but linked to the document indexing, that contains a very large entry vocabulary, with guidance to enable the searcher to select the best terms for a given search.[35]

Another device for helping users online, developed specifically for subject searching in an LCSH environment, is the system of search trees proposed by Drabenstott and Vizine-Goetz.[36] The search trees help users who have difficulty in matching input terms with the subject vocabulary by navigating the searching process from initial inquiries to valid, relevant subject headings. In this system, the user does not need to choose a particular approach, keyword, or controlled vocabulary. Rather, the system, based on the extent to which queries match the catalog's controlled vocabulary, responds by choosing the approach that produces the best results.

CONCLUSION

The Library of Congress subject headings system entered the online environment with features specifically designed for the card catalog and with many recognized shortcomings. In the past two decades, LCSH has been gradually adapted to the online environment, primarily through improvements in its vocabulary and syntax. Some of its shortcomings, such as limited access to each heading, were mitigated by online features and capabilities. In the online environment, features not available in manual systems remedy many of the shortcomings and insufficiencies of LCSH when used in manual catalogs. They also help to realize some of the potentials of the system that have not been fully explored in manual catalogs because of limitations such as linear access and the tedious process required for performing postcoordination manually.

Many of the principles that have governed the growth of the Library of Congress Subject Headings system take on different implications in the online context. The characteristics and features of online information handling increase the retrieval potential of the system, but at the same time they place different demands on it. The ever-expanding use of LCSH around the world adds another dimension in the consideration of the future directions of the system.

Even for measures for which there is widespread and enthusiastic support for the continuing improvement of LCSH throughout the profession and at the Library of Congress itself, it is unrealistic to expect changes to be effected rapidly. Delays are due not only to crushing financial constraints but also to the fact that the Library of Congress is still working within the limitations of its automated system, designed some 20 years ago.

The current Library of Congress Subject Headings system is far from ideal, but changes are being made continuously as the result of concerted efforts between the Library of Congress and the profession as a whole. In the future, we can expect this important and unique tool to continue to serve its functions in information retrieval as continuous improvements are being made.

NOTES

[1]Lois Mai Chan, *Library of Congress Subject Headings: Principles and Application*, 2nd ed. (Littleton, Colo.: Libraries Unlimited, 1986), 347-49.

[2]William E. Studwell, *Library of Congress Subject Headings Philosophy, Practice, and Prospects* (Binghamton, N.Y.: Haworth Press, 1990), 12.

[3]Karen Markey Drabenstott and Diane Vizine-Goetz, *Using Subject Headings for Online Retrieval: Theory, Practice, and Potential* (San Diego, Calif.: Academic Press, 1994), 331.

[4]Subject Subdivisions Conference (1991 : Airlie, Va.), *The Future of Subdivisions in the Library of Congress Subject Headings System: Report from the Subject Subdivisions Conference*, ed. Martha O'Hara Conway (Washington, D.C.: Cataloging Distribution Service, Library of Congress, 1992).

[5]For example, Sanford Berman, *Prejudices and Antipathies: A Tract on the LC Subject Heads Concerning People*, 1993 ed. (Jefferson, N.C.: McFarland, 1993); Doris Clack, *Black Literature Resources: Analysis and Organization* (New York: Marcel Dekker, 1975); Joan K. Marshall, *On Equal Terms: A Thesaurus for Nonsexist Indexing and Cataloging* (New York: Neal-Schuman, 1977); Margaret N. Rogers, "Are We on Equal Terms Yet? Subject Headings Concerning Women in *LCSH*, 1975-1991," *Library Resources & Technical Services* 37, no. 2 (April 1993): 181-96.

[6]Rogers, "Equal Terms," 181.

[7]Rogers, "Equal Terms," 195-96.

[8]Studwell, *Library of Congress Subject Headings*, 41.

[9]Drabenstott and Vizine-Goetz, *Using Subject Headings*, 148.

[10]Charles A. Cutter, *Rules for a Dictionary Catalog*, 4th ed., rewritten (Washington, D.C.: GPO, 1904), 69.

[11]Dagobert Soergel, *Organizing Information: Principles of Data Base and Retrieval Systems* (Orlando, Fla.: Academic Press, 1985), 230-37; Elaine Svenonius, "Design of Controlled Vocabularies," in *Encyclopedia of Library and*

Information Science, ed. Allen Kent, vol. 45, suppl. 10 (New York: Marcel Dekker, 1990).

[12]Barbara L. Berman, "Form Headings in Subject Cataloging," *Library Resources & Technical Services* 33, no. 2 (April 1989): 134-39.

[13]Subject Subdivisions Conference (1991: Airlie, Va.), *The Future of Subdivisions*.

[14]Berman, "Form Headings," 138.

[15]Marcia J. Bates, "Implications of the Subject Subdivisions Conference: The Shift in Online Catalog Design," in *The Future of Subdivisions*, 95.

[16]Karen M. Drabenstott with Celeste M. Burman and Marjorie S. Weller, *Enhancing a New Design for Subject Access to Online Catalogs* (Ann Arbor, Mich.: School of Information and Library Studies, University of Michigan, 1994), 95.

[17]Gerard Salton and Michael J. McGill, *Introduction to Modern Information Retrieval* (New York: McGraw-Hill, 1983), 4.

[18]Lois Mai Chan, "Alternatives to Subject Strings in the Library of Congress Subject Headings System: With Discussion," in *The Future of Subdivisions*, 46-56.

[19]Subject Subdivisions Conference (1991 : Airlie, Va.), *The Future of Subdivisions*, 6.

[20]Subject Subdivisions Conference (1991 : Airlie, Va.), *The Future of Subdivisions*, 8.

[21]Bates, "Implications," 97.

[22]Drabenstott and Vizine-Goetz, *Using Subject Headings*, 166.

[23]Drabenstott and Vizine-Goetz, *Using Subject Headings*, 334.

[24]In the early 1990s, the Cooperative Cataloging Council (CCC) was organized, under the aegis of the Library of Congress, for the purpose of increasing cataloging productivity at reduced costs. To achieve its goals, CCC established the international Program for Cooperative Cataloging (PCC), which includes overseas libraries in its membership.

[25]Karen M. Drabenstott, "Period Subdivisions in the Library of Congress Subject Headings System—Some Thoughts and Recommendations for the Future," *Cataloging & Classification Quarterly* 15, no. 4 (1992): 19-45.

[26]Karen M. Drabenstott, "Facilitating Geographic Subdivision Assignment in Subject Headings," *Library Resources & Technical Services* 36, no. 4 (October 1992): 412.

[27]Karen M. Drabenstott, "The Need for Machine-Readable Authority Records for Topical Subdivisions," *Information Technology and Libraries* 11, no. 2 (June 1992): 91.

[28]Mary Dykstra, "Can Subject Headings Be Saved?" *Library Journal* 113 (Sept. 15, 1988): 56.

[29]Drabenstott and Vizine-Goetz, *Using Subject Headings*, 338.

[30]Marcia J. Bates, "Factors Affecting Subject Catalog Search Success," *Journal of the American Society for Information Science* 28 (May 1977): 168.

[31]Sanford Berman, "Proposal for Reforms to Improve Subject Searching," in Pauline A. Cochrane, "Modern Subject Access in the Online Age: American Libraries' First Continuing Education Course: Lesson Three." *American Libraries* 15 (April 1984): 254.

[32]Studwell, *Library of Congress Subject Headings*, 82.

[33]Drabenstott and Vizine-Goetz, *Using Subject Headings*, 170.

[34]Drabenstott and Vizine-Goetz, *Using Subject Headings*, 125-32.

[35]Marcia J. Bates, "Rethinking Subject Cataloging in the Online Environment," *Library Resources & Technical Services* 33, no. 4 (October 1989): 400-412.

[36]Drabenstott and Vizine-Goetz, *Using Subject Headings*, 3, 301-41.

APPENDIXES

Appendix A:
Sample USMARC Records*

Subject Authority Records

PAGE sh93-98
02/18/93   [SUBJECTS]   [NCRD]   [MUMS]
0*FAC* DISPLAYED RECORD HAS BEEN VERIFIED.
VERIFIED   EVAL   SU
                                            MAY SUBD GEOG

```
010   001    ‡a    ‡ 93-98
020   040    ‡ac   ‡ DLC‡DLC
030   150 0  ‡a    ‡ Crop circles
031   450 0  ‡wa   ‡nnnn ‡ Circle formations in crops
032   450 0  ‡wa   ‡nnnn ‡ Circles, Corn
033   450 0  ‡wa   ‡nnnn ‡ Circles, Crop
034   450 0  ‡wa   ‡nnnn ‡ Corn circles
035   450 0  ‡wa   ‡nnnn ‡ Crop circle formations
036   450 0  ‡wa   ‡nnnn ‡ Crop field circles
037   450 0  ‡wa   ‡nnnn ‡ Cropfield circles
038   450 0  ‡wa   ‡nnnn ‡ Formations, Crop circle
040   550 0  ‡wa   ‡gnnn ‡ Curiosities and wonders
060   670    ‡ab   ‡Hennepin ‡(Crop circles x Crop field circles;
Cropfield circles)
062   670    ‡ab   ‡ LC data base, 1/8/9‡(crop circles)
064   670    ‡ab   ‡ Ox. dict. new words‡(crop circle: a (usually circular)
area of standing crops which has been inexplicably flattened, apparently
by a swirling, vortex-like movement (sometimes also called corn circles))
066   670    ‡ab   ‡ Crop circle enigma, 1990: ‡pp. 10, 12 (Circle
formations in crops, corn circles)
068   675    ‡a    ‡ IAC
070   952    ‡a    ‡ 2 bib. record(s) to be changed
100   005    ‡a    ‡ 19930218112433.0
110   FFD
```

01.n	02.i	03.0	04.n	05.a	06.n	07.n
08.n	09.a	10.a	11.a	12.a	13.a	14.
15.b	16.a	17.b	18.n	19.n	20.a	21.a
22.a	23.9306	24.te04	25.ta25	26.----	27.	28.-
29.-	30.-	31.-	32.-	33.7	34.!	35.7
36.!	37.!!!	38.j	39.j	40.1	41.z	42.93
43.a	44.n					

*Source: Library of Congress Information System (LOCIS).

PAGE sh85-109822
10/25/86   [SUBJECTS]   [NCRD]   [MUMS]
0*FAC* DISPLAYED RECORD HAS BEEN VERIFIED.
VERIFIED   EVAL   SU
                                MAY SUBD GEOG
010   001   ‡a   ‡ sh85-109822
020   040   ‡acd   ‡ DLC‡DLC‡DLC
030   150 -0 ‡a   ‡ Questione della lingua
040   680   ‡i   ‡ Here are entered works on the controversy in late
Medieval and early Renaissance literatures over the use of Latin versus
the use of the vernacular as a literary vehicle.
050   450 -0 ‡wa   ‡nnnn ‡ Language question in literature
060   550 -0 ‡wax   ‡gnnn ‡ Latin language, Medieval and modern
‡History
070   550 -0 ‡wax   ‡gnnn ‡ Literature, Medieval‡History and criticism
080   550 -0 ‡wayx ‡gnnn ‡ Literature, Modern‡15th and 16th
centuries‡History and criticism
090   005   ‡a   ‡ 19861025094216.2
100   FFD

01.n	02.!	03.0	04.a	05.a	06.n	07.n
08.n	09.a	10.a	11.a	12.b	13.a	14.
15.b	16.a	17.b	18.n	19.n	20.a	21.a
22.a	23.8030	24.fk07	25.----	26.----	27.	28.-
29.-	30.-	31.-	32.-	33.7	34.!	35.7
36.!	37.!!!	38.j	39.j	40.3	41.z	42.80
43.a	44.n					

PAGE sh85-149802
07/24/91   [SUBJECTS]   [NCRD]   [MUMS]
0*FAC* DISPLAYED RECORD HAS BEEN VERIFIED.
VERIFIED   NOT EVAL   SU
                                NOT SUBD GEOG
010   001   ‡a   ‡ sh85-149802
020   040   ‡acd   ‡ DLC‡DLC‡DLC
030   151 0 ‡a   ‡ Zimbabwe
040   451 0 ‡wa   ‡nnen ‡ Rhodesia, Southern
050   451 0 ‡wa   ‡nnnn ‡ Southern Rhodesia
055   451 0 ‡wa   ‡nnen ‡ Zimbabwe, Southern Rhodesia
060   681   ‡ia   ‡ Notes under ‡Rhodesia; Rhodesia and Nyasaland
070   005   ‡a   ‡ 19910724113949.9
080   FFD

01.n	02.-	03.0	04.a	05.a	06.n	07.n
08.n	09.a	10.a	11.a	12.b	13.a	14.
15.b	16.a	17.b	18.n	19.n	20.a	21.a
22.a	23.8024	24.fk03	25.----	26.fj28	27.	28.-
29.-	30.-	31.-	32.-	33.7	34.!	35.7
36.!	37.!!!	38.j	39.j	40.2	41.z	42.80
43.a	44.n					

PAGE n80-89998
05/06/91   [AUTH]   [NCRD] [MUMS]
0*FAC* DISPLAYED RECORD HAS BEEN VERIFIED.
VERIFIED   EVAL   RETRO M/AE

010 001   ‡a   ‡ n80-89998
020 040   ‡acd ‡ DLC‡DLC‡DLC
030 151 0 ‡a   ‡ Southern Rhodesia
040 670   ‡ab   ‡ Rhodesia, Southern. Central Statistical Office.
Monthly digest of statistics, Jan. 1979:‡t.p. (Rhodesia); Apr. 1979:
t.p. (Zimbabwe Rhodesia)
041 670   ‡ab   ‡ Standard encyc. S. Africa, 1974:‡v. 9, p. 324 (from
1953 to 1963 part of the Federation of Rhodesia and Nyasaland)
042 670   ‡ab   ‡ Africa S. of the Sahara, 1990‡(Zimbabwe:
Zimbabwe came into existence 4-18-80 as the successor to the colony
of Southern Rhodesia)
050 451 -0 ‡wa   ‡nnan ‡ Rhodesia, Southern
060 451 -0 ‡wa   ‡nnnn ‡ Rhodesia (1964-1980)
070 451 -0 ‡wa   ‡nnnn ‡ Zimbabwe Rhodesia
110 551 -0 ‡wa   ‡nnnn ‡ Rhodesia and Nyasaland
130 551 -0 ‡wa   ‡bnnn ‡ Zimbabwe
135 667   ‡a   ‡ SUBJECT USAGE: This heading is not valid for
use as a subject. Works about this place are entered under Zimbabwe.
155 952   ‡a   ‡ *bh99 041 042 110 130 06-04-90
160 005   ‡a   ‡ 19910506130239.5
170 FFD 01.n   02.n   03.0   04.n   05.a   06.b   07.c
          08.n   09.a   10.a   11.a   12.a   13.n   14.
          15.a   16.b   17.b   18.n   19.n   20.a   21.a
          22.a   23.   24.   25.---- 26.fj28 27.   28.-
          29.-   30.-   31.-   32.-   33.7   34.!   35.7
          36.!   37.!!! 38.a   39.a   40.   41.z   42.
          43.b   44.n

PAGE sh93-1113
04/21/93   [SUBJECTS]   [NCRD] [MUMS]
0*FAC* DISPLAYED RECORD HAS BEEN VERIFIED.
VERIFIED   EVAL   SU

```
010  001   ‡a   ‡ sh93-1113
020  040   ‡ac  ‡ DLC‡DLC
030  151 0 ‡a   ‡ Yazoo River Watershed (Miss.)
040  451 0 ‡wa  ‡nnnn ‡ Yazoo River Basin (Miss.)
050  550 0 ‡waz ‡gnnn ‡ Watersheds‡Mississippi
060  670   ‡ab  ‡ LC data base, 2/27/93‡(Yazoo River Watershed;
Yazoo River Basin)
070  952   ‡a   ‡ 2 bib. record(s) to be changed
080  952   ‡a   ‡ Made for existing bibliographic records
100  005   ‡a   ‡ 19930421110229.0
110  FFD   01.n  02.!     03.0    04.n    05.a  06.n  07.n
           08.n  09.a    10.a    11.a    12.a  13.a  14.
           15.b  16.a    17.b    18.n    19.n  20.a  21.a
           22.a  23.9314 24.te04 25.ta28 26.----  27.   28.-
           29.-  30.-    31.-    32.-    33.7  34.!  35.7
           36.!  37.!!!  38.j    39.j    40.2  41.z  42.93
           43.a  44.n
```

PAGE sh93-7668
11/26/93   [SUBJECTS]   [NCRD] [MUMS]
0*FAC*   DISPLAYED   RECORD   HAS   BEEN   VERIFIED.
VERIFIED   EVAL   SU

```
010  001   ‡a   ‡ sh93-7668
020  040   ‡ac  ‡ DLC‡DLC
030  150 0 ‡a   ‡ Tailhook Scandal, 1991-1993
050  550 0 ‡waz ‡gnnn ‡ Sexual harassment of women‡United
States
060  670   ‡a   ‡ Work cat.: 93-138159: Women in the military : the
Tailhook affair and the problem of sexual harassment, 1992.
070  670   ‡ab  ‡ Wash. Post index, 1992‡(Tailhook Association . . .
sexual harassment scandal)
080  670   ‡a   ‡ NYT index, Jan.-Mar. 1993.
090  670   ‡ab  ‡ MAGS‡(Tailhook scandal scars Naval aviation)
100  670   ‡ab  ‡ LC data base, 10/5/93‡(Tailhook Association)
110  952   ‡a   ‡ 0 bib. record(s) to be changed
120  005   ‡a   ‡ 19931126113620.5
130  FFD   01.n  02.!     03.0    04.n    05.a  06.n  07.n
           08.n  09.a    10.a    11.a    12.a  13.a  14.
           15.b  16.a    17.b    18.n    19.n  20.a  21.a
           22.a  23.9345 24.te05 25.yn47 26.----  27.   28.-
           29.-  30.-    31.-    32.-    33.7  34.!  35.7
           36.!  37.!!!  38.j    39.j    40.4  41.z  42.93
           43.a  44.n
```

Bibliographic Records

93-772
0*UPD* DISPLAYED RECORD HAS BEEN VERIFIED.

010 001 ‡a ‡ 93-772
030 050 00 ‡aba ‡ Z2401‡.K74 1993‡DH18
035 100 1 ‡aq ‡ Krewson, Margrit B.‡(Margrit Beran)
040 245 10 ‡ abc ‡ Hidden research resources in the Dutch-language collections of the Library of Congress :‡a selective bibliography of reference works = Verborgen onderzoeks-bronnen in de nederlandstalige collectie van de Library of Congress /‡Margrit B. Krewson.
050 260 ‡abc ‡ Washington, D.C. :‡Library of Congress,‡1993.
060 300 ‡ab ‡ 74 p. ;‡23 cm.
082 504 ‡a ‡ Includes bibliographical references and index.
084 651 0 ‡axx ‡ Benelux countries‡Bibliography‡Catalogs.
085 650 0 ‡axx ‡ Dutch literature‡Bibliography‡Catalogs.
086 610 20 ‡ax ‡ Library of Congress‡Catalogs.
087 740 01 ‡a ‡ Verborgen onderzoeks-bronnen in de nederlandstalige collectie van de Library of Congress.
089 082 00 ‡a2 ‡ 016.9492‡20
090 040 ‡acd ‡ DLC‡DLC‡DLC
093 043 ‡aa ‡ e1-----‡n-us-dc
095 051 ‡abc ‡ Z663‡.H53 1993‡Copy 3
100 005 ‡a ‡ 19931109145903.9
120 985 ‡a ‡ APIF/MIG
110 FFD

01.	02.	03.	04.x	05.	06.	07.
08.	09.	10.	11.	12.	13.	14.
15.eng	16.	17.	18.	19.	20.s	21.1993
22.	23.dcu	24.	25.	26.b	27.m	28.
29.	30.y	31.1	32.	33.7	34.f	35.7
36.a	37.	38.p	39.m	40.	41.a	

93-14085
0*UPD* DISPLAYED RECORD HAS BEEN VERIFIED.

```
010   001     ‡a    ‡ 93-14085
030   050 00 ‡aba  ‡ Z1601.A2‡G76 1968 Suppl. 5‡F1408
040   245 02 ‡abc  ‡ A Bibliography of Latin American and Caribbean
bibliographies, 1985-1989 :‡social sciences and humanities /‡Lionel
V. Lorona, editor.
050   260     ‡abc  ‡ Metuchen, N.J. :‡Scarecrow Press,‡1993.
080   300     ‡ac   ‡ xiv, 314 p. ;‡22 cm.
082   500     ‡a    ‡ "Supplement no. 5 to Arthur E. Gropp's A
Bibliography of Latin American bibliographies."
084   500     ‡a    ‡ Includes indexes.
090   020     ‡a    ‡ 0810827026 (alk. paper)
092   650   0 ‡axz  ‡ Bibliography‡Bibliography‡Latin America.
094   651   0 ‡ax   ‡ Latin America‡Bibliography.
096   700 10 ‡a    ‡ Lorona, Lionel V.
098   700 11 ‡adt  ‡ Gropp, Arthur E.,‡1902- ‡Bibliography of Latin
American bibliographies.
099   082 00 ‡a2   ‡ 016.01698‡20
100   040     ‡acd  ‡ DLC‡DLC‡DLC
102   043     ‡ a   ‡ cl-----
110   005     ‡a    ‡ 19930927071123.7
130   985     ‡a    ‡ APIF/MIG
120   FFD
01.      02.       03.       04.x    05.     06.      07.
08.      09.       10.       11.     12.     13.      14.
15.eng  16.       17.       18.     19.     20.s     21.1993
22.      23.nju    24.       25.     26.b    27.m     28.
29.      30.y      31.1      32.     33.7    34.      35.7
36.a     37.       38.p      39.m    40.     41.a
```

91-44881
0*UPD* DISPLAYED RECORD HAS BEEN VERIFIED.

```
010  001     ‡a   ‡ 91-44881
030  050 00 ‡ab  ‡ DB87‡.B5713 1992
033  100 1  ‡a   ‡ Bled, Jean-Paul.
035  240 10 ‡al  ‡ Francois-Joseph.‡English
040  245 10 ‡ac  ‡ Franz Joseph /‡Jean-Paul Bled ; translated by
Teresa Bridgeman.
050  260     ‡aabc‡ Oxford, UK ;‡Cambridge, Mass. :‡Blackwell
Publishers,‡1992.
060  300     ‡ac  ‡ 359 p. ;‡24 cm.
082  504     ‡a   ‡ Includes bibliographical references (p. 344-350)
and index.
086  020     ‡a   ‡ 0631167781
092  600 00 ‡abcd‡ Franz Joseph‡I,‡Emperor of Austria,
‡1830-1916.
093  651  0 ‡axx  ‡ Austria‡Kings and rulers‡Biography.
094  651  0 ‡axy  ‡ Austria‡History‡Francis Joseph, 1830-1918.
099  082 00 ‡a2   ‡ 943.6/04‡20
100  040     ‡acd  ‡ DLC‡DLC‡DLC
105  041 1  ‡ah   ‡ eng‡fre
106  043     ‡a   ‡ e-au---
120  005     ‡a   ‡ 19930617184454.1
140  985     ‡a   ‡ APIF/MIG
130  FFD
01.      02.      03.     04.x    05.     06.     07.
08.      09.      10.     11.     12.b    13.     14.
15.eng   16.      17.     18.     19.     20.s    21.1992
22.      23.enk   24.     25.     26.b    27.m    28.
29.      30.y     31.1    32.     33.7    34.     35.7
36.a     37.      38.p    39.m    40.     41.a
```

93-104356
0*UPD* DISPLAYED RECORD HAS BEEN VERIFIED.

```
010   001    ‡a    ‡ 93-104356
030   050 00 ‡ab   ‡ F868.S156‡T52 1992
050   100 1  ‡a    ‡ Thompson, Erwin N.
060   245 10 ‡ac   ‡ Presidio of San Francisco, Golden Gate National
```
Recreation Area, California /‡Erwin N. Thompson, Sally B. Woodbridge.
```
070   260    ‡abc  ‡ Denver, Colo. : ‡U.S. Dept. of the Interior, National
```
Park Service, Denver Service Center,‡1992
```
080   300    ‡abc  ‡ x, 250 p. :‡ill., maps ;‡28 cm.
081   440  0 ‡a    ‡ Special history study
082   500    ‡a    ‡ "Presidio of San Francisco, an outline of its
```
evolution as a U.S. Army post, 1847-1990."
```
090   500    ‡a    ‡ "August 1992."
100   504    ‡a    ‡ Includes bibliographical references (p. 245-250).
120   651  0 ‡ax   ‡ Presidio of San Francisco (Calif.)‡History.
130   651  0 ‡a    ‡ Golden Gate National Recreation Area (Calif.)
133   651  0 ‡ax   ‡ San Francisco (Calif.)‡Buildings, structures, etc.
148   700 10 ‡a    ‡ Woodbridge, Sally Byrne.
150   710 10 ‡abb  ‡ United States.‡National Park Service.‡Denver
```
Service Center.
```
180   040    ‡acd  ‡ DLC‡DLC‡DLC
182   043    ‡a    ‡ n-us-ca
210   922    ‡a    ‡ gs
220   985    ‡a    ‡ COPIED
230   005    ‡a    ‡ 19931014103235.0
250   985    ‡a    ‡ APIF/MIG
240   FFD
01.      02.       03.       04.      05.     06.     07.
08.      09.       10.       11.      12.     13.     14.
15.eng   16.       17.       18.      19.     20.s    21.1992
22.      23.cou    24.ab     25.      26.b    27.m    28.
29.      30.y      31.2      32.      33.7    34.f    35.7
36.a     37.       38.p      39.m     40.     41.a
```

93-34070
0*UPD* DISPLAYED RECORD HAS BEEN VERIFIED.

010	001	‡a	‡ 93-34070
030	050 00	‡ab	‡ PR2676‡.C48 1994
040	245 00	‡abc	‡ Christopher Marlowe :‡the plays and their

sources / ‡edited by Vivien Thomas and William Tydeman.

050	260	‡aabc	‡ London ;‡New York :‡Routledge,‡1994.
080	300	‡abc	‡ xii, 39 p. :‡map ;‡25 cm.
082	500	‡a	‡ One map on folded leaf inserted at end.
085	504	‡a	‡ Includes bibliographical references (p. 382-391)

and index.

090	020	‡a	‡ 0415040523
092	600 10	‡adx	‡ Marlowe, Christopher,‡1564-1593‡Sources.
093	650 0	‡ayx	‡ English drama‡Early modern and Elizabethan,

1500-1600‡Sources.

096	700 10	‡a	‡ Thomas, Vivien.
098	700 10	‡a	‡ Tydeman, William.
099	082 00	‡a2	‡ 822/.3‡20
100	040	‡acd	‡ DLC‡DLC‡DLC
103	043	‡a	‡ e-uk---
110	005	‡a	‡ 19940803145256.2
130	985	‡a	‡ APIF/MIG
120	FFD		

01.	02.	03.	04.x	05.	06.	07.
08.	09.	10.	11.	12.	13.	14.
15.eng	16.	17.	18.	19.	20.s	21.1994
22.	23.enk	24.b	25.	26.b	27.m	28.
29.	30.y	31.1	32.	33.7	34.	35.7
36.a	37.	38.p	39.m	40.	41.a	

Appendix B:
Free-Floating Form and Topical Subdivisions*

—Abbreviations
—Abbreviations of titles
—Ability testing
—Abstracting and indexing
—Abstracts
—Accidents *(May Subd Geog)*
—Accidents—Investigation
—Accounting
—Accreditation *(May Subd Geog)*
—Acronyms
—Administration
—Aerial photographs
—Air conditioning *(May Subd Geog)*
—Air conditioning—Control *(May Subd Geog)*
—Amateurs' manuals
—Analysis
—Anecdotes
—Anniversaries, etc.
—Archival resources
—Archives
—Art
—Atlases
—Audio-visual aids
—Audio-visual aids—Catalogs
—Audiotape catalogs
—Auditing
—Authorship
—Automatic control
—Automation
—Autonomous communities
—Awards *(May Subd Geog)*
—Biblical teaching

—Bibliography
—Bibliography—Catalogs
—Bibliography—Early
—Bibliography—Exhibitions
—Bibliography—Methodology
—Bibliography—Microform catalogs
—Bibliography—Union lists
—Bio-bibliography
—Biography
—Biography—Dictionaries
—Biography—History and criticism
—Book reviews
—Buildings
—Buildings—Conservation and restoration
—Buildings—Guidebooks
—By-laws
—By-products
—Calendars
—Calibration
—Cantons
—Capture, [date]
—Caricatures and cartoons
—Case studies
—Catalogs
—Catalogs and collections
—CD-ROM catalogs
—Censorship *(May Subd Geog)*
—Centennial celebrations, etc.
—Certification *(May Subd Geog)*
—Charitable contributions *(May Subd Geog)*
—Charts, diagrams, etc.

---

*The information presented in this section is based upon the *Subject Cataloging Manual: Subject Headings*, 4th ed. (Washington, D.C.: Library of Congress, Office of Subject Cataloging Policy, 1991), H1095. Many of the subdivisions included in this list are usable only under specific categories of headings. Consult the *Subject Cataloging Manual* for instructions on specific usage.

—Chronology
—Citizen participation
—Classification
—Cleaning
—Code numbers
—Code words
—Cold weather conditions
—Collectibles *(May Subd Geog)*
—Collection and preservation
—Collectors and collecting *(May Subd Geog)*
—Colonies
—Comic books, strips, etc.
—Communication systems
—Compact disc catalogs
—Comparative method
—Comparative studies
—Competitions *(May Subd Geog)*
—Composition
—Computer assisted instruction
—Computer programs
—Concordances
—Conduct of life
—Congresses
—Congresses—Attendance
—Conservation and restoration
—Constitution
—Control *(May Subd Geog)*
—Controversial literature
—Cooling
—Correspondence
—Corrosion *(May Subd Geog)*
—Corrupt practices
—Cost control
—Cost effectiveness
—Cost of operation
—Costs
—Costume *(May Subd Geog)*
—Cult *(May Subd Geog)*
—Curricula
—Data processing
—Data tape catalogs
—Databases
—Dating
—Decision making
—Defects
—Defects—Reporting *(May Subd Geog)*
—Defense measures *(May Subd Geog)*
—Departments
—Design
—Design and construction
—Designs and plans
—Deterioration

—Dictionaries
—Dictionaries—French, [Italian, etc.]
—Dictionaries—Polyglot
—Dictionaries, Juvenile
—Directories
—Discipline
—Discography
—Documentation *(May Subd Geog)*
—Drama
—Drawings
—Drying
—Dust control *(May Subd Geog)*
—Early works to 1800
—Econometric models
—Economic aspects *(May Subd Geog)*
—Electromechanical analogies
—Employees
—Encyclopedias
—Encyclopedias, Juvenile
—Endowments
—Energy conservation *(May Subd Geog)*
—Energy consumption *(May Subd Geog)*
—Environmental aspects *(May Subd Geog)*
—Equipment and supplies
—Estimates *(May Subd Geog)*
—Evaluation
—Examinations
—Examinations—Study guides
—Examinations, questions. etc.
—Exhibitions
—Experiments
—Facsimiles
—Fiction
—Field work
—Film catalogs
—Finance
—Fires and fire prevention *(May Subd Geog)*
—Folklore
—Food service
—Forecasting
—Foreign influences
—Forgeries *(May Subd Geog)*
—Forms
—Fume control *(May Subd Geog)*
—Government policy *(May Subd Geog)*
—Grading *(May Subd Geog)*
—Graphic methods
—Guidebooks
—Handbooks, manuals, etc.
—Health aspects *(May Subd Geog)*
—Heating and ventilation *(May Subd Geog)*

—Heating and ventilation—
  Control *(May Subd Geog)*
—Heraldry
—Historiography
—History
—History—16th century
—History—17th century
—History—18th century
—History—19th century
—History—20th century
—History—Chronology
—History—Philosophy
—History—Sources
—History and criticism
—History of doctrines
—History of doctrines—Early
  church, ca.30-600
—History of doctrines—Middle Ages,
  600-1500
—History of doctrines—16th century
—History of doctrines—17th century
—History of doctrines—18th century
—History of doctrines—19th century
—History of doctrines—20th century
—Hot weather conditions *(May Subd Geog)*
—Humor
—Identification
—Illustrations
—Indexes
—Industrial applications
—Influence
—Information services
—Insignia
—Inspection *(May Subd Geog)*
—Instruments
—International cooperation
—Interpretation
—Inventories
—Job descriptions *(May Subd Geog)*
—Juvenile drama
—Juvenile fiction
—Juvenile films
—Juvenile humor
—Juvenile literature
—Juvenile poetry
—Juvenile software
—Juvenile sound recordings
—Labeling *(May Subd Geog)*
—Labor productivity *(May Subd Geog)*
—Laboratory manuals
—Language
—Legends
—Lexicography

—Library resources
—Licenses *(May Subd Geog)*
—Lighting *(May Subd Geog)*
—Linear programming
—Literary collections
—Location *(May Subd Geog)*
—Longitudinal studies
—Maintenance and repair
—Management
—Manuscripts
—Manuscripts—Catalogs
—Manuscripts—Facsimiles
—Manuscripts—Indexes
—Manuscripts—Microform catalogs
—Maps
—Maps—Bibliography
—Maps—Early works to 1800
—Maps—Facsimiles
—Maps—Symbols
—Maps, Comparative
—Maps, Manuscript
—Maps, Mental
—Maps, Outline and base
—Maps, Physical
—Maps, Pictorial
—Maps, Topographic
—Maps, Tourist
—Maps for children
—Maps for the blind
—Maps for the visually handicapped
—Marketing
—Materials
—Mathematical models
—Mathematics
—Measurement
—Medals *(May Subd Geog)*
—Medical examinations *(May Subd Geog)*
—Meditations
—Membership
—Methodology
—Microform catalogs
—Miscellanea
—Models
—Moisture *(May Subd Geog)*
—Moral and ethical aspects
—Museums *(May Subd Geog)*
—Name
—Names
—Newspapers
—Noise
—Nomenclature
—Nomograms
—Notation
—Observations

—Observers' manuals
—Officials and employees
—Outlines, syllabi, etc.
—Packaging
—Packing *(May Subd Geog)*
—Papal documents
—Parodies, imitations, etc.
—Patents
—Periodicals
—Periodicals—Abbreviations of titles
—Periodicals—Bibliography
—Periodicals—Bibliography—Catalogs
—Periodicals—Bibliography—Union
  lists
—Periodicals—Indexes
—Personal narratives
—Personnel management
—Philosophy
—Photographs
—Photographs from space
—Physiological aspects
—Physiological effect
—Pictorial works
—Planning
—Poetry
—Political activity
—Political aspects *(May Subd Geog)*
—Popular works
—Posters
—Power supply *(May Subd Geog)*
—Practice *(May Subd Geog)*
—Prayer-books and devotions
—Prayer-books and devotions—
  History and criticism
—Preservation
—Prevention
—Prices *(May Subd Geog)*
—Prices—Government policy *(May
  Subd Geog)*
—Private collections *(May Subd Geog)*
—Privileges and immunities
—Problems, exercises, etc.
—Production control
—Production standards *(May Subd
  Geog)*
—Programmed instruction
—Programming
—Prophecies
—Protection *(May Subd Geog)*
—Provinces
—Psychological aspects
—Psychology
—Public opinion
—Publishing *(May Subd Geog)*
—Purchasing

—Quality control
—Quotations, maxims, etc.
—Rates
—Records and correspondence
—Recreational use
—Regions
—Registers
—Reliability
—Religion
—Remodeling
—Remote sensing
—Remote sensing maps
—Repairing
—Republics
—Research *(May Subd Geog)*
—Research grants *(May Subd Geog)*
—Reviews
—Romances
—Rules
—Rules and practice
—Safety appliances *(May Subd Geog)*
—Safety measures
—Safety regulations *(May Subd Geog)*
—Sanitation *(May Subd Geog)*
—Scholarships, fellowships, etc.
  (May Subd Geog)
—Scientific applications
—Security measures *(May Subd Geog)*
—Sermons
—Sex differences
—Siege, [date]
—Sieges
—Simulation methods
—Slang
—Slides
—Social aspects *(May Subd Geog)*
—Societies, etc.
—Sociological aspects
—Software
—Songs and music
—Sources
—Specifications *(May Subd Geog)*
—Specimens
—Spectra
—Speeches in Congress
—Stability
—Standards *(May Subd Geog)*
—State supervision
—States
—Statistical methods
—Statistical services
—Statistics
—Storage
—Study and teaching *(May Subd
  Geog)*

—Study and teaching—Activity programs *(May Subd Geog)*
—Study and teaching—Audiovisual aids
—Study and teaching—Simulation methods
—Study and teaching—Supervision
—Study and teaching (Continuing education) *(May Subd Geog)*
—Study and teaching (Early childhood) *(May Subd Geog)*
—Study and teaching (Elementary) *(May Subd Geog)*
—Study and teaching (Graduate) *(May Subd Geog)*
—Study and teaching (Higher) *(May Subd Geog)*
—Study and teaching (Internship) *(May Subd Geog)*
—Study and teaching (Preschool) *(May Subd Geog)*
—Study and teaching (Primary) *(May Subd Geog)*
—Study and teaching (Residency) *(May Subd Geog)*
—Study and teaching (Secondary) *(May Subd Geog)*
—Study guides
—Tables
—Taxation *(May Subd Geog)*
—Technique

—Technological innovations
—Telephone directories
—Terminology
—Territories and possessions
—Testing
—Textbooks
—Texts
—Themes, motives
—Therapeutic use
—Tombs
—Toxicology *(May Subd Geog)*
—Trademarks
—Translating
—Translations
—Translations into [name of language]
—Translations into [name of language]—Bibliography
—Transportation
—Tropical conditions
—Union lists
—Union territories
—Validity
—Valuation *(May Subd Geog)*
—Vibration *(May Subd Geog)*
—Video catalogs
—Vocational guidance *(May Subd Geog)*
—Waste disposal *(May Subd Geog)*
—Water-supply
—Weight
—Weights and measures

Appendix C:
Free-Floating Subdivisions Controlled By Pattern Headings*

LAW
Subdivisions Controlled By the
Pattern Heading for Legal Topics**

PATTERN: **Labor laws and legislation**

—Cases
—Codification
—Compliance costs *(May Subd Geog)*
—Criminal provisions
—Digests {Do not further subdivide by —**Periodicals**}
—Forms
—Interpretation and construction
—Language
—Legal research
    {used under inherently legal headings, including topical headings with the subdivision —**Law and legislation** or —**Legal status, laws, etc.** for works which discuss the use of legal research tools such as court reports, codes, digests, citators, etc., in determining the status of statutory, regulatory, or case law on a topic}
—Popular works
—Research *(May Subd Geog)*
    {used under legal topics for descriptions of proposed research, including such details as management, finance, personnel, special projects, methodology, goals, etc.}
—Trial practice

---

*The information presented in this section is based upon the *Subject Cataloging Manual: Subject Headings*, 4th ed. (Washington, D.C.: Library of Congress, Office of Subject Cataloging Policy, 1991).
**Library of Congress, *Subject Cataloging Manual*, H1154.5, H1550, H1710.

LITERATURE
Subdivisions Controlled by the Pattern Heading for Literatures (Including Individual Genres)*

PATTERN: **English literature**

Period subdivisions:
    Literatures and genres, except drama:

—Old English, ca. 450-1100
—Old English, ca. 450-1100—
    Modernized versions
—Middle English, 1100-1500
—Middle English, 1100-1500—
    Modernized versions

—Early modern, 1500-1700
—18th century
—19th century
—20th century

    Drama:

—To 1500
—Early modern and Elizabethan,
    1500-1600
—17th century

—Restoration, 1660-1700
—18th century
—19th century
—20th century

Topical and form subdivisions:

—Adaptations
—African influences
—American influences
—Anecdotes
—Appreciation (*May Subd Geog*)
—Arab influences
—Audio adaptations
—Bibliography
—Bibliography—Catalogs
—Bibliography—Early
—Bibliography—First editions
—Bibliography—Methodology
—Bio-bibliography
—Book reviews
—Brazilian influences
—Buddhist influences
—Celtic influences
—Censorship (*May Subd Geog*)
—Chinese influences
—Christian influences
—Chronology
—Classical influences
—Competitions (*May Subd Geog*)
—Concordances
—Criticism, Textual
—Dictionaries
—Discography

—Egyptian influences
—English influences
—European influences
—Examinations, questions, etc.
—Exhibitions
—Explication
—Explication—Dictionaries
—Film and video adaptations
—Foreign countries
—Foreign countries—History and criticism
—Foreign influences
—French influences
—Gallegan influences
—German influences
—Greek influences
—History and criticism
—History and criticism—Abstracts
—History and criticism—Bibliography
—History and criticism—Congresses
—History and criticism—Handbooks, manuals, etc.
—History and criticism—Periodicals
—History and criticism—Theory, etc.
—Humor
—Hungarian influences
—Illustrations
—Illustrations—Exhibitions

---

*Library of Congress, *Subject Cataloging Manual*, H1156.

—Indexes
—Indic influences
—Iranian influences
—Islamic influences
—Italian influences
—Japanese influences
—Latin American influences
—Manuscripts
—Manuscripts—Facsimiles
—Mediterranean influences
—Memorizing
—Microform catalogs
—Minangkabau influences
—Musical settings
—Mycenaean influences
—Oriental influences
—Outlines, syllabi, etc.
—Periodicals
—Periodicals—History
—Periodization
—Persian influences
—Philosophy
—Pictorial works
—Polish influences
—Political aspects
—Portuguese influences
—Problems, exercises, etc.
—Programmed instruction
—Psychological aspects
—Research *(May Subd Geog)*
—Roman influences
—Russian influences

—Sanskrit influences
—Scandinavian influences
—Scottish influences
—Shamanistic influences
—Social aspects *(May Subd Geog)*
—Societies, etc.
—Sources
—Spanish influences
—Stories, plots, etc.
—Study and teaching *(May Subd Geog)*
—Study and teaching—Audio-visual aids
—Study and teaching (Elementary)
  (May Subd Geog)
—Study and teaching (Graduate)
  (May Subd Geog)
—Study and teaching (Higher) *(May Subd Geog)*
—Study and teaching (Secondary)
  (May Subd Geog)
—Taoist influences
—Terminology
—Themes, motives
—Translations
—Translations—History and criticism
—Translations into French, [German, etc.]
—Translations into French, [German, etc.] —History and criticism
—Urdu influences
—West Indian influences
—Western influences
—Yiddish influences

Subdivisions Controlled By the Pattern Heading for Groups of Literary Authors*

PATTERN: **Authors, English**

Period subdivisions:

—Old English, ca. 450-1100
—Middle English, 1100-1500
—Early Modern, 1500-1700

—18th century
—19th century
—20th century

---

*Library of Congress, *Subject Cataloging Manual*, H1155.2.

Topical and form subdivisions:

—Aesthetics
—Anecdotes
—Archives
—Autographs
—Biography
—Biography—Dictionaries

—Biography—Exhibitions
—Biography—History and criticism
—Books and reading
—Caricatures and cartoons
—Chronology
—Correspondence

—Death
—Diaries
—Dictionaries
—Directories
—Economic conditions
—Family relationships
—Fees
—Fiction
—Health and hygiene
—Homes and haunts (May Subd Geog)
—Humor
—Indexes
—Interviews
—Journeys (May Subd Geog)
—Manuscripts
—Mothers

—Museums (May Subd Geog)
—Philosophy
—Pictorial works
—Political activity
—Political and social views
—Portraits
—Psychology
—Quotations
—Registers
—Relations with men
—Relations with women
—Religious life
—Sexual behavior
—Social conditions
—Tombs

Subdivisions Controlled By the Pattern Heading for Individual Literary Authors*

PATTERN: Shakespeare, William, 1564-1616

—Acting, see —Dramatic production; —Stage history
—Adaptations
—Aesthetics
—Allegory and symbolism, see —Symbolism
—Allusions
—Ancestry, see —Family
—Anecdotes
—Anniversaries, etc.
—Anonyms and pseudonyms
—Appreciation (May Subd Geog)
—Archives
—Archives—Catalogs
—Art
—Associates, see —Friends and associates
—Audio adaptations
—Authorship
—Authorship—Baconian theory, [Burton theory, etc.]
—Authorship—Collaboration
—Autobiography, see —Biography
—Autographs
—Autographs—Facsimiles
—Autographs, Spurious, see —Forgeries
—Bibliography
—Bibliography—Catalogs
—Bibliography—Exhibitions
—Bibliography—First editions
—Bibliography—Folios

—Bibliography—Folios. 1623, [1632, etc.]
—Bibliography—Methodology
Do not use. Use: 1. [author]. 2. Bibliography—Methodology
—Bibliography—Quartos
—Biography
—Biography—Birth, see —Birth
—Biography—Careers
—Biography—Chronology, see —Chronology
—Biography—Death and burial, see —Death and burial
—Biography—Exile, see —Exile
—Biography—Family, see —Family
—Biography—Health, see —Health
—Biography—Imprisonment, see —Imprisonment
—Biography—Last years and death, see —Death and burial; —Last years
—Biography—Marriage, see —Marriage
—Biography—Old age, see —Last years
—Biography—Psychology, see —Psychology
—Biography—Sources
—Biography—Youth, see —Childhood and youth
—Birth
—Birthday books, see —Calendars. Assign Birthday books as a second heading.

—*Bones*, see **—Relics**; **—Tomb**
—Books and reading
—Calendars
—*Canon*, see **—Authorship**; **—Chronology**; **—Criticism, Textual**
—*Careers*, see **—Biography—Careers**
—Caricatures and cartoons
—Censorship *(May Subd Geog)*
—*Centennial celebrations, etc.*, see **—Anniversaries, etc.**
—*Character*, see **—Ethics**; **—Psychology**; **—Religion**
—Characters
—Characters—Abandoned children
—Characters—Actors
—Characters—Afro-Americans
—Characters—Aged
—Characters—Angels
—Characters—Artists
—Characters—Children
—Characters—Clergy
—Characters—Comic characters
—Characters—Courtesans
—Characters—Criminals
—Characters—Daughters
—Characters—Dramatists
—Characters—Eccentrics
—Characters—Fairies
—Characters—Fathers
—Characters—Fools
—Characters—Gauchos
—Characters—Gentiles
—Characters—Ghosts
—Characters—Giants
—Characters—Gypsies
—Characters—Heroes
—Characters—Heroines
—Characters—Indians
—Characters—Intellectuals
—Characters—Irish
—Characters—Jews
—Characters—Kings and rulers
—Characters—Lawyers
—Characters—Men
—Characters—Mentally ill
—Characters—Messengers
—Characters—Minnesingers
—Characters—Monsters
—Characters—Mothers
—Characters—Muslims
—Characters—Novelists
—Characters—Physicians
—Characters—Poets
—Characters—Prisoners of war
—Characters—Revolutionaries

—Characters—Rogues and vagabonds
—Characters—Saints
—Characters—Satirists
—Characters—Scientists
—Characters—Servants
—Characters—Sick
—Characters—Singers
—Characters—Single people
—Characters—Slaves
—Characters—Soldiers
—Characters—Teachers
—Characters—Valets
—Characters—Villains
—Characters—Welsh
—Characters—Women
—Characters—Youth
—Characters—[name of individual character], e.g. **—Hamlet, [Margaret of Anjou, Sherlock Holmes, etc.]**
—Childhood and youth
—Chronology
—Cipher
—Comedies
—Comic books, strips, etc.
—*Commentaries*, see **—Criticism and interpretation**
—*Companions*, see **—Friends and associates**
—Concordances
—Congresses
—Contemporaries
—Contemporary England, [Contemporary America, Contemporary France, etc.]
—Correspondence
—Correspondence—Facsimiles
—Correspondence—Indexes
—*Costume*, see **—Dramatic production**; **—Stage history**
—Criticism, Textual
—Criticism and interpretation
—Criticism and interpretation—Congresses
—Criticism and interpretation—History
—Criticism and interpretation—History—17th century
—Criticism and interpretation—History—18th century
—Criticism and interpretation—History—19th century
—Criticism and interpretation—History—20th century
—Death and burial
—Death mask

—*Dialects*, see —**Language—Dialects**
—Diaries
—Dictionaries
—Discography
—*Diseases*, see —**Health**
—Drama
—Dramatic production
—Dramatic works
—*Dramaturgy*, see —**Dramatic production**; —**Dramatic works**; —**Technique**
—*Dwellings*, see —**Homes and haunts**
—*Editions*, see —**Bibliography**
—Editors
—*Education*, see —**Knowledge and learning**
—Encyclopedias
—Estate
—Ethics
—Exhibitions
—Exile *(May Subd Geog)*
—Family
—Fiction
—Fictional works
—Film and video adaptations
—*Forerunners*, see —**Sources**; —**Criticism and interpretation**
—Forgeries *(May Subd Geog)*
—Friends and Associates
—*Genealogy*, see —**Family**
—*Glossaries*, see —**Language—Glossaries, etc.**
—*Grammar*, see —**Language—Grammar**
—*Grave*, see —**Tomb**
—Handbooks, manuals, etc.
—*Handwriting*, see —**Autographs**
—*Haunts*, see —**Homes and haunts**
—Health
—Histories
—Homes and haunts *(May Subd Geog)*
—Homes and haunts—Guidebooks
—Humor
—*Iconography*, see —**Pictorial works**
—Illustrations
—Illustrations—Catalogs
—Illustrations—Exhibitions
—*Illustrations, Comic*, see —**Illustrations**
—*Imitations*, see **Parodies, imitations, etc.**
—Imprisonment
—In literature
—Indexes
—Influence

—Interviews
—*Itineraries*, see —**Journeys**
—*Journals*, see —**Diaries**
—Journeys *(May Subd Geog)*
—Journeys—Guidebooks
—Juvenile drama
—Juvenile fiction
—Juvenile films
—Juvenile humor
—Juvenile literature
—Juvenile poetry
—Juvenile sound recordings
—Knowledge—Agriculture, [America, etc.]
—*Knowledge—Aesthetics*, see —**Aesthetics**
—*Knowledge—Costume*, see —**Dramatic production**
—*Knowledge—Ethics*, see —**Ethics**
—*Knowledge—Philosophy*, see —**Philosophy**
—*Knowledge—Religion*, see —**Religion**
—Knowledge and learning
—Language
—Language—Dialects
—Language—Glossaries, etc.
—Language—Grammar
—Language—Pronunciation
—Language—Punctuation
—*Language—Style*, see —**Style**
—*Language—Versification*, see —**Versification**
—Language—Word frequency
—Last years
—Legends
—Library
—Library—Catalogs
—Library—Marginal notes
—Library resources
—Literary collections
—Manuscripts
—Manuscripts—Catalogs
—Manuscripts—Facsimiles
—*Marginalia*, see —**Scholia**
—Marriage
—*Men*, see —**Relations with men**
—Miscellanea
—Monuments *(May Subd Geog)*
—*Moral ideas*, see —**Ethics**
—Motion picture plays
—*Motion pictures*, see —**Film and video adaptations**
—*Moving-picture plays*, see —**Motion picture plays**
—Museums *(May Subd Geog)*

—*Musical settings*
—*Mysticism*, see **—Religion**
—Name
—Notebooks, sketchbooks, etc.
—On postage stamps
—Outlines, syllabi, etc.
—*Pageants*, see **—Anniversaries, etc.**; **—Dramatic production**
—*Paraphrases, tales, etc.*, see **—Adaptations**
—Parodies, imitations, etc.
—*Patriotism*, see **—Political and social views**
—Periodicals
—*Personality*, see **—Psychology**
—Philosophy
—Pictorial works
—*Plots*, see **—Stories, plots, etc.**
—Poetic works
—Poetry
—Political activity
—Political and social views
—Portraits
—*Prohibited books*, see **—Censorship**
—*Pronunciation*, see **—Language—Pronunciation**
—Prophecies
—Prose
—*Pseudonyms*, see **—Anonyms and pseudonyms**
—Psychology
—*Public opinion*, see **—Appreciation**
—Publishers
—Quotations
—Radio and television plays
—*Reading habits*, see **—Books and reading**
—*Relations with editors*, see **—Editors**
—*Relations with family*, see **—Family**
—*Relations with friends and associates*, see **—Friends and associates**
—Relations with men
—*Relations with publishers*, see **—Publishers**
—Relations with women
—Relics *(May Subd Geog)*
—Religion
—*Satire*, see **—Humor**
—Scholia
—*Screenplays*, see **—Motion picture plays**
—*Sepulchral monument*, see **—Tomb**
—Settings
—Sexual behavior

—*Sketchbooks*, see **—Notebooks, sketchbooks, etc.**
—*Social views*, see **—Political and social views**
—Societies, etc.
—Songs and music
—Songs and music-Discography
—Songs and music—History and criticism
—Sources
—Sources—Bibliography
—Spiritualistic interpretations
—Spurious and doubtful works
—Stage history *(May Subd Geog)*
—Stage history—To 1625
—Stage history—1625-1800
—Stage history—1800-1950
—Stage history—1950-
—*Stage presentation*, see **—Dramatic production**; **—Stage history**
—*Stage setting and scenery*, see **—Dramatic production**; **—Stage history**
—Statues
—Stories, plots, etc.
—Study and teaching *(May Subd Geog)*
—Study and teaching—Audio-visual aids
—Study and teaching—Audio-visual aids—Catalogs
—*Study and teaching—Outlines, syllabi, etc.*, see **—Outlines, syllabi, etc.**
—Style
—*Summaries, arguments, etc.*, see **—Stories, plots, etc.**
—Symbolism
—Technique
—*Textual criticism*, see **—Criticism, Textual**
—*Themes, motives*, see **—Criticism and interpretation**
—*Themes, motives—[specific topic]*, see **—Knowledge—[specific topic]**
—*Theology*, see **—Religion**
—*Tomb*
—Tragedies
—Tragicomedies
—Translations
—Translations—History and criticism
—Translations into French, [German, etc.]

—Translations into French, [German, etc.] —History and criticism
—*Translators*, see —**Translations— History and criticism**
—*Travesties*, see —**Parodies, imitations, etc.**
—Versification
—*Video adaptations*, see —**Film and video adaptations**

—*Voyages and travels*, see —**Journeys**
—Will
—*Women*, see —**Relations with women**
—*Yearbooks*, see —**Periodicals**
—*Youth*, see —**Childhood and youth**

*Library of Congress, *Subject Cataloging Manual*, H1155.4.

MUSIC
Subdivisions Controlled By the Pattern Heading for Music Compositions*

PATTERN: **Operas**

Period subdivisions:

—To 500
—500-1400
—15th century
—16th century

—17th century
—18th century
—19th century
—20th century

Music format subdivisions:

—2-piano scores
—3-piano scores
—Chorus scores with piano
—Chorus scores without accompaniment
—Parts
—Parts (solo)
—Piano scores
—Piano scores (4 hands)
—Scores
—Scores and parts

—Scores and parts (solo)
—Solo with harpsichord
—Solo with harpsichord and piano
—Solo with keyboard instrument
—Solo with organ
—Solo with piano
—Solo with pianos (2)
—Vocal scores with accordion
—Vocal scores with continuo

*Library of Congress, *Subject Cataloging Manual*, H1160.

Subdivisions Controlled By the Pattern Heading for Musical Instruments*

PATTERN: **Piano**

—Catalogs, Manufacturers'
—Catalogs and collections (*May Subd Geog*)
—Chord diagrams
—Construction (*May Subd Geog*)
—Customizing (*May Subd Geog*)
—Fingering

—Instruction and study (*May Subd Geog*)
—Instruction and study—Juvenile
—Methods
—Methods—Group instruction
—Methods—Juvenile
—Methods—Self-instruction

—Methods (Jazz, [Rock, Bluegrass, etc.])[1]
—Orchestra studies
—Pedaling
—Performance
—Religious aspects
—Studies and exercises
—Studies and exercises—Juvenile
—Studies and exercises (Jazz, [Rock, Bluegrass, etc.])[1]
—Tuning (*May Subd Geog*)

Note

[1]When assigning the subdivision —Methods or —Studies and exercises qualified by a particular style of popular music, assign as an additional heading the style of music subdivided by —Instruction and study, e.g.
  (1) Banjo—Methods (Bluegrass)   (1) Guitar—Studies and exercises (Rock)
  (2) Bluegrass music—Instruction   (2) Rock music—Instruction and study.
  and study.

*Library of Congress, *Subject Cataloging Manual*, H1161.

RELIGION
Subdivisions Controlled By the Pattern Heading for Religions*

PATTERN: **Buddhism**

—Apologetic works
—Apologetic works—History and criticism
—Catechisms
—Charities
—Controversial literature
—Controversial literature—History and criticism
—Creeds
—Customs and practices
—Discipline
—Doctrines
—Doctrines—Introductions
—Economic aspects (*May Subd Geog*)
—Essence, genius, nature
—Government
—History
—History—To ca. 100 A.D.
—History—19th century
—History—20th century
—History—Philosophy
—Influence
—Liturgical objects
—Missions (*May Subd Geog*)
—Origin
—Political aspects[1] (*May Subd Geog*)
—Prayer-books and devotions
—Prayer-books and devotions—English, [French, German, etc.]
—Prayer-books and devotions—History and criticism
—Psychology
—Relations
—Relations—Christianity, [Islam, etc.]
—Rituals[2]
—Rituals—Texts[2]
—Rituals—Texts—Concordances[2]
—Rituals—Texts—History and criticism[2]
—Sacred books[3]
—Sacred books—Hermeneutics
—Sacred books—Introductions
—Sacred books—Language, style
—Sacred books—Preservation
—Sacred books—Quotations
—Social aspects (*May Subd Geog*)
—Study and teaching (*May Subd Geog*)

Notes

[1]Not established under **Buddhism.** Use only under individual sects or denominations. For religions, assign a heading of the type: [*name of religion*] **and politics,** e.g. **Buddhism and politics.**

[2]Do not use the subdivision —**Rituals** and its further subdivisions under **Judaism** and sects of Judaism. Instead use the subdivision —**Liturgy** under **Judaism** and its sects. The latter subdivision may be further subdivided by —**Study and teaching; —Texts;** and —**Texts—History and criticism.**

[3]For subdivisions used under the uniform titles of individual sacred works, see H1188.

---

*Library of Congress, *Subject Cataloging Manual*, H1185.

Subdivisions Controlled By the Pattern Heading for Christian Denominations*

PATTERN: **Catholic Church**

—Adult education (*May Subd Geog*)
—Anniversaries, etc.
—Apologetic works
—Apologetic works—History and criticism
—Benefices (*May Subd Geog*)
—Bio-bibliography
—Bishops
—Bishops—Appointment, call, and election
—Catechisms
—Catechisms—English, [French, German, etc.]
—Catechisms—History and criticism
—Charities
—Clergy
—Clergy—Appointment, call and election
—Clergy—Degradation
—Clergy—Deposition
—Clergy—Deprivation of the clerical garb
—Clergy—Installation
—Clergy—Secular employment (*May Subd Geog*)
—Comparative studies
—Controversial literature
—Controversial literature—History and criticism
—Creeds
—Creeds—History and criticism
—Customs and practices
—Dioceses (*May Subd Geog*)
—Diplomatic service
—Discipline
—Doctrines
—Doctrines—History
—Doctrines—History—Modern period, 1500-
—Education (*May Subd Geog*)

—Employees
—Finance
—Foreign relations (*May Subd Geog*)
—Foreign relations—Treaties
—Government
—History
—History—Modern period, 1500-
—History—16th century
—History—17th century
—History—18th century
—History—19th century
—History—20th century
—History—1965-
—Hymns
—Hymns—History and criticism
—Hymns—Texts
—In literature
—Infallibility
—Influence
—Liturgy
—Liturgy—Calendar
—Liturgy—Texts
—Liturgy—Texts—Concordances
—Liturgy—Texts—History and criticism
—Liturgy—Texts—Illustrations
—Liturgy—Texts—Manuscripts
—Liturgy—Texts—Rubrics
—Liturgy—Theology
—Liturgy, Experimental
—Membership
—Missions (*May Subd Geog*)
—Museums (*May Subd Geog*)
—Name
—On postage stamps
—Pastoral letters and charges
—Political activity
—Prayer-books and devotions
—Prayer-books and devotions—English, [French, German, etc.]

—Prayer-books and devotions—History and criticism
—Publishing (*May Subd Geog*)
—Relations
—Relations—Anglican Communion, [Lutheran Church, etc.]

—Relations—Buddhism, [Judaism, etc.]
—Relations—Evangelicalism
—Relations—Protestant churches
—Sermons
—Sermons—History and criticism
—Teaching office

---

*Library of Congress, *Subject Cataloging Manual*, H1187.

Subdivisions Controlled By the Pattern Heading for Sacred Works*

PATTERN: **Bible**

TYPES OF HEADINGS COVERED BY THE PATTERN: Headings for the uniform titles of individual sacred works or scriptures from all religions, including their individual parts. Also included are apocryphal works. *Examples:* **Book of Mormon; Koran; Talmud; Tripitaka; Vedas; Bible. O.T. Apocrypha. Wisdom of Solomon; Bible. N.T. Gospels; Sermon on the mount; Beatitudes; Epistle of Barnabas**. The category does not include individual nonsacred liturgical or theological works. For subdivisions used under the uniform titles of secular classics, see H1155.8.

—Abridgments
—Accents and accentuation[1]
—Anecdotes
—Antiquities
—Appreciation (*May Subd Geog*)
—Authorship
—Authorship—Date of authorship
—Bahai interpretations
—Bibliography
—Biography
—Biography—Sermons
—Canon
—Canon, Catholic vs. Protestant
—Canonical criticism
—Caricatures and cartoons
—Children's sermons
—Children's use
—Chronology
—Chronology—Charts, diagrams, etc.
—Comic books, strips, etc.
—Commentaries
—Commentaries—Facsimiles
—Commentaries—History and criticism
—Comparative studies
—Concordances
—Concordances, English
—Concordances, English—American Revised
—Concordances, English—Douai
—Concordances, English—Geneva

—Concordances, English—Jerusalem Bible
—Concordances, English—Living Bible
—Concordances, English—Moffatt
—Concordances, English—New American Bible
—Concordances, English—New American Standard
—Concordances, English—New International
—Concordances, English—New Revised Standard
—Concordances, English—New World
—Concordances, English—Revised Standard
—Concordances, French, [German, etc.]
—Controversial literature
—Copies, Curious
—Criticism, Form
—Criticism, interpretation, etc. (*May Subd Geog*)
—Criticism, interpretation, etc.—Bibliography
—Criticism, interpretation, etc.—Censorship (*May Subd Geog*)
—Criticism, interpretation, etc.—Data processing
—Criticism, interpretation, etc.—History
—Criticism, interpretation, etc.—History—Early church, ca. 30-600

—Criticism, interpretation, etc.—
    History—Middle Ages, 600-1500
—Criticism, interpretation, etc.—
    History—Modern period, 1500-
—Criticism, interpretation, etc.—
    History—16th century
—Criticism, interpretation, etc.—
    History—17th century
—Criticism, interpretation, etc.—
    History—18th century
—Criticism, interpretation, etc.—
    History—19th century
—Criticism, interpretation, etc.—
    History—20th century
—Criticism, interpretation, etc., Jewish[1]
—Criticism, Narrative
—Criticism, Redaction
—Criticism, Textual
—Cross references
—Devotional literature
—Devotional use
—Dictionaries
—Dictionaries, Juvenile
—Editions, Curious
—Evidences, authority, etc.
—Evidences, authority, etc.—
    History of doctrines
—Examinations, questions, etc.
—Extra-canonical parallels
—Feminist criticism
—Folklore
—Geography
—Geography—Maps
—Geography—Maps—Early works to
    1800
—Handbooks, manuals, etc.
—Harmonies
—Harmonies—History and criticism
—Harmonies, English, [French, Ger-
    man, etc.]
—Harmonies, English, [French, Ger-
    man, etc.]—History and criticism
—Hermeneutics
—Hindu interpretations
—Historiography
—History
—History Bibles
—History of Biblical events
—History of Biblical events—Fiction
—History of Biblical events—Poetry
—History of contemporary events
—History of contemporary events—
    Fiction
—Homiletical use
—Humor

—Illustrations
—In literature
—Indexes
—Influence
—Influence—Medieval civilization
—Influence—Western civilization
—Inspiration
—Inspiration—History of doctrines
—Interlinear translations
—Interlinear translations, English,
    [French, etc.]
—Introductions
—Islamic interpretations
—Juvenile literature
—Juvenile poetry
—Language, style
—Legends
—Liturgical lessons, Dutch,
    [English, etc.]
—Liturgical use
—Manuscripts
—Manuscripts—Catalogs
—Manuscripts—Facsimiles
—Manuscripts—Paragraphs
—Manuscripts, English, [Latin,
    Aramaic, etc.]
—Manuscripts (Papyri)
—Marginal readings
—Meditations
—Memorizing
—Miscellanea
—Mnemonic devices
—Numerical division
—Outlines, syllabi, etc.
—Parables
—Paragraphs
—Parallel versions, English, [French, etc.]
—Paraphrases
—Paraphrases—History and criticism
—Paraphrases, English, [French,
    German, etc.]
—Paraphrases, English, [French,
    German, etc.]—History and
    criticism
—Periodicals
—Philosophy
—Picture Bibles
—Prayers
—Prayers—History and criticism
—Prefaces
—Prophecies
—Prophecies—Chronology
—Prophecies—[subject of prophecy]
—Psychology

—Publication and distribution
  (*May Subd Geog*)
—Publication and distribution—
  Societies, etc.
—Quotations
—Quotations, Early
—Quotations in rabbinical literature[1]
—Quotations in the New Testament[1]
—Reading (*May Subd Geog*)
—Reference editions
—Relation to Matthew, [Jeremiah, etc.][2]
—Relation to the Old Testament,
  [Mark, Psalms, etc.][3]
—Sermons
—Sermons—Outlines, syllabi, etc.
—Social scientific criticism
—Societies, etc.
—Sources

—Study and teaching (*May Subd Geog*)
—Study and teaching—Catholic Church
—Terminology
—Terminology—Pronunciation
—Textbooks
—Theology
—Thumb Bibles
—Titles of books
—Translating
—Use
—Use in hymns
—Versions[4]
—Versions, African, [Indic, Slavic, etc.][5]
—Versions, Baptist
—Versions, Catholic
—Versions, Catholic vs. Protestant
—Versions, Hussite
—Versions, Jehovah's Witnesses

*Library of Congress, *Subject Cataloging Manual*, H1188.

Notes

[1]Use only under **Bible. O.T.** or individual books of the Old Testament.

[2]Use only under individual books of the Old Testament. Make a duplicate entry under the reverse, e.g., 1. **Bible. O.T. Psalms—Relation to Jeremiah**. 2. **Bible. O.T. Jeremiah—Relation to Psalms.**

[3]Use only under individual books of the New Testament. Make a duplicate entry under the reverse, e.g., 1. **Bible. N.T. Matthew—Relation to Psalms.** 2. **Bible. O.T. Psalms—Relation to Matthew.**

[4]See H1300 for instructions on the use of the subdivision **—Versions.**

[5]Assign the adjectival qualifier for groups of languages only. For works on translations of the Bible into individual languages, assign: **Bible. [*language*]—Versions.** For works on particular translations, use **Bible. [*language*]—Versions—[*name of version*]**, e.g., **Bible. English—Versions—Authorized.**

Appendix D:
Free-Floating Subdivisions
Further Subdivided By Place*

—Abnormalities
—Abscess
—Abuse of
—Accidents
—Accreditation[1]
—Acupuncture
—Adaptation
—Adjuvant treatment
—Alcohol use
—Alternative treatment
—Ambrosian rite
—Ankylosis
—Antiochene rite
—Appreciation
—Appropriate technology
—Armed Forces
—Armenian rite
—Artificial insemination
—Artificial spawning
—Autopsy
—Awards[1,2,3]
—Balloons
—Basques
—Batteries
—Battlefields
—Bearings
—Behavior
—Benefices
—Beneventan rite
—Bioaccumulation
—Biological control
—Biological warfare
—Biopsy
—Biotechnology
—Blacks

—Blunt trauma
—Bonding
—Boundaries
—Brazing
—Breeding
—Byzantine rite
—Byzantine rite, Greek
—Byzantine rite, Melchite
—Byzantine rite, Romanian
—Byzantine rite, Ruthenian
—Byzantine rite, Ukrainian
—Calcification
—Calculi
—Campaigns
—Cancer
—Capital investments
—Capital productivity
—Care
—Care and hygiene
—Catalogs and collections
—Celtic rite
—Censorship
—Certification
—Chaldean rite
—Chaplains[4]
—Charitable contributions
—Chemical warfare
—Chemoprevention
—Chemotherapy
—Children[4]
—Chiropractic treatment
—Civil rights[5]
—Civilian relief
—Climatic factors
—Cold working

*The information presented in this section is based upon the *Subject Cataloging Manual: Subject Headings*, 4th ed. (Washington, D.C.: Library of Congress, Office of Subject Cataloging Policy, 1991), H860.

446

—Collaborationists
—Collectibles
—Collectors and collecting
—Collision damage
—Colonial forces
—Colonization[6]
—Commando operations
—Commerce[5]
—Competitions
—Complications
—Concentration camps
—Confiscations and contributions
—Conscientious objectors
—Conscript labor
—Conservation
—Conservation and restoration[7]
—Construction
—Contracting out
—Contraction
—Control
—Corrosion
—Corrosion fatigue
—Corrupt practices[1]
—Cost-of-living adjustments
—Counseling of
—Cracking
—Creep
—Crimes against
—Criticism, interpretation, etc.
—Cryopreservation
—Cryosurgery
—Cryotherapy
—Cult
—Cultural assimilation
—Cultural control
—Cultures and culture media
—Curing
—Customer services
—Customizing
—Cysts
—Decontamination
—Defects—Reporting
—Deinstitutionalization
—Dental care[5]
—Desertions
—Destruction and pillage
—Desulphurization
—Diagnostic use
—Dialects
—Diet therapy
—Dioceses
—Disease and pest resistance
—Diseases[5]
—Diseases and pests
—Disinfection

—Dislocation
—Dismissal of
—Disorders
—Dispersal
—Dissection
—Documentation
—Draft resisters
—Drug testing
—Drug use
—Dust control
—Eclectic treatment
—Ecology
—Economic aspects
—Ecophysiology
—Education[5]
—Education (Early childhood)
—Education (Elementary)
—Education (Graduate)
—Education (Higher)[5]
—Education (Preschool)
—Education (Primary)
—Education (Secondary)
—Effect of acid deposition on
—Effect of acid precipitation on
—Effect of air pollution on
—Effect of arsenic on
—Effect of automation on
—Effect of chemicals on
—Effect of cold on
—Effect of dams on
—Effect of drought on
—Effect of drugs on
—Effect of ethephon on
—Effect of explosive devices on
—Effect of ferrous sulphate on
—Effect of floods on
—Effect of fluorine on
—Effect of gamma rays on
—Effect of habitat modification on
—Effect of heat on
—Effect of heavy metals on
—Effect of implants on
—Effect of insecticides on
—Effect of light on
—Effect of logging on
—Effect of metals on
—Effect of minerals on
—Effect of noise on
—Effect of oil spills on
—Effect of oxygen on
—Effect of ozone on
—Effect of pesticides on
—Effect of pollution on
—Effect of radiation on
—Effect of salt on

—Effect of sediments on
—Effect of soil acidity on
—Effect of storms on
—Effect of stray currents on
—Effect of stress on
—Effect of technological innovations on
—Effect of temperature on
—Effect of thermal pollution on
—Effect of water level on
—Effect of water pollution on
—Effect of water quality on
—Eggs
—Electric equipment
—Electronic intelligence
—Employment
—Endoscopic surgery
—Environmental aspects
—Environmental engineering
—Estimates
—Etching
—Ethiopian rite
—Evacuation of civilians
—Exercise
—Exercise therapy
—Exile
—Extrusion
—Feed utilization efficiency
—Fertilizers
—Fibrosis
—Finance[4]
—Finishing
—First performances
—Food supply
—Foreign economic relations
—Foreign relations
—Foreign service
—Forgeries
—Fracture
—Fractures
—Frost damage
—Frost protection
—Frost resistance
—Fume control
—Gallican rite
—Gene therapy
—Geology
—Government ownership
—Government policy
—Grooming
—Gypsies
—Handling
—Health[2]
—Health and hygiene[5]
—Health aspects
—Health promotion services

—Health risk assessment
—Heating and ventilation
—Heirloom varieties
—Hemorrhage
—Herbicide injuries
—Hibernation
—Home care
—Homeopathic treatment
—Homes and haunts
—Hormone therapy
—Hospital care[5]
—Hospitals[5]
—Housing[5]
—Hypertrophy
—Imaging
—Immunotherapy
—Impact testing
—In-service training
—Induced spawning
—Industrial capacity
—Infections
—Infertility
—Insect resistance
—Inspection
—Institutional care
—Instruction and study
—Insurance
—Integrated control
—Jews
—Jews—Rescue
—Job descriptions
—Journalism, Military
—Journeys
—Kinship
—Labeling
—Labor productivity
—Laser surgery
—Law and legislation[8]
—Legal status, laws, etc.[5]
—Licenses
—Liturgy without a priest
—Logistics
—Long-term care
—Losses
—Magnetic resonance imaging
—Malabar rite
—Malankar rite
—Malpractice
—Manpower
—Maronite rite
—Massage
—Medals[1,2,5]
—Medical care[5]
—Medical examinations
—Mental health[2,5]

—Mental health services[5]
—Microbiology
—Micropropagation
—Microscopy
—Military aspects
—Military intelligence
—Military relations
—Missing in action
—Missions[5]
—Molecular diagnosis
—Monitoring
—Monuments[9]
—Motors—Cylinder heads
—Motors—Valves
—Mozarabic rite
—Museums[1,3,5]
—Mutation breeding
—Mutilation, defacement, etc.
—Needle biopsy
—Nursing
—Nursing home care
—Officials and employees[10]
—Oriental rites
—Palaces
—Parasites
—Pastoral counseling of
—Pathogens
—Patients
—Pensions[5,11]
—Performances
—Physical therapy
—Political aspects
—Pollution
—Pollution potential
—Postharvest losses
—Practice
—Press coverage
—Prices
—Private collections
—Production standards
—Professional ethics
—Propagation
—Promotions
—Prospecting
—Protection
—Protest movements
—Provincialisms
—Psychological testing
—Publication and distribution
—Publishing
—Purification
—Quenching
—Radiation injuries
—Radiography
—Radionuclide imaging

—Radiotherapy
—Ratings
—Reading
—Recruiting
—Regimental histories
—Registers of dead[4]
—Registration and transfer
—Rehabilitation
—Reinstatement
—Relapse
—Relations[10]
—Relics
—Relocation
—Reoperation
—Reporting
—Reporting to
—Research
—Research grants[1]
—Residence requirements
—Resignation
—Respite care
—Risk assessment
—Safety regulations
—Salaries, etc.[11]
—Scholarships, fellowships, etc.
—Search and rescue operations[4]
—Secret service
—Seeds—Viability
—Selection and appointment
—Services for[5,12]
—Shrines
—Side effects
—Skid resistance
—Skidding
—Social aspects
—Spawning
—Specifications
—Spectroscopic imaging
—Spoken English
—Spoken French, [Japanese, etc.]
—Stage history
—Standards
—Statues
—Storage—Diseases and injuries
—Stress corrosion
—Study and teaching
—Study and teaching (Clinical
  education)
—Study and teaching (Continuing
  education)
—Study and teaching (Early childhood)
—Study and teaching (Elementary)
—Study and teaching (Graduate)
—Study and teaching (Higher)
—Study and teaching (Internship)

—Study and teaching (Preceptorship)
—Study and teaching (Preschool)
—Study and teaching (Primary)
—Study and teaching (Residency)
—Study and teaching (Secondary)
—Subcontracting
—Substance use
—Suffrage[5]
—Summering
—Supplementary employment
—Supply and demand
—Surgery
—Suspension
—Syphilis
—Tactical aviation
—Taxation[5]
—Teacher training
—Tenure
—Territorial questions
—Thermotherapy
—Tobacco use
—Tournaments
—Toxicity testing
—Toxicology
—Training
—Training of
—Transmission
—Transplantation
—Transplanting
—Transportation—Diseases and
  injuries
—Travel
—Travel regulations
—Treatment

—Trypanotolerance
—Tuberculosis
—Tumors
—Tuning
—Type specimens
—Ulcers
—Ultrasonic imaging
—Underground literature
—Underground movements
—Underground movements, Jewish
—Underground printing plants
—Utilization
—Vaccination
—Valuation
—Variation
—Varieties
—Venom
—Vertical distribution
—Vertical integration
—Veterans
—Veterinary service
—Vibration
—Virus diseases
—Viruses
—Viscosity
—Vitality
—Vocalization
—Vocational education
—Vocational guidance
—War work
—Weed control
—Wintering
—Women[4]
—Wounds and injuries[5]

Notes

[1]Except when used under corporate bodies.

[2]Except when used under individual persons.

[3]Except when used under individual schools.

[4]Only when used under wars.

[5]Except when used under Indians.

[6]Except when used under places.

[7]Only when used under art objects.

[8]Except when used under topical subdivisions established under Indians, e.g.,
Indians of North America—Fishing—Law and legislation.

[9]Except when used under classes of persons and ethnic groups.

[10]Only when used under places.

[11]Except when used under individual legislative bodies.

[12]Except when used under types of schools.

Appendix E:
Free-Floating Subdivisions
Used Under Persons*

Subdivisions Used Under Classes of Persons**

—Abstracting and indexing
—Abstracts
—Abuse of *(May Subd Geog)*
—Alcohol use *(May Subd Geog)*
—Anecdotes
—Anniversaries, etc.
—Anthropometry
—*Appointment, qualifications, tenure, etc.,* see **—Selection and appointment**
—Archives
—Assaults against *(May Subd Geog)*
—Attitudes
—Autographs
—Bibliography
—Bibliography—Catalogs
—Bibliography—Microform catalogs
—Bibliography—Union lists
—Biography
—Biography—Dictionaries
—Biography—History and criticism
—Biography—Pictorial works
—Bonding *(May Subd Geog)*
—Book reviews
—Books and reading
—Care *(May Subd Geog)*
—*Care and hygiene,* see **—Care; —Health and hygiene**
—*Care and treatment,* see **—Care**
—Caricatures and cartoons
—Case studies
—Certification *(May Subd Geog)*
—Charitable contributions *(May Subd Geog)*

—Civil rights *(May Subd Geog)*
—Classification
—*Clothing,* see **—Costume; —Uniforms**
—*Clubs,* see **—Societies and clubs**
—Collectibles *(May Subd Geog)*
—Colonization *(May Subd Geog)*
—Comic books, strips, etc.
—Conduct of life
—Congresses
—Congresses—Attendance
—*Contributions, Charitable,* see **—Charitable contributions**
—Correspondence
—Costume *(May Subd Geog)*
—Counseling of *(May Subd Geog)*
—Crimes against *(May Subd Geog)*
—*Cultural life,* see **—Intellectual life**
—*Customs,* see **—Social life and customs**
—Death
—Deinstitutionalization *(May Subd Geog)*
—*Demand and supply,* see **—Supply and demand**
—Dental care *(May Subd Geog)*
—*Devotions,* see **—Prayer-books and devotions**
—Diaries
—Directories
—*Directories—Telephone,* see **—Telephone directories**
—Discipline
—Discography

---

*The information presented in this section is based upon the *Subject Cataloging Manual: Subject Headings,* 4th ed. (Washington, D.C.: Library of Congress, Office of Subject Cataloging Policy, 1991).
**Library of Congress, *Subject Cataloging Manual,* H1100.

451

—*Diseases and hygiene*, see **—Diseases; —Health and hygiene**
—Dismissal of *(May Subd Geog)*
—Drama
—Drug testing *(May Subd Geog)*
—Drug use *(May Subd Geog)*
—Dwellings *(May Subd Geog)*
—Early works to 1800
—Economic conditions
—Education *(May Subd Geog)*
—Education—[topic]
—Education (Continuing education) *(May Subd Geog)*
—Education (Early childhood) *(May Subd Geog)*
—Education (Elementary) *(May Subd Geog)*
—Education (Graduate) *(May Subd Geog)*
—Education (Higher) *(May Subd Geog)*
—Education (Preschool) *(May Subd Geog)*
—Education (Primary) *(May Subd Geog)*
—Education (Secondary) *(May Subd Geog)*
—Effect of automation on *(May Subd Geog)*
—Effect of technological innovations on *(May Subd Geog)*
—Employment *(May Subd Geog)*
—Employment—Foreign countries
—*Employment, Supplementary*, see **—Supplementary employment**
—*Ethics, Professional*, see **—Professional ethics**
—Examinations
—Examinations, questions, etc.
—Exhibitions
—Family relationships
—Fees
—*Fellowships*, see **—Scholarships, fellowships, etc.**
—Fiction
—Film catalogs
—Finance, Personal
—Folklore
—Genealogy
—Government policy *(May Subd Geog)*
—Handbooks, manuals, etc.
—*Haunts*, see **—Homes and haunts**
—Health and hygiene *(May Subd Geog)*
—Health risk assessment *(May Subd Geog)*
—Historiography
—History
—History—16th century
—History—17th century

—History—18th century
—History—19th century
—History—20th century
—*History—Anniversaries*, see **—Anniversaries, etc.**
—History—Sources
—Home care *(May Subd Geog)*
—Homes and haunts *(May Subd Geog)*
—Hospital care *(May Subd Geog)*
—Hospitals *(May Subd Geog)*
—Housing *(May Subd Geog)*
—Humor
—*Hygiene*, see **—Health and hygiene**
—*Iconography*, see **—Pictorial works**
—Identification
—In-service training *(May Subd Geog)*
—Indexes
—Information services
—*Injuries*, see **—Wounds and injuries**
—Institutional care *(May Subd Geog)*
—Insurance requirement
—Intellectual life
—Intelligence levels
—Intelligence testing *(May Subd Geog)*
—Interviews
—Job descriptions *(May Subd Geog)*
—Job stress *(May Subd Geog)*
—Juvenile drama
—Juvenile fiction
—Juvenile films
—Juvenile humor
—Juvenile literature
—Juvenile poetry
—Juvenile sound recordings
—Language
—*Law and legislation*, see **—Legal status, laws, etc.**
—Legal status, laws, etc.
—Library resources
—Licenses *(May Subd Geog)*
—Life skills guides
—Literary collections
—Long-term care *(May Subd Geog)*
—Longitudinal studies
—Manuscripts
—Medals *(May Subd Geog)*
—Medical care *(May Subd Geog)*
—Mental health *(May Subd Geog)*
—Mental health services *(May Subd Geog)*
—Miscellanea
—Monuments *(May Subd Geog)*
—Morality
—Museums *(May Subd Geog)*
—*Music*, see **—Songs and music**

—Nursing home care *(May Subd Geog)*
—Nutrition
—Obituaries
—Outlines, syllabi, etc.
—*Outside employment*, see **—Supplementary employment**
—Pastoral counseling of *(May Subd Geog)*
—Pensions *(May Subd Geog)*
—Pensions—Cost-of-living adjustments *(May Subd Geog)*
—Pensions—Effect of inflation on *(May Subd Geog)*
—Pensions—Unclaimed benefits
—Periodicals
—Periodicals—Bibliography
—Periodicals—Bibliography—Catalogs
—Periodicals—Bibliography—Union lists
—Periodicals—Indexes
—*Personal finance*, see **—Finance, Personal**
—Photographs
—Physiology
—Pictorial works
—*Place frequented*, see **—Homes and haunts**
—Poetry
—Political activity
—Portraits
—Posters
—Prayer-books and devotions
—Professional ethics *(May Subd Geog)*
—Promotions *(May Subd Geog)*
—Prophecies
—Protection *(May Subd Geog)*
—*Psychiatric care*, see **—Mental health services**
—Psychological testing *(May Subd Geog)*
—Psychology
—Public opinion
—*Qualifications*, see **—Rating of;** **—Selection and appointment**
—Quotations
—*Quotations, maxims, etc.*, see **—Quotations**
—Rating of *(May Subd Geog)*
—*Reading habits or interests*, see **—Books and reading**
—Recreation
—Recruiting *(May Subd Geog)*
—Registers
—Rehabilitation *(May Subd Geog)*
—Reinstatement *(May Subd Geog)*
—Religious life *(May Subd Geog)*
—Relocation *(May Subd Geog)*

—Reporting to *(May Subd Geog)*
—Research *(May Subd Geog)*
—Residence requirements *(May Subd Geog)*
—Respite care *(May Subd Geog)*
—*Salaries, allowances, etc.*, see **—Salaries, etc.**
—*Salaries, commissions, etc.*, see **—Salaries, etc.**
—Salaries, etc. *(May Subd Geog)*
—Scholarships, fellowships, etc.
—Selection and appointment *(May Subd Geog)*
—Services for
—Sexual behavior
—Social conditions
—Social life and customs
—Social networks *(May Subd Geog)*
—Societies, etc.
—Societies and clubs
—*Socioeconomic status*, see **—Economic conditions; —Social conditions**
—Songs and music
—Statistical services
—Statistics
—Substance use *(May Subd Geog)*
—Suffrage *(May Subd Geog)*
—Suicidal behavior *(May Subd Geog)*
—Supplementary employment *(May Subd Geog)*
—Supply and demand *(May Subd Geog)*
—Surgery *(May Subd Geog)*
—Surgery—Complications *(May Subd Geog)*
—Surgery—Risk factors *(May Subd Geog)*
—Taxation *(May Subd Geog)*
—Telephone directories
—Terminology
—Time management *(May Subd Geog)*
—Titles
—Tobacco use *(May Subd Geog)*
—Tombs
—Training of *(May Subd Geog)*
—Transfer
—Transportation
—Travel *(May Subd Geog)*
—Travel regulations *(May Subd Geog)*
—*Treatment*, see **—Care**
—Uniforms
—Vocational guidance *(May Subd Geog)*
—*Working conditions*, see **—Employment**
—Wounds and injuries *(May Subd Geog)*
—*Yearbooks*, see **—Periodicals**

Subdivisions Used Under Individual Persons*

—Abdication, [date]
—Abstracts
—Adaptations
—Adversaries
—Aesthetics
—Alcohol use
—*Allegory*, see —**Symbolism**
—*Ancestry*, see —**Family**
—Anecdotes
—*Anecdotes, facetiae, satire, etc.*, see
   —**Anecdotes**; —**Humor**
—Anniversaries, etc.
—Appreciation *(May Subd Geog)*
—Archaeological collections
—Archives
—Archives—Access control
—Archives—Catalogs
—Archives—Microform catalogs
—Art
—Art collections
—Art patronage
—Assassination
—Assassination attempt, [date]
—Assassination attempts
—*Associates*, see —**Friends and**
   associates
—*Attitude toward [specific topic]*, see
   —**Views on [specific topic]**
—Audiotape catalogs
—Authorship
—*Autobiography*, use **[name of person]**
—Autographs
—Autographs—Facsimiles
—*Autographs, Spurious*, see
   —**Forgeries**
—Awards
—Bibliography
—Bibliography—Catalogs
—Bibliography—Exhibitions
—Bibliography—Microform catalogs
—*Biography*, use **[name of person]**
—Birth
—*Bones*, see —**Relics**; —**Tomb**
—Bonsai collections
—Books and reading
—*Burial*, see —**Death and burial**
—Captivity, [dates]
—Career in [specific field or discipline]
—Caricatures and cartoons

—*Cartoons, satire, etc.*, see —**Carica-**
   tures and cartoons; —**Humor**
—Catalogs
—Catalogues raisonnés
—*Centennial celebrations, etc.*, see
   —**Anniversaries, etc.**
—*Character*, see —**Ethics**;
   —**Psychology**; —**Religion**
—Childhood and youth
—Chronology
—Claims vs. . . . .
—Clothing
—Coin collections
—Collectibles *(May Subd Geog)*
—Comic books, strips, etc.
—*Commentaries*, see —**Criticism**
   and interpretation
—Compact disc catalogs
—*Companions*, see —**Friends and**
   associates
—Concordances
—Congresses
—Contributions in [specific field or
   topic]
—Coronation
—Correspondence
—Correspondence—Catalogs
—Correspondence—Microform catalogs
—*Costume*, see —**Clothing**
—Criticism and interpretation
—*Crowning*, see —**Coronation**
—Cult *(May Subd Geog)*
—*Date of birth*, see —**Birth**
—Death and burial
—Death mask
—*Devotional literature*, see —
   Prayer-books and devotions
—Diaries
—Dictionaries
—Disciples
—Discography
—*Diseases*, see —**Health**
—Divorce
—Drama
—Dramaturgy
—Drug use
—*Dwellings*, see —**Homes and haunts**
—*Early life*, see —**Childhood and**
   youth

---

*Library of Congress, *Subject Cataloging Manual*, H1110.

—*Education*, see —**Knowledge and learning**
—Employees
—Encyclopedias
—*Enemies*, see —**Adversaries**
—Estate
—Ethics
—Ethnological collections
—Ethnomusicological collections
—Exhibitions
—Exile *(May Subd Geog)*
—Family
—Fiction
—Film catalogs
—Finance, Personal
—*Folktales*, see —**Legends**
—Forgeries *(May Subd Geog)*
—Freemasonry
—*Frequented places*, see —**Homes and haunts**
—Friends and Associates
—*Funeral*, see —**Death and burial**
—*Genealogy*, see —**Family**
—*Grave*, see —**Tomb**
—*Handwriting*, see —**Autographs**
—Harmony
—*Haunts*, see —**Homes and haunts**
—Health
—Herbarium
—Homes and haunts *(May Subd Geog)*
—Homes and haunts—Guidebooks
—Humor
—*Iconography*, see —**Pictorial works**
—*Imitations*, see **Parodies, imitations, etc.**
—Impeachment
—Imprisonment
—In literature
—Inauguration, [date]
—Indexes
—Influence
—Information services
—*Interment*, see —**Death and burial**
—*Interpretation*, see —**Criticism and interpretation**
—Interviews
—*Journals*, see —**Diaries**
—Journeys *(May Subd Geog)*
—Journeys—Guidebooks
—Juvenile drama
—Juvenile fiction
—Juvenile films
—Juvenile humor
—Juvenile literature
—Juvenile poetry
—Juvenile sound recordings
—Kidnapping, [date]
—Knowledge—Agriculture, [America, etc.]
—Knowledge and learning
—Language
—Language—Glossaries, etc.
—*Last illness*, see —**Death and burial**
—Last years
—*Leadership, Military*, see —**Military leadership**
—*Learning*, see —**Knowledge and learning**
—Legends
—*Letters*, see —**Correspondence**
—Library
—Library—Catalogs
—Library—Microform catalogs
—Library resources
—Literary art
—Literary collections
—*Litigation*, see —**Trials, litigation, etc.**
—Manuscripts
—Manuscripts—Catalogs
—Manuscripts—Facsimiles
—Manuscripts—Indexes
—Manuscripts—Microform catalogs
—Map collections
—Marriage
—Medals
—Meditations
—Mental health
—Military leadership
—Miscellanea
—Monuments *(May Subd Geog)*
—*Motives, themes*, see —**Themes, motives**
—Museums *(May Subd Geog)*
—*Music*, see —**Songs and music**
—Musical instrument collections
—Musical settings
—Name
—Natural history collections
—Notebooks, sketchbooks, etc.
—Notebooks, sketchbooks, etc.—Facsimiles
—Numismatic collections
—Numismatics
—*Old age*, see —**Last years**
—On postage stamps
—*Opponents*, see —**Adversaries**
—Oratory
—Outlines, syllabi, etc.

—Palaces *(May Subd Geog)*
—Pardon
—Parodies, imitations, etc.
—*Patronage of the arts*, see —**Art patronage**
—Performances *(May Subd Geog)*
—Periodicals
—*Personal finance*, see —**Finance, Personal**
—*Personality*, see —**Psychology**
—Philosophy
—Photograph collections
—*Pictorial humor*, see —**Caricatures and cartoons**
—Pictorial works
—*Place of birth*, see —**Birthplace**
—*Places frequented*, see —**Homes and haunts**
—Poetry
—Political and social views
—Portraits
—Poster collections
—Posters
—Prayer-books and devotions
—Prayer-books and devotions—English, [French, German, etc.]
—Pre-existence
—*Professional life*, see —**Career in [specific field or discipline]**
—Prophecies
—Psychology
—Public opinion
—*Public speaking*, see —**Oratory**
—Quotations
—*Reading habits*, see —**Books and reading**
—Relations with [specific class of persons or ethnic group]
—*Relations with employees*, see —**Employees**
—*Relations with family*, see —**Family**
—*Relations with friends and associates*, see —**Friends and associates**
—Relics *(May Subd Geog)*
—Religion
—*Residences*, see —**Homes and haunts**
—Resignation from office
—*Rhetoric*, see —**Literary art**; —**Oratory**
—Romances
—*Satire*, see —**Humor**
—*Sayings*, see —**Quotations**

—*Scholarship*, see —**Knowledge and learning**
—Scientific apparatus collections
—Seal
—Self-portraits
—*Sepulchral monument*, see —**Tomb**
—Sermons
—*Servants*, see —**Employees**
—Sexual behavior
—Shrines *(May Subd Geog)*
—*Sketchbooks*, see —**Notebooks, sketchbooks, etc.**
—Slide collections
—Slides
—Slides-Catalogs
—*Social views*, see —**Political and social views**
—Societies, etc.
—Songs and music
—Sources
—*Spiritual life*, see —**Religion**
—Statues *(May Subd Geog)*
—*Stories of operas*, see —**Stories, plots, etc.**
—Stories, plots, etc.
—Study and teaching *(May Subd Geog)*
—*Style, Literary*, see —**Literary art**
—Symbolism
—*Table-talk*, see —**Quotations**
—*Tales*, see —**Legends**; —**Romances**
—Teachings
—Thematic catalogs
—Themes, motives
—Titles
—Tomb
—*Travels*, see —**Journeys**
—Trials, litigation, etc.
—Video catalogs
—Views on [specific topic]
—*Views on aesthetics*, see —**Aesthetics**
—*Views on ethics*, see —**Ethics**
—*Views on politics and society*, see —**Political and social views**
—*Views on religion*, see —**Religion**
—*Views on society*, see —**Political and social views**
—*Voyages*, see —**Journeys**
—Will
—*Writing skill*, see —**Literary art**
—Written works
—*Yearbooks*, see —**Periodicals**
—*Youth*, see —**Childhood and youth**

Appendix F:
Free-Floating Subdivisions
Used Under Places

FREE-FLOATING SUBDIVISIONS:
NAMES OF PLACES*

TYPES OF HEADINGS COVERED: The subdivisions listed below may be used, within the limitations of the footnotes, as free-floating subdivisions under headings for geographic place names including continents; regions; islands; countries; states, provinces, and equivalent jurisdictions; counties and other local jurisdictions larger than cities; and headings for metropolitan areas, suburban areas, and regions based on names of cities. They may also be used, except as footnoted, under names of cities established as valid AACR 2 name headings, under names of extinct cities established as subject headings (in accordance with the provisions of H715), and under names of city sections, districts, or quarters (in accordance with the provisions of H720). Appropriate subdivisions may also be used under headings for geographic features or regions based on geographic features following the guidelines for the assignment of such headings given in H760. Appropriate subdivisions may also be used under names of bodies of water. For additional subdivisions used only under names of bodies of water, streams, etc., see H1145.5. This list does not cover international organizations and corporate bodies that are not jurisdictions, e.g., Commonwealth of Independent States.

—Abstracting and indexing
—Abstracts
—Administrative and political
  divisions
—Aerial exploration[1]
—Aerial photographs
—Aerial views
—Altitudes[1]
—Anecdotes
—Annexation to ...[1]
—Anniversaries, etc.
—Antiquities[2]
—Antiquities—Collection and
  preservation[2]

—Antiquities, Byzantine[2]
—Antiquities, Celtic[2]
—Antiquities, Germanic[2]
—Antiquities, Phoenician[2]
—Antiquities, Roman[2]
—Antiquities, Slavic[2]
—Antiquities, Turkish[2]
—Appropriations and expenditures
—Appropriations and expenditures—
  Effect of inflation on
—Archival resources
—Area[3]
—Armed Forces[4,5] (*May Subd Geog*)
—Audiotape catalogs

---

*The information presented in this section is based upon the *Subject Cataloging Manual: Subject Headings*, 4th ed. (Washington, D.C.: Library of Congress; Office of Subject Cataloging Policy, 1991), H1140.

—Bio-bibliography
—Biography
—Biography—Anecdotes
—Biography—Caricatures and cartoons
—Biography—Dictionaries
—Biography—History and criticism
—Biography—Humor
—Biography—Pictorial works
—Biography—Portraits
—Book reviews
—Boundaries (*May Subd Geog*)
—Buildings, structures, etc.[6]
—Calendars
—Capital and capitol[1]
—Census
—Census—Law and legislation
—Census, [*date*]
—Centennial celebrations, etc.
—Charters[7]
—Charters, grants, privileges[8]
—Church history
—Church history—16th century
—Church history—17th century
—Church history—18th century
—Church history—19th century
—Church history—20th century
—Civilization
—Civilization—16th century[1]
—Civilization—17th century[1]
—Civilization—18th century[1]
—Civilization—19th century[1]
—Civilization—20th century[1]
—Civilization—Foreign influences
—Civilization—Philosophy
—Claims
—Claims vs. . . . .
—Climate
—Climate—Observations
—Colonial influence
—Colonies[9]
—Colonization
—Commerce (*May Subd Geog*)
—Commercial policy[4]
—Commercial treaties[4]
—Compact disc catalogs
—Constitution[1]
—Constitution—Amendments[1]
—Constitution—Amendments—1st, [2nd, 3rd, etc.][1]
—Constitution—Signers[1]
—Constitutional history[1]
—Constitutional law[1]
—Constitutional law—Amendments[1]
—Constitutional law—Amend-ments—1st, [2nd, 3rd, etc.][1]

—Constitutional law—Amendments—Ratification[1]
—Constitutional law—Religious aspects[1]
—Constitutional law—Religious as-pects—Baptists, [Catholic Church, etc.][1]
—Constitutional law, State[1]
—Constitutional law, State—Amendments[1]
—Court and courtiers
—Court and courtiers—Costume
—Court and courtiers—Food
—Court and courtiers—Language
—Cultural policy
—Databases
—Defenses[4]
—Defenses—Economic aspects[4]
—Defenses—Law and legislation[4]
—Dependency on ...[4]
—Dependency on foreign countries[4]
—Description and travel
—Directories
—Discovery and exploration
—Discovery and exploration—French, [Spanish, etc.]
—Distances, etc.
—Drama
—Early works to 1800
—Economic conditions
—Economic conditions —Regional disparities[1]
—Economic integration[10]
—Economic policy
—Emigration and immigration
—Emigration and immigration—Economic aspects
—Emigration and immigration—Government policy
—Emigration and immigration—Religious aspects
—Emigration and immigration—Religious aspects—Baptists, [Catholic Church, etc.]
—Emigration and immigration—Social aspects
—Environmental conditions
—Eruption, [*date*][11]
—Eruptions[11]
—Ethnic relations
—Exiles[1]
—Fiction
—Folklore[12]
—Forecasting

—Foreign economic relations (*May Subd Geog*)
—Foreign public opinion[4]
—Foreign public opinion, British, [French, Italian, etc.][4]
—Foreign relations[13] (*May Subd Geog*)
—Foreign relations—Catholic Church[13]
—Foreign relations—Executive agreements[13]
—Foreign relations—Law and legislation[13]
—Foreign relations—Philosophy[13]
—Foreign relations—Treaties[13]
—Foreign relations administration[13]
—Gazetteers
—Genealogy
—Genealogy—Religious aspects
—Geography
—Gold discoveries[1]
—Guidebooks
—Handbooks, manuals, etc.
—Historical geography
—Historical geography—Maps
—Historiography
—History
—History—[*period subdivision, if established*]—Biography[14]
—History—[*period subdivision, if established*]—Biography—Anecdotes[14]
—History—[*period subdivision, if established*]—Biography—Portraits[14]
—History—[*period subdivision, if established*]—Chronology[14]
—History—[*period subdivision, if established*]—Philosophy
—History—[*period subdivision, if established*]—Sources
—History—Anecdotes
—History—Autonomy and independence movements[1]
—History—Blockade, [*date*]
—History—Bombardment, [*date*]
—History—Chronology
—History—Comic books, strips, etc.
—History—Errors, inventions, etc.
—History—Humor
—History—Partition, [*date*]
—History—Periodization[1]
—History—Philosophy
—History—Pictorial works
—History—Prophecies
—History—Religious aspects
—History—Religious aspects—Baptists, [Catholic Church, etc.]
—History—Religious aspects—Buddhism, [Christianity, etc.]
—History—Siege, [*date*]
—History—Sources
—History, Local[1,15]
—History, Local—Collectibles[1]
—History, Military
—History, Military—Religious aspects
—History, Naval
—Humor
—Imprints
—In literature
—Index maps
—Information services
—Intellectual life
—Intellectual life—16th century[1]
—Intellectual life—17th century[1]
—Intellectual life—18th century[1]
—Intellectual life—19th century[1]
—Intellectual life—20th century[1]
—International status
—Juvenile drama
—Juvenile fiction
—Juvenile humor
—Juvenile poetry
—Kings and rulers
—Kings and rulers—Art patronage
—Kings and rulers—Brothers
—Kings and rulers—Children
—Kings and rulers—Death and burial
—Kings and rulers—Dwellings
—Kings and rulers—Education
—Kings and rulers—Folklore
—Kings and rulers—Genealogy
—Kings and rulers—Heraldry
—Kings and rulers—Journeys (*May Subd Geog*)
—Kings and rulers—Mistresses
—Kings and rulers—Mothers
—Kings and rulers—Mythology
—Kings and rulers—Religious aspects
—Kings and rulers—Sisters
—Kings and rulers—Succession
—Kings and rulers—Tombs
—Languages[16]
—Languages—Law and legislation
—Languages—Political aspects
—Languages—Texts
—Library resources
—Literary collections
—Literatures[17]
—Manufactures
—Maps
—Maps—Bibliography
—Maps—Early works to 1800

—Maps—Facsimiles
—Maps, Comparative
—Maps, Manuscript
—Maps, Mental
—Maps, Outline and base
—Maps, Physical
—Maps, Pictorial
—Maps, Topographic
—Maps, Tourist
—Maps for children
—Maps for the blind
—Maps for the visually handicapped
—Military policy[4]
—Military policy—Religious aspects[4]
—Military relations (*May Subd Geog*)
—Military relations—Foreign countries
—Militia[1,5]
—Miscellanea
—Moral conditions
—Name
—National Guard[4,5]
—Naval militia[1]
—Newspapers
—Officials and employees (*May Subd Geog*)[18]
—Officials and employees—Accidents (*May Subd Geog*)
—Officials and employees—Foreign countries
—Officials and employees—Foreign countries—Foreign language competency
—Officials and employees—Furloughs
—Officials and employees—Leave regulations
—Officials and employees—Payroll deductions
—Officials and employees—Salaries, etc. (*May Subd Geog*)
—Officials and employees—Salaries, etc.—Regional disparities
—Officials and employees—Turnover
—Officials and employees, Alien
—Officials and employees, Honorary
—Officials and employees, Retired
—On postage stamps
—Photographs from space
—Pictorial works
—Poetry
—Politics and government
—Politics and government—[*period subdivision, if established*]—Philosophy
—Politics and government—Caricatures and cartoons
—Politics and government—Humor
—Politics and government—Philosophy
—Population
—Population policy
—Posters
—Proclamations[4]
—Quotations, maxims, etc.
—Race relations
—Registers
—Relations (*May Subd Geog*)
—Relations—Foreign countries
—Relief models
—Religion
—Religion—16th century
—Religion—17th century
—Religion—18th century
—Religion—19th century
—Religion—20th century
—Religion—Humor
—Religious life and customs
—Remote-sensing images
—Remote-sensing maps
—Research (*May Subd Geog*)
—Road maps
—Rural conditions[1]
—Seal
—Slides
—Social conditions
—Social life and customs
—Social policy
—Songs and music
—Statistical services
—Statistical services—Law and legislation
—Statistics
—Statistics, Medical
—Statistics, Vital
—Strategic aspects
—Study and teaching (*May Subd Geog*)
—Study and teaching—Law and legislation (*May Subd Geog*)
—Study and teaching (Continuing education) (*May Subd Geog*)
—Study and teaching (Early childhood) (*May Subd Geog*)
—Study and teaching (Elementary) (*May Subd Geog*)
—Study and teaching (Graduate) (*May Subd Geog*)
—Study and teaching (Higher) (*May Subd Geog*)

—Study and teaching (Internship)
  (*May Subd Geog*)
—Study and teaching (Preschool)
  (*May Subd Geog*)
—Study and teaching (Primary)
  (*May Subd Geog*)
—Study and teaching (Secondary)
  (*May Subd Geog*)
—Surveys

—Telephone directories
—Telephone directories—Yellow
  pages
—Territorial expansion[4]
—Territories and possessions[4,19]
—Tours
—Trials, litigation, etc.
—Zoning maps

Also free-floating:

. . . in art
. . . Metropolitan Area ([*geographic qualifier*])   (*based on names of cities*)
. . . Suburban Area ([*geographic qualifier*])   (*based on names of cities*)
. . . Region ([*geographic qualifier*])   (*based on names of cities*
    and geographic features)

Notes

[1]Do not use under cities.

[2]Do not use under names of ancient or early cities established as subject headings.

[3]Use for descriptions of the physical area of a place as well as for works on measurement of the area of a place.

[4]Use only under countries or under regions larger than countries.

[5]See H1159 for further subdivisions used under **—Armed Forces; —Militia;** and **—National Guard**.

[6]Use only under cities and city sections, as described in H1334 and H1334.5.

[7]Use only under states, counties, cities, etc. of the United States.

[8]Use under countries, etc. other than the United States, and under cities other than those of the United States.

[9]See H1149.5 for further subdivisions used under **—Colonies. [*name of country*]—Colonies** may also be used under topical headings, e.g., **Education—Great Britain—Colonies**.

[10]Use only under regions larger than countries.

[11]Use under names of volcanoes.

[12]Use only for works discussing folklore about the place. For works discussing folklore originating in the place, use **Folklore—[*place*]**.

[13]Use only under countries, or under regions larger than countries, as described in H1629.

[14]Use only under places where —**History—[*period subdivision*]** is established. If no period subdivision is established, use **[*place*]—Biography; [*place*]—Biography—Anecdotes; [*place*]—Biography—Portraits**.

[15]Use under names of regions, countries, states, etc., for the collective histories of several local units. For the history of a single locality, use the subdivision —**History** under the name of the locality.

[16]See H1154 for further subdivisions used under —**Languages**.

[17]See H1156 for further subdivisions used under —**Literatures**.

[18]See H1100 for further subdivisions used under classes of persons.

[19]**[*name of country*]—Territories and possessions** may also be used under topical headings, e.g., **Taxation—United States—Territories and possessions**.

FREE-FLOATING SUBDIVISIONS: BODIES OF WATER*

—Alluvial plain
—Channelization
—Channels
—Fertilization
—Navigation
—Navigation—Law and legislation
—Power utilization
—Recreational use
—Regulation
—Water rights

---

*Library of Congress, *Subject Cataloging Manual*, H1145.5.

Appendix G:
Patterns of Cross References
for Proper Names

Cross references for personal, corporate, and jurisdictional headings are made according to *Anglo-American Cataloguing Rules*, second edition, 1988 revision (*AACR2R*). References for individual subject headings are enumerated in LCSH. Following are patterns and examples of cross references of headings for certain types of proper names, gathered from LCSH, various parts of the *Subject Cataloging Manual*, and information provided by the Cataloging Policy and Support Office of the Library of Congress. Examples are taken from the Library of Congress Information System (LOCIS) through INTERNET.

PERSONS AND FAMILY NAMES

Gods and Goddesses

Pattern:
[Name of god *or* goddess] ([Ethnic adjective] deity)
    UF   [Alternate name] ([Ethnic adjective] deity)
    BT   **Gods, [Ethnic adjective]**

Example:
Ma-tsu (Chinese deity)
    UF   Ma-tsu (Chinese goddess)
    BT   **Gods, Chinese**

Gods and Goddesses from Classical Mythology

Pattern:
[Name of god *or* goddess] (...deity)
    UF   [Alternate name] (Greek or Roman deity)
    RT   **[Equivalent deity]**
    BT   **Gods, [Greek *or* Roman]**
           or **Goddesses, [Greek *or* Roman]**

Examples:
Neptune (Roman deity)
    UF   Neptunus
           Neptunus (Roman deity)
    RT   **Poseidon (Greek deity)**
    BT   **Gods, Roman**

463

Poseidon (Greek deity)
UF   **Poseidon**
RT   **Neptune (Roman deity)**
BT   **Gods, Greek**

Fictitious and Legendary Characters

Patterns:
[Name of character] (Fictitious character)
UF   [Alternate name] (Fictitious character)
BT   **Comic books, strips, etc.** {if appropriate}

[Name of character] (Legendary character) {*or* more specific qualifier}
UF   [Alternate name] (Legendary character)
BT   **Folklore—[Place]**
       Legends—[Place] {if appropriate}

Examples:
Fontana, Mac (Fictitious character)
UF   Fontana, MacKinley (Fictitious character)
       Mac Fontana (Fictitious character)
       MacKinley Fontana (Fictitious character)

Snooky (Fictitious character)
UF   Snooks (Fictitious character)
       Teenage Mutant Ninja Turtles (Fictitious characters)
BT   **Comic books, strips, etc.**

Huang-ti (Legendary ruler)
UF   Hsuan-yuan (Legendary ruler)
       Yellow Emperor (Legendary ruler)
       Yu-hsiung (Legendary ruler)
BT   **China—Kings and rulers**

John Henry (Legendary character)
BT   **Afro-Americans—Folklore**
       Folklore—United States

Royal Houses, Dynasties, Noble Houses

Patterns:
[Name], House of
UF   [Variant form of the name]
BT   **[Country of origin *or* Country most closely identified with**
       royal house]—Kings and rulers

[Name] dynasty
UF   [Variant form of the name]
BT   **[Country]—Kings and rulers**

[Name], [Title in English]
    UF   [Variant form of the name]
             [Title in English and Name in natural order]
    BT   **Nobility—[Country]**

Examples:
Vasa, House of
    UF   House of Vasa
             House of Wasa
             Wasa, House of
    BT   **Sweden—Kings and rulers**

Windsor, House of
    UF   House of Windsor
    RT   **Wettin, House of**
    BT   **Great Britain—Kings and rulers**

Achaemenid dynasty, 559-330 B.C.
    UF   Achaemenians
             Achaemenidae
             Achaemenids
             Hakhamanishiya
    BT   **Iran—Kings and rulers**

Sayyid dynasty, 1414-1451
    BT   **India—Kings and rulers**

Normandy, Dukes of
    UF   Dukes of Normandy
    BT   **Nobility—France**
             Nobility—Great Britain

Lippe-Biesterfeld, Counts of
    UF   Biesterfeld, Counts of
             Counts of Biesterfeld
             Counts of Lippe-Biesterfeld
    BT   **Nobility—Germany**

NAMES ASSOCIATED WITH PLACES

Archaeological Sites

Pattern:
[Name] Site ([Geographic qualifier])
    UF   [Alternate forms of name] ([Geographic qualifier])
    BT   **[Type of site, e.g. Caves; Kitchen-middens; Plantations; etc.]**
                 —[Modern country *or* First-order division]
             [Modern country *or* First-order division]—Antiquities

Examples:
Masada Site (Israel)
    UF   Horvot Metsadah (Israel)
             Horvot Mezada (Israel)
             Massada Site (Israel)
             Mazada Site (Israel)
             Metsada Site (Israel)
             Metsadah Site (Israel)
             Mezada (Fortress), Israel
             Mezada Site (Israel)
             Sabba Site (Israel)
             Sebbe Site (Israel)
    BT   **Israel—Antiquities**

Parque Lezama Site (Buenos Aires, Argentina)
    BT   **Argentina—Antiquities**

Texcal Cave (Mexico)
    UF   Cueva del Texcal (Mexico)
    BT   **Caves—Mexico**
             Mexico—Antiquities

Building Details

Pattern:
[Name of detail] ([Name of structure], [Geographic qualifier])
    UF   [alternate forms of name] ([Name of structure], [Geographic qualifier])
    BT   **[Name of structure]**
             [Type of detail]—[country]

Example:
Sistine Chapel (Vatican Palace, Vatican City)
    UF   Cappella pontificia (Vatican Palace, Vatican City)
             Cappella Sistina (Vatican Palace, Vatican City)
             Papal Chapel (Vatican Palace, Vatican City)
             Vatican Palace (Vatican City)—Sistine Chapel
    BT   **Chapels—Vatican City**
             Vatican Palace (Vatican City)

Buildings and Other Structures

Pattern:
[Name of structure] ([Geographic qualifier])
    UF   [Alternate forms of name] ([Geographic qualifier])
    BT   **[Type of structure]—[Country *or* First-order division]**

Examples:
Arlington House, the Robert E. Lee Memorial (Va.)
    UF   Arlington House (Va.)
           Custis-Lee Mansion (Va.)
           General Robert E. Lee Mansion (Va.)
           Lee Mansion (Va.)
           Robert E. Lee Mansion (Va.)
           Robert E. Lee Memorial (Va.)
    BT   **Dwellings—Virginia**
           Memorials—Virginia

Black Gate (Besançon, France)
    UF   Porta Nigra (Besançon, France)
           Porte noire (Besançon, France)
    BT   **Triumphal arches—France**

El Rancho Gumbo (Mont.)
    UF   Rancho Gumbo (Mont.)
    BT   **Ranches—Montana**

Forbidden City (Peking, China)
    UF   Imperial Palace (Peking, China)
           Ku-kung (Peking, China)
           Tzu-chin-ch'eng (Peking, China)
    BT   **Palaces—China**

Great Wall of China (China)
    UF   China—Great Wall
           China—Wall
           China, Great Wall of (China)
           Chinese Wall (China)
           Wall of China
           Wall of China (China)
    BT   **Fortification—China**
           Walls—China

Golden Gate Bridge (San Francisco, Calif.)
    BT   **Bridges—California**

John F. Shea Federal Building (Santa Rosa, Calif.)
    UF   Shea Federal Building (Santa Rosa, Calif.)
    BT   **Public buildings—California**

Robert F. Kennedy Memorial Stadium (Washington, D.C.)
    UF   D.C. Stadium (Washington, D.C.)
           District of Columbia Stadium (Washington, D.C.)
           Kennedy Stadium (Washington, D.C.)
           R.F.K. Stadium (Washington, D.C.)
           RFK Stadium (Washington, D.C.)
    BT   **Stadiums—Washington (D.C.)**

City Districts, Quarters, Sections

Pattern:
[Name of district *or* Section] ([Name of city])
    UF   [Alternate form of name] ([Geographic qualifier])
           [Alternate form of heading]

Examples:
North End (Boston, Mass.)
    UF   Boston (Mass.). North End

Rive gauche (Paris, France)
    UF   Left Bank (Paris, France)
           Paris (France). Rive gauche

Entities Within a City

Pattern:
[Name of entity] ([Name of city])
    UF   [Alternate name *or* form of name] ([Name of city])
    BT   **[Generic heading]—[Country *or* First-order division]**

Examples:
Central Park Heritage National Recreation Trail (New York, N.Y.)
    BT   **Central Park (New York, N.Y.)**
           Trails—New York (State)

City Park (Bridgeton, N.J.)
    BT   **Parks—New Jersey**

Fontana dei Mostri (Florence, Italy)
    UF   Mostri Fountain (Florence, Italy)
    BT   **Fountains—Italy**

Georgetown Waterfront (Washington, D.C.)
    UF   Washington (D.C.). Georgetown Waterfront
           Waterfront (Washington, D.C.)
    BT   **Waterfronts—Washington (D.C.)**

John F. Kennedy Park (Cambridge, Mass.)
    UF   Kennedy Park (Cambridge, Mass.)
    BT   **Parks—Massachusetts**

Extinct Cities

Pattern:
[City name] (Extinct city)
    UF   [Alternate modern name] ([Modern country])
           [Alternate early name] (Ancient city *or* City)
    BT   **Extinct cities—[Modern country]**
           [Modern country]—Antiquities

Examples:

Bibracte (Extinct city)
    UF   Bibracte (Ancient city)
    BT   **Extinct cities—France**
          France—Antiquities

Dor (Extinct city)
    UF   Dora (Extinct city)
          Dorah (Extinct city)
          Tel Dor (Israel)
    BT   **Extinct cities—Israel**
          Israel—Antiquities

Mstenice (Extinct city)
    UF   Mstenice (City)
    BT   **Czech Republic—Antiquities**
          Extinct cities—Czech Republic

Pompeii (Extinct city)
    UF   Pompei (Extinct city)
          Pompeii (Ancient city)
    BT   **Extinct cities—Italy**
          Italy—Antiquities

Geographic Features

Pattern:

[Distinctive name] [Generic term] ([Geographic qualifier])
    UF   [Alternate name] ([Geographic qualifier])—[Country *or*
          First-order division]
    BT   **[Type of feature]—[Country *or* First-order division]**

Examples:

Costa del Sol (Spain)
    UF   Sol, Costa del (Spain)
    BT   **Coasts—Spain**

Gallipoli Peninsula (Turkey)
    UF   Gelibolu Peninsula (Turkey)
    BT   **Peninsulas—Turkey**

Geysers, The (Calif.)
    UF   Big Geysers (Calif.)
          The Geysers (Calif.)
    BT   **Geysers—California**

Han River (Shensi Province and Hupeh Province, China)
    UF   Han Shui (Shensi Province and Hupeh Province, China)
    BT   **Rivers—China**

Han River (Kwangtung Province, China)
    UF   Han Chiang (Kwangtung Province, China)
             Han Jiang (Kwangtung Province, China)
             Han Kiang (Kwangtung Province, China)
    BT   **Rivers—China**

Islands or Island Groups

Pattern:
[Name of island *or* Island group] ([Geographic qualifier])
    UF   [Alternate name(s)] ([Qualifier])
             [Name in vernacular] ([Qualifier])
             [Uninverted form of name] ([Qualifier])
    BT   **[Name of group] ([Qualifier])**
             {omit if same as name of jurisdiction}
             Islands—[Country *or* First-order division]
             Islands of the [. . .]
             {if the island does not lie near its controlling jurisdiction}

Examples:
Madeira (Madeira Islands)
    UF   Ilha da Madeira (Madeira Islands)
             Madeira
    BT   **Islands—Madeira Islands**

Martin Garcia Island (Buenos Aires, Argentina)
    UF   Isla Martin Garcia (Buenos Aires, Argentina)
             Martin Garcia Island (Argentina and Uruguay)
    BT   **Islands—Argentina**

Snow Hill Island (Antarctica)
    BT   **Islands—Antarctica**

Parks, Reserves, National Monuments, Etc.

Pattern:
[Name of entity] ([Geographic qualifier])
    UF   [Alternate forms of name] ([Geographic qualifier])
    BT   **[Generic heading]—[Country *or* First-order division]**
             National parks and reserves—[Country *or* First-order division,
                 if a national park, etc.]
             [Name of larger entity of which entity in question forms a part]
             [Special topic]

Examples:
Sayward Forest (B.C.)
    BT   **Forest reserves—British Columbia**

Golden Gate National Recreation Area (Calif.)
    BT   **National parks and reserves—California**
             Recreation areas—California

Golden Gate Park (San Francisco, Calif.)
    BT   **Parks—California**

Streets and Roads

Pattern:
[Name of street *or* road] ([Geographic qualifier])
    UF   [Alternate name] ([Geographic qualifier])
    BT   **Streets *or* Roads *or* [More specific heading]—[Place]**

Examples:
Boulevard Saint-Laurent (Montreal, Quebec)
    UF   Boulevard St-Laurent (Montreal, Quebec)
            Main (Montreal, Quebec : Street)
            Saint-Laurent Boulevard (Montreal, Quebec)
            St-Laurent Boulevard (Montreal, Quebec)
            The Main (Montreal, Quebec : Street)
    BT   **Streets—Quebec (Province)**

Fifth Avenue (New York, N.Y.)
    UF   5th Avenue (New York, N.Y.)
    BT   **Streets—New York (State)**

Battle Road (Mass.)
    BT   **Roads—Massachusetts**

OTHER PROPER NAMES

Animals

Pattern:
[Name of animal] ([Generic qualifier])
    UF   [Alternate name] ([Generic qualifier])
    BT   **[Generic heading]**

Examples:
Millie (Dog)
    UF   Mildred Kerr Bush (Dog)
    BT   **Dogs**

Seattle Slew (Race horse)
    BT   **Horses**

National Groups in the United States

Pattern:
[Nationality] Americans *(May Subd Geog)*
    UF   [Alternate name]
            [Nationality] Americans—United States
    BT   **Ethnology—United States**
    BT   **[Nationality]—United States**

Examples:
Russian Americans *(May Subd Geog)*
    UF   Russian Americans—United States
    BT   **Ethnology—United States**
            Russians—United States

Mexican Americans *(May Subd Geog)*
    UF   Chicanos
            Hispanos
            Mexican Americans—United States
    BT   **Ethnology—United States**

National Groups in Other Countries

Pattern:
[Nationality] *(May Subd Geog)*
    NT   **[Name of subgroup, if any]**
    BT   **Ethnology — [Country of origin]**
            [Country of origin]
                  {if entry element is different from national group name}

Examples:
Russians *(May Subd Geog)*
    NT   **Russian Germans**
    BT   **Ethnology—Russia (Federation)**
            Slavs, Eastern

Mexicans *(May Subd Geog)*
    BT   **Ethnology—Mexico**

Indonesians *(May Subd Geog)*
    NT   **Indos**
    BT   **Ethnology—Indonesia**

Trials

Pattern:
[Name] Trial, [City], [Date(s)]
    UF   [Alternate name] Trial, [City], [Date(s)]
    BT   **Trials ([Topic])** *or* **[War crime trials]—[Place]**

Examples:
Central Park Jogger Rape Trial, New York, N.Y., 1990
    BT   **Trials (Rape)—New York (State)**

Watergate Trial, Washington, D.C., 1973
    BT   **Trials (Burglary)—Washington (D.C.)**
            Trials (Conspiracy)—Washington (D.C.)
            Watergate Affair, 1972-1974

Tokyo Trial, Tokyo, Japan, 1946-1948
    UF   Tokyo Trial, 1946-1948
             Tokyo War Crimes Trial, Tokyo, Japan, 1946-1948
             War crime trials—Tokyo, 1946-1948
    BT   **War crime trials—Japan**

WORKS ABOUT INDIVIDUAL WORKS OF ART BY KNOWN ARTISTS

Pattern:
[Name of artist]. [English title of work]
    UF   [English title] ([Type of art])
             [Vernacular title] ([Type of art])
    BT   **[Form of art], [Ethnic** *or* **National qualifier] {***or* **—[Place]}**
             [Name of person depicted]—Art {*or* **—Portraits, etc.**
                  or **—Portraits, caricatures, etc.}**

Examples:
Uccello, Paolo, 1397-1475. Battle of San Romano
    UF   Battaglia de San Romano (Painting)
             Battle of San Romano (Painting)
             Battle of Sant' Egidio (Painting)
             Battle piece (Painting)
             Battle scene (Painting)
             Rout of San Romano (Painting)
    BT   **Painting, Italian**

Agesander. Laocoon group
    UF   Athenodorus. Laocoon group
             Laocoon (Sculpture)
             Laocoon and his sons assailed by serpents (Sculpture)
             Polydorus. Laocoon group
    BT   **Sculpture, Greek**

Taketori monogatari emaki (Scrolls)
    NT   Tachibana, Moribe, 1781-1849. Taketori monogatari emaki
    BT   **Narrative painting—Japan**
             Scrolls, Japanese

WORKS ABOUT INDIVIDUAL WORKS OF ART BY UNKNOWN ARTISTS

Pattern:
[Vernacular title of work] ([Type of art])
    UF   [Variant of vernacular title] ([Type of art])
    BT   **[Form of art], [Nationality]**

Examples:
Genji monogatari emaki (Scrolls)
    BT   **Painting, Japanese**
            Scrolls, Japanese

Pai ho t'u (Painting)
    UF   100 cranes (Painting)
            One hundred cranes (Painting)
    BT   **Painting, Chinese**

Appendix H:
General Reference Sources Used in Establishing Headings*

GENERAL (AND CHILDREN'S LIT.) REFERENCE SOURCES

Title	Citation form
Academic American encyclopedia	Acad. Am. encyc.
The bookfinder / Dreyer	Bookfinder
Canada gazetteer atlas	Can gaz. atlas
Children's books in print	Child. BIP
Children's catalog	Child. cat.
Collier's encyclopedia	Collier's
The Columbia Lippincott gazetteer of the world	Lippincott
Compton's encyclopedia and fact-index	Compton's
Decisions on geographic names in the United States	Dec. geog. names
Dictionary of American slang / Wentworth	Dict. Am. slang
The Elementary school library collection	ESLC
The Encyclopedia Americana	Americana
Encyclopedia Britannica. [14th ed.]	Britannica 14
Encyclopedia Britannica. 15th ed. Micropaedia	Britannica Micro.
Encyclopedia Britannica. 15th ed. Macropaedia	Britannica Macro.
Encyclopedia international	Encyc. intl.
Hennepin County Library cumulative authority list	Hennepin
Information Access Company Resource File	IAC
Merit students encyclopedia	Merit
The national gazetteer	Nat. gaz.
National Geographic atlas of North America	Nat. Geog. atlas N. Am.

*The information presented in this section is based upon the *Subject Cataloging Manual: Subject Headings*, 4th ed. (Washington, D.C.: Library of Congress, Office of Subject Cataloging Policy, 1991), H203, pp. 7-8. For reference sources used in establishing headings in specific areas and subject fields, see H203, pp. 9-22.

GENERAL (AND CHILDREN'S LIT.) REFERENCE SOURCES

Title	Citation form
National Geographic atlas of the world	Nat. Geog. atlas
The New York times index	NYT index
9,000 words : a supplement to Webster's third new international dictionary	9000 words
The Oxford English dictionary	OED
Rand McNally commercial atlas and marketing guide	Rand McNally
The Random House dictionary of the English language	Random House
Readers' guide to periodical literature	Readers' guide
Scott, Foresman advanced dictionary / Thorndike, Barnhart	TB adv. dict.
Scott, Foresman beginning dictionary / Thorndike, Barnhart	TB beg. dict.
Scott, Foresman intermediate dictionary / Thorndike, Barnhart	TB inter. dict.
Sears list of subject headings	Sears
The Standard encyclopedia of the world's mountains	Encyc. world mts.
The Statesman's year-book	Statesman's yrbk.
The Times atlas of the world	Times atlas
The Third Barnhart dictionary of new English	BDNE
Websters' new geographical dictionary	Web. geog.
Webster's third new international dictionary of the English language, unabridged	Web. 3
The World Book encyclopedia	World Book

Appendix I:
First-Order Political Divisions of the Exceptional Countries*

First Order Division	*Form in Qualifier*
Australia	
Australian Capital Territory	(A.C.T.)
New South Wales	(N.S.W.)
Northern Territory	(N.T.)
Queensland	(Qld.)
South Australia	(S. Aust.)
Tasmania	(Tas.)
Victoria	(Vic.)
Western Australia	(W.A.)
Canada	
Alberta	(Alta.)
British Columbia	(B.C.)
Manitoba	(Man.)
New Brunswick	(N.B.)
Newfoundland	(Nfld.)
Northwest Territories	(N.W.T.)
Nova Scotia	(N.S.)
Ontario	(Ont.)
Prince Edward Island	(P.E.I.)
Québec (Province)	(Québec)
Saskatchewan	(Sask.)
Yukon Territory	(Yukon)

*The information presented in this section is based upon the *Subject Cataloging Manual: Subject Headings*, 4th ed. (Washington, D.C.: Library of Congress, Office of Subject Cataloging Policy, 1991), H810, pp. 8-11.

First Order Division	Form in Qualifier

Great Britain
England	(England)
Northern Ireland	(Northern Ireland)
Scotland	(Scotland)
Wales	(Wales)

Malaysia
Johor	(Johor)
Kedah	(Kedah)
Kelantan	(Kelantan)
Kuala Lumpur (Malaysia)	(Kuala Lumpur, Malaysia)
Malacca (State)	(Malacca)
Negeri Sembilan	(Negeri Sembilan)
Pahang	(Pahang)
Pinang	(Pinang)
Perak	(Perak)
Perlis	(Perlis)
Sabah	(Sabah)
Sarawak	(Sarawak)
Selangor	(Selangor)
Terengganu	(Terengganu)

United States
Alabama	(Ala.)
Alaska	(Alaska)
Arizona	(Ariz.)
Arkansas	(Ark.)
California	(Calif.)
Colorado	(Colo.)
Connecticut	(Conn.)
Delaware	(Del.)
Florida	(Fla.)
Georgia	(Ga.)
Hawaii	(Hawaii)
Idaho	(Idaho)
Illinois	(Ill.)
Indiana	(Ind.)
Iowa	(Iowa)
Kansas	(Kan.)
Kentucky	(Ky.)
Louisiana	(La.)
Maine	(Me.)
Maryland	(Md.)
Massachusetts	(Mass.)
Michigan	(Mich.)
Minnesota	(Minn.)

First Order Division	Form in Qualifier

United States *(Continued)*

Mississippi	(Miss.)
Missouri	(Mo.)
Montana	(Mont.)
Nebraska	(Neb.)
Nevada	(Nev.)
New Hampshire	(N.H.)
New Jersey	(N.J.)
New Mexico	(N.M.)
New York (State)	(N.Y.)
North Carolina	(N.C.)
North Dakota	(N.D.)
Ohio	(Ohio)
Oklahoma	(Okla.)
Oregon	(Or.)
Pennsylvania	(Pa.)
Rhode Island	(R.I.)
South Carolina	(S.C.)
South Dakota	(S.D.)
Tennessee	(Tenn.)
Texas	(Tex.)
Utah	(Utah)
Vermont	(Vt.)
Virginia	(Va.)
Washington (State)	(Wash.)
West Virginia	(W. Va.)
Wisconsin	(Wis.)
Wyoming	(Wyo.)

Yugoslavia

Montenegro	(Montenegro)
Serbia	(Serbia)

OTHER JURISDICTIONS THAT ARE ABBREVIATED WHEN USED AS QUALIFIERS

Jurisdiction	Form in Qualifier
British Virgin Islands	(V.I.)
New Zealand	(N.Z.)
Puerto Rico	(P.R.)
United States	(U.S.)
Virgin Islands of the United States	(V.I.)

Appendix J:
USMARC Coding for
Subject Information*

AUTHORITY DATA

Heading Usage in Authority Structures

A heading may be categorized as being suitable for either a **name** or a **subject authority structure**. Headings that are formulated using descriptive cataloging conventions (008/10) are suitable for a **name authority structure**. These headings encompass name, name/title, and uniform title headings in established heading and established heading and subdivision records and unestablished forms of these types of headings in reference records. Certain note and tracing and reference fields are used only in records for headings suitable for name authority structures.

Headings that are formulated using subject heading system/thesaurus building conventions (008/11) are suitable for a **subject authority structure**. These headings encompass name, name/title, uniform title, and topical term headings (and extended subject headings using these types of headings) in established heading and established heading and subdivision records; unestablished forms of these types of headings in reference and reference and subdivision records; and unestablished headings in subdivision and node label records. Certain note and tracing and reference fields in the format are used only in records for headings suitable for subject authority structures.

*USMARC Concise Formats, prepared by Network Development and MARC Standards Office (Washington, D.C.: Library of Congress Cataloging Distribution Service, 1991).

NLR

100 HEADING—PERSONAL NAME (NR)   *A*
An established personal name used in name, name/title, or extended
subject heading established heading records or an unestablished
personal name used in these types of headings in reference records.

<u>Indicators</u>
<u>First</u> Type of personal name entry element   *M*
    A value that indicates the form of the entry element of the
    heading.
 0   Forename   *A*
    The name is a forename or is a name consisting of words,
    initials, letters, etc., that are formatted in direct order.
 1   Single surname   *A*
    The name is a single surname formatted in inverted order
    or a single name without forenames that is known to be a
    surname.
 2   Multiple surname   *A*
    The name is a multiple surname formatted in inverted
    order or a multiple name without forenames that is known
    to be a surname.
 3   Family name   *A*
    The name represents a family, clan, dynasty, house, or
    other such group and may be formatted in direct or in-
    verted order.
<u>Second</u> Nonfiling characters   *M*
    A value that indicates the number of character positions
    associated with an initial definite or indefinite article at
    the beginning of a heading that are disregarded in sorting
    and filing processes.
 0-9 Number of nonfiling characters present   *M*
<u>Subfield Codes</u>
 ‡a Personal name (NR)   *M*
    A surname and/or forename; letters, initials, abbrevia-
    tions, phrases, or numbers used in place of a name; or a
    family name.
 ‡b Numeration (NR)   *A*
    A roman numeral or a roman numeral and a subsequent
    part of a forename when the first indicator value is 0.
 ‡c Titles and other words associated with a name (R) *A*
 ‡d Dates associated with a name (NR)   *A*
    Dates of birth, death, or flourishing, or any other date
    associated with a name.
 ‡e Relator term (R)   *O*
    A term that describes the relationship between a name and
    a work.
 ‡f Date of a work (NR)   *A*
    A date of publication used with a title of a work in a
    name/title heading.
 ‡g Miscellaneous information (NR)   *A*
    A data element not more appropriately contained in an-
    other defined subfield.
 ‡h Medium (NR)   *O*
    A media qualifier used with a title of a work in a name/title
    heading.
 ‡k Form subheading (R)   *A*

‡l	Language of a work (NR)	A
	The name of a language(s) used with a title of a work in a name/title heading.	
‡m	Medium of performance for music (R)	A
‡n	Number of part/section of a work (R)	A
	A number designation for a part or section of a work used with a title in a name/title heading.	
‡o	Arranged statement for music (NR)	A
	The abbreviation *arr.* used in a uniform title for a work in a name/title heading.	
‡p	Name of part/section of a work (R)	A
	A name designation of a part or section of a work used with a title in a name/title heading.	
‡q	Fuller form of name (NR)	A
	A more complete form of the name contained in subfield ‡a.	
‡r	Key for music (NR)	A
	The statement of key used in a uniform title for a work in a name/title heading.	
‡s	Version (NR)	A
	Version, edition, etc., information used with title of a work in a name/title heading.	
‡t	Title of a work (NR)	A
	A uniform title, a title page title of a work, or a series title used in a name/title heading.	
‡x	General subdivision (R)	A
‡y	Chronological subdivision (R)	A
‡z	Geographic subdivision (R)	A
‡6	Linkage (NR)	A
	The *linking tag* number of the associated field and a two-character *occurrence number* (right justified with a zero in the unused position) that link fields that are alternate graphic representations of each other. Subfield ‡6 is the first subfield in the field and is structured as follows: \<linking tag\>-\<occurrence number\>.	

110 HEADING—CORPORATE NAME (NR)   A

An established corporate name used in a name, name/title, or extended subject heading in established heading records or an unestablished corporate name used in these types of headings in reference records.

Indicators

First	Type of corporate name entry element	M
	A value that indicates the form of the entry element of the heading.	
0	Inverted name	A
	The corporate name begins with a personal name in inverted order.	
1	Jurisdiction name	A
	The entry element is a name of a jurisdiction that is also an ecclesiastical entity or is a jurisdiction name under which a corporate name, a city section, or a title of a work is entered.	
2	Name in direct order	A
Second	Nonfiling characters	M
0-9	Number of nonfiling characters present	M

See description of the second indicator under field 100.

NLR

<u>Subfield Codes</u>

‡a	Corporate name or jurisdiction name as entry element (NR)	*M*

A name of a corporate body, or the first entity when subordinate units are present; a jurisdiction name under which a corporate body, city section, or a title of a work is entered; or a jurisdiction name that is also an ecclesiastical entity.

‡b	Subordinate unit (R)	*A*

A name of a subordinate corporate unit, a name of a city section, or a name of a meeting entered under a corporate or jurisdiction name.

‡c	Location of meeting (NR)	*A*

A place name or a name of an institution where a meeting was held.

‡d	Date of meeting or treaty signing (R)	*A*

The date a meeting was held or, in a name/title field, the date a treaty was signed.

‡e	Relator term (R)	*O*
‡f	Date of a work (NR)	*A*
‡g	Miscellaneous information (NR)	*A*

The name of the *other party* to a treaty in a name/title heading; a subelement that is not more appropriately contained in subfield ‡c, ‡d, or ‡n in a heading for a meeting entered under a corporate name; or a data element that is not more appropriately contained in another defined subfield in any other type of corporate name heading.

‡h	Medium (NR)	*O*
‡k	Form subheading (R)	*A*
‡l	Language of a work (NR)	*A*
‡m	Medium of performance for music (R)	*A*
‡n	Number of part/section/meeting (R)	*A*

A number designation for a meeting entered under a corporate name or for a part or section of a work used with a title in a name/title heading.

‡o	Arranged statement for music (NR)	*A*
‡p	Name of part/section of a work (R)	*A*
‡r	Key for music (NR)	*A*
‡s	Version (NR)	*A*
‡t	Title of a work (NR)	*A*
‡x	General subdivision (R)	*A*
‡y	Chronological subdivision (R)	*A*
‡z	Geographic subdivision (R)	*A*
‡6	Linkage (NR)	*A*

See the descriptions of subfields ‡e, ‡f, ‡h, ‡l, ‡o, ‡p, ‡r, ‡s, ‡t, and ‡6 under field 100.

NLR

111 HEADING—MEETING NAME (NR)

A

An established meeting name used in a name, name/title, or extended subject heading in established heading records or an unestablished meeting name used in these types of headings in reference records.

Indicators

First   Type of meeting name entry element   *M*
A value that identifies the form of the entry element of the heading.

0   Inverted name   *A*
The meeting name begins with a personal name in inverted order.

1   Jurisdiction name   *A*
The entry element is a jurisdiction name under which a meeting name is entered.

2   Name in direct order   *A*

Second   Nonfiling characters   *M*

0-9   Number of nonfiling characters present   *M*

See the description of the second indicator under field 100.

Subfield Codes

‡a   Meeting name or jurisdiction name as entry   *M*
element (NR)
A name of a meeting, or the first entity when subordinate units are present; or a jurisdiction name under which a meeting name is entered in a pre-AACR 2 formulating heading.

‡c   Location of meeting (NR)   *A*

‡d   Date of meeting (NR)   *A*

‡e   Subordinate unit (R)   *A*
The name of a subordinate unit entered under a meeting name.

‡f   Date of a work (NR)   *A*

‡g   Miscellaneous information (NR)   *A*

‡h   Medium (NR)   *O*

‡k   Form subheading (R)   *A*

‡l   Language of a work (NR)   *A*

‡n   Number of part/section/meeting (R)   *A*

‡p   Name of part/section of a work (R)   *A*

‡q   Name of meeting following jurisdiction name   *A*
entry element (NR)
The name of a meeting that is entered under a jurisdiction name contained in subfield ‡a.

‡s   Version (NR)   *A*

‡t   Title of a work (NR)   *A*

‡x   General subdivision (R)   *A*

‡y   Chronological subdivision (R)   *A*

‡z   Geographic subdivision (R)   *A*

‡6   Linkage (NR)   *A*

See descriptions of subfields ‡g, ‡h, ‡l, ‡p, ‡s, ‡t, and ‡6 under field 100 and subfields ‡c and ‡n under field 110.

NLR

130 HEADING—UNIFORM TITLE (NR)   *A*
An established uniform title used in a title or extended subject
heading in established heading records or an unestablished title
used in these types of headings in reference records.

Indicators
First	Undefined; contains a blank (ƀ)	*M*
Second	Nonfiling characters	*M*
0-9	Number of nonfiling characters present	*M*

See the description of the second indicator under field 100.
Subfield Codes
ǂa	Uniform title (NR)	*M*
ǂd	Date of treaty signing (R)	*A*
ǂf	Date of a work (NR)	*A*
ǂg	Miscellaneous information (NR)	*A*
ǂh	Medium (NR)	*O*
	A media qualifier.	
ǂk	Form subheading (R)	*A*
ǂl	Language of a work (NR)	*A*
ǂm	Medium of performance for music (R)	*A*
ǂn	Number of part/section of a work (R)	*A*
ǂo	Arranged statement for music (NR)	*A*
ǂp	Name of part/section of a work (R)	*A*
ǂr	Key for music (NR)	*A*
ǂs	Version (NR)	*A*
ǂt	Title of a work (NR)	*A*
	A title-page title of a work.	
ǂx	General subdivision (R)	*A*
ǂy	Chronological subdivision (R)	*A*
ǂz	Geographic subdivision (R)	*A*
ǂ6	Linkage (NR)	*A*

See the descriptions of subfields ǂg and ǂ6 under field 100.

150 HEADING—TOPICAL TERM (NR)   *A*
An established topical term used in main or extended subject
headings in established heading records or an unestablished topical
term used in these types of headings in subdivision, reference, or
node label records.

Indicators
First	Undefined; contains a blank (ƀ)	*M*
Second	Nonfiling characters	*M*
0-9	Number of nonfiling characters present	*M*

See the description of the second indicator under field 100.

NLR

Subfield Codes

‡a   Topical term or geographic name as entry element (NR)   *M*
        A topical subject, a geographic name used as an entry
        element for a topical term, or a node label term.

‡b   Topical term following geographic name as entry   *A*
        element (NR)

‡x   General subdivision (R)   *A*

‡y   Chronological subdivision (R)   *A*

‡z   Geographic subdivision (R)   *A*

‡6   Linkage (NR)   *A*

See the description of subfield ‡6 under field 100.

151   HEADING—GEOGRAPHIC NAME (NR)   *A*

An established geographic name used in main or extended subject
headings in established heading records or an unestablished
geographic name used in these types of headings in subdivision
or reference records.

Indicators

First   Undefined; contains a blank (ƀ)   *M*

Second   Nonfiling characters   *M*

0-9   Number of nonfiling characters present   *M*

See the description of the second indicator under field 100.

Subfield Codes

‡a   Geographic name (NR)   *M*

‡x   General subdivision (R)   *A*

‡y   Chronological subdivision (R)   *A*

‡z   Geographic subdivision (R)   *A*

‡6   Linkage (NR)   *A*

See the description of subfield ‡6 under field 100.

BIBLIOGRAPHIC DATA

■ Subject Access Fields

The 6XX fields (with the exception of field 653 that is used for
uncontrolled index terms) contain subject headings or access terms
that provide additional access to a bibliographic record through a
heading or term that is constructed according to established subject
cataloging or thesaurus-building principles and guidelines. The standard list or authority file used is identified by the value in the second
indicator position or by the USMARC source code contained in subfield
‡2 that is used in conjunction with value 7.

The arabic number that precedes a subject access field in some
displays is not carried in the USMARC record. It may be generated
based on the field tag. The dash (—) that precedes a general subject
subdivision is not carried in the USMARC record; it may be generated
based on the presence of subfields ‡x, ‡y, and/or ‡z.

Format / NLR
B A C M M V S
K M F P U M E

600 SUBJECT ADDED ENTRY—PERSONAL   A A A A A A A
NAME (R)
A subject added entry in which the entry element
is a personal name.

Indicators
  First   Type of personal name entry element   *M M M M M M M*
    0   Forename   *A A A A A A A*
    1   Single surname   *A A A A A A A*
    2   Multiple surname   *A A A A A A A*
    3   Family name   *A A A A A A A*
  See the description of the first indicator under field
  100.
  Second   Subject heading system/thesaurus   *M M M M M M M*
                A value that indicates the subject heading
                system/thesaurus or authority file that
                was used to construct the subject heading.
                (Values 0-3 and 5-6 are authoritative-
                agency data elements.)
    0   Library of Congress Subject Headings/LC   A A A A A A A
                authority files
                The subject added entry conforms to and is
                appropriate for use in the *Library of Con-*
                gress Subject Headings (LCSH) and the LC
                authority files.
    1   LC subject headings for children's   A A A A A A A
                literature
                The subject added entry conforms to the
                "AC Subject Headings" section of the
                LCSH and is appropriate for use in the LC
                Annotated Card Program.
    2   Medical Subject Headings/NLM authority   A A A A A A A
                files
                The subject added entry conforms to the
                NLM authority files.
    3   National Agricultural Library subject   A A A A A A A
                authority file
                The subject added entry conforms to the
                NAL subject authority file.
    4   Source not specified   A A A A A A A
                The subject added entry conforms to a con-
                trolled list that cannot be identified by another
                defined value or by a code in subfield ‡2.
    5   Canadian Subject Headings/NLC authority   A A A A A A A
                file
                The subject added entry conforms to and is
                appropriate for use in the *Canadian Sub-*
                ject Headings and the NLC authority files.
    6   Répertoire des vedettes-matière/NLC   A A A A A A A
                authority file
                The subject added entry conforms to and is
                appropriate for use in the *Répertoire des*
                vedettes-matière and the NLC authority
                files.

		Format/NLR
		B A C M M V S
		K M F P U M E

7	Source specified in subfield ǂ2 The subject added entry conforms to the subject heading/thesaurus building conventions identified by the USMARC code contained in subfield ǂ2.	*A A A A A A A*

Subfield Codes

ǂa	Personal name (NR)	*M M M M M M M*
ǂb	Numeration (NR)	*A A A A A A A*
ǂc	Titles and other words associated with a name (R)	*A A A A A A A*
ǂd	Dates associated with a name (NR)	*A A A A A A A*
ǂe	Relator term (R)	*O O O O O O O*
ǂf	Date of a work (NR)	*A A A A A A A*
ǂg	Miscellaneous information (NR)	*A A A A A A A*
ǂh	Medium (NR) A media qualifier.	*O O O O O O O*
ǂk	Form subheading (R)	*A A A A A A A*
ǂl	Language of a work (NR)	*A A A A A A A*
ǂm	Medium of performance for music (R)	*A A A A A A A*
ǂn	Number of part/section of a work (R)	*A A A A A A A*
ǂo	Arranged statement for music (NR)	*A A A A A A A*
ǂp	Name of part/section of a work (R)	*A A A A A A A*
ǂq	Fuller form of name (NR)	*A A A A A A A*
ǂr	Key for music (NR)	*A A A A A A A*
ǂs	Version (NR)	*A A A A A A A*
ǂt	Title of a work (NR)	*A A A A A A A*
ǂu	Affiliation (NR)	*O O . . . . .*
ǂx	General subdivision (R)	*A A A A A A A*
ǂy	Chronological subdivision (R)	*A A A A A A A*
ǂz	Geographic subdivision (R)	*A A A A A A A*
ǂ2	Source of heading or term (NR) A USMARC code that identifies the source of the subject heading or access term when the second indicator position contains value 7. (The code is taken from the *USMARC Code List for Relators, Sources, Description Conventions* and is an authoritative-agency data element.)	*A A A A A A A*
ǂ3	Materials specified (NR) The part of the described materials to which the field applies.	*. O . . . O .*
ǂ4	Relator code (R)	*O O O . O O .*
ǂ6	Linkage (NR) The *linking tag* number of the associated field and a two-character *occurrence number* (right justified with a zero in the unused position) that link fields that are alternate graphic representations of each other. Subfield ǂ6 is the first subfield in the field and is structured as follows: <linking tag>-<occurrence number>.	*A A A A A A A*

See the descriptions of subfields ǂa, ǂb, ǂd, ǂe, ǂf, ǂg, ǂl, ǂn, ǂp, ǂq, ǂt, ǂu, and ǂ4 under field 100.

<table>
<tr><td></td><td></td><td colspan="7">Format/NLR</td></tr>
</table>

		B A C M M V S K M F P U M E

610 SUBJECT ADDED ENTRY—CORPORATE NAME (R)

A subject added entry in which the entry element is a corporate name.

		Format/NLR
610 SUBJECT ADDED ENTRY—CORPORATE NAME (R)		*A A A A A A A*

Indicators

First	Type of corporate name entry element	*M M M M M M M*
0	Inverted name	*A A A A A A A*
1	Jurisdiction name	*A A A A A A A*
2	Name in direct order	*A A A A A A A*

See the description of the first indicator under field 110.

Second	Subject heading system/thesaurus	*M M M M M M M*
0	Library of Congress Subject Headings/LC authority files	*A A A A A A A*
1	LC subject headings for children's literature	*A A A A A A A*
2	Medical Subject Headings/NLM authority files	*A A A A A A A*
3	National Agricultural Library subject authority file	*A A A A A A A*
4	Source not specified	*A A A A A A A*
5	Canadian Subject Headings/NLC authority file	*A A A A A A A*
6	Répertoire des vedettes-matière/NLC authority file	*A A A A A A A*
7	Source specified in subfield ǂ2	*A A A A A A A*

See the description of the second indicator under field 600.

Subfield Codes

ǂa	Corporate name or jurisdiction name as entry element (NR)	*M M M M M M M*
ǂb	Subordinate unit (R)	*A A A A A A A*
ǂc	Location of meeting (NR)	*A A A A A A A*
ǂd	Date of meeting or treaty signing (R)	*A A A A A A A*
ǂe	Relator term (R)	*O O O O O O O*
ǂf	Date of a work (NR)	*A A A A A A A*
ǂg	Miscellaneous information (NR)	*A A A A A A A*
ǂh	Medium (NR)	*O O O O O O O*
ǂk	Form subheading (R)	*A A A A A A A*
ǂl	Language of a work (NR)	*A A C A A A A*
ǂm	Medium of performance for music (R)	*A A A A A A A*
ǂn	Number of part/section/meeting (R)	*A A A A A A A*
ǂo	Arranged statement for music (NR)	*A A A A A A A*
ǂp	Name of part/section of a work (R)	*A A A A A A A*
ǂr	Key for music (NR)	*A A A A A A A*
ǂs	Version (NR)	*A A A A A A A*
ǂt	Title of a work (NR)	*A A A A A A A*
ǂu	Affiliation (NR)	*O O . . . . .*
ǂx	General subdivision (R)	*A A A A A A A*
ǂy	Chronological subdivision (R)	*A A A A A A A*

			Format/NLR
			B A C M M V S
			K M F P U M E

‡z	Geographic subdivision (R)	A A A A A A A
‡2	Source of heading or term (NR)	A A A A A A A
‡3	Materials specified (NR)	. O . . . O .
‡4	Relator code (R)	O O O . O O .
‡6	Linkage (NR)	A A A A A A A

See the descriptions of subfields ‡e, ‡f, ‡l, ‡p, ‡t, ‡u and ‡4 under field 100; subfields ‡a, ‡b, ‡c, ‡d, ‡g, and ‡n under field 110; and subfields ‡h, ‡2, ‡3, and ‡6 under field 600.

611 SUBJECT ADDED ENTRY—MEETING NAME (R)
A A A A A A A

A subject added entry in which the entry element is a meeting name.

Indicators

First	Type of meeting name entry element	M M M M M M M
0	Inverted name	A A A A A A A
1	Jurisdiction name	A A A A A A A
2	Name in direct order	A A A A A A A

See the description of the first indicator under field 111.

Second	Subject heading system/thesaurus	M M M M M M M
0	Library of Congress Subject Headings/LC authority files	A A A A A A A
1	LC subject headings for children's literature	A A A A A A A
2	Medical Subject Headings/NLM authority files	A A A A A A A
3	National Agricultural Library subject authority file	A A A A A A A
4	Source not specified	A A A A A A A
5	Canadian Subject Headings/NLC authority file	A A A A A A A
6	Répertoire des vedettes-matière/NLC authority file	A A A A A A A
7	Source specified in subfield ‡2	A A A A A A A

See the description of the second indicator under field 600.

Subfield Codes

‡a	Meeting name or jurisdiction name as entry element (NR)	M M M M M M M
‡c	Location of meeting (NR)	A A A A A A A
‡d	Date of meeting (NR)	A A A A A A A
‡e	Subordinate unit (R)	A A A A A A A
‡f	Date of a work (NR)	A A A A A A A
‡g	Miscellaneous information (NR)	A A A A A A A
‡h	Medium (NR)	O O O O O O O
‡k	Form subheading (R)	A A A A A A A
‡l	Language of a work (NR)	A A A A A A A

Format/NLR

| | | B A C M M V S |
		K M F P U M E
‡n	Number of part/section/meeting (R)	A A A A A A A
‡p	Name of part/section of a work (R)	A A A A A A A
‡q	Name of meeting following jurisdiction name entry element (NR)	A A A A A A A
‡s	Version (NR)	A A A A A A A
‡t	Title of a work (NR)	A A A A A A A
‡u	Affiliation (NR)	O O . . . . .
‡x	General subdivision (R)	A A A A A A A
‡y	Chronological subdivision (R)	A A A A A A A
‡z	Geographic subdivision (R)	A A A A A A A
‡2	Source of heading or term (NR)	A A A A A A A
‡3	Materials specified (NR)	. O . . . O .
‡4	Relator code (R)	O O O . O O .
‡6	Linkage (NR)	A A A A A A A

See the descriptions of subfields ‡f, ‡g, ‡l, ‡p, ‡t, ‡u, and ‡4 under field 100; subfields ‡c and ‡n under field 110; subfields ‡a, ‡e, and ‡q under field 111; and subfields ‡h, ‡2, ‡3, and ‡6 under field 600.

630 SUBJECT ADDED ENTRY—UNIFORM TITLE (R)

A A A A A A A

A subject added entry in which the entry element is a uniform title.

Indicators

First	Nonfiling characters	M M M M M M M
0-9	Number of nonfiling characters present	M M M M M M M

See the description of the first indicator under field 130.

Second	Subject heading system/thesaurus	M M M M M M M
0	Library of Congress Subject Headings/LC authority files	A A A A A A A
1	LC subject headings for children's literature	A A . A A A A
2	Medical Subject Headings/NLM authority files	A A A A A A A
3	National Agricultural Library subject authority file	A A A A A A A
4	Source not specified	A A A A A A A
5	Canadian Subject Headings/NLC authority file	A A A A A A A
6	Répertoire des vedettes-matière/NLC authority file	A A A A A A A
7	Source specified in subfield ‡2	A A A A A A A

See the description of the second indicator under field 600.

| | | Format/NLR |
| | | B A C M M V S
K M F P U M E |

Subfield Codes

Code	Description	B A C M M V S / K M F P U M E
‡a	Uniform title (NR)	M M M M M M M
‡d	Date of treaty signing (R)	A A A A A A A
‡f	Date of a work (NR)	A A A A A A A
‡g	Miscellaneous information (NR)	A A A A A A A
‡h	Medium (NR)	O O O O O O O
‡k	Form subheading (R)	A A A A A A A
‡l	Language of a work (NR)	A A A A A A A
‡m	Medium of performance for music (R)	A A A A A A A
‡n	Number of part/section of a work (R)	A A A A A A A
‡o	Arranged statement for music (NR)	A A A A A A A
‡p	Name of part/section of a work (R)	A A A A A A A
‡r	Key for music (NR)	A A A A A A A
‡s	Version (NR)	A A A A A A A
‡t	Title of a work (NR)	A A A A A A A
	The title-page title of an item.	
‡x	General subdivision (R)	A A A A A A A
‡y	Chronological subdivision (R)	A A A A A A A
‡z	Geographic subdivision (R)	A A A A A A A
‡2	Source of heading or term (NR)	A A A A A A A
‡3	Materials specified (NR)	. O . . . O .
‡6	Linkage (NR)	A A A A A A A

See the descriptions of subfields ‡f, ‡g, ‡l, ‡n, and ‡p under field 100; and subfields ‡h, ‡3, and ‡6 under field 600.

650 SUBJECT ADDED ENTRY—TOPICAL TERM (R)   A A A A A A A
A subject added entry in which the entry element is a topical term.

Indicators

		B A C M M V S / K M F P U M E
First	Level of subject	M M M M M M M
	A value that indicates whether the term is a primary or secondary descriptor of the content of the described material.	
b	No information available	A M A M M M M
0	No level specified	A . A . . . .
	The level of the term could be determined but is not specified.	
1	Primary	A . A . . . .
	The term describes the main focus or subject content of the material.	
2	Secondary	A . A . . . .
	The subject term describes a less important aspect of the content of the material.	
Second	Subject heading system/thesaurus	M M M M M M M
0	Library of Congress Subject Headings	A A A A A A A
	The subject added entry conforms to and is appropriate for use in the *Library of Congress Subject Headings* (LCSH).	

		Format/NLR B A C M M V S K M F P U M E
1	LC subject headings for children's literature	A A A A A A A
2	Medical Subject Headings The subject added entry conforms to the *Medical Subject Headings* (MeSH).	A A A A A A A
3	National Agricultural Library subject authority file	A A A A A A A
4	Source not specified	A A A A A A A
5	Canadian Subject Headings The subject added entry conforms to and is appropriate for use in the *Canadian Subject Headings*.	A A A A A A A
6	Répertoire des vedettes-matière The subject added entry conforms to and is appropriate for use in the *Répertoire des vedettes-matière*.	A A A A A A A
7	Source specified in subfield ‡2	A A A A A A A

See the description of the second indicator under field 600.

Subfield Codes

‡a	Topical term or geographic name as entry element (NR)	M M M M M M M
‡b	Topical term following geographic name as entry element (NR)	A A . A A A A
‡c	Location of event (NR)	. A . . . . .
‡d	Active dates (NR) The time period during which an event occurred.	. A . . . . .
‡e	Relator term (NR) A term that describes the relationship between the topical heading and the described materials.	. A . . . . .
‡x	General subdivision (R)	A A A A A A A
‡y	Chronological subdivision (R)	A A A A A A A
‡z	Geographic subdivision (R)	A A A A A A A
‡2	Source of heading or term (NR)	A A A A A A A
‡3	Materials specified (NR)	. O . . . O .
‡6	Linkage (NR)	A A A A A A A

See the descriptions of subfields ‡2, ‡3, and ‡6 under field 600.

651 SUBJECT ADDED ENTRY—GEOGRAPHIC NAME (R)   A A A A A A A

A subject added entry in which the entry element is a geographic name.

Indicators

First	Undefined; contains a blank (ƀ)	M M M M M M M
Second	Subject heading system/thesaurus	M M M M M M M
0	Library of Congress Subject Headings/LC authority files	A A A A A A A
1	LC subject headings for children's literature	A A A A A A A

		Format/NLR
		B A C M M V S
		K M F P U M E

2	Medical Subject Headings/NLM authority files	A A A A A A A
3	National Agricultural Library subject authority file	A A A A A A A
4	Source not specified	A A A A A A A
5	Canadian Subject Headings/NLC authority file	A A A A A A A
6	Répertoire des vedettes-matière/NLC authority file	A A A A A A A
7	Source specified in subfield ‡2	A A A A A A A

See the description of the second indicator under field 600.

Subfield Codes

‡a	Geographic name (NR)	M M M M M M M
‡x	General subdivision (R)	A A A A A A A
‡y	Chronological subdivision (R)	A A A A A A A
‡z	Geographic subdivision (R)	A A A A A A A
‡2	Source of heading or term (NR)	A A A A A A A
‡3	Materials specified (NR)	. O . . . O .
‡6	Linkage (NR)	A A A A A A A

See the descriptions of subfields ‡2, ‡3, and ‡6 under field 600.

653 INDEX TERM—UNCONTROLLED (R)   A . A A A A A
An index term added entry that is not constructed
by standard subject heading/thesaurus-building
conventions.

Indicators

First	Level of index term	M . M M M M
♭	No information available	A . A A A A
0	No level specified	A . A A A A
1	Primary	A . A A A A
2	Secondary	A . A A A A

See the description of the first indicator under field 650.

Second	Undefined; contains a blank (♭)	M . M M M M

Subfield Codes

‡a	Uncontrolled term (R)	M . M M M M
‡6	Linkage (NR)	A . A A A A

See the description of subfield ‡6 under field 600.

Format/NLR
B A C M M V S
K M F P U M E

654 SUBJECT ADDED ENTRY—FACETED   *A A A A A A A*
TOPICAL TERMS (R)
A topical subject constructed from a faceted vocabulary.

Indicators
  First   Level of subject   *M M M M M M M*
    ƀ   No information available   *A A A A A A A*
    0   No level specified   *A A A A A A A*
    1   Primary   *A A A A A A A*
    2   Secondary   *A A A A A A A*
  See the description of the first indicator under
  field 650.
  Second   Undefined; contains a blank (ƀ)   *M M M M M M M*
Subfield Codes
    ‡a   Focus term (NR)   *A A A A A A A*
    ‡b   Term (R)   *A A A A A A A*
         A term other than that considered the focus.
    ‡c   Facet/hierarchy designation (R)   *M M M M M M M*
         The designation used by the thesaurus
         specified by the USMARC code contained
         in subfield ‡2 to identify the facet/hierarchy
         for each term contained in subfields ‡a and
         ‡b.
    ‡2   Source of heading or term (NR)   *M M M M M M M*
    ‡3   Material specified (NR)   *O O O O O O O*
  See the descriptions of subfields ‡2 and ‡3 under
  field 600.

655 INDEX TERM—GENRE/FORM (R)   *O O . O O O O*
A genre or form term added entry. A *genre term*
designates the style or technique of the intellectual
content of textual materials or, for graphic materials,
aspects such as vantage point, intended purpose, or
method of representation. A *form term* designates
historically and functionally specific kinds of materials distinguished by their physical character, the
subject of their intellectual content, or the order of
information within them.

Indicators
  First   Undefined; contains a blank (ƀ)   *M M . M M M M*
  Second   Source of term   *M M . M M M M*
         A value that indicates that the source of
         the index term is the standard published
         list indicated by the USMARC code con-
         tained in subfield ‡2.
    7   Source specified in subfield ‡2   *M M . M M M M*

Format/NLR
B A C M M V S
K M F P U ME

Subfield Codes

‡a	Genre/form (NR)	*M*	*M*	.	*M*	*M*	*M*	*M*
‡x	General subdivision (R)	*A*	*A*	.	*A*	*A*	*A*	*A*
‡y	Chronological subdivision (R)	*A*	*A*	.	*A*	*A*	*A*	*A*
‡z	Geographic subdivision (R)	*A*	*A*	.	*A*	*A*	*A*	*A*
‡2	Source of term (NR)	*M*	*M*	.	*M*	*M*	*M*	*M*
‡3	Materials specified (NR)	.	*O*	.	.	.	*O*	.
‡6	Linkage (NR)	*A*	*A*	.	*A*	*A*	*A*	*A*

*See the descriptions of subfields ‡2, ‡3, and ‡6
under field 600.*

Appendix K: Abbreviations*

PROCEDURES:

1. Policy for headings established in the SUBJECTS file. Generally, do not include abbreviations when establishing new subject headings, except when specifically authorized in this instruction sheet.

2. Policy for headings established in the NAMES file and used as subject headings. When assigning personal, corporate body, or jurisdictional name headings as subject headings, assign them exactly as they appear in name authority records, including all abbreviations.

3. Correction of existing records and headings in the SUBJECTS file. When an error involving an abbreviation on a bibliographic record is encountered, update the record following standard corrections procedures. When an obsolete heading involving an abbreviation is encountered in the *SUBJECTS* file, change it according to the provisions of H193.

4. Form and topical subdivisions with abbreviations. Many standard subdivisions were formerly abbreviated on LC cards, and may still be encountered when working with pre-1970 records. Spell out in full all topical and form subdivisions when assigning headings to new works being cataloged. Use no abbreviations in form or topical subdivisions except **etc.** (cf. sec. 9, below). *Examples:*

—Description and travel	[*not* —Desc. & trav.]
—History and criticism	[*not* —Hist. & crit.]
—Periodicals	[*not* —Period.]
—Politics and government	[*not* —Pol. & govt.]
—Social life and customs	[*not* —Soc. life & cust.]

---

*The information presented in this section is based upon the *Subject Cataloging Manual: Subject Headings*, 4th ed. (Washington, D.C.: Library of Congress, Office of Subject Cataloging Policy, 1991), appendix A.

5. *Acronyms, initialisms, etc.* Establish concepts that are known primarily in an abbreviated form as such. Use the form of the abbreviation, acronym, etc., preferred in reference sources. Make a UF reference from the spelled out form to the abbreviated heading. *Examples:*

C.O.D. shipments
    UF   Cash on delivery shipments
    UF   Collect on delivery shipments

DBS/R (Computer system)
    UF   Datenbankbetriebssystem Robotron (Computer system)

DC-to-DC converters
    UF   Direct current-to-direct current converters

DDT (Insecticide)
    UF   Dichlorodiphenyltrichloroethane

MARC formats
    UF   Machine-readable cataloging formats

T-shirts
    UF   Tee shirts

6. *Ampersands.* Do not use ampersands in form or topical subdivisions, e.g. **—History and criticism** [*not* **—Hist. & crit.**]. Do not use ampersands to connect two elements in the qualifier of a geographic heading, e.g. **Harding, Lake (Ga. and Ala.)** [*not* **Harding, Lake (Ga. & Ala.)**]. Generally use the word **and** instead of an ampersand, except in the following situations:

a. *Name headings used as subjects.* Use the name heading with an ampersand, if it appears as such in the name authority record, e.g.

    Black & Decker Manufacturing Company (Towson, Md.)
    C.S. Wertsner & Son.
    Dow Jones & Co.

b. *UF references.* Use an ampersand in a UF reference if the heading is found in that form in sources consulted, e.g.

    Chesapeake and Ohio Canal (Md. and Washington, D.C.)
        UF   C & O Canal (Md. and Washington, D.C.)

7. *Coined plurals.* Form the plurals of letters and acronyms by adding the lowercase letters without an apostrophe, provided that the resulting construction is clear and unambiguous, e.g.

Biological response modifiers
    UF   BRMs (Biochemistry)

Threshold limit values (Industrial toxicology)
    UF   TLVs (Industrial toxicology)

8. *Dates.*

a. Anno Domini; Before Christ. Use the abbreviations **A.D.** and **B.C.**, when appropriate, but only after a specific year or span of years. Add **A.D.** to dates only if the dates in question span both B.C. and A.D. Add **B.C.** to all B.C. dates. If a date span is B.C., add **B.C.** only to the end of the span. *Examples:*

Egypt—History—332-30 B.C.
China—History—Han dynasty, 202 B.C.-220 A.D.

b. *[. . .] century.* Spell out the word **century** in full, e.g.

English literature—20th century
Twenty-first century

c. *Circa.* Use the abbreviation **ca.** in period subdivisions, placing it before the date to which it refers, e.g.

United States—History—Colonial period, ca. 1600-1775
Church history—Primitive and early church, ca. 30-600
Hoysala dynasty, ca. 1006-ca. 1346

d. *Names of months.* Spell out names of months in full, e.g.

Bulgaria—History—September Uprising, 1944

9. *Doctor; Doctor of [. . .].* Use the abbreviation used in the name authority record, e.g.

Dr. Williams's Library—Catalogs
Francis, John, Dr.—Art collections
Hartmann, Peter, Dr. jur.—Poster collections
Grant, David, M.D.

10. *Et cetera.* Use the abbreviation **etc.** in headings and subdivisions, e.g.

Law reports, digests, etc.—United States
Surveying—Handbooks, manuals, etc.

11. *Geographic qualifiers.* Most geographic headings are qualified by the name of the larger geographic unit. Jurisdictions that are to be abbreviated when used as geographic qualifiers are listed in H 810. *Examples:*

West (U.S.)
Harpers Ferry (W. Va.)
Harry S. Truman Dam (Mo.)
Kremlin (Moscow, Russia)
Red River (Tex.-La.)

12. Great Britain. Spell out in full. The abbreviation **Gt. Brit.** is not authorized by AACR 2. *Examples:*

Great Britain—History	[*not* Gt. Brit.—Hist.]
Women artists—Great Britain	[*not* Women artists—Gt. Brit.]
Labour Party (Great Britain)	[*not* Labour Party (Gt. Brit.)]
Great Britain. Royal Navy	[*not* Gt. Brit. Royal Navy]

13. Mount; Mountain; Mountains. Spell out in full; do not abbreviate in subject headings. *Examples:*

> Mount Zion Cemetery (Washington, D.C.)
> Signal Mountain (Tenn.)
> Appalachian Mountains

14. Mr.; Mrs. Use the abbreviation **Mr.** or **Mrs.** if used in the name authority record, e.g.

> Mr. A's Boys' Ranch—History
> Mr. Lucky. Trick dog training
> Downing, Clyde, Mrs.—Art collections—Catalogs

15. Numerals.

> *a. Cardinal and roman numerals.* Spell out cardinal and roman numerals, e.g.

> > One (The number)
> > Three-dimensional personality test
> > Zero (The number)

Exception: When reference sources indicate that a numeral in a specific phrase is not normally spelled out, establish and assign the heading in that form. *Examples:*

> 35mm cameras
> 4-H clubs
> TRS-80 Model III (Computer)

> *b. Ordinal numerals.* Spell out an ordinal numeral if it is the initial element of a heading, e.g.

> > First communion
> > Fourth of July
> > Fifteenth century
> > Twenty-first century

Exception: When reference sources indicate that a numeral in a specific phrase is not normally spelled out, establish and assign the heading in that form. *Example:*

> 20th Century Limited (Express train)

Record ordinal numerals not in the initial position in a heading in the form **1st, 2nd, 3rd, 4th**, etc., e.g.

> Dacian War, 1st, 101-102
> Dacian War, 2nd, 105-106
> Church history—3rd century
> United States—Social life and customs—20th century

16. *Saint (including foreign equivalents)*. Spell out in full, e.g.

> Bellini, Giovanni, d. 1516. Saint Francis in ecstasy
> Saint Lawrence River
> Saint Ninian's Island (Scotland)

However, when assigning name headings as subjects, use the headings exactly as they appear in name authority records, e.g.

> Federal Reserve Bank of St. Louis.
> Saint Louis Museum of Fine Arts.
> St. Louis post-dispatch.
> Eglise de St-Joachim (Saint-Joachim, Québec)
> *[no period after St]*

17. *United States*. Spell out in full, e.g.

> United States—Economic conditions
> France—Foreign relations—United States
> Progressivism (United States politics)
> Certificate of Merit (United States Army)

Exception: As a *geographic* qualifier, **United States** is abbreviated **(U.S.)**, e.g.

> Atlantic Coast (U.S.)
> West (U.S.)
> Coal Miners' Strike, U.S., 1949-1950
> Distinguished Service Cross (U.S.)

However, when assigning name headings as subjects, use the headings exactly as they appear in name authority records, e.g.

> United States. Congress. House.
> United States. Dept. of Agriculture.

> U.S. Army Engineer Topographic Laboratories.
> U.S. Nuclear Regulatory Commission.

> US Army Military Police School.
> US-USSR Joint Symposium on Myocardial Metabolism.

> Chemical Center and School (U.S.)
> Ryukyu Islands (United States Civil Administration, 1950-1972)

Appendix L: Capitalization*

PROCEDURES:

1. Policy for name headings used as subject headings. When using valid AACR 2 personal, corporate, and jurisdictional names and uniform titles as subject headings, transcribe them exactly as they appear on name authority records, including capital letters as indicated.

2. Policy for subject headings established in the SUBJECTS file. Transcribe existing headings and subdivisions in AACR 2 form exactly as they appear in subject authority records, using capital letters as indicated.

3. Proper nouns and adjectives. Capitalize proper nouns and adjectives in subject headings, subdivisions, or references regardless of whether they are in the initial position, e.g.

> !Kung (African people)
> *Naborr (Horse)
> 97 Sen (Fighter planes)
>
> Tariff on X-ray equipment and supplies
>
> Jesus Christ—Views on the Old Testament
>
> Gosannen kassen ekotoba (Scrolls)
>   UF   Hachiman Tarō ekotoba (Scrolls)

4. Initial words. Capitalize the first word of a subject heading, subdivision, or reference regardless of whether it is a proper name, e.g.

> Teenage boys
>   UF   Adolescent boys
>
> Writing—Materials and instruments
>
> Serbo-Croatian language—To 1500
>
> Beauce (France)
>   UF   La Beauce (France)
>
> Cévennes Mountains (France)
>   UF   Les Cévennes (France)

---

*The information presented in this section is based upon the *Subject Cataloging Manual: Subject Headings*, 4th ed. (Washington, D.C.: Library of Congress, Office of Subject Cataloging Policy, 1991), appendix B.

Exception: When a term is found in reference sources with the initial letter consistently lowercased, establish the heading (or reference) in that form. *Examples:*

> p-adic numbers
>
> p-divisible groups
>
> 35mm cameras
> > UF   35 mm cameras
>
> 3-dimensional manifolds (Topology)
> > USE   Three-manifolds (Topology)

5. Capitalize any letter within a heading that appears as such in reference sources. Use this rule in establishing named systems, computer languages, tests, etc. *Examples:*

4-H clubs	UNIMARC System
Agent Orange	Pac-Man (Game)
California Basic Educational Skills Test	PostScript (Computer program language)
DC-to-DC converters	RuneQuest (Game)
DDT (Insecticide)	SdKfz 251 (Half-track)
IJssel Lake (Netherlands)	SP/k (Computer program language)

6. Do not capitalize conjunctions, prepositions and the articles **a, an,** and **the** and their equivalents in other languages if they are not the first word in the heading, subdivision, or reference. *Examples:*

> Colors in the Bible
>
> Chesapeake and Ohio Canal (Md. and Washington, D.C.)

Exception: Capitalize **The** if it is the first word in a parenthetical qualifier, or the first word following a comma in an inverted heading, e.g.

> Jota (The Serbo-Croatian letter)
>
> Geysers, The (Calif.)

7. *Inverted headings and subdivisions.* Capitalize the word following a comma that would be in the initial position if the heading, subdivision, or reference were expressed as a phrase in direct word order. Capitalization is especially important to clarify inverted headings. *Examples:*

> Sculpture, Mandingo
>
> Medicine, Magic, mystic, and spagiric
>
> Merkem (Belgium), Battle of, 1918
>
> United States—History, Naval
>
> Measuring instruments
> > UF   Instruments, Measuring

8. Parenthetical qualifiers. Capitalize the first word in a parenthetical qualifier, as well as any proper nouns or adjectives within a parenthetical qualifier. Also capitalize the first word that follows a colon within a parenthetical qualifier. *Examples:*

> Chambri (Papua New Guinea people)
> Citizenship as point of contact (Conflict of laws)
> Wu (The Chinese word)
> Auschwitz (Poland : Concentration camp)
> Thebes (Egypt : Extinct city)

Note: In the past, certain headings and subdivisions were established with parenthetical qualifiers beginning with lowercased prepositions or with other lowercased words. Continue using headings of this type established in the SUBJECTS file, but do not establish new headings with parenthetical qualifiers beginning with a preposition. Example:

> English language—Conversation and phrase books (for secretaries)

9. Hyphenated compounds. When capitalizing the first part of a hyphenated compound, capitalize the second part also if it is a proper noun or proper adjective. Do not capitalize the second part of a hyphenated compound if it modifies the first or if the two parts constitute a single word. *Examples:*

> Ecuador-Peru Conflict, 1981
> Sabazius (Thraco-Phrygian deity)

> [*but* Twelve-tone system
> Twenty-first century]

10. Armed Forces. Capitalize the word **Forces** in the heading **Armed Forces** and in the subdivision **—Armed Forces,** e.g.

> Armed Forces—Civic action
> United States—Armed Forces—Foreign countries

11. [. . .] countries. Lowercase the word **countries** in phrase headings and subdivisions, e.g.

> Arab countries—History—20th century
> Canary Islanders—Foreign countries
> Communist countries
> European Economic Community countries—Economic conditions

12. Terms attached to dates.

> *a. Anno Domini; Before Christ.* Capitalize the abbreviations **A.D.** and **B.C.** (For details on the use of **A.D.** and **B.C.,** see App. A [i.e., appendix K of this book], sec. 8.a.) *Example:*

> China—History—Han dynasty, 202 B.C.-220 A.D.

b. *[. . .] century.* Do not capitalize the word **century,** e.g.

> English literature—20th century
> Twenty-first century

c. *Circa.* Do not capitalize the abbreviation **ca.** in period subdivisions, e.g.

> United States—History—Colonial period, ca. 1600-1775

13. *Named dynasties.* Do not capitalize the word **dynasty,** e.g.

> Achaemenid dynasty, 559-330 B.C.

14. *Family names.* Do not capitalize the word **family,** e.g.

> Miller family
> Pasêk Kayu Sêlêm family

15. *Family names with initial particles.* Headings for individual families derived from French, Spanish, Portuguese, Italian, German and Dutch may include the initial particles **De, Du, La, L', Von, Van,** etc. Capitalize initial particles in family names in both headings and references, e.g.

> Baden family
>   UF   Von Baden family
>
> De Groot family
>   UF   De Groote family

16. *Named events.* Capitalize all significant words in headings, subdivisions, or references that designate named events, e.g.

Watergate Affair, 1972-1974

Marinette Knitting Mills Strike, Marinette, Wis., 1951

Harpers Ferry (W. Va.)—History—John Brown's Raid, 1859
    UF   John Brown's Raid, Harpers Ferry, W. Va., 1859

Transylvania (Romania)—History—Peasant Uprising, 1784
    BT   Peasant uprisings—Romania

China—History—Ch'ing Dynasty Restoration Attempt, 1917
    UF   Ch'ing Dynasty Restoration Attempt, China, 1917

Exception: The generic terms in the following subdivisions have, by convention, been lowercased. Continue to follow this convention when establishing new headings for any of these events. Do not, however, propose any new subdivisions to be added to this list.

> -[. . .] colony, [date]
> -[. . .] conquest, [date]
> -[. . .] domination, [date]
> -[. . .] dynasties, [date]
> -[. . .] dynasty, [date]

-[. . .] intervention, [date]
-[. . .] movement, [date]
-[. . .] occupation, [date]
-[. . .] period, [date]
-[. . .] periods, [date]
-[. . .] rule, [date]

Examples:

Painting, Chinese—Three kingdoms-Sui dynasty, 200-618
Japan—History—Attempted Mongol invasions, 1274-1281
India—History—British occupation, 1765-1947
United States—History—Colonial period, ca. 1600-1775

17. *Cultural and archaeological periods.* Do not capitalize headings for cultural and archaeological periods, except for the initial word. *Examples:*

Bronze age
Iron age
Mesolithic period
Paleolithic period, Lower
Stone age

18. *Named movements.* Capitalize only the initial word of a named movement, e.g.

Anti-Nazi movement
China—History—Reform movement, 1898
Ecumenical movement
Gay liberation movement
Pro-life movement
Stakhanov movement
Symbolism (Literary movement)

19. *Named schools.* Capitalize only the initial word when establishing headings or subdivisions for named schools (i.e. groups of painters, economists, architects, etc., that are under a common local or personal influence producing a general similarity in their work). *Examples:*

Chicago school of theology
Classical school of economics
Marxian school of sociology
Flower arrangement, Japanese—Shōgetsudō Koryū school

Note: Some headings of this type have been established with the word school uppercased. Change these headings as they are encountered in the SUBJECTS file to the form specified above.

20. *Scientific names of plants and animals.* Capitalize only the initial word of the scientific name of a plant or animal, even if subsequent words include proper nouns or adjectives, e.g.

Anguilla japonica

Litchi chinensis
UF   Nephelium litchi

Pinus sibirica
UF   Pinus cembra sibirica

21. Geographic headings. Capitalize both generic and proper nouns and adjectives in names of places, regions, sites, metropolitan areas, and named geographic and geological features, including coasts, islands, rivers, valleys, watersheds, etc., in English headings or references. For non-English headings and references apply the appropriate capitalization rules according to Appendix A of AACR 2 and reference sources. *Examples:*

Alaska, Gulf of (Alaska)
Assateague Island National Seashore (Md. and Va.)
Atlantic Coast (Canada)
Beluga Lake (Alaska)
Boundary Waters Canoe Area (Minn.)
Dakota Aquifer
Death Valley (Calif. and Nev.)
Ionian Islands (Greece)
McKinley, Mount, Region (Alaska)
Peking Metropolitan Area (China)
Pennsylvania Dutch Country (Pa.)
Po River Valley (Italy)
Stone Creek Site (Alta.)
Tokyo Region (Japan)
Valley Forge National Historical Park (Pa.)
Washington Region

Parco nazionale della Maremma (Italy)
UF   Maremma, Parco nazionale della (Italy)
UF   Parco della Maremma (Italy)

Tatar Strait (Russia)
UF   Tatarskiĭ proliv (Russia)

Note: Lowercase the word **regions** *in the heading* **Arctic regions,** *e.g.*

Arctic regions—Aerial exploration

22. Capitalization rules for languages other than English. Use the current, appropriate rules for capitalization for the language concerned when establishing headings and making references. For guidance consult such sources as Appendix A of AACR 2 and reference sources. In cases of conflict, generally prefer the capitalization rule in Appendix A of AACR 2. *Examples:*

Tatar Strait (Russia)
UF   Tatarskiĭ proliv (Russia)

> *Strait is capitalized in the English heading **Tatar Strait (Russia)** in accordance with sec. 21 above. The Russian word for strait, **proliv,** as part of the vernacular UF reference, is lowercased because it appears as such in Russian encyclopedias and because lowercasing is consistent with the capitalization rules for Russian geographic names in Appendix A of AACR 2.*

Rite of spring (Ballet)
  UF   Sacre du printemps (Ballet)

> *Although **spring** appears uppercased in reference sources, both **printemps** and **spring** are lowercased because Appendix A of AACR 2 requires that names of seasons be lowercased in both English and French.*

Balkan Mountains (Bulgaria)
  UF   Stara planina (Bulgaria)

Bellini, Giovanni, d. 1516.   Saint Francis in ecstasy
  UF   Saint Francis in ecstasy (Painting)
  UF   San Francesco nel deserto (Painting)

Chang, Tse-tuan, fl. 1111-1120.   Going up the river at Ch'ing-ming Festival
        time
  UF   Ch'ing ming shang ho t'u (Scroll)

Parc provincial des Laurentides (Québec)
  UF   Laurentides Provincial Park (Québec)
  UF   Parc national des Laurentides (Québec)

Soester Scheibenkreuz (Sculpture)
  UF   Kreuztafel mit hölzener Scheibe (Sculpture)

Votivbild Kartause Cella Salutis zu Tückelhausen (Panel painting)

Appendix M: Punctuation*

PROCEDURES:

1. Period after subject tracing number. Place a period after the arabic numeral designating the subject heading number. Leave one space between the period and the first letter of the subject heading, e.g.

    1. Miniature books—United States—Bibliography.
    2. Miniature books—Specimens.

Do not input numerals to designate the order of subject headings when cataloging online.

2. Period at the end of a heading. Place a period at the end of a heading, e.g.

    1. Reagan, Ronald.
    2. Presidents—United States—Biography.

Exceptions: Omit the final period if the final element in the heading is a closing parenthesis, an open date, or a mark of ending punctuation, e.g.

    1. Seasonal variations (Economics)
    1. Education—Washington (D.C.)
    1. United States—Economic policy—1993-
    1. Capote, Truman, 1924-
    1. Sienkiewicz, Henryk, 1846-1916.   Quo vadis?

3. Dashes. When cataloging manually using a worksheet or printout, designate subdivisions by placing a dash before the subdivision.

When typing: Use two hyphens, one after the other, with no space before or after, e.g.

    1. Soviet Union--Foreign relations--United States--Bibliography.

---

*The information presented in this section is based upon the *Subject Cataloging Manual: Subject Headings*, 4th ed. (Washington, D.C.: Library of Congress, Office of Subject Cataloging Policy, 1991), appendix D.

When making handwritten annotations on a printout of a bibliographic or authority record: Make a single, unbroken line twice as long as a hyphen. Leave no space before or after.

When cataloging online, do not input any characters to represent dashes. Use a single delimiter (‡) to designate the beginning of a subfield.

4. *Hyphens.* When cataloging manually using a worksheet or printout, observe the following conventions in order to distinguish between hyphens and dashes:

When typing:

a. Use the standard hyphen on the typewriter. Leave no space before or after the hyphen, e.g.

> Afro-Americans
> X-rays
> High school teachers--In-service training
> St. Louis-San Francisco Railway Company

b. *Dates.* Use a single hyphen, even when the hyphen is the last element of a tracing, e.g.

> 1. United States--History--1945-
> 1. China--Civilization--1912-1949.

> For specific instructions on open dates and spacing if a subdivision or other information follows the open date, see sec. 6, below.

When making handwritten annotations on a printout of a bibliographic or authority record:

a. Make a short equal sign at the proper location. Leave no space before or after.

b. *Dates.* Use a short equal sign to represent a single hyphen, even when the hyphen is the last element of a heading.

5. *Spaces within abbreviations.*

> *Note: For general guidelines on the use of abbreviations in subject headings, see Appendix A [i.e., appendix K of this book].*

a. Leave no space after any periods within an abbreviation, e.g.

C.O.D. shipments	Egypt—History—To 332 B.C.
Bible. N.T. Matthew.	Washington (D.C.)

b. Leave no space within adjacent initials where a personal name forms part of a corporate name or part of a subject heading, e.g.

> C.S. Wertsner & Son

c. Leave no space after letters within an acronym, e.g.

DYNAMO (Computer program language)
MARC formats

d. Leave no space after an abbreviation and the dash designating a subdivision or after an abbreviation and the hyphen of a date span, e.g.

China—History—Han dynasty, 202 B.C.-220 A.D.—Bibliography

e. Leave one space between the final period of an abbreviated term and a word that follows, e.g.

C.O.D. shipments
Breakage, shrinkage, etc. (Commerce)
Church finance—History—Early church, ca. 30-600

However, if the word that follows an abbreviation is a subheading (see sec. 8), leave two spaces after the abbreviation when cataloging manually, or a delimiter with no space before or after when cataloging online, e.g.

Bible. O.T. Genesis.
Bible.‡N.T.‡Corinthians, 1st.

f. Leave one space within adjacent initials in personal name headings, e.g.

Manchester, P. W.   Smith, J. J., 1910-

g. Leave one space between preceding and succeeding initials if an abbreviation consists of more than a single letter, e.g.

Charleston (W. Va.)
Adelaide (S. Aust.)
Whitehead, David, Ph. D

h. Leave one space before and after an ampersand, e.g.

Columbus & Greenville Railway

6. *Open dates.* When cataloging manually, if an element ends with an open date, and a subdivision or other information (e.g. a title or free-floating phrase) follows it, leave one space after the hyphen before beginning the dash and subdivision or other information, e.g.

1. United States—Foreign relations—1989- —Periodicals.
1. Capote, Truman, 1924- —Criticism and interpretation.
1. Capote, Truman, 1924- In cold blood.
1. Wyeth, Andrew, 1917- Christina's world.
1. Dalí, Salvador, 1904- Homage to Goya.
1. Woods, Donald, 1933- , in motion pictures.

When cataloging online, use a delimiter to separate these subfields. If an open date is followed by a subject subdivision, i.e. an ‡x subfield, insert a blank space between the hyphen and the delimiter, e.g.

Wyeth, Andrew,‡1917- ‡Exhibitions

If an open date is followed by a ‡k subfield, insert a space and a comma between the hyphen and the delimiter, e.g.

Woods, Donald,‡1933- ,‡in motion pictures

If the open date is followed by a ‡t subfield, do not insert a space between the hyphen and the delimiter, e.g.

Michener, James A.‡(James Albert),‡1907-‡Centennial

7. *Name headings used as subject headings.* Use the same punctuation, capitalization, diacritics and spacing indicated on valid AACR 2 name authority records, e.g.

    1. Eglise de St-Joachim (Saint-Joachim, Québec) *[no period after St]*
    1. C.S. Wertsner & Son.
    1. Chung-kuo kung ch'an tang.

If a name heading ends with a closing parenthesis or mark of ending punctuation other than a period, retain this punctuation before adding the subdivision, e.g.

    1. Association of Flight Attendants (U.S.)—Periodicals.
    1. Sienkiewicz, Henryk, 1846-1916. Quo vadis?—Illustrations.

8. *Subheadings.* Subheadings are used in name headings to designate relationships between units and subunits, and function like subdivisions in subject headings. Subheadings are separated from the main heading by a period and two spaces when cataloging manually, or by a delimiter when cataloging online. For this discussion of punctuation, titles in author/title entries are also treated as subheadings. *Examples:*

Yale University. Library.
United States. Army. Chaplain Corps.
Shakespeare, William, 1564-1616.‡Sonnets.
Bible.‡N.T.‡Mark.

When cataloging manually:

    a. Leave a period and two spaces between a main heading and a subheading.

    b. Insert an em quad (a square) immediately after the period in question, if there is a possibility that the spacing would be unclear, such as when an abbreviation immediately precedes the subheading, e.g.

    1. Ssu-ma, Ch ien, ca. 145-ca. 86 B.C.□Shih chi.

c. If the name or unit before the subheading is qualified, place a period after the parentheses, even in those cases where the name authority record does not have the period, e.g.

    1. New York (N.Y.). Dept. of Social Services.

9. Breaking subject headings at the end of a line.

When cataloging manually:

a. Do not break a subject heading in the middle of a word or date or at the hyphen in a compound word. Instead, place the entire word or date or compound word on the next line, e.g.

1. High school teachers—
   In-service training.
	[*not* 1. High school teachers—In-ser-
	   vice training.]

1. High school teachers—
   In-service training.
	[*not* 1. High school teachers—In-
	   service training.]

1. Italy—Foreign relations—
   1914-1945.
	[*not* 1. Italy—Foreign relations—1914-
	   1945.]

b. Subheadings. Leave an em quad (a square) at the end of the first line, if the heading being transcribed goes on to a second line, e.g.

    1. United States.□ Army.□
      Chaplain Corps.

10. Use of commas before free-floating terms and phrases. See H362, sec. 2.

Glossary

AC Program. *See* Annotated Card Program.

Alphabetical subject catalog. A catalog containing subject entries based on the principle of specific and direct entry and arranged alphabetically. *Cf.* Alphabetico-classed catalog; Classed catalog; Dictionary catalog.

Alphabetico-classed catalog. A subject catalog in which entries are listed under broad subjects and subdivided hierarchically by topics. The entries on each level of the hierarchy are arranged alphabetically. *Cf.* Alphabetical subject catalog; Classed catalog; Dictionary catalog.

Analytical subject entry. Subject entry for part of a work. Also called subject analytic.

Annotated Card Program. A Library of Congress program for cataloging children's materials that differs from regular cataloging by the addition of a summary note and additional subject headings assigned from *Subject Headings for Children's Literature*. Also called AC Program.

Associative reference. *See* Related-term reference.

Authority record. *See* Name authority record; Subject authority record.

Biographical heading. A heading used with biographies that consists of the name of a class of persons with appropriate subdivisions, such as **Physicians—California—Biography**; **Poets, American—19th century—Biography**.

Biography. A special genre of works consisting of life histories of individuals, including those written by the individuals themselves (i.e., autobiographies). *Cf.* Collective biography; Complete biography; Individual biography; Partial biography.

Broader-term reference. A reference from a heading to a more comprehensive heading. It is indicated in *Library of Congress Subject Headings* by the letters BT. *Cf.* Hierarchical reference; Narrower-term reference.

BT reference. *See* Broader-term reference.

Chain. A series of subject terms from different levels of a hierarchy, arranged from general to specific or vice versa.

Chronological subdivision. A subdivision that shows the period or span of time treated in a work or the period during which the work appeared. Also called period subdivision. *Cf.* Form subdivision; Geographic subdivision; Topical subdivision.

Citation order. The order in which elements in a compound or complex subject heading, or in a heading with subdivisions, are arranged.

City doubling. The Library of Congress's policy to assign an additional entry under the name of a city when a work in certain subject categories has been assigned a heading of the type **[Topic]—[City]**.

City flip. The Library of Congress's previous practice of reversing the citation order between topic and place in some headings when the place involved was at the city level, as in **Fountains—California**, but *Los Angeles (Calif.)—Fountains*.

Class catalog. *See* Classed catalog.

Class entry. A subject entry consisting of a string of hierarchically related terms beginning with the broadest term leading to the subject in question.

Classed catalog. A subject catalog consisting of class entries arranged logically according to a systematic scheme of classification. Also called class catalog, classified subject catalog, systematic catalog. *Cf.* Alphabetical subject catalog; Alphabetico-classed catalog; Dictionary catalog.

Classified subject catalog. *See* Classed catalog.

Coextensive heading. A heading that represents precisely (not more generally or more specifically) the subject content of a work.

Collective biography. A work consisting of two or more life histories. *Cf.* Individual biography.

Complete biography. A biography that covers the entire life story of an individual. *Cf.* Partial biography.

Coordinate system. *See* Postcoordination.

Cross reference. A direction from one term or heading to another in the catalog. *Cf.* Equivalence reference; Explanatory reference; General reference; Hierarchical reference; Related-term reference; Specific reference.

Depth of indexing. The degree to which individual parts of a publication are represented in indexing. *Cf.* In-depth indexing.

Diaries. Registers or records of personal experiences, observations, thoughts, or feelings, kept daily or at frequent intervals.

Dictionary catalog. A catalog in which all the entries (e.g., author, title, subject, series) and cross references are interfiled in one alphabetical sequence. The subject entries in a dictionary catalog are based on the principle of specific and direct entry. The term, when used in reference to the subject entries, is sometimes used interchangeably with the term alphabetical subject catalog. *Cf.* Alphabetical subject catalog; Alphabetico-classed catalog; Classed catalog.

Direct subdivision. Geographic subdivision of a subject heading by the name of a place without interposition of the name of a larger geographic entity. *Cf.* Indirect subdivision.

Duplicate entry. (1) Entry of the same heading in two different forms (e.g., **United States—Foreign relations—France; France—Foreign relations—United States**); (2) Assignment of two headings to bring out different aspects of a work. Frequently, one of the headings is a specific heading and the other a general (also called generic) heading subdivided by an aspect (e.g., **Bluegrass** and **Grasses—Scandinavia** for a work about Bluegrass in Scandinavia).

Enumeration. Listing precombined subject headings or index terms for compound or complex subjects in a subject headings list or thesaurus. *Cf.* Precoordination; Synthesis.

Equivalence reference. A reference from a term or name not used as a heading to one that is used. It is indicated in *Library of Congress Subject Headings* by the symbols USE and UF (used for). *Cf.* Refer-from reference.

Exhaustive indexing. The practice of assigning indexing terms or subject headings to represent all significant concepts or aspects of a subject. *Cf.* In-depth indexing; Summarization.

Explanatory reference. A reference providing explanatory statements with regard to the heading involved. It is used when a simple reference does not give adequate information or guidance to the user.

Facet analysis. The division of a subject into its component parts (facets). Each array of facets consists of parts based on the same characteristic (e.g., language facet, space facet, time facet).

Festschrift. A collection of two or more essays; addresses; or biographical, bibliographical, and other contributions published in honor of a person, an institution, or a society, usually on the occasion of a birthday or anniversary.

Film. A generic term for any pictorial medium intended for projection, including motion pictures, filmstrips, slides and transparencies, videotapes, and video recordings.

First-order political division. A geographic unit representing a political division under the national level. The political divisions of countries are known as autonomous communities, cantons, departments, provinces, republics, states, and so on. The names of the first-order political divisions of certain countries are used in geographic qualifiers or indirect subdivisions instead of the name of the country.

Form heading. A heading representing the physical, bibliographical, artistic, or literary form or genre of a work (e.g., **Encyclopedias and dictionaries**; **Essays**; **Short stories**; **String quartets**).

Form subdivision. A division of a subject heading that brings out the form of the work (e.g., **—Bibliography**; **—Maps**; **—Periodicals**). *Cf.* Chronological subdivision; Geographic subdivision; Topical subdivision.

Free-floating phrase. A phrase that may be combined with a valid heading to form a new heading without establishing the usage editorially.

Free-floating subdivision. A subdivision that may be used under any existing appropriate heading without establishing the usage editorially.

General reference: A blanket reference to a group of headings rather than a particular heading. *Cf.* Specific reference.

Generic posting. The practice of assigning additional headings that are broader than the heading that represents precisely the content of the work.

Geographic heading. A name heading representing a place or an entity closely associated with a place (e.g., a park, a forest, a tunnel). *Cf.* Jurisdictional name heading; Non-jurisdictional name heading.

Geographic qualifier. The name of a larger geographic entity added to a local place name, such as **Cambridge (*Mass.*); Toledo (*Spain*)**.

Geographic subdivision. A subdivision by the name of a place to which the subject represented by the main heading is limited. Also called local subdivision. *Cf.* Chronological subdivision; Direct subdivision; Form subdivision; Indirect subdivision; Topical subdivision.

Hierarchical reference. A cross reference connecting headings on different levels of a hierarchy. *Cf.* Broader-term reference; Narrower-term reference; Related-term reference.

In-depth indexing. The practice of assigning indexing terms or subject headings to represent individual parts of a publication. *Cf.* Exhaustive indexing; Summarization.

Indirect subdivision. Geographic subdivision of a subject heading by name of country (or first-order political division in the case of Canada, Great Britain, and the United States), with further subdivision by name of a subordinate geographic unit. *Cf.* Direct subdivision.

Individual biography. A work devoted to the life of a single individual. *Cf.* Collective biography.

Inverted heading. An adjectival or prepositional phrase heading with the words rearranged in order to bring the significant noun to the initial position.

Jurisdictional name heading. A geographic heading representing a political or ecclesiastical jurisdiction. Entities that belong to this category include countries, principalities, territories, states, provinces, counties, administrative districts, cities, archdioceses, and dioceses. Jurisdictional name headings are established in accordance with *AACR2R*. *Cf.* Non-jurisdictional name heading.

Juvenile film. A film intended for children through the age of 15.

Juvenile work. A work intended for children through the age of 15 (or through the ninth grade).

Literary warrant. The use of an actual collection of material or body of literature as the basis for developing an indexing or classification system. In the case of LCSH, the literary warrant is the Library of Congress collection.

Liturgy. Prayers, rituals, acts, and ceremonies used in the official worship of a religion or denomination, public or private.

Local subdivision. *See* Geographic subdivision.

Model heading. *See* Pattern heading.

Multiple heading. A heading with a modifier followed by a bracketed series of similar modifiers ending with the word "etc.," such as *Authors, American, [English, French, etc.]*. This device was used previously by the Library of Congress to illustrate how a heading may be modified. The practice of establishing multiple headings was discontinued in 1979.

Multiple subdivision. A subdivision that incorporates bracketed terms, generally followed by the word "etc.," such as **Subject headings—Aeronautics, [Education, Latin America, Law, etc.]; Names, Personal—Scottish, [Spanish, Welsh, etc.]**. This device is used to indicate that similar subdivisions suggested by the terms enclosed in brackets may be created.

Name authority record. A record of a personal, corporate, or jurisdictional name heading that shows its established form and indicates the cross references made to the heading. *Cf.* Subject authority record.

Name-title heading. A heading consisting of the name of a person or corporate body and the title of an item. It is established according to *AACR2R* and used in both descriptive and subject cataloging.

Narrower-term reference. A reference from a heading to a less-comprehensive heading. It is indicated in *Library of Congress Subject Headings* by the letters NT. *Cf.* Broader-term reference; Hierarchical reference.

Non-jurisdictional name heading. A geographic heading representing an entity other than a jurisdiction. Typical non-jurisdictional name headings include those for rivers, mountains, parks, and roads.

Nonprint heading. *See* Unprinted heading.

NT reference. *See* Narrower-term reference.

Partial biography. A work that presents only certain details of a person's life. *Cf.* Complete biography.

Pattern heading. A heading that serves as a model of subdivisions for headings in the same category. Subdivisions listed under a pattern heading may be used whenever appropriate under other headings in the same category. For example, **Shakespeare, William, 1564-1616**, serves as a pattern heading for literary authors; **Piano** serves as a pattern heading for musical instruments. Also called model heading.

Period subdivision. *See* Chronological subdivision.

Political qualifier. *See* Type-of-jurisdiction qualifier.

Postcoordination. The representation of a complex subject by assigning separate single-concept terms at the input stage and the retrieval of that subject through combining the separate terms at the search or output stage. Also called a coordinate system. *Cf.* Precoordination.

Precoordination. The representation of a complex subject by means of combining separate elements of the subject at the input stage. *Cf.* Enumeration; Postcoordination; Synthesis.

Qualifier. A term (enclosed in parentheses) placed after a heading for the purpose of distinguishing between homographs or clarifying the meaning of the heading, such as **Indexing** *(Machine-shop practice)*; **Juno** *(Roman deity)*; **New York** *(State)*. *Cf.* Geographic qualifier; Type-of-jurisdiction qualifier.

Refer-from reference. An indication of the terms or headings from which references are to be made to a given heading. It is the reverse of the indication of a USE reference and is represented by the symbols UF (used for). *Cf.* Equivalence reference.

Reference. *See* Cross reference.

Related-term reference. A cross reference that connects headings related other than hierarchically. It is indicated in *Library of Congress Subject Headings* by the letters RT. *Cf.* Hierarchical reference.

RT reference. *See* Related-term reference.

Specific entry. Entry of a work under a heading that expresses its special subject or topic, as distinguished from an entry for the class or broad subject that encompasses that special subject or topic.

Specific reference. A reference from one heading to another. *Cf.* General reference.

Specificity. (1) The closeness of match between a term or heading and the document to which it is assigned; (2) Where a given term lies within a hierarchy of related terms—whether it is near the top and thus fairly general, or fairly far down and thus quite specific.

Split files. Separate files of subject entries in a catalog under headings represented by current and obsolete terms that refer to the same subject.

Subdivision. The device of extending a subject heading by indicating one of its aspects—form, place, period, topic. *Cf.* Chronological subdivision; Form subdivision; Geographic subdivision; Topical subdivision.

Subheading. A subordinate unit of a name heading that follows the main heading or another subheading and is separated from it by a period and two spaces (e.g., **United States. *Congress. Senate.***).

Subject. The theme or topic treated in a work, whether stated in the title or not.

Subject analysis. The process of identifying the intellectual content of a work. The results may be displayed in a catalog or bibliography by means of notational symbols as in a classification system, or verbal terms such as subject headings or indexing terms.

Subject analytic. *See* Analytical subject entry.

Subject authority record. A record of a subject heading that shows its established form, cites the authorities consulted in determining the choice and form of the heading, and indicates the cross references made to the heading. *Cf.* Name authority record.

Subject catalog. A catalog consisting of subject entries only; the subject portion of a divided book or card catalog.

Subject heading. The term (a word or group of words) denoting a subject under which all material on that subject is represented.

Subject-to-name reference. A reference from a subject heading to a name heading for the purpose of directing the user's attention from a particular field of interest to names of individuals or corporate bodies that are active or associated in some way with the field. Such references are no longer made by the Library of Congress.

Summarization. The practice of assigning indexing terms or subject headings to represent the overall content of a document rather than individual parts of it. *Cf.* Exhaustive indexing; In-depth indexing.

Syndetic device. The device used to connect related headings by means of cross references. *Cf.* Cross reference.

Synthesis. The representation of a subject by combining individual terms that are listed separately in a subject headings list or thesaurus. *Cf.* Enumeration; Precoordination.

Systematic catalog. *See* Classed catalog.

Thesaurus. A list of controlled indexing terms used in a particular indexing system.

Topical subdivision. A subdivision that represents an aspect of the main subject other than form, place, or period. *Cf.* Chronological subdivision; Form subdivision; Geographic subdivision.

Tracing. An indication of the access points that have been made for a particular cataloging record. These access points include descriptive and subject headings. On a Library of Congress record in a book or card catalog, they are recorded in a paragraph following the notes, with the subject headings listed first, each preceded by an Arabic numeral. In a MARC record, access points are indicated by codes.

Type-of-jurisdiction qualifier. A term (enclosed in parentheses) indicating type of jurisdiction, added to a geographic name in order to distinguish between places of the same name, such as **New York (*State*)**. Also called political qualifier.

Uniform heading. The representation of a given subject by one heading in one form only.

Uniform title. The title by which a work is identified for cataloging purposes. It is established according to *AACR2R* and used in both descriptive and subject cataloging.

Unique heading. The use of a heading to represent one subject or one concept only.

Unprinted heading. A heading that is used in catalog entries but not listed in LCSH. Most headings consisting of proper names (including personal and corporate headings) and many music headings are unprinted headings. Also called nonprint heading.

USE reference. *See* Equivalence reference.

UF reference. *See* Equivalence reference.

BiblioqRaphy

Aluri, Rao, D. Alasdair Kemp, and John J. Boll. *Subject Analysis in Online Catalogs*. Englewood, Colo.: Libraries Unlimited, 1991.

Angell, Richard S. "Library of Congress Subject Headings—Review and Forecast." In *Subject Retrieval in the Seventies: New Directions: Proceedings of an International Symposium*, edited by Hans (Hanan) Wellisch and Thomas D. Wilson. Westport, Conn.: Greenwood Publishing, 1972.

——. "Standards for Subject Headings: A National Program." In *Journal of Cataloging and Classification* 10 (October 1954): 193.

Anglo-American Cataloguing Rules. 2nd ed. 1988 revision. Prepared under the direction of the Joint Steering Committee for Revision of AACR, a committee of the American Library Association, the Australian Committee on Cataloguing, the British Library, the Canadian Committee on Cataloguing, the Library Association, and the Library of Congress, edited by Michael Gorman and Paul W. Winkler. Chicago: American Library Association, 1988.

Austin, Derek, with Mary Dykstra. *PRECIS: A Manual of Concept Analysis and Subject Indexing*. 2nd ed. London: British Library, Bibliographic Services Division, 1984.

Balnaves, John. "Specificity." In *The Variety of Librarianship: Essays in Honour of John Wallace Metcalfe*, edited by W. Boyd Rayward. Sydney: Library Association of Australia, 1976.

Bates, Marcia J. "Factors Affecting Subject Catalog Search Success." In *Journal of the American Society for Information Science* 28 (May 1977): 168.

——. "Implications of the Subject Subdivisions Conference: The Shift in Online Catalog Design." In Subject Subdivisions Conference (1991: Airlie, Va.): *The Future of Subdivisions in the Library of Congress Subject Headings System,* 92-98.

——. "Rethinking Subject Cataloging in the Online Environment." In *Library Resources & Technical Services* 33, no. 4 (October 1989): 400-412.

Berman, Barbara L. "Form Headings in Subject Cataloging." In *Library Resources & Technical Services* 33, no.2 (April 1989): 134-39.

Berman, Sanford. *Prejudices and Antipathies: A Tract on the LC Subject Heads Concerning People*. Metuchen, N.J.: Scarecrow Press, 1971; Jefferson, N.C.: McFarland, 1993.

——. "Proposal for Reforms to Improve Subject Searching." In "Modern Subject Access in the Online Age: American Libraries' First Continuing Education Course: Lesson Three," [edited] by Pauline A. Cochrane. *American Libraries* 15 (April 1984): 254.

Cataloging Service Bulletin 1- , Summer 1978- . Washington, D.C.: Library of Congress, Processing Services.

Chan, Lois Mai. "Alternatives to Subject Strings in the Library of Congress Subject Headings System: With Discussion." In Subject Subdivisions Conference (1991: Airlie, Va.): *The Future of Subdivisions in the Library of Congress Subject Headings System,* 46-56.

———. *Library of Congress Subject Headings: Principles of Structure and Policies for Application,* annotated version. Prepared by Lois Mai Chan for the Library of Congress. *Advances in Library Information Technology,* no. 3. Washington, D.C.: Cataloging Distribution Service, Library of Congress, 1990.

———. "Library of Congress Subject Headings As an Online Retrieval Tool: Structural Considerations: Paper Presented at the Symposium on Subject Analysis, 29-30 March 1985, Durham, N.C." In *Improving LCSH for Use in Online Catalogs,* edited by P. A. Cochrane. Littleton, Colo.: Libraries Unlimited, 1986.

Clack, Doris. *Black Literature Resources: Analysis and Organization.* New York: Marcel Dekker, 1975.

Coates, E. J. *Subject Catalogues: Headings and Structure.* London: Library Association, 1960; reissued with new preface, 1988.

Cochrane, Pauline A. *Improving LCSH for Use in Online Catalogs: Exercises for Self-help with a Selection of Background Readings.* Littleton, Colo.: Libraries Unlimited, 1986.

Cochrane, Pauline A., and Monika Kirtland. *I. Critical Views of LCSH . . . II. An Analysis of Vocabulary Control in the Library of Congress List of Subject Headings.* Syracuse, N.Y.: ERIC Clearinghouse on Information Resources, 1981.

Conway, Martha O'Hara. "Characteristics of Subject Headings in the Library of Congress BOOKSM Database." In *Library Resources & Technical Services* 37, no. 1 (January 1993): 47-58.

Conway, Martha O'Hara, and Karen M. Drabenstott. "The Expanded Use of Free-Floating Subdivisions in the Library of Congress Subject Headings System: With Discussion." In Subject Subdivisions Conference (1991 : Airlie, Va.): *The Future of Subdivisions in the Library of Congress Subject Headings System,* 26-35.

Cousins, S. A. "Enhancing Subject Access to OPACs: Controlled Vocabulary vs. Natural Language (Using PRECIS, LCSH and DDC)." In *Journal of Documentation* 48 (September 1992): 291-309.

Cutter, Charles A. *Rules for a Dictionary Catalog.* 4th ed., rewritten. Washington, D.C.: Government Printing Office, 1904.

Drabenstott, Karen M. "Facilitating Geographic Subdivision Assignment in Subject Headings." In *Library Resources & Technical Services* 36, no. 4 (October 1992): 411-25.

———. "The Need for Machine-Readable Authority Records for Topical Subdivisions." In *Information Technology and Libraries* 11, no. 2 (June 1992): 91-104.

———. "Period Subdivisions in the Library of Congress Subject Headings System—Some Thoughts and Recommendations for the Future." In *Cataloging & Classification Quarterly* 15, no. 4 (1992): 19-45.

Drabenstott, Karen M., with Celeste M. Burman and Marjorie S. Weller. *Enhancing a New Design for Subject Access to Online Catalogs.* Ann Arbor, Mich.: School of Information and Library Studies, University of Michigan, 1994.

Drabenstott, Karen Markey, and Diane Vizine-Goetz. *Using Subject Headings for Online Retrieval: Theory, Practice, and Potential.* San Diego, Calif.: Academic Press, 1994.

Dunkin, Paul S. *Cataloging U.S.A.* Chicago: American Library Association, 1969.

Dykstra, Mary. "Can Subject Headings Be Saved?" In *Library Journal* 113 (Sept. 15, 1988): 55-58.

———. "LC Subject Headings Disguised as a Thesaurus." In *Library Journal* 113 (March 1, 1988): 42-46.

Eaton, Thelma. *Cataloging and Classification: An Introductory Manual.* 4th ed. Ann Arbor, Mich.: Edwards Brothers, 1967.

El-Hoshy, Lynn M. "Introduction to Subdivision Practice in the Library of Congress Subject Headings System." In Subject Subdivisions Conference (1991 : Airlie, Va.): *The Future of Subdivisions in the Library of Congress Subject Headings System,* 117-29.

Enyingi, Peter, Melody Busse Lembke, and Rhonda Lawrence Mittan. *Cataloging Legal Literature: A Manual on AACR2 and Library of Congress Subject Headings for Legal Materials: With Illustrations.* 2nd ed. Littleton, Colo.: F.B. Rothman, 1988- .

Fountain, Joanna F. *Headings for Children's Materials: An LCSH / Sears Companion.* Englewood, Colo.: Libraries Unlimited, 1993.

Franz, Lori, John Powell, and Suzann Jude. "End-User Understanding of Subdivided Subject Headings (Study of Proposed LCSH Change)." In *Library Resources & Technical Services* 38 (July 1994): 213-26.

Frarey, Carlyle J. "Studies of Use of the Subject Catalog: Summary and Evaluation." In *Subject Analysis of Library Materials,* edited by Maurice F. Tauber. New York: School of Library Service, Columbia University, 1953.

———. *Subject Headings, The State of the Library Art.* Vol. 1, pt. 2. New Brunswick, N.J.: Graduate School of Library Science, Rutgers—The State University, 1960.

Hanson, J. C. M. "The Subject Catalogs of the Library of Congress." In *Bulletin of the American Library Association* 3 (July 1, 1909): 385-97.

Hayes, Susan. "Enhanced Catalog Access to Fiction: A Preliminary Study." *Library Resources & Technical Services* 36, no. 4 (October 1992): 441-59.

Haykin, David Judson. "Project for a Subject Heading Code." Revised. (Washington, D.C.: 1957.)

———. *Subject Headings: A Practical Guide*. Washington, D.C.: Government Printing Office, 1951.

———. "Subject Headings: Principles and Development." In *The Subject Analysis of Library Materials*, edited by Maurice F. Tauber. New York: School of Library Service, Columbia University, 1953.

Hemmasi, Harriette. "ARIS Music Thesaurus: Another View of LCSH." *Library Resources & Technical Services* 36, no. 4 (1992): 487-503.

Hemmasi, Harriette, Fred Rowley, and James D. Anderson. "Isolating and Reorganizing Core Vocabulary from Library of Congress Music Headings for Use in the Music Thesaurus." In *Proceedings of the 4th ASIS SIG/CR Classification Research Workshop, October 24, 1993*. Held at the 56th ASIS Annual Meeting, October 24-28, 1993, Columbus, Ohio, editors and workshop co-chairs: Philip J. Smith, Clare Beghtol, Raya Fidel, and Barbara H. Kwasnik. Silver Spring, Md.: American Society for Information Science, 1993, 89-101.

Hildreth, Charles R. *Online Public Access Catalogs: The User Interface*. Dublin, Ohio: OCLC, 1982.

Holley, Robert P. "Report on the IFLA Satellite Meeting 'Subject Indexing: Principles and Practices in the 90's,' August 17-18, 1993, Lisbon, Portugal." In *Cataloging & Classification Quarterly* 18, no. 2 (1993): 87-95.

Hulme, E. Wyndham. "Principles of Book Classification." *Library Association Record* 13 (1911): 445-47.

Kaiser, Julius O. *Systematic Indexing*. London: Pitman, 1911. (Card System Series, v. 2.)

Kirtland, Monika, and Pauline Cochrane. "Critical Views of LCSH—Library of Congress Subject Headings: A Bibliographic and Bibliometric Essay." In *Cataloging & Classification Quarterly* 1, no. 2/3 (1982): 71-94.

Lancaster, F. W. *Vocabulary Control for Information Retrieval*. 2nd ed. Arlington, Va.: Information Resources Press, 1986.

Larsgaard, Mary Lynette. *Map Librarianship*. 2nd ed. Littleton, Colo.: Libraries Unlimited, 1987.

Leighton, Lee William, Carol A. Mandel, and Bob Wolven. "Streamlining Subdivision Selection and Establishing Strings as Headings in the Library of Congress Subject Headings System: With Discussion." In Subject Subdivisions Conference (1991 : Airlie, Va.): *The Future of Subdivisions in the Library of Congress Subject Headings System*, 67-74.

Library of Congress. Cataloging Policy and Support Office. *Free-Floating Subdivisions: An Alphabetical Index.* 6th ed. Washington, D.C.: Cataloging Distribution Service, Library of Congress, 1994.

———. *Library of Congress Subject Headings.* 17th ed. Washington, D.C.: Library of Congress, 1994.

Library of Congress. Office for Subject Cataloging Policy. *LC Period Subdivisions Under Names of Places.* 5th ed. Washington, D.C.: Cataloging Distribution Service, Library of Congress, 1994.

———. *Revised Library of Congress Subject Headings: Cross-References from Former to Current Subject Headings.* Washington, D.C.: Cataloging Distribution Service, Library of Congress, 1991.

———. *Subject Cataloging Manual: Subject Headings.* 4th ed. Washington, D.C.: Cataloging Distribution Service, Library of Congress, 1991.

Library of Congress. Subject Cataloging Division. *Subject Headings Used in the Dictionary Catalogues of the Library of Congress.* Washington, D.C.: GPO, 1910/1914-.

Library of Congress Rule Interpretations. 2nd ed. Washington, D.C.: Cataloging Distribution Service, Library of Congress, 1989.

Lilley, Oliver Linton. "How Specific Is Specific?" *Journal of Cataloging and Classification* 11 (1955): 4-5.

List of Subject Headings for Use in Dictionary Catalogs. Prepared by a Committee of the American Library Association. Boston: Published for the ALA Publishing Section by the Library Bureau, 1895; 2nd ed. rev., 1898; 3rd ed. rev., 1911.

Mandel, Carol A., and Judith Herschman. "Subject Access in the Online Catalog." Report prepared for the Council on Library Resources, August 1981.

Markey, Karen. *Subject Searching in Library Catalogs: Before and After the Introduction of Online Catalogs.* Dublin, Ohio: OCLC, 1984. (OCLC Library, Information, and Computer Science Series, 4.)

Markey, Karen, and Diane Vizine-Goetz. "Untraced References in the Machine-Readable Library of Congress Subject Headings (General Explanatory References and Scope Notes)." In *Library Resources & Technical Services* 33 (January 1989): 37-53.

Marshall, Joan K. *On Equal Terms: A Thesaurus for Nonsexist Indexing and Cataloging.* New York: Neal-Schuman, 1977.

Matthews, Joseph R., Gary S. Lawrence, and Douglas K. Ferguson, eds. *Using Online Catalogs: A Nationwide Study.* New York: Neal-Schuman, 1983.

McCarthy, Constance. "The Reliability Factor in Subject Access." In *College and Research Libraries* 47, no. 1 (January 1986): 48-56.

McGarry, Dorothy, and Elaine Svenonius. "More on Improved Browsable Displays for Online Subject Access." In *Information Technology and Libraries* 10, no. 3 (September 1991): 185-91.

Metcalfe, John W. *Subject Classifying and Indexing of Libraries and Literature*. Sydney: Angus and Robertson, 1959.

Miksa, Francis. *The Subject in the Dictionary Catalog from Cutter to the Present*. Chicago: American Library Association, 1983.

National Library of Canada. *Canadian Subject Headings*. 2nd ed. Ottawa: National Library of Canada, 1985.

O'Neill, Edward T., and Rao Aluri. *Research Report on Subject Heading Patterns in OCLC Monographic Records*. Columbus: Ohio College Library Center, 1979. (OCLC Research Report Series OCLC/RDD/RR-79/1.)

Pietris, Mary K. "The Limited Use of Free-Floating Subdivisions in the Library of Congress Subject Headings System: With Discussion." In Subject Subdivisions Conference (1991 : Airlie, Va.): *The Future of Subdivisions in the Library of Congress Subject Headings System*, 11-25.

Prevost, Marie Louise. "An Approach to Theory and Method in General Subject Heading." In *Library Quarterly* 16, no. 2 (April 1946): 140-51.

Ranganathan, S. R. *Elements of Library Classification*. 3rd ed. Bombay: Asia Publishing House, 1962.

Répertoire de vedettes-matière. (Québec: Bibliothèque de l'Université Laval, 1989- , semiannual.)

Richmond, Phyllis Allen. "Cats: An Example of Concealed Classification in Subject Headings." In *Library Resources & Technical Services* 3 (Spring 1959): 102-12.

Rogers, Margaret N. "Are We on Equal Terms Yet? Subject Headings Concerning Women in *LCSH*, 1975-1991." In *Library Resources & Technical Services* 37, no. 2 (April 1993): 181-96.

Rolland-Thomas, Paule. "Thesaural Codes: An Appraisal of Their Use in the Library of Congress Subject Headings." In *Cataloging & Classification Quarterly* 16, no. 2 (1993): 71-91.

Salton, Gerard, and Michael J. McGill. *Introduction to Modern Information Retrieval*. New York: McGraw-Hill, 1983.

Salton, Gerard, and C. S. Yang. "On the Specification of Term Values in Automatic Indexing." In *Journal of Documentation* 29 (December 1973): 352.

Shera, Jesse H., and Margaret Egan. *The Classified Catalog: Basic Principles and Practices*. Chicago: American Library Association, 1956.

Shubert, Steven Blake. "Critical Views of LCSH—Ten Years Later: A Bibliographic Essay." In *Cataloging & Classification Quarterly* 15, no. 2 (1992): 37-97.

Soergel, Dagobert. *Organizing Information: Principles of Data Base and Retrieval Systems*. Orlando, Fla.: Academic Press, 1985.

Studwell, William E. *Library of Congress Subject Headings Philosophy, Practice, and Prospects*. Binghamton, N.Y.: Haworth Press, 1990.

————. "The 1990s: Decade of Subject Access: A Theoretical *Code* for LC Subject Headings Would Complete the Maturation of Modern Cataloging." In *American Libraries* 18 (December 1987): 958.

————. "On the Conference Circuit: The Subject Heading *Code*: Do We Have One? Do We Need One?" In *Technicalities* 10 (October 1990): 10-15.

Subject Indexing: Principles and Practices in the 90's. Proceedings of the IFLA satellite meeting held in Lisbon, Portugal, 17-18 August 1993, and sponsored by the IFLA Section on Classification and Indexing and the Instituto da Biblioteca Nacional e do Libro, Lisbon, Portugal, edited by Robert P. Holley et al. München: K.G. Saur, 1995.

Subject Subdivisions Conference (1991 : Airlie, Va.): *The Future of Subdivisions in the Library of Congress Subject Headings System: Report from the Subject Subdivisions Conference*, edited by Martha O'Hara Conway. Washington, D.C.: Cataloging Distribution Service, Library of Congress, 1992.

Svenonius, Elaine. "Design of Controlled Vocabularies." In *Encyclopedia of Library and Information Science*, edited by Allen Kent. Vol. 45, suppl. 10. New York: Marcel Dekker, 1990.

————. "Metcalfe and the Principles of Specific Entry." In *The Variety of Librarianship: Essays in Honour of John Wallace Metcalfe*, edited by W. Boyd Rayward. Sydney: Library Association of Australia, 1976.

Svenonius, Elaine, and Dorothy McGarry. "Objectivity in Evaluating Subject Heading Assignment." In *Cataloging & Classification Quarterly* 16, no. 2 (1993): 5-40.

Taube, Mortimer. "Specificity in Subject Headings and Coordinate Indexing." In *Library Trends* 1 (October 1952): 222.

USMARC Format for Authority Data, Including Guidelines for Content Designation. Prepared by Network Development and MARC Standards Office. Washington, D.C.: Cataloging Distribution Service, Library of Congress, 1987.

Vatican Library. *Rules for the Catalog of Printed Books*. Translated from the 2nd Italian edition by Thomas J. Shanahan, Victor A. Schaefer, and Constantin T. Vesselowsky, and edited by Wyllis E. Wright. Chicago: American Library Association, 1948.

Vickery, Brian C. "Systematic Subject Indexing." In *Journal of Documentation* 9, no. 1 (1953): 48-57.

Vizine-Goetz, Diane, and Karen Markey. "Characteristics of Subject Heading Records in the Machine-Readable Library of Congress Subject Headings." In *Information Technology and Libraries* 8 (June 1989): 203-9.

Weinberg, Bella Hass. "The Hidden Classification in Library of Congress Subject Headings for Judaica." In *Library Resources & Technical Services* 37 (October 1993): 369-79.

Wilson, Patrick, and Nick Robinson. "Form Subdivisions and Genre." In *Library Resources & Technical Services* 34, no. 1 (January 1990): 36-43.

Winkel, Lois, ed. *Subject Headings for Children: A List of Subject Headings Used by the Library of Congress with Dewey Numbers Added.* Albany, N.Y.: Forest Press, 1994.

Index

The designation "n. [number]" following a page number refers to a note reference(s) on that page.